LIBRARY OF
MARY BALDWIN COLLEGE

The Way of Philosophy

The Way of Philosophy

PHILIP WHEELWRIGHT

Professor of Philosophy at Dartmouth College
Visiting Professor, University of California at Riverside

The Odyssey Press  New York

COPYRIGHT, 1954
BY THE ODYSSEY PRESS, INC.

ALL RIGHTS RESERVED
PRINTED IN THE UNITED STATES

THIRD PRINTING

To
My Father

God offers to every man the choice between truth and repose. Take which you please; you can never have both.—EMERSON

Preface

The present volume, which has grown out of a long series of experiments in the teaching of introductory philosophy, combines two sorts of textbook into one. Its sixteen chapters contain the author's exposition of certain problems, arguments, and points of view which are commonly, and with good reason, regarded as constituting the main subject matter of philosophy. Supplementing the expository chapters are four groups of Readings, from sources ancient and modern, chosen both for their inherent worth and for their usefulness in throwing light upon the ideas presented. This combination of two kinds of material within the covers of a single book enables the student to come into direct and stimulating contact with philosophers of enduring greatness, while at the same time it furnishes him with a unified perspective in terms of which the different philosophies that he encounters can be interpreted and, tentatively at least, judged.

Not that an author's or a teacher's perspective can ever be handed over to a student ready-made. Indoctrination, even if it would work, is not philosophy. Nevertheless, a coherent point of view, alien though it may be to the student's predispositions, furnishes a model for the kind of intellectual construction and self-criticism which he must independently attempt if his philosophy is to be something more than prejudice and whim. The philosophy permeating these pages may be characterized as humanistic, existentialist, and realist—with such qualifications as the subsequent discussions may gradually reveal. Its implications come into clearest focus, probably, in the chapters on Free Will (X), on Other Minds (XI), and on Religious Values (XV). But both in the text and in the supplementary readings the student is furnished with ample arguments on which to take a contrary stand, if he should be so minded.

The translations from foreign sources are mostly my own, unless otherwise noted. The use of new translations is in line with my general wish to make philosophical problems as intelligible as possible in relation to living language. I say "in relation to" and not "in terms of," because our everyday forms of speech are generally too spineless for the uses of exact thought. But if popular language on the one hand needs to be employed with sharper precision of word and syntax, it is conversely true that the technical words and formulas of traditional philosophy require frequent overhauling in accordance with the changing intellectual climate of a given time.

Special thanks are due to Mrs. Burdette E. Weymouth, whose secretarial assistance, generously and multiformly bestowed, has been a large factor in producing the book as it now stands. Without the long help and patience of my wife there would have been no book at all. To name all those from whom I may have drawn ideas and criticisms at one time or another is hardly possible; but I should like to thank in particular Professor Jack C. Miller, of the Department of Physics at Pomona College, for his help on some of the technical problems discussed in Chapter V, and collectively my colleagues and students at Dartmouth College for their stimulation, help and forbearance during the many bright years I have spent with them.

PHILIP WHEELWRIGHT

The University of California at Riverside
January, 1954

Contents

PART ONE. THE MEANING AND METHOD OF PHILOSOPHY

I. WHAT IS PHILOSOPHY? — 3
  i. On Defining Philosophy — 3
  The philosophic attitude—The definition analyzed—Has philosophy a subject matter?—The concern for wholeness—The human factor—Order and growth
  ii. Types of Philosophical Problem — 12
  Contemplative vs. deliberative reason—Ethics and metaphysics
  iii. Formal Philosophy and Existential Philosophy — 14
  The existential approach—The formal approach
  iv. Three Philosophical Standpoints — 19
  Limits of the classification—Standpoint of the present book
  For Further Study — 22
  Questions for Discussion — 23

II. PROBLEMS OF KNOWLEDGE AND BELIEF — 24
  i. Knowledge, Acquaintance, and Belief — 25
  Two meanings of "know"—The certainty of pure acquaintance—The role of interpretation
  ii. Sources of Assurance — 28
  Hearsay and prejudice—Authority—Observation—Reason—Empirical method, or the method of hypothesis—Intuition
  For Further Study — 42
  Questions for Discussion — 43

III. PHILOSOPHICAL METHOD — 45
  i. Dialectic — 45
  Identity in difference—Difference in identity—Contextual amplification
  ii. Toward a Critical Metaphysics — 54
  Realms of discourse—The meaning of metaphysical—Primary terms of discourse—Postulates

CONTENTS

    ii. Toward a Critical Metaphysics   54
        Realms of discourse—The meaning of metaphysical—Primary terms of discourse—Postulates
    iii. The Value and Limits of Dialectic   61
        Ethical dialectic—Scientific dialectic—Criticism of criticism
    For Further Study   64
    Questions for Discussion   64

READINGS FOR PART ONE

Aristotle, *On Philosophical Wisdom*   66
William James, *The Spirit of Philosophy*   69
C. D. Broad, *The Relation of Philosophy to the Sciences*   70
Francis Bacon, *Aphorisms Concerning the Method of Philosophy*   80
René Descartes, *On the Method of Philosophy*   91
Arthur Schopenhauer, *The Way of Philosophy*   100
Arthur Schopenhauer, *The Nature of Abstraction*   102

PART TWO. THE WORLD AROUND US

IV. THE EVERYDAY WORLD   111
    i. Things: Their Qualities and Relations   112
        Things occupy space—Things have qualities—Things persist and change—Things have powers and capacities
    ii. Space and Time   117
        Space: perceptual and conceptual—Time: perceptual and conceptual
    iii. The Three Meanngs of "Why?"   122
        The causal "why"—The telic "why"—The structural "why"—Contingency
    For Further Study   126
    Questions for Discussion   127

V. THE CONCEPT OF PHYSICAL NATURE   128
    i. Pre-Kinetic Theories of Nature   129
        Hindu doctrine of the gunas—The Greek doctrine of contraries—Aristotle's doctrine of substances
    ii. The Classical Kinetic Theory   132
        Matter and motion—A world of pure chance—Universal causation—The homogeneity of cosmic space—Measurement—The conservation of mass—The conservation of energy—Mechanism
    iii. New Bearings in Physical Theory   146

CONTENTS   xi

       Entropy—Is the universe running down?—The first paradox of light: wave or bullet?—The second paradox of light: velocity—The Lorentz transformations—The field theory—The indeterminacy principle
       For Further Study   158
       Questions for Discussion   159

VI. THE PROBLEM OF REALITY   161
   i. Materialism   162
       Matter and motion—Determinism—The problem of secondary qualities—Cartesian dualism—Critique of materialism—The use and abuse of scientific objects
   ii. Idealism   169
   iii. Pragmatism   174
       Vaihinger's doctrine of "as-if"—Bridgman's doctrine of the instrument—Critique of pragmatism
   iv. Contextual Realism   181
       Characteristics of science—The non-scientific—Reality in context
       For Further Study   187
       Questions for Discussion   188

VII. THE WORLD OF LIVING THINGS   190
   i. The Meaning of Life   191
       The seeming properties of life—Bio-mechanism—Critique of mechanism
   ii. The Hypothesis of Evolution   196
       Distinction of problems—The evidences of evolution—The hypothesis of natural selection—Speculative problems
   iii. The Metaphysics of Evolution   203
       The three standpoints—The logic of emergence—Vitalism
       For Further Study   210
       Questions for Discussion   210

READINGS FOR PART TWO

Aristotle, *Philosophy of Nature*   212
William James, *The Thing and Its Relations*   221
Isaac Newton, *Rules of Scientific Philosophizing*   224
C. D. Broad, *Mechanism and Its Alternatives*   227
E. F. Caldin, *Empirical Laws and Theoretical Models*   234
A. S. Eddington, *The Status of Scientific Law*   236
D'Arcy W. Thompson, *On Teleology and Mechanism*   245
Arthur Schopenhauer, *Nature Interpreted as the Will to Live*   251

PART THREE. MIND, SOUL, AND SELF

VIII. WHAT IS A SELF? 261
    i. Subjective and Objective Approaches 261
        Behaviorism—Psychoanalytic theory—Cultural objectivism
    ii. The Unity of the Self 267
        The soul-substance docrine—Associationism—The concept of self-integration—Health of the soul—The Freudian concept of the self—Beyond Freud
    For Further Study 278
    Questions for Discussion 278

IX. THE MIND-BODY RELATION 280
    i. Interactionism 281
        Descartes' theory—First apriori objection: inconceivability—Second apriori objection: conservation of energy—Methodological basis of criticism
    ii. Behaviorism and Epiphenomenism 285
        The admission of subjectivity—The theory of epiphenomenism—Reasons against the theory
    iii. Parallelism 292
        Pansychism—Criticism
    For Further Study 297
    Questions for Discussion 298

X. FREEDOM OF CHOICE 299
    i. Clarification of the Problem 299
        Empirical vs. metaphysical freedom—Fatalism—Aristotle's doctrine of potencies—The theological issue—Historical determinism
    ii. The Case for Determinism 306
        Argument from causal invariability—Is determinism mechanistic?—Argument from reasonable expectancy
    iii. The Case for Libertarianism 311
        Pre-analytic arguments—Post-analytic arguments—Situational determinism examined—Universal determinism examined—Principle of deviations—The practice of freedom
    For Further Study 320
    Questions for Discussion 320

XI. OUR KNOWLEDGE OF OTHER SELVES 322
    i. Solipsism 323
        Radical solipsism—Objective solipsism—Criticisms

CONTENTS

ii. Rational Grounds of Belief ... 329
    The analogical arguments—A case of question-begging—Inference from the use of language—Is inference enough?
iii. Intuition through Response ... 336
    I-it and I-thou—Evolution of "thou" and "it"—The mystery of personhood—Conclusion
    For Further Study ... 341
    Questions for Discussion ... 342

READINGS FOR PART THREE

Plato, *The Nature of the Soul* ... 344
Aristotle, *The Nature of the Soul* ... 350
René Descartes, *On the Nature of the Mind* ... 353
René Descartes, *The Interrelation of Soul and Body* ... 357
William James, *The Consciousness of Self* ... 359
Bertrand Russell, *A Denial of Free Will* ... 372
William James, *The Belief in Free Will* ... 379
W. K. Clifford, *Our Knowledge of Other Selves* ... 389
Martin Buber, *I and Thou* ... 392

PART FOUR. VALUES

XII. THE NATURE OF VALUE ... 401
  i. Types of Value ... 401
     Having and being—Pleasure and pain—Axiological pluralism—The values of nonpossession—The aesthetic and the moral—The conditions of moral valuation
  ii. Absolutism vs. Relativism ... 413
     Absolutism—Extreme relativism—Semantic relativism—Meeting of extremes
  iii. Contextual Objectivism ... 420
     That values are objective—That value-statements are meaningful—That value-statements are contextual—Concluding comment
     For Further Study ... 428
     Questions for Discussion ... 429

XIII. AESTHETIC VALUES ... 432
  i. The Aesthetic Experience ... 433
     Pleasure and the aesthetic surface—Form—Participation—Significance—Psychic renewal

	ii. Artistic Creation	441
	Functional utility—Imitation—Self-expression—Formalization—Communication of meaning	
	For Further Study	452
	Questions for Discussion	453
XIV.	VALUES IN ACTION: THE REALM OF ETHICS	456
	The nature of ethical choice	
	i. The Ethics of Satisfactions	458
	The theory of hedonism—The social quandary—Is hedonism enough?	
	ii. The Idea of Duty	465
	The nature of temptation—Kant: duty as commitment to a universal—The worth of persons—Critical observations	
	iii. The Ethics of Self-Realization	470
	Good defined by function—The two functions of reason—The golden mean—Harmony and happiness	
	For Further Study	475
	Questions for Discussion	476
XV.	VALUE AND BELIEF: THE RELIGIOUS PROBLEM	477
	i. The Meaning of Religious Belief	477
	Two questions distinguished—Religion basically defined	
	ii. The Grounds of Disbelief	482
	The anthropological objection—The psychological objection	
	iii. The Religious Hypothesis	489
	The cosmological argument—The teleological argument—The moral argument—The ontological argument—The religious hypothesis existentially considered	
	For Further Study	505
	Questions for Discussion	506
XVI.	EPILOGUE: ON CHOOSING A PHILOSOPHY	508

READINGS FOR PART FOUR

Epicurus, *Letter to a Friend*	511
Jeremy Bentham, *The Nature and Sanctions of Moral Action*	513
Plato, *Crito*	523
Plato, *The Nature of Virtue*	536
Immanuel Kant, *Reason and Duty*	538
Aristotle, *The Philosophy of Happiness*	544
Aristotle, *On the Existence of God*	561

CONTENTS

Thomas Aquinas, *Five Arguments for God's Existence*	563
Baron d'Holbach, *A Plea for Atheism*	567
John Stuart Mill, *The Case for a Limited God*	573
William James, *The Nature and Validity of Religious Experience*	576
Martin Buber, *The Eternal Thou*	590

GLOSSARY 595

INDEX 611

PART ONE

The Meaning and Method of Philosophy

CHAPTER I

What Is Philosophy?

THEAETETUS. Yes, Socrates, I am amazed when I think of such questions; by the gods I am. I find myself wanting to know what they can mean; and there are times when I become almost dizzy with the contemplation of them.
SOCRATES. I see, my dear Theaetetus, that when Theodorus called you a philosopher he spoke with a true insight into your nature. For a feeling of wonder is what marks the philosopher, and philosophy begins in wonder. He was not a bad genealogist who said that Iris (the messenger of heaven) is the child of Thaumas (wonder). PLATO, *Theaetetus*

SOCRATES (*on trial*). The unexamined life is not worth living.
PLATO, *The Apology*

i. On Defining Philosophy

In beginning the study of any subject it is well to understand in a general way what the subject is about. Of course a fuller understanding must come gradually, as the study is systematically pursued. A definition offered at the outset is bound to be somewhat tentative—its purpose being to direct or invite the thoughts in one direction rather than another. So it is with philosophy: a student can only learn what it is by practicing it, yet he needs some preliminary definition to help him know when he *is* practicing it and when he is not.

The main trouble in trying to give an adequate definition of philosophy is this. We are accustomed to think of one science as distinguished from another by its subject matter. Physics deals with problems of mass and motion in a space-time continuum, biology with the structure and functioning of living organisms, sociology with the behavior of human beings taken collectively, and so on. It is natural that anyone reading a modern college or university catalogue and seeing these and many other subjects listed side by side with philosophy should assume that philosophy has a special subject matter too, and should ask what it is. No doubt there is a sense in which philosophy may be said to have subject matter; for the many volumes that philosophers write must be *about* something. Nevertheless what chiefly distinguishes philosophy from other pursuits is not a specific subject matter, but rather an attitude and method toward life and hence toward any given subject matter.

The philosophic attitude

In ordinary everyday situations we are accustomed to hear such statements as: "He took his defeat philosophically"; or, "Never worry!—that's *my* philosophy." The man whom we call philosophical, or in a spontaneous affectionate way "a philosopher," is one who can face the vicissitudes of life serenely and not be upset by reversals of fortune. Although this is only a part of the full meaning of philosophy, yet it is a real and important part of it. If a man's "philosophy of life" serves to free him from worry and vain regrets, it is clearly a most valuable thing to have.

But serenity is not the same as phlegmatic indifference, and to be above the battle is not to be ignorant that it is going on. You can be serene toward a situation, in the proper sense of the adjective, only by daring to look at it, and at its full implications for yourself, frankly and fearlessly. It is the subconscious, unexamined fears and irritations that destroy our serenity most of all. "Will there be a war?" "Will I be blown up?" "Is my financial security threatened?" "What is so-and-so's real opinion of me?" Even when we let the *words* of such questions play through our minds, the real question, which is to say the full nature of its impact upon all that we hold most dear, remains in large part below the surface of consciousness. We catch hurried, uneasy glimpses of it, and not liking what we see we force it back into the darkness of the unconscious again, where it continues to plague us in ways that escape our control. We instinctively try to deceive ourselves, and because self-deception is never complete (short of insanity) the result is likely to be an attitude of partially suppressed jitters. To be philosophical is to take the opposite course. The real philosopher neither ignores nor suppresses whatever is relevant to the full human situation. He makes, as William James has said, "an unusually obstinate attempt to think clearly and consistently." He tries to see life critically, yet appreciatively, and whole. Provisionally, then, let us define philosophy, or the philosophical attitude, as a *persistent attempt to see life critically, appreciatively, and whole*. There are three mutually conditioning ideas in this definition, and it is well to grasp the precise meaning and import of each.

The definition analyzed

To practice philosophy is to think *critically*; and this implies two things. First, the good philosopher is critical about *meanings*. He does not smudge over important or interesting distinctions, and he is not content with ideas that are confused and vague. On the contrary, he tries to make his ideas as clear as the nature of the subject matter will allow, and to mold language in such a way as to express and communicate those ideas with maximum precision. However, he must be critical even about the value of precision itself, recognizing that too much zeal for precision of a wrong kind may lead to irrelevance and superficiality. Secondly, besides being critical about meanings, the good philosopher is critical about *beliefs*. He does not accept opinions irresponsibly, but tries to understand the grounds on which they rest. In cases where one of his cherished beliefs involves an act of faith which goes beyond the objective evidence, he will frankly acknowledge this fact, and will then either suspend the belief as insufficiently grounded or else will make the act of affirmation deliberately, accepting full responsibility for what William James has called the "moral risk."

In the next place, to practice philosophy is to think *appreciatively*. Criticism alone is not enough. Although criticism is an indispensable element in all sound thinking, yet when practiced continually for its own sake, without reference to any larger and more affirmative aim, it finally becomes sterile and unsatisfying. The good philosopher takes joy in his apprehension of the world, in his discovery of himself, and in his many-sided relationships with fellow beings. His life is quickened by wonder. Philosophy for him is a continual adventure—an odyssey through strange seas. Other adventurers have preceded him, and he accepts gratefully whatever clues they can furnish, but the seas wear a subtly different aspect for every voyager, and are continually having to be charted anew. Experience offers unlimited possibilities of discovery and significant reinterpretation. The philosopher is one who delights in that manifoldness, whose heart and mind respond to each new situation, eagerly exploring its unknown depths of beauty, significance, and mystery.

Finally, to practice philosophy is to think *integrally*. To recognize and delight in the manifold is not enough. The philosophic mind seeks wholeness, and although an ultimate grasp of the World-All must ever elude our finite minds, we still accept the idea of it as an unreachable point of reference. To philosophize is to submit one's thought to the idea of a *cosmos*. Just what sort of cosmos is accepted as the guiding idea will depend partly on the individual philosopher's temperament and intellectual loyalties, partly on the climate of opinion in which he lives and has been reared. Materialists construct their cosmic idea on the analogy of bits of matter moving about in space. Idealists construct theirs on the analogy of rational minds. Whichever construction is preferred—and the history of philosophy records many intermediate possibilities—the materialistic philosopher and the idealistic philosopher are at any rate alike in this: that each of them finds particular happenings more intelligible when they are seen in the context of some large guiding idea to which its devotees give the honorific name "reality."

Has philosophy a subject matter?

So far we have been considering philosophy as an attitude rather than as a sphere of investigation. That is to say, we have been defining philosophy by reference to the philosopher who practices it rather than by reference to the nature of its subject matter. Let us now start on a new tack and see if we can find out anything distinctive about the subject matter with which philosophy is concerned. For while it is true that what chiefly distinguishes philosophy is the attitude of inquiry adopted toward any subject matter, it is also true that the significance of a thinker's attitude is inseparable from the nature of what he is thinking about.

What, then, is philosophy about? What kind of question do philosophers characteristically investigate? At first glance it would seem that philosophy has no specific subject matter of its own, inasmuch as it is possible to take any area of inquiry whatever—physical events, living organisms, mental phenomena, economic trends, historical occurrences, personal perplexities, moral codes, artistic forms, religious creeds—and deal with it philosophically. It is clear, then, that the subject matter of philosophy must differ from that of any particular science *in a different way* from that in which one science's subject matter differs from another's. Let us now consider what that peculiar difference is.

We must distinguish between two meanings of "subject matter." If the term is taken to mean a special area of factual investigation—as atomic research falls within the province of physics, chlorophyll analysis within that of botany or of biochemistry, exploration of the subconscious within that of psychology—then it is doubtful whether in this sense philosophy can be said to have a subject matter of its own. But subject matter may also be interpreted to mean any basic set of related questions. Anatomy and physiology both deal with animal bodies: the one with their structures, the other with their functions. Do they deal with the same subject matter or with two different ones? In a sense they deal with the same objects; in another and more analytic sense they have different subject matters in that they raise characteristically different types of questions, and therein deal with different *aspects* of the animal bodies. Anatomy deals with animal bodies in their static aspect, as structured; physiology deals with the same animal bodies in their dynamic aspect, as functioning.

Analogously, philosophy and science differ in the kind of approach they make to a situation, the kind of questions they raise, and hence the aspects of the situation which they accept as relevant. Atomic fission is of interest both to physicists and philosophers but in different ways. The atomic physicist inquires into the causes and physical effects of fission; the philosopher raises questions at longer range concerning its ulterior consequences for the happiness or wretchedness of mankind, and for our total conception of the nature and significance of the world. Philosophical inquiry may be directed toward anything whatever, but its aim will always be to behold and understand the object of inquiry (1) in its whole character and (2) in relation to man's most enduring and most deep-rooted interests. Let us consider these two points separately.

The concern for wholeness

Each of the sciences deals with a certain kind of fact and dismisses other kinds as irrelevant to its essential purposes. When a chemist discovers a new way of producing textiles or plastics or poison gas or fuel, he is not concerned, strictly as a chemist, either with the market value of his product or with the moral implications, for good or ill, of putting it to use. An economist, on the other hand, qua[1] economist, will regard the product solely as a commodity; which is to say, under the aspect of potential

[1] See Glossary for this and other technical terms when their meanings are not clear from the context.

marketability. No science faces all the facts suggested by a situation; each adopts a policy of systematic limitation, and this is the necessary price of its effectiveness. The logician F. B. Jevons has written:

> The strategy of science—the uniform method of all the sciences—consists in dividing the enemy's forces, as it were, and so beating them in detail. Every object has a host of various qualities, and each of these qualities is dealt with separately by a separate science—its color by optics, its weight by physics, its chemical constitution by chemistry, its organism by physiology, and so on. Of course, the color of a thing does not exist separately from the thing; nor can you take the weight out of a thing and carry off the weight into one room whilst you leave the thing without any weight in the other. All you can really do is to concentrate your attention on one of the many qualities that a thing possesses, and dismiss from attention all the other qualities. And when we do this, we are said to abstract that particular quality from the thing; and the quality itself is called an abstraction. These qualities—these abstract qualities—can be studied by themselves in one way only, and that is by pretending that they exist by themselves. And the study of such abstractions is what is called science.[2]

Philosophy, on the other hand, pays attention to the larger relatedness of things; it is the attempt at harmonizing and integrating the various provinces of human interests and activity. Thus where each of the sciences is abstract in its own characteristic way, philosophy is, or should be, concrete. Although an isolated system of knowledge such as astrophysics is undoubtedly valuable, it does not satisfy fully the human itch of rational wonder. We want to know how the different types of fact and systems of explanation fit into an intelligible view of life and existence as a whole. Our need of an ordered world is not satisfied if we think purely in terms of chemical reactions while in the laboratory, of economic pressures while reading the financial page of the newspaper, and of the dispensations of divine Provi-

[2] F. B. Jevons, *Philosophy—What Is It?* (1914), pp. 16-18.

dence while in church. To be philosophical is to have a concern for the relations among these different systems of relations. It is to be interested in discovering or surmising the pattern of the whole.

The human factor

There is another sense, too, in which science is abstract. Not only does a practitioner of one science ignore many of the qualities and relations which it is the business of other sciences to investigate. He also ignores (in his professional capacity) the role that he, the human scientist, plays in relation to his discoveries. Although both the student and the thing studied, the scientist and the objects he is investigating, must be present if any knowledge is to be attained, science dismisses the student from consideration and pretends that the thing under investigation is all that exists. The investigator's human concern with what he is doing, his hopes and fears, his elation or disappointment as his experiment succeeds or fails, are of no relevance whatever to the strictly scientific problem. Yet they matter a great deal in reality, and unless human purposes had been active no scientific investigation would ever have been begun. "Hence it is," Jevons concludes, "that science is doubly abstract. It is abstract in the first place because it dismisses from attention all qualities except the one under investigation, and pretends that that one alone exists; and it is abstract in the next place because it dismisses the student from attention and pretends that the thing under investigation alone exists."[3]

Thus there is this second way in which philosophy is more concrete than science: it takes account, in any investigation, of the human factor. Not only does the philosopher seek to understand the nature of the world in its wholeness. He also inquires how man, with his limited sense organs and powers of interpretation, can know the world as it really is. That is one way in which the human factor is involved in any investigation—as the

[3] Jevons, *op. cit.*, pp. 21-22.

sometimes forgotten but ever active human subject which seeks to know the nature and relatedness of the object. And there is another way. For assuming the object to be more or less correctly known, there always remains the further question of its *value*. Life constantly imposes on us the responsibility of making choices, and to choose is to put some value or other into operation. To reflect rationally upon the values which things have—in relation to other things and to ourselves—is an indispensable part of the exercise of philosophy.

When the two philosophic aims of wholeness and human relevance are actively interrelated we are being philosophical in something like a full sense. Such questions as whether and in what sense God exists, whether human consciousness outlasts the life of the body, the nature of good and evil, the relation of mind and brain, the validity of human knowledge, and so on, are philosophical rather than scientific questions by either or both of these criteria.

Order and growth

The wholeness at which philosophy aims is not a static wholeness, however. It should be conceived on the analogy of a growing organism, not on that of a prefabricated machine. A man's philosophy at the age of forty is likely to be different from what it was at the age of eighteen. One's beliefs mature through being challenged and tested by life's vicissitudes, even though the fundamental loyalties and the sense of general direction are preserved. To be philosophical is to be ever awake to the new testimonies which experience offers, and ever ready to reëxamine one's most cherished beliefs in their light. Frequently it involves the dismissal of intellectual orderings which, though they have served us in the past, are proving too restrictive and naive from the standpoint of our deepening experience and growing insights. Thus an intelligent child in growing toward adulthood learns to discard the old white-and-black, cowboy-and-Indian, hero-and-villain type of thinking, in order to adopt norms of judgment and of conduct that make fuller allowance for the complexity of human motives and the many-sidedness of situations.

ii. Types of Philosophical Problem

There are various ways of classifying philosophical problems—that is, of distinguishing and relating them according to some logical principle. Different treatises on philosophy are likely to proceed along quite different lines. For underlying the principle of classification that is chosen there is the author's sense of value —of what needs emphasizing and what can be overlooked, and of the relative importance of similarities and of differences in every comparison. Now since the aim of philosophy is to grasp things in their full relatedness, and since it is by the faculty[4] of reason that relatedness is understood, the initial distinction among philosophical problems should evidently be based upon the ways in which reason functions.

Contemplative vs. deliberative reason

Aristotle's demonstration of reason's twofold nature is as valid today as ever. Man is the rational animal, in that he can grasp the relationships of things more variously, more subtly, and more profoundly than any beasts can do. But he is still an animal, in that his instinctual and sensuous nature furnishes the substructure of his human existence. We are creatures of impulse, yet able within shifting limits to control and transform our impulses in the service of ideal ends. This double situation defines what Aristotle sometimes calls Practical Reason, or reason concerned with doing, and sometimes Deliberative Reason. We exercise our mental faculty in order to decide what course of action to follow. On the other hand, there are clearly situations where thought is employed without any apparent reference to action. We are often interested in discovering the truth without practical or moral aim; we simply wish to know what is really the situation and

[4] See Glossary for the exact meaning of this disputed word.

There are other types of inquiry which may acquire an existential character for this or that individual: a mathematician, for example, may undertake philosophical inquiries into the foundations of mathematics with truly existential concern. Nevertheless, the five types of inquiry listed above are probably those of most widely shared and sharable existential interest. For they are of basic and inescapable concern to man qua man.

The formal approach

Growing out of the existential questions are certain questions of a more formal and technical character, which we find ourselves having to face when we pursue the existential questions with sufficient persistence and care. The formal side of philosophy is important, and indeed indispensable for the serious student, having developed out of persistent attempts to define the existential problems with rigorous clarity and to explore their logical implications fully. Nevertheless its value is instrumental rather than final. The importance of technical questions in philosophy rests, in the long run, upon the importance of the existential questions which they help us to solve or at least to re-envisage in a more satisfactory light. The principal branches of formal inquiry in philosophy are these:

1. Problems of *ontology*. What is the nature of reality, and by what criterion, or by what criteria, do we distinguish it from mere appearance?

2. Problems of *cosmology*. What kind of order is most fundamental in the universe as a whole? A strictly interconnected order of cause and effect allowing of no exceptions? A loose order, which is never accurately described but only statistically approximated by scientific formulas? Or a telic order, involving the adaptation of means to ends, and inviting therefore the transference of organic concepts and types of explanation from the biological to the so-called inanimate world?

3. Problems of *epistemology*. How can we really know anything? Is the world really of the kind we think we discover it to

be, or is *any* set of beliefs about the nature of things merely a sort of wishful thinking, however disguised?

4. Problems of *semantics*. Are the words which we employ, and the syntactical relations between words, adequate to express and communicate the real nature of things? If not, then in what ways do the conventions of classification and of syntax misrepresent the real nature of what *is*?

5. Problems of *dialectic*. How are the various fields of human interest and investigation related to one another? What are the basic terms, or concepts, which each employs, and how are they related to those employed in other fields? What presuppositions, or postulates, are made in each field as an indispensable condition of getting any investigations under way in that field; and how are the presuppositions made in one field related to those made in another?

The foregoing classification is by no means intended as final. Its purpose is merely initiatory: to allow the student to envisage the kind of question that philosophy characteristically raises. In the following chapters the arrangement of problems will be somewhat different, as a glance at the Table of Contents will show; but the problems as there developed can generally be referred without much difficulty to some one or some combination of the foregoing types of inquiry.

Accordingly, when one or another problem in the study of philosophy seems abstract, dry, and remote from the real concerns of reflective living, it may be that it is still worth studying —for either of two reasons. Some problems—notably those in epistemology and semantics—although not existential in themselves, are valuably *propaedeutic*. That is to say, they are methodological disciplines, the mastery of which enables us to tackle the existential questions with greater effectiveness. On the other hand there may be found questions which appear dull and pointless on first encounter but which later, in the context of maturing experience, begin to be not only intellectually understood but existentially *encountered*. A student who has initially dismissed Parmenides' doctrine of being vs. non-being, and perhaps even Hamlet's "To be or not to be" soliloquy) as mere word-play, may come to think differently about it in later years if plagued by thoughts of suicide, or if tragically confronted with the death of one deeply beloved.

iv. Three Philosophical Standpoints

Now that the main types of philosophical question have been considered, what can be said about the principal ways of answering them? The classification of philosophical doctrines—or, less formally, of philosophical standpoints—will depend largely on what type of philosophical question is given priority. The most useful classification is one that has primary reference to man; one that is concerned with different views as to the status of man and his values in relation to everything that can be called, in the most comprehensive sense, his world. And on this basis the possible standpoints in philosophy are logically reducible to three: *materialism,* which takes something lower or less than man as the ultimate area of reference; *humanism,* which takes man himself, in his wholeness and in his distinctively human character, as that ultimate area; and *transcendentalism,* which looks ultimately to something—whether a divine Person or Persons or a realm of eternally valid Ideal Principles—higher and nobler than man. This may be regarded as an existential classification of philosophies, since it is based on considering the way in which any given philosophy interprets human existence and its ultimate cosmic role.

Limits of the classification

Two qualifications must be made concerning this existential classification of philosophies—one semantic, the other logical. Semantically, the three terms employed, like all highly general terms, are susceptible of ambiguity. Some philosophers who are materialists in the sense here defined reject the *word* "materialism" because of its pejorative and unpopular connotations; they prefer some more neutral word, such as "positivism" or "naturalism" or (in certain contexts) "realism." Nevertheless, while these other words are serviceable with respect to certain groups of problems, it seems that the word "materialism" is the best and most generally understood word for all-round use. A critical student of philosophy should of course use it descriptively and without derogatory overtones; for only in that way can the question of its truth and adequacy be objectively examined.

At the other end of the classification, the word "transcendentalism" may be questioned by some readers on the ground that it has been employed by such philosophers as Kant and Emerson in a more special sense. Well, almost any general word is likely to be limited by some writer or other to whatever usage his particular philosophy requires; let it be agreed that in the present book the word shall signify any philosophy which regards the supreme reality in the universe as something higher and better than man as we know and conceive him.

Finally, the word "humanism," while probably not objectionable to anyone, is persistently ambiguous, since a number of those who by my definition are either materialists on the one hand or transcendentalists on the other fly the humanist banner. To which it can only be replied that a student of philosophy should constantly practice looking beyond the label of any doctrine to the content of the doctrine itself.

The other qualification concerning our threefold scheme is a reminder that in this, as in virtually all classifications where general ideas are involved, there will be overlappings, border cases, and mixed cases. The chief cause of difficulty along this line consists in the fact that every philosophy has, potentially at least, both a contemplative and a practical aspect, and the two aspects sometimes get separated. Thus, a man who is a materialist in his theory about the nature of reality may be a practicing humanist, holding human rights sacred above all things and showing the most delicate and judicious sensitivity in his relationship with fellow men. On the other hand, a man who adopts a transcendental theory of the universe may be a practicing egoist, petty and callous toward others. Such anomalies do exist, but the important thing (from the existential standpoint) is to recognize that they *are* anomalies: they arise out of the familiar fact of human inconsistency. Perfect consistency is unattainable and perhaps even not altogether desirable: if an egoist holds transcendental beliefs, although they may be partly a hypocritical escape from the realities of his situation, they may also lead to an awakening of conscience and offer him an intellectual mirror in which eventually he will learn to see himself as he is. Generally speaking, in an existential problem the role of consistency is to guide rather than to restrict. Existential logic, as distinguished from mathematical, does not set up absolute rules of procedure, but it does demand an alertness to reconsider and revise whenever the presuppositions or the vital implications of one's philosophy fall too much into disharmony.

Standpoint of the present book

By and large the standpoint of the present book is humanistic. Such an avowal indicates an attitude and method toward problems rather than a prejudgment of answers. The one necessary humanistic postulate is that all deeply philosophical inquiries must not only start out from the human center but must be justified at each step by reference to the full range of human interests; therein they are distinguished from what is specialized, derivative, and abstract. A wise humanist accepts the factual discoveries of the sciences—so far as they are really discoveries and not theoretical speculations—and tries to discover in turn what their significance may be for the attainment of human goals; what he maintains is that human goals are autonomous and of first importance, that science is for the sake of man and not man for the sake of science. He will also recognize the vast importance of religion in the history of mankind, and will try to keep an open-minded attitude toward the possibility that the various religions of the world, however much encrusted with error and bias, represent real human insights into the mysterious heart of things. He will be ready to draw new insights from the ordinary, everyday activities—from working and playing and conversing with fellow human beings in whatever walk of life; but he will be no less ready to seek for clues and quickening suggestions in the records that man has left of the imaginative dimension of life—in literature, music, art and craftsmanship, and in the varied annals of history. Neither fact nor logic nor responsible authority are to be neglected; the question is one of proper focus. Humanism, in short, is the philosophy of the middle way, applied no less to problems of knowledge than to problems of deliberative choice.

For Further Study

WILLIAM JAMES, *Some Problems of Philosophy* (1911), Chap. I.
RALPH BARTON PERRY, *An Approach to Philosophy* (Scribner, 1905).
GEORGE S. FULLERTON, *An Introduction to Philosophy* (Macmillan, 1906), Chaps. I, II.
WILLIAM ERNEST HOCKING, *Types of Philosophy* (Scribner, rev. ed., 1939), Chap. I.
R. F. A. HOERNLÉ, *Matter, Life, Mind and God* (Harcourt, Brace, 1923), Lecture I.
A. C. EWING, *The Fundamental Questions of Philosophy* (Macmillan, 1952), Chap. I.
C. E. M. JOAD, *Philosophy* (London: Hodder and Stoughton, 1944), Chaps. I, II.
THOMAS V. SMITH, *The Philosophic Way of Life* (University of Chicago Press, 1929), Chap. I.
CLIFFORD BARRETT, *Philosophy* (Macmillan, 1925), Chap. I.
LEWIS W. BECK, *Philosophical Inquiry* (Prentice-Hall, 1952), Chap. I.
MARCUS LONG, *The Spirit of Philosophy* (Norton, 1953), Chap. I.
LOUIS O. KATTSOFF, *Elements of Philosophy* (Ronald Press, 1953), Chaps. I, IV.

Questions for Discussion

1. Recall the philosophical questions that have arisen from time to time in readings, discussions, other courses, or private reflections. Write down several of these in clear language, then see where they fit into the classification of problems in Section iii. Which of the questions you have formulated do you think most worth while for discussion in this course?

2. Is your personal philosophy at the present time closest to materialism, humanism, or transcendentalism, as these words are defined in Section iv? Has there been any important change in your outlook recently?

3. What answer could you give to a classmate who advised you to drop philosophy on the grounds:

a) that it is too abstract?

b) that unlike the sciences it has continued to ask the same questions for 2500 years without coming any nearer to answering them?

c) that science can give you all the answers you need?

4. What philosophical meaning, and how much truth or error, do you find in the following remarks?

a) "Men's souls take pleasure in getting wet, but the best soul is like a dry beam of light."—HERACLITUS (Greece, sixth century B.C.).

b) "Know thyself!"—Engraved on the grotto of the Oracle at Delphi.

c) "My only wisdom consists in knowing that I know nothing." —SOCRATES.

CHAPTER II

Problems of Knowledge and Belief

ONE of the most influential books in the development of philosophy since the Renaissance was John Locke's *An Essay Concerning Human Understanding* (1690). Dismayed by the confusions and irreconcilable oppositions of the many philosophies that attempted to answer the great philosophical riddles about the ultimate nature of things, Locke concluded that such direct attacks upon the problem were ill-advised, and that before setting ourselves inquiries of that nature it is wise to examine our own abilities and to see what problems our understandings are, or are not, fitted to deal with. Accordingly, his purpose in the *Essay* was "an inquiry into the origin, certainty and extent of human knowledge, together with the grounds and degrees of belief, opinion, and assent." And he adds:

If, by this inquiry into the nature of the understanding, I can discover the powers thereof, how far they reach, to what things they are in any degree proportionate, and where they fail us; I suppose it may be of use to prevail with the busy mind of man to be more cautious in meddling with things exceeding its comprehension; to stop when it is at the utmost extent of its tether; and to sit down in a quiet ignorance of those things which upon examination are found to be beyond the reach of our capacities.[1]

Locke's procedure embodies a cautionary wisdom, and it is valid in the main. But with a qualification. We cannot be alto-

---

[1] John Locke (1632-1704), *An Essay Concerning Human Understanding*, Bk. I, Chap. I, Sec. 4.

gether sure that we know just what our powers of knowing are. Locke's scepticism about our ability to answer ultimate questions about the nature of the universe might equally well apply to our ability to answer questions about the real nature of ourselves. "The understanding, like the eye," he writes, "whilst it makes us see and perceive all other things, takes no notice of itself; and it requires art and pains to set it at a distance, and make it its own object." Well, let us make the effort by all means; let us inquire carefully how the understanding works in acquiring its beliefs and in reaching out for knowledge, but let us not take for granted that such a method is bound to preserve us from error. With this qualification granted, the purpose of the present chapter is to make a critical beginning in the Lockian sense: to look a little way into the meaning of knowledge, to survey the principal sources by which knowledge and belief are arrived at, and to consider how far a sound philosophical method will make use of those sources.

i. *Knowledge, Acquaintance, and Belief*

Two meanings of "know"

The English word "knowledge" has two main senses: William James has called them Knowledge by Acquaintance and Knowledge About. In a rough way the distinction is amply familiar. If someone says, "I don't actually *know* him but I know who he is," we are not puzzled by the double usage. In certain other languages the ambiguity is avoided: German distinguishes acquaintance from knowledge by the words *kennen* and *wissen* respectively; French by *connaître* and *savoir*; Spanish by *conocer* and *saber*. But the linguistic parsimony of English in this respect has at least one virtue: it reminds us that the kinds of experience which the two words represent, though different, are continuous. Pure acquaintance is hard to isolate. As soon as you start to describe an experience, even to yourself, you begin to make comparisons and implicit judgments; which, in however elementary a way, is Knowledge About. For instance, suppose I feel a toothache. I know the ache by direct acquaintance. But in the very act of characterizing it as a toothache I make certain implicit judgments about it: that the source of the trouble is actually in a tooth, and that it is the sort of thing that a dentist can remedy. In conceptualizing and describing the ache I implicitly lay claim to a certain knowledge *about* it.

The certainty of pure acquaintance

Nevertheless, although Knowledge by Acquaintance and Knowledge About—or, as may be said, for simplicity, acquaintance and knowledge—are continuous and interrelated with each other, there is an important reason for distinguishing them. Pure acquaintance admits of no doubt, for it involves no interpretation, judgment, or belief about the datum; the datum with which we are acquainted simply *is*. But knowledge *about* a thing can go astray. I cannot err in the acquaintance I have of the present ache in the region of my jaw, but I may possibly err in calling it a toothache, for it is barely possible that no dentist could find anything wrong with my teeth and that the real cause would lie elsewhere, in some undiscovered psychoneural area.

The difference can be illustrated by considering the following paradox. Suppose that when I mention the toothache a Christian Scientist says to me, "You are mistaken. Pain does not exist; therefore you are deluded when you think you have a toothache. Change your way of thinking and the toothache (or what you take to be a toothache) will disappear." Now I am not concerned here with the truth or falsity of the Christian Science philosophy; I am only concerned with what the statement can possibly mean. *Some* experience is present to me that I call "the toothache": even the Christian Scientist acknowledges as much when he says that that experience will disappear. If he calls the pain unreal, then, he is not challenging the fact of bare acquaintance; he is challenging my beliefs *about* what I am acquainted with, and is proposing a counterbelief of his own—namely, that I can get rid of this thing that I am acquainted with if I will stop thinking of it as "pain" and will practice dismissing it from my thoughts altogether. He may possibly be right; the cure is worth trying. But the logical axiom here is that if there is a cure it is a cure of something—namely of what I was directly acquainted with, however I may choose to call it.

The role of interpretation

Both knowledge and belief share the foregoing difference with bare acquaintance: both of them add something in the way of interpretation and judgment to the immediate deliverances of awareness. How, then, do they differ? It is obvious, I dare say, that knowledge makes the greater claim. In accurate discourse I cannot be said to "know" that a proposition is true unless I assent to it because of unchallengeable grounds which support it. Otherwise my assurance is not knowledge but merely opinion, belief, or, if very strong, conviction. I can properly claim to *know* that there is a furnace in my cellar because I trust the evidence of my senses and memory, in addition to which my "common sense" (i.e., the spontaneous summation of numerous everyday observations and inferences) tells me that the furnace will not have moved. Hence, when the radiators fail to give forth heat I ask what is wrong with the furnace, I do not ask whether the furnace really exists. I can claim to know that there is an island called Puerto Rico in the Caribbean Sea, because I trust the authoritative consensus of mapmakers and informed visitors. And so on. Of course it may be that what seem adequate grounds to one man's judgment will seem inadequate to another's. A fundamentalist may declare: "I *know* that every word of the Old Testament is literally true"; to which a doubter is likely to reply, "You have a right to your own *opinion*." When it is desirable to avoid prejudging the question of whether knowledge or mere belief is present in a given case I shall employ the neutral word "assurance"; and the task of our next section is to survey the main sources from which assurances arise and acquire strength.

ii. Sources of Assurance

Hearsay and prejudice

We all base our views on one or both of these frail supports more than we like to admit. Prejudice is the wider of the two terms, for while any assurance based on hearsay without further validation may rightly be criticized as prejudiced, there are prejudices which are independent of hearsay, having their origin either in the temperamental predispositions of a given individual (What Francis Bacon has called Idols of the Cave[2]) or in the commonly shared predispositions that arise from the very character of the human understanding (what Bacon calls Idols of the Tribe). The latter kind of prejudice is subtler and therefore harder to eliminate; for, in Bacon's words, "the human understanding is like a false mirror, which, receiving rays irregularly, distorts and discolors the nature of things by mingling its own nature with it."

Prejudices arising from hearsay are called by Bacon Idols of the Market-place: they are the idols "formed by the intercourse and association of men with each other." Their source lies partly in the individual and tribal prejudices just mentioned, which are disseminated and given social solidarity by such intercourse. But there is a new factor that enters. For since it is by discourse that men associate with one another and exchange opinions, the errors of hearsay are greatly increased by the loose manner in which words are employed and the consequent inaccuracy of the ideas communicated. For "words, being commonly framed and applied according to the capacity of the vulgar, follow those lines of division which are most obvious to the vulgar understanding. And whenever an understanding of greater acuteness or a more diligent observation would alter those lines to suit the true divisions of nature, words stand in the way and resist the change."[3]

---
[2] Francis Bacon (1561-1626), *The Great Instauration,* Part II, "The New Organon." See Readings, pp. 80-91.
[3] Bacon, *op. cit.,* Sec. lix.

Confucius declared a first requirement of good government to be "the rectification of names." Such rectification falls within the province of *semantics*, the science of meaning; and it is an indispensable step in sound philosophical method.

Authority

Assurance based on authority should be distinguished from what is based on mere hearsay or prejudice. To accept any person, book, institution, or (it may be) supernatural revelation as authoritative means that we believe him or it to have good grounds for making statements in a certain sphere, which we ourselves lack. And rightly used authority is valuable and even indispensable. No one can verify for himself everything which he finds it useful to know: he appeals therefore to the testimony of men and of books which he supposes to possess a high degree of competence in their fields.

Of course we may be mistaken in attributing special competence in the field; which is to say, that what we take to be an authority is no real authority at all. Much contemporary advertising appeals to alleged authorities in bolstering the claims for its products; but whether the testimony thus given is really authoritative—i.e., based on firsthand, competent, and honest knowledge—or whether it is a matter of hearsay, snap judgment, and pecuniary stimulus, is for the wary consumer to judge. Advertising often makes the further implicit assumption that someone who is an acknowledged authority in one field is equally to be relied on in another—as when a golf champion or baseball star extols the superior merits of one brand of cigarettes. The fallacy is evident enough as soon as we look at it rationally, but the power of association is often strong enough to prevent reason from becoming active.

There is the error, too, into which many a reader falls, of attributing more authority to opinions printed in a book than to opinions of about the same objective validity which have not forced their way into print. What is printed in black and white looks so solid. From my own past experience I would predict that the words printed on these pages will be received more uncritically by a number of students than the same words were received by similar groups of students when published formerly on mimeographed sheets. Yet whatever degree of truth they may have or lack has not been altered by the passage from stencil to linotype.

Most important of all, for philosophical inquiry, is the role of authority with respect to the deepest questions that stir man's wonder. Can we rightly accept anyone's authority on questions concerning God, or human freedom of choice, or the intrinsic worth of anything of which we ourselves have intimate knowledge, or the best ultimate goals by which to live? Ideally we cannot, I think. In such matters every man must try to be his own philosopher: otherwise he is not functioning *as man*—he is wasting his human prerogative of being the animal who can think for himself. And yet in practice who of us can deny that he is affected in such matters by early home influences, by certain books, and by the opinions of his teachers, fellow students, and chance companions?

An opinion on existential matters which is proclaimed or accepted as authoritative and therefore not subject to critical examination is called a *dogma*. Three main types or spheres of dogmatic assertion may be noted: the religious, the political, and the metascientific. Religious dogmas are probably the easiest to recognize, for those who hold them usually admit that they are matters of faith, buttressed perhaps by revelation or ecclesiastical authority or a few stock arguments, and most such dogmas are explicitly formulated in the creed of one or another church. Political dogmas are easy to recognize when they are held by our opponents, civil or foreign; difficult when shared and taken for granted by all with whom we associate. But the dogmas hardest for many people to detect nowadays are those of the third class, arising from unwarranted extension of the concepts and hypotheses of the sciences. Properly considered, science has nothing to do with existential questions; what it does have to do with will be examined and defined in Chapters V and VI. But the prestige of science reaches farther than actual scientific procedures. Too often in popular writings the claim that "Science has proved this or that" is employed in the service of loose thinking and biased generalization. One of the philosopher's important critical tasks—and that is to say, the task of each individual who wishes to think about large matters with clarity and independence—is to distinguish authentic scientific discoveries and hypotheses from the metascientific dogmas and speculations that sometimes grow out of them. For example: To employ the theory of the electrical composition of the atom in order, on the one hand, to understand such a phenomenon as radioactivity and, on the other, to produce such a phenomenon as atomic fission, is scientific procedure and empirically justified. But to push on from there to the unlimited declaration that man and his purposes are "nothing but" various patterns of electrical energy is not science but irresponsible "scientizing." Again, the biological hypothesis of the evolution of species is a legitimately scientific one. If one were to conclude, however, that because men's ideas of God and their ideals of justice and universal brotherhood have had an evolutionary history they therefore lack objective validity, he would not be speaking as a scientist but as a scientizing metaphysician. Such illegitimate extensions of the thought-patterns of the sciences are the chief contemporary examples of what Bacon (with different applications in mind) called Idols of the Theatre—received systems of thought which "are but so many stage-plays, representing worlds of their own creation after an unreal and scenic fashion."

Observation

So far as it functions in producing assurance about any matter, observation is more than pure acquaintance as defined in Section i. What we commonly call observation involves some interpretation. This is proved by our speaking of certain observations as "erroneous"; whereas a pure datum of acquaintance cannot be erroneous, but only its interpretation. If you say, "I know that he is in town because I observed him sitting on his porch a short while ago," you are grounding belief upon observation, although it is possible that you may have mistaken your man.

Do we trust the observations of some senses more, on the whole, than those of others? The adage "Seeing is believing" testifies to the particular reliance we normally place in the sense of sight. But in cases where sight fails us (as in pitch-black darkness) or where its deliverances strike us as incredible (as in "seeing a ghost") we are likely to transfer our confidence to touch.

There is interpretation, which is to say implicit inference, in sight, no less than in the operations of the other senses, but as our visual interpretations are less subject to error, by and large, than our tactile, auditory, and olfactory interpretations, we habitually fail to notice their presence and regard the whole of a visual experience as if it were directly given—i.e., as if it were a datum of acquaintance. Compare the judgments, "I see a mouse," "I hear a mouse," and "I smell a mouse." The element of inference in the second and third judgments is evident, for we are accustomed to make mistakes in the interpretation of smell and sound. That odor in the cellar, or that scratchy noise in the walls, might perhaps have some other cause. When I actually *see* a mouse I feel much more assured of its presence, for I am not at all accustomed to hallucinations of that kind. All three statements represent combinations of direct acquaintance with inferential interpretation, but where the datum is visual the reliance upon the habitual and seemingly "natural" interpretation is usually much stronger.

We often apply the term "observation" to generalizations based upon a number of particular observations. To say, "I have *observed* that the temperature generally takes a sharp drop in the late afternoon," extends the meaning of "observe" in this way. In such observational generalizations two new kinds of error are to be guarded against: (*a*) Particularly when the generalization is a welcome one we are prone to overlook the "negative instances"—i.e., the exceptions, which would weaken or invalidate it. "The exception tests the rule"[4] is a good rule to remember. Or (*b*) it may be that our observations are not representative, that our samples have not been chosen fairly: as when someone condemns, say, all Lithuanians or all Peruvians because of unpleasant encounters with a few of them. His critical question ought to be: "Can there have been any constant factor in these encounters—something to do with my own attitude perhaps, or the stratum of society from which the samples were taken, or the kind of situation in which they found themselves at the time of being observed (frightened newcomers in a strange land, for instance)—to which the repetition of the unpleasant experience might logically be attributed?" Many unjust estimations of character are made because of such unrepresentative sampling. We describe a man as a dull companion on the basis of a number of meetings with him, but possibly he displays that character only when in our company.

Reason

A rationally self-evident proposition is one which it is impossible to doubt, provided its meaning is clearly understood. Consider the following propositions severally and see if you agree that each of them has this character of logical indubitability:

1. "The same thing cannot both exist and not exist at a given moment."
2. "A thing must either exist or not exist at a given moment."
3. "Quantities equal to the same quantity are equal to each other."

---

[4] The older wording of this adage, "The exception *proves* the rule," is frequently misused today, when the older meaning of "prove" as equivalent to "test" has been lost. To say that an exception can prove a rule in the modern sense of demonstrating that the rule is true, is of course silly.

4. "If A is larger than B and B is larger than C, then A is larger than C."

5. "If no elephants are invertebrates, then no invertebrates are elephants."

6. "If A is larger than B, then B is smaller than A."

7. "If something has color, it must have spatial extension."

8. "Every motion must have temporal duration."

9. "If I try to doubt my own existence, I prove that I exist by the very fact of my doubting."

Of these nine propositions (1) and (2) exemplify two fundamental exioms of logic: respectively the Law of Contradiction ("A is not both B and not-B") and the Law of Excluded Middle ("A is either B or not-B").[5] They are self-evidently true, provided we use the word "exists" univocally—that is, with a single meaning. Of course they do not exclude such a situation as that of Robin Hood, for instance, existing as a character in legend but not as an inhabitant of the real present-day world. The laws state nothing about what kind of existence any particular thing may have; they state simply two necessary relations between existing and not existing. Examples (3) and (4) illustrate the character of *transitivity* in relations: certain relations are such that we can discover from examination of their meaning alone their transitive function; i.e., if the relation holds between A and B and if it also holds between B and C, then it carries over from A to C and holds between them in that order. Transitive relations are of great importance in both mathematics and logic. Transitivity is inherent in the idea of series, or serial order, and therefore is at the basis of the number system. Transitivity characterizes the fundamental relation of *implication* and is therefore essential to the science of logic.

Propositions (5) and (6) are alike in another way. The for-

[5] In most books on logic these two axioms are generally supplemented by a third: the Law of Identity, A is A. However, in its abstract form it appears that "A is A" is a bare tautology. Its real utility is not descriptive but directive. It says, in effect: "The meaning of A *ought to be kept* the same throughout the entirety of a given logical context."

mer exemplifies the character of *symmetricality* in relations. We call a relation symmetrical when, if A bears that relation to B, B also bears it to A. Such inferences as "If A is near to B, then B is near to A" and "If C is remote from D, then D is remote from C" are discovered to be self-evident when the meaning of the relation expressed by "near to" or "remote from" is clearly understood. The inference in (6) is possible, on the other hand, because the relations expressed by "larger than" and "smaller than" are clearly seen, once their meaning is understood, to be inversely related to each other. The truth of (7) rests upon the necessary relation between color and spatial extension (whether both are real or both are imaginary); while that of (8) rests upon the necessary relation between any occurrence and the time in which it occurs.

Finally, the truth of (9) rests upon the logical principle of Presupposition by Denial—namely, that if it is impossible to deny a proposition without at the same time affirming it (whereas it *is* possible to affirm it without denying it) the truth of the proposition is thereby established.

The nine foregoing propositions are true *a priori:*[6] that is to say, they are independent of experience in the sense that *no possible experience can refute them.* An apriori truth, although it becomes realized in the experience of this or that individual, is not a hypothesis built out of the data of experience, but is *discerned as a property of a certain relation between meanings.* It is therefore self-evident to anyone who intellectually grasps the meanings and the relation between them.

Such intellectual understanding may be a single act, a single flash of rational insight, in which a certain relation between meanings—or, as in (4) and (6), a relation between relations

---

[6] The Latin phrase means literally, "from [what is true] before [experience]"—i.e., based on considerations that are independent of the particular findings of experience. When the term is used adverbially, as in this instance, it is customarily written as two words and italicized, since the usage is then closer to the original; when used adjectivally (as two lines below) it may more conveniently be treated as an ordinary English word, therefore written as one word not italicized.

between meanings—is instantaneously apprehended. This is probably the way in which your understanding of each of the nine given propositions has manifested itself; for the relational pattern which each of them represents is a simple one. The ability to grasp relations thus directly is called intuitive reason, or noetic reason (from the Greek *noêsis*, which was Plato's and Aristotle's word for the grasping of a truth by rational insight alone). The terms "rational intuition" and "rational noêsis" are sometimes employed. What all four terms signify is the direct act of discovering such truth as is implicit in a necessary meaning-relationship.

Where the relational pattern among meanings is more complex we often find ourselves obliged to think it out by a series of intellectual steps. The ability to do so is called *discursive reason*, and the activity of taking the necessary steps is called discursive reasoning. The science of valid relations by which such steps are guided is called *logic*. A conclusion reached by discursive reasoning is true with quite as much apriori certainty as a proposition grasped by direct rational intuition, provided the steps of the reasoning are logically valid. For instance, it is equally certain (A) that 2 plus 3 equals 5 and (B) that any six-digit number whose fourth, fifth, and sixth digits are the same respectively as the first, second, and third, must be divisible by 7, 11, and 13. The difference between (A) and (B) is not that the truth of the one is more certain than the truth of the other; it is that we can apprehend the truth of the first by an immediate act of rational intuition, whereas two steps of analysis are required for a grasp of the second. In the latter case we have first to realize that any number of the form *abcabc* (such as 463463, or 781781) is necessarily a multiple of 1001 (for every six-digit number which consists of a three-digit number occurring twice can be produced by multiplying 1001 by that three-digit number); and secondly we have to discover by actual multiplication (itself a discursive process) that 1001 is the product of 7, 11, and 13. Having taken these two steps separately we must then rationally intuit their logical connection. Putting them together we get a *syllogism*;[7] "Because every number of the form *abcabc* is a multiple of 1001 *and* because 1001 is a multiple of 7, 11, and 13, *therefore* every number of the form *abcabc* is a multiple of 7, 11, and 13."

Can a philosophy be built by rational method alone—that is, by a combination of intuitive reason and discursive reason exclusively? Not convincingly. Such philosophers as Thomas Aquinas, Descartes and Spinoza are called rationalists because in developing their systems of philosophy they have employed deduction at each step. Nevertheless their resultant philosophies are not identical with one another—and why? Because other elements than the purely rational are inevitably intermingled—personal insights, experiences, predispositions, and, in St. Thomas' case, explicit appeals to authority. Rational method is indispensable for philosophy, for without it a philosophy does not cohere and is merely a patchwork of loosely assembled and perhaps even contradictory opinions, but philosophy is more than a rational structure. A living philosophy must have flesh and blood as well as skeleton.

Empirical method, or the method of hypothesis

In the discovery and validation of facts that (*a*) have a public or potentially public character and (*b*) are not immediately evident, empirical method is indispensable. It is the method of experimental science, and in general may be conceived as consisting of the following five steps:[8]

1. *Formulation of a problem.* This of course is done upon the basis of previously made observations. But until the observations are envisaged in such a way as to suggest a problem to be solved and accordingly a certain procedure of investigation, empirical method cannot be said to have begun.

2. *Collection and classification of data.* The data must be

[7] From the Greek *syn*, "together," and *logos*, "rational proposition." Thus the word means "a logical conjunction of two propositions to yield a third, which is the conclusion." Cf. Glossary.

[8] The steps are substantially those given by John Dewey in *How We Think* (Heath, 1910).

chosen and arranged according to a standard of relevance, which is largely determined by the nature of the problem to be investigated. The same plant may be investigated by a gardener, whose interest lies in finding the right soil ingredients to improve its growth, and by a botanist interested in discovering its structural analogies to plants of another species. Both men's interests are of a scientific nature, but as their problems are different the kinds of datum which they emphasize will be somewhat different. In cases where the problem is such as to require a quantitative result the collection of data will involve, in some manner or other, enumeration.

3. *Formulation of a hypothesis, or of alternative hypotheses.* A hypothesis is a proposed solution of the problem. It is provisional. It may sometimes present itself to the investigator's mind in a sudden flash of insight, as is told of Archimedes' discovery of the amount of water displaced by floating bodies and of Newton's discovery of the general law of gravitation. But the circumstances of its discovery should not obscure the two fundamental conditions of its validity: (*a*) it is based upon previously assembled facts (by whatever mingling of conscious and subconscious associations in the mind of the scientist) and (*b*) it must not be accepted by reason of its own attractiveness or plausibility, but must be subjected to empirical verification.

4. *Deduction of consequences.* Where the hypothesis refers to a single event—e.g., that it will rain tomorrow—this fourth step is omitted; the hypothesis has simply to be verified by the event. But where a hypothesis has any degree of generality, its consequences in terms of concrete observations must be worked out by logical deduction. A hypothetical proposition is set up to express the relation of hypothesis to consequences: i.e., a proposition of the "If . . . then" type. *If* the law of gravitation applies to planetary motion, what observations should be possible? Newton proved mathematically that the gravitational pulls of the sun and of the neighboring planetary bodies together with the given planet's own force of inertia (i.e., its tendency to

move in a straight line at a uniform rate) must result in elliptical movements each of which he precisely described. Again, a detective engaged in solving a crime will doubtless frame several alternative hypotheses as to the identity of the guilty person. Assuming that he conducts the investigation rationally, he will then think out what logical entailments would follow from each in turn. *If* Mr. Black was the murderer *then it is entailed* that he must have been in that place and no other at a given hour, that he possessed or could have obtained possession of the knife with which the victim was stabbed, that he either left finger prints or had the foresight to rub them off or to wear gloves, that he had some kind of motive for the crime, etc.

5. *Verification.* Further observations or explorations are then requisite to discover whether the entailments thus deduced are true in actual fact. If even one of them can be proved false, and if it is an absolutely necessary entailment of the hypothesis, then the hypothesis is invalidated. An airtight alibi would establish Mr. Black's innocence: the only question would be whether the alibi were really as airtight as it looked. But what if all the entailments can be proved factually true? The hypothesis is then greatly strengthened, but not strictly proved. Obviously Mr. Black could have been near the scene of the crime, have possessed such a weapon, have had a grudge against the deceased, etc., without actually having committed the murder. Such evidence against him would be circumstantial: i.e., it is not conclusive, but is nevertheless cumulative, and a sufficient accumulation of it may convince a jury of Mr. Black's guilt "beyond a reasonable doubt."

When the hypothesis is more strictly a scientific one, on the other hand, and involves measurement, it may be the case that a positive verification of certain entailments of the hypothesis is sufficient to verify the hypothesis. This is because where measurement is involved the relation between the hypothesis and its entailment may become a relation of *logical equivalence*—which means that the entailment is mutual. Thus, when the existence of a planet outside the orbit of Neptune was still an unverified hypothesis it was necessary to compute just where in the sky the new planet would have to appear at a given time in order to account for the discrepancy between Neptune's actual orbit and the orbit which the gravitational force of the sun and the other planets would produce. The computation being made, telescopes were then directed on that spot, and the observation of a point of light there which exhibited planetary movements was sufficient to verify the theory conclusively.

It should be added that not all verification is directly observational. In the case of Newton's gravitational hypothesis, mentioned three paragraphs back, Newton's deductions showed that according to the hypothesis the planets should be moving in just such ellipses as Kepler had previously demonstrated to be the actual case. But of course neither Kepler nor anyone else can directly *observe* the planetary movements to be elliptical. Watch the course of Venus or Jupiter in the sky from night to night and see what their courses, relatively to the fixed stars, really look like. Kepler's description was a previously verified hypothesis, for which the requisite observations, deductions, and verifications had already been made. Many scientific discoveries, of course, interlock with other scientific discoveries in this way.

There are those who maintain that empirical method is the only valid method whereby truth can be established. Such a view generally goes by the name of *positivism*. For the purposes of valid scientific discovery and organization there is no need of going so far. It is enough to postulate that empirical method is the most generally valid (perhaps not the only valid) method for settling questions of fact (not necessarily all questions of "truth"). The meaning of this distinction will become clearer in Chapter VI.

Intuition

One kind of intuition has already been acknowledged—namely, *rational* intuition, where the truth of a proposition is validated solely by an examination of what the proposition *means*. The method of rational intuition produces results of unequivocal validity, but as the list on pp. 33-34 indicates, the propositions to which it is applicable are very much restricted in type.

There is a broader, looser, less firmly valid, but often very important and suggestive kind of intuition which does not proceed from strictly rational self-evidence but may be defined as a direct grasping of a situation by the whole mind, a final "sizing up" of evidences and values in a unitive mental commitment. The word "intuition," despite the partisan and crackpot uses to which it has sometimes been put, is doubtless the best word in English to denote that wholistic aspect of knowing. The word comes to us from the Latin verb *intueor*, "to look at," "to behold directly." What it connotes, however, is not a beholding of an object by the organ of vision but a beholding of a general situation by what we may call metaphorically "the eye of the mind." In practical matters one's conduct is often guided by intuitive judgments: here is a man who looks trustworthy, there is one who looks dishonest. Unfortunately such judgments are extremely prone to error. How, then, is intuition anything more than prejudice, and on what ground can it ever be accepted as contributing validly to human knowledge?

To answer these questions we must distinguish between *pre-ratiocinative* and *post-ratiocinative* intuition. To rely on intuition without any prior rational effort is ordinarily to make a snap judgment—which is to say, no real judgment at all but an arbitrary act of assertion. Whether all pre-ratiocinative intuitions are arbitrary, or whether some of them may, under special conditions, be deliverances from a higher source than man, is a question on which there will be differences of opinion. From the standpoint of purely human logic, at any rate, the deliverances of pre-ratiocinative intuition are notoriously unreliable.

Post-ratiocinative intuiting, on the other hand, is unavoidable as the crowning aspect of every process of discovery. When all the evidence is in hand, when all the rational deductions have been made, there is still the culminating step which may be expressed by the exclamation, "Oh, I see!" A train of reasoning must seem rational to the reasoner; the relevance and adequacy of the evidence must appear relevant and adequate to him;— otherwise he is accepting them irresponsibly, and what seems to be rational and empirical is but disguised hearsay. An authority, too,—whether person, book, or institution—must be accepted as authoritative by the believer's own intuitive judgment if it is to carry any validative weight. In short, intuition is important for the knowing process not in isolation but as a concomitant of the other contributing factors.

The six foregoing sources of intellectual assurance will have varying degrees of importance according to the nature of the problem considered. All of them, except the first—hearsay and prejudice—have a legitimate though limited place in a philosophic view of life, although different schools of philosophy distribute the emphasis differently. With respect to the various philosophical questions that are raised in the later chapters, a student will do wisely to consider not only what beliefs he holds but, more analytically and reflectively, how far those beliefs are grounded in one or another of these main sources of belief.

For Further Study

RENÉ DESCARTES, *Discourse on Method* (1637); *Meditations* (1641), especially I and II.
FRANCIS BACON, *Novum Organum* (1620).
JOHN LOCKE, *Essay Concerning Human Understanding* (1690), Bk. I.
WALTER LIPPMANN, *Public Opinion* (Macmillan, 1927).
WILLIAM ERNEST HOCKING, *Types of Philosophy* (Scribner, rev. ed., 1939), especially Part II.
A. E. MURPHY, *The Uses of Reason* (Macmillan, 1943).
WILLIAM PEPPERELL MONTAGUE, *The Ways of Knowing* (Macmillan, 1925), Part I.

Brand Blanshard, *The Nature of Thought* (Macmillan, 2 vols., 1939), Bk. III, "The Movement of Reflection."
John Laird, *Knowledge, Belief and Opinion* (Century, 1930).
A. C. Ewing, *Reason and Intuition* (Oxford University Press, 1942).
William Adams Brown, *Pathways to Certainty* (Scribner, 1931).
L. Susan Stebbing, *Thinking to Some Purpose* (London, 1939; reprinted in Penguin Books).

Questions for Discussion

1. Can there be pure acquaintance with a thing, without *any* knowledge about it? Can there be knowledge about a thing independently of any knowledge or acquaintance whatever? Consider what can be said on both sides of each question.

2. How adequate is the following explanation of how we form our ideas? Have you any ideas and beliefs which you would find difficult to explain in this manner? Do you detect any inconsistency between (*a*) and (*c*)?

  a) "Let us then suppose the mind to be, as we say, white paper, void of all characters, without any ideas; how comes it to be furnished? . . ."

  b) "First, our senses, conversant about particular sensible objects, do convey into the mind several distinct perceptions of things, according to those various ways wherein those objects do affect them; and thus we come by those ideas we have of yellow, white, heat, cold, soft, hard, bitter, sweet, and all those which we call sensible qualities; . . ."

  c) "Secondly, the other fountain, from which experience furnisheth the understanding with ideas, is the perception of the operations of our own minds within us, as it is employed about the ideas it has got."—John Locke, *op. cit.*, Bk. II, Chap. I.

3. What implicit warning is contained in the following statement? Can the danger be recognized and avoided in studying philosophy? Which of Bacon's Idols is involved here?

  "The understanding, like the eye, judging of objects only by its own sight, cannot but be pleased with what it discovers, having less regret for what has escaped it, because it is unknown."—John Locke, "Epistle to the Reader," in *op. cit.*

4. Examine the following statement by Francis Bacon of his qualifications as a philosopher. List them in what you think to be their order of importance for sound philosophizing.

"I found that I was fitted for nothing so well as for the study of Truth; as having a mind nimble and versatile enough to catch the resemblances of things (which is the chief point), and at the same time steady enough to fix and distinguish their subtler differences; as being gifted by nature with desire to seek, patience to doubt, fondness to meditate, slowness to assert, readiness to consider, carefulness to dispose and set in order; and as being a man that neither affects what is new nor admits what is old, and that hates every kind of imposture. So I thought my nature had a kind of familiarity and relationship with Truth."—From a fragment written about 1603, quoted by Gail Kennedy in his Odyssey Press edition of Bacon, Hobbes, Locke.

5. How far has your own intuition been active recently in such procedures as:

a) judging the evidence in your choice of courses?

b) accepting or rejecting the argument presented in a lecture or a book?

c) judging whether a certain course of action is or is not your duty?

d) judging whether a person, or book, or painting, or piece of music, which you initially dislike, is worth the trouble of further acquaintance?

CHAPTER III

Philosophical Method

SOCRATES used to declare that his only wisdom lay in knowing the limits of his own knowledge. Such, he added, is the one kind of wisdom possible to us mortals; for however extensive our knowledge may be it is as nothing compared to what we are ignorant of. Nor are the limits of knowledge merely quantitative. It is not a question primarily of how much we know, but of how modestly and self-critically, in short how *reflectively* we know it, and how ready and alert we are to accept every serious challenge to our supposed knowledge as new evidence and new insights become available.

i. Dialectic

Socrates gave to this reflective act the name *dialectic*—derived from a participle of a Greek verb meaning "to converse" and taken by Socrates to mean the *art of seeking truth through conversation*. Truth is never final, there is always another voice to be heard, and in reporting and developing the Socratic philosophy, therefore, Plato usually employed the form of a dialogue. Philosophic truth is not something to be captured in a formula, as a factual truth in chemistry for instance can be. It concerns experience as a whole, or some universal aspect of it. We seek to find out the truth, for instance, about the degree to which human selves can be independent of their material conditions; and by the very nature of human experience the evidence for beliefs about such a question can never be complete. For there is always a next moment, with new insights growing out of one's developing life and experience. As opposed to dogmatism, which slams the door upon truths or alleged truths already established, dialectic is a device for keeping the doors of the mind ajar and even finding new ones to open.

Three traits of dialectical method deserve particular attention. To think dialectically is (1) to examine differences with a view to discovering underlying identities; (2) to examine apparent identities with a view to discovering significant differences and so making relevant discriminations; (3) to see each given idea in larger context. The first and second of these traits are complementaries. The third is to some degree involved with them both; nevertheless it is important enough to be considered by itself. A passage from Plato's Dialogues, reporting Socrates' method of philosophizing, will be offered by way of exemplifying each of the three aspects in turn.

Identity in difference

The first passage is taken from Plato's Dialogue entitled *Meno*, where a question is raised about human excellence, for which the Greek word was *areté*, sometimes translated "virtue."

MENO. Can you tell me, Socrates, whether excellence can be taught, or is it acquired by practice rather than by teaching?

SOCRATES. I'm sorry to say I am ignorant of what you mean by "excellence," Meno; and if I do not know the meaning of it how can I know any of its attributes? So do, please, let me have your own definition of excellence.

MENO. Why, that's easy enough, Socrates. First of all, if you're asking about the excellence of a man, I would say it consists in this—that he should have the ability to manage public affairs in such a way as to benefit his friends, injure his enemies, and avoid suffering any injury himself. Or take the excellence of a woman: obviously it consists in the duties of keeping the household in order, taking care of everything indoors, and obeying her husband. Excellence in a child is something else again, and depends on whether it is a girl or a boy. Then there is the excellence of an elderly man, differing according as he is a freeman or a slave. In fact there are so many kinds of human excellence that one is never at a loss to say what excellence is. For the excellence of each one of us varies according to his age and mode of life, in each thing that we do. And the same holds true, I think, Socrates, of human failings.

SOCRATES. Decidedly I am in luck, Meno; for in seeking one excellence I have discovered a whole swarm of excellences in your keeping. Now, Meno, to carry on this figure of a swarm, suppose I were to ask you what is the real nature of the bee, and you replied that there are many different kinds of bees, and I retorted: Do you mean that it is by being bees that the many varieties differ from one another, or does their difference lie not in that but in something else—in their beauty or their size, for instance, or in some other such quality? Tell me, how would you answer my question?

MENO. I'd reply of course that they differ from one another in something else than the fact of being bees.

SOCRATES. And if I went on to say: Then tell me this please, Meno, what is the quality which, instead of differentiating them, unites them as one and the same thing, namely bees? You could give me an answer, couldn't you?

MENO. Yes.

SOCRATES. And similarly with human excellences. However many and various they are, they must all have some single common character whereby they are excellent, and which one would do well to keep in sight when expounding an answer to the question of what excellence really is. You grasp my meaning, don't you?

MENO. I think I understand you. But I don't see the point of the question as clearly as I should like.

SOCRATES. Take an analogy, Meno. Would you say it is only in the case of general excellence that there is one kind belonging to a man, another to a woman and so on, or do we find the same to be true of such qualities as health and size and strength? Do you think that there is one health for a man and another for a woman? Rather, does not health have a universal character wherever we find it, in a man or in anyone else?

MENO. I agree that health is one and the same thing, in man and in woman.

SOCRATES. Again, are not size and strength in similar case? If a woman is strong, the strength in her will have the same basic meaning (*eidos*) as it does in a man. That is to say, the strength of a man and the strength of a woman do not differ *as strength*. Or do you think otherwise?

MENO. By no means.

SOCRATES. Then will excellence, considered in its general character of excellence, be any different whether it is in a child or an old person, in a woman or in a man?

MENO. It strikes me though, Socrates, that this is not the same sort of case as the others.

SOCRATES. What! Were you not saying that a man's excellence is to manage public affairs well, and a woman's to manage a household?

MENO. I was.

SOCRATES. And is it possible to manage public affairs well, or a house, or anything at all, unless you manage it temperately and justly?

MENO. Surely not.

SOCRATES. So both the woman and the man must have the same qualities of justice and temperance if they are to be good?

MENO. Evidently.

SOCRATES. And what of a child? What of an elderly person? Can either of them be considered good if they are intemperate and unjust?

MENO. Surely not.

SOCRATES. But only if they are temperate and just?

MENO. Yes.

SOCRATES. Thus it turns out that all mankind are called good in the same basic sense; for they become good insofar as they acquire identical qualities.

MENO. So it would seem.

SOCRATES. And I suppose, if they had not the same excellence they would not be good in the same sense?

MENO. No.

SOCRATES. Then it appears that excellence is basically one and the same in all cases. . . .[1]

[1] Plato, *Meno*, 70A—73C (with omissions).

What does Socrates accomplish by such a dialectical maneuver? Let us see. At first sight it would seem that he is simply forcing Meno to define his principal term, *aretê*, human excellence. Even if that were all, it would be worth doing, for Meno had begun by asking how excellence is produced, and it is impossible to discuss a question significantly unless the meaning of its terms is understood.

But the act of definition here is something more than verbal—i.e., than recording how a word has been used or stipulating how it shall be used. It is an act of discovering identity in difference. The many instances of human excellence which Meno vaguely acknowledges (only two of which he has specified) are discovered to have some quality or qualities in common. One may take issue with Socrates on just what the common character is—Meno, in fact, does presently dispute the matter—but that there must be a common character is demonstrable. For unless the various qualities, functions, and relations called "excellent" had something in common to justify the use of an identical epithet, we would be guilty of equivocation—in the logician's strict sense of employing an identical sound or a written character for two distinct meanings. In every responsible use of a general word there is a common meaning attached to all instances to which the word is validly applied. And the discovery of general meanings exemplified in individual cases is one essential phase of dialectical procedure.

Difference in identity

The majority of men, Aristotle remarked, do not make careful distinctions. Partly this is due to intellectual sloth, a proneness to slipshod thinking; for in the celebrated metaphor of Heraclitus, men's souls tend ever to fall away from the active brightness of Fire into the messy dull inexactitude of Water and Mud. But there is another cause too. Where emotional interests are strongly involved there is a tendency to smudge over distinctions and use an emotively charged word as an unexamined instrument of attack and defense. In the emotional upheavals of Reformation Europe the words "heretic" and "Christian" were employed in violent attack and self-defense; in the emotional upheavals of twentieth century America such words as "radical" and "American" are often made to function analogously. But there is more than one way of being an American or a radical, even as there was more than one way of being a Christian or a heretic, and it is a basic requirement of clear thinking that such relevant differences be probed.

Plato's Dialogue the *Crito* represents Socrates in prison, condemned to death, discussing with his friend Crito the ethics of bribing the jailer in order to escape. One of Crito's arguments is an appeal to public opinion; he fears that he and Socrates' other friends will be thought remiss if their venerable leader is allowed to die without any attempt to save him. Socrates replies:

SOCRATES. My dear Crito, your zeal is most valuable if it should prove to be rightly directed; but if not, its very greatness would make it all the more troublesome. We must examine then whether we ought to do as you say or not; for I am still what I have always been—the kind of man who will not be persuaded to do anything but what on rational consideration appears best.

It used to be said, I think, by those of us who gave thought to what they were saying, that of men's opinions some ought to be highly esteemed and others not. Tell me please, Crito, don't you agree that we were right? For you in all human likelihood will not have to die tomorrow, and thus the exigencies of the moment will not lead you astray. Doesn't it strike you that we were right, then, in declaring that we ought not to esteem all human opinions but only some, and not those of all men but only of some? What would you say? Isn't this a sound principle?

CRITO. Yes, very sound.

SOCRATES. And isn't it the good opinions we should esteem, not the worthless ones?

CRITO. Yes.

SOCRATES. Now the good opinions are those of wise men, and the worthless are those of foolish men?

CRITO. Naturally.

SOCRATES. Then my excellent friend, we must not give any heed to what the multitude will say of us, but only to what will be said by one who has seriously reflected upon right and wrong, and to what is said by Truth herself.[2]

A subtler Socratic example of discovering differences within apparent identities sets in motion the central problem of Plato's *Republic*. The question has to do with the nature of justice, and one of the speakers, Polemarchus, has begun by defining it as "giving to each man his due." But there are different ways in which we can interpret a man's just due. Shall it be hereditary? Shall it be whatever an individual is able to get while keeping within the law? Shall it be determined by the extent of his social usefulness? Or is it best expressed by Louis Blanc's perfectionist formula, "From each according to his abilities, to each according to his needs"? Polemarchus' initial definition is not altogether worthless. It has the merit of recognizing that justice always connotes the idea of something being *due* a man; it implies a *norm*. So much is indisputable, but it is not enough. The ensuing argument of the *Republic* undertakes to discover what specific interpretation of dueness is the most acceptable.

Contextual amplification

The purpose of philosophy is to see things, so far as possible, in their wholeness. It involves the synoptic vision, which Lewis W. Beck has defined as "seeing everything in its bearing upon everything else, seeing things in their integral togetherness."[3] Naturally this is more than can ever actually be achieved; for no one's vision, unless God's, can comprehend the relatedness of all that is. Nevertheless the integral ideal points the way in which to direct our philosophic efforts; and we may distinguish two main aspects, or movements of thought, by which the building of a more integral philosophic standpoint takes place.

[2] Plato, *Crito*, 46B—48A (abridged).
[3] Lewis White Beck, *Philosophical Inquiry* (Prentice-Hall, 1952), p. 21.

1. *Intellectual consistency.* "Speculative philosophy," says Whitehead, "is the endeavor to frame a coherent, logical, necessary system of general ideas in terms of which every element of our experience can be interpreted."[4] The great systems of speculative philosophy—of Thomas Aquinas, Spinoza, and Hegel, for example—represent attempts, with patient thoroughness, to carry out this ideal. The most active principle in such an endeavor is the law of logical consistency, or non-contradiction. By this canon it is always illegitimate to hold two opinions which contradict each other. Either let one or the other of the opinions be renounced, or else find some way of reformulating and reinterpreting the conflicting views, establishing a new context in which they are shown to be mutually consistent.

The first of these methods—that of renunciation—is exemplified in Plato's *Phaedo*, where it has been propounded (p) that man's soul is a harmony of his bodily functions, and (q) that the soul is immortal. Socrates discloses the mutual inconsistency of these two propositions, p and q, by reminding his companions that a musical harmony, far from outlasting the instrument that produced it, dies away while the instrument lasts. To believe that the soul is a harmony produced by the body and to believe it immortal are logically inconsistent, and in the Dialogue the Pythagorean notion of the soul as a harmony is therefore dropped.

The second method—that of reconciliation—is exemplified by Thomas Aquinas' reconciliation of man's free will with God's foreknowledge of what man will choose. If another finite person could foreknow with perfect accuracy and certainty what I shall choose in the future, it follows by clear logic that I would not then be free to choose otherwise. In order to retain both doctrines —free will and divine foreknowledge—Aquinas postulates that the relation of an infinite being to time is radically different from the relation of a finite being to time. Infinite knowledge, being unlimited, would not limit the possibilities of future choice and realization as a finite knowledge of them would do.

[4] Alfred North Whitehead, *Process and Reality* (Macmillan, 1929), p. 4

2. *Vital consistency.* A philosophical belief must be consistent not only with other philosophical beliefs that are held, but also with one's actions, or at any rate with one's attempted program of action. In moral matters inconsistency between word and deed, or attempted deed, is hypocrisy; and we would have little respect for a man who talked much about justice while refusing to arbitrate with his employees or give heed to his neighbor's complaints, or who talked much about liberty and human rights while maligning and intimidating those who held widely different views from his own. When Socrates is reminding Crito of the principle they had formerly agreed on —that the opinions of wise men only, and not of the multitude, should be taken as guide—he adds: "Used we to be right in saying so before I was condemned to die, and has it now become evident that we were talking irresponsibly all the while, arguing for the sake of argument, and indulging in meaningless word-play?" The great crises of life put one's philosophy to the severest test; we have then to discover how genuine is our loyalty to the doctrines we like to profess.

In a broader way the criterion of vital consistency is applicable to metaphysical doctrines also. What good is a philosophy that makes no difference in the general quality and temper of one's life? Such was the question by which the voluntarist Nietzsche, the pragmatist William James, and more recently such existentialist philosophers as Jaspers, Marcel, and Sartre, have attacked the barrenness of vacuum-bred theorizing. More specifically, think of the problem of vital consistency in holding so uncompromising a doctrine as behavioristic determinism, or as solipsism. The behavioristic view that the human organism is really just a highly complex mechanism can be presented as a logical theory free from theoretical contradictions, but who either can or would want to act on that assumption throughout each day? Solipsism—the belief that everything I experience, persons and things alike, is simply my continuing dream, with no substantial existence of its own—can be accepted without contradiction as a theoretical possibility. But in practice no one acts upon it outside of a lunatic asylum. A consistency that is purely intellectual, not vital also, is too barren, too chronically abstract to be taken seriously as one's chosen philosophy.

From another standpoint, and seen in contemplative rather than practical perspective, the law of vital consistency takes the form of *the law of plenitude*—that aspects of reality are potentially infinite, and always more than any theory can specify. Intellectual, theoretical consistency is never achieved except at the cost of exclusion. The theorist tends to ignore or to undervalue those aspects of things which do not fit into his intellectual scheme. But life and experience are continually presenting us with something more than *any* theory, however comprehensive, is able to specify. A philosophical mind will be constantly alert to such evidences of ontological plenitude—such surplusages of the actual over the indicated. To recognize the limitations of a theory in this way is not necessarily to discredit the theory, but merely to specify its applicable range and thus to set the mind free to adopt alternative perspectives whereby the deliverances of experience may be envisaged and interpreted differently.

ii. Toward a Critical Metaphysics

Every problem, and likewise every term and proposition employed in stating the problem, has a certain *range of reference.* That is to say, an inquiry must be limited in scope; if it were not, it would be meaningless. To discuss anything satisfactorily we must know what is relevant and what is irrelevant to the subject under discussion; and this double aspect of acceptance and rejection is summarized by Spinoza's axiom, *Determinatio est negatio,* which can be paraphrased: "To say definitely what a thing is, is at the same time to say what it is not."

Realms of discourse

The range of reference of a group of related problems may be called their realm of discourse. Thus all problems concerning prices and costs, profits and losses, rents and mortgages and investments, fall within the economic realm of discourse; problems concerning the causal relations and mathematical correlations of space-time events fall within the physical realm of discourse; problems concerning the choice between good and evil, and the standards of right and wrong by which it is to be guided, fall within the ethical realm of discourse. Even though the boundary lines are not always clear and there is a great deal of overlapping, shifting, and vagueness in the relation between one realm and another, it is important to make our distinctions as firm as the subject matter and the context of discussion allow. To define the realm of discourse of a problem is simply a more formal and resolute way of knowing what is being spoken about.

A single concrete event may give rise to several types of inquiry, and thereby open up several realms of discourse. Suppose that a murder has been committed. As a step in his investigation of the crime a detective may have to discover the force and direction of the projected bullet. His problem, to that extent, falls within the realm of physics. Physical considerations are subsidiary, however; they are important only as means to the discovery of who fired the shot. Another group of problems fall within the realm of psychiatry: the murderer's motives, together with the previous experiences and acts, impulses, and repressions that may have contributed to them. These considerations, again, are quite secondary so far as the administration of public justice is concerned. The judge and jury must confine their attention to the nature of the act that has been committed, the identity of its perpetrator, and the penalty required by statute law. Their deliberations must take place primarily within the legal realm of discourse. Over and above all such special considerations an observer at the trial may find himself observing the accused as a fellow man, brooding upon the tragedy of his downfall, and speculating upon the kind of universe in which some men have so much more difficult a lot than others. These four directions of inquiry might be supplemented by others—the economic for example, and again the theological—but at all events they illustrate the way in which several overlapping realms of discourse may be opened up as ways of reflecting upon a simple concrete event or situation.

The meaning of metaphysical

Now since it is possible to be interested in several realms of discourse at once, questions may arise concerning their interrelations. Questions of this kind are called *metaphysical*; any reply that is formulated in answer to such a question is called a metaphysical judgment; and the embracing realm of discourse constituted by such questions is called metaphysics. Aristotle has demonstrated the need of metaphysics—or "first philosophy" as he called it—in the following passage:

> As there is a single science pertaining to whatever is healthful, so too in all analogous instances. For although the unity of a science need not consist in investigating all such objects as fall completely under a single definable concept, yet at the very least there must be some fundamental respect in which a single concept can be said to apply to them all. Clearly then, it belongs to a single science to take whatever *is* and study it solely under the aspect of its being. Now knowledge is always principally concerned with what is primary—i.e., with that on which other aspects depend and by which they are defined. If "essential thinghood" (*ousia*, sing.) has this sort of primacy, it must be of things-in-their-essential-character (*ousiai*, plur.) that the philosopher is to grasp the principles and explanations.[5]

While Aristotle's demonstration of the necessity of metaphysics is as valid as ever, we are inclined today to interpret "essence" and "essential" somewhat more flexibly than he was willing to do. What is essential and primary to a given inquiry depends largely upon the purposes which underlie it. The essential qualities of a landscape are one thing for a farmer, an-

[5] Aristotle, *Metaphysics*, Book Gamma (IV), Chap. ii.

other (though not totally different) for a painter, and yet another for a real-estate operator. The task of metaphysics must still be, as it was for Aristotle, to inquire into the being, the essence, the reality of each thing, but with the important qualification that what we conceive to be real and essential may vary somewhat with the total relevant context.

Consequently the question on which metaphysics was traditionally supposed to rest—"What is the ultimate nature of reality?"—will have to be modified. There are usually several senses in which a thing is said to be real, and a choice among them is likely to be somewhat arbitrary at best. Which is more real—the white chalk marks on the blackboard or the pure geometrical circle whose circumference has no thickness and whose radii are all exactly equal? One's answer (if he is not precommitted to some metaphysical theory) will depend on whether his task is to clean the blackboard or to solve the problem. What is "the real man"? Is he a bundle of reflex-mechanisms, or a stream of consciousness, or an economic unit whose services are worth just so much in a given market, or a citizen freely participating in a community of fellow citizens, or the creature and child of a divine Father, or an illusory individuation of the World Spirit? Every one of these answers has been seriously given by one thinker or another. Shall we be so immodest as to declare with finality that one of them is true and fundamental, the others false or derivative? Such has been the procedure of certain metaphysicians, and because their doctrines have often seemed arbitrary and mutually destructive, many people have superficially concluded that metaphysics is a worthless study. It is only against dogmatic metaphysics, however, that such a stricture is deserved—only against metaphysical judgments of the type, "x alone is real." The notion of metaphysics proposed and developed in this book is, on the contrary, *critical*.

Critical metaphysics may be defined as the study and comparison of the major realms of discourse which the human intelligence encounters, with a view to discovering their individual natures and their interrelations one with another. Now to understand the nature of a realm of discourse it is necessary to consider two things in particular: (1) the meaning of the basic terms which it employs, and (2) the truth-range of the basic propositions which it asserts. Let us examine these procedures separately.

Primary terms of discourse

In every realm of discourse, so far as it can be analyzed and expounded by logical method, there are certain fundamental or root terms on which the system of meanings constituting the realm of discourse in question is built. In mathematics, for instance, *unity* is a primary term, and the notions of *addition* and *equality* furnish primary relational terms by which, from unity, the system of integers is built up. In classical physics the terms *length*, *time*, and *mass* are fundamental. In contemporary physics more emphasis is given to events and intervals in an n-dimensional continuum; this modifies, although it does not wholly negate, the older concepts. In ethics there are the fundamental notions of *good* and *evil*, *right* and *wrong*, *ends* and *means*—some schools of thought preferring to take one pair as fundamental and some another.

Ordinarily these root terms, or at least some of them, are indefinable; other terms being defined by means of them. The mathematician does not define unity. He exemplifies it, by drawing his instances of unity from widely different kinds of experience. When the three terms *unity* ("1") *addition* ("+"), and *equality* ("=") are understood without formal definition by seeing them exemplified in a variety of ways, it then becomes possible to set up the formal definitions:

$$2 = 1 + 1,$$
$$3 = 2 + 1,$$
$$4 = 3 + 1, \text{ etc.}$$

In realms of discourse where the method and vocabulary are less formalized, and where human valuations play a larger role, there is likely to be some breadth of choice as to which of

PHILOSOPHICAL METHOD

the fundamental terms are taken as primary and undefined. Thus the main schools of ethics can be classified according to whether they set up the pair of terms *good* and *bad* (*evil*) or the pair of terms *right* and *wrong* as primary. The deontological type of ethics begins with *right* and *wrong* as the primary antithesis, exemplifiable, but indefinable, and relegates other ethical terms to a secondary place. The teleological type of ethics starts out with *good* and *bad* as primary notions, then defines right and wrong as applicable to actions which tend to produce good and bad respectively. Other types of ethical analysis may postulate some other pair of terms to be primary—e.g., pleasure vs. pain (hedonism), friend vs. foe (the Nazi philosopher Carl Schmidt), the strong, whole, healthy character, vs. the weak, divided, and sickly character (Nietzsche)—and insist that other ethical terms have valid meaning only so far as they can be derived from these.

Is it possible to push analysis to the limit and specify the root terms, the basic indefinables, of metaphysics itself? Many philosophers, starting with Plato in *The Sophist*, have attempted to say what are the ultimate categories of all knowledge. Perhaps as good an answer as any is that of Charles Renouvier, who in his *Essais de critique genérale* listed nine such categories: *relation* (which is at once the most general category and an abstract property of all the others), *number, spatial position, temporal succession, quality, becoming, causality, inherent tendency* (the telic principle), and *personhood*. Still, the list is not immune from criticism, and probably the best way of dealing with the problem of categories is not to seek a completely satisfactory list of them, but rather to be ready in dialectical reasoning to recognize categorial[6] differences and interrelations wherever they appear.

Postulates

As in each realm of discourse certain primary *terms* must be accepted without *definition*, so too certain primary *propositions*

---
[6] See Glossary under "Category."

must be accepted without *proof*. A few examples from several fields are as follows.

From mathematics: "For every finite value of x there is a finite value $x + 1$." "In the addition of quantities the order in which they are added is immaterial."

From traditional physics: "To every action there is always an equal and opposite reaction."

From relativity physics: "The trajectory of a light-ray is a geodesic of space."

From empirical science generally: "There is a uniformity among events, either absolute or approximate, such that probable predictions of future events can be made on the basis of events known to have occurred in the past."

From depth psychology: "There are unconscious as well as conscious states of mind."

From logic: "The relation of implication is transitive but not symmetrical." That is to say, if a implies b and b implies c, then a implies c; but if a implies b it does not follow that b implies a.

From ethics: "Some actions, or some results of action are better than others."

When such primary propositions appear to be self-evident, in the sense that it would be self-contradictory to deny them, they are called axioms. However, certain propositions which have seemed axiomatic at one time may later be challenged when looked at in a different intellectual perspective. Because of this unsettling fact there has been a tendency in recent years to be more cautious and regard all primary propositions as postulates, leaving undecided the question of whether in the last resort it would be theoretically possible to doubt them. Of the examples just given it seems clear that only the mathematical and logical postulates lay any firm claim to being axiomatic; and perhaps it would even be theoretically possible—as a game if nothing more—to set up a number system having a finite limit.

iii. The Value and Limits of Dialectic

It is doubtless clear by now that every realm of discourse can have meaning only by being somehow limited. And the same is true of every science, every theory, every proposition, and every idea that can be thought, experienced, or uttered. An idea is always about something *rather than* something else, a proposition asserts this *rather than* that, and a science involves one methodology and vocabulary *rather than* another. This is essentially what Spinoza meant by his principle quoted at the outset of the preceding section. Dialectic may now be redefined as the art of making such limitations explicit, thus enabling the mind to transcend them.

All genuine reasoning—as distinguished from mental repetition of an argument that has been learned—is dialectical to a large extent. Such reasoning is never purely linear, starting with clearly defined presuppositions and moving by distinct steps to a logically entailed conclusion. After the act of reasoning has achieved its goal, it can be expounded as consisting of formal relationships, and the discovery of that formal structure is necessary in testing whether or not the reasoning has been logically valid. But if we conceive reasoning in this way we are looking more to the results than to the active process.

Ethical dialectic

In thinking out a responsible course of action the dialectical procedure is usually evident. Shall I sacrifice a good dinner in order to afford to attend a concert? Suppose I wish both to dine in luxury and to attend the concert but that the present state of my purse prevents my doing both. How shall I choose between them? No simple "calculus of pleasures" such as Bentham recommended will serve, for the pleasures offered by the two courses of action differ not merely in degree but in kind. To deliberate between them consists largely in trying to imagine the two kinds of pleasurable experiences vividly and specifically, and to compare them with each other. One's imagination operates by dramatic projection: we envisage ourselves within each experience separately, attending to the goods that each one offers and then, by comparison with the other, what sacrifices it entails.

Scientific dialectic

Scientific reasoning, too, is dialectical, so far as in gathering data to establish a hypothesis the hypothesis is thereby given additional significance. Where an elementary student in a laboratory is working under direction, he doubtless knows pretty much in advance what sort of results he is expected to find, and his mental processes may be guided largely by the laboratory manual. Where, on the other hand, an authentic scientific discovery is made, there is not merely the grafting of an added fact on to preëxistent knowledge; there is also a newly critical attitude formed toward some aspect of the preëxistent knowledge itself. The apple which, according to legend, Newton saw drop was not for him merely a new fact; in any usual sense it was hardly a new fact at all. It seems unlikely that Newton first watched the apple drop and then reasoned by successive logical steps to his formulation of the law of gravitation. If such were the case, why had not Newton recognized the law as operative in previous instances of falling bodies that he had seen? From the standpoint of strict logic the law of gravitation is exemplified as much by one falling body as by another. What uniquely characterized the celebrated discovery was not a group of implicit logical relations, since these had been present in countless past situations without any discovery resulting; but a dialectical outreach of the mind, by which Newton became critical toward some of the presuppositions that had previously hedged and limited the kinds of theories it would occur to him to build.

Criticism of criticism

While we may perhaps grant that all reasoning is to some extent dialectical, it may be wondered how far philosophical thinking is genuine and how far it is merely a rationalization of certain habits, prejudices, and—in the case of a science—sets of postulates. How far can the dialectical method in philosophy be thoroughgoing? For must not every philosophical inquiry be limited by its own presuppositions? Hence, is not dialectical method self-contradictory at bottom, since it proceeds by criticizing this or that group of presuppositions while tacitly making presuppositions of its own? At the very least it is presupposing the validity of a critical approach to problems. And in practice it is likely to presuppose much more. Theological dogmas are critically examined often because we are predisposed to believe in the superior validity of scientific method; political conservatism is examined dialectically by one who takes for granted the superior virtues of a more liberal attitude; and in general we can recognize the prejudices of our neighbor only when they are set in relief by the different kind of prejudices that propel our own thinking. That being the case, is not dialectical method always somewhat partisan? And is not therefore the philosophical enterprise, with its claim to examine all points of view with dialectical objectivity, largely an illusion?

Well, granted that every exercise of philosophical criticism makes some presuppositions or other of its own, it is usually possible with care and patience to find out what these are, and thus, even without wholly discarding them, to recognize their limitations. I shall go on assuming that there is really an external world, that other persons besides myself have real existence, and that courage, justice, and good-will are intrinsically better than cowardice, tyranny, and hate; yet I can try to understand the contrary views held by subjectivists, solipsists, and totalitarian dictators respectively. To be philosophical is not to abandon all convictions; it is to know what one's really indispensable convictions are, and how they are related to the world in which we live; it is to find out why they are indispensable, and thus to distinguish them from other opinions which we are ready, if need be, to renounce.

For Further Study

WILLIAM ERNEST HOCKING, *Types of Philosophy* (Scribner, rev. ed., 1939), Chaps. III, VIII, IX, XI, XXXVII.

SUSANNE K. LANGER, *Philosophy in a New Key* (Harvard University Press, 1942; reprinted in Mentor Books).

A. C. EWING, *The Fundamental Questions of Philosophy* (Macmillan 1952), Chaps. II, III.

CLIFFORD BARRETT, *Philosophy* (Macmillan, 1935), Chap. II, especially the second half.

LOUIS O. KATTSOFF, *Elements of Philosophy* (Ronald Press, 1953), Chaps. II, III.

ERNST CASSIRER, *The Problem of Knowledge* (Yale University Press, 1950).

GUSTAV E. MUELLER, *Philosophy of Our Uncertainties* (University of Oklahoma Press, 1936).

Questions for Discussion

1. After studying the passages from Plato's *Meno* and *Crito* in Section i, what importance do you see in discovering hidden identities? in discovering hidden differences? How would one or both of the methods be employed in clarifying the meanings of:

a) nature?

b) justice?

c) God?

2. Read the excerpt from Descartes' *Discourse on Method*, given on pp. 91-99. Estimate fairly both the strength and weakness of the method of philosophizing which he proposes.

3. What is the danger of having intellectual consistency without vital consistency? Is there any comparable danger when the relation is reversed?

4. "It is clear that fixed concepts may be extracted by our thought from mobile reality; but there are no means of reconstructing the mobility of the real with fixed concepts."—HENRI BERGSON, *An Introduction to Metaphysics*.

What does this statement suggest about the limitations of:

a) everyday thought?

b) science?

c) philosophy?

5. In the study of *history,* can you point out one or more primary terms of discourse? one or more primary postulates?

6. How much truth and error do you judge there to be in each of the following statements? Why?

a) "What is real is rational, and what is rational is real."—Hegel.

b) "The last proceeding of reason is to recognize that there is an infinity of things which are beyond it."—Pascal.

c) "We know truth, not only by the reason, but also by the heart, and it is in this last way that we know first principles; and reason, which has no part in it, tries in vain to impugn them."—Pascal.

d) "The unrest which keeps the never stopping clock of metaphysics going is the thought that the non-existence of this world is just as possible as its existence."—Schopenhauer.

Readings for Part One

On Philosophical Wisdom*

ARISTOTLE

ALL MEN have a natural desire for knowledge. An indication of this is the joy we take in our perceptions; which we cherish for their own sakes, quite apart from any benefits they may yield us. It is especially true of sight, which we tend to prefer to all the other senses even when it points to no action, and even indeed when no action is in prospect; a preference explained by the greater degree to which sight promotes knowledge by revealing so many differences among things.

The evolution of reason

But while the other animals live by means of impressions and memories, with only a small amount of general experience, the human race lives also by art and reasoning. Memory is what gives rise to experience in men, for it is by having repeated memories of the same thing that our ability to have a single whole experience arises. At first sight experience seems much like knowledge and art, but it is truer to say that experience is the means through which science and art can be acquired; thus Polus rightly declares that "experience has produced art, inexperience chance."

No doubt the first discoverer of any art that went beyond man's ordinary sense-perceptions was admired by his fellows, not merely for whatever utility his discoveries may have had, but because his wisdom seemed to set him above others. And as further arts were discovered, some supplying the necessities of life, others its leisure

---

* From Aristotle (384-322 B.C.), *Metaphysics*, Bk. I, Chaps. i and ii; Bk. II, Chap. i; with omissions. Based on *Aristotle: Selections*, trans. and edited by Philip Wheelwright (Odyssey Press, rev. ed., 1951).

moments, the discoverers of the latter were always considered wiser than the discoverers of the former, because theirs was a sort of knowledge that did not aim at utility. The next step, when all such discoveries had been made, was the discovery of the sciences that do not aim either at pleasure or at the necessities of life; and this first occurred in those places where men enjoyed leisure: which explains why the mathematical disciplines first arose in Egypt, because in that country the priestly caste was permitted to live in leisure.

The nature of wisdom

The aim of our present discussion is to inquire about wisdom, which is generally understood to deal with the basic determining factors and initiating principles. For the man of experience is agreed to be wiser than one who is limited to mere sense-awareness, the artist than the man of experience, the master-craftsman than the manual worker, and the contemplative sciences to partake of more wisdom than the productive sciences. From this progressive relation it becomes clear that wisdom is that kind of knowledge which concerns ultimate principles and reasons-why.[1]

The motive of philosophy

It is through wonder that men begin to philosophize, whether in olden times or today. First their wonder is stirred by difficulties of an obvious sort, and then gradually they proceed to inquire about weightier matters, like the changes of the moon, sun and stars, and the origin of the universe. Now the result of wonderment and perplexity is to feel oneself ignorant. If, then, it was to escape ignorance that men began to philosophize, it is evident that they were pursuing this sort of study in order to know and not from any motive of utility. An incidental confirmation of this view is that thinking began to be undertaken as a pastime and recreation at a period when all the main necessities of life had been supplied. Clearly, then, knowledge of the kind that is under discussion is not sought for the sake of any external advantage; but rather, as we call that man free who exists in and for himself and not for another, so we pursue this as the one free and independent study, because it is the only one that exists for the sake of itself.

[1] See footnote on "reasons-why," p. 214.

The paradox of philosophy

Let it be noted, however, that the acquisition of such knowledge leads to a point of view which is in a way the reverse of that from which we began. Everyone begins, as we remarked earlier, by wondering that things should be as they are—whether the movements of marionettes, or the solstices, or the incommensurability of the diameter of a square with its side: because it seems remarkable to those who have not yet fathomed the reason-why, that there should exist no smallest common unit by which any two lengths could be measured. But in the end we come to the opposite point of view—which moreover is the better one, for surely the adage that "second thoughts are better thoughts" is most applicable in these cases where learning takes place. From the new standpoint there is nothing a geometer would so greatly wonder at as if the diameter *were* to be found commensurable.

The study of philosophic truth is difficult in one respect, easy in another. This is shown by the double fact that while no individual can grasp truth adequately, yet collectively we do not entirely fail. Each individual makes some report on the nature of things, and while this by itself contributes very little to the inquiry a combination of all such reports amounts to a good deal. That is to say, in so far as truth can be likened to the proverbial big door which even the poorest marksman cannot miss, it is easy; but the fact that we can know a large general truth and still not grasp some particular part of it shows how difficult truth-seeking really is. However, there are roughly two ways of accounting for a difficulty, and it may be that in the present case the reason for it lies not in the subject-matter but in ourselves, and that as bats' eyes are dimmed by daylight so the power of reason in our souls is dimmed by what is intrinsically most self-evident.

The Spirit of Philosophy*

WILLIAM JAMES

PHILOSOPHY is defined in the usual scholastic textbooks as "the knowledge of things in general by their ultimate causes, so far as natural reason can attain to such knowledge." This means that explanation of the universe at large, not description of its details, is what philosophy must aim at; and so it happens that a view of anything is termed philosophic just in proportion as it is broad and connected with other views, and as it uses principles not proximate, or intermediate, but ultimate and all-embracing, to justify itself. Any very sweeping view of the world is a philosophy in this sense, even though it may be a vague one. It is a *Weltanschauung*, an intellectualized attitude towards life. Professor Dewey well describes the constitution of all the philosophies that actually exist, when he says that philosophy expresses a certain attitude, purpose, and temper of conjoined intellect and will, rather than a discipline whose boundaries can be neatly marked off.

To know the chief rival attitudes towards life, as the history of human thinking has developed them, and to have heard some of the reasons they can give for themselves, ought to be considered an essential part of liberal education. Philosophy, indeed, in one sense of the term is only a compendious name for the spirit in education which the word "college" stands for in America. Things can be taught in dry dogmatic ways or in a philosophic way. At a technical school a man may grow into a first-rate instrument for doing a certain job, but he may miss all the graciousness of mind suggested by the term liberal culture. He may remain a cad, and not a gentleman, intellectually pinned down to his one narrow subject, literal, unable to suppose anything different from what he has seen, without imagination, atmosphere, or mental perspective.

* From William James (1842-1910), *Some Problems of Philosophy* (published posthumously by Longmans, Green in 1911). Reprinted by courtesy of the publisher.

Philosophy, beginning in wonder, as Plato and Aristotle said, is able to fancy everything different from what it is. It sees the familiar as if it were strange, and the strange as if it were familiar. It can take things up and lay them down again. Its mind is full of air that plays round every subject. It rouses us from our native dogmatic slumber and breaks up our caked prejudices. Historically it has always been a sort of fecundation of four different human interests —science, poetry, religion, and logic—by one another. It has sought by hard reasoning for results emotionally valuable. To have some contact with it, to catch its influence, is thus good for both literary and scientific students. By its poetry it appeals to literary minds; but its logic stiffens them up and remedies their softness. By its logic it appeals to the scientific; but softens them by its other aspects, and saves them from too dry a technicality. Both types of student ought to get from philosophy a livelier spirit, more air, more mental background. "Hast any philosophy in thee, Shepherd?"—this question of Touchstone's is the one with which men should always meet one another. A man with no philosophy in him is the most inauspicious and unprofitable of all possible social mates.

The Relation of Philosophy to the Sciences*

C. D. BROAD

A VERY LARGE number of scientists will begin such a book as this with the strong conviction that Philosophy is mainly moonshine, and with the gravest doubts as to whether it has anything of the slightest importance to tell them. I do not think that this view of Philosophy is true, or I should not waste my time and cheat my students by trying to teach it. But I do think that such a view is highly plausible, and that the proceedings of many philosophers have given the general public some excuse for its unfavorable opinion of Philosophy. I shall therefore begin by stating the case against

* From C. D. Broad, *Scientific Thought* (Harcourt, Brace, 1923; Humanities Press, 1949). Reprinted by courtesy of Humanities Press.

Philosophy as strongly as I can, and shall then try to show that, in spite of all objections, it really is a definite science with a distinct subject-matter. I shall try to show that it really does advance and that it is related to the special sciences in such a way that the cooperation of philosophers and scientists is of the utmost benefit to the studies of both.

The case against philosophy

I think that an intelligent scientist would put his case against Philosophy somewhat as follows. He would say: "Philosophers discuss such subjects as the existence of God, the immortality of the soul, and the freedom of the will. They spin out of their minds fanciful theories, which can neither be supported nor refuted by experiment. No two philosophers agree, and no progress is made. Philosophers are still discussing with great heat the same questions that they discussed in Greece thousands of years ago. What a poor show does this make when compared with mathematics or any of the natural sciences! Here there is continual steady progress; the discoveries of one age are accepted by the next, and become the basis for further advances in knowledge. There is controversy indeed, but it is fruitful controversy which advances the science and ends in definite agreement; it is not the aimless wandering in a circle to which Philosophy is condemned. Does this not very strongly suggest that Philosophy is either a mere playing with words, or that, if it has a genuine subject-matter, this is beyond the reach of human intelligence?"

Our scientist might still further strengthen his case by reflecting on the past history of Philosophy and on the method by which it is commonly taught to students. He will remind us that most of the present sciences started by being mixed up with Philosophy, that so long as they kept this connection they remained misty and vague, and that as soon as their fundamental principles began to be discovered they cut their disreputable associate, wedded the experimental method, and settled down to the steady production of a strapping family of established truths. Mechanics is a case in point. So long as it was mixed up with Philosophy it made no progress; when the true laws of motion were discovered by the experiments and reasoning of Galileo it ceased to be part of Philosophy and began to develop into a separate science. Does this not suggest that the subject-matter of Philosophy is just that ever-diminishing fragment of the universe in which the scientist has not yet discovered laws, and where we have therefore to put up with guesses? Are not such guesses the best that Philosophy has to offer; and will they not be swept aside as soon as some man of genius, like Galileo or Dalton or Faraday, sets the subject on the sure path of science?

Should our scientist talk to students of Philosophy and ask what happens at their lectures, his objections will most likely be strengthened. The answer may take the classical form: "He tells us what everyone knows in language that no one can understand." But, even if the answer be not so unfavorable as this, it is not unlikely to take the form: "We hear about the views of Plato and Kant and Berkeley on such subjects as the reality of the external world and the immortality of the soul." Now the scientist will at once contrast this with the method of teaching in his own subject, and will be inclined to say, if, e.g., he be a chemist: "We learn what *are* the laws of chemical combination and the structure of the benzene nucleus, we do not worry our heads as to what exactly Dalton thought or Kekule said. If philosophers really know anything about the reality of the external world why do they not say straightforwardly that it is real or unreal, and prove it? The fact that they apparently prefer to discuss the divergent views of a collection of eminent 'back-numbers' on the question strongly suggests that they know that there is no means of answering it, and that nothing better than groundless personal opinions can be offered."

How philosophy progresses

I have put these objections as strongly as I can, and I now propose to see just how much there is in them. First, as to the alleged unprogressive character of Philosophy. This is, I think, an illusion; but it is a very natural one. Let us take the question of the reality of the external world as an example. Common sense says that chairs and tables exist independently of whether anyone happens to perceive them or not. We study Berkeley and find him claiming to prove that such things can only exist so long as they are perceived by someone. Later on we read some modern realist, like Alexander, and we are told that Berkeley was wrong, and that chairs and tables can and do exist unperceived. We seem merely to have got back to where we started from, and to have wasted our time. But this is not really so, for two reasons.

(i) What we believe at the end of the process and what we believed at the beginning are by no means the same, although we express the two beliefs by the same form of words. The original belief of common sense was vague, crude and unanalyzed. Berkeley's arguments have forced us to recognize a number of distinctions and to define much more clearly what we mean by the statement that chairs and tables exist unperceived. What we find is that the original crude belief of common sense consisted of a number of different beliefs, mixed up with each other. Some of these may be true and others false. Berkeley's arguments really do refute or throw grave doubt on some of them, but they leave others standing. Now it may be that those which are left are enough to constitute a belief in the independent reality of external objects. If so this final belief in the reality of the external world is much clearer and subtler than the *verbally* similar belief with which we began. It has been purified of irrelevant factors, and is no longer a vague mass of different beliefs mixed up with each other.

(ii) Not only will our final belief differ in content from our original one, it will also differ in certainty. Our original belief was merely instinctive, and was at the mercy of any sceptical critic who chose to cast doubts on it. Berkeley has played this part. Our final belief is that part or that modification of our original one that has managed to survive his criticisms. This does not of course *prove* that it is true; there may be other objections to it. But, at any rate, a belief that has stood the criticisms of an acute and subtle thinker, like Berkeley, is much more likely to be true than a merely instinctive belief which has never been criticized by ourselves or anyone else. Thus the process which at first sight seemed to be merely circular has not really been so. And it has certainly not been useless; for it has enabled us to replace a vague belief by a clear and analyzed one, and a merely instinctive belief by one that has passed through the fire of criticism.

Analysis of meanings

The above example will suggest to us a part at least of what Philosophy is really about. Common-sense constantly makes use of a number of concepts, in terms of which it interprets its experience. It talks of *things* of various kinds; it says that they have *places* and *dates*, that they *change,* and that changes in one *cause* changes in others, and so on. Thus it makes constant use of such concepts or categories as thinghood, space, time, change, cause, etc. Science takes over these concepts from common-sense with but slight modification, and uses them in its work. Now we can and do *use* concepts without having any very clear idea of their meaning or their mutual relations. I do not of course suggest that to the ordinary man the words *substance, cause, change,* etc., are mere meaningless noises, like *Jabberwock* or *Snark.* It is clear that we mean something, and something different in each case, by such words. If we did not we could not use them consistently, and it is obvious that on the whole we do consistently apply and withhold such names. But it is possible to apply concepts more or less successfully when one has only a very confused idea as to their meaning. No man confuses place with date, and for practical purposes any two men agree as a rule in the places that they assign to a given object. Nevertheless, if you ask them what exactly they mean by *place* and *date,* they will be puzzled to tell you.

Now the most fundamental task of Philosophy is to take the concepts that we daily use in common life and science, to analyze them, and thus to determine their precise meanings and their mutual relations. Evidently this is an important duty. In the first place, clear and accurate knowledge of anything is an advance on a mere hazy general familiarity with it. Moreover, in the absence of clear knowledge of the meanings and relations of the concepts that we use, we are certain sooner or later to apply them wrongly or to meet with exceptional cases where we are puzzled as to how to apply them at all. For instance, we all agree pretty well as to the place of a certain pin which we are looking at. But suppose we go on to ask: "Where is the image of that pin in a certain mirror; and is it in this place (whatever it may be) in precisely the sense in which the pin itself is in *its* place?" We shall find the question a very puzzling one, and there will be no hope of answering it until we have carefully analyzed what we mean by *being in a place.*

Again, this task of clearing up the meanings and determining the relations of fundamental concepts is not performed to any extent by any other science. Chemistry *uses* the notion of substance, geometry that of space, and mechanics that of motion. But they assume that you already know what is meant by *substance* and *space* and *motion*. So you do in a vague way; and it is not their business to enter, more than is necessary for their own special purposes, into the meaning and relations of these concepts as such. Of course the special sciences do in some measure clear up the meanings of the concepts that they use. A chemist, with his distinction between elements and compounds and his laws of combination, has a clearer idea of substance than an ordinary layman. But the special sciences only discuss the meanings of their concepts so far as this is needful for their own special purposes. Such discussion is incidental to them, whilst it is of the essence of Philosophy, which deals with such questions for their own sake. Whenever a scientist begins to discuss the concepts of his science in this thorough and disinterested way we begin to say that he is studying, not so much Chemistry or Physics, as the *Philosophy* of Chemistry or Physics. It will therefore perhaps be agreed that, in the above sense of Philosophy, there is both room and need for such a study, and that there is no special reason to fear that it will be beyond the compass of human faculties.

At this point a criticism may be made which had better be met at once. It may be said: "By your own admission the task of Philosophy is purely verbal; it consists entirely of discussions about the meanings of words." This criticism is of course absolutely wide of the mark. When we say that Philosophy tries to clear up the meanings of concepts we do not mean that it is simply concerned to substitute some long phrase for some familiar word. Any analysis, when once it has been made, is naturally *expressed* in words; but so too is any other discovery. When Cantor gave his definition of Continuity, the final result of his work was expressed by saying that you can substitute for the word "continuous" such and such a verbal phrase. But the essential part of the work was to find out exactly what properties are present in objects when we predicate continuity of them, and what properties are absent when we refuse to predicate continuity. This was evidently not a question of words but of things and their properties.

Examination of beliefs

Philosophy has another and closely connected task. We not only make continual use of vague and unanalyzed concepts. We have also a number of uncriticized beliefs, which we constantly assume in ordinary life and in the sciences. We constantly assume, e.g., that every event has a cause, that nature obeys uniform laws, that we live in a world of objects whose existence and behavior are independent of our knowledge of them, and so on. Now science takes over these beliefs without criticism from common-sense, and simply works with them. We know by experience, however, that beliefs which are very strongly held may be mere prejudices. [African] Negroes find it very hard to believe that water can become solid, because they have always lived in a warm climate. Is it not possible that we believe that nature as a whole will always act uniformly simply because the part of nature in which the human race has lived has happened to act so up to the present? All such beliefs then, however deeply rooted, call for criticism. The first duty of Philosophy is to state them clearly; and this can only be done when we have analyzed and defined the concepts that they involve. Until you know exactly what you mean by *change* and *cause* you cannot know what is meant by the statement that *every change has a cause*. And not much weight can be attached to a person's most passionate beliefs if he does not know what precisely he is passionately believing. The next duty of Philosophy is to test such beliefs; and this can only be done by resolutely and honestly exposing them to every objection that one can think of oneself or find in the writings of others. We ought only to go on believing a proposition if, at the end of this process, we still find it impossible to doubt it. Even then of course it may not be true, but we have at least done our best.

The role of critical philosophy

These two branches of Philosophy—the analysis and definition of our fundamental concepts, and the clear statement and resolute criticism of our fundamental beliefs—I call *Critical Philosophy*. It is obviously a necessary and a possible task, and it is not performed by any other science. The other sciences *use* the concepts and *assume* the beliefs; Critical Philosophy tries to analyze the former and to criticize the latter. Thus, so long as science and Critical Philosophy keep to their own spheres, there is no possibility of conflict between them, since their subject-matter is quite different. Philosophy claims to analyze the general concepts of substance and cause, e.g.; it does not claim to tell us about particular substances, like gold, or about particular laws of causation, as that *aqua regia* dissolves gold. Chemistry, on the other hand, tells us a great deal about the various kinds of substances in the world, and how changes in one cause changes in another. But it does not profess to analyze the general concepts of substance or causation, or to consider what right we have to assume that every event has a cause.

It should now be clear why the method of Philosophy is so different from that of the natural sciences. Experiments are not made, because they would be utterly useless. If you want to find out how one substance behaves in presence of another you naturally put the two together, vary the conditions, and note the results. But no experiment will clear up your ideas as to the meaning of *cause* in general or of *substance* in general. Again, all conclusions from experiments rest on some of those very assumptions which it is the business of Philosophy to state clearly and to criticize. The experimenter assumes that nature obeys uniform laws, and that similar results will follow always and everywhere from sufficiently similar conditions. This is one of the assumptions that Philosophy wants to consider critically. The method of Philosophy thus resembles that of pure mathematics, at least in the respect that neither has any use for experiment.

There is, however, a very important difference. In pure mathematics we start either from axioms which no one questions, or from premises which are quite explicitly assumed merely as hypotheses; and our main interest is to deduce remote consequences. Now most of the tacit assumptions of ordinary life and of natural science claim to be true and not merely to be hypotheses, and at the same time they are found to be neither clear nor self-evident when critically reflected upon. Most mathematical axioms are very simple and clear, whilst most other propositions which men strongly believe are highly complex and confused. Philosophy is mainly concerned, not with remote conclusions, but with the analysis and appraisement of the original premises. For this purpose analytical power and a certain kind of insight are necessary, and the mathematical method is not of much use.

The role of speculative philosophy

Now there is another kind of Philosophy; and, as this is more exciting, it is what laymen generally understand by the name. This is what I call *Speculative Philosophy*. It has a different object, is pursued by a different method, and leads to results of a different degree of certainty from Critical Philosophy. Its object is to take over the results of the various sciences, to add to them the results of the religious and ethical experiences of mankind, and then to reflect upon the whole. The hope is that, by this means, we may be able to reach some general conclusions as to the nature of the Universe, and as to our position and prospects in it.

There are several points to be noted about Speculative Philosophy.

(i) If it is to be of the slightest use it must presuppose Critical Philosophy. It is useless to take over masses of uncriticized detail from the sciences and from the ethical and religious experiences of men. We do not know what they mean, or what degree of certainty they possess until they have been clarified and appraised by Critical Philosophy. It is thus quite possible that the time for Speculative Philosophy has not yet come; for Critical Philosophy may not have advanced far enough to supply it with a firm basis. In the past people have tended to rush on to Speculative Philosophy, because of its greater practical interest. The result has been the production of elaborate systems which may quite fairly be described as moonshine. The discredit which the general public quite rightly attaches to these hasty attempts at Speculative Philosophy is reflected back on Critical Philosophy, and Philosophy as a whole thus falls into undeserved disrepute.

(ii) At the best Speculative Philosophy can only consist of more or less happy guesses, made on a very slender basis. There is no hope of its reaching the certainty which some parts of Critical Philosophy might quite well attain. Now speculative philosophers as a class have been the most dogmatic of men. They have been more certain of everything than they had a right to be of anything.

(iii) A man's final view of the Universe as a whole, and of the position and prospects of himself and his fellows, is peculiarly liable to be biased by his hopes and fears, his likes and dislikes, and his judgments of value. One's Speculative Philosophy tends to be influenced to an altogether undue extent by the state of one's liver and the amount of one's bank-balance. No doubt livers and bank-balances have their place in the Universe, and no view of it which fails to give them their due weight is ultimately satisfactory. But their due weight is considerably less than their influence on Speculative Philosophy might lead one to suspect. But, if we bear this in mind and try our hardest to be "ethically neutral," we are rather liable to go to the other extreme and entertain a theory of the Universe which renders the existence of our judgments of value unintelligible.

A large part of Critical Philosophy is almost exempt from this source of error. Our analysis of truth and falsehood, or of the nature of judgment, is not very likely to be influenced by our hopes and fears. Yet even here there is a slight danger of intellectual dishonesty. We sometimes do our Critical Philosophy, with half an eye on our Speculative Philosophy, and accept or reject beliefs, or analyze concepts in a certain way, because we feel that this will fit in better than any alternative with the view of Reality as a whole that we happen to like.

(iv) Nevertheless, if Speculative Philosophy remembers its limitations, it is of value to scientists, in its methods, if not in its results. The reason is this. In all the sciences except Psychology we deal with objects and their changes, and leave out of account as far as possible the mind which observes them. In Psychology, on the other hand, we deal with minds and their processes, and leave out of account as far as possible the objects that we get to know by means of them. A man who confines himself to either of these subjects is likely therefore to get a very one-sided view of the world. The pure natural scientist is liable to forget that minds exist, and that if it were not for them he could neither know nor act on physical objects. The pure psychologist is inclined to forget that the main business of minds is to know and act upon objects; that they are most intimately connected with certain portions of matter; and that they have apparently arisen gradually in a world which at one time contained nothing but matter. Materialism is the characteristic speculative philosophy of the pure natural scientist, and subjective idealism that of the pure psychologist. To the scientist subjective idealism seems a fairy tale, and to the psychologist materialism seems sheer lunacy. Both are right in their criticisms, but neither sees the weakness of his own position. The truth is that both these doctrines commit the fallacy of over-simplification; and we can hardly avoid falling into some form of this unless at some time we make a resolute attempt to think *synoptically* of all the facts. Our *results* may be trivial; but the *process* will at least remind us of the extreme complexity of the world, and teach us to reject any cheap and easy philosophical theory, such as popular materialism or popular theology.

Aphorisms Concerning the Method of Philosophy*

FRANCIS BACON

i

Man, being the servant and interpreter of Nature, can do and understand so much, and so much only, as he has observed in fact or in thought of the course of nature: beyond this he neither knows anything nor can do anything.

ii

Neither the naked hand nor the understanding left to itself can effect much. It is by instruments and helps that the work is done, which are as much wanted for the understanding as for the hand. And as the instruments of the hand either give motion or guide it, so the instruments of the mind supply either suggestions for the understanding or cautions.

iii

Human knowledge and human power meet in one; for where the cause is not known the effect cannot be produced. Nature to be commanded must be obeyed; and that which in contemplation is as the cause is in operation as the rule.

iv

Towards the effecting of works, all that men can do is to put together or put asunder natural bodies. The rest is done by nature working within.

*From Francis Bacon (1561-1626), *The Great Instauration* (1620), Part II, "Which is called The New Organon; or, True Directions Concerning the Interpretation of Nature."

XXXV

It was said by Borgia of the expedition of the French into Italy, that they came with chalk in their hands to mark out their lodgings, not with arms to force their way in. I in like manner would have my doctrine enter quietly into the minds that are fit and capable of receiving it; for confutations cannot be employed, when the difference is upon first principles and very notions and even upon forms of demonstration.

xxxvi

One method of delivery alone remains to us, which is simply this: we must lead men to the particulars themselves, and their series and order; while men on their side must force themselves for awhile to lay their notions by and begin to familiarize themselves with facts.

xxxvii

The doctrine of those who have denied that certainty could be attained at all, has some agreement with my way of proceeding at the first setting out; but they end in being infinitely separated and opposed. For the holders of that doctrine assert simply that nothing can be known; I also assert that not much can be known in nature by the way which is now in use. But then they go on to destroy the authority of the senses and understanding, whereas I proceed to devise and supply helps for the same.

xxxviii

The idols and false notions which are now in possession of the human understanding, and have taken deep root therein, not only so beset men's minds that truth can hardly find entrance, but even after entrance obtained, they will again in the very instauration of the sciences meet and trouble us, unless men being forewarned of the danger fortify themselves as far as may be against their assaults.

xxxix

There are four classes of Idols which beset men's minds. To these for distinction's sake I have assigned names—calling the first class Idols of the Tribe; the second, Idols of the Cave; the third, Idols of the Market-place; the fourth, Idols of the Theater.

xli

The *Idols of the Tribe* have their foundation in human nature itself, and in the tribe or race of men. For it is a false assertion that the sense of man is the measure of things. On the contrary, all perceptions, as well of the sense as of the mind, are according to the measure of the individual and not according to the measure of the universe. And the human understanding is like a false mirror, which, receiving rays irregularly, distorts and discolors the nature of things by mingling its own nature with it.

xlii

The *Idols of the Cave* are the idols of the individual man. For everyone (besides the errors common to human nature in general) has a cave or den of his own, which refracts and discolors the light of nature—owing either to his own proper and peculiar nature; or to his education and conversation with others; or to the reading of books, and the authority of those whom he esteems and admires; or to the differences of impressions, accordingly as they take place in a mind preoccupied and predisposed or in a mind indifferent and settled; or the like. So that the spirit of man (according as it is meted out to different individuals) is in fact a thing variable and full of perturbation, and governed as it were by chance. Whence it was well observed by Heraclitus that men look for sciences in their own lesser worlds, and not in the greater or common world.

xliii

There are also idols formed by the intercourse and association of men with each other, which I call *Idols of the Market-place,* on account of the commerce and consort of men there. For it is by discourse that men associate; and words are imposed according to the apprehension of the vulgar. And therefore the ill and unfit choice of words wonderfully obstructs the understanding. Nor do the definitions or explanations, wherewith in some things learned men are wont to guard and defend themselves, by any means set the matter right. But words plainly force and overrule the understanding, and throw all into confusion, and lead men away into numberless empty controversies and idle fancies.

xliv

Lastly, there are Idols which have immigrated into men's minds from the various dogmas of philosophies, and also from wrong laws of demonstration. These I call *Idols of the Theater;* because in my judgment all the received systems are but so many stage-plays, representing worlds of their own creation after an unreal and scenic fashion. Nor is it only of the systems now in vogue, or only of the ancient sects and philosophies, that I speak; for many more plays of the same kind may yet be composed and in like artificial manner set forth; seeing that errors the most widely different have nevertheless causes for the most part alike. Neither again do I mean this only of entire systems, but also of many principles and axioms in science, which by tradition, credulity and negligence have come to be received.

But of these several kinds of Idols I must speak more largely and exactly, that the understanding may be duly cautioned.

xlv

The human understanding is of its own nature prone to suppose the existence of more order and regularity in the world than it finds. And though there be many things in nature which are singular and unmatched, yet it devises for them parallels and conjugates and relatives which do not exist. Hence the fiction that all celestial bodies move in perfect circles; spirals and dragons being (except in name) utterly rejected. Hence too the element of Fire with its orb is brought in, to make up the square with the other three which the sense perceives. Hence also the ratio of density of the so-called elements is arbitrarily fixed at ten to one. And so on of other dreams. And these fancies affect not dogmas only, but simple notions also.

xlvi

The human understanding when it has once adopted an opinion (either as being the received opinion or as being agreeable to itself) draws all things else to support and agree with it. And though there be a greater number and weight of instances to be found on the other side, yet these it either neglects and despises, or else by some distinction sets aside and rejects; in order that by this great and pernicious predetermination the authority of its former conclusions may remain inviolate. And therefore it was a good answer that was made by one who, when they showed him hanging in a temple a picture of those who had paid their vows as having escaped shipwreck, and would have him say whether he did not now acknowledge the power of the gods,—"Aye," asked he again, "but where are they painted that were drowned after their vows?" And such is the way of all superstition, whether in astrology, dreams, omens, divine judgments, or the like; wherein men, having a delight in such vanities, mark the events where they are fulfilled, but where they fail, though this happen much oftener, neglect and pass them by. But with far more subtlety does this mischief insinuate itself into philosophy and the sciences; in which the first conclusion colors and brings into conformity with itself all that come after, though far sounder and better. Besides, independently of that delight and vanity which I have described, it is the peculiar and perpetual error of the human intellect to be more moved and excited by affirmatives than by negatives; whereas it ought properly to hold itself indifferently disposed towards both alike. Indeed in the establishment of any true axiom, the negative instance is the more forcible of the two.

xlvii

The human understanding is moved by those things most which strike and enter the mind simultaneously and suddenly, and so fill the imagination; and then it feigns and supposes all other things to be somehow, though it cannot see how, similar to those few things by which it is surrounded. But for that going to and fro to remote and heterogeneous instances, by which axioms are tried as in the fire, the intellect is altogether slow and unfit, unless it be forced thereto by severe laws and overruling authority.

xlviii

The human understanding is unquiet; it cannot stop or rest, and still presses onward, but in vain. Therefore it is that we cannot conceive of any end or limit to the world; but always as of necessity it occurs to us that there is something beyond. Neither again can it be conceived how eternity has flowed down to the present day: for that distinction which is commonly received of infinity in time past and in time to come can by no means hold; for it would thence follow that one infinity is greater than another, and that infinity is wasting away and tending to become finite. The like subtlety arises touching the infinite divisability of lines, from the same inability of thought to stop. But this inability interferes more mischievously in the discovery of causes: for although the most general principles in nature ought to be held merely positive, as they are discovered, and cannot with truth be referred to a cause; nevertheless the human understanding being unable to rest still seeks something prior in the order of nature. And then it is that in struggling towards that which is further off it falls back upon that which is more nigh at hand,— namely, on final causes; which have relation clearly to the nature of man rather than to the nature of the universe, and from this source have strangely defiled philosophy. But he is no less an unskilled and shallow philosopher who seeks causes of that which is most general, than he who in things subordinate and subaltern omits to do so.

xlix

The human understanding is no dry light, but receives an infusion from the will and affections; whence proceed sciences which may be called "sciences as one would." For what a man had rather were true he more readily believes. Therefore he rejects difficult things from impatience of research; sober things, because they narrow hope; the deeper things of nature, from superstition; the light of experience, from arrogance and pride, lest his mind should seem to be occupied with things mean and transitory; things not commonly believed, out of deference to the opinion of the vulgar. Numberless in short are the ways, and sometimes imperceptible, in which the affections color and infect the understanding.

lii

Such then are the idols which I call *Idols of the Tribe*; and which take their rise either from the homogeneity of the substance of the human spirit, or from its preoccupation, or from its narrowness, or from its restless motion, or from an infusion of the affections, or from the incompetency of the senses, or from the mode of impression.

liii

The *Idols of the Cave* take their rise in the peculiar constitution, mental or bodily, of each individual; and also in education, habit, and accident. Of this kind there is a great number and variety; but I will instance those the pointing out of which contains the most important caution, and which have most effect in disturbing the clearness of the understanding.

liv

Men become attached to certain particular sciences and speculations, either because they fancy themselves the authors and inventors thereof, or because they have bestowed the greatest pains upon them and become most habituated to them. But men of this kind, if they betake themselves to philosophy and contemplations of a general character, distort and color them in obedience to their former fancies. . . .

lv

There is one principal and as it were radical distinction between different minds, in respect of philosophy and the sciences; which is this: that some minds are stronger and apter to mark the differences of things, others to mark their resemblances. The steady and acute mind can fix its contemplations and dwell and fasten on the subtlest distinctions; the lofty and discursive mind recognizes and puts together the finest and most general resemblances. Both kinds, however, easily err in excess, by catching the one at gradations the other at shadows.

lvi

There are found some minds given to an extreme admiration of antiquity, others to an extreme love and appetite for novelty; but few so duly tempered that they can hold the mean, neither carping at what has been well laid down by the ancients, nor despising what is well introduced by the moderns. This, however, turns to the great injury of the sciences and philosophy: since these affectations of antiquity and novelty are the humors of partisans rather than judgments; and truth is to be sought for not in the felicity of any age, which is an unstable thing, but in the light of nature and experience, which is eternal. These factions therefore must be abjured, and care must be taken that the intellect be not hurried by them into assent.

lviii

Let such then be our provision and contemplative prudence for keeping off and dislodging the Idols of the Cave, which grow for the most part either out of the predominance of a favorite subject, or out of an excessive tendency to compare or to distinguish, or out of partiality for particular ages, or out of the largeness or minuteness of the objects contemplated. And generally let every student of nature take this as a rule—that whatever his mind seizes and dwells upon with peculiar satisfaction is to be held in suspicion, and that so much the more care is to be taken in dealing with such questions to keep the understanding even and clear.

lix

But the *Idols of the Market-place* are the most troublesome of all: idols which have crept into the understanding through the alliances of words and names. For men believe that their reason governs words; but it is also true that words react on the understanding; and this it is that has rendered philosophy and the sciences sophistical and inactive. Now words, being commonly framed and applied according to the capacity of the vulgar, follow those lines of division which are most obvious to the vulgar understanding. And whenever an understanding of greater acuteness or a more diligent observation would alter those lines to suit the true divisions of nature, words stand in the way and resist the change. Whence it comes to pass that the high and formal discussions of learned men end oftentimes in disputes about words and names; with which (according to the use and wisdom of the mathematicians) it would be more prudent to begin, and so by means of definitions reduce them to order. Yet even definitions cannot cure this evil in dealing with natural and material things; since the definitions themselves consist of words, and those words beget others: so that it is necessary to recur to individual instances, and those in due series and order. . . .

lx

The Idols imposed by words on the understanding are of two kinds. They are either names of things which do not exist (for as there are things left unnamed through lack of observation, so likewise are there names which result from fantastic suppositions and to which nothing in reality corresponds), or they are names of things which exist, but yet confused and ill-defined, and hastily and irregularly derived from realities. Of the former kind are Fortune, the Prime Mover, Planetary Orbits, Element of Fire, and like fictions which owe their origin to false and idle theories. And this class of idols is more easily expelled, because to get rid of them it is only necessary that all theories should be steadily rejected and dismissed as obsolete.

But the other class, which springs out of a faulty and unskillful abstraction, is intricate and deeply rooted. Let us take for example such a word as *humid*, and see how far the several things which the word is used to signify agree with each other; and we shall find the word *humid* to be nothing else than a mark loosely and confusedly applied to denote a variety of actions which will not bear to be reduced to any constant meaning. For it both signifies that which easily spreads itself round any other body; and that which in itself is indeterminate and cannot solidize; and that which readily yields in every direction; and that which easily divides and scatters itself; and that which easily unites and collects itself; and that which readily flows and is put in motion; and that which readily clings to another body and wets it; and that which is easily reduced to a liquid, or being solid easily melts. Accordingly when you come to apply the word—if you take it in one sense, flame is humid; if in another, air is not humid; if in another, fine dust is humid; if in another, glass is humid. So that it is easy to see that the notion is taken by abstraction only from water and common and ordinary liquids, without any due verification.

lxi

But the *Idols of the Theater* are not innate, nor do they steal into the understanding secretly, but are plainly impressed and received into the mind from the play-books of philosophical systems and the perverted rules of demonstration. To attempt refutations in this case would be merely inconsistent with what I have already said: for since we agree neither upon principles nor upon demonstrations there is no place for argument. And this is so far well, inasmuch as it leaves the honor of the ancients untouched. For they are no wise disparaged—the question between them and me being only as to the way. For as the saying is, the lame man who keeps the right road outstrips the runner who takes a wrong one. Nay it is obvious that when a man runs the wrong way, the more active and swift he is the further he will go astray.

But the course I propose for the discovery of sciences is such as leaves but little to the acuteness and strength of wits, but places all wits and understandings nearly on a level. For as in the drawing of a straight line or a perfect circle, much depends on the steadiness and practice of the hand, if it be done by aim of hand only, but if with the aid of rule or compass, little or nothing; so is it exactly with my plan. But though particular confutations would be of no avail, yet touching the sects and general divisions of such systems I must say something; something also touching the external signs which show that they are unsound; and finally something touching the causes of such great infelicity and of such lasting and general agreement in error; that so the access to truth may be made less difficult, and the human understanding may the more willingly submit to its purgation and dismiss its idols.

lxii

Idols of the Theater, or of Systems, are many, and there can be and perhaps will be yet many more. For were it not that now for many ages men's minds have been busied with religion and theology; and were it not that civil governments, especially monarchies, have been averse to such novelties, even in matters speculative; so that men labor therein to the peril and harming of their fortunes, not only unrewarded but exposed also to contempt and envy: doubtless there would have arisen many other philosophical sects like to those which in great variety flourished once among the Greeks. For as on the phenomena of the heavens many hypotheses may be constructed, so likewise (and more also) many various dogmas may be set up and established on the phenomena of philosophy. And in the plays of this philosophical theater you may observe the same thing which is found in the theater of the poets, that stories invented for the stage are more compact and elegant, and more as one would wish them to be, than true stories out of history.

In general, however, there is taken for the material of philosophy either a great deal out of a few things, or a very little out of many things; so that on both sides philosophy is based on too narrow a foundation of experiment and natural history, and decides on the authority of too few cases. For the rational school of philosophers snatches from experience a variety of common instances, neither duly ascertained nor diligently examined and weighed, and leaves all the rest to meditation and agitation of wit.

There is also another class of philosophers, who having bestowed much diligent and careful labor on a few experiments, have thence made bold to educe and construct systems; wresting all other facts in a strange fashion to conformity therewith.

And there is yet a third class, consisting of those who out of faith and veneration mix their philosophy with theology and traditions; among whom the vanity of some has gone so far aside as to seek the origin of sciences among spirits and genii. So that this parent stock of errors—this false philosophy—is of three kinds; the *sophistical,* the *empirical,* and the *superstitious.*[1]

lxvii

A caution must also be given to the understanding against the intemperance which systems of philosophy manifest in giving or withholding assent; because intemperance of this kind seems to establish Idols and in some sort to perpetuate them, leaving no way open to reach and dislodge them.

This excess is of two kinds: the first being manifest in those who are ready in deciding; and render sciences dogmatic and magisterial; the other in those who deny that we can know anything, and so introduce a wandering kind of inquiry that leads to nothing: of which kinds the former subdues, the latter weakens the understanding. . . .

[1] Bacon's particular examples of Idols of the Theater have less relevance today. There is no use flogging dead snakes. The student is advised, therefore, to seek examples of these three types of philosophical fallacy—the sophistical, the empirical, and the superstitious—in systems of thought that are current in our own time.

lxviii

So much concerning the several classes of Idols, and their equipage: all of which must be renounced and put away with a fixed and solemn determination, and the understanding thoroughly freed and cleansed; the entrance into the kingdom of man, founded on the sciences, being not much other than the entrance into the kingdom of heaven, whereinto none may enter except as a little child.

On the Method of Philosophy*

RENÉ DESCARTES

On examining one's own opinions

It is true that we do not destroy all the houses in a town merely in order to rebuild in another fashion, with more beautiful streets; yet it is not unusual for private owners to have their own houses demolished in order to erect new ones, and sometimes indeed they are forced to do so when there is danger of collapse from insecure foundations. By analogy I argued to myself that a private individual should never try to reform the whole of a society by altering and overturning everything in order to reconstruct it anew; nor should he try to reform the entire body of the sciences, or the established way of teaching them. But so far as private opinions are concerned I thought myself fully justified in trying to sweep away all that I had held up to this time, in order that I might be in a position either to replace them by others more correct, or to reinstate these original opinions after I had determined their place in a rational system.

I firmly believed that in this way I should succeed in conducting my life much better than if I built only on old foundations, and relied upon principles which in youth I had taken wholly upon trust. Although I recognized various difficulties in the undertaking, they

* From René Descartes (1596-1650), *Discourse on Method* (1637), Parts II and III.

did not seem insurmountable, nor comparable to those that beset even the mildest attempt at reform in public affairs. For public institutions are like huge edifices, which are not easy to raise again when they have collapsed, nor even to keep erect when their foundations have begun to totter; and their fall is bound to be violent. Granted that established institutions are often defective (as indeed the very diversity of them attests), nevertheless it would seem that custom partly inures us to their faults, and partly manages to avoid or correct them more effectively than deliberate planning could do. In any case the imperfections are almost always more endurable than the process of removing them would be; just as highways winding among the mountains gradually become so smooth from frequent use that it is better for a traveler to follow them than to take short cuts over rocks and precipices.

That is why I wholly disapprove of those restless and busy meddlers, who although called neither by birth nor fortune to take part in the management of public affairs, are yet ever devising new reforms. In fact, if I thought that anything in this treatise would offer the slightest justification for such folly, I would never allow it to be published. The most I have ever intended has been to reform my own beliefs and base them on a foundation which would be entirely my own. If my work has given me such satisfaction that I am now publishing a draft of it, that does not mean that I advise others to make a similar attempt. Those whom God has endowed with greater genius will doubtless entertain more exalted designs; whereas even my present one is likely to seem too venturesome to the majority. The simple resolve to strip oneself of all past beliefs should not be taken up lightly by everyone. In particular there are two classes of men who should not attempt it. On the one hand there are those who, overestimating their own cleverness, substitute impulse for judgment and lack the patience to arrange their thoughts in proper order; so that when a man of this description has taken the liberty of doubting the principles he formerly accepted, and has deviated from the beaten track, he is unable to stay on the path which must be followed in order to arrive at the goal, and thus he remains wandering astray all through his life. On the other hand there are those who, having enough sense or modesty to realize that there may be others who excel them in the power of distinguishing truth from falsehood, content themselves with following the opinions of those others instead of searching out better ones for themselves.

For my own part, I would doubtless have been one of these last if I had never had more than a single teacher, or if I had never discovered what wide diversities of opinion prevail among men of the greatest learning. But I had become aware, even in my college days, that nothing can be imagined so strange and incredible but that some philosopher or other has maintained it. Moreover, in the course of my travels I had observed that men whose opinions are utterly the reverse of ours are not necessarily barbarians and savages on that account, but sometimes show themselves our equals if not our superiors in the use they make of their reason. I also considered how different is the character developed in a person reared from infancy in France or Germany from what that same individual would have had, assuming the same natural capacities, if he had passed his entire life among Chinese or cannibals. In respect of clothing, too, I noticed how the fashions which pleased us ten years ago, and which will perhaps please us again before another ten years have passed, seem at present extravagant and ridiculous. From all this I concluded that our opinions are much more influenced by custom and example than by any assured knowledge. Nor could I settle the matter, in questions of any real difficulty, by accepting the opinion of the majority, for in such cases the truth is more likely to be discovered by a thoughtful individual than by a large group. I could not, however, single out anyone whose opinions struck me as superior to those of his fellows, and hence I found that I was obliged to undertake the investigation for myself.

But like one who walks alone in the dark I resolved to go slowly, and with such constant circumspection, that although my progress might be slow I would at least be on guard against falling. Even those opinions which had slipped into my mind without rational examination I did not wish to repudiate on the spot, but thought that I should first take ample time to plan out the task I had set myself, and to ascertain the true method of obtaining knowledge of everything within the power of my mind to grasp.

Where the formal sciences are limited

Among the different branches of philosophy I had, in my younger days, turned my mind to logic, and among those of mathematics to analytic geometry and algebra—three arts or sciences which I thought should contribute something to the design I had in view. But on examining them I found, in the case of logic, that its syllogisms and most of its other operations enable us better to communicate what we already know—or even, as in the Art of Lully, to speak without judgment of what we do not know—than to learn anything new. Granted that the science of logic contains many precepts both true and good, yet these are intermingled with so many others which are superfluous or even downright misleading, that it is almost as hard to separate the two groups as to hew a Diana or a Minerva out of a rough block of marble.

As to the "analysis" of the ancients and the algebra of the moderns, besides the fact that they deal only with what is highly abstract and seemingly of no real use, the former is always so restricted to the consideration of figures that it cannot exercise the understanding without greatly fatiguing the imagination; while the latter depends so much on certain rules and formulas that it has become a dark and mysterious art which confuses the mind instead of a science fitted to cultivate it.

These considerations induced me to seek some other method which, while combining the advantages of the three just mentioned, would be free of their defects. Moreover, just as too many laws often furnish an excuse for lawlessness, a state being much better governed when there are a few laws strictly enforced, so in like manner, instead of the large number of precepts which constitute the science of logic, I thought that I would be amply served by the four which follow, provided that I made a firm and unwavering resolve not to violate them on any occasion whatever.

The four rules of method

The first of my rules was to accept nothing as true which I did not clearly recognize to be so; that is, carefully to avoid precipitancy and prejudice, and to admit nothing more into my judgments than what was presented to my mind so clearly and distinctly as to allow no room for doubt.

The second was to divide each of the difficulties which I encountered into as many parts as possible and as might be requisite for its best solution.

The third was to conduct my thoughts in due order, beginning with what is simplest and easiest to understand, and so rising gradually, step by step, to the knowledge of what is more complex, and assigning an order in thought even to topics which do not stand to one another in any clear natural order of their own.

The last was always to make my enumerations so complete and my reviews so broad, that I would be certain of having omitted nothing.

How mathematics can serve

Those long chains of reasoning, so simple and easy when understood, by which geometers arrive at the most difficult demonstrations, had led me to imagine that perhaps all things to which human knowledge can attain might be mutually connected in much the same way. If so, then our minds could reach out to even the most remote matters, and probe even the most recondite, provided only that we would refrain from accepting anything as true which is not so, and would always direct our thoughts in the order necessary for deducing certain truths from certain others. Nor was it difficult to discover where I should properly begin, for I was already aware that one should begin with what is simplest and easiest to know. And when I reflected that of all those who have hitherto sought truth by way of science it is only mathematicians who have succeeded in producing demonstrations, by discovering reasons which are certain and evident, I had no doubt that they, too, must have begun in that way. In following their example I had no other purpose in view than that of accustoming my mind to an active love of truth and a distaste for unsound reasoning. Not that I had any intention of trying to learn all the branches of mathematics; for I observed that however much they might differ in detail they are all at one in confining themselves to the various relations and proportions that subsist among objects, and I therefore judged that it would be better to examine those proportions in their most general aspect, without referring them to particular objects except by way of necessary illustration. By not limiting them to any objects in particular I would be better able to extend their application afterwards to any class of objects for which they might prove suitable. Furthermore, having perceived that in order to understand such relations I would sometimes have to consider them singly and sometimes only in the aggregate, I concluded that when considering them in detail I had better picture them in the form of lines and figures, whereby they could be most simply and distinctly represented to my imagination and senses, but that in order to retain them in memory or to grasp several of them in combination I had better express them in formulas as succinctly as possible. In this way I considered that I was taking over all that was best in both geometrical analysis and algebra, correcting the defects of each by the help of the other. . . .

Maxims of conduct

In setting out to rebuild one's house it is not enough to tear down the old structure and provide materials and builders for the new—or, it may be, to engage in the work ourselves according to carefully drawn plans of our own. There is also the need to prepare some other house where we can be comfortably lodged during the reconstruction. Similarly, in order that I might not remain irresolute in my actions while reason obliged me to suspend my judgment, and that I might in the interval carry on my life as happily as I could, I drew up for myself a provisional code of morals, consisting of three or four maxims, which I should now like to set forth.

The first was to obey the laws and customs of my country, remaining constant to the religion in which by God's grace I had been educated from childhood, and in all other matters to avoid extremes, guiding my conduct by the most moderate opinions which I should find operative in the lives of the most judicious of my fellow-citizens. For having resolved to attach no value to my own opinions, in order to examine them more objectively, I felt sure that the best plan for the present was to follow the opinions of those on whose judgment the greatest reliance could be placed. Granted that there may be judicious men among the Persians and Chinese no less than among ourselves, yet it seemed to me more expedient to bring my conduct into harmony with the opinions of those with whom I would have to live. Furthermore, in order to ascertain what their real opinions were, I thought I should observe what they did rather than what they said: not only because in the corrupt state of our manners nowadays there are few disposed to speak exactly as they believe, but also because many are not aware of what they really do believe; for the act of believing a thing is different from the act of knowing that we believe it, and can occur without the latter.

Among various opinions held in equal repute I resolved to choose always the most moderate: partly because these are always better suited to daily living than excess, which is usually bad; partly because I would then be less in danger of straying far from the true road than if, having adopted one extreme, it should turn out that I ought to have chosen quite differently. Especially I included under the notion of excess all promises which involve any substantial abridgment of our future liberty. Not that I disparaged these laws which, as a prop to our feeble and vacillating natures, uphold the vows and contracts by which we bind ourselves to persevere in some course of action where a good end is in view; nor even those laws which, for the security of commerce, sanction other agreements where the end in view is morally indifferent. But since I perceived that nothing in the world is unchanging, and since in my own case I was undertaking to improve my judgments more and more rather than allow them to deteriorate, it would have been a grave sin against good sense if, because I happened to approve of something at one time, I should obligate myself to approve of it in the future, when either its actual character or the light in which it appeared to me might be less favorable.

My second maxim was to be as firm and resolute in my actions as I was able, and to hold no less steadfastly to the most doubtful opinions, when once I had made up my mind to adopt them, than if they had been absolutely certain. In this I was imitating the example of travelers who, finding themselves lost in a forest, know that they must not wander first one way and then another, still less remain where they are, but must walk as straight as they can in a single direction, not altering it for any slight reasons, even though it may have been sheer chance that first determined them in their choice. By this means, even if they do not arrive exactly where they had wished, they will at length come out somewhere, which is doubtless preferable to remaining in the middle of the forest. In like manner, since there are many situations in life that require prompt decision, we ought always, when we cannot discover which opinion is most true, to act on whatever one is most probable; and in cases where we can discover no more probability in one opinion than in another we ought nonetheless to settle upon some one of them and thenceforth to regard it, so far as practice is concerned, as though there were no doubt about its being true and excellent. For even if the opinion should turn out later to be wrong, our motive in thus choosing it is not. This principle served to deliver me from all the backward looks and regrets which affect the mind and agitate the conscience of those vacillating creatures who are always adopting some course of action as worthwhile which they afterwards judge to be bad.

My third maxim was to try always to conquer myself rather than fortune, to alter my desires rather than the order of the world, and more generally to accustom myself to believe that there is nothing entirely within our control except our thoughts: so that after we have done our best in regard to external arrangements any lack of success is regarded not as a failure on our part but as something quite beyond our power. This maxim by itself seemed sufficient to prevent my desiring anything in the future beyond what I could actually achieve, thereby rendering me contented; for since our will does not normally induce us to desire anything save what our understanding represents to it as somehow possible of attainment, it is plain that if we consider all external goods as equally outside our power we shall no more regret the accidental loss of such as seem to be our due than we would regret not possessing the kingdoms of China or Mexico. In the same way, making necessity into a virtue so to speak, we shall no more desire to be well if ill, or free if in prison, than we now desire to have our bodies formed of a substance as incorruptible as diamonds, or to have wings to fly with like birds. It must be admitted that to accustom oneself to regard all things from this point of view requires long exercise and meditation frequently repeated; but I believe that it is principally in this that the secret of those philosophers is to be found who, in ancient times, were able to free themselves from the tyranny of fortune and, despite suffering or poverty, to rival the gods in their happiness. For by schooling themselves ceaselessly to consider the limitations prescribed to them by nature they became so entirely convinced that nothing was really at their disposal save their own thoughts, that this conviction alone sufficed to dispel any longing toward outward objects; and over their thoughts they acquired so absolute a mastery that they had good ground for esteeming themselves more rich and more powerful, freer and happier than other men, who, however much they might be favored by nature and fortune, could never, without this philosophy, become masters of all their desires.

Finally (to conclude this moral code) I thought I should review the different occupations of men which life offers, in order to pick out the best. Without wishing to disparage any other occupations I decided that I could not do better than continue in the one in which I was engaged—that is to say, go on devoting my entire life to the cultivation of my reason, and advancing as much as possible in the knowledge of truth by following the method I had prescribed myself. This method, from the time I began to apply it, was a source of such deep satisfaction to me that I felt sure no greater or more innocent joy could be found in this life. As I went on each day discovering by means of it new truths which seemed to me important although ignored by other men, the delight I took in it so filled my mind that all else seemed of no account. Besides, the three preceding maxims had been founded solely on this design I had of continuing the search for truth. For since God has endowed each of us with some mental light whereby to distinguish true from false, I could not have contented myself with accepting other people's opinions for a single moment if I had not been resolved to use my own judgment in examining them at the proper time. Nor could I have followed doubtful opinions without scruple unless I had planned to take every opportunity of finding better ones, should such exist. And finally, I could not have restrained my desires and drawn happiness from such discipline, had I not been following a path by which I expected to attain all the knowledge of which I was capable and secure for myself in the end the best of all possible goods. For inasmuch as we neither seek nor shun any action except so far as our understanding represents it to us as good or bad, it is enough to judge wisely in order to act well, and the wisest judgment leads to the best action—that is to say, to the acquisition of all the virtues and therewith all other goods within our reach. Once we are assured of having reached that stage, we cannot fail to be happy.

The Way of Philosophy*

ARTHUR SCHOPENHAUER

THE TWO first conditions of philosophizing are these: first, to have the courage to set one's heart upon no question; and, secondly, to bring all that which is obvious in itself to clear consciousness in order to comprehend it as problem. Finally, in order, properly speaking, to philosophize, the mind must be truly at leisure. It must pursue no purposes, and thus not be led by the Will, but give itself over undividedly to the teaching which the perceptive world and its own consciousness impart to it. Now professors of philosophy are concerned as to their personal use and advantage, and what leads thereto; there the serious point for them lies. For this reason they fail altogether to see so many obvious things, indeed do not so much as once come to reflection on the problems of philosophy.

Philosopher and poet contrasted

The poet brings pictures of life, human character, and situations before the imagination, sets everything in motion, and leaves it to everyone to think into these pictures, as much as his intellectual power will find for him therein. On this account he can satisfy men of the most divine capacities, even fools and wise men at the same time. Now the philosopher does not bring in the same way life itself, but the completed thoughts which he has abstracted from it, and demands that his reader should think just in the same way, and just as far as he himself, and his public is, in consequence, very small. The poet may therefore be compared to him who brings the flowers, the philosopher to him who brings the quintessence.

Another great advantage which poetical achievements have over philosophical is this, that all poetical works can stand without

---

* From Arthur Schopenhauer (1788-1860), "On Philosophy and Its Method" in *Parega and Paralipomena* (1851), described by him as "Detached yet systematically arranged thoughts on many different subjects."

hindrance to each other side by side; while a philosophical system has hardly come into the world, but it contemplates the destruction of all its brothers, like an Asiatic sultan on ascending the throne. For as there can only be one queen in a beehive, so there can only be one philosophy on the order of the day. Systems are of as unsociable a nature as spiders, of which each sits alone in its web, and sees how many flies will let themselves be caught in it, but only approaches another spider in order to fight it. Thus, while the works of poets pasture peacefully next each other like lambs, those of philosophers are born ravening beasts, and their destructive impulses are even directed primarily against their own species, like those of scorpions, spiders, and the larvae of certain insects. They come into the world like the armed men from the seed of Jason's dragons' teeth, and have till now like these mutually exterminated each other. This battle has already lasted more than 2,000 years. Will a final victory and lasting peace ever result from it?

Private meditation superior to discussion

Conversation with another is related to serious meditation and inward contemplation of the things, as a machine to a living organism. For only in the latter case is everything cut from one piece, or as it were played in one key, whereby alone it can acquire clearness, intelligibility, and true coherence—in fact, unity. Otherwise, heterogeneous pieces of very different origin are stuck together, and a certain unity of movement is forced, which often unexpectedly stops. It is only oneself that one understands perfectly; others only half, for one can at most attain to community of concepts, but never to the perceptual point of view lying at their foundation. Hence deep philosophical truths are never brought to light by way of common thinking in dialogue. Such, however, is very serviceable as practice to the hunting up of problems, to their ventilation, and afterwards to the testing, controlling, and criticizing of the proposed solution. . . .

Neither our knowledge, nor our insight, will be ever specially increased by the comparison and discussion of what has been said by others; for that is always like pouring water from one vessel into another. Only by the contemplation of things oneself, can insight and knowledge be really increased; for it alone is the living source, always ready, and always at hand. It is curious to see how would-be philosophers are for ever occupied with the first method, and seem not to know the other at all, being always concerned with what this one has said and with what that one may have meant. So that they are, as it were, perpetually turning old casks upside down in order to see whether some drop may not have remained behind, while the living well-spring lies neglected at their feet. Nothing so much as this betrays their incapacity, or gives the lie more to their assumed mien of importance, depth, and originality.

The Nature of Abstraction*

ARTHUR SCHOPENHAUER

The value of abstraction

The outward impression upon the senses, together with the mood which it specifically awakens in us, vanishes when the thing itself vanishes. Therefore these two cannot of themselves constitute experience proper, whose teaching is to guide our conduct for the future. The image of that impression, which the imagination preserves, is originally weaker than the impression itself, and becomes weaker and weaker daily, until in time it disappears altogether. There is only one thing which is not subject either to the instantaneous vanishing of the impression or to the gradual disappearance of its image, and which is therefore free from the power of time. This is the *concept*. In it, then, the teaching of experience must be stored up, and it alone is suited to be a safe guide to our steps in life. Therefore Seneca says rightly, *"Si vis tibi omnia subjicere, te subjice rationi"* ("If you wish to subjugate all things to yourself, first subjugate yourself to reason"—Epistle 37). And I add to this that the essential condition of surpassing others in actual life is that

---

* From Arthur Schopenhauer, *The World as Will and Representation* (1819), "Supplements to the First Book," Chaps. VI, VII. A revision of the Haldane and Kemp translation.

we should reflect or deliberate. Such an important tool of the intellect as the *concept* evidently cannot be identical with the *word*, this mere sound, which as an impression of sense passes with the moment, or as a phantasm of hearing dies away with time. Yet the concept is a representation the distinct consciousness and preservation of which are bound up with the word. Hence the Greeks called word, concept, relation, thought, and reason by the name of the first, the *Logos*. The concept is altogether different, however, both from the word to which it is joined, and from the perceptions out of which it has originated. It is of an entirely different nature from these sensuous impressions. Nevertheless it is able to take up into itself all the results of perception, and give them back again unchanged and undiminished even after a very long period of time; thus alone *experience* arises.

But the concept preserves not what is perceived nor what is thereupon felt, but only what is essential in these, in an entirely altered form and yet as an adequate representative of them; in the same way that flowers cannot be preserved, but their ethereal oil, their essence, with the same smell and the same virtues, can be. Action that has been guided by right conceptions will, in the outcome, coincide with the reality that was aimed at.

We may judge of the inestimable value of concepts, and consequently of the reason, if we glance for a moment at the infinite multitude and variety of the things and conditions that coexist and succeed each other, and then consider that speech and writing (the signs of concepts) are capable of affording us accurate information as to everything and every relation when and wherever it may have been; for a comparatively small number of concepts can contain and represent an infinite number of things and conditions. In my own view abstraction is a throwing off of useless baggage for the sake of more easily handling the cognitions which must be compared and must therefore be turned about and looked at this way and that. We allow much that is unessential, and therefore only confusing, to fall away from the real things, and work with few but essential characteristics conceived in the abstract.

The limits of abstraction

But just because general concepts are only formed by thinking away and leaving out existing qualities, and are therefore the emptier the more general they are, the use of this procedure is confined to the working up of knowledge which we have already acquired. This working up includes the drawing of conclusions from premises contained in such knowledge. New insights, on the contrary, can only be obtained from what is intuitively perceived (and this alone is full and rich knowledge) aided by the power of judgment. Further, because the denotative extent and the meaningful content of concepts stand in inverse relation to each other—so that the more is thought *under* a concept, the less is thought *in* it—concepts form a graduated series, a hierarchy, from the most special to the most general, at the lower end of which scholastic realism is almost true, and at the upper end nominalism. For the most special concept is almost the individual, thus almost real; and the most general concept (e.g., *being,* which is the noun formed from the copula) is scarcely anything but a word. Therefore philosophical systems which confine themselves to such very general concepts, without getting down to the real, are little more than mere juggling with words. For since all abstraction consists in thinking away, the further we push it the less we have left over. Therefore, when I read those modern philosophizings which move constantly in the widest abstractions, I am soon quite unable, in spite of all attention, to think almost anything more in connection with them. For I receive no material for thought, but am supposed to work with mere empty shells, which gives me a feeling like that which we experience when we try to throw very light bodies; the strength and the exertion are both there, but there is no object to receive them and thus supply the pole complementary to mental movement.

The importance of language

The close connection of the concept with the word and hence of speech with reason, touched on above, rests ultimately upon the following ground. Our entire consciousness, in both its inward and outward apprehension, has *time* as its form throughout. Concepts, on the other hand, which originate through abstraction and are representations of a perfectly general kind, different from all particular things, have in this very property a certain degree of objective existence, which does not belong to any series of events in time. Therefore in order to enter the immediate present of an individual consciousness, and thus to admit of being introduced into a series of events in time, they must to a certain extent be reduced again to the nature of individual things, and thus, through being individualized, become linked to an idea of sense.

Such an idea is the *word*. It is accordingly the sensible sign of the concept, and as such the necessary means of *fixing* it—that is, of presenting it to the consciousness, which is bound up with the form of time—and thus of establishing a connection between the reason, whose objects are merely general universals knowing neither place nor time, and consciousness, which is bound up with time, is sensuous, and so far purely animal. Only by this means is the voluntary reproduction of concepts, and thus their recollection and preservation, possible and open to us; and only by means of this, again, are operations with concepts possible—judgment, inference, comparison, specification, etc. It is true that it sometimes happens that concepts occupy consciousness without their signs, as when we run through a train of reasoning so rapidly that we could not think the words in the time. But such cases are exceptions, which presuppose great exercise of reason, which they could only have obtained by means of language. How much the use of reason is bound up with speech we see in the case of the deaf and dumb, who, if they have learnt no kind of language, show scarcely more intelligence than the ourang-outang or the elephant. For their reason is almost entirely potential, not actual.

Words and speech are thus the indispensable means of distinct thought. But as every means, every machine, at once burdens and hinders, so also does language; for it forces the fluid and modifiable thoughts, with their infinitely fine distinctions of difference, into certain rigid, permanent forms, and thus in fixing also fetters them. This hindrance is to some extent got rid of by learning several languages. For in these the thought is poured from one mold into another, and somewhat alters its form in each, so that it becomes more and more freed from all form and clothing, and thus its own proper nature comes more distinctly into consciousness, and it recovers again its original capacity for modification. The ancient languages render this service very much better than the modern, because, on account of their great difference from the latter, the same thoughts are expressed in them in quite another way, and must thus assume a very different form; besides which, the more perfect grammar of the ancient languages makes possible a more artistic and more perfect construction of the thoughts and their connection. Thus a Greek or a Roman might perhaps content himself with his own language, but he who understands nothing but some single modern patois will soon betray this poverty in writing and speaking; for his thoughts, firmly bound to such narrow stereotyped forms, must appear awkward and monotonous.

The hazard of reason

In the case of all things in this world new drawbacks or disadvantages cleave to every source of aid, to every gain, to every advantage; and thus reason also, which gives to man such great advantages over the brutes, carries with it its special disadvantages, and opens for him paths of error into which the brutes can never stray. Through it a new species of motives, to which the brute is not accessible, obtains power over his will. These are the *abstract* motives, the mere thoughts, which are by no means always drawn from his own experience, but often come to him only through the talk and example of others, through tradition and literature. On becoming accessible to thought he is at once exposed to error.

The brute can never stray far from the path of nature; for its motives lie only in the world of perception, where only the possible, indeed only the actual, finds room. On the other hand, all that is only thinkable, and therefore also the false, the impossible, the absurd, and senseless, enters into abstract conceptions, into thoughts and words. Since now all partake of reason, but few of judgment, the consequence is that man is exposed to delusion, for he is abandoned to every conceivable chimaera which anyone talks him into, and which, acting on his will as a motive, may influence him to perversities and follies of every kind, to the most unheard-of extravagances, and also to actions most contrary to his animal nature. True culture, in which knowledge and judgment go hand in hand, can only be brought to a few; and still fewer are capable of receiving it. For the great mass of men a kind of *training* everywhere takes its place. It is effected by example, by custom, and the very early and firm impression of certain conceptions, before any experience, understanding, or judgment were there to disturb the work. Thus thoughts were implanted, which afterward cling as firmly, and are as incapable of being shaken by any instruction, as if they were inborn.

Ordinary men show even in the smallest affairs want of confidence in their own judgment, just because they know from experience that it is of no service. With them prejudice and imitation takes its place; and thus they are kept in a state of continual adolescence, from which scarcely one in many hundreds is delivered. Certainly this is not avowed, for even to themselves they appear to judge; but all the time they are glancing stealthily at the opinion of others, which is their secret standard. While each one would be ashamed to go about in a borrowed coat, hat, or mantle, they all have nothing but borrowed opinions, which they eagerly collect wherever they can find them, and then strut about giving them out as their own. Others borrow from them again and do the same thing. This explains the wide and rapid spread of errors, and also the prestige of what is bad; for the professional purveyors of opinion, such as journalists and the like, give as a rule only false wares, as those who hire out masquerading dresses give only false jewels.

PART TWO

The World Around Us

CHAPTER IV

The Everyday World

PHILOSOPHICAL speculations and scientific hypotheses alike have their starting point in the common-sense world, the world of everyday experience. This is none other than the familiar world around us that we see, touch, feel, taste, smell, and to which we respond emotively and kinaesthetically. It is the world we discover when we first begin to look reflectively about us. Interpretation has already entered into it, but for the most part our interpreting has taken place unconsciously and in accordance with natural needs and cultural habits. The more explicit interpretations of the world offered by science, theology and philosophy are sometimes strikingly different and remote from this world of daily familiarity. Sometimes their departures from it are justified either by utility or by the greater degree of intellectual systematizing that they represent. Nevertheless, such systems of interpretation become unduly abstract and begin to lose their human relevance unless they maintain intelligible relationships to what is directly experienced. The question of the present chapter, then, is this: What are the characteristics of our world as it offers itself to our experience at firsthand, independently of whatever theories—scientific, philosophical, sociological, or theological—may be adduced to interpret and explain it? The first step in any soundly based philosophy is to discover not what we think about experience, but what in its sheer presented actualness we discover it to *be*.

i. Things: Their Qualities and Relations

The most obvious starting-point for an inventory of the main elements in the everyday world is *things*. The word has a pretty broad coverage, but I am using it here in its literal sense as when we refer to the "things" in a room, not in the idiomatic sense as when we say, "The thing that bothers me is . . ." Even in the literal sense there are many borderline cases. Are atoms things? No, not in the present experiential sense. Atoms are *scientific objects*, and a knowledge of them depends upon methods other than direct experience. You cannot see, touch, or hear an atom; you can only see, touch, and hear what you take to be a result or manifestation of atomic movement. Our problem at present is to discipline our minds into describing the world as we actually experience it. What, then, of air? It is not seen directly, we feel its touch only when it becomes a breeze or in breathing it in and out of our lungs. Apart from those oblique ways of detecting it our knowledge of air comes by inference and experiment, not by direct experience,—a point confirmed by the fact that ancient languages generally have words for breath and breeze, which can be felt, and for sky, which can be seen, but no word for air as such.

The variety of borderline cases need not deter us, however. Their presence is a useful reminder that an experiential inventory can never be complete and that a broad experiential concept such as "thing" can never be altogether exact. Scientific objects, on the one hand, have another kind of thinghood from that now under discussion: they will be discussed under a later topic. On the other hand, even things as we familiarly experience them may turn out to be less real in one way or another than we had supposed: a problem also to be examined. But admitting that we cannot be entirely exact, let us be as exact as we can. What are the main characteristics which things, in our everyday experience, seem to have? How are things distinguishable from such non-things as ideas, qualities, relations?

Things occupy space

Every *thing,* in the commonly recognized physical sense, has some shape and size (its intrinsic spatial character) and position (representing its extrinsic spatial relations). Reflection on the last characteristic yields the experiential axiom that *two things cannot have the same position simultaneously:* i.e., two things cannot occupy the same space at the same time. This law is by no means an induction from experience. Experientially we sometimes find cases that appear to challenge it: where two things which were separate in space afterward coalesce. When that happens, however,—e.g., when rain is absorbed by the soil—our mind tends strongly to interpret the phenomenon in either of two ways. The older and generally more primitive way is to accept the new appearance—mud—as a new thing, born of our union of the two old things, rain and soil, which died in giving it birth. Even nowadays we find it natural enough to employ that thought-form in receiving the phenomenon into our intelligence: we say, "There is nothing but mud where formerly was dry soil." In early Greek times, two generations before Socrates, it was Heraclitus of Ephesus who elevated this type of interpretation into a philosophy of flux: things never remain fixed, but are ever dying and being reborn. Mud is born out of the death of water and earth. The alternative thought-form is that of mixture. We can interpret the mud as a composite, in which particles of soil and particles of water exist side by side, so that again, by a quite different expedient, we are excused from having to think of two things existing in the very same space. When this way of thinking is adopted as a universal principle of explanation it leads to the atomic theory of Democritus and Epicurus in ancient times and to the molecular and atomic theories of our own day. It seems likely that the second way of interpreting coalescence involves a greater degree of conceptualization than the first, and that it accordingly moves farther away from the experiential data themselves.

Things have qualities

The stone is gray, heavy, rough; the feather is white, light, and fuzzy. Thinghood and quality are in fact complementary categories. We cannot think of a thing without some qualities or other; and conversely when we think of qualities—blue, soft, dry, etc.—our tendency is to relate them to a subject (grammatically speaking) and thus think of the subject as a thing. Our minds seemingly have a strong disposition toward such substantive thinking. Sometimes qualities appear in our experience without any definite substantive reference, but our habit of substantive thinking is so ingrained that we devise a suitable noun for them to inhere in. Suppose I look upward on a clear day and see blue. What is it that is blue? Nothing that I can verify independently by touch. Needing a subject-noun, however, I pronounce, "The *sky* is blue." Again if you remark that it is warm today and some quibbler challenges you, "What is warm?" you may retort, "The weather." The addition of neither subject, "sky" or "weather," supplies any new knowledge, merely a verbal resting place. (At least that would be true in most contexts.)

The situation is quite different when I see something blue on a chair, inquire what it is, and am told "a sweater." Here the reply is a real one, not merely verbal. For a sweater has other qualities than color. To say that the appearance represents a sweater is to indicate that it will be soft and woolly to the touch, pliant to the kinaesthetic sense, and of a certain shape when held up and examined. That is why we think of the sweater as a thing; for it is characterized not by one property but by various properties, particularly such as are discoverable by sight, touch, and kinaesthesis.

Things persist and change

Persistence and change are complementary aspects of thinghood. In the flow of experience we sometimes regard things as keeping their essential identity even though their qualities are altered; sometimes we regard things themselves as coming into existence and perishing. We may say, "That is the same milk that you bought last week, but it is now sour." Or, when the process of transformation has gone farther, we are likely to say, "The milk has turned into curds and whey." When a boy grows up we think, on the one hand, of the boy being transformed into a man—i.e., the boy gradually ceases to exist and a man comes into being; while on the other hand we also think of this changing phenomenon as a single person who remains himself amid all the changes that mark his growth.

A sheet of paper lies before me as I write. There was a time when it did not exist, and eventually it will be burned and converted into ash. But until it is burned we normally regard it as one and the same thing even though some of its qualities may be altered drastically. If it is crumpled (changed from smooth to rough) or painted (changed from white to green) or doused in water (changed from stiff to limp) most of us would agree that it is still the same paper, although the look and feel and utility of it are now quite different. Why then not speak in the same way when it is burnt? Why not say of the ash, "This is still the same paper but it has now become gray, crumbly, and semivolatile"? Because we follow a recognized verbal convention to extend the word "paper" so far and no farther; and the convention is partly pragmatic, partly conventional. When the changes become so very extreme or fundamental it is no longer convenient or useful in most situations to hold on to the concept of "the same thing." However, there can be special situations where we would regard the matter differently. A detective examining the ash for evidence of writing would be interested in knowing whether this is the ash *of* the paper on which the incriminating message was written. Whatever form of words he uses, he is thinking in terms of the persistent element in the situation. He is implicitly using the category of thinghood on a deeper level of analysis.[1]

There is another way, too, in which thinghood involves persistence. The persistence must be continuous. I look at a chair,

[1] Cf. Aristotle's analysis of physical change: Readings, pp. 212-214.

shut my eyes, and then look and see it again. There was a time lapse in my experience of it, but I feel confident that the chair has persisted during that interval. Obviously such confidence goes beyond the specific evidence; it is implicit in our ascription of thinghood to a collection of experiential data. If I were really to believe that the chair ceased to exist whenever I ceased to see and feel it, I would no longer be regarding it as a real thing, a real chair, but either as an idea or figment of my imagination or as a collection of separate things.

The continuity which we normally ascribe to a thing is spatial too. When objects are separated I am more likely to call them a cluster than a single thing. If I declare them to be "pieces of the same thing"—e.g., the fragments of a broken pot—is it not because I think of them as once having formed an experiential continuity?

Another form of continuity which we normally ascribe to things is continuity of movement—in which both spatial and temporal continuity are implied. We tend to believe that a thing cannot pass from point A to point B without passing over a continuous route between them. The conception is not universal, to be sure, for sixteenth-century treatises on the supernatural declare that angels and demons can disappear at one place and instantaneously appear at another far distant; and the quantum theory in physics postulates an analogous property in electrons. All such, however, are borderline cases which do not invalidate the general semantic practice.

Things have powers and capacities

All things have powers of a sort, but the powers of some are more obvious, because exercised more frequently or more grossly in our experience, than those of others. Ordinarily, no doubt, we think of dynamite as having more power than a stone, since it can explode under familiar conditions. But powers are never absolute: they require suitable conditions for their exercise. The dynamite has the power of exploding only if certain conditions of heat, percussion, etc. are supplied; and on the other hand a large stone has the power of cracking a man's skull, given the condition that it is dropped on his head.

Capacities are the passive or receptive form of powers. Things differ not only in what they can do (given suitable conditions) but in what can be done to them or with them. Wood can be carved, stone can be hewn, clay can be moulded. Using Aristotle's word "potentialities" for powers and capacities taken together, we may say that it is usually quite as much by their potentialities as by their qualities that things are distinguished from one another.

ii. Space and Time

Our discussion of "things" has already had to involve some consideration of space and time. Let us now investigate these familiar entities a bit further. And please keep in mind that I am speaking of space and time as you and I experience them and intend them in our concrete living existence. The physicist's conception of a four-dimensional space-time is foreign to this point of view; it does not report or affect our experience directly. Putting aside all theories about them we have no difficulty in recognizing space and time as clearly distinguishable aspects of our experience: the one being characterized by such relations as *above, below, near to, distant from, inside of, outside of*; the other by such relations as *before* and *after, early* and *late, long ago* and *soon*.

Space: perceptual and conceptual

As immediately experienced, space appears to us in the concrete guise of shape, size, and distance, and more dynamically as movement. "Keep plenty of space between you and me," "How much more space there is in the room with the furniture rearranged!" "What a spacious vista!" "The wide open spaces of the western plains"—remarks like these illustrate the concrete character of ordinary spatial experience. An art critic will speak of a sculptor's "plastic use of space," or of the "flowing space" of a Romanesque interior. And one of a child's first tasks in learning to draw is to forget the somewhat geometrical conception of space which he has previously built up in response to life's practical demands and to draw what he directly sees. He *knows* that the road keeps the same width as you travel along it—such knowledge being essential to the practical requirements of travel —but he *sees* its outlines as converging in the distance. The character which space actually has for us varies somewhat with the context. The sides of the road are convergent—to anyone in his role of passive motionless spectator; they remain parallel—to anyone in his role of active traveler or surveyor.

Philosophers accordingly often distinguish between perceptual and conceptual space. Perceptual space is the spatial impression which we get, prior to conceptualization, by the interplay of visual and kinaesthetic perceptions—i.e., of looking and implicitly reaching; it is therefore qualitative and pluralistic, different spaces appearing to us with individualities by which we distinguish them. My room is to me a familiar enclosed space which draws its character from such things as the wallpaper, the furniture, and all the associations that have developed in my mind out of past acquaintance with it and present purposes. Experientially it is quite different from the space I see as I look down a street, or again when I look off from a mountain top, or when I am watching a movie screen or peering into a microscope. Conceptual space, on the other hand, is the formalized concept, abstracted from all particular qualities and transcending all boundaries. It is all one (particular spaces being a part of it) and isomorphic (each piece of it having identical properties with every other piece).[2] It is the ideal space to which the theorems of geometry apply.

[2] These two characteristics are challenged by certain developments in contemporary physics, but they still firmly hold good of the classical concept of space which is most people's objective standard of reference.

The distinction is by no means sharp, however. There are various degress and forms of conceptualization. The baby in learning to discriminate between things it can successfully reach for and things it cannot is already conceptualizing in an elementary way.

Moreover, when we turn from the childhood of the individual to the childhood of the race we see halting and still largely concrete attempts at conceptualizing space. Ernst Cassirer cites the African Joruba tribe, for whom each of the main regions of their known world is thought and spoken of in terms of a particular color. A more highly organized cosmology is found among the Zuñi Indians, for whom the four cardinal directions are correlated with the four elements, the four seasons, the four main types of occupation, and other fourfold groups. The north, for them, is more essentially of the nature of air, the south of fire, the west of earth, and the east of water. North also means winter, south summer, west spring, and east fall. In addition to the four directions on the earth's surface there are the directions of above and below, carrying various overtones of religious and mythological suggestion, and there is also the central point from which all six directions start—the "here." These seven spatial directions, constituting as they do a natural mode of orienting oneself spatially in the world, may possibly, Cassirer suggests, have contributed originally to the sacred character which the number seven acquired in so many widely separate localities.

Even today our direct experience of space is likely to have more in common with the primitive view than with the purified scientific concept. Each of us naturally feels himself to be the central locus from which space stretches away in all directions, although he may piously "correct" this experiential view by a more objectively astronomical picture of the universe when he stops to think about it. The little boy who when asked if he was lost replied sobbingly, "No, but my home is!" was being true to his central intuition.

As we begin to think about space critically and thus conceptualize it, drawing however upon our own intellectual intuitions and not yet upon scientific theory, we discover certain apriori characteristics of space—i.e., characteristics which at this stage of conceptualization assert themselves as self-evident. (*a*) Space is *one*: particular spaces are all parts of Space. (*b*) Space is *infinite*: we cannot form a clear and distinct idea of a space that is limited, for to think of a limit is necessarily to think of space beyond the limit—into which, if I stood on that limit, I could stretch my hand. (*c*) Space is *continuous*: we cannot think of a break or gap between two pieces of space, for to do so would be to think of a space between the two pieces, thereby reëstablishing the continuity. (*d*) Space is *three-dimensional.* On the one hand we cannot imagine a two-dimensional universe, a world of infinitely thin pancake creatures, for when we try to do so we find ourselves obliged to imagine a third dimension of space above and below it. Nor can we think of space as four-dimensional, unless we resort to a further abstraction of the space-concept into sheer algebraic relations. (*e*) Finally, it is impossible to think of space without things in it. We can think of empty space between things, and we can think of empty space extending indefinitely beyond the periphery of actual things. Things there must be, however, if space is to have meaning. Try to think of an absolutely empty space and you'll find yourself thinking your own body into it as the central point of reference.

Time: perceptual and conceptual

Like space, time has both a perceptual and a conceptual aspect. Here, however, the word "perceptual" may be misleading, for outer perceptions play no necessary part in our sense of time; the internal ones are the more important—the feeling of the body's pulsative beats. Hence I am inclined to speak rather of "experiential time."

Experiential time is centered in *now*. Always whenever I pay attention to my time-experience I think of past and future as extensions of the "now"—the past as the potentiality of all memories, the future as the potentiality of all expectancies. Each of us lives in what for him is the present. But the experiential present is not a mathematical instant, such as can be postulated in the scientific view of time; it is a moving and eventful present, always in process of being born out of what has just been and in process of giving way to what is just about to be. Such time, moreover, is heteromorphic, not isomorphic. That is to say, each moment has its own total character, which is not identical with the total character of any other moment, being drawn from the entire sum of memories and expectancies, whether conscious or subconscious, which constitute the living past and future of just that moment and no other.

Experiential time need not be entirely subjective. It is centered in subjectivity, yet it acquires a sort of objectivity, rough but effectual, so far as it is shared by more persons than one. When two men keep in step while walking together, or swing their axes in concerted rhythm while chopping wood, or sing and play in the same musical rhythm, they are objectifying their directly enjoyed time experiences in a manner suited to their purpose.

In civilizations that live closer to the pulse of nature than ours do, time is characteristically apprehended in ways analogous to those just cited. The Quiche Mayan Indians of Guatemala, for instance, even today use neither clocks nor calendars, but are able to date a fiesta by such indications as "When the corn is green" or "Soon after the rainy season begins." As preparations for the fiesta are undertaken everyone participates one way or another, and a common time sense develops through shared activity and shared feeling. Moreover, in the life of comparatively primitive peoples a large place is given to ritual, and the time sense in ritual is qualitatively configured, for there is a recognized order, pace, and duration. Such a time sense, moreover, makes less of a clear distinction between past and present than we find it natural to do. As distinguished from our quasi-linear view of time the primitive mind envisages a relationship that is not primarily serial but exemplifies what Cassirer has called the

Law of Concrescence: the tendency of events, perhaps remote if measured by standards of systematic historiography, to coalesce on the basis of some similarity or felt congruity or recurrent tribal ritual.

As we take the first steps toward conceptualizing time, we notice two basic ways in which it differs from space: it has only one dimension and it is irreversible. On the other hand it is analogous to space in at least four respects: it is one, infinite, continuous, and it contains events. Apart from some kind of succession of events, outer or inner, actual or imagined, one cannot even think of time.

In raising such questions as these last we are conceptualizing time to some degree. As the process of conceptualization goes on, an interesting phenomenon emerges: we find ourselves giving time more and more of a spatial character. As human societies became more cosmopolitan, both the size and the increasing differentiation of functions tended to weaken the collective sense of time. External aids were needed; practical convenience required that time should be measured. To say, "I'll meet you in a little while," admits of too much variety of interpretation. How can it be made definite enough for two individuals to reconvene simultaneously? The chances of success are slight if each relies on his own private time sense. To agree on exactly when they will meet, the two individuals must agree on a common measure for time. And time can be accurately measured only by spatializing it. "When shall we meet?" "When the sun is at the zenith"; "When the water in the water clock has sunk to the third notch"; "When the shadow on the sundial has moved just so far." As men move more and more toward a scientific world view, a conception of time develops that makes it little more than an appendage of space.

iii. *The Three Meanings of "Why?"*

As man confronts his world he feels an itch to explain it—to ask why things happen as they do. His questionings would be futile unless there were certain relational characteristics in the world which give a basis for at least partial answers. A clue can be found to certain of the world's main relational characteristics by considering in what ways men ask the question "Why?"

The causal "why"

Often our "why" means that we want to know what preceding event or events have brought the given phenomenon about. "Why does it thunder?" "Because of the electrically caused collision of columns of air." "Why do you limp?" "Because I have hurt my ankle." The discovery and generalization of causal relations is properly carried out by empirical method, on the basis of observed past frequencies of sequential occurrence under controlled conditions.

Spontaneity. This defines the limits of the causal "why." Experientially considered, some events "just happen." We say, "He just flared up at me for no reason at all"—and this may well describe the way it seemed. By a further effort of analysis we may admit that there were probably hidden causes for his anger, for we assume the applicability of the causal postulate even where its working is not immediately evident; nevertheless we cannot be entirely sure that there is no aspect of spontaneity whatever in a situation.

The telic "why"

If you put the question, "Why are you going downtown?" you probably expect some such answer as, "In order to buy a newspaper." If the person questioned were to reply by offering you an account of the stimuli that had aroused in him the idea of going downtown, and of his own psychophysical condition that disposed him to respond in that way to the stimuli, you might think him evasive, or at any rate long-winded. He would have misinterpreted your telic "why" as a causal "why." And in a case like this one the explanatory factor that really counts is the telic one. You can have no relevant understanding of why a person goes downtown unless you know his purpose in doing so.

When you ignore that, you are treating him not as a person but as a thing.

Vestigial remains of telic thinking in the natural sciences are found in such terms as "attraction" and "repulsion" in physics, "affinity" in chemistry, "tropism" in botany, "adaptation to environment" and "instinct" in zoölogy. Some of these are merely linguistic survivals; others represent deep-rooted ways of envisaging a certain type of phenomenon. "Why do the plant's roots reach toward moisture?" "Because it needs the water in order to live." That is a common and not unnatural use of the telic "why" in everyday botanical experience. There is simply a recognition that certain things in our world are not only pushed into activity by what has just occurred, but may also be drawn into activity *by a not-yet existent situation which is aimed at as a good.* Telic explanations enter somewhat into our study of plants, more insistently and elaborately into our dealings with the higher animals, and most fully and explicitly of all when we consider our fellow men. A certain type of philosophical question— "What is the purpose of the universe, or of human life?"—extends the telic category to the world as a whole; but it is doubtful whether such a question has any clear meaning, and in any case finite mortals cannot successfully answer it.

Accident and chance. These terms define the limits of the telic "why." "I smashed into his car by accident" means that I did not do it purposely. It has nothing to do with denial of a cause of the accident. Indeed, if someone asks, "How did it happen?" we take that to represent the causal "why" and describe all the factors that were present—that the other car swerved suddenly, that the road was slippery, and the like. When an accidental occurrence pertains to an end previously envisaged, it may be described as a matter of chance or luck.

The structural "why"

Sometimes the question "why?" is answered by giving the structure into which the challenged phenomenon falls. The simplest case of this (the one mentioned by Aristotle in this connection) consists of stating *what* a thing is, and hence by implication what properties and tendencies it might be expected to show. "Naturally it's cold; it's winter, isn't it?" "He talks that way because he's a professor." Or one's answer may be given in terms of a much more complex structure, set up by scientific postulation—"He behaves that way because he has an inferiority complex."

Contingency

However comprehensive any theory or system of explanation may be, there is always something left over—qualities and aspects not fully accounted for by that system. Although sound, for example, may be satisfactorily "explained" by the theory of waves undulating through the air, there remain over and above these *the heard sounds* themselves, which are auditory in nature, as the air-waves which produce them are not. Suppose we ask, "*Why* does one shape imprinted in the groove of a phonograph record produce the sound of the human voice, another shape the sound of a trumpet?" There is no answer to such a question. The science of acoustics investigates empirically what sounds are produced by what shapes; it does not recognize as valid the question why the connection should be thus and not otherwise. The philosopher describes such relations, which pertain to but are not explained by a given system of explanation as *contingent* to that system. More colloquially we might speak of them as *incidental* to it.

Even mathematics shows elements of contingency. Suppose one were to ask, for example, "Why is 38 the only number under 100 whose square (1444) has a digit occurring three times?" There are many mathematically significant relations into which the fact of 1444 being the square of 38 does fit: for instance, that its increment over the square of 37 is 2 units less than the increment of the square of 39 over the square of 38—as follows from the familiar algebraic law of progressive squares. But there is no significant mathematical relation to which the question just cited can refer. Nor is there any characteristic of the number 38, as distinguished from other two-digit numbers, whereby we could tell in advance that its square must have a special property. It is only when we have actually computed the square of 38— whether by multiplying, or by the law of progressive squares, or in some other manner—that we empirically discover the triply occurring digit. The relation of the square of 38 to 1444 is necessary, but its relation to the special property of having a triply occurring digit is contingent.

The foregoing survey of characteristics of the everyday world is intended as suggestive rather than complete. Indeed there are at least two noteworthy omissions: *persons* and *values*. No account of the world is philosophically adequate which omits some account of these two indispensable facts of common experience. Just because they are so important, however, they are reserved for discussion in later sections of the book: persons in Part Three, and especially in Chapter XI; values in Part Four, and especially in Chapter XII. The scientific view of nature, which it will be our next task to investigate, is more closely related to the categories discussed in the present chapter: to space and time, substance and power, cause and law. For the evolution of physical science has consisted largely—on the ideological as distinguished from the operational side—in a sharpening and transformation of the popular ways of conceiving these entities, into exact concepts that increasingly meet the double scientific need of intellectual understanding and practical control.

For Further Study

HENRI BERGSON, *An Introduction to Metaphysics* (Putnam, 1912; reprinted in Liberal Arts Press, 1949).
CLARENCE I. LEWIS, *Mind and the World-Order* (Scribner, 1929), Chap. II.

Brand Blanshard, *The Nature of Thought* (Macmillan, 2 vols., 1939), Bk. I, "Thought in Perception."
George S. Fullerton, *The World We Live In* (Macmillan, 1912), especially Chaps. I, II.
R. F. A. Hoernlé, *Studies in Contemporary Metaphysics* (Harcourt, Brace, 1920), Chaps. IV, V.

Questions for Discussion

1. When you say, "It was raining but now it has become clear," is the double use of "it" merely a convention of syntax, or does it connote a real identity of any kind?

2. Duns Scotus declares that the "haecceities" of things, i.e., their hereness and nowness, are ultimate. Charles Peirce accepts this statement and comments: "Why this which is here is such as it is; how, for instance, if it happens to be a grain of sand, it came to be so small and so hard, we can ask; we can also ask how it got carried here; but the explanation in this case merely carries us back to the fact that it was once in some other place, where similar things might naturally be expected to be. Why IT, independently of its general characters, comes to have any definite place in the world, is not a question to be asked; it is simply an ultimate fact."

Can you offer other examples of such haecceities in daily experience? (Remember that every haecceity can be explained *in some respect*. To show its ultimate character, therefore, requires careful statement, not casual mention.)

3. Compare the meanings that *time* has to a physicist; to yourself as you wonder how soon the lecture will end; to yourself as you recall experiences you had as a child; to a historian; to a musician. Can you specify any element of identity that runs through these diverse manifestations?

4. Analyze what you mean when you speak of someone as getting or not getting "the breaks." Is this epithet simply a synonym for "chance" as defined in Section iii, or does it vaguely connote an unknown force? Is the expression "playing your luck" inconsistent with the notion of luck as pure chance?

CHAPTER V

The Concept of Physical Nature

THE IDEA of physical nature has undergone a long process of growth. To understand both the power and the limits of this idea in interpreting human experience—i.e., to understand it philosophically—we must be able to see it in historical perspective. Even in its elementary phases it has a kind of primitively scientific character. For the aim of science, broadly speaking, is to discover order and connection among the indefinitely numerous and diverse data of public experience. Where a private, unshared datum is in question, such as a dream, the scientific procedure is to conceive it in publicly intelligible terms—ignoring such ephemeral qualities and nuances of it as the dreamer cannot share or communicate—and then to explain it by a hypothesis that can somehow be publicly tested. Unless a mode of investigation has this doubly public character it cannot rightly be called scientific.

However, the standards of public intelligibility and the criteria of public validation are not the same for every age and every culture. Modern science has sharpened and restricted its notions of the intelligible and the valid in a way that will be indicated in Section ii, and it is the usual custom today to conceive of science only in this more special sense. To attain a broader perspective we shall first look, in Section i, at several earlier, protoscientific ways of envisaging and explaining the universe. Such theories may be collectively described as pre-kinetic, inasmuch as they do not yet take spatial movement as the type and explanation of all other kinds of process.

i. Pre-Kinetic Theories of Nature

A child who knows nothing of the theory of light waves can readily learn that a blending of blue and yellow produces green. His thinking is scientific up to a point, for it involves an explanation which is publicly verifiable and which, moreover, gives him a control over his instruments and materials. On the other hand, it is by no means scientific in the characteristically modern sense of the word, for it has no recourse to any such kinetic concepts as light waves or corpuscular movements.

In prescientific cultures men have sought to explain things somewhat in the manner of an observant child. The colors, sounds, and emotional qualities—hatefulness, ruggedness, friendliness, etc.—that we find in, or ascribe to, the things of everyday life are taken by them at face value, as belonging to the real world instead of to man's subjective interpretation of it. They go beyond the child's naive acceptance in that they seek to systematize their findings, and to that extent they have taken a further step toward a scientific conception of things. But their systematizing is likely to be *in terms of the qualities themselves,* or of some of them, and thus their theories (whatever their defects) generally stay closer to the actualities of the concrete everyday world than the theoretical science of our own day cares to do. Three examples from ancient science will illustrate this character.

Hindu doctrine of the gunas

What might be called, in a very broad sense, the problem of theoretical chemistry presented itself to the ancient Hindus in terms of the question: What are the *primary experienced qualities* which, by blending together, produce all the diverse manifestations of experience? To understand the question as the

Hindu thinkers understood it we should avoid the modern tendency to distinguish between "inner" and "outer," mental and physical. No such cleavage exists at this stage of Hindu thought. The qualities to be explained, and the qualities designated as their ground of explanation, pertain to self and not-self alike. This difference creates a semantic problem in translating the Sanskrit words into English, for most English words refer either to the physical or to the mental aspect but not to both at once unless by conscious metaphor. The ancient meanings therefore have to be identified by the combined connotations of several English words.

The Hindus called their three root-qualities the *gunas*. The meaning of them may be indicated roughly as follows:

>*sattva:* the bright, balanced, serene
>*rajas:* the fiery, active, passionate
>*tamas:* the dark, dull, inert

Every object and every action, every human or animal character, and every condition of society is distinguished, the Hindus believed, by one ratio rather than another in which the three gunas are blended together.

The Greek doctrine of contraries

The early philosopher-scientists of Greece tended to think of qualities not triadically, like the Hindus, but dyadically, in terms of such familiar antitheses as warm vs. cool, dry vs. moist, light vs. dark and so on. Another intellectual tradition among them distinguished four basic substances—fire, air, water, and earth. Much of the early Greek speculation about natural phenomena took the form of trying to explain how opposites (which seem like natural enemies) could either intermingle or change into one another.

Anaxagoras, a scientific philosopher who was still alive during Socrates' young manhood, forced the qualitative way of thinking to its limit. Everything is mixed up in everything else, but to different degrees. If meat and wine are transformed in the stomach into blood, bone, and waste products (so he reasoned), there must be "seeds" of blood, bone, etc. already in the foods themselves. Likewise the blood and bone must still contain, in small amounts, the seeds of meat, of wine, and of everything else that has contributed to the human organism. For what *are* meat and wine, bone and blood? Not absolutely different from one another, but formed by different ratios of the different main pairs of opposites: thus, there is more of the dry in meat and bone, more of the moist in wine and blood. Anaxagoras' speculations were highly regarded in ancient times. From the modern standpoint their defect is not so much an inherent implausibility (once their strangeness is overcome) as an indifference to the demands of controlled experiment.

Aristotle's doctrine of substances

Aristotle worked out a more mature account of natural process than Anaxagoras had given. As a biologist he began with a belief that the locus of reality is to be found in concrete things and in their process of development. To explain process by changes from opposite to opposite, or from one pattern of opposites to another, is unsatisfactory, he argues; for "it is hard to conceive how density and rarity, for instance, each retaining its essential nature, could in any way act upon each other."[1] Qualitative change is never adequately described by such a statement as "Warm becomes cold." There is always a *something*, a "substance," which was warm and which becomes cold, remaining itself throughout the change.

Moreover, every substance has an inherent tendency, or set of inherent tendencies, which is an expression of its own nature. The word *entelecheia*, by which Aristotle expresses this idea of inherent tendency, connotes that the end or goal toward which the thing tends (*telos*) is "in" the thing itself—i.e., derived from its own nature—and not imposed upon it by an outside force. Thus the Aristotelian world is *telic*—not in the monistic sense

[1] *Natural Science* (the so-called *Physics*), Bk. I, Sec. vi (p. 9 of the Odyssey Press edition of selections from Aristotle).

that there is one governing cosmic purpose, but in the pluralistic sense that each thing has a natural potency (*dynamis*) of its own, which tends, so far as surrounding conditions allow, toward its own most perfect fulfillment.

ii. The Classical Kinetic Theory

In opposition to the qualitative and teleological theory of nature inherited from ancient Greece, the theory which came into prominence in the sixteenth and seventeenth centuries, and which today is a dominant influence on both scientific and popular thinking, is based upon five leading principles:

1. *The kinetic principle*: Every process of nature can be explained in terms of matter and motion.
2. *The principle of telic neutrality*: Any given process, and the motions of which it consists, are to be explained by reference to previous spatial motions, never by reference to a tendency inherent in the process itself (an "entelechy") nor to a cosmic mind or purpose.
3. *The causal principle*: All process takes place according to fixed law.
4. *The principle of homogeneity*: The same laws of motion are operative in all regions of space.
5. *The principle of measurement*: "All significant differences can eventually be stated in quantitative, and therefore potentially measurable terms."

In addition to these five most fundamental assumptions of traditional physics, three derivative principles are important enough to be mentioned: (6) the conservation of mass, (7) the conservation of energy, and (8) the principle of mechanical reciprocity.

Matter and motion

By "motion" is meant—as current usage confirms—*movement in space*, and the corresponding adjective is "kinetic." The original Greek word *kinesis* had a broader meaning, to be sure, and Aristotle used it to designate any kind of observable process whatever, with no special preference given to movement from point to point in space. But because of the importance of spatial motion in post-Renaissance physics, the more restricted meaning of "kinetic" has subsequently prevailed. Similarly, by "matter" is meant not natural potency, as with Aristotle, but what Descartes defined as "extended substance"—i.e., anything so far as it is conceived as spread out in space. The meaning of the kinetic principle, then, is this: That every kind of process—including changes of quality, organic processes of assimilation and maturing and all else—can be represented with symbolic adequacy by the spatial movements of the spatially extended matter composing it. In short, kinetic interpretation is postulated as permissible for all physical phenomena.

An outstanding seventeenth-century example of kinetic reduction is Robert Boyle's theory of heat. The interrelation of observation and postulation is strikingly shown in a recent article by Marie Boas.[2] Boyle observed that a nail struck by a hammer remains cool as long as the hammer blows continue to force it into the wood, but that when the nail has been driven in up to its head a continuance of hammer blows causes it to become hot. How explain the phenomenon? Boyle reasoned that the impetus of the blows, being no longer able to impart a forward motion to the entire nail, imparts its motion instead to the molecular particles of the nail. The increased motion of the component molecules must therefore, he argues, be the cause of the increased heat. From this and other such experiments he draws the generalization that molecular movement is the cause of heat.

To a modern reader Boyle's reasoning seems valid enough. Nevertheless it is not self-evident. A typical ancient Greek observer, if he had been confronted with the same set of data, would not have felt impelled to explain in the same way. Anaximander, early Greek philosopher-scientist of the sixth century

[2] "Boyle as a Theoretical Scientist," *Isis*, vol. 41 (1950).

B.C., accepting qualities as the irreducible terms of his reasoning, would have explained the appearance of heat by his principle of "reparation"—that the cold, having "committed injustice" by occupying the nail for so long a time, was finally dislodged by the hammer blows (as a tyrant might be dislodged by a revolution), enabling the hostile quality of hot to rush in and seize its place. However odd Anaximander's explanation may seem to a mind steeped in modern ideas, there is nothing inherently wrong with it. It is not self-contradictory, and it is not inconsistent with the observed facts. From a logical standpoint it is one possible explanation. Why, then, would neither Boyle in the seventeenth century nor we in the twentieth century be willing to give it serious consideration?

The answer is that Boyle, like ourselves, was intellectually committed to a kinetic interpretation of natural process. In a relatively early work (*The Origin of Forms and Qualities*) he had affirmed his belief in what he called "the corpuscular philosophy" and "the mechanical hypothesis"—the basis of which is that all things are composed of, and therefore can only be understood in terms of, "those two most grand and most catholic principles of bodies, matter and motion." These two principles are "catholic" in the sense that they suffice by themselves to explain all the properties of the universe.

By this very thing, that the mechanical principles are so universal, and therefore so applicable to so many things, they are rather fitted to include, than necessitated to exclude, any other hypothesis that is founded in nature, as far as it is so.[3]

A world of pure chance

It will be recalled that in Chapter IV "chance" was defined by logical opposition not to "cause" but to "purpose." When we speak of an event as happening by chance we mean that it was *not aimed at*, that it came about independently of what anyone

[3] Robert Boyle, *Works,* Vol. IV, p. 72 ("On the Excellency of the Mechanical Principle").

wanted. Now the classical kinetic theory of the universe holds that the only valid scientific explanation of any natural process —or (by Principle 1) of any set of spatial motions—must be by reference to previous spatial motions. Such telic categories as "purpose," "tendency," "fulfillment" are held to be confused substitutes for the true explanation, which ultimately always takes the form of showing a relation between later motions and earlier. The late R. G. Collingwood, in his thoughtful book, *The Idea of Nature,* has written:

> The naturalistic philosophies of the fifteenth and sixteenth centuries attributed to nature reason and sense, love and hate, pleasure and pain, and found in these faculties and passions the causes of natural process. So far their cosmology resembled that of Plato and Aristotle; and even more that of the pre-Socratics. But this animism or hylozoism was a recessive factor even in the early Renaissance cosmologies, whereas it had been a dominant one in Greek thought; as time went on it was submerged by the mathematical tendency which from the first had accompanied it; and as this tendency got the upper hand, the idea of nature as an organism was replaced by the idea of nature as a machine.[4]

The work of Gilbert and Kepler on magnetism in the early seventeenth century strongly confirmed the revolt against teleology. The so-called father of Greek philosophy, Thales, had declared: "The lodestone evidently has a soul, for it attracts and is attracted to the iron." The ideas of attraction and repulsion are metaphorical borrowings from conscious, purposive motives within ourselves. They connote a natural disposition toward or away from certain objects. Johannes Kepler repudiated the Greek and early conception of inherent tendencies (what Aristotle had called "entelechies") and posited in its place the principle of inertia—that the natural state of a body is to remain stationary except so far as its rest is disturbed by the presence of a neighboring body. Kepler still spoke of a gravitational "affection" draw-

[4] R. G. Collingwood, *The Idea of Nature* (Oxford University Press, 1945), p. 95.

ing bodies together, but with two important differences. Such affection is not special to certain bodies but is found in the relation of every physical body to every other. Therefore it is nothing individual and qualitative, but mechanical and quantitative, and Kepler accordingly took a momentous step for the development of physics by replacing the older word *anima* (soul) by the word *vis* (energy). A parallel emphasis is found in Boyle's description of the universe as a "self-moving engine" and as "a great piece of clockwork."

But although the new science has disallowed purpose as an explanation of particular events, most of its adherents in the seventeenth and to a lesser extent in the eighteenth century were willing (as contemporary materialists are usually not) to face the implication that a self-moving engine or clock requires an original designer and maker. Both Boyle and Kepler accept the agency of God in creating the physical universe, although they insist as scientists that it is illegitimate to explain particular occurrences by recourse to theology. Boyle writes:

> It more sets off the wisdom of God in the fabric of the universe, that he can make so vast a machine perform all those things which he designed it should, by the mere contrivance of brute matter managed by certain laws of local motion and upheld by his ordinary and general concourse.[5]

Universal causation

"The cause, philosophically speaking," says John Stuart Mill, "is the sum total of the conditions positive and negative taken together, . . . which being realized, the consequent invariably follows."[6] In ordinary discourse we are apt to use the term more loosely. We might readily say, for instance, that exposure to cold and wet was the cause of a certain case of pneumonia, yet

---

[5] Robert Boyle, *Works*, Vol. V, p. 162 ("Vulgarly Receiv'd Notions of Nature").

[6] J. S. Mill, *A System of Logic:* Bk. III, Chap. V, "On the Law of Universal Causation," Section 3. By negative conditions he means "the absence of preventing or counteracting causes."

THE CONCEPT OF PHYSICAL NATURE 137

pneumonia does not invariably follow a similar degree of exposure. Other factors, such as degree of bodily resistance, are also relevant to the causal relation explanation here; and when we speak of cause with careful accuracy ("philosophically," as Mill puts it) we must have reference to the *totality* of relevant factors which is invariably followed by a certain event or set of events which we call the effect.

Mill's definition raises, however, a further question. *Is there any* combination of factors which is always—absolutely without exception—followed by a given effect? In the section of his *Logic* preceding the one just quoted Mill answers with a resounding affirmative:

> For every event there exists some combination of objects or events, some given concurrence of circumstances, positive and negative, the occurrence of which is always followed by that phenomenon. We may not have found out what this concurrence of circumstances may be; but we never doubt that there is such a one, and that it never occurs without having the phenomenon in question as its effect or consequence.

How is the truth of this principle known? Evidently not by observation, for (as Mill's second statement confirms[7]) there are many cases where no one knows just *what* combination of circumstances would be needed to produce a given effect. Yet we tend to go on believing that *some* such combination exists, if only we could find it. We go on believing in some kind of necessary causal connection in the universe, even though our specific knowledge of the precise forms which that causal connection takes is far from complete and achieves at best a high degree of probability, never absolute certainty. The principle that causal connections are in the last resort necessary and universal is not verifiable by experience, but is a *postulate* on which traditional physics bases its procedures.

[7] Mill is not always consistent however. See Question 5 at the end of the chapter.

Principle 2, which pertained to the telic "why," was first stated negatively (as denying any purpose in nature) and afterward positively (as affirming a world of pure chance). So now Principle 3, which pertains to the causal "why" and which has so far been stated positively (as affirming that causation operates universally in nature) may also be stated negatively (as a denial of sheer spontaneity).

The homogeneity of cosmic space

Homogeneity means that all units of which a thing is composed are essentially identical. Principle 2 has already applied the idea of homogeneity to the category of Substance; for in requiring that all qualitative differences be translated into differences of position and motion in space it declares, in effect, that not the heterogeneous individuals of daily life but the homogeneous objects got by analysis are fundamental. The significance of substantive homogeneity will be further clarified in Principle 5. Again, Principle 3 has applied the idea of homogeneity to the category of Time, as seen in causal perspective; for it declares, in effect, that the ultimately fundamental causal relations (if we could only discover them) are the same for all time, and hence that every span of time is essentially homogeneous with every other.

The principle now to be considered applies the idea of homogeneity to the category of Space. It might be expressed: The efficacy of a causal connection among events is not affected by the region of space in which it transpires. Space is thus conceived as a neutral three-dimensional infinite container, *in* which events take place and causally affect one another, but which does not in any way, as space, affect the course of their activity. Isaac Newton stated the principle forcibly in his *Principia* (1686): "Absolute space, in its own nature, without relation to anything external, remains always similar and immovable."[8]

[8] Isaac Newton (1642-1727), *Philosophiae Naturalis Principia Mathematica*, Bk. I, Scholium ii. Translated from the Latin by Andrew Motte in 1729, revised by Florian Cajori (University of California Press, 1934).

This principle that the mere spatial position of an event (considered in abstraction from the other events occurring in the region) is indifferent to its behavior, may seem obvious to most readers today. Nevertheless it is by no means self-evident. It is a postulate of classical kinetic theory, and neither the Aristotelian physics which preceded it nor the relativistic physics which has followed accepts it without qualification.

Ancient theories nearly all conceived space as having an absolute center. A majority located that center somewhere on or within the earth, a few Pythagoreans located it in a counter-earth (*anti-chthon*) hung out in space off the opposite side of our own earth and hence invisible, while one or two radicals even suggested that it might be located in the sun. At any rate, wherever they supposed the center specifically to be, most ancient thinkers agreed that things tended to behave differently according as they were nearer the center or farther away. Plato taught that space is the cosmic Nurse—thereby symbolizing its radically organic, and hence differentiated character. Aristotle observed that "earth" (i.e., solids) is uncomfortable when it is dislodged from the earth-center where it naturally belongs, and tends by its own inherent spontaneity to return—as we see when a stone that has been hurled into the air hurries back to earth again—that fire, whose natural habitat is at the periphery of the universe, tends to fly upward. It was a plausible corollary of that way of thinking, that the sun, moon, and other skyey orbs tend to move in circles about the cosmic center; for as a circular orbit is everywhere equidistant from the center, the same laws will operate on all arcs of it, but not quite identically elsewhere.

The qualitative, organic conception of space, although it underwent many modifications, was not fundamentally challenged until the middle of the sixteenth century. Copernicus' epoch-making work on the solar system, *On the Revolution of the Celestial Orbs* (1543), put forward the helio-centric hypothesis —that the sun rather than the earth is the center around which the planets revolve. The real importance of Copernicus for later science and philosophy consisted not in shifting the cosmic center from one point to another, but in *implicitly denying that the universe has a center at all.* Copernicus opened up the logical possibility of regarding *any* point as the center; the practicing astronomer was thus made free to select the sun as his point of reference, which he has found it convenient to do because the mathematical computation of planetary movements is thereby simplified.

The denial that the world had an absolute center involved a drastic change in philosophical outlook. It destroyed the long prevailing view of the natural world as an organism. Its importance for the principle of spatial homogeneity, and hence by extension for homogeneity of essential natures, is well shown by Collingwood:

> An organism implies differentiated organs; in the spherical world-organism of Greek thought there was earth in the middle, then water, then air, then fire, and lastly, for Aristotle, the *quinta essentia* of the world's outermost envelope. Now, if the world has no center, the very basis of these differentiations disappears; the whole world is made of the same kind of matter, the law of gravitation applies not only in the sublunary regions as Aristotle thought but everywhere, and the stars, instead of having a divine substance of their own, are homogeneous with our earth.
>
> This idea, so far from diminishing the scope of man's powers, vastly enlarged it; for it taught him that scientific laws established by him on earth would hold good throughout the starry heavens. It was directly owing to Copernicus' denial of geometric astronomy that Newton could imagine the force which kept the moon in its orbit to be the same that drew his apple to the ground. For Aristotle, nature is made of substances differing in quality and acting heterogeneously: earth naturally moves towards the center, fire away from the center, and so forth. For the new cosmology there can be no natural differences of quality; there can only be one substance, qualitatively uniform throughout the world, and its only differences are therefore differences of quantity and of geometrical structure.[9]

[9] Collingwood, *op. cit.*, pp. 97-98. By courtesy of Oxford University Press.

Measurement

A result of the kinetic principle is that the measurement of the data becomes inherently possible; a result of the causal principle is that such measurement becomes methodologically necessary. Let us examine these two propositions separately.

So far as you think of natural processes entirely in terms of qualitatively homogeneous bits of matter moving about in space there is no inherent obstacle (practical difficulties apart) to measuring them. Purple, wine red, scarlet, crimson, and pink are manifestly different qualities as a person with normal eyesight beholds them. But just how different they are, and how the difference between purple and scarlet compares with the difference between crimson and pink, no one can say, and if he did manage to express the differences to his own satisfaction he could not be sure of precise understanding or full agreement on the part of anyone else. If, however, for the shades of purple and red which he sees directly he substitutes the corresponding light waves revealed by a photometer, he will be able to state the difference between one shade and another with mathematical exactitude. Moreover he can be confident of securing agreement among all other observers who can read the data which the photometer supplies.

Similarly with tones, flavors, odors, and the rest. Two musicians may be able to agree with great precision about differences of pitch and timbre, but such agreement is not likely to be widespread. Perhaps nearly everyone will agree that a drink tastes sweeter after sugar has been added, but who can say *how much* sweeter? When, however, not sounds but sound-waves are in question, and not the flavor as privately experienced but the accompanying discharge of saliva, we are then dealing with properties that can be described quantitatively.

Consider now the second point—that a strict adherence to the causal principle makes the use of measurement necessary. For to declare that an event a causes an event e is to declare (speaking strictly) that an *exact* repetition of *a* (relevant circumstances remaining equal) will always be followed by an *exact* repetition of *e*. Such exactitude cannot be discovered unless *a* and *e* can be measured.

The importance of quantitative analysis for scientific method began to be fully recognized in the early seventeenth century, as is indicated by an often cited statement of Galileo:

> Philosophy is written in that vast book which stands ever open before our eyes, I mean the universe; but it cannot be read until we have learnt the language and become familiar with the characters in which it is written. It is written in mathematical language, and the letters are triangles, circles and other geometrical figures, without which means it is humanly impossible to comprehend a single word.[10]

Galileo's statement should be interpreted somewhat guardedly. That the universe is written in mathematical language is a truth not of observation alone, but of observation and interpretation combined. We certainly discover qualitative differences—of color, auditory tone, etc.—in any perceptual observations we make of the surrounding world. The physical scientist, being a man with normal organs of perception, is also aware of such differences; but he is committed by the needs of his science to translate them into differences of quantity with which experience has shown them to be somewhat regularly associated. Such translation is an important part of the step from common-sense thinking to scientific.

The conservation of mass

It was an axiom of most early Greek speculative science that "Nothing can be absolutely created or destroyed." The phenomenon of *apparent* creation and destruction in so many areas of human experience required, therefore, to be interpreted in the light of the principle. The created and vanishing aspects,

---

[10] Quoted by Collingwood, *op. cit.*

Plato argued, *could not* be real, by reason of the very fact that they are impermanent. The demand for permanence has been a strong motive in scientific as in religious thought.

But to declare for permanence is one thing; to demonstrate it, another. How is it possible to give objective evidence that nothing has been gained or lost in a physical transformation? Evidently only if a quantitative type of analysis has been carried out. To discover whether we have gained or lost in money or in weight, we take the proper measurements. The same condition holds for natural objects. Thus it is that Principle 5 offers a basis and an implementation for Principle 6. Conservation can be established only by comparing two answers to the question "How much?" and finding them identical.

Now it is self-evident that in any given process the identity cannot hold true of all aspects. If it did so, there would be no change. A transformation takes place; its latter phase, then, is different from its former. But the question now confronting us is, *What* remains quantitatively unchanged throughout the changing process? An early and somewhat speculative answer to this question was: the amount of matter. Which leads at once to the question, How is the amount of matter to be determined? Evidently not by size, for some matter seems to be more dense than other. By weight then? That seems to be getting closer to what is wanted. But the weight of an object does not stay quite constant: it varies slightly between measurements taken at sea level and at the top of a mountain—a difference readily explained by reference to the law of gravitation. By the introduction of a factor called "the gravitational constant" an abstract property called *mass* becomes mathematically expressible as equal to measured weight divided by the gravitational constant for the place where the measurement is taken.

Clearly, then, mass is a more abstract concept than weight—although weight, too, involves both a perceptual and a conceptual element. Thus our perception tells us that a heavy suitcase "weighs more" after we have been lugging it several blocks;

our reason, however, corrects this perceptual judgment, distinguishing between the "weight" which stays the same throughout the journey and the feeling of greater heaviness induced by fatigue.

The transition from weight to mass is but another stage of the same objectifying journey. Why do we insist that the suitcase is still of the same weight six blocks later? Because we need an objective standard that will hold good for all persons in all conditions of fatigue; the scale provides such a standard. But the scale, in turn, reports the weight of a given object differently according to its height above sea level; hence the physicist's attention is turned to the concept "mass," which is objective with respect not only to persons but also to degrees of elevation. The mass of a thing is postulated to remain identical throughout, unless a part of that mass has been removed kinetically.

The conservation of energy

The function of theory in correcting an apparent anomaly of experience is seen again in the development of the idea of energy. To an ancient man observing a pendulum, its energy might have appeared to die down as it comes to an end of its arc, and to gather momentum again as it begins to swing back. In order to set up a conservation law which will hold good for all phases of the pendulum's movement, a physicist finds it necessary to distinguish between *kinetic* and *potential* energy. At the bottom of its swing the pendulum displays a maximum of kinetic energy; as it travels ever more slowly up the arc its kinetic energy diminishes, and finally (for the barest moment) ceases altogether. But the conservation law preserves the theoretical identity by postulating that the increase of potential energy at each moment exactly compensates for the diminished amount of kinetic energy; at all times during the swing the summation of the two forms of energy is equal.

Yet there is still a further qualification needed. If the amount of energy thus remained constant, the pendulum would go on swinging forever—which it does not do. The conservation law explains this by the concept of *friction.* Through friction a certain amount of mechanical energy (kinetic and potential) is transformed into radiant energy, heat. Thus although the power of motion in the pendulum gradually slows down, it is still postulated that the total amount of energy—motion plus potential energy plus heat—remains constant. It will be observed, then, that the validity of the law of conservation of energy is purchased at a price. At the price, namely, of conceiving the term "energy" abstractly enough to include the metric aspects of three very diverse kinds of experience—namely, motion, remaining at rest while having the power to move, and heat.

Mechanism

The kinetic principle and the causal principle taken together yield the principle of mechanism, namely: Given the mass, position, and velocity of every particle in the universe at a certain moment, it is theoretically possible to compute the mass, position, and velocity of every particle at any previous moment or at any later moment. In fact, the reason for the kinetic principle becomes clearer in this context; for by translating all qualitative processes into terms of matter and motion we are better able to implement the principle of universal causation. For example, it is roughly true that the same white granular substance that we call "sugar," when put on the tongue, more or less invariably produces the same sweet flavor. But our perceptions of color and taste are too shifting to allow of an exact judgment of causal connection between them. Our memory cannot perfectly assure us that this is precisely the same flavor as we tasted yesterday. But when the white granular qualities of the sugar are theoretically replaced by rapidly moving molecules, and when the flavor is replaced by the motion of molecules composing the tongue's taste buds together with motions along the nerves leading to the cerebral cortex, then, since the relation is conceived as between one set of motions and another, it can be conceived with greater exactitude. The point has been further examined under Principle 5.

iii. New Bearings in Physical Theory

Within a little more than the last half century the basic concepts and postulates of physics have been radically transformed. Some of these transformations are philosophically significant; others may be too technical, too remote from the familiarities of daily experience, to arouse philosophical concern. And in any case we should not make the mistake of seeing only the differences and ignoring the pervasive identities between the new and the old.

To use a comparison, we could say that creating a new theory is not like destroying an old barn and erecting a skyscraper in its place. It is rather like climbing a mountain, gaining a new and wider view, discovering unexpected connections between our starting point and its rich environment. But the point from which we started out still exists and can be seen, although it appears smaller and forms a tiny part of our broad view gained by the mastery of the obstacles on our adventurous way up.[11]

The account that follows is not of the new physics as a whole, for that would be beyond the present writer's competence, and in any case would not promote the aims of the book. A few major ideas are chosen for discussion because of the interesting philosophical questions to which they give rise.

Entropy

The first concept to be considered antedates by nearly three-quarters of a century the major beginnings of contemporary physics. In 1824 a captain of French military engineers named Sadi Carnot published a memoir entitled *Reflexions sur la puissance motrice du feu* ("Reflections on the Motive Power of Fire"). Carnot was investigating an engineering problem: "What

---

[11] Einstein and Infeld, *The Evolution of Physics* (Simon and Schuster, 1938), pp. 158-159.

actually happens in a steam engine at work?" And the crucial point of his solution was that "the production of motive power in the steam engine is not due to a real consumption of the caloric [i.e., the heat-energy], but to its transfer from a hotter to a colder body—that is to say, to the reëstablishment of its equilibrium."

The equilibrium has been established by the simultaneous cooling of a relatively hot body and heating of a relatively cool body. The hot and the cool body have thus affected each other because of their difference of temperature at the outset. High temperature alone will not perform work; a difference between two temperatures is required. A locomotive runs not merely because the temperature inside the boiler is high but because it is higher than the temperature outside the boiler, where the work is to be done. In the process of performing the work, the high temperature of the steam becomes reduced; there is partial neutralization of temperature.

Carnot's younger German contemporary, Clausius, worked out an important generalization and consequence of this behavior of steam. Clausius starts with the axiom (which seems self-evident from the standpoint of kinetic physics) that "Heat cannot pass from a cold body to a hot body." In physical processes, therefore, the direction of heat transference is always one-way. If two blocks of iron, one cold and one red hot, are placed surface to surface, then (ignoring effects from the surrounding medium) it is an observable fact that the hotter block will warm the colder one and that (as the reverse side of the same process) the colder block will cool the hotter one. No one thinks for a moment—so far as the described situation goes—that the hot block will get hotter while the cold block gets colder. Evidently, then, the process is irreversible; when the hot and cold blocks have neutralized each other's temperature, no further change of temperature can take place in them unless a new temperature differential is introduced from outside. Carnot and Clausius generalized the principle and set up the Second Law of Thermodynamics, sometimes called Carnot's Law—that in any system of physical processes the temperature tends to reach an equilibrium, with the result that, so far as the system itself is concerned, no more work can be done. To the neutralization factor, Clausius gave the name *entropy*, and accordingly he restated the Law in obverse form: "The entropy of any physical system tends always to a maximum." In this form it has been named the Law of Entropy.

Is the universe running down?

In its most generalized form the Law of Entropy has been interpreted to mean that the amount of energy available for work in the universe is steadily decreasing. While it does not contradict the First Law of Thermodynamics (the conservation of energy) it does emphasize the highly abstract character of that earlier law. To say, "The same amount of energy still exists but less of it is available for work," sounds somewhat like an old man's idle boast, "I can run as fast as when I was thirty years younger—but I just don't feel like trying it any more." The question of most nearly human concern is not of energy in the abstract but of *available* energy. And the Law of Entropy announces that the cosmic supply of available and hence significant energy is continually running down.

Philosophically, then, we are faced with the question: How was that supply of free energy created? By what process or from what source did it originate? By what means (if at all) is it being replenished? So long as the Newtonian concept of a homogeneous time held sway, the question of cosmic origins could be ignored. The events of each moment could be postulated as having been caused by the events of the preceding moment, and so on in turn without end. But the concept of entropy, when generalized, implies that cosmic time is basically heterogeneous. In plainer terms, the universe is running down. It is (so far as this one type of investigation goes) inherently self-destructive. If natural process involves continual self-destruction, must we postulate an original process of creation? Or a counteractive and continuing one? And can such a creative process be adequately explained in physical terms, or must our thought here speculatively transcend the categories and methods of physics?

The first paradox of light: wave or bullet?

The theory of light that is most familiar to the common reader is the wave theory. The classical argument for it was stated by Huygens two centuries ago. Light, he argues, "spreads, as sound does, by spherical surfaces and waves; for I call them waves from resemblance to those which are seen to be formed in water when a stone is thrown into it, and which present a successive spreading as circles—though these arise from another cause, and are only a flat surface."

Newton, however, who was contemporary with Huygens and fully understood his argument, defended a corpuscular theory of light, rejecting the wave theory. Huygens' analogy, he thinks, will not stand up under examination. Sound waves spread in air; the ripples caused by a stone plashing into a lake have the water as their medium. But there is no discoverable medium through which light spreads out. And to assume a wave in empty space is self-contradictory; it is not a wave you are talking about, but a corpuscle.

Huygens sought to overcome the difficulty by assuming (he was not the first to do so) the existence of a hypothetical substance called *ether*—a transparent medium permeating everything in the universe. But Newton objected to such an assumption as gratuitous, since there seems to be no way either of verifying the presence of ether or of explaining it kinetically. Furthermore Newton argues that light rays travel along straight lines and cast sharp shadows, whereas the waves of familiar experience bend around an obstacle.

During the nineteenth century, as corroborative evidences in favor of the wave theory accumulated, Newton's objections got brushed aside. But with Max Planck's discovery of the quantum theory in 1900 the question, "Wave or corpuscle?" was reopened.

The point of the quantum principle of interest to the layman is that the energy which bodies emit in radiation comes forth not in a continuous stream, as the laws of classical physics require, but in tiny discontinuous amounts called *quanta.* How does this discovery affect the physicist's understanding of light? Let Planck himself reply. In a communication to the Franklin Institute in 1927 he wrote:

> The classical theory recognizes and treats only the two extreme cases: on the one side, corpuscular motions, on whose outermost border lies the uniform motion of a particle in a straight line; on the other side, wave-motions, on whose outer limit lies the static, homogeneous field. Looked upon from the newly established point of view, there is neither pure corpuscular motion, nor any pure wave-motion. Rather, every corpuscular motion includes something of wave-motion and every wave-motion something of corpuscular motion. The difference is only gradual and quantitative.[12]

Planck proceeds to explain that in the motion of a particle, when the ratio of the impulse to the curvature of the path—which of course is infinite when the path is a straight line, making the curvature zero—sinks to a certain order of magnitude (represented by Planck's constant, h) the laws of wave-motion begin to play an appreciable part. In the case of monochromatic light, on the other hand, when the ratio of its energy to its frequency—which is infinite in a static field, where the frequency is zero—sinks to that same order of magnitude, then the corpuscular laws begin to be appreciable.

Is there any philosophical inconsistency in admitting that light is partly wave and partly bullet? The properties of waves and bullets as we know them in ordinary experience are quite distinct; we certainly cannot *picture* what their combination would be like. But for the progress of physical theory, mental pictures are nonessential and may prove distracting. Light is light, and its immediate nature, as a datum of direct experience,

---

[12] *Science,* n. s., Vol. 113 (1951), p. 78.

THE CONCEPT OF PHYSICAL NATURE 151

is well known to all but the blind. To describe it in terms of waves or of bullets is merely an analogy in either case, and it is philosophically naive to mistake an analogy for an identity. Sentences of the form, "Light is waves" or "Light is bullets," are inexact at best, and to accept them uncritically is to fall into what Bacon has called an Idol of the Theatre. The resurgence of the corpuscle theory of light is a valuable reminder that no imagined model of physical reality should ever be taken as final. Such models are not empirical facts; they are *theoretical constructs,* which serve a usefully integrative purpose at a given stage of science.

The second paradox of light: velocity

An even more startling property of light, in the context of contemporary physics, is its constant velocity for all observers. If you were driving a car at 40 miles an hour and another car passed you going in the same direction at 55 miles an hour, the second car would be pulling *away from you* at the rate of 15 miles an hour. This relation of velocities will appear self-evident to most motorists, and it can be verified by measuring the distances traveled by the two vehicles after a given span of time.

Now suppose that instead of a motorcar your vehicle is a body moving through space at a very high rate of speed—let's say, for the sake of illustration, 36,284 miles per second in relation to the earth from which it started. And let's suppose, further, that a ray of light passes you, traveling (as it has been measured to do) at the rate of 186,284 miles per second in relation to the earth. By analogy with the relation between the motor cars you would infer that the light is drawing away from you at the rate of 150,000 miles per second. Such, however, is not the case. In the new physics the speed of light is taken to move always at the rate of 186,284 in relation to all moving bodies whatever!

How can such a paradox be swallowed? In the perspective of ordinary notions of space and time it obviously cannot. If we are to accept the hypothesis of the *constant velocity of light in rela-*

tion to all moving objects—regardless of in what direction or with what velocity they are moving—a change of perspective is logically inevitable. On the classical assumptions velocity is taken as a function of distance and time. That is to say, our familiar way of calculating runs like this: If you travel a given distance (say one mile) in a given time (say 10 minutes) you are thereby defined as traveling at such and such a velocity—in this case 6 miles per hour. If you halve the distance (half a mile in 10 minutes) you halve the velocity (it now becomes 3 miles per hour), but if instead you halve the time (a mile in 5 minutes) you double the velocity (which now becomes 12 miles per hour). All of that is both plain and familiar.

Mathematically, however, it is equally possible to work backwards: i.e., given the velocity, to compute an equation of relationships between distance and time. And that is what has to be done, once the velocity of light is taken as an invariant. Thus it is that whereas both Newtonian physics and "common sense" accept the three dimensions of space and the one dimension of time as irreducible and clearly homogeneous, the new physics regards them as different dimensional aspects of space-time.

A corollary of the foregoing is that the size of anything is affected by its rate of motion relatively to something else. The length of a measuring rod is affected by its direction and rate of movement. It is shorter when it moves in the dimension of its length than when it moves at right angles to it. This alteration is known as the FitzGerald contraction. In ordinary mundane velocities the contraction is so extremely slight that it may be ignored. When, on the other hand, the velocities are enormously high, as in the case of intra-atomic particles, or the distances enormously great, as in the case of inter-stellar distances, the contraction becomes of substantial importance.

The Lorentz transformations

The paradox can be seen in another perspective by considering one of the transformation equations first computed by H. A.

Lorentz, representing the relation between the measurements of distance which two observers in different moving frames of reference will make. The equation, when the two frames of reference are moving at uniform velocities in straight lines with respect to each other, is as follows:

$$x' = \frac{x-vt}{\sqrt{1-\frac{v^2}{c^2}}}$$

In this equation x' and x stand for the distance measurements which the two moving observers will make respectively; v for their velocity relative to each other; c for the velocity of light; and t for whatever time interval is chosen. Although the full mathematical implications of the formula transcend the understanding of the layman, a moment's close inspection will show what a radical idea is here involved. According to our ordinary notions, an increase in time would involve an increase in the distance traveled. This familiar relation would be indicated by the Lorentz equation if only the numerator were retained and the denominator ignored. For we would then have the simple equation: $x' = x - vt$, which can be transposed to read: $x - x' = vt$. It says that the difference between the distance measurement made by a passenger in the automobile moving at 55 miles per hour and one in the automobile moving at 40 miles per hour is equal to v, the velocity of the two cars relative to each other, multiplied by the time-interval t. This is precisely what we should expect. For v in this case is 15 miles per hour, and if we take a time-span of 20 minutes or one third of an hour, and thus set t equal to $1/3$, the value of vt becomes 5. Now to write

$$x' = x - 5$$

is simply to express the familiar fact that in 20 minutes the slower car (x') will have traveled 5 miles less than the faster car. There is no difficulty so far.

And this is virtually what the Lorentz equation actually says for ordinary velocities. For examine the denominator:

$$\sqrt{1-\frac{v^2}{c^2}}.$$

In everyday situations the fraction is extremely small. Even the fastest modern jet planes travel only about a third of a mile per second. A numerator of $\frac{1}{3}^2$ over a denominator of $(186,284)^2$ is so very minute as to be virtually zero; hence the larger denominator becomes virtually 1, and the simple equation $x'=x-vt$ is all that remains. The theory of relativity does not affect our technique of measurement in the context of ordinary life.

When very great velocities are in question, however, the distance measurements of the two observers is no longer a simple affair. If we start by knowing or assuming the distance measurement of one observer, x, to have a certain value, then the distance measurement of the other observer, x', will be greater than we would expect it to be by ordinary means of computation (the two moving cars, for example); and it will go on being greater to just the extent that their velocity relative to each other, v, increases. The relative standards of distance measurement become increasingly paradoxical as the velocity relative to two moving systems increases.

The field theory

What Einstein has called the most important discovery in physics since Newton may be put briefly thus: "It is not the charges nor the particles, but the field in the space between the charges and the particles, which is essential for the description of physical phenomena."[13] This is a difficult concept for the layman to grasp; it is epitomized best, perhaps, by Hilbert's statement that gravitation acts so as to make the total curvature of space-time a minimum, or by E. T. Whittaker's "Gravitation

[13] Einstein and Infeld, *op. cit.*, p. 259.

simply represents a continual effort of the universe to straighten itself out," or by the often repeated remark that gravitation has become a metric property of space-time.

Philosophically the theory is important not because of any logical consequences, but because it seems to have furnished the germ of one of the most important and suggestive ideas in contemporary philosophy—namely, Alfred North Whitehead's theory of the physical universe as *organism,* growing out of his attack upon what he calls the "fallacy of simple location." Things and events cannot be defined in isolation, Whitehead argues, for they are not two kinds of entity but inseparable parts of an "actual occasion," and each "actual occasion" is spread over space and goes through time. Points and instants are merely abstractions derived from contemplating actual occasions in terms of geometrical problems. There is nothing corresponding to them in the world of physical actualities. Physical nature is *process,* and it is *organism.* Being process, it never stops to have its picture taken. Being organism, it can only be known in its togetherness. The statement of field theory quoted above—"not the charges nor the particles but the field in the space between" —becomes for Whitehead "not the events nor the substances, but their ever-changing interconnectedness"—as essential for the description of physical phenomena.

On this basis, then, traditional materialism with its corollary of absolute determinism—"cause exactly equal to the effect"— cannot be maintained. To verify the deterministic hypothesis would require a comparison of an earlier state of the cosmos with a later state; but "the philosophy of organism" (as Whitehead calls his metaphysical extension of the field theory) declares that no such comparison is possible, inasmuch as there is no such thing as an earlier state sharply distinct from a later state.

The older point of view enables us to abstract from change and to conceive of the full reality of Nature *at an instant,* in abstraction from any temporal duration and characterized as to its interrelations solely by the instantaneous distribution of matter in space. . . . For the modern view process, activity, and change are the matter of fact. At an instant there is nothing. Each instant is only a way of grouping matters of fact. Thus since there are no instants, conceived as simple primary entities, there is no Nature at an instant.[14]

The causal laws of classical physics, most clearly stated in the *Logic* of John Stuart Mill, are criticized by the eminent Swiss mathematician Hermann Weyl, as "no more than a rough attempt to describe the methodology of inductive research." Their main shortcoming, Professor Weyl adds, "lies in the failure to explain how the various given 'instances' to which the rules refer are to be isolated from a situation given as a whole."[15] And Professor F. A. Lindemann emphasizes the paradoxical nature of the situation when he writes:

There is no sense in discussing the co-ordinates of particles unless they are in principle observable. There is no way of observing them without altering the essential quantities. Each time a particle is observed we render its future uncertain.[16]

The indeterminacy principle

Evidently related to the changed perspective brought about by the field theory is the emphasis on indeterminacy as an essential and irreducible element in nature. D'Abro's exposition of the matter is so exact that I offer the following passage in his own words:

In Minkowski's four-dimensional space-time, a measurement of position and of time may be represented by a point which, on being joined to the origin, determines a four-dimensional vector called a space-time vector. A measurement of momentum and of

---

[14] Alfred North Whitehead, *Nature and Life* (Cambridge University Press, 1934), pp. 47-48.
[15] Hermann Weyl, *Philosophy of Mathematics and Natural Science* (Princeton University Press, 1949), p. 193.
[16] F. A. Lindemann, *The Physical Significance of the Quantum Theory* (Oxford University Press, 1932), p. 146.

energy determines another vector called the momentum-energy vector. Heisenberg's uncertainty relations, which connote the impossibility of obtaining a simultaneous knowledge of the space-time position of a particle and of its momentum and energy, may therefore be expressed by the statement: The space-time vector and the energy-momentum vector cannot be focused simultaneously; the better the one is focused, the more blurred does the other become. Now, the rigorous conservation of momentum and of energy has a meaning only insofar as momentum and energy can be accurately defined, and this is possible only when the momentum-energy vector is rigorously focused. The space-time position then becomes utterly uncertain, so that the rigorous laws of conservation are incompatible with an accurate localization in space-time. Thus, the rigorous conservation laws, which illustrate rigorous causal connections, may be retained but only when an accurate space-time localization is relinquished. Conversely, when an accurate localization is secured, rigorous conservation laws cease to hold. These results may be generalized into the statement: A rigorous space-time description and a rigorous causal sequence for individual processes cannot be realized simultaneously—the one or the other must be sacrificed. This statement expresses Bohr's Principle of Complementarity.[17]

We can, to be sure, ascribe both position and velocity to a particle if we are willing to accept a certain margin of inaccuracy in our statements. If, however, we insist on a more accurate statement of position, the greater accuracy is attained at the cost of less accuracy in the statement of the velocity; and vice versa.

Although the metaphysical implications of the uncertainty principle are still in dispute among physicists, there seems to be a growing recognition that the old exactitudes which could be postulated for a Newtonian universe no longer have application to the world that contemporary physics has opened up. The English physicist, Charles Galton Darwin (not to be confused with the older and more widely known biologist of that name) has summed up the contemporary outlook as follows:

[17] A. d'Abro, *The Rise of the New Physics* (Dover Publications, 1951), Vol. II, pp. 950-951. By courtesy of the publisher.

In the old days it looked as if the world had hard outlines, and the old logic was the appropriate machinery for its discussion. Things went wrong when it was found necessary to call in the help of the principle of probability; this appeared at first as an alien, but there was hope in the old days that the alien might be naturalized. It has resisted the process and we now recognize that it cannot be assimilated. . . . Nature has no sharp edges, and if there is a slight fuzziness inherent in absolutely all the facts of the world, then we must be wrong if we attempt to draw a picture in hard outline.[18]

For Further Study

James B. Conant, *Science and Common Sense* (Yale University Press, 1951).

G. Burniston Brown, *Science, Its Method and Philosophy* (Norton, 1950).

A. G. Ramsperger, *Philosophies of Science* (Crofts, 1942).

W. H. Werkmeister, *A Philosophy of Science* (Harper, 1940).

A. C. Benjamin, *An Introduction to the Philosophy of Science* (Macmillan, 1937).

Karl Pearson, *The Grammar of Science* (1892; republished in Everyman's Library).

E. F. Caldin, *The Power and Limits of Science* (London, Chapman and Hall, 1949).

James H. Jeans, *Physics and Philosophy* (Macmillan, 1948).

Arthur S. Eddington, *The Nature of the Physical World* (Macmillan, 1937).

Henry Morgenau, *The Nature of Physical Reality* (McGraw-Hill, 1950). Many of the chapters presuppose technical knowledge, but particularly Chapters 4 and 5 (on Constructs) and 16 ("The Breakdown of Physical Models") can be read with profit by an attentive philosophy student.

C. F. von Weizsäcker, *The World View of Physics* (University of Chicago Press, 1952), especially Chapter Five, on the role of symbolism in natural science.

[18] Charles Galton Darwin, in his presidential address to the mathematical and physical science section of the British Association for the Advancement of Science, in *Science*, n.s., Vol. 88 (1938). What is here the final sentence comes earlier in the address.

P. W. Bridgman, *A Philosophy of Science* (Harper, 1940).
Bertrand Russell, *The ABC of Relativity* (Harper, 1925).
Albert Einstein and Leopold Infeld, *The Evolution of Physics* (Simon and Schuster, 1938).
Herbert Butterfield, *The Origins of Modern Science* (Macmillan, 1951).
William Cecil Dampier, *A History of Science and Its Relations with Philosophy and Religion* (Cambridge University Press, rev. ed., 1949).
Edmund T. Whittaker, *From Euclid to Eddington: A Study of Conceptions of the External World* (Cambridge University Press, 1949).

Questions for Discussion

1. Would your confidence in a competent mechanic's ability to discover the cause of trouble in your car be lessened if you believed that the ultimate laws of nature are not certain but only highly probable?

2. Caldin writes (*op. cit.*) that although measurement of time by clocks is indirect, since it employs measurements of length, it is possible to measure time directly also, by reference to the swings of a pendulum.
    a) What unverifiable assumption is made in measuring a time-interval by comparison with the swing of a pendulum?
    b) Does this way of measuring time really escape the necessity of measuring lengths?

3. Richard Wistar sums up "the kinetic-molecular of an ideal gas" as follows: (*a*) A gas is made up of molecules in rapid motion. (*b*) They undergo frequent collisions. (*c*) They move in straight lines between collisions. (*d*) The molecules are negligibly small in comparison with the space occupied by a gas. (*e*) They have no attraction for each other. (*f*) The collisions are perfectly elastic, in that no loss of kinetic energy results. (*Man and his Physical Universe*, Wiley, 1953).
    From what you know of physics, could you identify some of these propositions as more empirically verifiable than others? If so, what scientific justification have the others?

4. "Common sense imagines that when it sees a table it sees a table. This is a gross delusion."—BERTRAND RUSSELL.

a) Reconstruct what you suppose to have been Mr. Russell's grounds for this remark. Then verify your supposition by consulting pp. 213-214 of *The ABC of Relativity*.

b) Is Mr. Russell's second sentence an over-statement? If so, how would you rephrase it?

5. Is John Stuart Mill's statement that "invariability of succession is found *by observation* to obtain between every fact in nature and some other fact which has preceded it" consistent or inconsistent with the passage quoted on p. 137 of the text and with Mill's reference to "the undoubted assurance we have that there is a law to be found if only we knew how to find it"? (*A System of Logic,* Bk. III, Chap. V, Sec. 2.)

CHAPTER VI

The Problem of Reality

THE QUESTION of reality is the basic question of philosophy on its metaphysical as distinguished from its ethical side. Generally speaking there are two ways of asking the question: it can be asked dogmatically, and it can be asked critically. To ask bluntly, "What constitutes pure reality, as opposed to mere appearance?" is to invite a closed answer, and a partisan mode of argument. *Materialists* and *idealists* (both terms to be taken in their philosophical, not their popular sense) give contrary answers to the question, but in their more extreme forms both doctrines agree as to the propriety of asking the question in such terms. The failure of philosophers during twenty-five hundred years to solve the question as thus formulated has forced certain of their number, more candid or less optimistic than the rest, into a position of scepticism. Even a sceptic, however, must act, and therefore on the positive side of his philosophy the sceptic is likely to be a *pragmatist,* holding that the only meaning of "real" is what, in the long run, "works."

But materialism, idealism, and pragmatism are not the only possible answers to the problem of basic reality. It is quite possible to formulate the metaphysical question in such a way as to avoid the assumption that the answer should be of a closed and doctrinaire type. This is done by asking not "What is real and what is mere appearance?" but *"In what precise sense* may this and that object or aspect of experience be considered real?" The

161

philosophy which results from putting the question of reality always in the second form rather than the first, has been called by several names; the most suitable of which is doubtless *contextualism,* or still better, *contextual realism.* The present chapter will therefore examine the claims and the shortcomings of materialism, idealism and scepticism in turn, and will then illustrate the method by which contextual realism can overcome the difficulties which inhere in each of them.

i. Materialism

Materialism is the metaphysical theory which takes the kinetic concept of nature (expounded in the last chapter) as the very standard of *reality,* and declines to regard other aspects of experience as real except so far as they can be translated into kinetic terms. The following passages from three materialists living at different periods of history will indicate the persistent power of the idea.

Matter and motion

(1) Some four centuries before the beginning of the Christian era the Greek philosopher Democritus taught as follows:

There are two kinds of knowledge: real knowledge and obscure knowledge. To obscure knowledge belong all things of sight, sound, odor, taste and touch; real knowledge is distinct from this. . . . We perceive nothing true in what concerns the thing itself unless it is modifications of the position of the body and the things which fall upon or resist us. . . . Sweet and bitter, heat and cold, and color, are only opinions; there is nothing true but atoms and the void.

(2) In the seventeenth century of our era a vigorous expression of materialism was embodied in Thomas Hobbes' treatise, *Leviathan.* In the first chapter he declares:

All of which qualities [color, sound, savor, heat, feeling, etc.] called *sensible,* are, in the object that causeth them, but so many

THE PROBLEM OF REALITY 163

several motions of the matter, by which it presseth our organs diversely. Neither in us that are pressed, are they any thing else but divers motions; for motion produceth nothing but motion.

(3) Finally a twentieth-century materialist, Hugh Elliot, has written as follows:

All that really exists is the material particles of the substance of the nervous system. When these particles enter upon a certain kind of chemical activity, the effect is to suggest the existence of some new kind of elusive non-material entity called mind. But this entity has no more real existence than has fire. In each case we have to do exclusively with molecules undergoing disintegration or combination. This chemical activity suffices in itself to account for the whole of the phenomena flowing from the center of activity, and the belief in any additional independent entity is a fallacy which itself can be expressed in physico-chemical terms. The flames of a fire flash out swiftly in all directions and vanish again, to reappear instantly in a closely similar form. So, too, the ideation or emotion of the individual may open up new avenues of mind for a brief moment, as they travel on to a new position. In each case the fluctuations of form are due to the constantly changing area of chemical activity; and just as the fire maintains for short periods a relative constancy of size and shape, so the mental content of an individual is apt to remain for a time at about the same value of intensity, and fastened to the same subjects of attention. At times the fire burns low; at other times it bursts forth into exuberant activity. The accuracy of the analogy is due to the fact that both phenomena are based upon the same foundation; the one is a manifestation from inorganic matter, while the other is a manifestation from organic matter, and therefore immeasurably more complex as to its chemistry.[1]

In short, the metaphysical principle which Elliot puts forward is "the denial of any form of existence other than those envisaged by physics and chemistry, that is to say, other than existences that have some kind of palpable material characteris-

[1] Hugh Elliot, *Modern Science and Materialism* (Longmans, Green, 1919), pp. 196-197.

tics and quality." The kinetic principle has here been raised to the status of a metaphysical absolute.

Determinism

The principle of causal uniformity, too, is given absolute status by modern materialists. Every occurrence, the materialist holds, is predetermined in every last detail by what has occurred previously. Hence in a basic sense there is truly nothing new under the sun. Older materialists did not always adhere to this principle. Epicurus, in particular, while insisting that the motion of atoms through space is the only real kind of occurrence, attempted to account for the diversity of the world and man's apparent freedom by postulating that from time to time one atom or another—quite spontaneously, from no cause at all—deviates ever so slightly from the straight line in which it has been traveling; whence collisions occur, and interminglings, and the long slow evolution of the complex world. Modern materialists repudiate that aspect of the older theory as naive. A slight deviation, they argue, is as much a violation of the causal principle as a great one would be. Later occurrences are predetermined by earlier occurrences not grossly but minutely. There are no real spontaneities. When we are surprised it is always merely the result of our ignorance. Hence the modern materialist declares with the astronomer Laplace:

> If for a single instant an intelligence were to be acquainted with all the forces by which nature is animated and with the positions of all the particles that compose it, and if this intelligence should be capable of submitting all these data to rational analysis, it would represent by one and the same formula the movements of the largest bodies in the universe and those of the smallest atom. Nothing would be uncertain for it; the future as well as the past would be open to its inspection.

Anyone who possessed such powers and who ten billion years ago possessed complete knowledge of every movement occurring in the nebular universe which then presumably existed, would have been able to predict every minutest action which anyone of us living today is now performing or is going to perform. Man, in the last analysis, is entirely a product of circumstance.

The problem of secondary qualities

To conceive of physical nature in strictly kinetic terms raises a troublesome philosophical conundrum. What is to be the metaphysical status—that is to say, the status in terms of reality and unreality—of the *non*-kinetic aspects of things? If warmth (as felt) is to be "explained" by a visual model, namely colliding molecules; if music (as heard) is to be "explained" by another visual model, namely air-vibrations within a certain range of frequencies; then what kind of entities are the heard sounds and the felt warmth themselves? To explain them is to relate them to something else, but you can only relate them if they somehow exist. The philosophically thoughtful scientists of the seventeenth century had therefore to face the question: In what sense can existence be attributed to the experienced qualities which are not accepted as terms of scientific explanation? If by Boyle's mechanical hypothesis the colors and sounds and warmth and coolness which seem to characterize nature are "really" not in nature at all, then where and what are they?

Cartesian dualism

The answer that won widest acceptance was expressed in the dualism of Descartes and afterwards of John Locke. In one of the most influential books in modern philosophy, *An Essay concerning Human Understanding* (1690) Locke distinguishes between the *primary qualities* of bulk, figure, number, situation, and motion, which our senses discover as actually existing in the physical world, and *secondary qualities* which "are nothing but the powers those substances have to produce several ideas in us by our senses." Color and sound, warmth and chill, flavor and fragrance, taken as we directly experience them, are not qualities in objects, but are "ideas in us produced"; the corresponding qualities in the objects are the powers of producing them. Thus Locke postulates a dualism between the "qualities," both primary and secondary, which really characterize the world of nature (all of them expressible as quantities) and the "ideas" which those objectively real characteristics produce in sentient minds. Some ideas (the ideas of spatial location and movement, for instance) resemble the corresponding qualities of objects, while other ideas (e.g., of red and blue) do not. This type of dualism, which has been strongly influential on much subsequent philosophy, is sometimes called *epistemological dualism,* because it is offered as an answer to the problem of epistemology —the problem of valid knowledge; sometimes *representative dualism,* because the ideas of red and blue are said to "represent" the physical motions that cause them; sometimes *Cartesian dualism,* after the seventeenth-century French philosopher Des Cartes or Descartes, who advocated and defended it.

Descartes himself was not a materialist. He was interested in both sides of the dualism; but he insisted on their sharp ontological cleavage.

> Extension in length, breadth and depth, constitutes the nature of corporeal substance; and thought constitutes the nature of thinking substance. For all else that may be attributed to body presupposes extension, and is merely a mode of this extended thing; as everything we find in mind is merely so many diverse forms of thinking. Thus, for example, we cannot conceive of figure except in an extended thing, nor of movement except in an extended space: so imagination, feeling, and will, only exist in a thinking thing.[2]

The material world, the world of matter, he defined as consisting of geometrical qualities exclusively—shape, size, and motion; thereby giving philosophical support to the development of the kinetic theory in science. On the other hand, his treatise on the "passions" (i.e., feelings and other mental states) of the soul

[2] Descartes, *Principia Philosophiae,* Part I, Principle 53.

gave impetus to the development of modern psychology. Moreover he believed that soul and body could *mutually* affect each other's activity; this is the theory of interactionism, which will be examined in Chapter IX.

But it was Descartes' geometrical definition of matter, as "extended substance," not his belief in the mind's independent reality, that proved to have the stronger influence. The idea of "mind," which he defined as "thinking substance," had only a negative utility for physical scientists: as a convenient intellectual receptacle to which they might relegate all those aspects of experience which have no place in the kinetic view of things. The Cartesian philosophy encouraged physicists to consider light-waves as "physical," the blues and greens produced by them as "mental." The physicist who is also a materialist goes a step farther: light-waves, being physical, are objectively "real"; the blues and greens are mere subjective "appearances." Descartes, moreover, allowed that man might play some part in directing the actions of his body and hence in controlling the universe that surrounds him; the materialist denies that he can ever be anything more than a mere product of all that has gone before.

Critique of materialism

Is out-and-out materialism of this sort an inevitable result of the straightforward advance of scientific thinking? Is it the price of scientific progress that man as an independent, willing, aspiring, thinking self or soul must be conceived as a zero, a kind of presumptuous illusion, a mere ghostly excrescence on the pattern of a mechanically ordered universe? No such consequence necessarily follows. Some practicing scientists have tended toward materialism, many others have not; if materialism followed logically from an examination of scientific practice, how would such diversity be explained? Materialism is only one of several ways of fitting the facts of science into a world-picture; three other main ways are presently to be examined. One's judgment of the claims of materialism must be made partly in the light of these alternative views, partly in the context of the problems developed in later chapters, and partly from the maturing of one's attitude toward the experiences of actual living. Two preliminary criticisms, however, can be offered at this time.

The use and abuse of scientific objects

What is a scientific object? Consider an atom, for example. By the postulates of the kinetic theory, an atom has only primary qualities, and is therefore colorless. But in any picture we form of an atom it obviously must have some color—a shade of gray at least—or it could not be visually distinguished from what is adjacent. The atom as a scientific object, then, is fundamentally different from the mental pictures that are appealed to when thinking about it—when it is likened to billiard balls, for instance.

Suppose someone began to talk seriously of a man seeing an atom through a microscope, or better perhaps of cutting one in half with a knife. There are a number of non-analytical people who would be quite prepared to believe that an atom could be visible to the eye or cut in this manner. But anyone at all conversant with physical conceptions would almost as soon think of killing the square root of two with a rook rifle as of cutting an atom in half with a knife. One's conception of an atom is reached through a process of hypothesis and analysis, and in the world of atoms there are no knives and no men to cut. If you have thought with a strong consistent mental movement, then when you have thought of your atom under the knife blade, your knife blade has itself become a cloud of swinging grouped atoms, and your microscope lens a little universe of oscillatory and vibratory molecules. If you think of the universe, thinking at the level of atoms, there is neither knife to cut, scale to weigh, nor eye to see. The universe *at that plane to which the mind of the molecular physicist descends* has none of the shapes or forms of our common life whatever.[3]

Dogmatic materialism is based upon the fallacy of confusing scientific objects with real things. Contemporary scientists, by

[3] H. G. Wells, *First and Last Things* (London: Cassell), pp. 39-40.

and large, are less prone to the fallacy than the scientists of a generation ago: thanks largely to the paradoxes (mentioned in the last chapter) which recent physics has discovered in such scientific objects as light, space, and matter. Nevertheless the tendency toward materialistic thinking is still strong.

If metaphysical beliefs were fully consistent with the actual practices of those who hold them, no scientist would be a hard-and-fast materialist. In its most characteristic manifestations science does not stop with theory. The scientist develops his theories, and as a technologist he constructs instruments and machines because of human purposes to be satisfied. Think concretely and there is always some human purpose directing every scientific thought and every technological application; to construct a philosophy in which human purposes are forgotten or explained away as mere by-products is to stand the actual evidence on its head, and to think in abstractions. Science has been developed by man and for man, not man by and for science!

ii. Idealism

An ingenious and revolutionary reply to the materialists was devised by Bishop George Berkeley in the early eighteenth century. In *An Essay towards a New Theory of Vision*, his first important work and a major contribution to the science of optics, Berkeley showed what a different scientific perspective could be got by starting not with the assumption of space but with our way *of knowing* space. His refutation of epistemological dualism is classic in its brevity:

At this time it seems agreed on all hands, by those who have had any thoughts of that matter, that colors, which are the proper and immediate object of sight, are not without the mind. But then it will be said, by sight we have also the ideas of extension, and figure, and motion; all which may well be thought without, and at some distance from the mind, though color should not. In answer to this, I appeal to any man's experience whether the visible extension of any object doth not appear as near to him as the color of that object; nay, whether they do not both seem to be in the very same place. Is not the extension we see colored, and is it possible for us, so much as in thought, to separate and abstract color from extension? Now, where the extension is, there surely is the figure, and there the motion too.[4]

Berkeley has cannily pointed his attention at the one type of secondary quality which is least easily fitted into the theory of epistemological dualism. Color, to a much greater degree than sounds, fragrances, etc., is inseparable from space; and vice versa. Imagine a color, and you imagine it as extended; imagine any extended object, and you necessarily imagine it as distinguished from the surrounding medium by some difference of color or color tone.

To which the materialist is likely to reply that such color differences pertain only to our way of perceiving the object, not to the object itself in its own nature. In his *Principles of Human Knowledge* (1710) Berkeley counterreplies:

> If we thoroughly examine this tenet, it will, perhaps, be found at bottom to depend on the doctrine of *abstract ideas*. For can there be a nicer strain of abstraction than to distinguish the existence of sensible objects from their being perceived, so as to conceive them existing unperceived? Lights and colors, heat and cold, extension and figures, in a word the things we see and feel, what are they but so many sensations, notions, ideas, or impressions on the sense; and is it possible to separate, even in thought, any of these from perception? For my part I might as easily divide a thing from itself.
> I may indeed divide in my thoughts or conceive apart from each other those things which, perhaps, I never perceived by sense so divided. Thus I imagine the trunk of a human body without the limbs, or conceive the smell of a rose without thinking on the rose itself. So far I will not deny I can abstract, if that may properly be called *abstraction* which extends only to the conceiving separately

---

[4] George Berkeley (1685-1753) *Essay towards a New Theory of Vision* (1709). Sec. xviii.

such objects as it is possible may really exist or be actually perceived asunder. But my conceiving or imagining power does not extend beyond the possibility of real existence or perception. Hence as it is impossible for me to see or feel any thing without an actual sensation of that thing, so is it impossible for me to conceive in my thoughts any sensible thing or object distinct from the sensation or perception of it.[5]

Thus Berkeley has succeeded in rejoining the two kinds of quality, secondary and primary, which Descartes and Locke had regarded as ontologically separate. But only at the cost of denying that the physical world has any independent existence whatever!

Some truths there are so near and obvious to the mind, that a man need only open his eyes to see them. Such I take this important one to be, to wit, that all the choir of heaven and furniture of the earth, in a word all those bodies which compose the mighty frame of the world, have not any subsistence without a mind, that their being (*esse*) is their being perceived or known (*percipi*); that consequently so long as they are not actually perceived by me, or do not exist in my mind or that of any other created spirit, they must either have no existence at all, or else subsist in the mind of some eternal spirit: it being perfectly unintelligible and involving all the absurdity of abstraction, to attribute to any single part of them an existence independent of a spirit.[6]

Esse est percipi: to be is nothing else than to be perceived. Such is the challenging subjective principle to which Berkeley's argument leads. "The absolute existence of unthinking things are words without a meaning." That is to say, the materialist's supposition of objects existing apart from some mind's actual engagement in knowing them is meaningless in the sense of being a barren abstraction, for which no relevant evidence has been, or ever can be, adduced. All evidence about the nature

---

[5] George Berkeley, *Principles of Human Knowledge,* Sec. v.
[6] *Ibid.,* Sec. vi, with one small grammatical emendation for clarity.

of things is mental evidence; it is something perceived and known to a mind which interprets and judges it and uses it in the establishment of theories. To talk of nonmental objects is to cut the evidence in two, and ignore one half of it. Berkeley caps the argument by his celebrated dilemma:

> In short, if there were external bodies, it is impossible we should ever come to know it; and if there were not, we might have the very same reasons to think there were that we have now. Suppose, what no one can deny possible, an intelligence, without the help of external bodies, to be affected with the same train of sensations or ideas that you are, imprinted in the same order and with like vividness in his mind. I ask, whether that intelligence hath not all the reason to believe the existence of corporeal substances, represented by his ideas, and exciting them in his mind, that you can possibly have for believing the same thing? Of this there can be no question; which one consideration is enough to make any reasonable person suspect the strength of whatever arguments he may think himself to have for the existence of bodies without the mind.[7]

The materialist, however, might retort: "If nothing exists save someone's ideas, how can there be valid scientific prediction? Our ideas are notoriously sometimes wayward; the scientific discipline undertakes to correct that waywardness by discovering an ordered world independent of the ideas, to serve as their standard of truth. How can there be any distinction between truth and error if ideas are all? How can one idea be truer than another, unless there is an external standard by reference to which they are to be compared and judged? More specifically, what basis can there be (once the world of matter is denied) for distinguishing ideas of sense from ideas of fancy? Berkeley's reply to this crucial question takes place upon two levels—the one, phenomenological, the other transcendental.

On the first level Berkeley comes close to the position taken by John Stuart Mill, who in the next century was to define an

---

[7] *Ibid.*, Sec. xx.

"object" as a *permanent possibility of sensation*. That is to say, it is our permanent, or better our ordered and coherent sensations (or "ideas"), that we take as constitutive of the real world —not because they give us mental copies of a real world that exists apart from the mind, but because by "the real world" we *mean* the pattern of orderly relations among ideas which, with care and selection, we can discover. Berkeley puts the point as follows:

> The ideas of sense are more strong, lively, and *distinct* than those of the imagination; they have likewise a steadiness, order, and coherence, and are not excited at random, as those which are the effects of human wills often are, but in a regular train or series. Now *the set rules or established methods, wherein the mind we depend on excites in us the ideas of sense, are called the laws of nature:* and these we learn by experience, which teaches us that such and such ideas are attended with such and such other ideas, in the ordinary course of things.
>
> This gives us a sort of foresight, which enables us to regulate our actions for the benefit of life. And without this we should be eternally at a loss: we could not know how to act anything that might procure us the least pleasure, or remove the least pain of sense. That food nourishes, sleep refreshes, and fire warms us; that to sow in the seed-time is the way to reap in the harvest, and, in general, that to obtain such or such ends, such and such means are conducive, all this we know, *not by discovering any necessary connection between our ideas,* but only by the observation of the settled laws of nature, without which we should be all in uncertainty and confusion, and a grown man no more know how to manage himself in the affairs of life than an infant just born.[8]

But Berkeley does not stop there. The observed fact that there is a "consistent, uniform working among our ideas," and that ideas are constantly borne in upon us which are clearly not altogether the result of our own agency, proves, to his view, that there is "some other will or spirit that produces them." Such evi-

---

[8] *Ibid.,* Secs. xxx, xxxi.

dences of order testify to "the goodness and wisdom of that governing Spirit whose will constitutes the laws of nature." Note that Berkeley says "constitutes" instead of "produces." God (by the logic of this argument) is not an agent acting upon a world of matter distinct from himself. He is the perfect mind, eternally engaged in the activity of thinking a perfect world; the world has no other existence than in God's thought; and the laws of nature are therefore the ways in which God *thinks*. Man's thinking does, therefore, have a standard of objective validity, although that standard is not to be found in a world inertly material. What distinguishes a true idea from a false—whether in the empirical sciences, in morality, theology, or whatever else—is the correspondence of that idea (so far as its limited context allows) with an idea in the mind of God. Science and theology are thus two branches of the same intellectual enterprise; for science is the ordering of our ideas according to one set or another of intelligible principles, and the perfect orderer, the perfect scientist, is God.

iii. Pragmatism

The philosophy which in different contexts has been called *pragmatism, instrumentalism, functionalism,* and (with a negative emphasis) *fictionalism,* reflects a familiar double aspect of the modern temper. On the one hand, a disillusionment with lofty theories which prove impossible to substantiate in detail. On the other hand, a zest to get things done, and consequently a willingness to judge the worth and even the "truth" of a theory or a philosophy by its success or failure in practice. Generally speaking, the pragmatic philosophy defines "reality" and "truth" in terms of the values that inhere in action successfully performed —although there is admittedly some difference of conviction among pragmatists as to the standards by which success should be judged.

Vaihinger's doctrine of "as-if"

Perhaps the most systematic treatment of the pragmatic philosophy is contained in Hans Vaihinger's volume, *The Philosophy of "As If."* All theories, Vaihinger argues,—whether scientific, metaphysical, theological, or whatever else—are products of thought; and thought, which has evolved as a biological function in man's struggle for existence, belongs properly "in the service of the will to live and dominate." But since things which originate to serve a certain purpose often undergo a fuller development than is necessary for the attainment of their purpose, finally even becoming ends in themselves, so it has been with the evolution of thought. As men acquire more leisure to theorize, the original practical purpose of thought is lost sight of, and theories become interesting and important in themselves. A result of this artificial development, Vaihinger holds, is that emancipated thought "sets itself problems which are impossible, not only to human thought, but to every form of thought." All metaphysical thinking he regards as falling into this error. Even science, he argues, has a larger fictional element than is generally realized. Take, for example, the concept of *force*.

If two events, one preceding and the other following, are united by a constant bond, we call that peculiarity of the antecedent event, which consists in its being followed by another event, its "force," and we measure this force in terms of the magnitude of its effect. In reality only sequences and coexistences exist, and we ascribe "forces" to things, by regarding the actual phenomena as already possible and then hypostasizing these possibilities and peculiarities, and separating them from the rest as real entities.[9]

From this and associated instances Vaihinger concludes that "theoretical mechanics is for the most part a tissue of purely arbitrary ideas." Roughly the same conclusion holds for all scientific thinking. For science does two things at once. (1) It

[9] Hans Vaihinger (1852-1933), *The Philosophy of "As If"* (Harcourt, Brace, 1924), p. 197.

determines the sequences and co-existences of actually perceived phenomena; and to this extent Vaihinger considers it to be dealing with reality. (2) It "weaves" its discoveries into concepts which give them a more concise, more picturable, and seemingly more intelligible form. These concepts are "the additions of man, and constitute merely the frame in which man encloses the treasure of reality in order that he may manipulate it better. . . . Without their aid we could admittedly not deal with the world, nor would we be able to act; they are, in fact, a necessary evil." We need such "discursive aids" in the practical business of thinking and calculating, and of communicating our thoughts to others. Without them "we would be disarmed, and there would be nothing left for us to do but remain silent and stare vacantly into space, after the manner of certain sceptics." Nevertheless, when the moment of practical necessity has passed we can lay these supplements aside again, just as in mathematics we drop an imaginary quantity that has been introduced in order to facilitate the computation. Or, in another simile, just as a builder removes the scaffolding, which has outlasted its usefulness when the building is completed.[10]

Bridgman's doctrine of the instrument

A physicist who has applied pragmatic method to the interpretation of his own science is Professor P. W. Bridgman. The basis of his argument is his principle of the operational character of concepts, which he defines as follows:

> In general, we mean by any concept nothing more than a set of operations; *the concept is synonymous with the corresponding set of operations.*[11]

Take the concept of length, for example. When we first hear of the relativistic hypothesis that the length of an object is af-

---
[10] Vaihinger, *op. cit.,* pp. 67-68.
[11] P. W. Bridgman, *The Logic of Modern Physics* (Macmillan, 1927), p. 5.

fected by the direction and velocity of its movement, and that the very instruments by which to measure lengths are themselves affected similarly, we are likely to find the situation uncomfortably paradoxical. What *is* length? we may ask in bewilderment. Professor Bridgman's reply is that the question itself is invalid. Absolute existence is a fiction; belief in it is a habit of mind that can only impede the physicist's pursuit of his proper task. That task is always a matter of certain operations. Certain physical operations are performed in finding what we call the length of an object. The concept of length is fixed when the operations of measuring it are fixed; whence Bridgman concludes that "the concept of length involves as much as and nothing more than the set of operations by which length is determined."

In measuring ordinary lengths the operations are usually simple and familiar enough—like applying a yardstick—to give no trouble. But in measuring the length of bodies moving at a high velocity relatively to ourselves (such as stars or cathode particles), the operations have to be quite different. Consequently, Bridgman argues, the length which is spoken of in relativity physics "does not mean the same as" the length which is spoken of in Newtonian physics.

More fundamental than the concept of length is the concept of identity. We feel an imperious demand to know what's what; and even if the length of a thing is unstable we want to know whether it is "the same thing" that has the different lengths. Now there can be no question, Bridgman concedes, that "the concept of identity is a tool perfectly well adapted to deal approximately with nature in the region of our ordinary experience." But what happens when we bring our thought-processes to bear upon the problems of theoretical physics? Our mental habits, with their demand for the idea of identifiable things, are still strong. As a result "we are continually surprising ourselves in the invention of discrete structures further and further down in the scale of things, whose sole *raison d'être* is to be found entirely within ourselves." When the atom is broken down into the positive and negative charges composing it, there is a strong urge (not only in laymen but in many scientists) to form a *picture* of the components, or at least of the orbits on which they move. The simile of the atom as a miniature solar system is the result. But "what physical assurance have we that an electron in jumping about in an atom preserves its identifiability in anything like the way that we suppose, or that the identity concept applies here at all?" The motive for applying the identity concept on this level of investigation is not experimental, but psychological. The concept here becomes an empty one; in terms of the physicist's actual operations Bridgman declares it to be without meaning. The valid meanings corresponding to the ideas of identity and continuity are found in a precise description of the operations undertaken in finding experimental evidences of them.

An associated conundrum is that of ultimate component parts. The mind habitually seeks a stopping place where its work of analysis may theoretically come to rest: if atoms are not ultimate, then we tend to think that there must be some components of atoms, or components of the components, that are so. There must be some material entities, we argue, out of which all larger structures are formed. Bridgman replies that not only does present experimental evidence suggest the probability that there are structures within the electron and the quantum, but moreover that "there is no experimental evidence that the sequence of phenomena in nature as we go to ever smaller scales is a terminated sequence, or that a drop of water is not in itself essentially infinite." In short, "there is no evidence that nature reduces to *simplicity* as we burrow down into the small scale."[12]

Critique of pragmatism

Pragmatists have performed a good service in emphasizing the derivative and instrumental character of abstract theories, and thereby destroying their dogmatic claims. Theories were made

---

[12] Bridgman, *op. cit.*, p. 207. Cf. the humanistic application which Dr. Hocking makes of this idea: Chap. X, p. 318.

by men for men's use. When they are so formulated that they seem to contradict men's clearest and best insights into the real nature of things, we had better ask whether the proper function of a theory—which is to elucidate experience rather than to negate it—has not been forgotten.

Nevertheless, the pragmatist, in restricting the role of theory, may have gone too far in the opposite way. To describe only the operations performed and the perceptual findings of the experiment is laboratory hackwork, not science in the full sense. Science is more than manipulation and observation; it involves interpretation also. It seeks not only to report nature but to understand her. In what sense can scientific interpretation be more than "as if" thinking? A chemist-philosopher, E. F. Caldin, replies as follows.

Suppose that the scientist's problem is to interpret the empirical generalization that, for a gas at constant temperature, pressure and volume vary inversely. Can we imagine any visual model of the gas such that it would exhibit this law? Professor Caldin writes:

> Classical kinetic theory in its simplest form pictured the gas as a swarm of minute particles, hard and elastic, moving in all directions. These particles, according to the theory, collide with each other and with the walls of the vessel at intervals, and on these occasions behave exactly as billiard balls behave when they collide with each other or with the cushions; or, rather, as billiard balls would behave if they and the cushions were perfectly smooth and elastic, so that no energy were lost by friction. This behavior is presumed to obey the same laws of mechanics as those found for ordinary bodies. The pressure of a gas on the vessel walls is then paralleled by the pressure due to the innumerable impacts of the particles on the walls of the enclosure. If we reduce the volume of the enclosure, the frequency of impact increases (because on the average a particle meets the wall more often) and so the pressure increases. Exact calculation by the methods of ordinary dynamics shows that for this model the product pv would indeed be a constant, just as we found by experiment for actual gases. . . .

So far, then, the theoretical model is in accord with the observations. The gas behaves *as if* it consisted of hard elastic particles obeying the laws of Newtonian mechanics. But this alone would not be sufficient support for the theory. For it might be possible to devise many other models that would agree equally well with our observations. However, the pressure-volume relation is not the only one that this model can reproduce. For instance, if we assume that increase of temperature may be represented by increase in the average velocity of the particles, we find that we can deduce for the model a relation between temperature, pressure and volume that is very close to that found experimentally for gases. And many other properties of gases—diffusion, viscosity, and so on—are likewise quantitatively represented. The theoretical interpretation suggested does not agree merely with one observed property of the gas; it is in harmony with many observed properties of very diverse kinds. One single model accounts for a variety of observations; many different experiments are unified by a single theory.[13]

To be "in harmony with many observed properties of very diverse kinds" is admittedly proof of the usefulness of a theoretical interpretation; is it a proof of its truth as well? Is it a ground for judging that we have gotten intellectually closer to the heart of things—to actual reality—than we had done by earlier and less adequate theories? The pragmatist says "No." We are vaporizing when we talk about reality; let us stick to the criterion of utility, which we can understand.

But utility for what? The pragmatist's usual reply is: for ordering our sensations and thereby serving the total needs of the human organism coping with its manifold environment. Vaihinger subscribes to this ulterior justification, although in consistency he can mean by "human organism" only the complex of sensations, internal and external, which it yields us. Thus it becomes evident that a pragmatist such as Vaihinger has his own standard of reality—despite his attempt to regard "reality" as no more than a fiction and instrument of thought. For he,

[13] E. F. Caldin, *The Power and Limits of Science* (London: Chapman and Hall, 1949), p. 19. By courtesy of the publisher.

too, is making a metaphysical judgment in declaring that sensations as we receive them, prior to theoretical interpretation, constitute the real stuff of experience and hence the only reality we can know; that all other alleged realities—whether God or vital force or atoms and electrons—are but the fictitious products of "logical activity" carried on for the sake of ordering, comparing, predicting, and perhaps controlling sensations.

It would appear, then, that Vaihinger's philosophy is tangent to Berkeley's in its sensate aspect, despite different vocabularies and different ulterior reaches. Unlike the Bishop he cannot have recourse to God as an explanatory principle; for the theoretical constructs of theology he rejects quite as decisively as those of science. He is left, then, with a philosophy of *immediatism*, or (in the technical sense) *sensationalism*. He is committed to the proposition that the advance of modern science over Greek and Arabian science does not consist in its giving a more truthful account of reality, but solely in the fact that its fictions have proved more useful than theirs in enabling us to predict and control (not to understand!) our sensuous life. Is such scepticism the last word?

iv. *Contextual Realism*

Can there be a metaphysical standpoint which neither reduces all other aspects of human experience to mere appearances or symbols of a natural universe, nor yet, on the other hand, deprecates the scientific picture of the universe as a set of fictions? To find such a middle ground is a part of the great contemporary task of bridging the gap between the sciences and the humanities, and thus of reaffirming the essential wholeness of man's intellectual interests. To do this requires a double effort of criticism. On the one hand humanistic wisdom should take full account of scientifically established truths—estimating cannily the degree to which, and the sense in which, they really *are* established. On the other hand, the discoveries and the theoretical constructs of science should be interpreted and evaluated in large humanistic context—that is, in relation to all that deeply and persistently concerns man as an intellectual, vital, and aspirational being.

Characteristics of science

Let us begin by recapitulating the principal characteristics of the scientific outlook, for (remembering Spinoza's *Determinatio est negatio*)[14] the way to see beyond the perspective of science is to understand very precisely what that perspective involves. Six characteristics of science will prove especially illuminating in this respect.

1. Science *describes* phenomena; it does not, explicitly at least, evaluate them. Of course the scientist is also a man and a citizen, he may be a husband, a father, an artist, a moral idealist, and much else. In each of these roles he serves certain values. Moreover, these are the values of science itself—the value of intellectual integrity, above all else. But scientific procedure, although conditioned by such values, does not deal with them. It is the function of each science to discover, in the field it has staked out, what is actually the case, regardless of what the scientist's or anyone else's wishes in the matter might be.

2. Scientific descriptions are *selective*. The different sciences are distinguished from one another by the specific principles of selection they adopt. Thus a physicist, a chemist, an anatomist, and a psychologist select different, though overlapping, types of problem to investigate, and accept correspondingly different sets of data as relevant to their inquiries. Nevertheless, there is a more abstract sense in which all natural sciences employ an identical principle of selection: they tend to accept as proper data only those aspects of things that are *publicly verifiable*. Thus the somewhat private experiences of the religious mystic, the lover, and the artist are not accepted as directly evidential. In a sense they are of interest to the psychologist; but only as offering clues to the nature of the "subject"—the psychophysical

[14] Cf. Chap. III, p. 54.

organism—not as offering clues to the nature of the world with which the subject thinks himself to be in contact. Moreover, the scientific psychologist does not rest content with the subject's verbal testimony as to what he has experienced, but seeks confirmatory evidence in overt behavior. Thus to the scientific psychologist the "subject" becomes an *object* of investigation. The aim in science is to eliminate as far as possible the subjective and personal element from the problem.

3. Science is guided by the principle of parsimony. This finds expression at the very threshold of the modern era in "Occam's razor" as it has become called—the rule of good explanation formulated by the English Fransciscan philosopher William of Occam (or Ockham) early in the fourteenth century: *Entia non multiplicanda est praeter necessitatem.* That is to say, of two explanations, both of which account for the known facts, choose the one which requires the fewer additional assumptions.

4. Science is not interested in an individual as such, but only as *representative of a class,* and as indicating something about the nature of that class. There are, to be sure, overlapping classes, and a part of the scientist's task with respect to each datum is classificatory—deciding of what class or classes it is representative, and in what way.

Physics is concerned with general laws. It is not interested in individual events as such. It is true that some unique occurrence, such as an eclipse, might conceivably be of physical interest, but only in so far as it exemplified general laws. Physics is concerned with events following one another according to a general rule, in invariable sequence (such as the cooling and freezing of water); or events always occurring together (such as the heating of an axle by friction when it rotates); or with properties found always together in invariable association (such as the lustre of metals and their high electrical conductivity); or indeed the properties of any definite and stable chemical substance, whether element or compound.[15]

---

[15] Caldin, *op. cit.,* p. 10.

5. As science advances, it puts increased emphasis upon data that can be *measured*. This is a natural corollary of the principle of public verifiability. A scientist wishes to have his discoveries and hypotheses verified—by other scientists and by his own later experiments—not only in a rough loose way, but as exactly as possible; and therefore, other considerations equal, he prefers measurable results. Hence, although measurement is given more prominence in some sciences than in others—e.g., in physics than in biology—nevertheless it may be said generally that science, particularly in its more developed stages, tends to stress the quantitative aspect of things, and either to ignore or to regard as mere by-products the radically qualitative aspects.

6. Science is *deterministic*. It accepts the postulate of causal determinism (whether for every individual event, as in classical mechanics, or for statistically determined classes, as in some branches of modern physics) as a regulative ideal—that is, as holding good even in situations where its validity cannot be empirically tested.

The non-scientific

Now by recognizing these characteristics as essential to the meaning of "scientific objects" and hence of the scientific world view, it becomes possible, by simple dialectical antithesis, to discover the apriori possibilities of realms of discourse that are *not* scientific. Briefly, it may be said: Experiences so far as they are (1) evaluated, (2) private, (3) full, (4) individual, (5) qualitative, (6) fortuitous, are not accepted as material for science. Sometimes it is not recognized how many aspects of a situation a scientific inquiry ignores; for the translation of raw materials of experience into scientific forms may go on almost unconsciously in an age where the prestige of science is so high. Nevertheless, if our attitude toward science is to be a humanistically intelligent one we shall be aware of the *experiential difference* between the Newtonian or Einsteinian view of space and the freer spatial perspectives that are found in dreams, in a painting by Cezanne, in the "flowing" space of an architectural interior, or even in just gazing at the sky and seeing the stars as moderately distant pin points of light. Or again, between time as measured by clocks and calendars and time as the slow boredom of crawling hours or as the brisk exciting pulse of living adventure. Or again, between the physicist's analysis of matter into patterns of electrical charges and our familiar acquaintance with matter as something more or less hard, pushable, and impenetrable. Or once again, between the scientist's postulate of a deterministic universe and our own frequent experience of chance events, of novelty, of being taken by surprise, and above all of exerting our own unique and individual power in such a way as to bring about a situation of our own making.

In all these cases we are up against a major division of categories: those defining the scientist's "world" or realm of discourse and those defining realms of discourse which (in a non-pejorative sense) are non-scientific. That the non-scientific categories somehow *are*, and do somehow have meaning, is demonstrated by the dialectical principles already laid down: for if science is more than an empty word it must have definite characteristics; and a set of characteristics can be definite only by being semantically limited—i.e., only by not being some other meaningful set.

Still the partisan of science may protest that the aspects of experience which he emphasizes are somehow more *real* than those which he ignores. Such a partisan will do well to reflect upon Professor C. I. Lewis' sagacious reply:

> The word "real" has a single meaning, of course, in the same sense that "useful" or any other such elliptical term has a single meaning. Nothing is useful for every purpose, and perhaps everything is useful for some purpose. A definition of "useful" *in general* would not divide things into two classes, the useful and the useless. Nor could we arrive at such a definition by attempting to collect all useful things into a class and remark their common characters, since we should probably have everything in the class and nothing outside it

to represent the useless. Instead, we should first have to consider the different types of usefulness or of useful things and then discover, if possible, what it is that characterizes the useful as contrasted with the useless in all these different cases. We should find, of course, that it was not some sense-quality but a relation to an end which was the universal mark of usefulness. Similarly, to arrive at a general definition of "the real" it would not do to lump together all sorts of realities in one class and seek directly for their common character. Everything in this class would be at once real, in some category, and unreal in others. And nothing would be left outside it. The subject of our generalization must be, instead, the distinction real-unreal in all the different categories.[16]

Reality in context

Instead of defining "real" and "unreal" dogmatically, then, let us rather consider *in what sense* each thing, each quality, each relationship is real, and then by analogy attempt to say what common core of meaning all these uses of the words "real" and "reality" share. The most general answer that can be given is: *relevance to the context* (or realm of discourse) *in terms of which the judgment of reality is made.* Black coffee and coffee with cream in it look virtually the same through a photospectroscope: we see, as a matter of fact, a complete spectrum, all the colors of the rainbow. Are we to conclude from this that there is "no real difference" between coffee in those two states? In the context of breakfast the difference is real enough; the theoretical identities which a physicist can point out are relatively unreal. Again, if our problem is the behavioristic one of discovering how a human organism will react to given stimuli, then the private mental awareness of the individual thus investigated is "unreal" —i.e., not germane to the kind of inquiry undertaken—hence, out of context. But how equally irrelevant and "unreal" are, perhaps, a behaviorist's report on a young lady's reflexes to a young man in love! Love generates its own intuitions of reality, and the

[16] Clarence I. Lewis, *Mind and the World-Order* (Scribner, 1929), pp. 15-16. By courtesy of the publisher.

wise lover will not confuse these with the definitions of "real" that serve other purposes, in quite other contexts.

Perhaps there is an ascription of value implicit in every metaphysical judgment. To declare something "real" is to declare, in a given context, its *worth*. When the normative, which is to say the valuational element in metaphysical judgments is recognized, the partisanship of philosophers—and this includes scientists in their capacity of philosopher—is better understood. Every philosophy is no doubt a somewhat limited attempt to give systematic expression to what someone intuits to be the most worthwhile aspects of things. It is an individual's declaration of his cosmic allegiance.

For Further Study

RALPH BARTON PERRY, *Present Philosophical Tendencies* (Longmans, Green, 1912), especially Chaps. III, IV; XIII.

C. D. BROAD, *The Mind and its Place in Nature* (1925; Humanities Press, 1951), Chap. II, "Mechanism and its Alternatives."

CLARENCE I. LEWIS, *Mind and the World-Order* (Scribner, 1929), Chaps. IV-VI.

STEPHEN C. PEPPER, *World Hypotheses* (University of California Press, 1942).

FREDERICK J. E. WOODBRIDGE, *An Essay on Nature* (Columbia University Press, 1940).

GEORGE P. ADAMS, *Man and Metaphysics* (Columbia University Press, 1948).

W. T. STACE, *The Nature of the World; An Essay in Phenomenalist Metaphysics* (Princeton University Press, 1940).

WILLIAM JAMES, *Pragmatism* (Longmans, Green, 1907).

D. W. GOTSHALK, *Structure and Reality* (Dial Press, 1937).

PAUL WEISS, *Reality* (Princeton University Press, 1938).

WILLIAM ERNEST HOCKING, *Types of Philosophy* (Scribner, 1929), especially Part III.

W. A. SINCLAIR, *An Introduction to Philosophy* (Oxford University Press, 1944).

Questions for Discussion

1. Hugh Elliot in *Modern Science and Materialism* has defined the materialistic view of nature as involving three main principles: the absolute uniformity of law, the denial of all teleological explanation, and "the denial of any form of existence other than those envisaged by physics and chemistry." Can you construct a reasonable idea of nature by accepting all his principles? By rejecting them all? By partly accepting and partly rejecting?

2. Ernst Haeckel declares that the passion which draws two lovers together is "the same powerful unconscious attractive force" as that which impels a spermatozoon to force an entrance into the ovum, and as that which unites two atoms of hydrogen with one atom of oxygen in forming a molecule of water. (*The Riddle of the Universe*, 1901, p. 224.)

Is there any ambiguity in his use of the word "same"?

3. Can you discover any significant sense in which the moss on a secluded rock, where no animals with organs of vision have ever seen it, is really green?

4. Zeno of Elea offered four famous demonstrations that physical movement is illusory. Examine critically the following two of them:

a) Assume that Achilles, pursuing a tortoise, runs ten times as fast. He can never overtake it, for when he reaches the point where the tortoise was, the tortoise will have moved a tenth of their original distance further along; when Achilles reaches that new point, the tortoise will have proceeded one hundredth of their original distance still further; and so *ad infinitum*. Since Achilles does appear to overtake the tortoise, and since it is logically evident that he cannot do so, it must be that his movement is merely apparent, not real.

b) An arrow shot from a bow is seemingly in motion. But at each instant it must be in a given place—i.e., instantaneously at rest in that place. A series of rests, however many, cannot produce movement. Therefore the arrow does not really move.

5. Reflect on Berkeley's challenging dilemma: "In short, if there were external bodies [i.e., external to our "ideas," or impressions of them] it is impossible we should ever come to know it; and if there were not, we might have the very same reasons to think there were that we have now."—Dr. Samuel Johnson's answer was to vigorously

THE PROBLEM OF REALITY

kick a stone, exclaiming, "Thus, Sir, do I refute Berkeley." Is it a refutation? Can you furnish a better one?

6. Reconsider Professor Wistar's analysis of the properties of an ideal gas (Question 3 of Chapter 5) in the light of (*a*) Vaihinger's *as-if* philosophy; (*b*) contextual realism. How "real" would you consider the molecules thus described, as compared with the fluid gas which we perceive?

CHAPTER VII

The World of Living Things

EVERYONE understands in a rough way the difference between the living and the lifeless. A tree, a dog, a man are alive; a stone and a cloud are inanimate. In primitive times, to be sure, and among such nature-peoples as survive today, the dividing line is drawn somewhat differently. To the primitive mind everything emotionally interesting is alive or has the potency of life. And among more developed peoples there have been individual philosophers and poets espousing the philosophy of panpsychism—that soul or life is in all things. Nevertheless, despite minority opinions and despite possible borderline instances that might be hard to classify, it is pretty widely agreed in our society as to what things are alive and what are not.

Within the past century, however, two developments in biological science have disturbed the complacency of the common attitude. The one has been the furtherance of laboratory techniques in testing, controlling, and so "explaining" life processes; even, it is claimed, of synthetically producing some of the more elementary of them out of non-living constituents. Such experimental success, however limited, suggests the question whether it is possible—in principle if not in practice—to control and produce all life processes, even the highest, the most distinctively human, by experimental techniques. If that were really possible—by a scientist incomparably more skilled and in a laboratory incomparably better equipped than any that now exist—then it would seem to follow that there is no unique difference between living and non-living, but only incidental differences of complexity and arrangement of parts.

The other development has been the establishment and general acceptance of the hypothesis of the evolution of species. For if higher species have evolved from lower species, the question naturally presents itself whether the so-called higher species is anything more than a rearrangement, a re-configuration, of the same elements that made up the lower. Moreover, the idea of more complex forms developing out of simpler ones suggests the further question, where the simpler ones came from originally. Did they originate, way way back, out of non-living things? If so (a very big *if*, incidentally) does that mean that they are essentially no more than non-living things?

Let us first, then, examine the meaning of life directly, without help or hindrance from evolutionary considerations; and afterwards inquire what evolution means and how it may affect the central issue.

i. *The Meaning of Life*

The seeming properties of life

Instead of classifying the properties of a living organism as biologists do whose purpose is to differentiate and study the various particular functions, the present chapter invites your attention to those aspects which have most philosophic import. Nutrition, for example, will not be considered separately, for so far as nutrition is a differentiating factor of the living organism it involves *metabolism*. Now metabolism, as generally understood in biological discussions and as defined in a recent edition of Webster's *New International Dictionary*, is simply "the sum of the processes concerned in the building up of protoplasm and its destruction incidental to the manifestation of vital phenomena." While this definition is not wholly circular—for it expands the idea of metabolism into the complementary processes of building up (anabolism) and breaking down (katabolism), it is partly so, inasmuch as it leaves unexplained the essential terms "protoplasm" and "vital phenomena."

In part, the complementary processes of anabolism and katabolism themselves supply the required explanation. For they are always co-present, simultaneously operative, although the organism may have the gross appearance of either developing or decaying according as the one or the other is dominant. So long as the organism is alive there is always some kind of *dynamic equilibrium* between the opposing processes; and what we call *health* is (generally speaking) a dynamic equilibrium in which the anabolic forces are somewhat stronger than the katabolic.

Health and sickness, indeed, are a pair of categories which everyone is likely to recognize as applying to living and not to lifeless things. We have a general and more or less workable idea of what is meant by describing a man or a horse as healthy or ill, and we extend the terms, without any sharp sense of unfitness, to a caterpillar or a tree or a flower. In ancient Greek medicine, in the writings grouped around the name of Hippocrates, health is described as a right blending (*krasis*) of the body's elements. Never mind that the elements were not then conceived in the same way as a modern chemist would conceive them. What is important, and what largely confirms Hippocrates' right to his acknowledged title of father of Western medicine, is his enunciation of the principle that, whatever the nature of the elements themselves may be, health consists in the "right proportion" in which they are mixed. In the philosophical teachings of Socrates, Plato, and Aristotle the idea of right proportion becomes a guiding principle of life: for the health of the soul, even more than but not excluding the health of the body, is at stake.

Another important aspect of health—inseparable from the former two but worth a moment's focused attention—is *effective wholeness*. Even in English idiom, until recently, "whole" could be understood to mean healthy, as its use in the King James translation of the Bible shows. In a healthy organism there is some degree of mutuality between the various parts, as well as between each part and the whole organism. When some part is injured, healing processes begin to operate elsewhere in the organism and bring aid to the injured part. And the operation of the parts shows a constant tendency to be for the service of the whole. The action of a mammal's lungs in mixing air with blood and the action of its stomach in digesting food are relatively meaningless processes if regarded in isolation; they can be understood and significantly described only when they are seen as contributing in different ways to the good, which is to say the health, of the entire organism.

As the parts cannot be properly understood apart from the whole, so the earlier stages of an organism cannot be properly understood apart from some reference to what the organism will be at maturity. Botanists and gardeners are led to study seeds because of the different plants into which past observations have shown that the seeds will grow. Nor is the attitude an arbitrary one. For the objective fact is that very slight differences in the seeds—sometimes indistinguishable under a microscope—develop into large, complex, and organically patterned differences in the flower. Similarly, two indistinguishable embryos will develop, the one into a man, the other into a pig. In studying any species of plant or animal it is customary, and with good objective reason, to fix upon the stage of maturity—when the anabolic and katabolic processes are in approximate equilibrium—as the stage by which the other stages are to be judged and understood.

Besides the organic phenomena just examined we may briefly note three others. The closely related functions of irritability (the power to respond to stimuli, both external and internal) and adaptability (the consequent power to adjust to environmental situations) give further evidence of the natural subordination of parts to whole. Organic memory (the power of modifying later responses according as earlier responses turned out satisfactory or no) gives analogous evidence in the time dimension: for in this process one moment of the organism's life is seen as modifying another moment for the good, or health, of the whole. Finally, reproduction carries beyond the individual life cycle of birth, maturity, and death, and ensures that the life of the species shall continue, though the individual die.

Bio-mechanism

The bio-mechanist is one who maintains that the apparent differences between organic and inorganic are not real; that all processes, the so-called organic and inorganic alike, are reducible in the last analysis to movements of inorganic particles in space. He argues that since every organic process is made up of component chemical processes, and since these in turn depend upon the physical laws of molecular movement, it follows that an organism could be satisfactorily explained both as a whole and down to the smallest detail, if the entire complex of molecular movements could be plotted. Biology thus becomes conceived as a makeshift kind of chemistry, and chemistry in turn as a makeshift kind of physics. The objects studied by biology are distinguished by greater complexity of structure and function, but there is no other respect in which they are distinguished from the simplest inorganic movements. Jacques Loeb, who was an extreme mechanist, declares:

> Living organisms have the peculiarity of developing and reproducing themselves automatically, and it is this automatic character of reproduction and development which differentiates them *for the time being* from machines made of inanimate matter.[1]

In short, it is held that if a scientist's observational powers, instruments, memory, and computing ability were adequate to the strain, he could give a more exact and therefore truer description of organic behavior by attending not to the gross organic manifestations themselves but exclusively to the molecular movements involved.

---

[1] Jacques Loeb, "The Chemical Character of the Process of Fertilization and its Bearing upon the Theory of Life Phenomena." Italics added.

Critique of mechanism

There are two distinct but related questions raised by the theory of mechanism. The first centers in the issue of determinism. It asks, in the words of J. Arthur Thomson, "whether there are irreducible peculiarities in vital activities—peculiarities which cannot be adequately accounted for in terms of physico-chemical or ideally mechanical description? Or is the usually admitted incompleteness of the physico-chemical description of, let us say, a reflex action merely temporary, and likely soon to disappear?"[2] Jacques Loeb unhesitatingly affirms the latter alternative: "We may, therefore, say that it is now proved beyond all doubt that the variables in the chemical processes in living organisms are identical with those with which the chemist has to deal in the laboratory."[3] The words "proved beyond all doubt," when applied to so universal a proposition as the one in question, are a pretty sure indication that the utterance is rhetorical rather than scientific. No less a scientist than Alfred North Whitehead has offered the suggestive and cautionary hypothesis that chemical processes may perhaps be subtly affected and modified, in ways which at present we have no instruments for testing, when brought within an organic context. And in any case, the potent doubts which recent advances in physics have raised against the mechano-deterministic hypothesis even as applied to the behavior of inorganic masses in motion, makes it a very shaky support on which to build a general proof of mechano-determinism in biology.

The second question concerns direction and emphasis. Independently of whether a complete mechanical description of organic processes were *possible*, would it be *significant*? J. Arthur Thomson expands the question as follows:

Supposing there were available a complete mechanical account of, say, the opening of a Yucca flower, would that be all that is wanted

[2] J. Arthur Thomson, *The System of Animate Nature* (Holt, 1920), Vol. I, p. 109.
[3] Jacques Loeb, *The Recent Development of Biology*.

in Biology? Would light have been thrown, for instance, on the fact that only one Yucca flower opens on each plant each evening, that the flowers begin to open when the Yucca moths begin to emerge from their cocoons, that the life of the flower and the life of the moth are closely bound up together, so that the one without the other is not made perfect? The Yucca flower and the Yucca moth are organisms with a history; they have come to work into one another's hands. Are their adaptive relations only different in degree from the dynamical relations between Earth and Moon, or must we admit that the answers to distinctively biological questions do not follow from even a complete ledger (were that available) of the chemical and physical transactions?[4]

In other words, regardless of whether or not an exhaustive mechanical explanation of vital phenomena is abstractly possible, would it ever be fully relevant to the kind of question which the biologist qua biologist must ask?

ii. *The Hypothesis of Evolution*

Evolution, as a general concept, connotes development from the relatively simple to the relatively complex. The term is applied today in a great many fields. Books have been written on the evolution of the solar system, the evolution of culture, evolution of medicine, evolution of the university, and so on indefinitely. According to its Latin etymology the word "evolve" means "unroll" or "roll out." But this meaning had better be ignored for the present; for to insist on it would be to prejudge the question raised in the next section, which is whether the evolution of life is essentially an unrolling of what was already covertly present in the nature of things, or involves rather the successive introduction into existence of factors that are absolutely new. If the latter view is taken, evolution would seem to be not so much an unrolling as a kind of rolling up.

---

[4] Thomson, *loc. cit.*

Distinction of problems

Evolution in the narrower sense, or biological evolution, is the hypothesis that the many species of relatively complex organisms which exist are descended from fewer species of relatively simpler organisms. The resulting organisms have been more manifold and they have been, structurally and functionally, more complex. Note that the hypothesis is here stated, and should be stated, without involving the assumption of a single common ancestry for all existing species; and also without assuming that the line of ancestry of present-day organisms necessarily goes all the way back to the simplest pre-cellular protoplasm. It may well be the case that both of these additional propositions are true; they offer interesting subjects for speculation, as will be noted presently. But a scientific hypothesis should be formulated with a reasonable economy, and with a distinction between what the available evidence strongly confirms as most probably true and what it tantalizingly suggests to the imagination as a likely but at present unverifiable possibility.

Accordingly, it is well to distinguish clearly three different types of problem connected with the general concept of biological evolution. The first concerns empirical evidence for the scientific hypothesis in the limited sense just defined. It may be said without fear of serious rebuttal that the hypothesis in this limited form has been established beyond reasonable doubt. Next, if it is true that there has been an evolution of species from fewer and simpler to more manifold and more complex forms, the question arises of *how* the process has taken place—what causes have been principally operative. This is a question partly of fact and partly of philosophical interpretation; the factual aspect will be mentioned in the present section, the question of philosophical interpretation reserved for the next. On both aspects of the question there has been, ever since Darwin's day, and continues to be, lively disagreement. Those biologists who disagree with Darwin are, almost without exception, disagreeing on the second question and not on the first. Lastly, there are such speculative questions as how life originated on the planet and what, if any, the next step in evolution will be. These, like most other speculative questions, are scarcely profitable to dwell upon in the present state of our knowledge; but as they sometimes appeal strongly to the wayward imagination, they will be considered briefly at the end of the present section.

The evidences for evolution

Why is it permissible to regard the restricted hypothesis of evolution as true beyond reasonable doubt? The evidence is not of the kind, so often available in dealing with the inanimate world, where a single crucial experiment can be made which virtually settles the issue then and there. Of the several kinds of evidence adduced in support of the hypothesis not a single one would be accepted by all investigators as conclusive. Taken collectively, however, their evidential validity accumulates. Let us survey briefly the principal types of such evidence.

a) From fossil remains. Geological research has supplied evidence that the earth's surface has been built up in layers by slow deposit. The science of paleontology studies the fossils of animals found in the various layers, and is able to estimate their approximate age from the stratum in which they are found. Such evidence discloses that various animal forms once existed which are now extinct; and it strongly suggests that in certain cases there has been a gradual development of anatomical structure through successive ages—e.g., from the small five-toed *eohippus* to later organisms which bear an ever increasing resemblance to the modern horse.

b) From geographical distribution. Geological research has supplied evidence that lands now separated by ocean were in some cases once continuous stretches. In those cases it is found, with a fairly high degree of correlation, that flora and fauna which for other reasons can be supposed to have evolved more recently are strikingly different.

c) From comparative anatomy. Aristotle had observed instances of analogy among diverse animal structures: he mentions specifically the relation of bones to a spiny structure, of nail to hoof, hand to claw, and scale of fish to feather of bird.[5] But he drew no evolutionary consequences from these observations; instead, he used them as evidence for the classification of what he supposed were essentially static types. Clearly, then, their evidential value is subsidiary; they may be considered as strengthening the evolutionary hypothesis when it has been set up, but they do not necessarily suggest it by themselves.

d) From embryology. A similar qualification must be observed in the use of embryological evidence. Aristotle knew a good deal about animal embryos, although considerably less than the microscope and controlled surgery have revealed in recent years. But his recognition that at certain stages the embryos of higher forms show likenesses to adult lower forms did not suggest to him the evolutionary hypothesis. In fact, it supports that hypothesis only if the additional assumption is made that an organism in embryo tends to *recapitulate* the main stages through which its ancestors have passed in their long racial history.

e) From vestigial remains. Most organisms contain certain organs, such as the human appendix and the wings of the female gypsy moth, which seem to be functionally superfluous. Their presence would be understandable, however, if they could be supposed to have served a useful function in some ancestral animal of a different type.

f) From artificial breeding. By selective breeding and suitable crossbreeding it has been possible experimentally to produce certain animals and plants that differ considerably from previously known varieties. Dogs, for example, appear to have been developed by early man's ingenuity in domesticating the wolf. Luther Burbank developed the grapefruit by crossing the orange and the lemon. Is it not possible that nature may have acted

---

[5] *Description of Animals (Historia Animalium)*, Bk. I, Sec. i, (p. 109 of the Odyssey Press revised edition of selections from Aristotle).

over long ages as man has done more briefly and with deliberate foresight?

How much does this evidence prove? It is a useful intellectual discipline to examine each separate item of evidence by itself, and reflect how far it would suggest and logically support the hypothesis of evolution to a person who had no other ground for believing in it. It can be seen that the real power of the evidence here is not linear, as in a geometrical demonstration, but *cumulative* and roughly similar to the way in which a physician diagnoses an ailment from a variety of symptoms or in which a detective builds up a circumstantial case against a suspect. The hypothesis of evolution has been "proved"—not with absolute finality, but as immeasurably more probable than any competing explanation that has been offered.

The hypothesis of natural selection

While Darwin's chief claim to lasting remembrance rests upon the painstaking research with which he collected the evidences cited above and the clear scientific status which he thus gave to a hypothesis which up to then had been somewhat vague and speculative, he did not confine himself to establishing the overwhelming probability that an evolution of species has taken place; he offered also a hypothesis *to explain how* one species may have evolved into another. This secondary hypothesis is widely known as the hypothesis of natural selection, and it involves four steps: *variation*—that in any generation there will be accidental[6] differences of structure and function differentiating each organism from its brother organisms; *struggle for existence*—that because more organisms are produced in any generation than can possibly survive (a single ordinary housefly, for example, lays millions of eggs), there is a continual life-and-death struggle among them; *survival of the fittest* (natural selection in the narrower sense)—that those organisms whose accidental variations adapt them most favorably to environ-

---

[6] Remember that "accidental" does not mean uncaused. See the distinction between *spontaneous* and *accidental* in Chapter IV, p. 124.

mental conditions are the ones which, by and large, will survive; *heredity*—that the more favorably adaptive traits of the surviving organisms will, by and large, be transmitted to their offspring.

Two remarks are in order concerning the hypothesis of natural selection. The first is that natural selection does not rest upon anything like so strong a body of interconfirmatory evidence as the hypothesis of evolution itself. Whereas nearly all contemporary biologists accept evolution as established beyond dispute, they differ widely in their attitudes toward natural selection as an explanation of how it occurred. And in the second place, whereas the question of evolution involves a sharp antithesis, an either-or—for either present-day species did evolve from simpler and fewer species or they did not—the question of natural selection allows of partial and qualified assent. It can be accepted as one of the factors operating in the evolutionary process without being upheld as the only factor. It may have been a contributory cause but not the sufficient cause. In the opinion of many biologists the real mystery, which natural selection does nothing to dispel, lies in the phenomenon of variation; especially since, as Hugo DeVries argued in 1900, some of the variations, in order really to increase an organism's survival powers, must have been large and abrupt. Thus two eminent biologists, Thompson and Geddes, write:

> Natural selection remains still a *vera causa* in the origin of species, but the function ascribed to it is practically reversed. It exchanges its former supremacy as the supposed sole determinant among practically indefinite possibilities of structure and function, for the more modest position of simply accelerating, retarding or terminating the process of otherwise determined change. It furnishes the brake rather than the steam or the rails for the journey of life; or in better metaphor, instead of guiding the ramifications of the tree of life, it would in Mivert's excellent phrase, do little more than apply the pruning-knife to them.[7]

---

[7] J. Arthur Thomson and Patrick Geddes, *Evolution* (Holt, 1911), p. 248.

Speculative problems

A speculative question may be defined as one which is factual rather than interpretive or valuational in type, but for which no actual means of verification is available or likely to be available. It is not profitable to dwell for long upon purely speculative questions; nevertheless they do obtrude themselves upon our curiosity, and it is well to have a look at them in order to distinguish them clearly from questions of other types. Three speculative questions in particular are suggested by the idea of biological evolution.

a) The unity of life. Do all existing forms of life, both plant and animal, share a common ancestry? Are they all descended from an original protoplasmic source? Evolutionists usually assume that such has been the case, for any alternative account would introduce needless complications. But as simple protoplasm and one-celled animals do not leave any fossil-record in the rocks, there is not likely to be any positive evidence for the assumption.

b) The origin of life. Since the earth was once a molten mass thrown off by the sun, there must have been a time when there was no life upon it. How, then, did earthly life originate? Did it evolve out of inanimate beginnings? That is the answer which most evolutionists regard as inherently most likely. An exception, however, was the biologist and chemist Arrhenius, who suggested that life in a very simple form might be, like the basic physical elements, or basic energy-constituents, an eternal component in the universe, wandering here and there throughout interstellar space; and that germs of this primordial life might have struck the earth under conditions suitable for their development.

c) The direction of evolution. Is there any evidence that biological evolution is still continuing today? And if so, are there any indications of what new forms are likely to evolve in the future? Tales of a coming "superman" may be dismissed as mere fantasy; we simply have no evidence whatever of what a biological species beyond the human might be. The only reasonable sense in which the continuing evolution of mankind can be discussed is in terms of *social* evolution.

iii. The Metaphysics of Evolution

How is evolution to be conceived philosophically? As entirely a set of material processes, or as the manifestation of a cosmic will? As merely *redistributive,* involving rearrangement of particles and forces that had always existed, or as genuinely *creative,* involving the coming-into-existence, at various stages, of entities entirely new? Man's ambivalent attitude toward spontaneity, mentioned in Chapter IV, comes into play here. On the one hand, as we survey the evolutionary process there do appear to be real novelties created which had never existed before; on the other hand, the human intelligence tends always to look for some kind of identity persisting through change, and even to postulate an identity when it cannot be empirically discovered.

The three standpoints

One's conception of what an organism *is* (the question discussed in Section i) will naturally influence one's philosophical interpretation of the evolutionary process. A mechanist will have no new problem when confronted with the fact of evolution. Since he postulates that there is nothing significant about organic behavior except what can be restated in terms of chemical, and so ultimately of physical laws, he will take the transformation of species to be completely explainable—in principle if not in practice—by those laws. An organicist, on the other hand, can interpret evolution in either of two ways. Since he regards organisms as motivated telically, and since the only model for an understanding of telic motivation is one's personal everyday experience of willing certain means for the sake of a purposed end, the organicist conceives organisms, or at any rate the higher organisms, as moved by something analogous to will, or telic striving, as we experience and exercise it in ourselves. This inner urge, this self-determined striving toward a goal appropriate to one's own nature has been designated, it will be recalled, by the Aristotelian word "entelechy." The question then arises whether the kind of entelechy which each of us recognizes in his own person has existed eternally and supplies the basic moving principle of the evolutionary process from its very inception, or whether entelechy is itself a product of evolution. Has the will, which is to say aspirational striving, come into existence as a real and absolute novelty in the course of evolution? That is the answer given by the theory of emergence. Or has it always existed, even in the things we call inanimate, so that the evolving structures and functions are a slow product of its unfolding—much as a human individual, in a briefer span of time, can exert his personal will to control his posture or his gestures? This is the answer given by vitalism, or evolutionary transcendentalism.

Such, then, are three main types of evolutionary metaphysic. The *mechanist* takes his starting point in the inanimate world, conceived as a set of interacting and potentially calculable movements in space. Applying the principle of continuity he reasons that man, having evolved out of those inanimate movements, is merely a product, an end-result, and not at all an independent contributor. Such is the type of argument pursued, for example, by Ernst Haeckel in *The Riddle of the Universe*. The *vitalist* takes his starting point in the experiential center, in human experience as each of us knows it through living it; here he finds striving and purposive aspiration to be a central fact; therefore, applying the principle of continuity he reasons that something of the same essence must be present, in one degree or another, all the way down the evolutionary scale, and even (by the same logic) in the blazing ball of fire which the earth once was. The *emergent evolutionist* (no simpler name for him having found currency) takes issue with both the foregoing theories by discarding their shared assumption of continuity, which he finds to be at variance with the apparent facts. The apparent fact is, he argues, that long ago, when the earth was newly discharged from the sun, there could not have been any life upon it, and therefore no will, purpose, aspiration; it appears too, and even more forcibly, that will, purpose, aspiration do exist in men today. Very well, then, why not follow the plain indications? There was a time when no will or consciousness existed; today they do exist; therefore they must have "emerged" in the process of animal evolution—which is to say, there must have been real discontinuities, real novelties, in the progress from nebula to protoplasm to fish to ape to man.

Mechanism, since it postulates no more than an elaborate regrouping of physicochemical elements, requires no further explanation. The character of the theory is sufficiently indicated by the quotations from Jacques Loeb in Section i and the evolutionary argument summarized in the foregoing paragraph. Some further characterization of the other two theories, however, may be desirable.

The logic of emergence

Let us imagine a universe in which hydrogen and oxygen had always existed apart from each other, until at a certain moment of time they came together in suitably proportionate amounts and under suitable conditions of pressure and temperature, so as to form water. Something new will have been generated—a liquid having characteristics that never before existed and so could not have been deduced from the characteristics of the gases that preceded it. A modern chemist knows in advance what will happen when hydrogen and oxygen meet in such a manner, but that is because he has made, or someone has made, previous observations of the phenomenon. Without someone's previous experience of the outcome, or something like the outcome, no prediction of it is possible. The peculiar characteristics of water, then—in our supposed universe—are strictly emergent; which is to say that they are not present in, and could not have been deduced from, the characteristics of the two ingredients that went into their making. The characteristics of water were a genuine novelty in that supposed universe.

In our actual universe, the emergent evolutionist holds that something analogous appears to have happened, not once but repeatedly. When mass-particles came together in such a way as to produce protoplasm, the life-phenomena which protoplasm exhibits were new characteristics which had not previously existed. Metabolism was a new kind of behavior, a new emergent; it operated according to new laws, which could not have been deduced from the simpler laws governing the movements of inanimate mass-particles. Again, at some stage or other in animal evolution there emerged the rudiments of psychic life. Do we not all take it as likely that dogs, for example, are capable of feeling pain whereas one-celled animals without a nervous system are not? If our common supposition is true, then pain—or, what is the same thing, feelings of pain—must have emerged somewhere along the evolutionary scale. The nature of pain cannot be understood by one who has never felt it, and its presence in the higher animals could not have been deduced from studying the properties of metabolism. Finally man, with his powers of reflective self-consciousness, cannot be explained as a mere regrouping of elements and characteristics found in the lower animals; he exhibits, as Lloyd Morgan puts it, *new types of effective relatedness*.[8] New qualities and new kinds of relationship appear in man; his behavior, although limited and thus partly conditioned by the laws of inanimate nature (he is still bound by the law of gravitation, for instance) cannot be entirely explained or predicted by them. With the emergence of man new types of laws become operative: notably, those which involve the moral "ought." Conscience and reflective self-examination

[8] C. Lloyd Morgan, *Emergent Evolution* (Holt, 1923), p. 204. Morgan, however—as Samuel Alexander has done in *Space, Time and Deity*—carries the principle of emergence a step farther and speaks of the evolutionary emergence of God as the highest step.

represent a genuine novelty in the evolutionary sequence. Thus the theory of emergence, as Morgan declares, "accepts the 'more' at each ascending stage as that which is given, and accepts it to the full.... It does not interpret the higher in terms of the lower only; for that would imply denial of the emergence of those new modes of natural relatedness which characterize the higher and make it what it is. Nor does it interpret the lower in terms of the higher."[9]

Vitalism

The two best known vitalistic philosophers in the West have probably been Arthur Schopenhauer and Henri Bergson. Schopenhauer, in the second Book of *The World as Will and Idea*, declares that "the inner nature of everything is will"; that "what makes itself known to us in our most immediate self-knowledge as *will* is also what objectifies itself at different grades in all the phenomena of the world."

That which, in us, pursues its ends by the light of knowledge, strives in nature blindly and dumbly in a one-sided and unchangeable manner. Yet in both cases it may be brought under the conception of will; just as the first dim light of dawn must share the name of sunlight with the rays of full midday.[10]

A substantially similar view, though with different emphasis, vocabulary, and arguments, is developed in Bergson's *Creative Evolution*.

In the East, particularly in India, it is by giving a vitalistic and spiritual interpretation to cosmic process that the leading modern philosophers succeed in bringing the empirical data of evolution into harmony with their own philosophical traditions. Hindu philosophy has accepted the broad principle of evolution from very ancient times, regarding it as an unfolding of Brahma

[9] *Ibid.*, pp. 297-298.
[10] Schopenhauer, *The World as Will and Representation*, Bk. II. Schopenhauer's view is represented more fully in the excerpt on pp. 251-257 of the present volume.

(the World-Ground), an irradiating of the Divine Nature into the infinitely numerous forms of things. But evolution, to the Hindu mind, must be complemented by *involution*: the "outbreathing" of the World Spirit into successively more individuated forms has as its counterpart an "inbreathing," in which individuals, as they come to self-realization and understand their real nature, seek to re-identify themselves with the universal Spirit that is their source.

Thus one of the leaders of contemporary Hindu philosophy, Sri Aurobindo,[11] invites us to imagine a single observer of the universe as it looked, say, a billion years ago. Such a one would have seen only an array of apparently dead galaxies stretched around him in infinite space, "a tireless creation of nebulae and star-clusters and suns and planets, existing only for itself, without a sense in it, empty of cause or purpose. It might have seemed to him a stupendous machinery without a use, a mighty meaningless movement, an aeonic spectacle without a witness, a cosmic edifice without an inhabitant; for he would have seen no sign of an indwelling Spirit, no being for whose delight it was made."

After some aeons, had our hypothetical observer surveyed the cosmic scene again, he might have noticed, in one small corner of the universe at least, that Matter had become organized, its cohesions and repulsions stabilized, in such a way as to produce a new phenomenon: the emergence of life. But still the real secret of the phenomenon would have remained veiled. Nature at this stage would have appeared to him as "a wanton and abundant creatrix busy scattering the seed of her new power and establishing a multitude of forms in a beautiful and luxurious profusion or, later, multiplying endlessly germs and species for the pure pleasure of creation: a small touch of lively color and movement would have been flung over the immense cosmic desert and nothing more."

[11] Sri Aurobindo Ghose, *The Life Divine* (Calcutta: Arya Publishing House, 3 vols., 1939-1940. A later one-volume edition is published by Greystone Press, in the Sri Aurobindo Library, 1949.)

And even if he had looked again, aeons later, when Mind had emerged from the evolutionary process—when *man* had evolved, creating tools, building cities, carving beauty out of stone, discovering the mathematical and physical structure of the world, developing a love of reflection and a quest for truth, and even, "as a supreme defiance to the reign of Matter," awakening to the mystery of the hidden Godhead and becoming the seeker after invisible things of the spirit,—even then our observer might still not have understood that all this remarkable development was anything more than "a little bubbling of sensitive grey stuff of brain, a queer freak in a bit of inanimate Matter moving about on a small dot in the Universe." For he would have based his understanding upon the appearance of things at the earliest stage of cosmic development, interpreting the later stages by the more elementary manifestations that had preceded them.

In short, evolution as Aurobindo interprets it is not a mere rearrangement of material elements (the view of mechanism) nor is it a sheer self-creation of absolute novelties at higher and higher levels of organization and significance (the emergence theory). Nothing, he declares, has come out of the evolutionary development that had not previously gone into it. There can be evolution from Matter into Spirit only because there has been and continues to be the complementary process—the involution of Spirit into Matter.

No conclusive test can settle the issue here raised. All three metaphysical interpretations of evolution are consistent with the known facts. One of them, emergentism, is more cautious than the others; for what it amounts to is little more than a generalized description of what appears, from the evidence, to have actually taken place. The other two are more hardily speculative, but represent characteristically different philosophic tempers, and hence different notions as to what kinds of experience should receive primary attention and hence be taken as representative of all else. The emergentist does not insist on the primacy of a single type. For him experience is obdurately manifold, hospitality of attention to all types of experience is the supreme intellectual virtue, and the law of plenitude is more appropriate to the spirit of philosophic inquiry than the law of parsimony.

For Further Study

J. S. HALDANE, *The Philosophy of a Biologist* (Oxford University Press, 1935).
L. T. HOBHOUSE, *Development and Purpose* (Macmillan, 1913).
HENRI BERGSON, *Creative Evolution* (Holt, 1911; reprinted in The Modern Library).
C. LLOYD MORGAN, *Emergent Evolution* (Holt, 1923).
C. LLOYD MORGAN, *Life, Mind and Spirit* (Holt, 1925), Chaps. III-V.
PIERRE LECOMTE DU NOÜY, *Human Destiny* (Longmans, Green, 1947).
J. C. SMUTS, *Holism and Evolution* (Macmillan, 1926).
HANS DRIESCH, *The Science and Philosophy of the Organism* (London: 1908).
EDMUND SINNOTT, *Cell and Psyche; the Biology of Purpose* (University of North Carolina Press, 1950).
AGNES ARBER, *The Natural Philosophy of Plant Form* (Cambridge University Press, 1950).
WILLIAM McDOUGALL, *Modern Materialism and Emergent Evolution* (Van Nostrand, 1929).
C. JUDSON HERRICK, *The Thinking Machine* (University of Chicago Press, 1932). Defense of mechanism by a neurologist.
JACQUES LOEB, *The Mechanistic Conception of Life* (University of Chicago Press, 1912).
J. H. WOODGER, *Biological Principles* (Harcourt, Brace, 1929).

Questions for Discussion

1. "The scientific temperament feels much more comfortable when it is breaking down a complex phenomenon into simpler parts than when it is trying to pull together a series of diverse facts into a unity of relationship. For a solution of ultimate riddles, however,

synthesis is more important than analysis. . . . It is
know that a living plant is composed of cellular units,
more important to understand how, through the m
interrelation of these units, the orderly development
is assured."—EDMUND W. SINNOTT, "The Cell and the ₁ᵢ₀
Organization" (address given as retiring president of the Botanical
Society of America; published in *Science,* Vol. LXXXIX).

Against what tendency in contemporary biology is this warning urged? What biologist quoted in the chapter does in fact claim to solve ultimate riddles by analysis? In what way is synthesis more satisfactory? In what way less so?

2. Which of the evidences for biological evolution strike you as the strongest? Which play no more than a confirmatory role?

3. What influence has the theory of evolution had in other fields than biology? In social studies? In educational theory? In the study and practice of religion?

4. The theory of evolution has been offered on the one hand as proof that mankind has progressed; on the other, that human traits are merely one set of variations, neither better nor worse (in the long view) than the tusks and claws, the speed and strength, of other animals.

Is either of these inferences justified?

5. It has been said that the theory of emergence gives no answer, but merely restates the question. Discuss.

6. It has been said that the trans-empirical assumption which vitalism makes is justified on the same ground as that on which a psychologist justifies the hypothesis of an unconscious mind. What is that ground? Do you agree with the comparison?

Readings for Part Two

Philosophy of Nature*

ARISTOTLE

Analysis of becoming

When one thing is spoken of as "coming to be" out of another thing, or out of another kind of thing, the process may be interpreted in both a simple and a compound sense. Here is what I mean. There is a sense in which (1) a man becomes cultured, another in which (2) his previous state of unculture passes into a state of being cultured, and still another in which (3) an uncultured man becomes a cultured man. The terms that are regarded as undergoing change in the first two cases (*i.e.*, the man and the state of being cultured) as well as what each of them becomes (*i.e.*, cultured) I call simple; but when an uncultured man is regarded as becoming a cultured man, both terms of the process are compound. In some cases of becoming, moreover, we can speak of something as coming into existence "out of" some previously existing state—*e.g.*, being cultured comes into existence out of the state of unculture; while there are other cases where this mode of expression is inapplicable—*e.g.*, we do not say that the state of being cultured comes into existence "out of" a man, but simply that a man becomes cultured. Again, as regards the two ways in which a simple thing can be said to "become something," in the one case the thing persists through the process of becoming, in the other it does not: thus, a man is still a man on becoming cultured; but his state of unculture, *i.e.*, his not being cultured, does not persist either singly or in combination with the subject.

* From Aristotle, *Natural Science* (the so-called *Physics*), Bk. I, Chaps. vii, ix; Bk. II, Chaps. iii, viii, ix (with omissions). Based on *Aristotle: Selections* (Odyssey Press, 1951).

These distinctions and the several types of becoming that they reveal enable us to conclude that there must be in all cases a subject which, as we say, "becomes something"—a subject which, though one numerically, is more than one in form. By its form I mean here the specific ways in which the subject is expressed; its two aspects, man and the state of unculture, being of course distinguishable. The one aspect, man, which has not the character of an opposite, survives the process of becoming; while the other aspect—the lacking culture, or the state of being uncultured, or the compound form "uncultured man"—does not.

Hence it appears that whatever "becomes" is always composite: there is something (a new element of form) that comes into existence, and something else that becomes it. This "something else" can be conceived in a double sense: as the enduring substratum, or as the original qualification which in the process is replaced by its opposite. In the example previously employed, "uncultured" is the original qualification, "man" is the subject; in the making of a statue the lack of form, shape and order are the original qualification, while the bronze or stone or gold is the subject. If we grant, then, that all things are determined by basic principles and responsible conditions, of which they are the essential, not the accidental result, it plainly follows that everything comes into existence from the subject and from a certain form simultaneously.

The subject of any change is numerically one, but with a duality of form. From one point of view it might seem enough to take as principles some pair of opposites such as cultured vs. uncultured, hot vs. cold, joined vs. unjoined; but there is another point of view from which this interpretation is inadequate, inasmuch as opposites cannot be acted on by each other. We therefore solve the difficulty by postulating a substratum which is distinct from either of the opposites that successively inhere in it, and is not itself the opposite of anything.

What the underlying substratum is, can be understood by analogy. As bronze is to a completed statue, wood to a bed, and the still unformed materials to the objects fashioned from them, so the underlying substratum is to anything substantial, particular, and existent.

Matter may be regarded from one point of view as becoming and perishing, from another as not. Considered as that in which there is incompleteness, it perishes in its very nature, because the incompleteness which perishes is a part of it. Considered as a potentiality of change, however, it does not perish essentially, but must be regarded as uncreated and imperishable. For what I mean by matter is just this: the ultimate substratum of things, on which their origination and their existence essentially depend. By this argument, then, matter in the sense of basic potentiality cannot perish; for if it did it could only pass into itself, and so after perishing it would continue to exist.

The four types of explanation

We have next to consider the question of the factors that make a thing what it is:[1] what they are and how they are to be classified. For knowledge is the object of our studies, and we can hardly be said really to know a thing until we have grasped the "why" of it —i.e., until we have grasped the factors that are most directly responsible for it. Clearly, then, this must be our aim also with regard to the phenomena of becoming and perishing and all forms of physical change, so that having grasped the underlying principles we may employ them in the explanation of particular phenomena.

1. *Material factor.* In one sense, then, the reason for anything means the material out of which an object is generated and which is immanent in the generated object—e.g., the bronze of a statue, the silver of a bowl, and also the generic classes to which such materials belong.

2. *Formal factor.* Next, it may mean the form or pattern—i.e., what the thing is defined as being essentially; and also the genus to which this essence belongs. Thus the ratio 2:1 is a formal condition of the musical octave. Generally speaking, number and the factors that make up the definition of a thing are what constitute its formal condition.

3. *Propelling factor.* A third meaning is the immediate source of change or of cessation from change. In this sense a man who gives advice acts as determining agency on him who receives it, a father on his offspring, and generally speaking whatever produces or changes anything on the product or on the thing changed.

[1] Aristotle's four basic factors or reasons-why of anything have been traditionally referred to in English as "the four causes"—the material cause, formal cause, efficient cause, and final cause. It is no longer idiomatic, however, to use the word "cause" so broadly.

4. *Telic factor.* Finally, the reason for anything may mean the end (*telos*) or purpose for the sake of which a thing is done: *e.g.*, health may be a determining factor in going for a walk. "Why is he taking a walk?" we ask. "In order to be healthy": having said this we think we have given a sufficient explanation. Under this category must also be put all the intermediate steps which the agent must take as means to the end—*e.g.*, taking off weight, loosening the bowels, also drugs and surgical instruments, as means to health. All these are for the sake of an end, although they differ in that some are actions to be performed while others are instruments to be used.

Thus we have enumerated the various ways in which one thing can determine another. Frequently it happens that more than one type of determining factor bears an essential (not merely an incidental) relation to a single thing. It is qua statue, and not by virtue of an incidental aspect, that a statue owes its existence both to the sculptor who makes it and to the bronze from which it is made; although these of course are related to it in different ways—the one as the force that produces it, the other as its material. Again, some things may be regarded as determining each other reciprocally—*e.g.*, exercise and physical fitness—but not in the same sense, for while exercise is the actual source from which physical fitness proceeds, physical fitness is rather the end toward which exercise is directed. Again, a given factor will often account for quite opposite results: if a certain result can be attributed to its presence, we may blame the opposite result on its absence. Thus we attribute a shipwreck to the absence of the pilot whose presence would have brought the ship to safety.

But all of the determining factors just mentioned come under our fourfold classification. In the sense of "that out of which," letters are the determinants of syllables, raw materials of manufactured goods, fire and the like of physical bodies, the parts of the whole, and the premises of the conclusion. In each of these cases the first of the related terms is a substratum (*i.e.*, material factor) as parts are to a whole; while the second is the essential character which the substratum receives—its whole or synthesis or form (formal factor). Again, the seed or sperm, the doctor, the man who gives advice—in short, any agent—is the source from which the starting or stopping of a motion or change originates (the propelling factor).

And finally, there are those things which determine in the sense of being a goal, *i.e.*, a good toward which other things tend (the telic factor); for the phrase "for the sake of" connotes both a goal and a highest good—whether the good be real or apparent.

Evidence that nature is telic

We must now explain in what sense nature belongs to the class of telic entities. Then, in what follows, we shall consider what is meant by necessity when spoken of with reference to natural phenomena.

With reference to the former question it may be objected that nature does not act with reference to a goal or by reason of the fact that one thing is better than another, but for the same reason that it rains—not to make the corn grow, but out of necessity. When rain falls, so the argument runs, it is simply because the rising vapor has become cooled, and being cooled turns to water, which descends, causing the corn to grow; on the same basis as, when rain spoils the crops on the threshing-floor, we do not suppose that it fell for the sake of spoiling them but that it merely happened to do so. Why, then, should it not be the same with the organic parts of nature? Take the case of our teeth, for example—the front teeth sharp and suitable for tearing the food, the back ones broad and flat, suitable for grinding it—may they not have grown up thus by simple necessity, and their adaptation to their respective functions be purely a coincidence? The same argument can be offered about any organic structure to which purpose is commonly ascribed; and it is further explained that where the organic structures happen to have been formed *as if* they had been arranged on purpose, the creatures which thus happen to be suitably organized have survived, while the others have perished—as Empedocles relates of his "man-faced ox-creatures."

While these and similar arguments may cause difficulties, they certainly do not represent the truth. For in the first place, (1) teeth and all other natural phenomena come about in a certain way if not invariably at least normally, and this is inconsistent with the meaning of chance.[2] We do not appeal to chance or coincidence in explaining the frequency of storm in winter nor of heat in mid-

---

[2] Observe that Aristotle conceives of *chance* as the contrary of *goalfulness*, not as opposed to (indeed, rather as implied by) *necessity*. Cf. p. 124.

summer; we would, however, if the situation were to be reversed. As every occurrence must be ascribed either to coincidence or to purpose, if such cases as the foregoing cannot be ascribed to coincidence or chance they must be ascribed to purpose.

(2) Furthermore, in any human art or technique, where there is an end to be achieved, the first and each succeeding step of the operation are performed for the sake of that end. As in human operations, so in the processes of nature; and as in nature, so in each human undertaking—unless there is something to interfere. Human operations, however, are for the sake of ends; hence natural processes must be so too. If a house, for example, had been a natural product it would have been made by the same successive stages as it passed through when made by human technique; and if natural objects could be duplicated artificially it would be by the same series of steps as now produce them in nature. In art and in nature alike each stage is for the sake of the one that follows; for generally speaking, human art either gives the finishing touches to what nature has had to leave incomplete, or else imitates her. Hence, if the operations that constitute a human art are for the sake of an end, it is clear that this must be no less true of natural processes. The relation of earlier to later terms of the series is the same for both.

(3) This is most clearly true in the case of the lower animals, whose behavior is admittedly independent of any conscious art or experiment or deliberation—so much so, in fact, that it is debated whether the work of spiders, ants, and the like is due to intelligence or to some other faculty. Passing gradually down the scale we find that plants too produce organs subservient to their natural ends: leaves, for instance, are put forth to provide shade for the fruit. Hence, if it is both by nature and also for a purpose that the swallow builds its nest and the spider its web, and that plants put forth leaves for the sake of the fruit and push down rather than up with their roots for the sake of nourishment, it is evident that the type of determining factor which we have called telic is operative in the objects and processes of nature.

The meaning of telic determination

What, then, is a telic determinant? Consider first that nature exists under a twofold aspect—as composed of materials [lit., "as matter"] and as consisting in the ways in which things are shaping up [lit., "as form"]; that by the second of these aspects is meant the *telos*, the perfected results at which processes tend to arrive, and that all the earlier stages in any process are for the sake of such perfected results—i.e., are telically determined by them. It follows from all this that the telic determinant of a thing is nothing else than the way in which it tends to shape up.

Mistakes in nature

No human art is free from error: the man of letters makes mistakes in grammar, and the physician may administer a wrong dose. Hence it is not surprising that there should be errors in the processes of nature too. Just as in the arts and other human techniques there are certain procedures which correctly serve their specific ends, while to aim at such ends and miss them is to fail; so it presumably is with nature, and what we call freaks are simply failures or errors in respect of nature's proper ends.

The processes of nature are best illustrated by the case of a doctor who doctors himself. Nature similarly is agent and patient at once.

The meaning of necessity in nature

As for necessity, does it exist conditionally or unconditionally? People tend to think of necessity as something inherent in the process of production; which is pretty much as if they should suppose that a wall might be built by an accidental conjunction of necessary forces—i.e., that as heavy things are naturally borne downward and light things toward the top, so the stones and foundations would necessarily fall to the lowest place, the earth more lightly rising above, and the wood, because it was the lightest of all, forming the roof. But while it is true that the wall cannot be built unless these materials with their respective properties are present; still, being only its material conditions, they will not suffice to account for the completed wall, which is brought into existence for the sake of sheltering us and protecting our goods. And so with all other cases of working toward an end: although the end cannot be attained without certain materials possessing definitive properties, these are only the material precondition of its attainment; properly speaking, what brings it into existence is a certain purpose. Suppose, for example, we were to ask why a saw is what it is. In order that it may perform a certain work and thereby serve a certain end, we should reply. But let us suppose this work cannot be performed unless the saw is made of iron. We may then declare that if it is to be truly a saw and perform its function it "must necessarily" be made of iron. Necessity, then, is conditional. It is not of the same order as the end; for while necessity resides only in the material preconditions, the end or purpose is found in the definition.

From the foregoing analogy it is plain that when we speak of necessity we are referring to the material aspect of nature and the changes proper to that aspect. While the natural scientist must deal with the material aspect too, his primary concern is with the purposive or goalful aspect; for the goal may determine the material changes, but these do not determine the goal. The principle that determines the goal, or inherent purpose, of a thing is to be found in its meaning (*logos*) and definition. In the case of human techniques, when we have determined what kind of a house we want, certain materials must then "of necessity" be either had or got in order to build it; and when we have determined what we mean by health, certain things become necessary in order to secure it. So it is with nature: if man, for instance, has a certain meaning, certain antecedent conditions are requisite to his existence, and these conditions will in turn presuppose others.

Right attitude of the zoölogist[3]

Of things which hold together by nature there are two kinds: those that are unborn, imperishable and eternal, and those that are subject to generation and decay. The former, although of highest worth and even divine, are less accessible to our investigation, inasmuch as the findings of sense-experience throw very little light on the questions which we most desire to answer about them. It is much easier to learn about things that perish—*i.e.*, plants and animals —because we live in their midst, and anyone who cares to take the trouble can acquire abundant information about them. In any case, having discussed elsewhere the apparent nature of divine objects, our present task is to speak about the nature of animals.

---

[3] The remaining paragraphs are taken from Aristotle's zoölogical treatises: *The Parts of Animals*, I, v; and *Description of Animals*, VIII, i.

So far as possible we shall omit no species of animal from consideration, however mean its condition. For even animals that are not attractive to sense offer, to the contemplative vision, the immeasurable joy of discovering creative nature at work in them. It would be strangely paradoxical if we enjoyed studying mere likenesses of nature, because of the painter's or carver's art that they embody, while ignoring the even greater delight of studying nature's own works where we are able to discern the formative factors. So we should not childishly refuse to study the meaner animals, for in all works of nature there is something of the marvellous. A story is told of Heraclitus, that when some visitors desired to see him but hesitated when they found him in the kitchen warming himself by the fire, he bade them: "Come in, don't be afraid! for here, too, are gods." In like manner, boldly and without distaste, we ought to pursue the investigation of every sort of animal, for every one of them will reveal to us something both of nature and of beauty. I say beauty, because in nature it is purpose, not haphazard, that predominates; and the purpose which directs and permeates her works is one type of the beautiful.

Whatever part or structure happens to be under discussion is not important in itself, as a material thing, but only in relation to the whole conformation of which it is a part. Just as the real interest of architecture lies not in the bricks, mortar, and timber, but in the whole house, so the study of nature is properly concerned not with the material parts (which have no independent existence) but with the precise character of the composite whole.

Man compared with the other animals

While certain traits in men differ only in degree from those in animals—man exhibiting more of one trait and certain animals more of another—there are also traits in man to which the corresponding traits in animals are related only by the principle of analogy. For as men exhibit art and wisdom and intelligence, animals possess other kinds of natural ability which serve much the same purpose. This view of the matter is confirmed by considering human children: for in them can be seen the indications and seeds of their future dispositions, yet their psychic traits at that age are virtually the same as those of the lower animals. Accordingly it is not unreasonable to regard animals as exhibiting traits analogous to those in man, even where no identity or similarity is apparent. Nature passes from lifeless things up to the highest animal life by such gradual degrees that the continuity obscures boundaries and puzzles us how to classify intermediate forms.

The Thing and Its Relations*

WILLIAM JAMES

What pure experience is

"Pure experience" is the name which I gave to the immediate flux of life which furnishes the material to our later reflection with its conceptual categories. Only new-born babes, or men in semi-coma from sleep, drugs, illnesses, or blows, may be assumed to have experience pure in the literal sense of a *that* which is not yet any definite *what,* though ready to be all sorts of whats; full both of oneness and of manyness, but in respects that don't appear; changing throughout, yet so confusedly that its phases interpenetrate and no points, either of distinction or of identity, can be caught. Pure experience in this state is but another name for feeling or sensation. But the flux of it no sooner comes than it tends to fill itself with emphases, and these salient parts become identified and fixed and abstracted; so that experience now flows as if shot through with adjectives and nouns and prepositions and conjunctions. Its purity is only a relative term, meaning the proportional amount of unverbalized sensation which it still embodies.

Far back as we go, the flux, both as a whole and in its parts, is that of things conjunct and separated. The great continua of time, space, and the self envelop everything, betwixt them, and flow together without interfering. The things that they envelop come as separate in some ways and as continuous in others. Some sensations coalesce

---

* From William James, *Essays in Radical Empiricism* (Longmans, Green, 1912), Chapter III. By courtesy of the publisher.

with some ideas, and others are irreconcilable. Qualities compenetrate one space, or exclude each other from it. They cling together persistently in groups that move as units, or else they separate. Their changes are abrupt or discontinuous; and their kinds resemble or differ; and, as they do so, they fall into either even or irregular series.

In all this the continuities and the discontinuities are absolutely co-ordinate matters of immediate feeling. The conjunctions are as primordial elements of "fact" as are the distinctions and disjunctions. In the same act by which I feel that this passing minute is a new pulse of my life, I feel that the old life continues into it, and the feeling of continuance in no wise jars upon the simultaneous feeling of a novelty. They, too, compenetrate harmoniously. Prepositions, copulas, and conjunctions—*is, isn't, then, before, in, on, beside, between, next, like, unlike, as, but*—flower out of the stream of pure experience, the stream of concretes or the sensational stream, as naturally as nouns and adjectives do, and they melt into it again as fluidly when we apply them to a new portion of the stream.

Why we conceptualize

If now we ask why we must thus translate experience from a more concrete or pure into a more intellectualized form, filling it with ever more abounding conceptual distinctions, rationalism and naturalism give different replies.

The rationalistic answer is that the theoretic life is absolute and its interests imperative; that to understand is simply the duty of man; and that who questions this need not be argued with, for by the fact of arguing he gives away his case.

The naturalist answer is that the environment kills as well as sustains us, and that the tendency of raw experience to extinguish the experient himself is lessened just in the degree in which the elements in it that have a practical bearing upon life are analyzed out of the continuum and verbally fixed and coupled together, so that we may know what is in the wind for us and get ready to react in time. Had pure experience, the naturalist says, been always perfectly healthy, there would never have arisen the necessity of isolating or verbalizing any of its terms. We should just have experienced inarticulately and unintellectually enjoyed. This leaning on "reaction" in the naturalist account implies that, whenever we intellectualize a relatively pure experience, we ought to do so for the sake of redescending to the purer or more concrete level again; and that if an intellect stays aloft among its abstract terms and generalized relations, and does not reinsert itself with its conclusions into some particular point of the immediate stream of life, it fails to finish out its function and leaves its normal race unrun.

Most rationalists nowadays will agree that naturalism gives a true enough account of the way in which our intellect arose at first, but they will deny these latter implications. The case, they will say, resembles that of sexual love. Originating in the animal need of getting another generation born, this passion has developed secondarily such imperious spiritual needs that, if you ask why another generation ought to be born at all, the answer is: "Chiefly that love may go on." Just so with our intellect: it originated as a practical means of serving life; but it has developed incidentally the function of understanding absolute truth; and life itself now seems to be given chiefly as a means by which that function may be prosecuted. But truth and the understanding of it lie among the abstracts and universals, so the intellect now carries on its higher business wholly in this region, without any need of redescending into pure experience again.

If the contrasted tendencies which I thus designate as naturalistic and rationalistic are not recognized by the reader, perhaps an example will make them more concrete. Mr. Bradley, for instance, is an ultra-rationalist. He admits that our intellect is primarily practical, but says that, for philosophers, the practical need is simply Truth. Truth, moreover, must be assumed "consistent." Immediate experience has to be broken into subjects and qualities, terms and relations, to be understood as truth at all. Yet when so broken it is less consistent than ever. Taken raw, it is all undistinguished. Intellectualized, it is all distinction without oneness. "Such an arrangement may *work,* but the theoretic problem is not solved." The question is *"how the diversity can exist in harmony with the oneness."* To go back to pure experience is unavailing. "Mere feeling gives no answer to our riddle." Even if your intuition is a fact, it is not an *understanding.* "It is a mere experience, and furnishes no consistent view." The experience offered as facts or truths "I find that my intellect rejects because they contradict themselves. They offer a complex of diversities conjoined in a way which it feels is not its way and which it can not repeat as its own. . . . For to be satisfied, my intellect must understand, and it can not understand by taking a congeries in the lump."[1] So Mr. Bradley, in the sole interests of "understanding" (as he conceives that function), turns his back on finite experience forever. Truth must lie in the opposite direction, the direction of the Absolute; and this kind of rationalism and naturalism, or (as I will now call it) pragmatism, walk thenceforward upon opposite paths. For the one, those intellectual products are most true which, turning their face towards the Absolute, come nearest to symbolizing its ways of uniting the many and the one. For the other, those are most true which most successfully dip back into the finite stream of feeling and grow most easily confluent with some particular wave or wavelet. Such confluence not only proves the intellectual operation to have been true (as an addition may "prove" that a subtraction is already rightly performed), but it constitutes, according to pragmatism, all that we mean by calling it true. Only in so far as they lead us, successfully or unsuccessfully, back into sensible experience again, are our abstracts and universals true or false at all.

Rules of Scientific Philosophizing*

ISAAC NEWTON

Rule 1

We should not admit more causes of natural occurrences than are at once true and sufficient to explain them.

Thus scientific philosophers agree that nature does nothing in vain, and the operation of a greater number of causes would be vain where

[1] The quotations are from F. H. Bradley, *Appearance and Reality*.
* From Isaac Newton (1642-1727), *Philosophiae Naturalis Principia Mathematica (The Mathematical Principles of Natural Philosophy)*, Bk. III, the section entitled *"Regulae Philosophandi."* The work was first published

a less would serve. For nature is simple and does not luxuriate in superfluous causes.

Rule ii

Therefore to natural effects of the same type we should assign the same causes, so far as possible.

E.g., in explaining respiration in man and in beast; the fall of meteors found in Europe and America; the phenomenon of light in a bonfire and in the sun; the reflection of light on the earth and on the planets.

Rule iii

Such qualities of bodies as cannot be intensified or diminished, and as are found to belong to all bodies on which experiments can be made, should be taken as the qualities of all bodies whatever.

For the qualities of bodies become known only through experiments, and we should therefore accept as universal all such as universally tally with experiments. Moreover, if they cannot be diminished they cannot be altogether removed. Surely we ought not to follow dreams of our own making which contradict the evidence of experiments, nor should we depart from the principle of analogy, according to which nature is habitually simple and always consistent with herself. Thus the spatial extension of bodies becomes known only by means of the senses; but although in some bodies this quality is not perceived directly, yet because it is found in all bodies that can be perceived, we ascribe it to all bodies universally. Again, we discover by experience many cases of bodies that are hard. Now the hardness of a totality arises from the hardness of its parts, and hence we rightly conclude that the elementary particles are hard not only in the bodies whose hardness is directly perceived but in all others also. That all bodies are impenetrable, too, we infer not from reason but from sensation. Those that we handle are found to be impenetrable, and thence we conclude that impenetrability is a property

---

in 1686; the third edition, on which the present translation is based, in 1726. The Latin word *hypotheses* is here translated "theories." When Newton made his celebrated remark, *"Hypotheses non fingo,"* he obviously did not mean that he was avoiding all hypotheses in the present-day sense of the word.

of all bodies whatsoever. That all bodies are moveable and endowed with certain forces of enduring in motion and in rest (which we call the forces of inertia) we likewise infer from the corresponding properties of bodies that we have seen. Inasmuch as the extension, hardness, impenetrability, mobility, and force of inertia of a whole arise from the extension, hardness, impenetrability, mobility, and force of inertia of its parts, we therefore conclude that all the smallest component particles of bodies must likewise be extended, hard, impenetrable, moveable, and endowed with the forces of inertia. This is the foundation of all natural philosophy.

Moreover, we have learned from observable instances that the adjacent parts of bodies, when divided, can be separated from one another; hence it is mathematically certain that the parts which we have not been able to divide are rationally distinguishable into smaller parts. It is uncertain, to be sure, whether those parts which we can distinguish but not yet actually divide can be divided and separated from one another by natural forces. But if it could be established by a crucial experiment, by the breaking of a hard and solid body, that some elementary particle actually underwent division, we might then conclude, by virtue of our rule, not only that the divided parts are separable but also that the particles not yet divided are capable of being divided to infinity.

Finally, if it is universally established, through experiments and astronomical observations, that all bodies about the earth gravitate toward the earth, and that they do so in proportion to the quantity of matter which each contains; that the moon gravitates toward the earth in proportion to the quantity of its matter; that our ocean, in turn, gravitates toward the moon; that all the planets gravitate toward one another; and that there is a similar gravitation of comets toward the sun: then by our rule we shall have to conclude that *all* bodies gravitate toward one another mutually. The argument from what is observed to what is unobserved applies even more forcibly to universal gravitation than to the impenetrability of bodies, since we cannot employ any experiment or extended mode of observation to establish the presence of this latter property in astronomical bodies. On the other hand, I do not affirm by any means that gravitation is *essential* to bodies. By their inherent force I understand only the force of inertia. This is immutable, whereas their gravity is diminished as they recede from the earth.

Rule iv

Whatever propositions have been inferred by induction from observed phenomena we should accept in experimental philosophy as either accurately or approximately true, notwithstanding contrary theories, until other phenomena occur which establish them either as more accurate or as liable to exceptions.

This must be done in order that the argument by induction may not be evaded by a reliance on theories.

Mechanism and Its Alternatives*

C. D. BROAD

The ideal of pure mechanism

Let us first ask ourselves what would be the ideal of a mechanical view of the material realm. I think, in the first place, that it would suppose that there is only one fundamental kind of stuff out of which every material object is made. Next, it would suppose that this stuff has only one intrinsic quality, over and above its purely spatio-temporal and causal characteristics. The property ascribed to it might, e.g., be inertial mass or electric charge. Thirdly, it would suppose that there is only one fundamental kind of change, viz., change in the relative positions of the particles of this stuff. Lastly, it would suppose that there is one fundamental law according to which one particle of this stuff affects the changes of another particle. It would suppose that this law connects particles by pairs, and that the action of any two aggregates of particles as wholes on each other is compounded in a simple and uniform way from the actions which the constituent particles taken by pairs would have on each other. Thus

---

* From C. D. Broad, *Mind and Its Place in Nature* (Harcourt, Brace, 1925; Humanities Press, 1951). Reprinted by courtesy of the Humanities Press.

the essence of Pure Mechanism is (*a*) a single kind of stuff, all of whose parts are exactly alike except for differences of position and motion; (*b*) a single fundamental kind of change, viz., change of position. Imposed on this there may of course be changes of a higher order, *e.g.*, changes of velocity, of acceleration, and so on; (*c*) a single elementary causal law, according to which particles influence each other by pairs; and (*d*) a single and simple principle of composition, according to which the behavior of any aggregate of particles, or the influence of any one aggregate on any other, follows in a uniform way from the mutual influences of the constituent particles taken by pairs.

A set of gravitating particles, on the classical theory of gravitation, is an almost perfect example of the ideal of Pure Mechanism. The single elementary law is the inverse-square law for any pair of particles. The single and simple principle of composition is the rule that the influence of any set of particles on a single particle is the vector-sum of the influences that each would exert taken by itself. An electronic theory of matter departs to some extent from this ideal. In the first place, it has to assume at present that there are two ultimately different kinds of particle, viz., protons and electrons. Secondly, the laws of electro-magnetics cannot, so far as we know, be reduced to central forces. Thirdly, gravitational phenomena do not at present fall within the scheme; and so it is necessary to ascribe masses as well as charges to the ultimate particles, and to introduce other elementary forces beside those of electro-magnetics.

On a purely mechanical theory all the apparently different kinds of matter would be made of the same stuff. They would differ only in the number, arrangement and movements of their constituent particles. And their apparently different kinds of behavior would not be ultimately different. For they would all be deducible by a single simple principle of composition from the mutual influences of the particles taken by pairs; and these mutual influences would all obey a single law which is quite independent of the configurations and surroundings in which the particles happen to find themselves. The ideal which we have been describing and illustrating may be called "Pure Mechanism."

When a biologist calls himself a "Mechanist" it may fairly be doubted whether he means to assert anything so rigid as this. Probably all that he wishes to assert is that a living body is composed only of constituents which do or might occur in non-living bodies, and that its characteristic behavior is wholly deducible from its structure and components and from the chemical, physical and dynamical laws which these materials would obey if they were isolated or were in non-living combinations. Whether the apparently different kinds of chemical substance are really just so many different configurations of a single kind of particles, and whether the chemical and physical laws are just the compounded results of the action of a number of similar particles obeying a single elementary law and a single principle of composition, he is not compelled as a biologist to decide. I shall later on discuss this milder form of "Mechanism," which is all that is presupposed in the controversies between mechanistic and vitalistic biologists. In the meanwhile I want to consider how far the ideal of Pure Mechanism could possibly be an adequate account of the world as we know it.

Limitations of pure mechanism

No one of course pretends that a satisfactory account even of purely physical processes in terms of Pure Mechanism *has* ever been given; but the question for us is: How far, and in what sense, *could* such a theory be adequate to all the known facts? On the face of it external objects have plenty of other characteristics beside mass or electric charge, *e.g.*, color, temperature, etc. And, on the face of it, many changes take place in the external world beside changes of position, velocity, etc. Now of course many different views have been held about the nature and status of such characteristics as color; but the one thing which no adequate theory of the external world can do is to ignore them altogether. I will state here very roughly the alternative types of theory, and show that none of them is compatible with Pure Mechanism as a complete account of the facts.

(1) There is the naive view that we are in immediate cognitive contact with parts of the surfaces of external objects, and that the colors and temperatures which we perceive quite literally inhere in those surfaces independently of our minds and of our bodies. On this view Pure Mechanism breaks down at the first move, for certain parts of the external world would have various properties different from and irreducible to the one fundamental property which

Pure Mechanism assumes. This would not mean that what scientists have discovered about the connection between heat and molecular motion, or light and periodic motion of electrons would be wrong. It might be perfectly true, so far as it went; but it would certainly not be the whole truth about the external world. We should have to begin by distinguishing between "macroscopic" and "microscopic" properties, to use two very convenient terms adopted by Lorentz. Colors, temperatures, etc., would be macroscopic properties, *i.e.*, they would need a certain minimum area or volume (and perhaps, as Dr. Whitehead has suggested, a certain minimum duration) to inhere in. Other properties, such as mass or electric charge, might be able to inhere in volumes smaller than these minima and even in volumes and durations of any degree of smallness. Molecular and electronic theories of heat and light would then assert that a certain volume is pervaded by such and such a temperature or such and such a color if and only if it contains certain arrangements of particles moving in certain ways. What we should have would be laws connecting the macroscopic qualities which inhere in a volume with the number, arrangement, and motion of the microscopic particles which are contained in this volume.

On such a view how much would be left of Pure Mechanism? (i) It would of course not be true of macroscopic properties. (ii) It might still be true of the microscopic particles in their interactions with each other. It might be that there is ultimately only one kind of particle, that it has only one non-spatio-temporal quality, that these particles affect each other by pairs according to a single law, and that their effects are compounded according to a single law. (iii) But, even if this were true of the microscopic particles in their relations *with each other,* it plainly could not be the *whole truth* about them. For there will also be laws connecting the presence of such and such a configuration of particles, moving in such and such ways, in a certain region, with the pervasion of this region by such and such a determinate value of a certain macroscopic quality, *e.g.*, a certain shade of red or a temperature of 57° C. These will be just as much laws of the external world as are the laws which connect the motions of one particle with those of another. And it is perfectly clear that the one kind of law cannot possibly be reduced to the other; since color and temperature are irreducibly different characteristics from figure and motion, however close may be the causal connection between the occurrence of the one kind of characteristic and that of the other. Moreover, there will have to be a number of different and irreducible laws connecting microscopic with macroscopic characteristics, for there are many different and irreducible determinable macroscopic characteristics; *e.g.*, color, temperature, sound, etc. And each will need its own peculiar law.

(2) A second conceivable view would be that in perception we are in direct cognitive contact with parts of the surfaces of external objects, and that, so long as we are looking at them or feeling them, they do have the colors or temperatures which they then seem to us to have. But that the inherence of colors and temperatures in external bodies is dependent upon the presence of a suitable bodily organism, or a suitable mind, or of both, in a suitable relation to the external object.

On such a view it is plain that Pure Mechanism cannot be an adequate theory of the external world of matter. For colors and temperatures would belong to external objects on this view, though they would characterize an external object only when very special conditions are fulfilled. And evidently the laws according to which, *e.g.*, a certain shade of color inheres in a certain external region when a suitable organism or mind is in suitable relations to that region cannot be of the mechanical type.

(3) A third conceivable view is that physical objects can seem to have qualities which do not really belong to any physical object, *e.g.*, that a pillar-box can seem to have a certain shade of red although really no physical object has any color at all. This type of theory divides into two forms. (*a*) It might be held that, when a physical object seems to have a certain shade of red, there really is *something* in the world which has this shade of red, although this something cannot be a physical object or literally a part of one. Some would say that there is a red mental state—a "sensation"—; others that the red color belongs to something which is neither mental nor physical.[1] On either of these alternatives it would be conceivable that Pure Mechanism was the whole truth about matter con-

---

[1] (*b*) It might be held that *nothing* in the world really has color, though certain things *seem* to have certain colors. The relation of "seeming to have" is taken as ultimate.

sidered in its relations with matter. But it would be certain that it is not the whole truth about matter when this limitation is removed. Granted that bits of matter only *seem* to be red or to be hot, we still claim to know a good deal about the conditions under which one bit of matter will seem to be red and another to be blue and about the conditions under which one bit of matter will seem to be hot and another to be cold. This knowledge belongs partly to physics and partly to the physiology and anatomy of the brain and nervous system. We know little or nothing about the mental conditions which have to be fulfilled if an external object is to seem red or hot to a percipient; but we can say that this depends on an unknown mental factor x and on certain physical conditions a, b, c, etc., partly within and partly outside the percipient's body, about which we know a good deal. It is plain then that, on the present theory, physical events and objects do not merely interact mechanically with each other; they also play their part, along with a mental factor, in causing such and such an external object to seem to such and such an observer to have a certain quality which really no physical object has. In fact, for the present purpose, the difference between theories (2) and (3) is simply the following. On theory (2) certain events in the external object, in the observer's body, and possibly in his mind, cause a certain quality to inhere in the external object so long as they are going on. On theory (3) they cause the same quality to *seem* to inhere in the same object, so long as they are going on, though *actually* it does not inhere in any physical object. Theory (1), for the present purpose, differs from theory (2) only in taking the naive view that the body and mind of the observer are irrelevant to the *occurrence* of the sensible quality in the external object, though of course it would admit that these factors are relevant to the *perception* of this quality by the observer. This last point is presumably common to all three theories.

I will now sum up the argument. The plain fact is that the external world, as perceived by us, seems not to have the homogeneity demanded by Pure Mechanism. If it *really* has the various irreducibly different sensible qualities which it *seems* to have, Pure Mechanism cannot be true of the whole of the external world and cannot be the whole truth about any part of it. The best that we can do for Pure Mechanism on this theory is to divide up the external world first on a macroscopic and then on a microscopic scale; to suppose that the macroscopic qualities which pervade any region are causally determined by the microscopic events and objects which exist within it; and to hope that the latter, in their interactions with *each other* at any rate, fulfill the conditions of Pure Mechanism. . . . We must remember, moreover, that there is no *a priori* reason why microscopic events and objects should answer the demands of Pure Mechanism even in their interactions with each other; that, so far as science can tell us at present, they do not; and that, in any case, the laws connecting them with the occurrence of macroscopic qualities *cannot* be mechanical in the sense defined.

If, on the other hand, we deny that physical objects have the various sensible qualities which they seem to us to have, we are still left with the fact that some things *seem* to be red, others to be blue, others to be hot, and so on. And a complete account of the world must include some explanation of such events as "seeming red to me," "seeming blue to you," etc. We can admit that the ultimate physical objects may all be exactly alike, may all have only one non-spatio-temporal and non-causal property, and may interact with each other in the way which Pure Mechanism requires. But we must admit that they are also cause-factors in determining the *appearance,* if not the *occurrence,* of the various sensible qualities at such and such places and times. And, in these transactions, the laws which they obey *cannot* be mechanical.

We may put the whole matter in a nutshell by saying that the appearance of a plurality of irreducible sensible qualities forces us, no matter what theory we adopt about their status, to distinguish two different kinds of law. One may be called "intra-physical" and the other "trans-physical." The intra-physical laws may be, though there seems no positive reason to suppose that they are, of the kind required by Pure Mechanism. If so, there is just one ultimate elementary intra-physical law and one ultimate principle of composition for intra-physical transactions. But the trans-physical laws cannot satisfy the demands of Pure Mechanism; and, so far as I can see, there must be at least as many irreducible trans-physical laws as there are irreducible determinable sense-qualities.

Empirical Laws and Theoretical Models*

E. F. CALDIN

SCIENCE, however, is not complete with the formulation of empirical laws. For though these express compactly the behavior of physical systems they give us small understanding of them, and science is essentially directed towards the understanding of nature. . . . The observational part of science needs to be completed by a theoretical scheme, and this is the task of theoretical construction.

Thus, for instance, we have to interpret the empirical law that, for gas at constant temperature, $pv = c$. Can we imagine any model of a gas such that it would exhibit this law? Classical kinetic theory in its simplest form pictured the gas as a swarm of minute particles, hard and elastic, moving in all directions. These particles, according to the theory, collide with each other and with the walls of the vessel at intervals, and on these occasions behave exactly as billiard balls behave when they collide with each other or with the cushions; or, rather, as billiard balls would behave if they and the cushions were perfectly smooth and elastic, so that no energy were lost by friction. This behavior is presumed to obey the same laws of mechanics as those found for ordinary bodies. The pressure of a gas on the vessel walls is then paralleled by the pressure due to the innumerable impacts of the particles on the walls of the enclosure. If we reduce the volume of the enclosure, the frequency of impact increases (because on the average a particle meets the wall more often) and so the pressure increases. Exact calculation by the methods of ordinary dynamics shows that for this model the product pv would indeed be a constant, just as we found by experiment for actual gases. . . .

So far, then, the theoretical model is in accord with the observa-

* From E. F. Caldin (Professor of Chemistry at the University of Leeds, England), *The Power and Limits of Science* (London: Chapman and Hall, 1949). Reprinted by courtesy of the publisher.

tions. The gas behaves *as if* it consisted of hard elastic particles obeying the laws of Newtonian mechanics. But this alone would not be sufficient support for the theory. For it might be possible to devise many other models that would agree equally well with our observations. However, the pressure-volume relation is not the only one that this model can reproduce. For instance, if we assume that increase of temperature may be represented by increase in the average velocity of the particles, we find that we can deduce for the model a relation between temperature, pressure and volume that is very close to that found experimentally for gases. And many other properties of gases—diffusion, viscosity, and so on—are likewise quantitatively represented. The theoretical interpretation suggested does not agree merely with one observed property of the gas; it is in harmony with many observed properties of very diverse kinds. One single model accounts for a variety of observations; many different experiments are unified by a single theory.

What do we mean by "unifies" and "accounts for" in this connection? I think we simply mean that by reasoning about the hypothetical entities (particles) with their hypothetical properties (such as elasticity and Newtonian behavior), we can deduce the laws of their behavior in various circumstances; and that the laws so deduced agree, within experimental error, with those derived from observations on actual gases. The empirical laws are "unified" because they are all reproduced by deductions about a single model. A given law —say the relation $pv = c$—is "accounted for" because it can be deduced from this model. This agreement between deductions from a set of hypothetical entities and relations, on the one hand, and the laws derived from observation on the other, seems to me to be the essence of scientific "explanation."

The Status of Scientific Law*

A. S. EDDINGTON

Identical laws

Energy, momentum and stress, which we have identified with the ten principal curvatures of the world, are the subject of the famous laws of conservation of energy and momentum. Granting that the identification is correct, *these laws are mathematical identities*. Violation of them is unthinkable. Perhaps I can best indicate their nature by an analogy.

An aged college Bursar once dwelt secluded in his rooms devoting himself entirely to accounts. He realized the intellectual and other activities of the college only as they presented themselves in the bills. He vaguely conjectured an objective reality at the back of it all—some sort of parallel to the real college—though he could only picture it in terms of the pounds, shillings and pence which made up what he would call "the common-sense college of everyday experience." The method of account-keeping had become inveterate habit handed down from generations of hermit-like bursars; he accepted the form of accounts as being part of the nature of things. But he was of a scientific turn and he wanted to learn more about the college. One day in looking over his books he discovered a remarkable law. For every item on the credit side an equal item appeared somewhere else on the debit side. "Ha!" said the Bursar, "I have discovered one of the great laws controlling the college. It is a perfect and exact law of the real world. Credit must be called plus and debit minus; and so we have the law of conservation of £. s. d. This is the true way to find out things, and there is no limit to what may ultimately be dis-

---

* From Arthur S. Eddington, *The Nature of the Physical World*. (The Gifford Lectures for 1927; published by Cambridge University Press, 1928.) Reprinted by courtesy of the publisher.

covered by this scientific method. I will pay no more heed to the superstitions held by some of the Fellows as to a beneficent spirit called the King or evil spirits called the University Commissioners. I have only to go on in this way and I shall succeed in understanding why prices are always going up."

I have no quarrel with the Bursar for believing that scientific investigation of the accounts is a road to exact (though necessarily partial) knowledge of the reality behind them. Things may be discovered by this method which go deeper than the mere truism revealed by his first effort. In any case his life is especially concerned with accounts, and it is proper that he should discover the laws of accounts whatever their nature. But I would point out to him that a discovery of the overlapping of the different aspects in which the realities of the college present themselves in the world of accounts, is not a discovery of the laws controlling the college; that he has not even begun to find the controlling laws. The college may totter but the Bursar's accounts still balance.

The law of conservation of momentum and energy results from the overlapping of the different aspects in which the "non-emptiness of space" presents itself to our practical experience. Once again we find that a fundamental law of physics is no controlling law but a "put-up job" as soon as we have ascertained the nature of that which is obeying it. We can measure certain forms of energy with a thermometer, momentum with a ballistic pendulum, stress with a manometer. Commonly we picture these as separate physical entities whose behavior towards each other is controlled by a law. But now the theory is that the three instruments measure different but slightly overlapping aspects of a single physical condition, and a law connecting their measurements is of the same tautological type as a "law" connecting measurements with a meter-rule and a foot-rule.

I have said that violation of these laws of conservation is unthinkable. Have we then found physical laws which will endure for all time unshaken by any future revolution? But the proviso must be remembered, "granting that the identification (of their subject matter) is correct." The law itself will endure as long as two and two make four; but its practical importance depends on our knowing that which obeys it. We think we have this knowledge, but do not claim infallibility in this respect. From a practical point of view the law would be upset, if it turned out that the thing conserved was not that which we are accustomed to measure with the above-mentioned instruments but something slightly different.

Selective influence of the mind

This brings us very near to the problem of bridging the gulf between the scientific world and the world of everyday experience. The simpler elements of the scientific world have no immediate counterparts in everyday experience; we use them to build things which have counter-parts. Energy, momentum and stress in the scientific world shadow well-known features of the familiar world. I feel *stress* in my muscles; one form of *energy* gives me the sensation of warmth; the ratio of *momentum* to mass is velocity, which generally enters into my experience as change of position of objects. When I say that I feel these things I must not forget that the feeling, in so far as it is located in the physical world at all, is not in the things themselves but in a certain corner of my brain. In fact, the mind has also invented a craft of world-building; its familiar world is built not from the distribution of relata and relations but by its own peculiar interpretation of the code messages transmitted along the nerves into its sanctum. . . .

The law of conservation is a truism for the things which satisfy it; but its prominence in the scheme of law of the physical world is due to the mind having demanded permanence. We might have built things which do not satisfy this law. In fact we do build one very important thing "action" which is not permanent; in respect to "action" physics has taken the bit in her teeth, and has insisted on recognizing this as the most fundamental thing of all, although the mind has not thought it worthy of a place in the familiar world and has not vivified it by any mental image or conception. You will understand that the building to which I refer is not a shifting about of material; it is like building constellations out of stars. The things which we might have built but did not, are there just as much as those we did build. What we have called building is rather a selection from the patterns that weave themselves. . . .

Perhaps it will be objected that other things besides mind can appreciate a permanent entity such as mass; a weighing machine can appreciate it and move a pointer to indicate how much mass there is. I do not think that is a valid objection. In building the physical world we must of course build the measuring appliances which are part of it; and the measuring appliances result from the plan of building in the same way as the entities which they measure. If, for example, we had used some of the "lumber" to build an entity x, we could presumably construct from the same lumber an appliance for measuring x. The difference is this—if the pointer of the weighing machine is reading 5 lbs. a human consciousness is in a mysterious way (not yet completely traced) aware of the fact, whereas if the measuring appliance for x reads 5 units no human mind is aware of it. Neither x nor the appliance for measuring x have any interaction with consciousness. Thus the responsibility for the fact that the scheme of the scientific world includes mass but excludes x rests ultimately with the phenomena of consciousness.

Perhaps a better way of expressing this selective influence of mind on the laws of Nature is to say that *values* are created by the mind. All the "light and shade" in our conception of the world of physics comes in this way from the mind, and cannot be explained without reference to the characteristics of consciousness.

The world which we have built from the relation-structure is no doubt doomed to be pulled about a good deal as our knowledge progresses. The quantum theory shows that some radical change is impending. But I think that our building exercise has at any rate widened our minds to the possibilities and has given us a different orientation towards the idea of physical law. The points which I stress are:

Firstly, a strictly quantitative science can arise from a basis which is purely qualitative. The comparability that has to be assumed axiomatically is a merely qualitative discrimination of likeness and unlikeness.

Secondly, the laws which we have hitherto regarded as the most typical natural laws are of the nature of truisms, and the ultimate controlling laws of the basal structure (if there are any) are likely to be of a different type from any yet conceived.

Thirdly, the mind has by its selective power fitted the processes of Nature into a frame of law of a pattern largely of its own choosing; and in the discovery of this system of law the mind may be regarded as regaining from Nature that which the mind has put into Nature. . . .

The nature of exact science

One of the characteristics of physics is that it is an exact science, and I have generally identified the domain of physics with the domain of exact science. Strictly speaking the two are not synonymous. We can imagine a science arising which has no contact with the usual phenomena and laws of physics, which yet admits of the same kind of exact treatment. It is conceivable that the Mendelian theory of heredity may grow into an independent science of this kind, for it would seem to occupy in biology the same position that the atomic theory occupied in chemistry a hundred years ago. The trend of the theory is to analyze complex individuals into "unit characters." These are like indivisible atoms with affinities and repulsions; their matings are governed by the same laws of chance which play so large a part in chemical thermodynamics; and numerical statistics of the characters of a population are predictable in the same way as the results of a chemical reaction.

Now the effect of such a theory on our philosophical views of the significance of life does not depend on whether the Mendelian atom admits of a strictly physical explanation or not. The unit character may be contained in some configuration of the physical molecules of the carrier, and perhaps even literally correspond to a chemical compound; or it may be something superadded which is peculiar to living matter and is not yet comprised in the schedule of physical entities. That is a side-issue. We are drawing near to the great question whether there is any domain of activity—of life, of consciousness, of deity—which will not be engulfed by the advance of exact science; and our apprehension is not directed against the particular entities of physics but against all entities of the category to which exact science can apply. For exact science invokes, or has seemed to invoke, a type of law inevitable and soulless against which the human spirit rebels. If science finally declares that man is no more than a fortuitous concourse of atoms, the blow will not be softened by the explanation that the atoms in question are the Mendelian unit characters and not the material atoms of the chemist.

The elephant on the grassy hillside

Let us then examine the kind of knowledge which is handled by exact science. If we search the examination papers in physics and natural philosophy for the more intelligible questions we may come across one beginning something like this: "An elephant slides down a grassy hillside . . ." The experienced candidate knows that he need not pay much attention to this; it is only put in to give an impression of realism. He reads on: "The mass of the elephant is two tons." Now we are getting down to business; the elephant fades out of the problem and a mass of two tons takes its place. What exactly is this two tons, the real subject-matter of the problem? It refers to some property or condition which we vaguely describe as "ponderosity" occurring in a particular region of the external world. But we shall not get much further that way; the nature of the external world is inscrutable, and we shall only plunge into a quagmire of indescribables. Never mind what two tons *refers* to; what *is* it? How has it actually entered in so definite a way into our experience? Two tons *is* the reading of the pointer when the elephant was placed on a weighing-machine. Let us pass on. "The slope of the hill is 60°." Now the hillside fades out of the problem and an angle of 60° takes its place. What is 60°? There is no need to struggle with mystical conceptions of direction; 60° *is* the reading of a plumb-line against the divisions of a protractor. Similarly for the other data of the problem. The softly yielding turf on which the elephant slid is replaced by a coefficient of friction, which though perhaps not directly a pointer reading is of kindred nature. No doubt there are more roundabout ways used in practice for determining the weights of elephants and the slopes of hills, but they are justified because it is known that they give the same results as direct pointer readings.

And so we see that the poetry fades out of the problem, and by the time the serious application of exact science begins we are left with only pointer readings. If then only pointer readings or their equivalents are put into the machine of scientific calculation, how can we grind out anything but pointer readings? But that is just what we do grind out. The question presumably was to find the time of descent of the elephant, and the answer is a pointer reading on the seconds' dial of our watch.

Correlation of pointer-readings

The triumph of exact science in the foregoing problem consisted in establishing a numerical connection between the pointer reading of the weighing-machine in one experiment on the elephant and the pointer reading of the watch in another experiment. And when we examine critically other problems of physics we find that this is typical. The whole subject-matter of exact science consists of pointer readings and similar indications. We cannot enter here into the definition of what are to be classed as similar indications. The observation of approximate coincidence of the pointer with a scale-division can generally be extended to include the observation of any kind of coincidence—or, as it is usually expressed in the language of the general relativity theory, an intersection of world-lines. The essential point is that, although we seem to have very definite conceptions of objects in the external world, those conceptions do not enter into exact science and are not in any way confirmed by it. Before exact science can begin to handle the problem they must be replaced by quantities representing the results of physical measurement.

Perhaps you will object that although only the pointer readings enter into the actual calculation it would make nonsense of the problem to leave out all reference to anything else. The problem necessarily involves some kind of connecting background. It was not the pointer reading of the weighing-machine that slid down the hill! And yet from the point of view of exact science the thing that really did descend the hill can only be described as a bundle of pointer readings. (It should be remembered that the hill also has been replaced by pointer readings, and the sliding down is no longer an active adventure but a functional relation of space and time measures.) The word elephant calls up a certain association of mental impressions, but it is clear that mental impressions as such cannot be the subject handled in the physical problem. We have, for example, an impression of bulkiness. To this there is presumably some direct counterpart in the external world, but that counterpart must be of a nature beyond our apprehension, and science can make nothing of it. Bulkiness enters into exact science by yet another substitution; we replace it by a series of readings of a pair of calipers. Similarly the greyish black appearance in our mental impression is replaced in exact science by the readings of a photometer for various wave-lengths of light. And so on until all the characteristics of the elephant are exhausted and it has become reduced to a schedule of measures. There is always the triple correspondence—

(*a*) a mental image, which is in our minds and not in the external world;

(*b*) some kind of counterpart in the external world, which is of inscrutable nature;

(*c*) a set of pointer readings, which exact science can study and connect with other pointer readings.

And so we have our schedule of pointer readings ready to make the descent. And if you still think that this substitution has taken away all reality from the problem, I am not sorry that you should have a foretaste of the difficulty in store for those who hold that exact science is all-sufficient for the description of the universe and that there is nothing in our experience which cannot be brought within its scope.

I should like to make it clear that the limitation of the scope of physics to pointer readings and the like is not a philosophical craze of my own but is essentially the current scientific doctrine. It is the outcome of a tendency discernible far back in the last century but only formulated comprehensively with the advent of the relativity theory. The vocabulary of the physicist comprises a number of words such as length, angle, velocity, force, potential, current, etc., which we call "physical quantities." It is now recognized as essential that these should be *defined* according to the way in which we actually recognize them when confronted with them, and not according to the metaphysical significance which we may have anticipated for them. In the old textbooks mass was defined as "quantity of matter"; but when it came to an actual determination of mass, an experimental method was prescribed which had no bearing on this definition. The belief that the quantity determined by the accepted method of measurement represented the quantity of matter in the object was merely a pious opinion. At the present day there is no sense in which the quantity of matter in a pound of lead can be said to be equal to the quantity in a pound of sugar. Einstein's theory makes a clean sweep of these pious opinions, and insists that each physical quantity should be defined as the result of certain operations of measurement and calculation. You may if you like think of mass as something of inscrutable nature to which the pointer reading has a kind of relevance. But in physics at least there is nothing much to be gained by this mystification, because it is the pointer reading itself which is handled in exact science; and if you embed it in something of a more transcendental nature, you have only the extra trouble of digging it out again.

It is quite true that when we say the mass is two tons we have not specially in mind the reading of the particular machine on which the weighing was carried out. That is because we do not start to tackle the problem of the elephant's escapade *ab initio* as though it were the first inquiry we had ever made into the phenomena of the external world. The examiner would have had to be much more explicit if he had not presumed a general acquaintance with the elementary laws of physics, *i.e.*, laws which permit us to deduce the readings of other indicators from the reading of one. *It is this connectivity of pointer readings, expressed by physical laws, which supplies the continuous background that any realistic problem demands.* . . .

Whenever we state the properties of a body in terms of physical quantities we are imparting knowledge as to the response of various metrical indicators to its presence, *and nothing more.* . . .

Symbolic knowledge and intimate knowledge

We have two kinds of knowledge which I call symbolic knowledge and intimate knowledge. I do not know whether it would be correct to say that reasoning is only applicable to symbolic knowledge, but the more customary forms of reasoning have been developed for symbolic knowledge only. The intimate knowledge will not submit to codification and analysis; or, rather, when we attempt to analyze it the intimacy is lost and it is replaced by symbolism.

For an illustration let us consider Humor. I suppose that humor can be analyzed to some extent and the essential ingredients of the different kinds of wit classified. Suppose that we are offered an alleged joke. We subject it to scientific analysis as we would a chemical salt of doubtful nature, and perhaps after careful consideration of all its aspects we are able to confirm that it really and truly is a joke. Logically, I suppose, our next procedure would be to laugh.

But it may certainly be predicted that as the result of this scrutiny we shall have lost all inclination we may ever have had to laugh at it. It simply does not do to expose the inner workings of a joke. The classification concerns a symbolic knowledge of humor which preserves all the characteristics of a joke except its laughableness. The real appreciation must come spontaneously, not introspectively. I think this is a not unfair analogy for our mystical feeling for Nature, and I would venture even to apply it to our mystical experience of God. There are some to whom the sense of a divine presence irradiating the soul is one of the most obvious things of experience. In their view a man without this sense is to be regarded as we regard a man without a sense of humor. The absence is a kind of mental deficiency. We may try to analyze the experience as we analyze humor, and construct a theology, or it may be an atheistic philosophy, which shall put into scientific form what is to be inferred about it. But let us not forget that the theology is symbolic knowledge whereas the experience is intimate knowledge. And as laughter cannot be compelled by the scientific exposition of the structure of a joke, so a philosophic discussion of the attributes of God (or an impersonal substitute) is likely to miss the intimate response of the spirit which is the central point of the religious experience.

On Teleology and Mechanism*

D'ARCY W. THOMPSON

As SOON AS we adventure on the paths of the physicist, we learn to *weigh* and to *measure,* to deal with time and space and mass and their related concepts, and to find more and more our knowledge

---

* From D'Arcy W. Thompson, *On Growth and Form* (Cambridge University Press, 1917). Corrected according to the revised edition, 1942, but without its additions. Reprinted by courtesy of the publisher.

expressed and our needs satisfied through the concept of *number,* as in the dreams and visions of Plato and Pythagoras; for modern chemistry would have gladdened the hearts of those great philosophic dreamers.

But the zoologist or morphologist has been slow, where the physiologist has long been eager, to invoke the aid of the physical or mathematical sciences; and the reasons for this difference lie deep, and in part are rooted in old traditions. The zoologist has scarce begun to dream of defining, in mathematical language, even the simpler organic forms. When he meets with a simple geometrical construction, for instance in the honeycomb, he would fain refer it to psychical instinct or to skill and ingenuity rather than to the operation of physical forces; when he sees in snail, or nautilus, or tiny foraminiferal or radiolarian shell, a close approach to the perfect sphere or spiral, he is prone, of old habit, to believe that it is after all something more than a spiral or a sphere, and that in this "something more" there lies what neither mathematics nor physics can explain. In short he is deeply reluctant to compare the living with the dead, or to explain by geometry or by mechanics the things which have their part in the mystery of life. Moreover he is little inclined to feel the need of such explanations or of such extension of his field of thought. He is not without some justification if he feels that in admiration of nature's handiwork he has an horizon open before his eyes as wide as any man requires. He has the help of many fascinating theories within the bounds of his own science, which, though a little lacking in precision, serve the purpose of ordering his thoughts and of suggesting new objects of inquiry. His art of classification becomes an endless search after the blood-relationships of things living, and the pedigrees of things dead and gone. The facts of embryology record for him (as Wolff, von Baer and Fritz Müller proclaimed) not only the life-history of the individual but the ancient annals of its race. The facts of geographical distribution or even of the migration of birds lead on and on to speculations regarding lost continents, sunken islands, or bridges across ancient seas. Every nesting bird, every ant-hill or spider's web displays its psychological problems of instinct or intelligence. Above all, and in things both great and small, the naturalist is rightfully impressed, and finally engrossed, by the peculiar beauty which is manifested in apparent fitness or "adaptation"—the flower for the bee, the berry for the bird.

Time out of mind, it has been by way of the "final cause," by the teleological concept of "end," of "purpose," or of "design," in one or another of its many forms (for its moods are many), that men have been chiefly wont to explain the phenomena of the living world; and it will be so while men have eyes to see and ears to hear withal. With Galen, as with Aristotle, it was the physician's way; with John Ray, as with Aristotle, it was the naturalist's way; with Kant, as with Aristotle, it was the philosopher's way. It was the old Hebrew way, and has its splendid setting in the story that God made "every plant of the field before it was in the earth, and every herb of the field before it grew." It is a common way, and a great way; for it brings with it a glimpse of a great vision, and it lies deep as the love of nature in the hearts of men. . . .

It is retained, somewhat crudely, in modern embryology, by those who see in the early processes of growth a significance "rather prospective than retrospective," such that the embryonic phenomena must be "referred directly to their usefulness in building the body of the future animal":[1] which is no more, and no less, than to say, with Aristotle, that the organism is the *telos*, or final cause, of its own processes of generation and development. It is writ large in that Entelechy which Driesch rediscovered, and which he made known to many who had neither learned of it from Aristotle, nor studied it with Leibnitz, nor laughed at it with Rabelais and Voltaire. And, though it is in a very curious way, we are told that teleology was "refounded, reformed and rehabilitated" by Darwin's theory of natural selection, whereby "every variety of form and color was urgently and absolutely called upon to produce its title to existence either as an active useful agent, or as a survival" of such active usefulness in the past. But in this last, and very important case, we have reached a teleology without a *telos*, as men like Butler and Janet have been prompt to show, an "adaptation" without "design," a teleology in which the final cause becomes little more, if anything, than the mere expression or resultant of a sifting out of the good from the bad, or of the better from the worse, in short of a process of

---

[1] Edwin G. Conklin, "Embryology of Crepidula," *Journal of Morphology*, XIII (1897), p. 203.

mechanism. The apparent manifestations of purpose or adaptation become part of a mechanical philosophy, according to which "chaque chose finit toujours par s'accommoder à son milieu."[2]. . .

But the use of the teleological principle is but one way, not the whole or the only way, by which we may seek to learn how things came to be, and to take their places in the harmonious complexity of the world. To seek not for ends but for antecedents is the way of the physicist, who finds "causes" in what he has learned to recognize as fundamental properties, or inseparable concomitants, or unchanging laws, of matter and of energy. In Aristotle's parable, the house is there that men may live in it; but it is also there because the builders have laid one stone upon another: and it is as a *mechanism,* or a mechanical construction, that the physicist looks upon the world. Like warp and woof, mechanism and teleology are interwoven together, and we must not cleave to the one and despise the other; for their union is "rooted in the very nature of totality."[3]. . .

The search for differences or fundamental contrasts between the phenomena of organic and inorganic, of animate and inanimate things has occupied many men's minds, while the search for community of principles, or essential similitudes, has been pursued by few; and the contrasts are apt to loom too large, great though they may be. M. Dunan, discussing the "Problem of Life" in an essay which M. Bergson greatly commends, declares: "The physico-chemical laws are blind and brutal; where they operate exclusively, there is not order and harmony, but only incoherence and chaos."[4] But the physicist proclaims aloud that the physical phenomena which meet us by the way have their forms, not less beautiful and scarce less varied than those which move us to admiration among living things. The waves of the sea, the little ripples on the shore, the sweeping curve of the sandy bay between the headlands, the outline of the hills, the shape of the clouds, all these are so many riddles of form, so many problems of morphology, and all of them the physicist can more or less easily read and adequately solve: solving them by reference to their antecedent phenomena, in the material system of mechanical

---

[2] Pierre Janet, *Les causes finales* (1876), p. 350. "Everything ends up by accommodating itself to its environment."

[3] Bernard Bosanquet, "The Meaning of Teleology," *Proceedings of the British Academy,* 1905-1906, pp. 235-245.

[4] "Le problème de la vie," *Revue Philosophique,* XXXIII (1892).

forces to which they belong, and to which we interpret them as being due. They have also, doubtless, their *immanent* teleological significance; but it is on another plane of thought from the physicist's that we contemplate their intrinsic harmony and perfection, and "see that they are good."

Nor is it otherwise with the material forms of living things. Cell and tissue, shell and bone, leaf and flower, are so many portions of matter, and it is in obedience to the laws of physics that their particles have been moved, molded and conformed. They are no exception to the rule that "God always geometrizes." Their problems of form are in the first instance mathematical problems, and their problems of growth are essentially physical problems; and the morphologist is, *ipso facto,* a student of physical science. . . .

It behooves us always to remember that in physics it has taken great men to discover simple things. They are very great names indeed that we couple with the explanation of the path of a stone, the droop of a chain, the tints of a bubble, the shadows in a cup. It is but the slightest adumbration of a dynamical morphology that we can hope to have, until the physicist and the mathematician shall have made these problems of ours their own, or till a new Boscovich shall have written for the naturalist the new *Theoria Philosophiae Naturalis.*

How far, even then, mathematics will *suffice* to describe, and physics to explain, the fabric of the body no man can foresee. It may be that all the laws of energy, and all the properties of matter, and all the chemistry of all the colloids are as powerless to explain the body as they are impotent to comprehend the soul. For my part, I think it is not so. Of how it is that the soul informs the body, physical science teaches me nothing; and that living matter influences and is influenced by mind is a mystery without a clue. Consciousness is not explained to my comprehension by all the nerve-paths and neurones of the physiologist; nor do I ask of physics how goodness shines in one man's face, and evil betrays itself in another. But of the construction and growth and working of the body, as of all else that is of the earth earthy, physical science is, in my humble opinion, our only teacher and guide.

Often and often it happens that our physical knowledge is inadequate to explain the mechanical working of the organism; the phenomena are superlatively complex, the procedure is involved and entangled, and the investigation has occupied but a few short lives of men. When physical science falls short of explaining the order which reigns throughout these manifold phenomena—an order more characteristic in its totality than any of the phenomena in themselves—men hasten to invoke a guiding principle, an entelechy, or call it what you will. But all the while no physical law, any more than that of gravity itself, not even among the puzzles of stereo-chemistry or of physiological surface-action or osmosis, is known to be transgressed by the bodily mechanism. . . .

Physical science and philosophy stand side by side, and one upholds the other. Without something of the strength of physics, philosophy would be weak; and without something of philosophy's wealth, physical science would be poor. But there are fields where each, for a while at least, must work alone; and where physical science reaches its limitations, physical science itself must help us to discover. Meanwhile the appropriate and legitimate postulate of the physicist, in approaching the physical problems of the living body, is that with these physical phenomena no alien influence interferes. But the postulate, though it is certainly legitimate, and though it is the proper and necessary prelude to scientific enquiry, may some day be proven to be untrue; and its disproof will not be to the physicist's confusion, but will come as his reward. In dealing with forms which are so concomitant with life that they are seemingly controlled by life, it is in no spirit of arrogant assertiveness that the physicist begins his argument. . . .

Nature Interpreted as the Will to Live*

ARTHUR SCHOPENHAUER

WE CAN never arrive at the real nature of things from without. However much we investigate, we can never reach anything but images and names. We are like a man who goes round a castle seeking in vain for an entrance, and sometimes sketching the façades. And yet this is the method that has been followed by all philosophers before me.

Man's dual aspect

In fact, the meaning for which we seek, of that world which is present to us only as our representation, or the transition from the world as mere representation for the knowing subject to whatever it may be besides this, would never be found if the investigator himself were nothing more than the pure knowing subject—a winged cherub without a body. But he is himself rooted in that world. He finds himself in it as an *individual*—that is to say, his knowledge, which is the necessary supporter of the whole world as representation, is yet always given through the medium of a body, whose affections are, as we have shown, the starting-point for the understanding in the perception of that world. His body is, for the pure knowing subject, a representation like every other representation, an object among objects. Its movements and actions are, from that standpoint, so far known to him in precisely the same way as the changes of all other perceived objects, and would be just as strange and incomprehensible as they if their meaning were not explained for him in an entirely different manner. Otherwise he would see his actions follow upon given motives with the constancy of a law of nature, just as the changes of other objects follow upon causes, stimuli, or motives. But

---

* From Arthur Schopenhauer, *The World as Will and Representation*, Bk. II and "Supplement to the Second Book," Chap. XXVIII. Based on the Haldane and Kemp translation, but with *Vorstellung* translated "representation," and *Idee* translated "form" or "idea" according to the context.

he would not understand the influence of the motives any more than the connection between every other effect which he sees and its cause. He would then call the inner nature of these manifestations and actions of his body which he did not understand a force, a quality, or a character, as he pleased, but he would have no further insight into it. But all this is not the case; indeed the answer to the riddle is given to the subject of knowledge who appears as an individual, and the answer is *will*. This and this alone gives him the key to his own existence, reveals to him the significance, shows him the inner mechanism of his being, of his action, of his movements. The body is given in two entirely different ways to the subject of knowledge, who becomes an individual only through his identity with it. It is given as a representation in intelligent perception, as an object among objects and bound by the laws of objects. And it is also given in quite a different way as that which is immediately known to everyone, and is signified by the word *will*. Every true act of his will is also at once and without exception a movement of his body. The act of will and the movement of the body are not two different things objectively known, which the bond of causality unites; they do not stand in the relation of cause and effect; they are one and the same, but they are given in entirely different ways,—immediately, and again in perception for the understanding. The action of the body is nothing but the act of the will objectified, *i.e.*, passed into perception.

* * *

Meaning of the will to live

Every glance at the world, to explain which is the task of the philosopher, confirms and proves that *will to live,* far from being an arbitrary hypostasis or an empty word, is the only true expression of its inmost nature. Everything presses and strives towards *existence,* if possible *organized existence,* i.e., *life,* and after that to the highest possible grade of it. In animal nature it then becomes apparent that *will to live* is the keynote of its being, its one unchangeable and unconditioned quality. Let any one consider this universal desire for life, let him see the infinite willingness, facility, and exuberance with which the *will to live* presses impetuously into existence under a million forms everywhere and at every moment, by means of fructification and of germs, nay, when these are wanting, by means of *generatio aequivoca,* seizing every opportunity, eagerly grasping for itself every material capable of life; and then again let him cast a glance at its fearful alarm and wild rebellion when in any particular phenomenon it must pass out of existence, especially when this takes place with distinct consciousness. Then it is precisely the same as if in this single phenomenon the whole world would be annihilated forever, and the whole being of this threatened living thing is at once transformed into the most desperate struggle against death and resistance to it. Look, for example, at the incredible anxiety of a man in danger of his life, the rapid and serious participation in this of every witness of it, and the boundless rejoicing at his deliverance. Look at the rigid terror with which a sentence of death is heard, the profound awe with which we regard the preparations for carrying it out, and the heart-rending compassion which seizes us at the execution itself. We would then suppose there was something quite different in question than a few less years of an empty, sad existence, embittered by troubles of every kind, and always uncertain: we would rather be amazed that it was a matter of any consequence whether one attained a few years earlier to the place where after an ephemeral existence he has billions of years to be. In such phenomena, then, it becomes visible that I am right in declaring that *the will to live* is that which cannot be further explained, but lies at the foundation of all explanations, and that this, far from being an empty word, like the absolute, the infinite, the idea, and similar expressions, is the most real thing we know, the kernel of reality itself.

Maintenance of universal types

But if now, abstracting for a while from this interpretation drawn from our inner being, we place ourselves as strangers over against nature, in order to comprehend it objectively, we find that from the grade of organized life upwards it has only one intention—that of the *maintenance of the species.* To this end it works, through the immense superfluity of germs, through the urgent vehemence of the sexual instinct, through its willingness to adapt itself to all circumstances and opportunities, even to the production of bastards, and through the instinctive maternal affection, the strength of which is so great that in many kinds of animals it even outweighs self-love, so that the mother sacrifices her life in order to preserve that of the young. The individual, on the contrary, has for nature only an indirect value, only so far as it is the means of maintaining the species. Apart from this its existence is to nature a matter of indifference; indeed nature even leads it to destruction as soon as it has ceased to be useful for this end. Why the individual exists would thus be clear; but why does the species itself exist? That is a question which nature when considered merely objectively cannot answer. For in vain do we seek by contemplating her to find an end of this restless striving, this ceaseless pressing into existence, this anxious care for the maintenance of the species. . . . The whole thing, when regarded thus from a purely objective standpoint, as extraneous to ourselves, looks as though nature were only concerned that of all her universal and permanent Forms none should be lost. For the individuals are fleeting as the water in the brook, the Forms, on the contrary, are permanent, like its eddies: but the exhaustion of the water would also do away with the eddies.

We would have to stop at this unintelligible view if nature were known to us only from without, thus were given us merely *objectively*, and we accepted it as comprehended by knowledge, and also as sprung from knowledge, *i.e.*, in the sphere of the representation, and were therefore obliged to confine ourselves to this province in solving it. But the case is otherwise, and a glance at any rate is afforded us into the *interior of nature;* inasmuch as this is nothing else than *our own inner being,* which is precisely where nature, arrived at the highest grade to which its striving could work itself up, is now by the light of knowledge found directly in self-consciousness. Here the will shows itself to us as something absolutely different from the representation, in which nature appears unfolded in all her universal Forms; and it now gives us, at one stroke, the explanation which could never be found by the objective study of representations. Thus the subjective here gives the key for the exposition of the objective. In order to recognize, as something original and unconditioned, that exceedingly strong tendency of all animals and men to retain life and carry it on as long as possible—a tendency which was set forth above as characteristic of the subjective, or of the will—it is necessary to make clear to ourselves that this is by no means the result of any objective *knowledge* of the worth of life, but is independent of all knowledge; or, in other words, that those beings exhibit themselves, not as drawn from in front, but as impelled from behind.

Evidences of the will to live

If with this intention we first of all review the interminable series of animals, consider the infinite variety of their types, as they exhibit themselves always differently modified according to their element and manner of life, and also ponder the inimitable ingenuity of their structure and mechanism, which is carried out with equal perfection in every individual; and finally, if we take into consideration the incredible expenditure of strength, dexterity, prudence, and activity which every animal has ceaselessly to make through its whole life; if, approaching the matter more closely, we contemplate the untiring diligence of wretched little ants, the marvelous and ingenious industry of the bees, or observe how a single burying-beetle buries a mole of forty times its own size in two days in order to deposit its eggs in it and insure nourishment for the future brood, at the same time calling to mind how the life of most insects is nothing but ceaseless labor to prepare food and an abode for the future brood which will arise from their eggs, and which then, after they have consumed the food and passed through the chrysalis state, enter upon life merely to begin again from the beginning the same labor; and also how, like this, the life of the birds is for the most part taken up with their distant and laborious migrations, then with the building of their nests and the collecting of food for the brood, which itself has to play the same role the following year; and so all work constantly for the future, which afterwards makes bankrupt;—then we cannot avoid looking round for the reward of all this skill and trouble, for the end which these animals have before their eyes, which strive so ceaselessly. In short, we are driven to ask: What is the result? What is attained by the animal existence which demands such infinite preparation? And there is nothing to point to but the satisfaction of hunger and the sexual instinct, or in any case a little momentary comfort, as it falls to the lot of each animal individual, now and then in the intervals of its endless need and struggle. If we place the two together, the indescribable ingenuity of the preparations, the enormous abundance of the means, and the insufficiency of what is thereby aimed at and attained, the insight presses itself upon us that life is a business, the proceeds of which are very far from covering the cost of it.

This becomes most evident in some animals of a specially simple manner of life. Take, for example, the mole, that unwearied worker. To dig with all its might with its enormous shovel claws is the occupation of its whole life; constant night surrounds it; its embryo eyes only make it avoid the light. It alone is truly a nocturnal animal; not cats, owls, and bats, who see by night. But what, now, does it attain by this life, full of trouble and devoid of pleasure? Food and the begetting of its kind; thus only the means of carrying on and beginning anew the same doleful course in new individuals. In such examples it becomes clear that there is no proportion between the cares and troubles of life and the results or gain of it. The consciousness of the world of perception gives a certain appearance of objective worth of existence to the life of those animals which can see, although in their case this consciousness is entirely subjective and limited to the influence of motives upon them. But the blind mole, with its perfect organization and ceaseless activity, limited to the alternation of insect larvae and hunger, makes the disproportion of the means to the end apparent. In this respect the consideration of the animal world left to itself in lands uninhabited by men is also specially instructive.

A beautiful picture of this, and of the suffering which nature prepares for herself without the interference of man, is given by Humboldt in his *Ansichten der Natur*; nor does he neglect to cast a glance at the analogous suffering of the human race, always and everywhere at variance with itself. Yet in the simple and easily surveyed life of the brutes the emptiness and vanity of the struggle of the whole phenomenon is more easily grasped. The variety of the organizations, the ingenuity of the means, whereby each is adapted to its element and to its prey contrasts here distinctly with the want of any lasting final aim; instead of which there presents itself only momentary comfort, fleeting pleasure conditioned by wants, much and long suffering, constant strife, a war of all, each one both a hunter and hunted, pressure, want, need, and anxiety, shrieking and howling; and this goes on through endless centuries, or till once again the crust of the planet breaks. Yunghahn relates that he saw in Java a plain far as the eye could reach entirely covered with skeletons, and took it for a battlefield; they were, however, merely the skeletons of large turtles, five feet long and three feet broad, and the same height, which come this way out of the sea in order to lay their eggs, and are then attacked by wild dogs, who with their united strength lay them on their backs, strip off their lower armor, that is, the small shell of the stomach, and so devour them alive. But often then a tiger pounces upon the dogs. Now all this misery repeats itself thousands and thousands of times, year out, year in. For this, then, these turtles are born. For whose guilt must they suffer this torment? Wherefore the whole scene of horror? To this the only answer is: it is thus that the will to live objectifies itself. Let one consider it well and comprehend it in all its objectifications, and then one will arrive at an understanding of its nature and of the world; but not if one frames general conceptions and builds card houses out of them.

PART THREE

Mind, Soul, and Self

CHAPTER VIII

What Is a Self?

EVERYONE speaks and thinks a good deal in the first person singular. "I think . . .," "I want . . .," "I feel . . ." are familiar everyday expressions. They assert one's personal point of view and one's personal rights; they are reminders that subjectivity is an ineradicable component in all human intercourse. Too great an emphasis on the "I" is a mark of egoism, and encourages biased interpretations of things. Nevertheless, even the most objective attempts to reason and carry on experiments betray the personal slant of the reasoner and experimenter; indeed, they are worth making, in the final analysis, only because their results and the evidence on which they are based commend themselves to the experience and judgment of various individual *I*'s. What, then, am I? What do I mean when I speak of my *self*?

i. *Subjective and Objective Approaches*

At first sight it would appear that the question, "What am I?" must be approached subjectively, by introspection. For this is the one investigation where the investigator and his subject matter are identical. Why, then, not simply close my organs of sense to the outer world, banish memories, hopes, and prefabricated interpretations, and attend entirely to the *me* that remains? Such is the method of classical introspection formulated in Descartes' second Meditation:

I will suppose that all the things which I see are false; I will persuade myself that none of the things which my fallible memory presents to me as having happened ever really existed; that my senses tell me nothing about a world beyond myself; that body, figure, extension, movement, and place are but fictions of my mind. What, then, can be esteemed as true? Nothing?

But I myself—am I not something? Even if I am deceived in thinking that I have senses and a body, am I so dependent on body and senses that I cannot exist without them? But I have said I will persuade myself that nothing in the world has the existence that I attribute to it; hence that my body with its sense organs is but a figment of my imagination—much as if I were to dream that I had some entirely different kind of body. If I am persuaded that all these things have no real existence, may I not further persuade myself that I, too, do not exist? No, that is impossible. I most surely exist so long as I am persuading myself of something. Grant that I may be deceived about as much else as you will, there is one thing about which I cannot possibly be deceived, and that is that at the moment of being deceived I must exist. The proposition, "I am," "I exist," is necessarily true each time that I mentally conceive it.[1]

Up to a point Descartes stands upon irrefutable ground. There is a sense in which I most certainly do exist at the moment when I am questioning my existence. But the logic of the situation does not carry me any farther than that one abstract admission. Descartes proceeds in his later Meditations to "deduce," as he thinks, certain further characteristics of the self whose existence has been demonstrated by this logical *tour de force*. But his alleged deductions have by no means the same self-evident character as his original theorem. *That* I am is entirely certain at the moment when I reflect upon it; *what* I am is a question of labyrinthine complexity, which, when answered on introspection, allows of any amount of error, doubt, and self-deception. The chronic uncertainty of introspective method has stimulated, particularly in the present century, the search for a

[1] Paraphrased from the second of Descartes' *Meditations*. A more literal translation is included among the Readings, pp. 353-357.

method that can yield objectively verified results. Two such methods are particularly influential in psychological discussions today: behaviorism and psychoanalysis.

Behaviorism

Behaviorism is a special form of materialism, derived from the technique employed in modern laboratory psychology for certain types of problem. Like other species of materialism it declares the methods of the experimental sciences to be necessary and sufficient for solving all personal problems; in other words, that if the problem is one to which experimental method cannot be applied in principle, then it is no real problem, it is a pseudo-problem. Any question concerning consciousness the behaviorists dismiss on this ground as a pseudo-problem. Accordingly, in *Psychology from the Standpoint of a Behaviorist,* the book which may be regarded as the first forthright statement of behavioristic method and doctrine, John B. Watson declares that in his exposition "the reader will find no discussion of consciousness and no reference to such terms as sensation, perception, attention, will, image and the like." He rejects such concepts and the problems arising from them, on two grounds: that he does not need them in carrying out the type of investigation that interests him, and that he finds it impossible to use them with rigorous clarity and consistency. Consequently:

Behavioristic psychology attempts to formulate, through systematic observation and experiment, the generalizations, laws and principles which underlie man's behavior. When a human being acts—does something with arms, legs or vocal cords—there must be an invariable group of antecedents serving as a "cause" of the act. . . . Psychology is thus confronted immediately with two problems—the one of predicting the probable causal situation or stimulus giving rise to the response; the other, given the situation, of predicting the probable response.[2]

[2] John B. Watson, *Psychology from the Standpoint of a Behaviorist* (Lippincott, 1919), p. 5.

Two sentences of this quoted passage raise problems to be dealt with in later chapters. The second sentence makes explicit the deterministic assumption underlying behaviorism: that for any given action in an individual organism (assuming that the description of it could be complete) there "must be" an invariable cause; and conversely, from a given set of causes (assuming again the possibility of a total description) there must result an invariable behavioral effect. The arguments for and against this belief will be examined in Chapter X. The third sentence, tacitly recognizing that our knowledge of the given effect or of the given cause is never actually complete, combines with the first sentence to define the scope of behavioristic method in terms of probable rather than certain results. But notice in the first and third sentences the attitude toward fellow men that is involved. Behavioristic method is interested in explaining them, discovering what makes them tick, and consequently—as Watson frankly admits—in controlling them, conditioning them, manipulating them:

> Give me a dozen healthy infants, well-formed, and my own specified world to bring them up in and I'll guarantee to take any one at random and train him to become any type of specialist I might select —doctor, lawyer, artist, merchant-chief and, yes, even beggar-man and thief, regardless of his talents, penchants, tendencies, abilities, vocations, and race of his ancestors.[3]

Whether Watson or any other behaviorist can make good so sweeping a boast is open to question. But in any case the boasting reveals the intent that lies behind the method. Behaviorism treats human beings as things to be manipulated—complex things no doubt, but still *things* rather than self-governing persons. There is a deep moral and metaphysical issue here—the problem of the right relation between self and self—which will be examined in Chapter XI.

In the present context we need only observe the limited conception of selfhood which behaviorism implies. Its method *ex-*

---

[3] Watson, *Behaviorism* (Norton, rev. ed., 1930), p. 82.

cludes from consideration any part of what I think of as "myself" other than what can be detected in the form of bodily movements. Hence, as its basic concepts are geared to its method, behaviorism dismisses my conscious states as "unreal," or at any rate inconsequential. My toothache, to the behaviorist, is nothing more than its publicly observable manifestations—the vibrating dental nerves, the clenched fists, the laryngeal disturbances as the so-called "cries of pain" are suppressed, etc. And thus he artificially limits his conception of selfhood to those aspects of it which his method is capable of handling.

Psychoanalytic theory

The psychoanalytic interpretation of the self seeks objectivity in another way. It is less doctrinaire than behaviorism: instead of denying so immediately obvious a fact as consciousness it regards consciousness as something actual but incomplete—as the changing surface of a deep well of unconscious mentality in which the real causes of the surface ripples are to be found. The conscious mind has its overt intentions and makes its own excuses when they are not carried out. But slips of the tongue, slips of the pen, the sudden impulses that betray the most carefully laid plans, all testify to some more powerful set of causes than those found in the conscious awareness and intent. Freud even goes so far, in *The Psychopathology of Everyday Life,* as to declare that the woman who loses her wedding ring "really" wishes that she never had it, and that the physician who forgets the name of his rival "really" wishes that name blotted out of existence. The conscious mind shies away from admitting such unpleasant explanations of its quirks, and consoles itself with "rationalizations"—that is, rationally plausible explanations which seem to justify the dubious action or omission but have no basis in determinable fact.[4]

---

[4] The student of philosophy is advised to avoid using the word "rationalization" so broadly as to cover all reasoning of a personal or moral sort. The word should be restricted to cases where there is some evidence that self-deception is being practiced.

Since introspection is no trustworthy guide as to the character and motives of the unconscious part of the psyche, Freud successively tried out three other methods of investigation. His earliest experiments, influenced by the success of the French neurologist Charcot in treating hysteria patients, was with hypnosis. Often under hypnosis a patient's memory can be tapped and the origin of the symptoms discovered. But Freud encountered two difficulties: many neurotic patients could not be hypnotized, and hypnosis did not in all cases effect a cure. He next came under the influence of the Viennese physician Josef Breuer, and tried out the possibilities of "free association"—i.e., of encouraging the patient to talk out his emotional difficulties, thereby tapping his unconscious memory through mental associations made when he is fully relaxed. It is a slower method, but Freud found that it was effective for more patients and generally led to a more thorough catharsis. Thirdly, he employed dream analysis, on the hypothesis that a dream is a symbolic expression of the dreamer's libido, or unconscious desire. The idea of the self which resulted from these procedures will be mentioned in Section ii.

Cultural objectivism

The nature of selfhood cannot be adequately understood unless it is envisaged in relation to the cultural milieu in which it has grown up. In recent writings there has been increased recognition of how deeply the self becomes molded by such cultural factors as family organization, community life, manner of daily employment, literary and artistic heritage, prevalent religious attitudes and beliefs, dominant social and political loyalties. Sometimes these factors are defined over-narrowly—as in the doctrine of Karl Marx, which virtually reduces man to a product of economic forces, or as in that of certain sociologists who "explain" man and human ideals as entirely the product of folkways. Such one-track interpretations are not very enlightening. The individual's partial autonomy, his limited but real freedom to make what he will of himself, should not be ignored. It is true that every man is deeply rooted in and largely conditioned by the folkways and standards of the culture in which he is reared. But the relation of selfhood to its environmental conditions is too subtly modulated and ambiguous to be adequately represented by any single theory.

ii. *The Unity of the Self*

Each of us speaks of himself as though he were quite sure of continuing to be the same person—yesterday, today, and tomorrow. At least that is our more usual conception. Occasionally we complicate matters by a remark such as, "I was not myself when I spoke so rudely," but it is doubtful if we mean this quite literally. At any rate it is hard to be sure in what way and to what extent I am a unified being. In what sense am I the same person that I was as a child? What, if anything, am "I" during a deep and dreamless sleep? What, if anything, remains of me after death? All such questions cluster around the central question, "*What am I?*" Not "What is my body?"—the only question which strict behaviorists recognize as valid—but "What am I who knows and manages this body?" What is this self whom I encounter immediately and inescapably in moments of introspection?

The soul-substance doctrine

To such questions the average man would doubtless exclaim, "Oh, you're asking about my *soul!*" And according to the current of opinions in which he happened to be moving he would express either conviction or disbelief in this supposed entity. But what does the word "soul" mean? Sometimes it is spoken lightly, to connote no more than the generally acceptable word "self"—as when we say, "A bit of hardship is good for the soul," or as when we read that some character in a novel felt joy or grief or shame "in the very depths of his soul." Historically, however, the word has connoted much more than that, and the fuller meaning has always been a part of the orthodox tradition in Christian teaching. Christian thinkers have traditionally regarded the soul as a substance—not, of course, as a material substance having its existence in space, but as a permanent something which underlies and supports the various psychic phenomena which belong to it.

The most celebrated pre-Christian expression of this view is found in Plato's Dialogue, *Phaedo*. Socrates, who is in prison and enjoying the company of certain friends for the last time before he must drink the hemlock, discusses the possibility of continuing to live after the body's death—i.e., whether the soul, or self, can survive the body. The discussion naturally involves the questions of the nature of the soul or self, and its relation to the body during what we call life. Socrates deals with the last question first, drawing from Simmias the following admission:

> SOCRATES. When does the soul attain to truth? For we have agreed, have we not, that when she seeks to investigate anything in collaboration with the body she is deceived?
> SIMMIAS. True.
> SOCRATES. Then if she is to attain truth at all, it must become known to her by thought?
> SIMMIAS. Yes.
> SOCRATES. And can she not think best when none of the senses, whether of sound or sight or pleasure or pain, is distracting her? That is to say, when she draws herself away from the body and frees herself so far as she can from all contact with it, striving to be wholly alone with herself in order to seek what is really true?
> SIMMIAS. Certainly.

Later in the discussion, with Cebes now as interlocutor, Socrates proceeds to a consideration of the soul's real nature:

> SOCRATES. Should we not ask ourselves what kind of thing it is that is subject to dispersion, and hence in danger of being destroyed? And should we not then proceed to inquire whether the soul is that

kind of thing? And should not our hopes and fears for our own souls be governed by our answer?

CEBES. That is true.

SOCRATES. Now it is compound things that are naturally capable of being broken up; for having been put together they can be taken apart. But merely what is uncompounded must be the one kind of thing that is indissoluble, if anything is?

CEBES. Yes, I should think so.

The uncompound, then, is that which we need not fear will be destroyed. But Socrates' second question is still to be answered: Is the soul composite or simple? Socrates begins by distinguishing sharply between the ever-changing things and occurrences of the visible world, which are perceived through the ever-changing sense-channels of the body; and the changeless "forms" of things, the enduring standards by which they can be compared and appraised, such as equality and beauty, which must be known by a part of ourselves that is equally unchanging, and this is the soul.

SOCRATES. Now then, Cebes: does it not follow from all we have been saying, that the soul is of the nature of the divine—in that it is immortal, and has the power of thought, and is indissoluble and unchangeable? And that the body is of the nature of the human—being mortal, and without the power of thought; and multiform, and so dissoluble and changeable? Can there be any reasonable denial of this, my dear Cebes?

CEBES. None whatever.

SOCRATES. Then if that is true, shall we not say that while the body is liable to rapid dissolution, the soul is wholly or at least very nearly indissoluble?

CEBES. Yes, indeed.[5]

Associationism

The argument that man's soul must be immortal because it is not composite and therefore not liable to change or dissolu-

[5] The three passages are from Plato's *Phaedo*, 65, 78-80.

tion, was revived by various theological writers in the seventeenth and eighteenth centuries, notably by Bishop Butler in his widely read *Analogy of Religion*. The dubious logic of the argument stirred David Hume, a generation later, to a diametrically opposite avowal:

> For my part, when I enter most intimately into what I call *myself*, I always stumble on some particular perception or other, of heat or cold, light or shade, love or hatred, pain or pleasure. I never can catch *myself* at any time without a perception, and never can observe anything but the perception. When my perceptions are removed for any time, as by sound sleep, so long am I insensible of *myself*, and may truly be said not to exist. And were all my perceptions removed by death, and could I neither think nor feel nor see nor love nor hate after the dissolution of my body, I should be entirely annihilated, nor do I conceive what is farther requisite to make me a perfect non-entity.

Hume concludes, therefore, that a self is "nothing but a bundle or collection of different perceptions, which succeed each other with an inconceivable rapidity, and are in a perpetual flux and movement." And sparing no pains to avoid being misunderstood, he adds this carefully qualified simile:

> The mind is a kind of theatre, where several perceptions successively make their appearance; pass, re-pass, glide away, and mingle in an infinite variety of postures and situations. There is properly no *simplicity* in it at one time, nor *identity* in different—whatever natural propension we may have to imagine that simplicity and identity. The comparison of the theatre must not mislead us. They are the successive perceptions only, that constitute the mind; nor have we the most distant notion of the place where these scenes are represented, or of the materials of which it is composed.[6]

Thus an associationistic theory, such as Hume's, regards the mind, and indeed the entire self, as nothing more than a product

---

[6] David Hume, *A Treatise of Human Nature*, Part IV, Sec. 6 (pp. 350-351 of the Odyssey Press edition of selections from Berkeley and Hume).

of sensations and ideas, which follow or accompany one another according to the laws of mental association. Indeed, the very words "mind" and "self" are no more than convenient labels for the activity of such association. Hence, although associationism does do ampler justice than behaviorism to the qualitative diversity of psychic phenomena, it ignores quite as flagrantly the humanistic postulate that a man is somehow more than the sum of his parts—that within modest limits he is an initiator and director.

The concept of self-integration

It seems fairly evident that the truth about selfhood must lie somewhere between the two extreme views just cited. The soul-substance doctrine not only alleges a degree of unity that goes far beyond any possibility of experiential verification; it also is hard to reconcile with certain data of abnormal psychology, such as split personality, schizophrenia, and the like. Associationism, on the other hand, in stressing exclusively the flow and succession of psychic moments through time, does no justice to the integrative activities of the self and furnishes no standard whereby to distinguish a more unified self from a less. What of a man who makes a resolve early in life, plans a career or some other program of coherent action, and carries it out over the years? Is such a one a mere victim of time, a mere congeries of successive mental states and acts? Not exhaustively, it would seem. To some degree he molds time; for by his foresight and his resolute fidelity to that foresight he brings present and future together into an intelligible whole. And everyone of us has explored his power to do this in some measure. What appears to be wanted, then, is the concept of a kind of unity that is not static but dynamic, not absolute but relative to the purposes and life-context of the individual, yet effectively real.

As a matter of fact, Plato, in other Dialogues than the *Phaedo,* makes various suggestions that appear to stem from such a concept. In the *Symposium* he describes the soul as a lover, always somehow incomplete and seeking completion and fulfillment by joining with the object that it loves. The object of love may be one of several kinds, which Plato summarizes under three heads—physical, social (inter-personal), and intellectual. What they have in common is that, to the soul that aspires to know them, each of them is *kalos*—the principal Greek word connoting intrinsic value; it may be translated "fine," "splendid," "beautiful." The simile of the lover suggests the further consideration that the aspiring soul desires not only to possess the beautiful and so far as possible to become one with it, but also to "create in the beautiful." As the physical lover consummates his love by creating flesh-and-blood offspring, the lover of beautiful forms is inspired by them to create a new spiritual vision and make it somehow effective in the integration of his own person and of the world around him.

What is it in one's own person that needs to be integrated? In both the *Phaedrus* and the *Republic* Plato analyzes the soul into three "parts," or functional aspects: it has carnal desires (*epithymia*), spiritual energies (*thymos*), and mental illumination (*noêsis*). A man is pulled both by appetites (to eat and drink, to gratify the sex urge, to indulge in idle forms of amusement) and by aspirations (the zest of action and accomplishment). In a celebrated simile Plato likens these two kinds of motivation to a pair of horses drawing a chariot, the one both sluggish and lascivious, the other so spirited that he can hardly be restrained. But fortunately the chariot (the soul) has a driver (the conscious mind) who manages the inferior horse by alternately spurring it on and sharply checking it when its evil desires threaten to pull the chariot off the road; while he treats the nobler horse as an ally, guiding rather than commanding him.

Whereas Plato's philosophy contains an unresolved tension between two concepts of the soul, the substantial and the functional, his pupil and independent follower Aristotle stressed the functional aspect exclusively. Aristotle defines soul as the primary *entelecheia* of a natural body possessing organs, and as the "determining principle" of a living body.[7] Since the Greek word *telos* means an end or aim, the word *en-telecheia* connotes that the end toward which the bodily movements are directed is essentially an end given by the nature of the organism itself. Soul, in short, is the basic faculty[8] of organization of an organic body. In man it may become rational—i.e., a conscious intention of self-direction; whereas in lower animals it is more or less blindly instinctive. But in no case is it something separate or separable from the body. Although superior to the body during life, it vanishes into nothingness when the body dies.

Health of the soul

What is the "end given by the nature of the organism itself"? The natural end of any organism is *health* in the broadest sense of the word. Health involves maximal fullness of life, the most harmonious fulfillment of such life processes as a given species of organism is capable of. Health consists—not only to Aristotle but to virtually all the Greeks—in right proportion and due measure. The importance of right proportion and right blending for the health of the body is stressed by the Greek medical writers, particularly by those belonging to the school of the great Hippocrates:

> The human constitution contains the salty and the bitter, the sweet and the acid, the astringent and the insipid, and many other elements possessing properties that vary both in number and in strength. These, when mixed and compounded with one another, are not noticed and do not injure their possessor; but when one of them is separated off and stands alone, then it becomes both noticeable and injurious.[9]

Socrates extended the idea of health from the body to the soul, the Greek word for which is *psyche*. Thus when Crito solicits him to break the law by letting his friends bribe the

---
[7] Aristotle, *De Anima*, II. i, iv.
[8] Consult Glossary for the precise meaning of the word "faculty."
[9] From the Hippocratic treatise, *On Ancient Medicine*, Chap. xiv.

jailor and escaping from prison where he is under sentence of death, Socrates replies:

> SOCRATES. If by following the advice of those who do not understand such matters we cripple that part of us which is improved by health and injured by disease, would life thus crippled be worth living? The reference here is to the body, is it not?
> CRITO. Yes.
> SOCRATES. Would life be worth living with the body in a crippled and bad condition?
> CRITO. Of course not.
> SOCRATES. Similarly, will life be worth living if we cripple that part of us which is improved by justice and injured by injustice? Do we regard the part of ourselves that has to do with justice and injustice as less important than the body?
> CRITO. By no means.
> SOCRATES. But even more worthwhile?
> CRITO. Yes, far more.[10]

In Socrates, Plato, and Aristotle alike, notwithstanding metaphysical differences, the practical emphasis is on the soul's health; and they agree, too, that health consists in a harmonization and rightly proportioned blending of the soul's several faculties under the guidance of reason.

The Freudian concept of the self

Freud, as has been said above, extended the investigation of the self by taking more explicit and detailed account of the unconscious aspects of the self—or psyche—than had been done before. Freud draws heavily upon the data of abnormal psychology, on the hypothesis that the psychotic (the insane) and the psychoneurotic (the emotionally unbalanced) are not sharply different from so-called normal persons, but exhibit a more marked form of tendencies that all of us share. In such abnormal individuals the psyche may behave in such a way that it can best be conceived as splitting, or tending to split, into its com-

---

[10] Plato, *Crito*, 47E–48A.

ponent parts. In a relatively normal psyche the split is less obvious, but the concept of a multiple-structured self is still applicable.

Freud conceives the psyche, whether normal or abnormal, to consist of three dynamical components, or interacting forces. The *ego* is the conscious intelligence, the discriminating part of the self. Freud postulates that the ego is entirely selfish, egoistic, always calculating for its own supposed benefit; that it acts with forethought and seeks to satisfy its individual wants by taking account of and consciously manipulating or coming to terms with the social and physical environment. The *id* is the blind unconscious driving power of the self. In his earlier writings Freud tended to identify it with the sex instinct. In his more mature thought he conceives of it as formed of two opposing drives—*eros* and *arakne,* the life and death instincts. These move us without foresight of consequences; they strive peremptorily for satisfaction except so far as they are controlled by one of the other main elements. Freud interprets the newborn babe as being almost entirely *id;* the ego develops from it in the process of meeting social reality. The *superego* (earlier called the "censor") provides the sense of *ought.* It is the seat of the "ego ideal," and is the great socializing force. It corresponds roughly to what we ordinarily call conscience; with the proviso that, in Freud's theory, it is entirely developed out of the child's early conflicts, both his fears and his admirations, toward the environing world.

Freud, somewhat analogously to the Greeks, conceives psychic health as a harmonious state of balance and nonconflict among the ego, the id, the superego, and external reality. The balance, however, is continually being upset or threatened, and much human behavior is a resultant of such conflicts or of their resolutions. The aim of psychoanalysis is to use associational techniques, such as were described in Section i, in order to bring unconscious conflicts into the open and so destroy their power, thus delivering the individual from psychic illness to psychic health.

Beyond Freud

Despite Freud's fame, neither his concepts nor his presuppositions should be taken as the last word. He has made valuable contributions to psychotherapy. But the conceptual scheme from which he works is open to critical disagreement. One avenue of disagreement is opened up by comparing the Freudian triad with the Platonic. In Plato's simile of the charioteer and his two horses it is evident that the sluggish horse corresponds roughly to the Freudian id. But elsewhere the correspondence is inexact and obscure. The charioteer is like the ego in being fully conscious, and the spirited horse is like the superego in providing the aspirational force in action directed toward ideal goals. But in Plato's view it is not the spirited horse that discerns the goals, it is the charioteer, which is to say the conscious mind. For the charioteer as Plato conceives him is the rightful master who utilizes the nobler horse's spiritual energy but reserves to himself the right and the responsibility of saying how that energy should be directed.

Again, Freud's identification of the id with the Love and Death instincts and his sexual or quasi-sexual interpretation of these has been regarded by many psychologists as too narrow and doctrinaire. Particularly Freud's one-time disciple Alfred Adler came early to the conclusion that there is something more fundamental than sexuality at the root of human neuroses. The primary source of conflict, he maintained, is a feeling of inferiority. The most powerful human urge is the will to power, the will to dominate, and to be recognized. This instinct takes many forms, but each individual must either make himself superior in some way or, if frustrated in that, build up fantasies of superiority. The first and healthier way is illustrated by Demosthenes who overcame his stuttering by learning to speak with pebbles in his mouth and eventually developed into the greatest orator in Greece, or by a boy poor at sports who learns to draw satisfaction from success in his studies or in debating or in social popularity. The other way, the way of fantasy, is memorably represented in James Thurber's short story, *The Secret Life of Walter Mitty*, where an intimidated husband meets every fresh assault of a nagging wife by an elaborate daydream of self-gratification. Thus Adler regards the self-assertive impulse and not the sex impulse as the dominant force in the human psyche. It is the source of all great achievement on the one hand, but when it is frustrated either by circumstance or by the individual's own hypersensitiveness it becomes the main cause of maladjustment and misconduct.

Finally, one may challenge Freud's interpretation of the super-ego—the conscience—as merely the product of frustrations arising out of conflicts between the id and the external world. The Freudian case is put with considerable strength by the British psychologist J. C. Flügel, who analyzes the superego as partly (1) an "introjection" into the subconscious mind of the precepts and attitudes of one's fellowmen; partly (2) a development out of childhood aggressive impulses against one's parents, which later turn against one's self and become masochistic; and partly (3) a compensation for the defects of one's actual self by building up an ego-ideal which one would like to attain. The third component in Flügel's analysis is characteristically Adlerian. It becomes evident that Freud, Adler, and Flügel are alike in taking for granted that the super-ego must be exhaustively explainable in terms of calculable elements in the individual's organism and environment.

Now whether you accept or reject the adequacy of their common presupposition, it is well at least to recognize that there is another possible and indeed widely held view which these psychoanalysts refuse even to take seriously. That is the view that conscience does not entirely originate in the natural world —i.e., in the struggles and frustrations of the individual psyche in itself and its physico-social environment, although admittedly it is greatly modified and individuated by these; but that its real source and therefore its basis of moral authority is transcendental.

More comprehensively, the neglected view is that man's psyche is not exhaustively understandable in terms of its material and environmental conditions, but must be considered also, and perhaps more basically, in its relation to the world of spirit, with which it has a natural but too seldom remembered affinity. No survey of views concerning the nature of selfhood would be complete without mention of this possibility; its examination, however, must be reserved for Chapter XV.

For Further Study

WILLIAM JAMES, *The Principles of Psychology* (Holt, 2 vols., 1890).
G. T. W. PATRICK, *What Is the Mind?* (Macmillan, 1929).
CHARLES W. MORRIS, *Six Theories of Mind* (University of Chicago Press, 1933).
EDNA HEIDBREDER, *Seven Psychologies* (Appleton-Century, 1933).
RALPH BARTON PERRY, *Present Philosophical Tendencies* (Longmans, Green, 1912), Chap. XII, "A Realistic Theory of the Mind."
WILLIAM JAMES, *Essays in Radical Empiricism* (Longmans, Green, 1912), Chap. I, "Does Consciousness Exist?"
JOHN LAIRD, *Problems of the Self* (Macmillan, 1917).
GILBERT RYLE, *The Concept of Mind* (Barnes and Noble, 1949).
CARROLL C. PRATT, *The Logic of Modern Psychology* (Macmillan, 1939).
R. F. A. HOERNLÉ, *Studies in Contemporary Metaphysics* (Harcourt, Brace, 1920), Chaps. VIII, IX.
PETER LASLETT, ed., *The Physical Basis of Mind* (Macmillan, 1939).
CHARLES S. SHERRINGTON, *Man on His Nature* (Gifford Lectures for 1937-1938; Macmillan, 1941).
CURT JOHN DUCASSE, *Nature, Mind and Death* (Open Court, 1951).

Questions for Discussion

1. What different ideas and questions suggest themselves according as you speak of your innermost self by the names *self, ego, psyche, soul?*

2. Regarding Watson's claim, quoted on p. 264, that he could train any normal infant into any type of specialist he might select:

a) Do you think his claim can probably be substantiated, or not?

b) If such power could be acquired, do you think it should be exercised? What can be said on both sides of this question?

c) If exercised at all, by whom? With what limitations?

3. "Of what use would it be to you, Sir, to become King of China on condition of forgetting all that you have been? Would it not be the same as if God, at the same time as he destroyed you, created a king in China?"—Leibniz.

How important is memory, then, in the unity of the self?

What bearing does this have on the question of the soul's immortality?

4. Study the passage from Plato's *Laws* (Readings, pp. 347-350) and explain why self-motion is so essential an attribute of selfhood.

5. After studying the two passages quoted from Hume (p. 270) and the critical comments that follow, do you see any reasonable sense in which *you* are anything more than successive perceptions which "pass, re-pass, glide away, and mingle"?

6. How are the ideas of psychic health and self-integration interrelated? Can you have one without the other?

7. How do you estimate both the value and the limitations of Freud's method?

CHAPTER IX

The Mind-Body Relation

IN EVERYDAY experience we normally take for granted that mind and body affect each other in a diversity of ways. When a pin pricks your hand you feel the pain. Stimulants excite, sedatives lull not only pulse and heartbeat but, as a rule, one's mental outlook and zest. Experimental studies in visual perception show that when an object is presented to the eye there occurs an excitation of the retinal nerves: the perceiver thereupon sees the object and can contemplate it. Analogously with the other senses. To be sure there are some bodily changes that appear not to register upon the mind of the person to whom they belong. A physician may say, "My stethoscope reveals a disturbance in your chest," and the patient reply, "I wasn't aware of it." But in general the cases are numerous and familiar where activities set up in a human body are known to the body's possessor in mental and qualitatively diverse forms.

Equally familiar are many apparent evidences that the mind can affect the body, by initiating activities in it. We sometimes pause in order to think before acting; and we do this in the belief that our thoughts can have some influence upon how we act. Where voluntary acts are concerned the influence takes the form of decision: I deliberate whether to turn east or west, and when I have mentally compared the advantages to be had from each I decide that west is the direction I want, and it is no occasion for surprise when my legs respond physically to my decision by carrying me where I want to go. The influence takes involuntary forms too. The man who allows himself to become angry by reflecting on some imagined injury may find his hands trembling, his heart pumping, and his throat constricted. Lustful thoughts manifest themselves in other bodily ways. Long continued worry may cause dyspepsia or even stomach ulcers. Contrariwise, a serene outlook and joyful disposition seem to be important contributors to bodily health, and most physicians agree that a patient's recovery from illness is likely to be accelerated if he can be persuaded to keep up his courage and confidence.

In short, the assumption on which many, perhaps most, of our day-by-day activities are postulated is that mind and body at least sometimes interact. Whether they really do so or only appear to do so is the question to be considered in the present chapter.

i. Interactionism

The rough-and-ready view that mind and body sometimes interact must be formulated as a more precise and detailed hypothesis in order that its merits and difficulties can be examined. Let us begin by looking at a typical situation where *apparently* some interaction takes place. Suppose that I see a book, and because its title suggests a connection with certain of my interests I pick it up. Using B for "bodily event" and M for "mental event," we may interpret the ordinary way of conceiving the occurrence as a causal linkage of four different events, two bodily and two mental. The book lying on the table (B_1) causes my mental consideration of the book in connection with my other thoughts and interests (M_1), which causes my resolve to look into it (M_2), which causes the motion of my arm and hand in picking it up (B_2). Experimental analysis of the physical process of sense perception shows that between B_1 and M_1 there are intermediary connecting events: certain vibratory movements passing with unimaginable swiftness from the object to the retina of my eye, and other such movements passing from the retina along the afferent nerves to the optical center of the brain, presumably setting up appropriate vibrations in that region. It would appear, then, that the book itself, as a set of physical events, is several steps removed in the causal chain from the mental awareness of the book; and that the more immediate cause of that awareness is a particular pattern of cerebral vibration. Again, it can be shown experimentally that there are connecting events between M_2 and B_2: vibratory movements from the brain along the efferent nerves to the muscles of the arm and hand, causing a pattern of muscular flexions which results in those movements described as "picking up the book."

Descartes' theory

The classical statement of interactionist theory was formulated by Descartes, who postulated that matter and mind were entirely independent natures, or, in the language of his day, substances. Matter he defined as *extended* substance: it exists only so far as it is spread out in space. Mind he defined as *thinking* substance: it lacks spatial extension altogether and exists only so far as it thinks, consciously or unconsciously. Observe that Descartes is not stating any paradox. He is simply formulating in clear terms the view of mind and matter that most of us hold. What we mean by mind is not a ghost or shadow or aerated something in or around the body. "Mind" is merely a convenient noun for the verb "to think." To say that I have a mind is equivalent to saying that I have the faculty of forming ideas about things.

How are mind and body connected? Descartes believed the medium of connection to be the pineal gland at the base of the brain—a physical organ, since it is spatially extended through a part of the head, yet possessing "animal spirits," which are an "active" ingredient in that they are of the nature of thought but yet move through the body. Quite possibly if Descartes had been writing in the idiom of today he would have used the term "subconscious" for what he called "animal spirits." On that interpretation Descartes was espousing the highly suggestive theory that the body affects the conscious mind by acting first upon the subconscious (conceived as a physical movement) and that the conscious mind affects the body through the same medium. The first half of the theory might explain why, for example, when you "didn't hear" something that was said to you, it can be proved by hypnosis that you nevertheless took it into, and stored it up in, your subconscious memory. The second half of the theory might explain the familiar phenomenon of weak will power. When a person resolves again and again to get up out of bed on a dark frosty morning and yet goes on lying there even while he makes new resolves, the explanation might be that although his conscious will declares its intent it fails to receive confirmation and aid from the subconscious.

But however natural a view interactionism may be, and however ingenious Descartes' elaboration of it, certain difficulties become evident when it is subjected to analytic examination. The principal objections that have been urged against it are briefly as follows.

First apriori objection: inconceivability

There are some who repudiate interactionism because of the alleged inconceivability of a causal connection between two such radically different entities as a bodily movement and a conscious thought. How, they ask, can an *idea* produce a *movement* in the brain cells? W. K. Clifford remarks sarcastically that it is as though we supposed that two carriages of a railway train were kept together by feelings of amity between the engineer and the brakeman. And in a similar tone Charles Mercier asks whether we can imagine the idea of a beefsteak either binding together or loosening the attractive force of two molecules of the brain.

Second apriori objection: conservation of energy

A more definite objection than the foregoing rests upon an appeal to the principle of conservation of physical energy, which for several centuries has been a basic assumption of physical science; for in classical modern physics it is postulated that the amount of energy in the universe is always fixed and constant. On the assumption that a mental act is utterly different in kind from physical energy, how can it affect the brain without thereby changing the amount of physical energy present? Wilhelm Wundt has offered the counter-suggestion that a mental act might delay or accelerate the transformation of potential energy into kinetic, and thus affect the processes of the brain and change the course of behavior without adding to the total amount of energy in existence. But this is no real solution, for some quantity of energy would be required in order to transform potential energy into kinetic, and therefore if the mind were to accomplish a transforming which the brain by itself had not been going to do, the mind would thereby be injecting some energy, physically unaccounted for, into the brain.

Methodological basis of criticism

Since the law of conservation of energy is no longer quite so unchallengeable an axiom as it appeared to be some decades ago, contemporary scientists are likely to base their objection to interactionism on more modest grounds. Their argument is a pragmatic one. A study of the brain and motor reflexes is quite possible and indeed much simpler without bringing consciousness into the picture. Regardless of whether any new physical energy is ever created, a scientist engaged in studying the brain finds it convenient to accept the methodological postulate (not necessarily with the dogmatic finality of an axiom) that *so far as he can succeed in isolating his field of observation,* the law of conservation of energy holds good within that field. In actual fact he can never be altogether certain of having isolated it, and therefore his conclusions are legitimately stated not as certainties but as probabilities. His predictions allow for a certain average "margin of error," which is to say of deviation from the calculated outcome; and what precisely causes such deviations he does not inquire beyond a certain point, because any investigation must accept certain limits. But as a practicing scientist he would prefer to accept the fact of unexplained small deviations rather than introduce such a scientifically unmanageable concept as that of consciousness. It simply does not fit in with the type of method he has chosen. It violates the law of parsimony—the principle of intellectual economy.

ii. *Behaviorism and Epiphenomenism*

Mechanistic-behavioristic theories of human nature are likely to ignore the phenomenon of consciousness as far as possible, or to declare that it represents simply another vocabulary for a certain type of bodily process: "fear" and "anger" being taken as convenient *words* for summarizing certain recognizable patterns of change of heartbeat, muscular contraction, breathing, etc., and "thought" for certain incipient speech tendencies in the throat and larynx with more obscure ramifications in the brain and chest. When the behaviorist speaks in this way he is adopting an attitude not only toward his immediate subject matter, the human organism, but also toward language. He is raising a semantic question, a question of meanings; and his answer to it rests on the semantic theory known as *logical positivism,* which states that the only kind of object to which language can meaningfully refer is some aspect of the physical world. If a behaviorist adheres rigidly to this position he is impregnable; because to any mention of conscious thought as something other than the laryngeal vibrations which his instruments can detect, or of the experience of joy as something other than the specifiable changes in eyes, lungs, muscles, glands, and whatever else, all he need reply is, "I don't know what you're talking about. Such words convey no meaning to me other than the specific sets of physical meanings which I can test operationally." No discussion is possible with any person who denies the very meaning of what would be discussed.

The admission of subjectivity

However, behaviorists rarely manage to be perfectly consistent in their denial of consciousness. John B. Watson, for instance, after elsewhere identifying thought and emotion with their physical correlates, comes up with occasional such statements as the following:

> He [the introspective psychologist] might as well have tried to catch the changing scenes in a kaleidoscope or the shift of colors on a Maine coast at sunset as to try to lay verbal hold of the "stuff" emotions are made of.[1]

Here Watson seems to be acknowledging that emotions can be felt emotionally (not merely seen as bodily movements) and that they therefore do subjectively exist; his objection to them is that the qualities which they have for the person who feels them cannot be articulated ("laid verbal hold of") by the linguistic techniques of science. And that is true. A novelist, dramatist, or poet, or for that matter a vivid conversationalist, can describe the subjective character of emotional experience with partial success by using language with color and fire; but a scientist, using strictly scientific language, cannot. The limitation follows as a corollary from the requirements of scientific thinking, discussed in Chapter VI.

And yet, however hard it may be to describe a subjective experience, the experience certainly does exist for the experiencer and is something different from what can be observed objectively of the corresponding bodily processes. The felt pain of a toothache is real enough, and is clearly distinguishable from what the dentist sees when he looks into the mouth—clearly distinguishable even from all that he *could* see if he were able to make the fullest conceivable observations of all the intricate and minute motions of the dental nerves. It is possible that there might be

[1] John B. Watson, *The Ways of Behaviorism* (Harper, 1928), pp. 46-47.

a dentist who knew his job thoroughly but had never experienced a toothache of his own. Such a dentist would probably have only a vague idea of what a toothache *felt* like, although he might have a very clear and well founded idea of what the inflamed dental nerves *looked* like. The question inevitably suggests itself, then: What is the relation between the visible or instrumentally detectable nerve movements and the felt pain? The behaviorist, so far as he recognizes this question at all, gives the answer known as epiphenomenism.

The theory of epiphenomenism

Epiphenomenism declares, in brief, that conscious states—thoughts, feelings, doubts, decisions, and all other experiences in their character of being experienced—exist subjectively, privately, and unsharably; but are ineffectual, having no power whatever to initiate or affect physical events. Consider a statement of the position written by Thomas Huxley nearly a century ago:

> The consciousness of brutes would appear to be related to the mechanism of their body simply as a collateral product of its working, and to be as completely without any power of modifying that working as a steam-whistle which accompanies the work of a locomotive engine is without influence on its machinery. Their volition, if they have any, is an emotion *indicative* of physical changes, not a *cause* of physical changes.... The soul stands related to the body as the bell of a clock to the works, and consciousness to the sound which the bell gives out when it is struck.
>
> It is quite true that, to the best of my judgment, the argumentation which applies to brutes holds equally good of men; and, therefore, that all states of consciousness in us, as in them, are immediately caused by molecular changes of the brain-substance. It seems to me that in men, as in brutes, there is no proof that any state of consciousness is the cause of change in the motion of the matter of the organism. If these positions are well based, it follows that our mental conditions are simply the symbols in consciousness of the changes which take place automatically in the organism; and that, to take an extreme illustration, the feeling we call volition is not the cause of a

voluntary act, but the symbol of that state of the brain which is the immediate cause of that act. We are conscious automata.[2]

Huxley differs from Descartes on the one hand, and from such extreme behaviorists as Watson on the other, in his willingness to admit the likelihood that animals, or at least the higher animals, enjoy some degree of consciousness. Being a reasonable man on the whole, he was no doubt led to that admission by two considerations, the one popular, the other scientific. In the first place, all of us normally take for granted that dogs, for instance, are capable of feeling. Their behavior strongly encourages the belief, and that we believe it is shown by our unwillingness to hurt a dog unnecessarily—a compunction which we do not feel toward a worm. If the dog were nothing but a reacting mechanism there would be no more reason to avoid stepping on its paw than to avoid stepping on a twig. Its squeal would be merely a squeak in the machinery. But in actual fact we regard him as something more than that. Even if his reactions are mechanical, at the very least he is a machine that can feel joy and pain.

In the second place, Huxley was influenced, as Descartes had not been, by evolutionary considerations. If men have evolved from the lower animals and if men enjoy conscious experiences, then it is awkward to suppose that such conscious enjoyment appeared suddenly, in its full human form, with the emergence of man; it would seem more likely that the simian vertebrates from which man evolved were conscious in a more elementary way than man, but yet somehow conscious. And by analogical extension the argument would apply to dogs, horses, elephants, and other species of higher vertebrates.

But the evolutionary argument is a two-edged weapon with Huxley. If, when carried downward from man to beast, it confirms his instinctive belief that some subhuman species have a capacity for feeling, yet when carried upward from beast to man it yields a complementary conclusion. As a practicing scientist

[2] Thomas Huxley, quoted in William James, *Psychology*, Vol. I, p. 131.

Huxley believed that beasts were, and could and should be investigated as, reacting mechanisms. Any pain or other feeling which they might display can be acknowledged as a probable fact and then (he maintained) be dismissed from scientific consideration—since if it really exists it is a mere by-product of evolution which in no way affects the pattern of physical reactions that the scientist studies. And if the emergent consciousness has no function, plays no effectual role in beasts, then it must be likewise ineffectual in the human race which has evolved from beasts. Thus evolutionary considerations persuaded Huxley on the one hand that states of consciousness exist in beasts as well as in men, and on the other hand that they are nugatory and impotent in men as well as in beasts.

What is the conception of man that results? How does the epiphenomenist regard you or me as a whole—that is, as a totality of observable behavior and private experience, of objective and subjective aspects? The answer is a curious sort of dualism, in which the two sets of terms are related asymmetrically. Bodily events produce mental events and determine at each moment exactly what they are to be and how they are to follow one another. Mental events on the other hand have absolutely no effect upon bodily events; they are merely a symbolic and inexact record of them. Bodily events are reactions to previous bodily events and to outer physical events which affect the body through sense organs and in other ways. Some of these bodily events, probably those involving the cerebral hemispheres, produce certain mental experiences—we do not know how or why. The mental experiences, in turn—which may be called mental events, since they occur in a time-sequence—are barren. They are born and die without issue. They include among themselves feelings of effort, and such feelings *seem* to have some effect upon the body, for the legs and arms usually move in the way that the mental effort intends. But to suppose that the mental effort and intention really move the body is to confuse cause and effect. The conscious purpose is an *epiphenomenon*—an effect of the bodily reflex arc that eventuates in the movements of arms or legs, but is in no sense a cause of those movements. "So the melody floats from the harp-string, but neither checks nor quickens its vibrations; so the shadow runs alongside the pedestrian, but in no way influences his step."[3]

Reasons against the theory

The most natural objection to be raised against epiphenomenism, and the one that will doubtless first occur to the reader who thinks as he reads, is its incongruity with men's daily experiences normally interpreted. We seem to ourselves to make decisions mentally and to carry them out in physical movements; it would appear very odd from a common-sense standpoint if all such experiences of mental efficacy were delusive. To be sure, we are sometimes deceived in other matters, and we may possibly be deceived in this. It *could* be that the universal testimony of human experience is false in this respect. It could be that our apparent mental grip on the world is a mistaken reading of the deliverances of consciousness, and that physical process, including all that our own bodies do, proceeds along its metalled ways inflexibly, without the least influence from a specifically mental source. In that case all man's actions would be determined by the preëxisting arrangement of mass-particles and energies in the physical universe; and man would have no ability to change anything except as it was already bound to be changed. This aspect of the matter will turn up again in the next chapter as the problem of free will. All that needs to be said in the present context is that the evidence of much ordinary and ordinarily trusted experience supports the view that mind does sometimes make a difference in bodily behavior, and that we should not dismiss such evidence without excellent reasons for doing so.

A more positive argument against epiphenomenism is offered by William James, who appeals, like Huxley but with a different emphasis and a contrary result, to the principle of evolution as a premise:

[3] James, *op. cit.*, p. 133. James disagrees with the position, however.

It is very generally admitted, though the point would be hard to prove, that consciousness grows the more complex and intense the higher we rise in the animal kingdom. That of a man must exceed that of an oyster. From this point of view it seems an organ, superadded to the other organs which maintain the animal in the struggle for existence; and the presumption of course is that it helps him in some way in the struggle, just as they do. But it cannot help him without being in some way efficacious and influencing the course of his bodily history.[4]

James' meaning is essentially an argument by inductive analogy. In the course of evolutionary development it is pretty safe to generalize that most, if not all, structures and distinctive functions come into existence because they are of some use to the organism. Why then should consciousness be an exception? Why should consciousness have arisen in the evolutionary process unless it served the needs of the organism? If it is a mere "walking shadow," such that the body could carry on just as well without it, there would seem to be no reason for its having emerged into existence, or, once it had emerged, for persisting (if we may credit the circumstantial evidence) over so many generations.

More specifically, consider pleasure and pain. It is admitted by the epiphenomenists themselves that pleasures are generally associated with beneficial, pains with detrimental experiences. Burns, wounds, suffocation, long deprivation of food or drink, are injurious to the organism *and* psychically disagreeable; preserving a healthy body, filling a hungry stomach, and relaxing after work are useful to the organism *and* psychically pleasant. There are exceptions, to be sure, but they do not invalidate the general rule. A man may take pleasure in drinking more alcohol than is good for him, but such pleasures are incidental and sporadic outgrowths of the more normal ones that keep mankind alive. One physiologist has speculated that if all rivers and springs were filled with alcohol instead of water, then by the operation of natural selection men would either have come to hate the stuff or would have developed an immunity to its more

[4] James, *op. cit.*, p. 38.

noxious effects. Now why should there be this general correlation between our conscious feelings of pleasure and pain and the utility or injuriousness of bodily actions unless the consciousness of pleasure and of pain had some effective role to play? If pleasures and pains have no efficacy, "one does not see," James remarks, "why the most noxious acts, such as burning, might not give thrills of delight, and the most necessary ones, such as breathing, cause agony." The correspondence between pleasurable and useful, and between painful and harmful, while by no means perfectly exact, is too widespread, especially in relation to the most vitally important activities, to be ascribed to pure chance.

iii. Parallelism

The logical weaknesses which philosophical analysis reveals in interactionism and in epiphenomenism have stirred certain philosophers to formulate the theory called parallelism. The aim of the parallelist is twofold; he approaches his task with cautionary glances in two opposite directions. On the one hand he is concerned to "save the laws of nature": i.e., to stand by the postulate of physical causality—that every physical event, the behavior of men no less than the collisions of molecules or the falling of stones, must be entirely explicable in terms of other physical events and of the laws which describe their collective activity. Therein the parallelist escapes the difficulties of interactionism. On the other hand he wishes to retain the human prerogative of understanding human consciousness not just as an accidental by-product of the physical processes but as something with a life and rationale of its own, such that the worth which it attributes to itself is not necessarily ruled out as specious.

Parallelism's ingenious solution is this. A particular mental event is caused not by an immediately preceding physical event in the brain or elsewhere, but by an immediately preceding mental event. As there is a stream of self-contained causal activity in the physical world, so likewise there is a stream of self-contained causal activity in the mental world. The two streams are parallel. There is no interchange of causal activity between them, but there is a strict concomitance, a one-to-one correspondence. For every link in the chain of bodily causes and effects there is a corresponding link in the chain of mental causes and effects, and vice versa. But there is no linkage between the one chain and the other. It is simply their nature to exist in perfect mutual correspondence. An eminent nineteenth century parallelist, Friedrich Paulsen, writes as follows:

> The physical processes in the brain form a closed causal nexus. There is no member that is not physical in its nature. One would see as little of psychical processes, of ideas and thoughts, as in the movements of the mill. A man crosses the street. Suddenly his name is called; he turns around and walks toward the person who called him. The omniscient physiologist would explain the whole process in a purely mechanical way. He would show how the physical effect of the sound-waves upon the organ of hearing excited a definite nervous process in the auditory nerve, how this process was conducted to the central organ, how it released certain physical processes there which finally led to the innervation of certain groups of motor nerves, the ultimate result of which was the turning and movement of the body in the direction of the sound-waves. All these occurrences together combine into an unbroken chain of physical processes. Alongside of this, another process occurred of which the physiologist as such sees nothing and needs to know nothing, with which, however, he is acquainted as a thinking being who interprets his percepts; there are auditory sensations, which aroused ideas and feelings. The person called heard his name; he turned around in order to discover who called him and why he was addressed; he perceived an old acquaintance and went to greet him. These occurrences accompany the physical series without interfering with it; perception and presentation are not members of the physical causal series.[5]

Now if one's thoughts and feelings constitute a causal chain which has no causal dependence on the events taking place in the

---

[5] Friedrich Paulsen, *Introduction to Philosophy* (Eng. tr., 1895), p. 84.

body, how are we to explain such a phenomenon as the birth of consciousness in an infant? Or the familiar everyday phenomenon of waking up? Everyone has experienced the momentary bewilderment of being awakened suddenly. The first waking experiences usually appear to be an interruption, not a continuation of the previous dream states. Light streaming in the window, the jangling alarm clock, the hand that prods us: these appear as discontinuities in the sequence of our awarenesses—as intruders from an exterior world. If, as the parallelist declares, they are not to be explained by physical impingements on eye, ear, and limb, how can they be accounted for at all? When the man in Paulsen's illustration heard his name called, what was the immediate cause of his mental awareness of the sounds? The auditory experience is, by hypothesis, parallel to certain motions in the lobe of the brain; these motions are caused by other motions in the afferent nerves from the eardrums, and those in turn by vibrations in the outer air, coming from the source of the sound. If the postulate of strict correspondence between the psychic and the physical is developed logically, there must be some kind of mentality corresponding to each of these outward physical conditions. Just as the brain movements have their outer physical causes, so the auditory experience must have its "outer" mental causes. In short, we arrive at the paradox that there must somehow be mental states corresponding to the sound waves in the air!

Panpsychism

The parallelist boldly accepts this consequence of his theory. The very logic of the situation requires him to universalize his parallelism. Paulsen affirms plainly: "No psychical process anywhere without concomitant movement, no process of movement anywhere without a concomitant psychical process." When a bell rings, the physical movements which proceed from it have *as their sole effects* certain excitations of nerves and brain. Simultaneously there are, Paulsen declares, certain "inner processes" which cause the sensation of sound that is experienced. He adds, however—what is perhaps obvious—that we can have no *direct* evidence of these inner processes; they are "given only at one point, in self-consciousness," whereas the physical world is given to us at many more points in the form of motion. The psychic concomitants of the movements of inanimate nature are unconscious and very elementary; their reality is established by rational deduction, not by direct acquaintance.

Thus Paulsen's parallelism leads logically into panpsychism—the theory that there is a psychic inner side to everything that exists. The position is virtually the same as that which was examined under the name of vitalism in Chapter VII. In fact, one and the same philosophy customarily goes by the name vitalism when in answer to the question, "How has evolution taken place?" and panpsychism when in answer to the question, "How can the mind affect and be affected by its world?"

Criticism

It is hard to give a brief statement of parallelism that does justice to the seriousness and intelligence of some of its defenders. Such able metaphysicians as Spinoza, Fechner, Schopenhauer, and Paulsen cannot be lightly dismissed; and either Schopenhauer's *The World as Will and Idea* or Paulsen's *Introduction to Philosophy* might well be studied and and their arguments fully weighed before the theory is decisively judged. Nevertheless there are two weaknesses in the theory which have perhaps already begun to suggest themselves to the reader's mind.

The first and more general defect has already been mentioned in the critical discussion of vitalism. To recapitulate: The theory is highly speculative; it has to postulate, by the supposed demand of intellectual consistency, the existence of something—an omnipresent psychic life in all things—for which there is no possibility, by ordinary standards, of actual verification. In this respect parallelism is more remote from human experience than either interactionism or epiphenomenism.

Secondly, while parallelism differs from epiphenomenism in regarding mind as having some effectuality—namely upon other mental states—it insists quite as firmly as epiphenomenism that the mental can have no influence whatever upon the physical. In this respect it is as stubbornly opposed as epiphenomenism is to our ordinary way of interpreting human volition.

Finally, the parallelist has not solved the problem of human freedom any more satisfactorily than the epiphenomenist: a given mental event is theoretically "caused" by a preceding mental event, but it must be "parallel to" a certain neuro-cerebral condition, which has been strictly caused by previous physical events in the body and its environment. Paulsen's distinction between the relations "parallel to" and "caused by" dwindles to zero on examination. The mental state must be just what it is by virtue of a previous mental state: he calls that relation "causal." The mental state also must be just what it is by virtue of a simultaneous brain state: he describes these relations by the word "parallel." Whichever word is employed, the mind is still conceived as tightly bound by its physical *and* mental preconditions.

The last of these criticisms throws the body-mind controversy into a new perspective. Underlying the arguments for and against the three main positions—not to mention the many variants which careful analysis can disclose or invent—there is the efficacy of mind in relation to matter. That the material world has a considerable power over our minds is evident to everyone. A blow on the head, a sleeping pill, a few cocktails, an organic illness—each of these in its particular way demonstrates the limiting conditions which matter imposes upon mind. That limits exist is certain; but are they rigid or flexible? Cocktails affect the quality of one's consciousness, it is true; but a man of strong character learns the art of controlling his psychic forces as he drinks, and through them his bodily responses. A victim of illness can exert his will to achieve a state of inner serenity and thereby, up to a point, can sometimes even change the course of the illness itself. Are such evidences of mind's occasional power over matter as real as they seem? Both epiphenomenism and parallelism, for different reasons, declare them essentially illusions. Whatever the mind thinks, feels, or wills they hold to be strictly a result of previous causes—notwithstanding their different theories as to the nature of those causes. Interactionism therefore stands over against them both in this important respect, of allowing for the reality of the mind's partial and occasional control of the body and thereby of the environing world. The metaphysics of mind in its active aspect, as will, becomes the theme of the next chapter.

For Further Study

WILLIAM JAMES, *Principles of Psychology* (1890), Chaps. II, V, XXV.
JAMES B. PRATT, *Matter and Spirit* (Macmillan, 1922).
JAMES B. PRATT, "The Present Status of the Mind-Body Problem," *The Philosophical Review*, Vol. XLV (1936), pp. 144 ff.
WILLIAM MCDOUGALL, *Body and Mind* (Macmillan, 1911).
C. A. STRONG, *Why the Mind Has a Body* (1903).
HELEN FLANDERS DUNBAR, *Mind and Body; Psychosomatic Medicine* (Random House, 1947).
C. D. BROAD, *The Mind and its Place in Nature* (1925; Humanities Press, 1951), Chap. III.
JOSEPH B. RHINE, *The Reach of the Mind* (William Sloane Associates, 1947).
CHARLES S. SHERRINGTON, *The Integrative Action of the Nervous System* (Scribner, 1906).
WILLIAM ERNEST HOCKING, *The Self, Its Body and Freedom* (Yale University Press, 1928).
A. C. EWING, *The Fundamental Questions of Philosophy* (Macmillan, 1952), Chap. VI.
GEORGE S. FULLERTON, *A System of Metaphysics* (Macmillan, 1904), Part III.
GEORGE S. FULLERTON, *An Introduction to Philosophy* (Macmillan, 1921), Chap. X.

Questions for Discussion

1. What seem to you the main reasons for accepting interactionism? For rejecting it? How far are your reasons drawn from experience, and how far from theory?

2. What bearing, if any, might the new developments in physical science (discussed in Chapter 5, Section iii) have upon the question of interactionism?

3. If you were to accept Huxley's epiphenomenism (p. 287) and believe yourself a "conscious automaton," would it make any difference in your practical attitudes and choices? How would your belief that other people are automata affect your dealings with them?

4. Form your own judgment of William James' two criticisms of epiphenomenism.

5. Examine the parallelist assumption that some form of mind is present as another aspect of every process of nature. Does it seem to you a possible view, or quite absurd? What bearing might it have upon any of your other beliefs if you were to accept it seriously?

CHAPTER X

Freedom of Choice

The so-called problem of free will has long been a favorite topic of controversy. It comes up repeatedly in student "bull sessions," and of all questions concerning the nature of selfhood it is the one most likely to stir heated argument. Nor is this surprising. For on the one hand we all perform many actions each day on the supposition that we are choosing them and that it would be possible to choose otherwise. The possession of such freedom, in some matters at least, seems to us of great and even unique importance, and to lose it would imply a degradation from the rank of persons to that of mere things. On the other hand, strong considerations can be adduced for the view that man, like everything else in nature, is entirely subject to natural law, and that human choices therefore are entirely predetermined by what has gone before. Is men's familiar sense of freedom real or illusory? This is the problem of *metaphysical freedom* more popularly known as free will.

i. *Clarification of the Problem*

Empirical vs. metaphysical freedom

There is a loose but indispensable sense in which everyone knows what freedom is. To be free is to be unhindered from doing what we wish. Such freedom may be trivial, as when a spoilt child wants to have his way in trifles, or when we mutter,

"I'm damned if I'll let him tell me what to do," and so do the opposite whether we really want to or not. Where the end is shortsighted or unreflectively impulsive the freedom to attain it is of correspondingly small importance. But in other cases, where the purpose is far-reaching and deeply rooted in one's sense of personal integrity, the freedom to attain it—and therefore freedom from obstacles or agencies that would prevent its attainment—becomes of paramount importance. The great political freedoms guaranteed by the Bill of Rights in our American Constitution recognize the inviolate importance of worshiping according to one's conviction, of thinking and speaking according to one's conscience, and of pursuing happiness in a manner most truly expressive of one's integral self. But both these classes of freedom, the trivial and the morally significant, are alike in one respect: they both have to do with external hindrances. And as we can verify pretty well by experience whether there is or is not external interference with what we consciously desire to attain, the term *empirical freedom* may be used for freedom of such sort. That is to say, when you find yourself ostensibly unhindered in the pursuit of a given aim, you are empirically free in that respect.

Empirical freedom offers problems of a different kind from the question posed in the present chapter. There is the practical question of how to attain freedom from certain persistent obstacles—poverty, ill-health, awkward situations, unpleasant duties, and the like. Looked at in social perspective this question gives rise to one of the important questions of political philosophy: viz., how the basic freedoms of one person or group can be upheld without unduly curtailing equally basic freedoms of other persons or groups. And there is the further question—demanding great psychological and sociological insight—of how much freedom, and what kinds of freedom, are of maximum benefit to men; for nowadays in a luxury economy, amid all the freedoms which labor-saving devices, new forms of entertainment, and the loosening of moral restraints have combined to promote, it is well to review from time to time the standards by which such freedoms can be reflectively appraised.

But such questions do not concern us here; they will be touched on in Chapter XIV. The present issue is a metaphysical one, in the sense which has been given to the word in Chapter III; for it asks whether human freedom is ever *real*. That is to say, in those actions where you seem to yourself most free in the empirical sense—where you enjoy a strong and clear sense of being able to take *either* of two courses of action and reject the other—is the openness of the situation as real as it looks, or is your choice entirely determined by preëxistent causes and is the freedom therefore only apparent? This is the problem of metaphysical freedom, and when it is clearly understood there are two and only two possible answers: determinism and libertarianism. *Determinism* is the position that every human choice is, in the last analysis, completely and undeviatingly prescribed by what has gone before; whereas its contradictory, *libertarianism,* declares that some human choices, to some degree, are genuine, in the sense that they are *not entirely* engineered by past events.

Fatalism

Determinism in the sense just defined should be clearly distinguished from the looser, older, and superstitious credo which is properly called fatalism. A fatalist does not necessarily deny that real freedom of choice exists; he merely says that at best it is trivial, inasmuch as all roads lead to the same outcome. A man's final destiny, the main eventualities of his life are what is fixed, not necessarily every step toward their attainment. When anyone says, "It doesn't matter what you do, you're safe so long as your luck holds out," he is speaking as a fatalist. The implication of "It doesn't matter what you do" is that there is more than one thing you *can* do, although the eventual outcome will not be affected by what course you choose. Fatalism is therefore only loosely, not strictly, deterministic.

In ancient Greek tragedy Fate is conceived as a vaguely impersonal force, operating implacably behind the scenes and catching up the human protagonists in its toils. The old Theban story which Sophocles employed as the plot of *Oedipus Tyrannus* is an excellent example. Laius, king of Thebes, having been warned by an oracle that his infant son would some day take his life, ordered a herdsman to expose the child to death on Mount Ida. But it was rescued by a shepherd and taken to King Polybus of Corinth, who adopted the infant and named it Oedipus. When Oedipus grew up he learned from an oracle that he was destined to kill his father and unite in marriage with his mother. Ignorant of his birth, he sought to escape so evil a destiny by fleeing from Corinth. On a narrow road he met Laius driving with an attendant to Delphi. A quarrel arose over the right of way, and the upshot was that Oedipus slew both the other travelers. Later he arrived at Thebes and eventually married the now widowed Jocasta, neither of them suspecting that they were mother and son. Thus the oracles' prophecies were fulfilled. And even if Oedipus had stayed in Corinth or taken a different route the ultimate outcome would have been the same. For Oedipus was doomed, his fate was fixed, and no particular choice of action could alter it.

Aristotle's doctrine of potencies

It was Aristotle who, of all Greek thinkers, brought the question of real freedom into clearest focus; although his vocabulary and his different manner of contextualizing the problem sometimes cause the importance of his contribution to be overlooked. Aristotle uses the word "potency" for the power in a thing to become something other than what it is at a given moment. Since everything in the mundane world is in process of change, everything has potency to some degree. But there is an essential difference between non-rational potencies and rational ones.

The difference between the two types is that every rational potency admits of contrary outcomes, whereas a non-rational potency admits of only one outcome. . . . For as man's rational understanding pertains in different ways to both of two contrary outcomes, and as the initiating principle of motion with regard to them resides in his soul (*psyche*), it follows that the soul can produce either of two contrary courses of action by linking them up with this one initiating source.[1]

In the *Nicomachean Ethics,* similarly, where he is discussing the nature of moral deliberation, Aristotle lays down the twin principles: (1) that "man is the originating principle of his actions" and (2) that "deliberation is concerned with things within the subject's own power to accomplish." To deliberate is to think about the question, "What shall I do?" and it involves more than merely asking, "What is the actual situation?"—which involves purely factual reasoning. And it is a familiar fact that we do sometimes deliberate. But it is impossible and meaningless to deliberate, he argues, about occurrences that are entirely independent of our will—"regardless of whether their regularity is due to mechanical necessity (i.e., sheer physical impact) or to organic nature or to some other cause. . . . For what we deliberate about are things within our control and attainable by action."[2]

On the whole, then, Aristotle appears to be plainly on the side of libertarianism, as indeed Socrates and Plato had been before him. And such is the dominant note in his writings. Nevertheless it must be admitted that he does not always keep the issue crystal clear. For even in the case of rational potencies, he writes, the agency that makes the decision between one set of effects and another is desire:

For whichever of two things a creature decisively desires to do, that thing it will do, when the existing circumstances permit and when there is an object at hand capable of being acted upon by the potency in question. In short, when a creature which has a rational

[1] Aristotle, *Metaphysics,* Bk. IX, Chap. ii (based on p. 88 of the Odyssey Press edition of selections from Aristotle).
[2] *Nicomachean Ethics,* Bk. III, Chap. iii (pp. 207-209 of the Odyssey Press edition of selections from Aristotle).

potency desires that for which it has the potency, and when the circumstances are appropriate, it must act accordingly.[3]

Thus there is an unresolved ambiguity in Aristotle's conception and treatment of the freewill problem, even though his prevailing attitude is strongly libertarian. At all events, the analysis of the problem requires to be carried further.

The theological issue

Christian theology has had a hard time, by and large, reconciling the concept of God's omnipotence and omniscience on the one hand with the concept of man's real moral responsibility and guilt on the other. If God is *all*-powerful, how can man's power be real? If it were real would it not be capable in some degree of hindering God's purposes? To this it has traditionally been replied that God freely willed to bestow on man the gift of freedom; that he is free to withdraw it if he chooses, but that he evidently does not choose.

St. Augustine (353-430 A.D.) elaborated the doctrine by declaring that although God bestowed on man the gift of freedom, man forfeited what was most essential to it by his first sin, for ever since that original disobedience which Adam committed man has had no power to save himself but can be saved only by divine grace. Furthermore, Augustine said, God has exercised his own unconditioned power of choice by "electing" certain men to be saved and not others. Each man's salvation or damnation is therefore, in the Augustinian theology, predestined. The doctrine of predestination was later to receive its strongest and most uncompromising expression in the teachings of John Calvin in the sixteenth century.

If the belief in predestination rested entirely upon the postulate of divine omnipotence it would not necessarily involve a strict determinism. You could hold that each man's destiny is predetermined with reference to the central issue of salvation or

---

[3] Aristotle, *Metaphysics*, loc. cit.

damnation without necessarily supposing that he has no power of independent choice at all. But there is another attribute of God to be considered—his omniscience. If, as orthodox Christians believe, God's omniscience extends without limit into the future, then he knows in advance every choice that each of his creatures is going to make, and since his knowledge cannot err it clearly allows the creature no possibility of choosing differently. If God's infinite knowledge includes, as it must, the particular item of knowledge that at four o'clock on a certain Thursday I am going to "decide" to go skating, then it is obviously impossible that I should *not* decide to go skating at that time—which is to say that I am not free in the matter, for it is already settled which way my "decision" will go. In short it is only an apparent decision, not a real one. Those Christian creeds which declare that God is omniscient (in the precise sense of the word) *and* also that man has free will (also in the precise sense) are trying to digest a hard logical contradiction.

Historical determinism

When the word "determinism" is preceded by the adjective "historical," or when the context shows that such a qualification is to be understood, no strict determinism is meant, but only a loose determinism of large-scale events, leaving room for some degree of individual self-determination in small matters. Marxism, on its theoretical side, involves a determinism of this kind. Thus Marx's famous disciple Leon Trotsky writes, in *The History of the Russian Revolution*, that he does "not at all pretend to deny the significance of the personal in the mechanics of the historic process, nor the significance in the personal of the accidental." Although he believes that the Russian Revolution of 1917 was inevitable, being a necessary outcome of economic conflicts within czarist and European bourgeois society, he admits that particular events composing the Revolution could have been otherwise than they were. Lenin, the Revolution's prime leader, might have chosen to cross a street at a different corner from where he actually did, and so might have been struck by an assassin's bullet which in actual fact missed him. What then? The Revolution might have been managed somewhat less ably, but in Trotsky's view it would have taken place successfully nevertheless, and the main pattern of history would have been virtually unaffected.

The issues which have just been sketched are obliquely related to the issue of metaphysical determinism vs. libertarianism, and they use enough of the same vocabulary to confuse an unwary reader. But let us be clear about it. The central issue confronting us is whether or not a man has any power, however small, of genuine choice—genuine self-determination. If metaphysical determinism is true, then every choice I make has been absolutely necessitated by previous happenings in my body and environment, and those by yet prior happenings, and so on endlessly. I could not have chosen otherwise than as I actually did choose, and at the present moment I cannot choose otherwise than as I actually am choosing. The future is as settled as the past. If, on the other hand, libertarianism is true, there are limited but real choices presented to me: limited because external circumstances on the one hand and my own interests and reflex patterns on the other set up a framework of available and meaningful possibilities, but real because within that framework it is not yet altogether prescribed by the nature of things how I shall choose. The choice is genuinely up to me, the alternatives are real ones, and when I have chosen one alternative it remains true that *I could have chosen the other instead*. To the arguments supporting both sides of this metaphysical issue we now turn.

ii. *The Case for Determinism*

Argument from causal invariability

The concept to which the theory of determinism principally appeals is that of the uniformity of causal relations. "Given the same cause (in all its relevant ramifications), the same effect (ditto) must follow." Hugh Elliot puts the case succinctly when he writes:

> If oxygen and hydrogen in the proportion by weight of eight to one are mixed together, and an electric spark is passed through them, water is formed; and on every occasion where precisely the same conditions are realized precisely the same result ensues. This truth is the basis of experimental method. If from similar conditions it were possible that dissimilar results should follow on various occasions, then experiments would be useless for advancing knowledge.[4]

The first step in Elliot's argument should be noted closely: that in order for scientific experiments to be carried out in such a way as to advance human knowledge, the principle of uniformity must operate universally and with no variation whatever. It isn't enough to suppose that there is a general uniformity, a rough-and-ready uniformity allowing of minor deviations here and there. It must be supposed that if exactly the same cause were to occur twice, then *exactly* the same effect would necessarily follow. In other words, at any given moment of time the character of subsequent moments is strictly determined. If A stands for the state of the universe at nine o'clock on a certain morning, then there will be a certain other state of the universe, B, which *must* come into existence at 9:01 in every minutest detail. It is granted, of course, that actually to know what A or what B is in its entirety vastly transcends our human powers. But Elliot continues:

> Nevertheless, we shall be led to adopt the proposition of Laplace, to the effect that if we knew the precise disposition at any moment of all the matter and energy existing in the Universe, and the direction of motion of every moving particle, and if we were armed with a mathematics of infinite power, we should be able to prophesy the exact disposition of all the matter and energy in the Universe at any future time.

[4] Hugh Elliot, *Modern Science and Materialism* (Longmans, Green, 1919), p. 139.

Any being who possessed such powers, and who, a myriad ages ago, had acquired absolute knowledge at some moment of the nebula from which the solar system arose, would have been able to prophesy that at this present moment there would exist a being identical with myself who would be writing the words that are now flowing from my pen; he would have been able to prophesy that a little later other beings, identical with my readers, would be perusing those words, and he would be aware of what emotions would be excited within them by the perusal. In other words, the uniformity of Nature and the paramountcy of law are universal and without exception.[5]

In short, according to the determinist, the permanent possibility remains: *if* there existed a wizard-scientist with an exhaustively complete knowledge of past events, such a one could predict with unerring accuracy every event, of whatever kind, still to come.

But what evidence can there be for physical determinism if, so far as we know, the omniscient wizard-scientist does not exist, and if admittedly our human powers are infinitely inadequate to cope with an equation involving the totality of everything? The determinist replies that the evidence is inductive and cumulative. He points to the conspicuous progress of the experimental sciences in discovering the causes of phenomena that had previously been unexplained. Comets and solar eclipses were once believed to depend upon the caprices of malignant deities; they are now explained by precise astronomical laws. Great advances have been made too in the explanation of certain aspects of animal and even human behavior. Insanity, for example, which once was regarded as a supernatural visitation, can now be shown to have a material basis in the precipitation of colloids in the brain cells by an alkaloid in the blood. Admittedly the science of psychology is at present far less accurate in most respects than physics and astronomy, for the movements of a human being are incomparably more complex than those of planets and comets. But in all fields of investigation, whatever their present state of advancement, the direction is essentially the same—away from an accept-

[5] Elliot, *op. cit.*, pp. 139-140.

ance of obscurity, mystery, and caprice, toward the ever expanding discovery of hidden laws at work.

And indeed, if the deterministic principle holds good rigidly and exactly for all nature, then it obviously holds good rigidly and exactly for every particular part of nature. Is man, then, part and parcel of nature? He obviously is to some degree, as our daily experience makes abundantly clear; but is he so entirely and absolutely? The determinist answers yes—that there is no respect whatever in which any man or any part or aspect of him can be an exception to the laws that govern nature as a whole. From this it follows that a man must at each moment act just as he is acting, choose just as he is choosing; and his consciousness of being somewhat free to act differently is an illusion.

But how, it may be asked, does so widespread an illusion originate? Spinoza has given a classical statement of the determinist's usual reply to this question. "Men think themselves free just because they are conscious of their own volitions and desires, and never give any thought in their ignorance, to the causes which have disposed them so to wish and desire." And he offers the following illustration:

Conceive, I beg, that a stone, while continuing in motion, should be conscious of a feeling of endeavor to keep in motion. Such a stone, being conscious merely of its own endeavor and interested in the result, would believe itself to be completely free, and would think that it continued in motion solely because of its own wish. Such is that human freedom, which all boast that they possess, and which consists solely in the fact that men are conscious of their own desires but are ignorant of the causes whereby that desire has been determined.[6]

Is determinism mechanistic?

In Section iii it will be argued that strict determinism must be mechanistic, and that therefore it must take an epiphenomenist view of mind. It should be noted, however, that certain writers have tried to reconcile determinism with an admission that the

---

[6] The first quotation is from Spinoza's *Ethics,* Appendix to Part I; the second from his Correspondence. Both are based upon Elwes' translation.

human mind has some degree of real efficacy in the determination of human behavior. In short, they sometimes try to be interactionists and determinists at once. This appears to be the position taken by the biologist C. Judson Herrick, who declares on the one hand that "the prevision of possible consequences of an act is a causal factor in determining present action," and, on the other, that "the causal sequence is woven through this whole complex pattern without a break."[7] Professor Herrick calls himself a believer in "real freedom," but his actual stand on the controversy can be judged by such a statement as the following:

> The original nature of man includes his inherited bodily form, his reflexes and instincts, and certain potentialities for further development *whose exact patterns will be determined* by the environment in which he lives, that is, by the educative processes to which he is subjected. On the structural side, his inner nature at any stage of his life is his protoplasmic organization at that moment. His conduct is determined by the reaction of that inner nature to the environmental conditions then prevailing.[8]

Clearly, if his words mean what they appear to mean, Herrick believes that at any given moment there is only one possible course of action for a person. On the other hand, he believes that one's awareness of a situation is itself a causal factor in the situation, affecting to some degree how one will act. But, he insists, at any given moment the precise character of every conscious state—every perception, desire, thought, will, etc.—(1) is strictly caused by previous bodily and environmental forces, (2) is strictly correlated with the agent's "protoplasmic organization at that moment," and (3) can affect the future in only one possible way—for Herrick regards the law of strict causation as applying to consciousness also.

---

[7] C. Judson Herrick, *Fatalism or Freedom* (Norton, 1926), pp. 61 and 81. Professor Herrick uses the word "fatalism" for determinism that does not involve mind as a real causative factor, and "determinism" for a determinism that does.

[8] *Ibid.*, p. 59-60. Italics supplied.

For the present let this much be said for Herrick's position: that it makes a laudable attempt to do justice to the evidence that consciousness is an actually functioning part of man's total being. But can such interactionism—for that is plainly what it is, although Herrick does not employ the term—be held consistently with a strict determinism? In the next section I shall argue that it cannot.

Argument from reasonable expectancy

One final argument for determinism may be briefly mentioned. It is sometimes declared that unless a strict and universal determinism is accepted there can be no ground for any reasonable expectancy whatever. Half a century ago John Fiske interpreted libertarianism to mean that "volitions arise without cause"; and he argued that if this were the case we could not make any reliable judgments of human character. In his somewhat sardonic illustration, if a murder were committed we could have no more reason to suspect the worst enemy of the murdered man than his best friend. The consequence of such a doctrine would be, he argued, that "nothing which anyone may do ought ever to occasion surprise. The mother may strangle her first-born child, the miser may cast his long-treasured gold into the sea, the sculptor may break in pieces his lately finished statue, in the presence of no other feelings than those which before led them to cherish, to hoard, and to create." And this consequence seems to Fiske so manifestly absurd that he considers it an effective refutation of the existence of free will. Need so extreme a set of consequences be accepted, or is that merely a caricature of the libertarian position?

iii. The Case for Libertarianism

The case for free will may be stated on two levels: pre-analytic and post-analytic. The pre-analytic evidence is, in legal language, *prima facie*: it is confined to preliminary reasons for taking the claims of libertarianism in full seriousness. The post-analytic evidence can be introduced only after the arguments for the opposing side have been met and appraised.

Pre-analytic arguments

The main pre-analytic arguments are two: experiential and moral. They represent the principal motives which people in general are likely to have for believing in free will.

1. *Experiential evidence.* At first sight nothing seems more obvious to a person than that he is, at some times and in some respects, free. And if he is at all reflective he does not mean by this merely that he is free from external obstacles. He believes himself to be free in the intrinsic sense of facing a future whose character is not entirely predetermined, and which may become one thing *or* another according as he now decides. Who has not had the experience of choosing to act in a certain way while clearly conscious that he could have acted differently? What distinction in the entire range of human experience is more fundamental and more apparently real than the distinction between what lies within our power to choose and what does not? Is Spinoza right in insisting that this is sheer delusion? Is introspection entirely untrustworthy on such a point?

We are forced back to a more fundamental question, concerning the validity and scope of introspective evidence. There is a rightful use for the subjective private evidence of introspection. In questions pertaining to the nature of the questioner's own self, subjective evidence is indispensable, because any description of the self which omits such evidence turns out to be talking about peripheral aspects of the self—its bodily manifestations, which can be seen or tested experimentally by all—and not its most intrinsic nature.

But *how far*, it may be asked, can we rely on introspection? May it not often deceive us? Undoubtedly it may, but what is to be our criterion for judging whether it does or not? Let it be admitted that introspective evidence is not valid when it clearly and demonstrably contradicts any empirically verifiable fact. Thus, if I should become subjectively convinced that I can win a bout with a heavyweight champion, I have only to put my subjective belief to an objective test, and the fact of the champion's superiority will demonstrate itself in a concrete and decisive manner. But if, on the other hand, I become subjectively convinced that I am free to choose between A and B—i.e., that the issue is not yet settled—there is no analogous test by which I can be proved wrong. Whichever one I actually do choose, I can still believe without empirical contradiction that I have chosen it freely and that I might equally well have chosen the alternative. So far, then, the evidence from introspection cannot be empirically discredited. The eminent physicist Arthur H. Compton calls attention to the fact that "one's ability to move his hand at will is much more directly and certainly known than are even the well-tested laws of Newton, and that if these laws deny one's ability to move his hand at will the preferable conclusion is that Newton's laws require modification."[9] Compton intends his argument to be independent of whether physicists may find it necessary to modify Newton's laws on other grounds.

2. *The moral argument.* Can there be genuinely moral issues without some degree of real freedom? Suppose that the apparent choice between lying and telling a difficult truth lies before me. Suppose further, I am convinced that to tell the truth is in this instance the better course of action, but that I am tempted to lie because it is easier. In such a situation there is a clear meaning to the word "ought." I feel that I *ought* to tell the truth even though I am tempted to lie, and I may still feel that I *ought to have told* the truth even after the lie is spoken. To say that I "ought" to do something seems virtually meaningless unless I have the power to do or leave undone. "Ought" is not applicable to a situation where either "must" or "cannot" holds true. Genuine moral responsibility is inconsistent with strict

---

[9] Arthur H. Compton, *The Freedom of Man* (Yale University Press, 1935), p. 26.

determinism; for how can you be genuinely responsible for seeing that a certain job gets done if there is really not the slightest possibility of the job failing to get done?

Post-analytic arguments

It should be remembered throughout the present controversy that determinism and libertarianism stand on different logical footings. Determinism makes a universal claim, libertarianism does not. Determinism declares that *all* events, and particularly all human actions, are *entirely* predetermined by antecedent events; libertarianism only declares that there are *sometimes* cases where *in some respects* and within reasonable limits a human action may be genuinely free. Hence the determinist, to make good his claim, must prove beyond reasonable doubt that there are no exceptions to his universal proposition; whereas the libertarian could establish his case by demonstrating (1) that there *can* be cases of genuine freedom, and (2) that on the basis of this possibility there is good reason to believe that there *are some* such cases *to a limited degree*. Now to prove that there can be cases of genuine freedom is equivalent to disproving that there cannot be any such. Accordingly, the libertarian's first analytic step must be to demonstrate that the determinist's main arguments are invalid.

Situational determinism examined

The most basic argument for determinism, as was shown in the last section, rests upon an appeal to the absolute uniformity of the laws of nature. It is argued that as all causal sequences take place in a perfectly uniform manner there is no room for freedom in the sense here under discussion. Now the assertion of causal uniformity can take either of two forms: situational or universal. Suppose that a certain man, after a moral struggle with himself, has committed theft. Afterward he thinks, "Oh, if only I could live those moments over again, so that I might choose differently." Situational determinism replies: "If you could live those moments over again knowing what you know now, then it might be that you would choose differently. But if time could be rolled back so that you were placed in exactly the same situation as before, and with exactly the same set of dispositions as before, without any of the new 'wisdom after the event' which you now enjoy, you would then most certainly go through exactly the same stages of temptation as in the first instance and you would necessarily end up by committing the theft at the same moment and in the same way. For if the *total* cause were exactly the same, the total effect would have to be the same also."

Situational determinism can never be either proved or disproved—as must be evident to anyone who gives real thought to the problem. For time cannot be rolled back. No man can live through the same experience twice. To speak of recapturing a certain experience, is to overlook one inherent difference between the old experience and the new: the second experience contains a memory of the first, and is enriched or otherwise modified thereby. And in other ways, too, the lapse of time will have changed the disposition of the experiencer. In any situation involving human choice the odds are strictly *infinity to one* against the exactly identical recurrence of that situation. Consequently there can never be any way of verifying situational determinism: it remains, and must remain, a purely speculative theory.

Universal determinism examined

Since determinism can thus never be empirically verified with direct reference to a human situation, the determinist is forced back upon a deductive argument: situational determinism is true, he maintains, because universal determinism is true. In a given situation you are bound to act in one and only one way because you are part of the universal web of nature, and nature is entirely lawful. Here, then, are two premises: (*a*) that man is entirely of a piece with nature, and (*b*) that nature is strictly lawful in the sense that it can be analyzed down to causal processes which are invariable. Let us examine the premises separately.

a) Is man of a piece with nature? In a rough sense, yes; he has evolved out of more elementary natural processes and his body consists of recognized chemical elements which are distinguished from one another by different molecular patterns. If, then, the molecular movements take place according to strict natural causation, must not the actions of man, who is constituted out of them, do likewise?

The libertarian replies that the conclusion does not follow. There is an unexamined assumption in the argument. It is assumed that molecules follow the same laws in a living body—particularly in a human brain—as in an inorganic situation. There is no empirical evidence that this assumption is correct. Indeed, the late Alfred North Whitehead, speaking out of a profound knowledge of physics, was fond of challenging the assumption, maintaining that the very properties which the chemist ascribes to carbon, phosphorus, etc., on the basis of inorganic experiments with them, may be altered in ways quite unknown to us when functioning in an organ such as the human brain.

b) Now as to the second premise. Is nature strictly lawful in the sense that its ultimate component processes follow unvarying causal patterns? The libertarian answers (i) that the word "ultimate" in this connection no longer has any real meaning in science, and (ii) that on any *given* level of analysis known to science there are always found to occur some deviations from strict regularity. Let us examine these points in reverse order.

Principle of deviations

Consider the operational meaning of equality in empirical science. Absolute equality is an abstraction confined to pure mathematics. In any physical application the most that can be said is that there is approximate equality; for no measuring instruments are perfect. Some of the approximations are, to be sure, very close indeed: the margin of error can be made very small. In other cases the observable deviations are considerable.

But, it may be asked, with the advance of science do we not learn more and more about the exact causes of such deviations and thus explain apparent deviations by appealing to hidden uniformities? Yes and no. As physical science has advanced during the past half century it is true that some apparent deviations have been shown to be based on hidden uniformities, but it is also true that *some apparent uniformities have been shown to conceal hidden deviations.* The outstanding instance of the latter type of development has been in the field of intra-atomic physics. The relatively simple principles of mechanics, based on the laws of mass and motion applicable to larger inert bodies, do not hold for the component parts of the atom. The electron, proton, and neutron, into which the atom has been analyzed, show such unpredictable variation of behavior that the principle of mechanical causality has had to be abandoned and methods of statistical approximation have taken its place. Thus the German physicist Werner Heisenberg declares:

> The resolution of the paradoxes of atomic physics can be accomplished only by renunciation of old and cherished ideas. Most important of these is the idea that natural phenomena obey exact laws—the principle of causality.[10]

And Dr. Arthur H. Compton, whose experiments have been partly responsible for the dramatic reversal of viewpoint in contemporary physics, declares: "Natural phenomena do not obey exact laws. This statement marks perhaps the most significant revolution in the history of scientific thought."[11]

To be sure, there are certain other eminent physicists, such as Max Planck, who deny that the principle of causality should be abandoned in the light of the new discoveries. However seemingly erratic the deviations, they argue, there must be an

[10] Werner Heisenberg, *The Physical Principles of the Quantum Theory* (1930), p. 62.
[11] Compton, *op. cit.*, p. 7.

ultimate explanation for them. To this the libertarian replies that such a view is merely a speculation, a shadowy hope without empirical backing. For while it is possible that some future advance of science may break down the electron and proton into still more minute components and thereby discover causes of certain deviations now unexplained, there are just as likely to be found some new, as yet unguessed deviations along with them. And why may not such a process of discovery go on forever? William Ernest Hocking writes:

> What, then, if there *are no ultimate physical units*? If the atom gives way to the electron, shall the electron or the proton be the last outpost of nature's subtlety because it stands at the limit of our present powers of analysis? Physics will not be dogmatic here. Beyond each new stage of penetration into nature's detail, it will surmise other stages. And if there is no assignable limit to the analysis of the physical event, there is no physical law which we can assume to be *the* law of change.[12]

The practice of freedom

If we accept the principle of indeterminism as ontologically real, do we thereby give up the right to make reasonable predictions? Must we then expect men to act without any motivation whatever? By no means. We shall go on predicting as we have always done—with greater or less probability, never with absolute certainty. And in the case of human beings we neither need nor desire absolute predictability. A person whose every action could be foretold would be a mere mechanism—and altogether boring after we got to know him. What we want in a friend is *not perfect predictability, but a general moral reliability,* which is quite consistent with a good deal of unpredictability in detail. We want and expect our friend to vary in incidental ways; and if we feel we can always rely on him in a crisis it is not because he is a mechanism, it is because he is one who can

---

[12] William Ernest Hocking, *The Self; Its Body and Freedom* (Yale University Press, 1928), p. 160.

discriminate between right and wrong, good and evil, and who has built the character we admire by the repeated exercise of free choice in these fundamental matters.

And in any case the greater part of our day by day activities are based upon the libertarian assumptions. We become determinists when the problem confronting us is a technical one, such as discovering the cause of a stalled motor; for if we examine the carburetor and find nothing amiss we must look elsewhere for the cause, and it is the implicit deterministic postulate that encourages us to keep on looking. Whether determinism is exactly and undeviatingly true even in so-called mechanical phenomena no man can be altogether sure. No matter; it is exact enough and predictable enough for a garage mechanic to base his actions on. But when we leave problems of the motor-car and attend to problems of ourselves and fellow-men, our normal assumption is the libertarian one of *limited* causal determination. Whether by our own efforts or with the help of friends or in more special cases by the aid of psychoanalysis, we seek to discover our previous causal patterns in order to win a certain freedom from bondage to them in the future. No doubt future examinations will reveal still other causal patterns conditioning this or that part of our behavior. Freedom is never absolute; at best it is a freedom won from this or that particular set of determining circumstances. But when we *act*—that is, make choices and self-directive efforts—it is on the implicit assumption that some new winning of freedom, however small, is possible; and that the effort is worth while. Thus it was that William James, when emerging as a young man from a period of illness and mental despondency, wrote in his diary: "My first act of free will shall be to believe in free will." The assumption is not provable, to be sure, but neither is it disprovable. It is an ultimate metaphysical dilemma—an "antinomy," as Kant said, to which no categorical solution is possible on rational and evidential grounds. If Kant is right, and if (as the libertarian maintains) *it is demonstrable that there can be no demonstration of either of the contending positions,* then the only reasonable solution would seem to be in terms of the existential question: Which hypothesis, the deterministic (which is absolute) or the libertarian (which is non-absolute) really governs the most significant acts and relationships and insights of human life? And to *that* question the greater validity of the libertarian answer seems plain.

For Further Study

WILLIAM ERNEST HOCKING, *The Self, its Body and Freedom* (Yale University Press, 1928).

WILLIAM JAMES, *Principles of Psychology* (1890), Vol. II, Chap. XXVI.

GEORGE H. PALMER, *The Problem of Freedom* (Houghton, Mifflin, 1911).

ARTHUR H. COMPTON, *The Freedom of Man* (Yale University Press, 1935). A defense of freedom by an outstanding physicist.

C. JUDSON HERRICK, *Fatalism or Freedom; A Biologist's Answer* (Norton, 1926).

JOHN MACMURRAY, "Freedom in a Personal Nexus," in *Freedom: Its Meaning,* edited by Ruth Nanda Ashen (Harcourt, Brace, 1940).

MORTIMER TAUBE, *Causation, Freedom and Determinism* (London: Allen and Unwin, 1936).

M. DAVIDSON, *Free Will or Determinism* (London: Watts, 1937).

HERMAN HAROLD HORNE, *Free Will and Human Responsibility* (Macmillan, 1912).

H. WILDON CARR, *The Unique Status of Man* (Macmillan, 1928).

PAUL WEISS, *Man's Freedom* (Yale University Press, 1950), Chaps. VII, XVI.

A. C. EWING, *The Fundamental Questions of Philosophy* (Macmillan, 1952), Chap. V.

Questions for Discussion

1. Soldiers in battle often believe that "somewhere there's a bullet with my number on it." Comment on (*a*) the psychological benefits and (*b*) the logical reasonableness of this type of fatalism.

2. After examining *both* of the quotations from Aristotle's *Metaphysics* (pp. 302-304) would you consider him a determinist or a libertarian?

3. "In the least of substances eyes as piercing as God's could read the whole sequel of things in the universe."—Leibniz.

a) If you accept this statement must you be a determinist?

b) If you are a determinist must you accept this statement?

4. Would a belief in free will tend to diminish your confidence in the regularity of nature? Would a disbelief in free will tend to diminish your sense of responsibility?

5. "If we are free, the self that is free must be outside the flow of events, and itself timeless."—Dean Inge (*Proceedings of the Aristotelian Society*, Vol. XXI).

Does this attempt to reconcile man's freedom with physical determinism strike you as promising, or not?

CHAPTER XI

Our Knowledge of Other Selves

EACH of us assumes, in the ordinary practices of living, that other persons exist independently of himself. This is quite different from the assumption, previously discussed, of the independent existence of matter. If we can agree—as we implicitly do in our behavior and attitudes—that the material world continues to exist when it is not observed, then of course there is no further reason to doubt that human bodies exist continuously also. But the question that now arises is not whether John's body continues to exist when John is fast asleep and no other watcher is present, but whether John himself enjoys conscious existence at those times when his body is awake.

To believe that each other person enjoys a conscious life of his own, an area of privacy into which no one else can wholly enter, is not only usual, it is a necessary basis for social life. For if anyone were really to believe that other persons were unconscious mechanisms or even mere colored shapes moving across his own private range of vision, he obviously would feel no compunction about injuring them or exploiting them at will. A workable society is possible only if each member respects, to some degree at least, the point of view of his fellow members; and to respect another's point of view is to accept the fact that he, too, has a private way of looking at things, of forming judgments, of making choices, of enjoying and suffering—in short, that he, like one's own self, is conscious. The problem now before us is,

How do we know this? More accurately—since the word "we" begs the question—How do *I* know that you, he, they, exist in conscious independence of me? On what grounds can I justify to myself the assumption that other persons enjoy conscious experiences which I do not share, or which I only partially share?

Put in this last way the metaphysical difficulty becomes plainer. To believe in something more than meets the eye—or rather the eye, ear and other senses combined—naturally suggests the question, On what grounds do I believe it? And when this challenge is raised with respect to the belief in the independent existence of other minds, other conscious selves, there are three main possible replies: One may be a solipsist (in theory at least) and declare that there are no valid grounds at all for the belief. Or, more moderately, one may justify the belief either on grounds of rational analogy or by direct, intuitive response. We shall now consider these three positions in turn.

i. *Solipsism*

The logical possibility of solipsism has been remarked by many a thinker who is not himself a solipsist. The Archbishop Fénelon, for instance, writes:

Not only all the bodies which I seem to perceive, but also all the spirits which appear to constitute a society of which I am a member . . . —all these beings, I say, may possibly have no reality and not be anything but a pure illusion which takes place entirely within myself alone. In short, it may be that I myself constitute the whole of nature.[1]

To be sure, Fénelon's motive in stressing this logical possibility was to advance his general argument that the beliefs by which we live, secular as well as sacred, go beyond the reach of justification by strict evidence; that it is an act of faith to believe in Bill Smith's existence no less than to believe in God's. However

[1] From François Fénelon (1651-1715), *Traité de l'existence et des attributs de Dieu*, Pt. II, Chap. i.

that may be, philosophically we cannot stop there. Faith is a needful element in belief but not the whole of it. We still have to ask, Why faith in this rather than in that? Why do I believe that the cries of an injured man indicate a conscious feeling of pain in him, whereas I hold no such belief about the squeaks and rumbles of an automobile?

Radical solipsism

A more recent philosopher, the biologist Hans Driesch, pushes Fénelon's argument a step farther. Not only is solipsism logically possible, it is "the only basis of philosophy that is not dogmatic." That is to say, it is the only philosophical starting point that makes no assumptions. To avoid making assumptions it is necessary, however, to define the starting point very carefully. Descartes' famous starting point—"I think, therefore I exist"—assumes too much. Descartes is right in declaring "I cannot, without self-contradiction, doubt that I am doubting, hence existing *at this moment*." He is wrong in concluding "I exist as a substance"—i.e., as one who has had a history—as one whose memories and introspective discoveries can be generally relied on. No, the one "fundamental pre-phenomenon," as Driesch calls it, is the certainty: "I am something (I can't be sure what) at this very moment when I raise the question." And such is the only fact—though not a fact in the usual public sense of the word—that is beyond any doubt. Driesch concludes:

> Solipsism, then, is not dogmatic, not even in a negative manner. It does not say: What I consciously have is *nothing but* my phenomenon. It merely says: What I consciously have is *certainly* my phenomenon—whether it be anything else or not.[2]

The views expressed (not, as a matter of fact, actually held) by Fénelon and Driesch are alike in being solipsistic and subjectivist as well. The word "solipsism" usually carries this double implication; but in order to analyze the problem clearly I pro-

---

[2] Hans Driesch, *The Problem of Individuality* (1914), p. 75.

pose that we distinguish between the two notions. Where both notions are present together I shall employ the term "radical solipsism." Let us examine this position first, and afterward the type of solipsism that rejects subjectivism.

The radical solipsist is committed not to transcend the actually and immediately given. As long as he remains silent he cannot be refuted. But the immediately given—the pure *this, here, now, such*—cannot be spoken. To say "this" is to imply "this vs. that"; "here and now" means "as distinguished from there and then"; "such" means "not otherwise." Even by significant monosyllables the radical solipsist must belie himself. And if he attempts to formulate his belief in solipsism the contradiction is even more glaring. "Only *my* sensations exist" means "Mine do, but no one else's do." How can this be said or meant unless there is already some implicit notion of a "someone else"?

Objective solipsism

Unlike the radical solipsist, who takes his stand in purely subjective experience, the behaviorist (as discovered in Chapter VIII) puts his trust in the physical world of matter and motion. Although he is not a solipsist in the radical and full sense just described, it seems that he is solipsistic in the way that counts for most. For when the behaviorist denies the existence of mind as anything other than certain types of bodily behavior-patterns, *whose* mind is he denying? The answer seems plain: *Always someone else's*. It is only on other people that the behaviorist can operate effectively and consistently. The behaviorist's observation of himself is necessarily confused by the element of introspection —of subjectivity. For if he were not conscious the behaviorist would not be able to make any observations, and there would be no problem; all would be silence. But since he is conscious he is certainly more than the object of his investigations; he is also the subject who investigates.

The point here is the familiar one that one knows oneself differently from the way in which one knows others. Suppose that

Tom is suffering from a toothache and that he communicates this fact to his behaviorist friend Bill. To Tom the sentence "I have a toothache" means primarily the pain he *feels*; to Bill it means primarily Tom's facial twinges, etc. that he *sees*. As a behaviorist Bill is not interested in Tom's feelings, but only in the visible twitchings and other such bodily reactions. But to Tom there is manifestly something more than visible twitchings going on in him; there is pain. Moreover, if Bill were to acquire a severe toothache of his own he could not remain the pure behaviorist. His own pain would be real for him, and would give another dimension of significance to the objectively observable twitchings. The conclusion is evident: No one can take a purely behavioristic attitude towards himself, but only towards others. The behaviorist says in effect: "I myself exist in a special sense, in which other people do not. They are automatons, whereas I am the engineer who consciously decides how to operate them. They are puppets; I am the puppeteer who pulls the strings." Behaviorism is thus incorrigibly partisan.

Examine, for instance, Gilbert Ryle's statement that "to find that most people have minds" (he makes exception of idiots and newborn infants) "is simply to find that they are able and prone to do certain sorts of things, and this we do by witnessing the sort of thing they do."[3] Obviously Professor Ryle knows more about his own mind than merely the things his body does which can be publicly "witnessed." He knows himself from the inside, so to speak,—as one who has the direct experience of thinking, feeling, striving, etc. This is at least a part of what "having a mind" means as applied to himself. But as applied to others he declares that "having a mind" can mean *merely* that their bodies perform in certain ways.

In considering Professor Ryle's statement let us attend to its full import. It would be entirely reasonable if he were to say: (A) "I cannot know another person's existence in the same way that I know my own." It is quite true, and generally acknowl-

---

[3] Gilbert Ryle, *The Concept of Mind* (London: Hutchinson, 1949), p. 61.

edged, that one cannot know another person in quite the same way that he knows himself. But Ryle is not speaking only about one's way of knowing another person. He is taking a stand on the metaphysical question that is central to this chapter: *"What does it mean to know that other people have minds?"* It is the object of the verb "to know" that is in question, not the verb itself. And on this more fundamental question Professor Ryle takes a negative stand. He commits himself, in effect, to the proposition: (B) "I cannot know that other persons exist in the same way that I exist—namely as conscious beings." This is quite a different proposition from A, and much more doubtful. Whereas A says that the path by which I discover another person's existence (as a conscious being) is different from the path by which I discover my own, B says that I cannot discover another person's existence in that sense at all. The position of B, therefore, is that of objective solipsism.

Criticisms

How important is it, really, not only to believe in the existence of other persons as "able and prone to do certain things" but to believe in them as enjoying conscious experiences of their own? What interest would a man have in a wife or child or friend unless he held the second belief in addition to the first? Who would care to live in a society of the most ingeniously contrived puppets? Each reader will have to answer these questions for himself, but the general tenor of the answer is not much in doubt. Jean Paul Richter has vividly portrayed the dreary situation of the solipsist who reflects on his isolated condition:

Truly I wish that there were men, and that I was one of them. If there exists, as I very much fear, no one but myself, unlucky dog that I am, then there is no one at such a pass as I. The only enthusiasm left me is logical enthusiasm—all my metaphysics, chemistry, technology, botany, entomology, are summed up in the old adage: Know Thyself. I am not merely my own Savior, but also my own Devil, Executioner, and Master of the Knout. Around me stretches humanity turned to stone. In the gloomy uninhabited void glows no love, no admiration, no prayer, no hope, no aim. I am so wholly alone; nowhere a heart-beat; no life, nothing, about me; and without me nothing but nothing. Who hears my wail, and who knows me now? Ego. Who will hear it, and who will know me to all eternity? Ego.[4]

Of course the *worthlessness* of a puppet society such as Mr. Ryle's objective solipsism implies, or of Richter's cosmic void, is no disproof of its *actuality*. Nevertheless it may well give us pause. To live perpetually with the nihilistic vision of a Richter would presumably paralyze action. But even the solipsist must act. And he will find it impossible to make all his actions jibe with his beliefs. To treat other human beings as though they had no conscious existence of their own would be to cut oneself off from social relationships, and thereby to frustrate the deep social promptings of one's nature. The life of an individual seems to be variously involved with the independent lives of others; and our everyday activities are based upon the assumption that our environment is at once really physical and really social—that is, that we are surrounded not only by other material bodies, but also, as another aspect or dimension of certain of those bodies, by other conscious minds functioning much like our own. To deny this assumption in theory while constantly expressing it in practice seems a poor way to philosophize.

The objective solipsist, moreover, might be accused of a fallacy of misplaced credulity. Unlike the more extreme type of solipsist he believes in the independent existence of the outer material world. He believes that physical bodies go on existing and behaving according to natural laws, whether he is present to observe them or not. And such a belief (as Berkeley among others has demonstrated) goes beyond any possible amount of actual evidence. So there is a leap of faith in the one case as in the other. An extreme solipsist has the dry merit of consistency: he

---

[4] Jean Paul Richter (1763-1865). The passage is translated by George S. Fullerton in *A System of Metaphysics*.

refuses to take any leap of faith whatever. The objective or behavioristic solipsist, on the other hand, takes the leap of faith in the one case while refusing to take it in the other. He steps beyond the certitude of his actual experience in accepting the existence of the material world; he refuses to step beyond the certitude of his actual experience and accept the existence of other selves. He is credulous where he gains less by his credulity, and refuses to be credulous where he would gain more.

ii. Rational Grounds of Belief

The most traditional opinion, among philosophers who have dealt with the problem, is that we arrive at a belief in the existence of other minds, other selves, by a process of inference. Assuming that we do know, or at least firmly believe that other minds exist, then since we are evidently not conscious of them in the same way that we are conscious of our own, namely by introspection, and since we do not perceive them as physical objects in the same way that we perceive human bodies, it is concluded that our belief must be based not upon direct but upon indirect, which is to say inferential evidence. More briefly the argument might be put: We do not discover the existence of other minds by introspection (which is internal observation) nor by perception (which is external observation), and since these are the only kinds of direct evidence that are possible, we must therefore make the discovery by indirect means—i.e., by rational inference.

The analogical arguments

The form of inference to which the belief in other minds has been most widely attributed is *analogy*. I observe that other human organisms exist (so the argument is supposed to run) which resemble my own in general characteristics of appearance and behavior. Since my own organism, particularly when it behaves in certain identifiable ways, is accompanied by conscious states which I speak of as "I," "myself," "the real me," etc., I infer by analogy that every other such organism is animated by a mind more or less like my own. John Stuart Mill has amplified the argument as follows:

> I conclude that other human beings have feelings like me, because, first, they have bodies like me, which I know, in my own case, to be the antecedent condition of feelings; and because, secondly, they exhibit the acts, and other outward signs, which in my own case I know by experience to be caused by feelings. I am conscious in myself of a series of facts connected by a uniform sequence, of which the beginning is modifications of my body, the middle is feelings, the end is outward demeanor. In the case of other human beings I have the evidence of my senses for the first and last links of the series, but not for the intermediate link. I find, however, that the sequence between the first and last is as regular and constant in those other cases as it is in mine. In my own case I know that the first link produces the last through the intermediate link, and could not produce it without. Experience, therefore, obliges me to conclude that there must be an intermediate link; which must either be the same in others as in myself, or a different one. I must either believe them to be alive, or to be automatons; and by believing them to be alive, that is, by supposing the link to be of the same nature as in the case of which I have experience, and which is in all respects similar, I bring other human beings, as phenomena, under the same generalizations which I know by experience to be the true theory of my own existence. And in doing so I conform to the legitimate rules of experimental inquiry.[5]

The view which Mill puts forward has an initial plausibility, no doubt. In many specific cases where the question of another person's particular experiences—i.e., of the particular content of his mind—is raised, we find ourselves employing analogical inference. We infer that someone is in pain by the nature of his behavior—whether by an outcry, or a spasmodic movement, or

---

[5] From John Stuart Mill (1806-1873), *An Examination of Sir William Hamilton's Philosophy*, Chapter XII.

other physical indications. Other things equal, a person who has had little or no experience of acute pain will probably be less alert to perceive and interpret the marks of suffering in another. Contrariwise, if feelings of pain in my own case have sometimes been attended by such phenomena as a groan or a clenched jaw, I am quite likely to attribute pain to another person when I perceive a similar bodily phenomenon in him. The reasoning (like all reasoning from analogy) can be schematized as a proportion. If F stands for my feelings, B for certain of my bodily movements, and B' for the like movements of another human body, the proportion would run:

$$B : F : : B' : x$$

Naturally, F' suggests itself at once as the missing term. Just as my muscular spasm when iodine is applied to an open wound (B) is accompanied by a feeling of sharp local pain (F), so a similar spasm in another body (B') is probably accompanied by a similar feeling of pain in the other person to whom that body belongs (F'). The inference is frequently valid, and at any rate is a possible one to make, *provided the reasoner already has a conception of another person as existing.*

A case of question-begging

But in Mill's more general application of the inference it is supposed that the reasoner does not start with the conception of another person as existing. If he did so there would be no need of the inference. Since he does not do so, he must supplement the inference by analogy (*Step 1*) with an inference by elimination (*Step 2*). After inferring that as B is attended by F, so B' is probably attended by F', he must make the following inferential interpretation of what F' means. He must be supposed to argue: "Since the inferred feeling of pain (F') is in no instance ever felt by me, it must be felt by someone else." (*Step 2*). Now how can he possibly (I don't say legitimately, but even *possibly*) make such an inference unless he already has some notion of what the words "someone else" can mean? But if he already has such a notion, then the entire act of inference begs the question at issue. A. E. Taylor writes:

> If I once have good ground for the conviction that similarity of inner experience is attended by similarity of physical structure, then of course I can in any special case treat the degree of structural resemblance between one organism and another as a sufficient reason for inferring a like degree of resemblance between the corresponding inner experiences. But upon what grounds is the general principle itself based? Obviously, if my own inner experience is the only one known to me originally, I have absolutely no means of judging whether the external resemblances between my own organism and yours afford reason for crediting you with an inner experience like my own or not. If the inference by analogy is to have any force whatever in a particular case, I must already know independently that likeness of outward form and likeness of inner experience at least in some cases go together.[6]

From the sudden disturbance among a flock of birds I infer that my neighbor's cat is stalking them. My inference is based on a memory of former occasions, when I have observed the birds to behave in the same way and have actually seen the neighbor's cat. Such is the familiar procedure of inference by analogy. But the argument for other minds is essentially different from this. I have observed the neighbor's cat; I have not observed (so the argument assumes) any other mind than my own. Moreover I can verify the presence of the cat by direct observation when conditions are favorable; but *ex hypothesi* I cannot directly observe the presence of another mind under any conditions at all.

Thus although inference by analogy from bodily behavior is frequently used, with fair success, to gauge the particular forms which another person's consciousness is taking, such an act of inference is possible only if there is already some belief, or disposition to believe, in that other person's independent existence.

[6] A. E. Taylor, *Elements of Metaphysics* (London: Methuen, 1920), p. 205.

Hence the use of that same method of inference, to support the proposition that other persons do exist independently, would be to presuppose what has to be proved—which is a flagrant begging of the question. We may conclude, I think, that although inference by analogy is frequently employed in judging what the content of another mind at a given moment may be, it is by no means an adequate explanation of why we believe in other minds in the first place.

Inference from the use of language

But it is still possible that our belief in other persons' conscious existence might be based on some form of inference other than analogy. The English philosopher H. H. Price has proposed the theory that the belief can be inferred from the nature of a communicative situation.[7] Suppose, for instance, I hear another body than my own utter the noises, "Here comes the bus." This set of noises has a symbolic character for me; which is to say, I understand its meaning. Now the meaning in this case is an assertion, and, like every significant assertion, a potential object of belief. But it may be that on hearing and understanding the sentence I do not believe the proposition it asserts. However, I now look around; and there, sure enough, is the bus, which I had not been expecting yet. "This simple occurrence, of hearing an utterance, understanding it and then verifying it for oneself, provides some evidence that the foreign body which uttered the noises is animated by a mind like my own." I may reasonably deduce, in short, that those words were prompted by another state of consciousness which consisted in seeing or hearing the bus, or in observing some related phenomenon from which its advent was inferred.

Suppose now (Professor Price's argument continues) that I am often in the neighborhood of that same vociferating body, and that it repeatedly produces utterances or gestures which I

[7] H. H. Price, "Our Evidence for the Existence of Other Minds," in *Philosophy*, Vol. XIII (1938), pp. 425-456.

can understand, and which I then proceed to verify for myself. Suppose this to take place in various kinds of situation. Would I not then think I had very strong evidence for believing that the other body was animated by a mind like my own? To be sure the evidence would never amount to demonstration. That is to say, the conclusion is only probable, not certain. But probability is the best we can ever hope for in matters of fact. In view of the large number of such experiences I have had, with many human-shaped bodies in many different kinds of situation, the probability that other minds exist in some sort of connection with those bodies becomes so high as to amount to a practical certainty, even though not a mathematical one.

Is inference enough?

Unquestionably Mr. Price has pointed out an indispensable factor in one's knowledge of other minds. The fact of significant communication with another body is more important than the likenesses, structural and functional, between that other body and one's own; although it involves some functional similarity as its condition. And the importance becomes greater in proportion to the degree of one's intelligence. A stupid or naive man can hardly believe that foreigners, people with different appearance and habits from his own, are fully human. Likeness and familiarity are the traits upon which his judgment relies. To be minded is, for him, to be like-minded. An intelligent man, on the other hand, seeks to freshen his experience by adventures into the strange and unknown. The greatest of such adventures, potentially, is that of coming to know other minds—not superficially and perfunctorily, but with communicative depth and penetration. Communication takes place when A utters or writes or gesticulates *symbols,* which B interprets. To say that B interprets them as symbols, instead of as mere signs (e.g., a thundercloud as a sign of coming storm) is to say that he takes them as the expression of another mind, partly but not wholly like his own. Not only in flesh-and-blood relationships but in such indirect ways as reading books does the symbolizing and communicating process take place. The joy of reading a great book comes in large part from the sense of being spoken to, at whatever remove, by a great mind. And we come to know and respect that other mind not solely, not perhaps even mainly, by its likeness to us, but by the new thoughts and new imaginings to which its many-sided communication prompts us.

But although we can infer much about the nature of another mind from the communicative relationships in which it and we participate, the same critical doubt may be raised here as was done with respect to analogy. Granted that both kinds of inference—from likeness and from communicative activity—are important factors in the process of getting to know other minds, they do not seem to offer a full explanation taken by themselves. The argument from communication begs the question much as the argument from resemblance was shown to do. To hear a two-legged body utter the noise, "Look! There's the bus!"; to consequently expect a bus and then verify that a bus is really there; to have the same thing happen with other two-legged bodies and other noise-patterns in other situations;—what does all this really prove? Simply that there are certain regularities of sequence in my private experience. Just as I discover that a lightning flash is usually followed by the sound of thunder, so I discover, but with a more complex set of qualifications, that certain noise-patterns produced by two-legged bodies are often followed by visual perceptions of certain kinds. Theoretically I could still discover this and remain a solipsist. In that event the noise-patterns, like the lightning, would be *signs* (not, of course, infallible ones) that a certain further experience was to be expected; they would not be *symbols*. That some events (as experienced by me) are signs of other events (probably to be experienced by me) is all that inductive inference can prove. Even when those first events are the vociferatings of another biped, they do not furnish evidence that other minds are producing them. Our belief in the existence of other minds, then, however much it may be aided and particularized by the development of communication with them, must rest upon something more than pure logical inference.

iii. Intuition through Response

Is there a sense in which we know other minds directly? Is there what Professor Price (in rejecting it) has called *extrospective* acquaintance? In short, has each of us a direct and intuitive apprehension of other minds in much the same way as he has of his own? This is the answer to which the foregoing stages of the chapter's argument have necessarily led. If we do have an assured conviction that other conscious selves exist, and if indirect (inferential) evidence is not enough to account for it, then it must be that the evidence for the belief is at least partly direct and preratiocinative—which is to say *intuitive*.

The word "intuitive" is nothing to boggle at. Each of us knows intuitively that he himself exists. To doubt it would be self-contradictory and absurd. When in *Through the Looking-Glass* Tweedledum tells Alice that she is merely a sort of thing in the snoring Red King's dream, Alice begins to cry. "You won't make yourself one bit realer by crying," Tweedledum tells her severely. If the reader smiles, is it because while he, like Tweedledum, finds it easy enough to disbelieve in Alice's existence, he sees the plain absurdity of expecting Alice to admit to herself (if she were capable of admitting anything to herself) that she does not exist?[8] Each person's own existence is introspectively self-evident to that person. Is there such a thing as extrospective self-evidence too? The analytic certainties of pure logic and mathematics do not fall under either head, since they have to do with abstract relations only, not with questions of concrete existence. But what of the conviction that an external world exists? And what of the conviction that here and there in that world

---

[8] Lewis Carroll, *Through the Looking-Glass and What Alice Found There;* the sequel to *Alice in Wonderland.* Both of these little masterpieces of metaphysical fantasy are recommended to the reader who enjoys experimenting with ideas.

—or in some relation to it—there exist other conscious minds like our own? Are not these basic certainties intuited as self-evidently as the certainty that one's self exists? Is not each of us extrospectively sure of a real world and of real persons in it, even as he is introspectively sure of himself?

To say that intuitive extrospection is essential to the knowledge of other minds, is not to say that it is all. If it were all, then as Professor Price rightly points out in the article already referred to, we would "never be deceived by waxworks; we could tell at a glance whether the man we see lying by the roadside is unconscious, or dead, or only shamming; and we should know at once whether the words we hear are uttered by a gramophone or by an animate and conscious human organism." Undoubtedly intuition can go wrong in detail. This is true of introspective and extrospective forms alike. A wise man will admit that he may sometimes be deceived as to the character of himself, of the world, and of other persons. But that is quite a different thing from admitting that he can be deceived in thinking that he, the world, and other persons somehow exist. The basic certainties are always with us, but they have to be educated and empirically particularized.

I-it and I-thou

If it is equally certain that in some way or other one's self, one's world, and one's fellow beings exist, why has existence of the last type, existence of fellow beings, sometimes been supposed to require special proof? Certain contemporary existentialist philosophers—notably Martin Buber, Gabriel Marcel, and Eugen Rosenstock-Huessy[9]—have offered a valuable kind of analysis which not only answers this question but goes far toward solving the riddle of what one *means* by another person's existence. Briefly their argument is this. All real knowledge begins as knowledge of acquaintance. Now the way of being acquainted

---

[9] The present exposition follows mainly Buber and Marcel. For Professor Rosenstock-Huessy's contribution, see bibliography, p. 342.

with a person is essentially different from the way of being acquainted with a thing. A person I know as a "thou"; a thing, as an "it." The difference however does not lie exclusively in the object, but in one's attitude toward the object. The real difference is between the two basic kinds of relation in which it is possible for one to stand. Man adopts a twofold attitude toward his world, according to the "primary word" which he speaks: *I-thou* or *I-it*. To speak one or the other of these primary pairs of words is not a matter of saying it with one's vocal chords, but of standing in a certain relation to the world and to one's fellow beings that constitute it.

The *I-it* relation is essentially manipulative. I draw myself apart from some fragment of experience in order to know it, measure it, control it, label it, and form a theory about it. Thus I treat that fragment as a *thing,* an *it.* The *things* of experience are of many kinds, and I can look at them in various ways, but in any case they stand apart from me, each bounded off from the others and myself bounded off from all of them.

When I face a human being as a *thou,* on the other hand, and adopt the primary relationship *I-thou* to him, he is not a thing among things, and does not consist of things. "The human being," Buber writes, "is not *he* or *she,* bounded from every other *he* or *she,* a specific point in space and time within the net of the world, nor is he a nature able to be discursively experienced and described, a loose bundle of named qualities." He is not to be explained by anything else. In that existential moment "all else lives in his light."[10]

The *I-thou* relation differs from the *I-it* relation in an important way. It is inherently mutual. When I treat someone or some element of my world as an *it,* I do not thereby recognize that other's right to treat me as an *it* in return. In fact I try to avoid that consequence if I can. To accept someone as a *thou,* on the other hand, is to recognize him as having real being—that is

---

[10] Martin Buber, *I and Thou.* See the passages from this work in the Readings, pp. 392-397.

to say, as being an *I* in his own right. Now to accept another's *I*-hood is to adopt, or stand ready to adopt, the role of *thou* in his presence. I not only speak; I invite response, and stand ready to listen. The *I-thou* attitude is thus at the same time a *thou-I* attitude. To respect another's personhood is to accept a relationship of essential reciprocity.

Evolution of "thou" and "it"

Such reciprocity was more spontaneous, Buber holds, among more "primitive" peoples than among ourselves. Their stock of objects is more meagre and their circle of acts is more narrowly prescribed by custom, but within that more limited range their lives are "highly charged with presentness." Their very language shows evidences of this; for the nuclei of their speech—pre-grammatical word forms which do much of the work of sentences—tend to indicate the wholeness of a relation. Thus, in one of Buber's most memorable examples, the Zulu expresses the idea of "far away" by a word which means, when analyzed, *"There where someone cries out: 'O mother, I am lost!'"*

Probably the earliest human attitude is more rudimentary than either *I-thou* or *I-it*. It is a sort of undifferentiated *we*, a consciousness of the flock. Although it can hardly have existed in pure form, it was probably more characteristic of men at a time when their social functions required relatively little division of labor. A nomadic tribe which trekked together, hunted together, fought together against a common enemy, worshiped and sacrificed together in the presence of tribal gods, would doubtless feel their tribal *we*-hood as the dominant stress of their life. But in the slow process of tribal evolution men's activities gradually became more differentiated. When two primitive hunters close in on their quarry from different directions, there is the beginning of mutual confidence and mutual respect. When the boys of the tribe emulate certain of the elders not by blind adherence to custom but because they admire them and consciously want to be like them, and when the elders in turn see the boys not as potential rivals and expropriators but as potential successors in upholding the military renown of tribe and family, there is again such a beginning. When the male experiences moments of tenderness toward his mate, there is a third. Of course there are the beginnings of *I-it* relations too—as one tribesman tries to cheat or slay another, or as he enslaves his enemy, or treats his wife as a chattel. But the point is that the *I-thou* relation has fully as much claim to primacy in human evolution. The idea of another person eventually develops out of that relation; it is not derived by inference from the ideas—of matter, cause, etc.—which eventually develop out of the *I-it* relation. In this sense and in some such evolutionary context it can be plausibly maintained that our belief in other persons' existence arises intuitively and not by inference.

The mystery of personhood

Each of us demands some area of privacy in which his thoughts and feelings are his own, in which he is safe from snoopers. Some of our most intimate reflections we are perhaps willing to share, when the occasion is apt, with a close friend or two; but even when willing we cannot totally succeed, for our media of communication are always too gross. Here again is reciprocity; for as I recognize an area of privacy in myself, so too I admit the existence of one in each other person. He is he, and I am I. His entire inward nature I can never know; my perspective is never totally his perspective. All our communication, our coöperative enterprises, our shared experiences, our conversational give-and-take of feelings and thought stop short of full knowledge. A person is a mystery, not merely a set of problems. Nor can we reasonably wish it otherwise. One can flourish as a person only if there is something inviolably his own at the heart of him.

To say that the essential person is a mystery rather than a problem is to say—according to Gabriel Marcel's analysis—that he is essentially not an object, he is a *presence*. Objects raise problems—of existence, classification, and causal connection. We formulate these problems as definitely as we can, for the sake of explaining and perhaps of controlling the objects. A presence has no such clean-cut properties. It is objective in the sense that it is really there; it is not objective, for it cannot be handled, measured, and predicted in the manner of objects. The difference between a presence and an object is, for Marcel as for Buber, a difference between two kinds of utterly fundamental relationship, which involve different ways of responding on our part. We grasp at an object, define it, try to explain it; whereas "a presence is something which can only be gathered to oneself or shut out from oneself, only be welcomed or rebuffed."[11]

Conclusion

The real question about other persons, then, is not so much how we know they exist, as how and why we erect a wall of mental concepts which shuts out the plain evidences that persons exist and the more desultory evidence that elements of personhood may perhaps be found in other areas of experience than that of human society. The ultimate boundaries of heaven and earth we can never know; what counts is our readiness to gather in or shut out, to welcome or rebuff. The evidence that other persons exist is not abstract, it is concrete—a continual demand by other *thous* upon the *thou* in us to keep the mutuality of the *I-thou* relationship alive. In those recurrent mutualities of friendship, love, and loyalty of coöperation we have all the evidence we can want, and the only evidence that is relevant, that we live in a society of fellows and not in a solipsistic vacuum.

For Further Study

W. W. Spencer, *Our Knowledge of Other Minds* (Yale University Press, 1930).
John Wisdom, *Other Minds* (London: Blackwell, 1952). Advanced.
William Ernest Hocking, *The Meaning of God in Human Experience* (1912), Chap. XVII-XXI.

[11] Gabriel Marcel, *The Mystery of Being*. (The Gifford Lectures for 1949-1950; published in America by the Henry Regnery Co.) The discussion of presence and mystery vs. objects and problems is in Vol. I, Chap. X.

GEORGE S. FULLERTON, *A System of Metaphysics* (1904), Chap. XXVII, "The Existence of Other Minds."

C. D. BROAD, *The Mind and its Place in Nature* (Harcourt, Brace, 1925), Chap. VII, "The Mind's Knowledge of Other Minds."

A. E. TAYLOR, *Elements of Metaphysics* (London, 1903), Bk. III, Chap. II, "The Problem of Matter," particularly Sec. 3. The next two sections, 4 and 5, develop certain consequences of this view for the interpretation of the universe as a whole. Cf. Chap. 15 of the present book.

SAMUEL ALEXANDER, *Space, Time and Deity* (Macmillan, 1920), Bk. III, Chap. I. B., "The Apprehension of Other Minds" (pp. 31-37 of the second volume).

GEORGE SANTAYANA, *Reason in Common Sense* (Vol. I of the series, *The Life of Reason*, Scribner 1906), Chap. VI, "Discovery of Fellow-Minds."

JOHN STUART MILL, *Examination of Sir William Hamilton's Philosophy* (1865), Chap. XII. Standard defense of the analogical theory.

EUGEN ROSENSTOCK-HUESSY, *Out of Revolution* (New York: William Morrow, 1938), "Epilogue." A strongly individual approach.

NATHALIE A. DUDDINGTON, "Our Knowledge of Other Minds," in *Aristotelian Society Proceedings,* Vol. 19 (1918-1919), pp. 147-178.

H. H. PRICE, "Our Evidence for the Existence of Other Minds," in *Philosophy,* Vol. 13 (1938), pp. 425-456.

J. R. JONES, "Our Knowledge of Other Persons," in *Philosophy,* Vol. 25 (1950), pp. 134-148.

MARTIN BUBER, *I and Thou* (German original, 1923; Eng. tr. Edinburgh, 1937, distributed in America by Charles Scribner's Sons).

———, *Between Man and Man* (London: Routledge, 1947): especially Part I, "Dialogue," written in 1929, to amplify the teaching of *I and Thou.*

Questions for Discussion

1. Is it easier to doubt another person's existence than to doubt your own? If so, is this due to the same kind of prejudice as when you think your own needs more important than another's? Or is it essentially different?

2. Which would you find it easier to doubt—the existence of the material world independent of our impressions of it, or the existence of other conscious selves? In other words, would you find it easier to take the position of Berkeley or of the solipsist described by Richter?

3. Which of the following statements seems to you to explain best our knowledge of other minds?

a) "The logical justification of our belief in other minds can only be by way of bodily behavior."—W. T. STACE.

b) "Our fellow human beings excite in us the social or gregarious instinct, and to feel socially towards another being is to be assured that it is something like ourselves. We do not first apprehend that another being is a mind and then respond to him, whether positively as in affection or negatively as in aversion; but in our tenderness or dislike we are aware of him as like ourselves."—S. ALEXANDER.

c) "Personality is neutral in its very being. The self is one term in a relation between two selves. . . . The self exists only in the communion of selves."—JOHN MACMURRAY.

4. It has been suggested that in telepathy one mind knows another, and that thus the telepathic relation, even though rare, may show in a more striking form the manner in which one mind gets to know another naturally. Professor Price (*op. cit.*) replies: "The telepathic relation appears to be causal, not cognitive; it is more like infection than like knowledge. . . . just as, when you have scarlet fever and I catch it from you, my fever is not a knowing of yours."

Assuming that there are authentic cases of telepathy (i.e., where the thinking of a thought by one mind causes that thought to arise in another mind), what is your opinion as to the above suggestion?

5. How far do you think that each of the following factors limits and falsifies our knowledge of other selves:

a) the fact that people sometimes feign feelings and thoughts which are not really theirs?

b) the fact that people sometimes conceal their feelings and thoughts?

c) our own lack of sensitivity?

Readings for Part Three

The Nature of the Soul*

PLATO

The soul as self-moved

Anything which receives from an outside source the motion which it imparts to other things, may lose that motion and thereby cease to live. It is only that which moves itself, inasmuch as it never quits itself, that never ceases moving, but is a source and fountain of motion for everything else.

Now a primary source cannot come into being. For whatever comes into being must originate out of a primary source, but the latter cannot originate out of anything whatever: if it had done so, it would not be really a primary source. Furthermore, since it has not come into being, it must be indestructible. For if a primary source could be destroyed, then, since there would be no higher source out of which it could be recreated, and since no other becoming could take place without it, the entire cosmic process would collapse and come to a standstill.

So now that we have found that what is moved by itself is immortal, none will hesitate to affirm that this power of self-motion is implied in the very essence and definition of soul. A body which receives its motions from outside is called inanimate, but one that derives its motions from a source within itself is said to be animate or "besouled."[1] Thus common speech supports our view that self-motion defines the soul's very nature.

---

* The first two sections are from Plato (427-347 B.C.), *Phaedrus*, 245C-246 A. Based in part on the translation by J. Wright (1888).

[1] Our word "animate" is from the Latin parallel to Plato's Greek word *empsychon*. Both connote the presence of an *anima, psyche,* soul.

Analogy of the winged charioteer

To explain the soul's nature in detail would be an endless task, which only a god could accomplish. As men we must be content to say what it resembles. Let us say, then, that the soul resembles the union of combined powers in a pair of winged steeds and a winged charioteer. In the souls of the gods the horses and the driver are all alike good and of good extraction; but the breed of other souls is mixed. In the souls of men the charioteer finds, in managing his two steeds, that one of them is generous and of generous breed, while the other is of opposite descent and opposite character. And thus it comes about that driving, for us humans, is a difficult and troublesome task.

Our next task is to distinguish the mortal and the immortal components in a living being: All that is soul has the care of all that is inanimate, and traverses the entire universe, now manifesting itself in one form, now in another. When it is perfect and fully feathered, it roams the upper air and directs the stars in their courses; but the soul that has lost its feathers is borne down until it can fasten on something solid. That is to say, it enters an earthy body, which now, by reason of its new inhabitant, seems capable of self-motion. This compound of soul and body is called an animal, and is further described as mortal. The term "immortal" is applied not on rational grounds, but because, without having seen or formed any adequate conception of the god within, we picture him to ourselves as an immortal animal, possessed of a soul and body eternally conjoined.

The bodily seats of the soul[2]

As we said at the outset, the elements [of soul and body] were in disorder until the creator-god introduced measure and proportion both within and among them, so far as they were severally capable of receiving it. For at first there was no proportion to be found anywhere, unless by chance, nor was there anything that could properly be called by such names as fire, water, and the others now in use. It was the Creative Power who first set all these elements in order, and then out of them constructed our universe—a single living organism containing within itself all living creatures both mortal and

---

[2] From Plato, *Timaeus,* 69 B-71 A.

immortal. Of divine things he himself was the artificer, but the task of fashioning mortal creatures he laid upon his offspring. And they, on receiving an immortal principle of soul, imitated him by framing around it a mortal body, the whole of which they gave to be its vehicle.

Now in the body they housed also another form of soul, the mortal, containing dreadful and compelling passions: first pleasure, which is evil's greatest lure; next pains, which are barriers against the good; and besides these rashness and fear, a pair of unwise counsellors; anger hard to persuade, and hope, too easily led astray. Mingling these with irrational sensation and all-daring desire, they compounded the mortal element as it had to be.

Having done this and being unwilling to pollute the divine any more than necessary, they housed the mortal part away from it in another abode within the body, setting the neck as an isthmus and boundary between the head and the chest, to keep them apart. And they implanted the mortal part within the chest and in what is called the trunk. Since one part of the mortal soul is better and one inferior, they built a partition within the hollow trunk, as though marking off the men's apartment from the women's, by placing the midriff between them as a fence. Accordingly that part of the soul which is courageous and spirited they housed nearer to the head, between the midriff and the neck, in order that it might hearken to the reason and collaborate with it in forcibly subduing the tribe of desires, whenever these should refuse willing obedience to the word of command from the citadel. . . .

That part of the soul which consists in the desire for food and drink and all the other appetites that proceed from the nature of the body, they housed in the region extending from the midriff down to the navel as its lower boundary. This area they arranged as a manger for feeding the body as a whole. Here they tethered the appetitive part of the soul, like a savage beast which they had to keep on hand and feed if the race of mortals was to go on existing. Their purpose for stationing it here was to let it feed at its trough and dwell as far as possible from the seat of counsel, in order that its fuss and clamor might not disturb that highest part of the soul but allow it to be at peace while deliberating what is best for the entire organism.

The soul's self-motion[3]

The speakers are an Athenian Stranger, probably spokesman for Plato's own views, and Cleinias.

ATHENIAN. When someone asks me, "Are all things at rest, Stranger, and does nothing move? Or is the very opposite the case? Or are some things in process of change while others stay the same?" I shall reply: "Some things are in process, while others stay the same."

After enumerating eight different kinds of process—rotary motion, forward movement, a combination of these, separation, composition, growth, decay, and perishing—the Athenian continues:

ATHENIAN. And now, my friends, have we not enumerated all the different types of process with the exception of two?
CLEINIAS. What two?
ATHENIAN. The very two, good sir, with which the whole of our present inquiry is concerned.
CLEINIAS. Speak more clearly.
ATHENIAN. We are inquiring about the soul, are we not?
CLEINIAS. Certainly.
ATHENIAN. Well now, you'll agree that there is one kind of motion which can impart its motion to other things but not actually start a process going within itself; while there is another principle of motion which can produce in itself as well as in other things the processes of combination and separation, of increase and decrease, of birth and destruction. Surely we must include this last as one of the several kinds of motion?
CLEINIAS. Yes, granted.
ATHENIAN. The ninth on our list, then, is the kind of process which is moved by something other than itself, and in turn imparts its motion to something other; while the tenth is that which initiates a process both in itself and in other things, fitting in with every action and every feeling in things, and therefore called the real principle of process and motion in all that exists.
CLEINIAS. I agree fully.

[3] From Plato, *The Laws,* Bk. X, 893 B-896 D.

ATHENIAN. Now of these ten kinds of motion, which would we most rightly judge to be the mightiest and most effective?

CLEINIAS. We are bound to say that the power of producing motion in oneself [literally, "the motion which is able to move itself"] is vastly superior to all the others.

ATHENIAN. Well said. But in that case we must make one or two corrections in what has just been said.

CLEINIAS. What do you mean?

ATHENIAN. What we said about the tenth kind of motion was not quite accurate.

CLEINIAS. In what way?

ATHENIAN. Logically it should come first, since it is first both in order of becoming and in degree of power. And what we foolishly called the ninth just now should really be second.

CLEINIAS. How do you mean?

ATHENIAN. Just this. If we postulate that one thing brings about change in another, and that in yet another, and so on, will there ever be any prime cause of that process of change? How can any one of the steps in such a process be the cause of the rest? It is impossible. But when that which has stirred itself into motion makes a change in something else, and that again in something else, so that the process is spread through countless other things, will not the prime source of all this activity have to be the change that was originally self-moved?

CLEINIAS. Admirably put, and I am in full agreement.

ATHENIAN. Or let me put the question in another way, and answer it myself.—Suppose, as certain thinkers have ventured to affirm, that the entirety of everything was once united and at rest: which of the principles of motion we have named would become operative first? Clearly the self-moving. The first process to come into being could not have been caused by anything other than itself, for by hypothesis no previous force was operating. Therefore since self-motion is demonstrably the starting-point of all other processes—the first to arise among things at rest and the first to exist among the various kinds of process—we must conclude that self-motion is necessarily the eldest and most potent sort of change, and that the motion which is altered by something else and thereby has effects upon other things is the second in rank.

CLEINIAS. Perfectly true.

ATHENIAN. And now we have reached a stage of the argument where we can answer the following question.

CLEINIAS. What?

ATHENIAN. If we should see this power of self-motion in any material thing—earth or water or fire—or in some combination of material elements, how should we describe its condition?

CLEINIAS. Are you asking me whether we should speak of something as *alive* when it moves itself?

ATHENIAN. Yes.

CLEINIAS. Why, yes, it is alive, of course.

ATHENIAN. Now stop a moment please, and reflect. Are there not three things you wish to know about every object?

CLEINIAS. What do you mean?

ATHENIAN. There is the *essence,* there is the *definition* of the essence, and there is the *name.* . . . Now what is the definition of that which we name "soul"? Can there be any other definition than the one we have just stated—"the motion which is able to produce itself"?

CLEINIAS. You mean to say that "self-movement" is the definition of that very same essence to which we all give the name "soul"?

ATHENIAN. That is just what I mean. And if this is true can we still complain of any lack of proof that soul is identical with the prime source and moving power of all that is, has been, and shall be—and indeed of all that is opposite to these? For we have clearly demonstrated that it is responsible for all process and movement whatever?

CLEINIAS. No, we can no longer complain. For soul, being the prime source of motion, has been sufficiently proven to be the eldest of all things that exist.

ATHENIAN. And what about the process which is produced in one object by the activity of another, having no power of moving itself, but being simply the change of a soulless, inanimate body? Should not that be rated second—or as far down the list as you prefer?

CLEINIAS. Yes.

ATHENIAN. Then we are fully justified in declaring that soul is prior to body, and that body is secondary and dependent—the soul governing and the body being governed according to the ordinance of nature?

CLEINIAS. Entirely justified.

ATHENIAN. And do you recall our previous admission that if soul could be proved older than body, then the attributes belonging to soul must be older than those of the body?

CLEINIAS. Yes, I recall.

ATHENIAN. Then, if soul is prior to body, it follows that men's characters and dispositions, their wishes and reasonings, their responsible opinions and reflections and memories will be prior to the length, breadth, depth, and physical power of bodies?

CLEINIAS. Most certainly.

The Nature of the Soul*

ARISTOTLE

Definition of soul

The most generally recognized class of things is that of bodies—especially natural bodies, which are the originals of all others. Some natural bodies possess life, others do not; life signifying the power of self-nourishment, and of growth and decay. Accordingly, every natural body possessing life must be not only a specific thing but one comprising both matter and form. But because body thus possesses a certain attribute, namely life, it is not on that account to be identified with the soul; for body is not itself an attribute but simply the subject and the material basis of attributes. Soul, therefore, must be a specific thing in the sense that it is the form of a natural body endowed with the capacity of life. Specific thinghood in this sense is actuality; and soul, therefore, is the actuality of body as just defined. Further, as the word actuality has two senses, illustrated respectively by the possession and exercise of knowledge, it is evident that soul is actuality in the former of these senses; for sleep as well as waking is

* From Aristotle, *Psychology* (*De Anima*), Bk. II, Chap. i; Bk. I, Chap. i; Bk. III, Chap. iv. Based on *Aristotle: Selections* (Odyssey Press, 1951).

a state of the soul, and whereas waking is analogous to the exercise of knowledge, sleep is analogous to its mere possession. Moreover, since the possession of knowledge must precede its exercise, the soul may be defined as *the initial actuality of a natural body endowed with the capacity of life.*

This definition of soul is applicable to whatever body possesses organs. The term organs is here extended to include the parts of plants; for these, in spite of their rudimentary structure, exhibit certain analogies to animal organs: the leaf, for instance, serves as protective covering for the pericarp, and the pericarp for the fruit; while again, the roots are analogous to mouth, since like them they ingest food. Hence if we require a general definition applicable to every type of soul, we may define the soul as *the initial actuality of a natural body possessing organs.* The question whether soul and body are identical, therefore, is as superfluous as to ask whether wax and the shape imprinted on it are identical, or, in general whether the material of a thing is identical with the thing of which it is the material.

Soul's relation to body

A further problem respecting the attributes of the soul is whether they all belong to body and soul together or whether any of them are peculiar to the soul alone—a difficult question but unavoidable. Apparently in a majority of cases, such as anger, courage, desire, and all sensation, the soul neither acts nor is acted upon apart from the body. Thinking is perhaps the most likely exception; yet if thinking consists in a succession of mental images, or at least is impossible without such images, it is plain that even thinking cannot be carried on independently of the body. If we can discover any functions or other characteristics peculiar to the soul alone, we may regard the soul as capable of existing apart from the body; whereas if it possesses no such functions or characteristics of its own, separate existence will be impossible to it. In the latter case the soul will be comparable to the straightness of a line. The line, qua straight, has many properties, such as that of touching a bronze sphere at a point; but this does not mean that straightness by itself will have such a property. For, in fact, straightness never exists by itself, but is always found existing as an aspect of body. Similarly we may take it that the affections of the soul—angry passion and gentleness, fear, pity, courage, and even joy, love, and hate—always involve body; for their occurrence is accompanied by some specific affection of the body. This is shown by the fact that violent and striking things may happen to us without our being either frightened or irritated; while at other times, when the body is already perturbed and in a condition like that of anger, our emotions may be aroused by faint and trifling occurrences. Even better evidence is found in the fact that men sometimes fall into a state of terror without anything terrible having occurred. This being so, it is evident that *the affections of the soul are simply meanings subsisting in matter,* and ought therefore to be defined accordingly: anger, for instance, as a certain way in which a body, or some organ or faculty of a body, is moved by such and such a cause with reference to such and such an end.

The functional nature of mind

Coming now to that aspect or faculty of the soul whereby it knows and takes counsel, and putting aside the question of whether this aspect can be separated from the rest of the soul in fact or only in thought, we must investigate both its distinguishing characteristics and the way in which its thinking occurs.

If thinking is analogous to perceiving it will be a process wherein the intellectual aspect of the soul is acted upon by an object capable of being thought; or at any rate, something similar to that. It follows that this aspect of the soul, although itself impassive, must be capable of receiving the form of the intelligible object: that is to say, it must be at once potentially like its object and actually distinct from it. In short, as the faculty of sense is related to sensible objects, so thought must be related to intelligible objects. And since everything is a possible object of thought, Anaxagoras was right in declaring that this aspect of the soul, in order to have authority over the things it knows, must be unmixed with any of them; for its functioning is hindered and impaired by the intrusion of anything alien. Accordingly, the intellectual faculty, like the sensitive, has no other intrinsic nature than that of being a certain capacity; from which it follows that mind, as we may call this aspect of the soul—I mean its thinking and judging aspect—has no actual existence before it thinks. This is another reason why we cannot properly regard it as containing an alloy of anything physical; for if it did, it would have had to take on particular qualities, such as coldness and warmth, and perhaps would even, like the sensitive faculty, have acquired a special organ of its own. But in fact nothing of the sort occurs. Hence the Platonists are justified in calling the soul the place of forms; although it should be recognized that this description applies not to the entire soul but only to its intellective aspect, and that the forms do not reside there actually but only potentially.

On the Nature of the Mind*

RENÉ DESCARTES

YESTERDAY's meditation has filled my mind with so many doubts that I am no longer able to forget them, and yet I do not see any way in which they can be resolved. It is as though I had suddenly fallen into deep water, too much bewildered either to set my feet securely on the bottom or to swim and so support myself on the surface. Nevertheless I will make an effort and try anew the same path as the one I entered upon yesterday: that is to say, I will proceed by setting aside all that admits of the slightest doubt, just as if I had discovered it to be utterly false; and I will follow steadfastly along this road until I have met with something which is certain, or at least, if I can do nothing more, until I have learned for certain that nothing certain is to be found. Archimedes required, as a condition of moving the earth from one place to another, only that one point in the universe should be immovably fixed. Analogously I shall be entitled to the highest hopes if I am lucky enough to discover a single thing that is certain and indubitable.

Accordingly I will suppose that all the things which I see are false: I will persuade myself that nothing which my fallacious memory represents to me has ever existed; I will pretend that I possess no senses; I will imagine that body, figure, extension, move-

* From René Descartes, *Meditations* (1641), Meditation II. Newly translated.

ment and place are but fictions of my mind. What, then, can be accepted as true? Perhaps only this—that nothing whatever is certain.

But how can I be sure there is not something altogether different from the aspects I have been enumerating—something of which it is impossible to have the slightest doubt? Is there not a God—or at any rate, some Being, call it what you will—who causes these thoughts to arise in my mind? The assumption is not a necessary one, for conceivably I might be capable of producing such thoughts by myself. Myself, then! am not I at least something? But in what way? I have found myself able to deny that I possess senses and a body. But here I hesitate, for what follows from that? Am I so dependent on body and senses that I cannot exist without them? I have succeeded in persuading myself that neither heaven nor earth, neither minds nor bodies exist: does that mean I am persuaded that I, too, do not exist? Surely not. I must have existed in order to persuade myself of something. Nevertheless, what if there were some diabolical being, of the greatest power and cunning, who constantly employed his ingenuity in deceiving me? Well, supposing it were so: I would obviously have to exist in order to be deceived by him; and let him deceive me as he will, he can never bring it about that I am nothing so long as I have the thought that I am something. Thus after careful and mature examination of the matter we are obliged to conclude that the proposition, *I am, I exist,* is necessarily true each time that I pronounce it, or that I mentally conceive it.

But I do not yet know clearly enough *what* I am, even though absolutely certain *that* I am; and hence I must be careful to see that I do not inadvertently mistake some other object for myself and thereby go astray in respect to this very knowledge that I hold to be the most certain and most evident of all. That is why I shall now consider afresh what it was I had believed myself to be before I entered upon the present train of reflections; and of my former opinions I shall suspend all that might be invalidated to the slightest degree by the critical scrutiny I have undertaken, in order that nothing but what is absolutely certain and indubitable may remain.

What, then, did I formerly take myself to be? Undoubtedly I believed I was a man. But what is a man? Shall I say here a rational animal? Definitely not; for then I would have to inquire what an animal is, and what is rational, thus passing insensibly from a single question into others more and more difficult; and my leisure is not so abundant that I care to waste it trying to unravel subtleties like these. I would rather confine myself to the thoughts that sprang up in my mind of themselves, inspired solely by my own nature when I was applying myself to the question of my very being. Let me think back.[1] In the first place I supposed myself to possess a face, hands, arms, and all that system of members composed of bones and flesh which constitute the corpse I call my body. In addition to all this I reflected that I was nourished, that I walked, perceived, felt, and reasoned, and I ascribed all these actions to the soul; but I did not stop to consider what the soul was—or, if I did, I supposed it to be something extremely rarefied and elusive like wind or flame or aether, spread throughout my grosser parts. The body, on the other hand, caused me no doubts at all, for I believed I had a very clear knowledge of it. If I had wished to describe just how I conceived it I would have proceeded thus: "By the body I understand all that which can be enclosed within a certain shape; something which can occupy a certain place, and so fill the spatial extent of it as to exclude all other bodies; which can be perceived either by touch, sight, hearing, taste, or smell; which can be moved in various ways, but always by something other than and external to itself, something touching and impressing it—for I did not regard the power of self-movement, any more than that of feeling or of thinking, to pertain to the nature of bodies; in fact I was always a little astonished to find such faculties displaying themselves in bodies of a certain kind.

But *what am I*, now that I have supposed that there is a certain powerful and presumably malicious being who spends all his powers in deceiving me? Can I affirm that I possess any one of all those attributes that I have just mentioned as pertaining to the nature of body? After considering them attentively one by one I must confess there is none of them that can properly be said to belong to myself. To show this in detail would be tedious and unnecessary. Let us pass, then, to the attributes of the soul: can any one of them be regarded as indubitably and essentially my own? What of nutrition and voluntary locomotion? But if it is true that I have no body, it must also be true that I am not capable either of walking or of taking nourishment. Or what of perception? But that, too, is impossible without the body; and besides, I have frequently, during

[1] This short sentence is interpolated by the present translator, since Descartes is referring to his first Meditation.

sleep, believed that I perceived objects which I afterwards came to acknowledge I had not really perceived at all. What, then, of thinking? Here at last I discover what properly belongs to and cannot be separated from myself. I am, I exist: granted this is certain, but how often? As often as I think; for it might conceivably be the case that if I should wholly cease to think, I would at the same time utterly cease to be. I am here admitting as true only what is absolutely necessary; and to speak accurately in this vein, I am nothing more than a thing which thinks. It is in this precise sense that I may now call myself a mind, or soul, or understanding, or reason—terms whose real meaning was hitherto unknown to me. Granted that I am something real, that I really exist; but what am I? My answer has been given: a thinking being.

Now what is a thing that thinks? It is a thing that doubts, understands, conceives, affirms, denies, wills and refuses; also that imagines and perceives. Surely it is no trifling matter if all these functions belong to my nature. And why should they not? Am not I—the very being who now doubts of nearly everything—also one who understands and conceives certain things, who affirms one of them to be true and denies the rest, who feels averse to being deceived, who imagines many things, sometimes despite his will, and who likewise perceives many, in such a way as to suggest that the bodily organs intervene? Is there nothing in all this which is as securely true as the fact of my existence, and which would remain so even though I might be always dreaming and subject to the deceptions of him who had created me? On the contrary, are not these attributes really all one with my thinking, and hence inseparable from myself? For it is so evident from simple inspection that it is I who doubt, I who understand, and I who desire, that it is unnecessary to belabor the point any further. Likewise it must be this same I who imagine; for even though it may be true (as I postulated at the outset) that none of the things which I imagine really exist, still the power of imagination continues to operate in me and to form part of my thought. Finally, I am the same being who perceives—that is, who apprehends certain objects as though by organs of sense—since it is a plain fact that I see light, hear a noise, and feel heat. But it may be objected that these presentations are false and that I am dreaming. Let it be granted. Still it is at least quite certain that I seem to myself to see light, hear a noise, and feel heat. This much cannot be false, and it constitutes what is usually called my feeling or awareness (*sentire*), which is nothing else than thinking (*cogitare*) in the sense here defined. From this train of reasoning I begin to know what I am with a little more clarity and distinctness than heretofore.

The Interrelation of Soul and Body*

RENÉ DESCARTES

Article xxx

Union of the soul with the entire body

In order to understand the matter more adequately we should realize that the soul is joined with the entire human body. We cannot say without qualification that it is located in one part of the body exclusively. For it is one and indivisible, in the sense that its functions are so arranged and related to one another that the failure of any one of them renders the entire body somewhat defective. Moreover, its very nature is such that it bears no relation to the extension, dimensions, and other component properties of the material body, but only to the body so far as it operates as an organic whole. This is evident from the fact that we cannot possibly conceive of a half or a third of a soul, nor of the space it occupies. Nor is the soul made smaller when some portion of the body is cut off; on the contrary, it is set entirely free when the union of bodily organs is finally dissolved.

Article xxxi

The pineal gland

Nevertheless, although the soul is joined with the entire body, there is one part of the body in which it exercises its functions more

* From René Descartes, *The Passions of the Soul* (1649), the last work published by Descartes before his death a few months later.

particularly than elsewhere. Some take this special part to be the brain, others the heart: the brain because of its connection with the organs of sense, and the heart because it appears to be the place where our deepest feelings are centered. But it seems to me quite clear, after carefully examining the matter, that the part of the body where the soul operates most directly is not the heart, nor is it the entire brain, but only the innermost portion of the brain—a tiny gland situated in the very middle of it, and suspended above the duct through which the animal spirits in the forward passages can communicate with those in the rear ones, so that the slightest movements which occur in it can greatly alter the course of those spirits, and conversely the smallest changes occurring in the animal spirits may greatly affect the movement of this gland.

Article xxxii

Evidence of its function

The reason why I feel sure, on reflection, that this gland must be the one place where the soul operates directly upon the body is as follows. All the other parts of the brain are found in pairs, just as all the organs of our outer senses are double—*e.g.*, two eyes, two hands, two ears. Now our awareness of a particular thing is single and undivided. Hence there must necessarily be some place where the double visual image and the other double impressions, which proceed from the several pairs of sense-organs acted on by a single object, can unite before reaching the soul and thus represent to it not two objects but one. It is easy to understand how these images and other impressions can unite in this gland by the agency of the animal spirits which fill the passages of the brain; but there is no other place in the body where they can be so united if not here.

Article xxxiv

Interaction of soul and body

The theory here set forth, then, is that the soul operates most directly upon the little gland which is poised in the middle of the brain. From here it radiates through all the rest of the body by means of the animal spirits, the nerves, and even the blood, which, receiving impressions from the animal spirits, carries them via the arteries into all the body's members. I have already explained, in discussing the machinery of the body, that the tiny nerve-filaments are so distributed that according as one or another movement is excited in them by sense-objects they open in one or another way the pores of the brain, causing the animal spirits contained in these passages to enter in different ways into the muscles, and thereby they move the limbs in one or another of the ways in which they are capable of being moved. Any other causes, likewise, which affect the movement of the animal spirits, will have similar results. I must now add that the small gland with which the soul is most directly connected functions in the following double way. It is so suspended between the passages containing the animal spirits that it can be moved by them in as many different ways as there are sense-differences in the object; and it carries this motion on to the soul, whose nature is such that she receives as many different perceptions as there are diverse movements in the gland. Conversely, the bodily machine is so constituted that whenever the gland is moved in one or another by the soul—or for that matter by any other cause—it pushes the animal spirits which surround it toward the pores of the brain, through which they are conducted along the nerves to the muscles, thereby producing movement in the limbs.

The Consciousness of Self*

WILLIAM JAMES

The first fact for us, then, as psychologists, is that thinking of some sort goes on. I use the word thinking, for every form of consciousness indiscriminately. If we could say in English "it thinks," as we say "it

---

* From William James, *Principles of Psychology* (2 vols., Henry Holt & Co., 1890), parts of Chaps. IX and X. Reprinted by courtesy of the publisher.

rains" or "it blows," we should be stating the fact most simply and with the minimum of assumption. As we cannot, we must simply say that *thought goes on.*

Five Characters in Thought

How does it go on? We notice immediately five important characters in the process, of which it shall be the duty of the present chapter to treat in a general way:

1) Every thought tends to be part of a personal consciousness.

2) Within each personal consciousness thought is always changing.

3) Within each personal consciousness thought is sensibly continuous.

4) It always appears to deal with objects independent of itself.

5) It is interested in some parts of these objects to the exclusion of others, and welcomes or rejects—*chooses* from among them, in a word—all the while.

In considering these five points successively, we shall have to plunge *in medias res* as regards our vocabulary, and use psychological terms which can only be adequately defined in later chapters of the book. But every one knows what the terms mean in a rough way; and it is only in a rough way that we are now to take them. This chapter is like a painter's first charcoal sketch upon his canvas, in which no niceties appear.

(1) *Thought tends to personal form*

When I say *every thought is part of a personal consciousness,* "personal consciousness" is one of the terms in question. Its meaning we know so long as no one asks us to define it, but to give an accurate account of it is the most difficult of philosophic tasks. This task we must confront in the next chapter; here a preliminary word will suffice.

In this room—this lecture-room, say—there are a multitude of thoughts, yours and mine, some of which cohere mutually, and some not. They are as little each-for-itself and reciprocally independent as they are all-belonging-together. They are neither: no one of them is separate, but each belongs with certain others and with none beside. My thought belongs with my other thoughts, and your thought with your other thoughts. Whether anywhere in the room there be a mere thought, which is nobody's thought, we have no means of ascertaining, for we have no experience of its like. The only states of consciousness that we naturally deal with are found in personal consciousnesses, minds, selves, concrete particular I's and you's.

Each of these minds keeps its own thoughts to itself. There is no giving or bartering between them. No thought even comes into direct *sight* of a thought in another personal consciousness than its own. Absolute insulation, irreducible pluralism, is the law. It seems as if the elementary psychic fact were not *thought* or *this thought* or *that thought*, but *my thought*, every thought being *owned*. Neither contemporaneity, nor proximity in space, nor similarity of quality and content are able to fuse thoughts together which are sundered by this barrier of belonging to different personal minds. The breaches between such thoughts are the most absolute breaches in nature. Everyone will recognize this to be true, so long as the existence of *something* corresponding to the term "personal mind" is all that is insisted on, without any particular view of its nature being implied. On these terms the personal self rather than the thought might be treated as the immediate datum in psychology. The universal conscious fact is not "feelings and thoughts exist," but "I think" and "I feel." No psychology, at any rate, can question the *existence* of personal selves. The worst a psychology can do is so to interpret the nature of these selves as to rob them of their worth. A French writer, speaking of our ideas, says somewhere in a fit of anti-spiritualistic excitement that, misled by certain peculiarities which they display, we "end by personifying" the procession which they make—such personification being regarded by him as a great philosophic blunder on our part. It could only be a blunder if the notion of personality meant something essentially different from anything to be found in the mental procession. But if that procession be itself the very "original" of the notion of personality, to personify it cannot possibly be wrong. It is already personified. There are no marks of personality to be gathered elsewhere, and then found lacking in the train of thought. It has them all already; so that to whatever farther analysis we may subject that form of personal selfhood under which thoughts appear, it is, and must remain, true that the thoughts which psychology studies do continually tend to appear as parts of personal selves. . . .

(2) Thought is in constant change

I do not mean necessarily that no one state of mind has any duration—even if true, that would be hard to establish. The change which I have more particularly in view is that which takes place in sensible intervals of time; and the result on which I wish to lay stress is this, that *no state once gone can recur and be identical with what it was before.* . . .

We all recognize as different great classes of our conscious states. Now we are seeing, now hearing; now reasoning, now willing; now recollecting, now expecting; now loving, now hating; and in a hundred other ways we know our minds to be alternately engaged. But all these are complex states. The aim of science is always to reduce complexity to simplicity; and in psychological science we have the celebrated "theory of *ideas*" which, admitting the great difference among each other of what may be called concrete conditions of mind, seeks to show how this is all the resultant effect of variations in the *combination* of certain simple elements of consciousness that always remain the same. These mental atoms or molecules are what Locke called "simple ideas." Some of Locke's successors made out that the only simple ideas were the sensations strictly so called. Which ideas the simple ones may be does not, however, now concern us. It is enough that certain philosophers have thought they could see under the dissolving-view-appearance of the mind elementary facts of *any* sort that remained unchanged amid the flow.

And the view of these philosophers has been called little into question, for our common experience seems at first sight to corroborate it entirely. Are not the sensations we get from the same object, for example, always the same? Does not the same piano-key, struck with the same force, make us hear in the same way? Does not the same grass give us the same feeling of green, the same sky the same feeling of blue, and do we not get the same olfactory sensation no matter how many times we put our nose to the same flask of cologne? It seems a piece of metaphysical sophistry to suggest that we do not; and yet a close attention to the matter shows that *there is no proof that the same bodily sensation is ever got by us twice.*

What is got twice is the same OBJECT. We hear the same *note* over and over again; we see the same *quality* of green, or smell the same objective perfume, or experience the same *species* of pain. The realities, concrete and abstract, physical and ideal, whose permanent existence we believe in, seem to be constantly coming up again before our thought, and lead us, in our carelessness, to suppose that our "ideas" of them are the same ideas. . . .

(3) Within each personal consciousness, thought is sensibly continuous

I can only define "continuous" as that which is without breach, crack, or division. I have already said that the breach from one mind to another is perhaps the greatest breach in nature. The only breaches that can well be conceived to occur within the limits of a single mind would either be *interruptions, time-*gaps during which the consciousness went out altogether to come into existence again at a later moment; or they would be breaks in the *quality,* or content, of the thought, so abrupt that the segment that followed had no connection whatever with the one that went before. The proposition that within each personal consciousness thought feels continuous, means two things:

1. That even where there is a time-gap the consciousness after it feels as if it belonged together with the consciousness before it, as another part of the same self;
2. That the changes from one moment to another in the quality of the consciousness are never absolutely abrupt. . . .

When Paul and Peter wake up in the same bed, and recognize that they have been asleep, each one of them mentally reaches back and makes connection with but *one* of the two streams of thought which were broken by the sleeping hours. As the current of an electrode buried in the ground unerringly finds its way to its own similarly buried mate, across no matter how much intervening earth; so Peter's present instantly finds out Peter's past, and never by mistake knits itself on to that of Paul. Paul's thought in turn is as little liable to go astray. The past thought of Peter is appropriated by the present Peter alone. He may have a *knowledge,* and a correct one too, of what Paul's last drowsy states of mind were as he sank into sleep, but it is an entirely different sort of knowledge from that which he has of his own last states. He *remembers* his own states, whilst he only *conceives* Paul's. Remembrance is like direct feeling; its object is suffused with a warmth and intimacy to which no object of mere conception ever attains. This quality of warmth and intimacy and immediacy is what Peter's *present* thought also possesses for itself. So sure as this present is me, is mine, it says, so sure is anything else that comes with the same warmth and intimacy and immediacy, me and mine. What the qualities called warmth and intimacy may in themselves be will have to be matter for future consideration. But whatever past feelings appear with those qualities must be admitted to receive the greeting of the present mental state, to be owned by it, and accepted as belonging together with it in a common self. This community of self is what the time-gap cannot break in twain, and is why a present thought, although not ignorant of the time-gap, can still regard itself as continuous with certain chosen portions of the past.

Consciousness, then, does not appear to itself chopped up in bits. Such words as "chain" or "train" do not describe it fitly as it presents itself in the first instance. It is nothing jointed; it flows. A "river" or a "stream" are the metaphors by which it is most naturally described. *In talking of it hereafter, let us call it the stream of thought, of consciousness, or of subjective life.* . . .

Substantive vs. transitive parts of thought

This difference in the rate of change lies at the basis of a difference of subjective states of which we ought immediately to speak. When the rate is slow we are aware of the object of our thought in a comparatively restful and stable way. When rapid, we are aware of a passage, a relation, a transition *from* it, or *between* it and something else. As we take, in fact, a general view of the wonderful stream of our consciousness, what strikes us first is this different pace of its parts. Like a bird's life, it seems to be made of an alternation of flights and perchings. The rhythm of language expresses this, where every thought is expressed in a sentence, and every sentence closed by a period. The resting-places are usually occupied by sensorial imaginations of some sort, whose peculiarity is that they can be held before the mind for an indefinite time, and contemplated without changing; the places of flight are filled with thoughts of relations, static or dynamic, that for the most part obtain between the matters contemplated in the periods of comparative rest.

Let us call the resting-places the "*substantive parts,*" and the *places of flight* the "*transitive parts,*" *of the stream of thought.* It then appears that the main end of our thinking is at all times the attainment of some other substantive part than the one from which we have just been dislodged. And we may say that the main use of the transitive parts is to lead us from one substantive conclusion to another.

Now it is very difficult, introspectively, to see the transitive parts for what they really are. If they are but flights to a conclusion, stopping them to look at them before the conclusion is reached is really annihilating them. Whilst if we wait till the conclusion *be* reached, it so exceeds them in vigor and stability that it quite eclipses and swallows them up in its glare. Let anyone try to cut a thought across in the middle and get a look at its section, and he will see how difficult the introspective observation of the transitive tracts is. The rush of the thought is so headlong that it almost always brings us up at the conclusion before we can arrest it. Or if our purpose is nimble enough and we do arrest it, it ceases forthwith to be itself. As a snowflake crystal caught in the warm hand is no longer a crystal but a drop, so, instead of catching the feeling of relation moving to its term, we find we have caught some substantive thing, usually the last word we were pronouncing, statically taken, and with its function, tendency, and particular meaning in the sentence quite evaporated. The attempt at introspective analysis in these cases is in fact like seizing a spinning top to catch its motion, or trying to turn up the gas quickly enough to see how the darkness looks.

But . . . if there be such things as feelings at all, *then so surely as relations between objects exist in rerum naturâ, so surely, and more surely, do feelings exist to which these relations are known.* There is not a conjunction or a preposition, and hardly an adverbial phrase, syntactic form, or inflection of voice, in human speech, that does not express some shading or other of relation which we at some moment actually feel to exist between the larger objects of our thought. If we speak objectively, it is the real relations that appear revealed; if we speak subjectively, it is the stream of consciousness that matches each of them by an inward coloring of its own. In either case the relations are numberless, and no existing language is capable of doing justice to all their shades.

We ought to say a feeling of *and*, a feeling of *if*, a feeling of *but*, and a feeling of *by*, quite as readily as we say a feeling of *blue* or a feeling of *cold*. Yet we do not: so inveterate has our habit become of recognizing the existence of the substantive parts alone, that language almost refuses to lend itself to any other use. . . .

Feelings of tendency

Suppose three successive persons say to us: "Wait!" "Hark!" "Look!" Our consciousness is thrown into three quite different attitudes of expectancy, although no definite object is before it in any one of the three cases. Leaving out different actual bodily attitudes, and leaving out the reverberating images of the three words, which are of course diverse, probably no one will deny the existence of a residual conscious affection, a sense of the direction from which an impression is about to come, although no positive impression is yet there. Meanwhile we have no names for the psychoses in question but the names hark, look, and wait.

Suppose we try to recall a forgotten name. The state of our consciousness is peculiar. There is a gap therein; but no mere gap. It is a gap that is intensely active. A sort of wraith of the name is in it, beckoning us in a given direction, making us at moments tingle with the sense of our closeness, and then letting us sink back without the longed-for term. If wrong names are proposed to us, this singularly definite gap acts immediately so as to negate them. They do not fit into its mould. And the gap of one word does not feel like the gap of another, all empty of content as both might seem necessarily to be when described as gaps. When I vainly try to recall the name of Spalding, my consciousness is far removed from what it is when I vainly try to recall the name of Bowles. Here some ingenious persons will say: "How *can* the two consciousnesses be different when the terms which might make them different are not there? All that is there, so long as the effort to recall is vain, is the bare effort itself. How should that differ in the two cases? You are making it seem to differ by prematurely filling it out with the different names, although these, by the hypothesis, have not yet come. Stick to the two efforts as they are, without naming them after facts not yet existent, and you'll be quite unable to designate any point in which they differ." Designate, truly enough. We can only designate the difference by borrowing the names of objects not yet in the mind. Which is to say that our psychological vocabulary is wholly inadequate to name the differences that exist, even such strong differences as these. But namelessness is compatible with existence. There are innumerable consciousnesses of emptiness, no one of which taken in itself has a name, but all different from each other. The ordinary way is to assume that they are all emptinesses of consciousness, and so the same state. But the feeling of an absence is wholly other than the absence of a feeling. It is an intense feeling. The rhythm of a lost word may be there without a sound to clothe it; or the evanescent sense of something which is the initial vowel or consonant may mock us fitfully, without growing more distinct. Every one must know the tantalizing effect of the blank rhythm of some forgotten verse, restlessly dancing in one's mind, striving to be filled out with words. . . .

The truth is that large tracts of human speech are nothing but *signs of direction* in thought, of which direction we nevertheless have an acutely discriminative sense, though no definite sensorial image plays any part in it whatsoever. . . .

The Empirical Self

The Empirical Self of each of us is all that he is tempted to call by the name of *me*. But it is clear that between what a man calls *me* and what he simply calls *mine* the line is difficult to draw. We feel and act about certain things that are ours very much as we feel and act about ourselves. Our fame, our children, the work of our hands, may be as dear to us as our bodies are, and arouse the same feelings and the same acts of reprisal if attacked. And our bodies themselves, are they simply ours, or are they *us*? Certainly men have been ready to disown their very bodies and to regard them as mere vestures, or even as prisons of clay from which they should some day be glad to escape.

We see then that we are dealing with a fluctuating material. The same object being sometimes treated as a part of me, at other times as simply mine, and then again as if I had nothing to do with it at all. *In its widest possible sense,* however, *a man's Self is the sum total of all that he* CAN *call his,* not only his body and his psychic powers, but his clothes and his house, his wife and children, his ancestors and friends, his reputation and works, his lands and horses, and yacht and bank-account. All these things give him the same emotions. If they wax and prosper, he feels triumphant; if they dwindle and die away, he feels cast down—not necessarily in the same degree for each thing, but in much the same way for all. . . .

The material self

(a) The body is the innermost part of *the material Self* in each of us; and certain parts of the body seem more intimately ours than the rest. The clothes come next. The old saying that the human person is composed of three parts—soul, body and clothes—is more than a joke. We so appropriate our clothes and identify ourselves with them that there are few of us who, if asked to choose between having a beautiful body clad in raiment perpetually shabby and unclean, and having an ugly and blemished form always spotlessly attired, would not hesitate a moment before making a decisive reply. Next, our immediate family is a part of ourselves. Our father and mother, our wife and babies, are bone of our bone and flesh of our flesh. When they die, a part of our very selves is gone. If they do anything wrong, it is our shame. If they are insulted, our anger flashes forth as readily as if we stood in their place. Our home comes next. Its scenes are part of our life; its aspects awaken the tenderest feelings of affection; and we do not easily forgive the stranger who, in visiting it, finds fault with its arrangements or treats it with contempt. All these different things are the objects of instinctive preferences coupled with the most important practical interests of life. We all have a blind impulse to watch over our body, to deck it with clothing of an ornamental sort, to cherish parents, wife and babies, and to find for ourselves a home of our own which we may live in and "improve."

An equally instinctive impulse drives us to collect property; and the collections thus made become, with different degrees of intimacy, parts of our empirical selves. The parts of our wealth most intimately ours are those which are saturated with our labor. There are few men who would not feel personally annihilated if a life-long construction of their hands or brains—say an entomological collection or an extensive work in manuscript—were suddenly swept away. The miser feels similarly towards his gold, and although it is true that a part of our depression at the loss of possessions is due to our feeling that we must now go without certain goods that we expected the possessions to bring in their train, yet in every case there remains, over and above this, a sense of the shrinkage of our personality, a partial conversion of ourselves to nothingness, which is a psychological phenomenon by itself. We are all at once assimilated to the tramps and poor devils whom we so despise, and at the same time removed farther than ever away from the happy sons of earth who lord it over land and sea and men in the full-blown lustihood that wealth and power can give, and before whom, stiffen ourselves as we will by appealing to anti-snobbish first principles, we cannot escape an emotion, open or sneaking, of respect and dread.

The social self

(*b*) *A man's Social Self* is the recognition which he gets from his mates. We are not only gregarious animals, liking to be in sight of our fellows, but we have an innate propensity to get ourselves noticed, and noticed favorably, by our kind. No more fiendish punishment could be devised, were such a thing physically possible, than that one should be turned loose in society and remain absolutely unnoticed by all the members thereof. If no one turned round when we entered, answered when we spoke, or minded what we did, but if every person we met "cut us dead," and acted as if we were non-existing things, a kind of rage and impotent despair would ere long well up in us, from which the cruellest bodily tortures would be a relief; for these would make us feel that, however bad might be our plight, we had not sunk to such a depth as to be unworthy of attention at all.

Properly speaking, *a man has as many social selves as there are individuals who recognize him* and carry an image of him in their mind. To wound any one of these his images is to wound him. But as the individuals who carry the images fall naturally into classes, we may practically say that he has as many different social selves as there are distinct *groups* of persons about whose opinion he cares. He generally shows a different side of himself to each of these different groups. Many a youth who is demure enough before his parents and teachers, swears and swaggers like a pirate among his "tough" young friends. We do not show ourselves to our children as to our club-companions, to our customers as to the laborers we employ, to our own masters and employers as to our intimate friends. From this there results what practically is a division of the man into several selves; and this may be a discordant splitting, as where one is afraid to let one set of his acquaintances know him as he is elsewhere; or it may be a perfectly harmonious division of labor, as where one tender to his children is stern to the soldiers or prisoners under his command.

The most peculiar social self which one is apt to have is in the mind of the person one is in love with. The good or bad fortunes of this self cause the most intense elation and dejection—unreasonable enough as measured by every other standard than that of the organic feeling of the individual. To his own consciousness he *is* not, so long as this particular social self fails to get recognition, and when it is recognized his contentment passes all bounds.

A man's *fame*, good or bad, and his *honor* or dishonor, are names for one of his social selves. The particular social self of a man called his honor is usually the result of one of those splittings of which we have spoken. It is his image in the eyes of his own "set," which exalts or condemns him as he conforms or not to certain requirements that may not be made of one in another walk of life. Thus a layman may abandon a city infected with cholera; but a priest or a doctor would think such an act incompatible with his honor. A soldier's honor requires him to fight or to die under circumstances where another man can apologize or run away with no stain upon his social self. A judge, a statesman, are in like manner debarred by the honor of their cloth from entering into pecuniary relations perfectly honorable to persons in private life. Nothing is commoner than to hear people discriminate between their different selves of this sort: "As a man I pity you, but as an official I must show you no mercy; as a politician I regard him as an ally, but as a moralist I loathe him"; etc., etc. What may be called "club-opinion" is one of the very strongest forces in life. The thief must not steal from other thieves; the gambler must pay his gambling-debts, though he pay no other debts in the world. The code of honor of fashionable society has throughout history been full of permissions as well as of vetoes, the only reason for following either of which is that so we best serve one of our social selves. You must not lie in general, but you may lie as much as you please if asked about your relations with a lady; you must accept a challenge from an equal, but if challenged by an inferior you may laugh him to scorn: these are examples of what is meant.

The spiritual self

(c) By the *Spiritual Self*, so far as it belongs to the Empirical Me, *I mean a man's inner or subjective being,* his psychic faculties or dispositions, taken concretely; not the bare principle of personal Unity, or "pure" Ego, which remains still to be discussed. These psychic dispositions are the most enduring and intimate part of the self, that which we most verily seem to be. We take a purer self-satisfaction when we think of our ability to argue and discriminate, of our moral sensibility and conscience, of our indomitable will, than when we survey any of our other possessions. Only when these are altered is a man said to be alienated from himself.

Now this spiritual self may be considered in various ways. We may divide it into faculties, as just instanced, isolating them one from another and identifying ourselves with either in turn. This is an *abstract* way of dealing with consciousness, in which, as it actually presents itself, a plurality of such faculties are always to be simultaneously found; or we may insist on a concrete view, and then the spiritual self in us will be either the entire stream of our personal consciousness, or the present "segment" or "section" of that stream, according as we take a broader or a narrower view—both the stream and the section being concrete existences in time, and each being a unity after its own peculiar kind. But whether we take it abstractly or concretely, our considering the spiritual self at all is a reflective process, is the result of our abandoning the outward-looking point of view, and of our having become able to think of subjectivity as such, *to think ourselves as thinkers.*

A Denial of Free Will*

BERTRAND RUSSELL

Motivation of the belief

The problem of free will is so intimately bound up with the analysis of causation that, old as it is, we need not despair of obtaining new light on it by the help of new views on the notion of cause. The free-will problem has, at one time or another, stirred men's passions profoundly, and the fear that the will might not be free has been to some men a source of great unhappiness. I believe that, under the influence of a cool analysis, the doubtful questions involved will be found to have no such emotional importance as is sometimes thought, since the disagreeable consequences supposed to flow from a denial of free will do not flow from this denial in any form in which there is reason to make it. It is not, however, on this account chiefly that I wish to discuss this problem, but rather because it affords a good example of the clarifying effect of analysis and of the interminable controversies which may result from its neglect.

Let us first try to discover what it is we really desire when we desire free will. Some of our reasons for desiring free will are profound, some trivial. To begin with the former: we do not wish to feel ourselves in the hands of fate, so that, however much we may desire to will one thing, we may nevertheless be compelled by an outside force to will another. We do not wish to think that, however much we may desire to act well, heredity and surroundings may force us into acting ill. We wish to feel that, in cases of doubt, our choice is momentous and lies within our power. Besides these desires, which are worthy of all respect, we have, however, others not so respectable, which equally make us desire free will. We do not like to think that other people, if they knew enough, could predict our actions, though

*From Bertrand Russell (1872—), *Our Knowledge of the External World* (W. W. Norton, 1929), pp. 247–256. Reprinted by courtesy of the publisher.

we know that we can often predict those of other people, especially if they are elderly. Much as we esteem the old gentleman who is our neighbor in the country, we know that when grouse are mentioned he will tell the story of the grouse in the gun-room. But we ourselves are not so mechanical: we never tell an anecdote to the same person twice, or even once unless he is sure to enjoy it; although we once met (say) Bismarck, we are quite capable of hearing him mentioned without relating the occasion when we met him. In this sense, everybody thinks that he himself has free will, though he knows that no one else has. The desire for this kind of free will seems to be no better than a form of vanity. I do not believe that this desire can be gratified with any certainty; but the other, more respectable desires are, I believe, not inconsistent with any tenable form of determinism.

We have thus two questions to consider: (1) Are human actions theoretically predictable from a sufficient number of antecedents? (2) Are human actions subject to an external compulsion? The two questions, as I shall try to show, are entirely distinct, and we may answer the first in the affirmative without therefore being forced to give an affirmative answer to the second.

(1) Are human actions theoretically predictable from a sufficient number of antecedents?

Let us first endeavor to give precision to this question. We may state the question thus: Is there some constant relation between an act and a certain number of earlier events, such that, when the earlier events are given, only one act, or at most only acts with some well-marked character, can have this relation to the earlier events? If this is the case, then, as soon as the earlier events are known, it is theoretically possible to predict either the precise act, or at least the character necessary to its fulfilling the constant relation.

To this question, a negative answer has been given by Bergson, in a form which calls in question the general applicability of the law of causation. He maintains that every event, and more particularly every mental event, embodies so much of the past that it could not possibly have occurred at any earlier time, and is therefore necessarily quite different from all previous and subsequent events. If, for example, I read a certain poem many times, my experience on each occasion is modified by the previous readings, and my emotions are never repeated exactly. The principle of causation, according to him, asserts that the same cause, if repeated, will produce the same effect. But owing to memory, he contends, this principle does not apply to mental events. What is apparently the same cause, if repeated, is modified by the mere fact of repetition, and cannot produce the same effect. He infers that every mental event is a genuine novelty, not predictable from the past, because the past contains nothing exactly like it by which we could imagine it. And on this ground he regards the freedom of the will as unassailable.

Bergson's contention has undoubtedly a great deal of truth, and I have no wish to deny its importance. But I do not think its consequences are quite what he believes them to be. It is not necessary for the determinist to maintain that he can foresee the whole particularity of the act which will be performed. If he could foresee that A was going to murder B, his foresight would not be invalidated by the fact that he could not know all the infinite complexity of A's state of mind in committing the murder, nor whether the murder was to be performed with a knife or with a revolver. If the *kind* of act which will be performed can be foreseen within narrow limits, it is of little practical interest that there are fine shades which cannot be foreseen. No doubt every time the story of the grouse in the gun-room is told, there will be slight differences due to increasing habitualness, but they do not invalidate the prediction that the story will be told. And there is nothing in Bergson's argument to show that we can never predict what *kind* of act will be performed.

Again, his statement of the law of causation is inadequate. The law does not state merely that, if the *same* cause is repeated, the *same* effect will result. It states rather that there is a constant relation between causes of certain kinds and effects of certain kinds. For example, if a body falls freely, there is a constant relation between the height through which it falls and the time it takes in falling. It is not necessary to have a body fall through the *same* height which has been previously observed, in order to be able to foretell the length of time occupied in falling. If this were necessary, no prediction would be possible, since it would be impossible to make the height exactly the same on two occasions. Similarly, the attraction which the sun will exert on the earth is not only known at distances for which it has been observed, but at all distances, because it is known to vary as the inverse square of the distance. In fact, what is found to be repeated is always the *relation* of cause and effect, not the cause itself; all that is necessary as regards the cause is that it should be of the same *kind* (in the relevant respect) as earlier causes whose effects have been observed.

Another respect in which Bergson's statement of causation is inadequate is in its assumption that the cause must be *one* event, whereas it may be two or more events, or even some continuous process. The substantive question at issue is whether mental events are determined by the past. Now in such a case as the repeated reading of a poem, it is obvious that our feelings in reading the poem are most emphatically dependent upon the past, but not upon one single event in the past. All our previous readings of the poem must be included in the cause. But we easily perceive a certain law according to which the effect varies as the previous readings increase in number, and in fact Bergson himself tacitly assumes such a law. We decide at last not to read the poem again, because we know that this time the effect would be boredom. We may not know all the niceties and shades of the boredom we should feel, but we know enough to guide our decision, and the prophecy of boredom is none the less true for being more or less general. Thus the kinds of cases upon which Bergson relies are insufficient to show the impossibility of prediction in the only sense in which prediction has practical or emotional interest. We may therefore leave the consideration of his arguments and address ourselves to the problem directly.

The law of causation, according to which later events can theoretically be predicted by means of earlier events, has often been held to be *a priori,* a necessity of thought, a category without which science would be impossible. These claims seem to me excessive. In certain directions the law has been verified empirically, and in other directions there is no positive evidence against it. But science can use it where it has been found to be true, without being forced into any assumption as to its truth in other fields. We cannot, therefore, feel any *a priori* certainty that causation must apply to human volitions.

The question how far human volitions are subject to causal laws is a purely empirical one. Empirically it seems plain that the great majority of our volitions have causes, but it cannot, on this account, be held necessarily certain that all have causes. There are, however, precisely the same kinds of reasons for regarding it as probable that they all have causes as there are in the case of physical events.

We may suppose—though this is doubtful—that there are laws of correlation of the mental and the physical, in virtue of which, given the state of all the matter in the world, and therefore of all the brains and living organisms, the state of all the minds in the world could be inferred, while conversely the state of all the matter in the world could be inferred if the state of all the minds were given. It is obvious that there is *some* degree of correlation between brain and mind, and it is impossible to say how complete it may be. This, however, is not the point which I wish to elicit. What I wish to urge is that, even if we admit the most extreme claims of determinism and of correlation of mind and brain, still the consequences inimical to what is worth preserving in free will do not follow. The belief that they follow results, I think, entirely from the assimilation of causes to volitions, and from the notion that causes *compel* their effects in some sense analogous to that in which a human authority can compel a man to do what he would rather not do. This assimilation, as soon as the true nature of scientific causal laws is realized, is seen to be a sheer mistake. But this brings us to the second of the two questions which we raised in regard to free will, namely, whether, assuming determinism, our actions can be in any proper sense regarded as compelled by outside forces.

(2) *Are human actions subject to an external compulsion?*

We have, in deliberation, a subjective sense of freedom, which is sometimes alleged against the view that volitions have causes. This sense of freedom, however, is only a sense that we can choose which we please of a number of alternatives: it does not show us that there is no causal connection between what we please to choose and our previous history. The supposed inconsistency of these two springs from the habit of conceiving causes as analogous to volitions—a habit which often survives unconsciously in those who intend to conceive causes in a more scientific manner. If a cause is analogous to a volition, outside causes will be analogous to an alien will, and acts predictable from outside causes will be subject to compulsion. But this view of cause is one to which science lends no countenance.

Causes, we have seen, do not *compel* their effects, any more than effects *compel* their causes. There is a mutual relation, so that either can be inferred from the other. When the geologist infers the past state of the earth from its present state, we should not say that the present state *compels* the past state to have been what it was; yet it renders it necessary as a consequence of the data, in the only sense in which effects are rendered necessary by their causes. The difference which we *feel*, in this respect, between causes and effects is a mere confusion due to the fact that we remember past events but do not happen to have memory of the future.

The apparent indeterminateness of the future, upon which some advocates of free will rely, is merely a result of our ignorance. It is plain that no desirable kind of free will can be dependent simply upon our ignorance; for if that were the case, animals would be more free than men, and savages than civilized people. Free will in any valuable sense must be compatible with the fullest knowledge. Now, quite apart from any assumption as to causality, it is obvious that complete knowledge would embrace the future as well as the past. Our knowledge of the past is not wholly based upon causal inferences, but is partly derived from memory. It is a mere accident that we have no memory of the future. We might—as in the pretended vision of seers—see future events immediately, in the way in which we see past events. They certainly will be what they will be, and are in this sense just as determined as the past. If we saw future events in the same immediate way in which we see past events, what kind of free will would still be possible? Such a kind would be wholly independent of determinism: it could not be contrary to even the most entirely universal reign of causality. And such a kind must contain whatever is worth having in free will, since it is impossible to believe that mere ignorance can be the essential condition of any good thing. Let us therefore imagine a set of beings who know the whole future with absolute certainty, and let us ask ourselves whether they could have anything that we should call free will.

Such beings as we are imagining would not have to wait for the event in order to know what decision they were going to adopt on some future occasion. They would know now what their volitions were going to be. But would they have any reason to regret this knowledge? Surely not, unless the foreseen volitions were in themselves regrettable. And it is less likely that the foreseen volitions would be regrettable if the steps which would lead to them were also foreseen. It is difficult not to suppose that what is foreseen is fated, and must happen however much it may be dreaded. But human actions are the outcome of desire, and no foreseeing can be true unless it takes account of desire. A foreseen volition will have to be one which does not become odious through being foreseen. The beings we are imagining would easily come to know the causal connections of volitions, and therefore their volitions would be better calculated to satisfy their desires than ours are. Since volitions are the outcome of desires, a prevision of volitions contrary to desires could not be a true one. It must be remembered that the supposed prevision would not create the future any more than memory creates the past. We do not think we were necessarily not free in the past, merely because we can now remember our past volitions. Similarly, we might be free in the future, even if we could now see what our future volitions were going to be. Freedom, in short, in any valuable sense, demands only that our volitions shall be, as they are, the result of our own desires, not of an outside force compelling us to will what we would rather not will. Everything else is confusion of thought, due to the feeling that knowledge *compels* the happening of what it knows when this is future, though it is at once obvious that knowledge has no such power in regard to the past. Free will, therefore, is true in the only form which is important; and the desire for other forms is a mere effect of insufficient analysis.

The Belief in Free Will*

WILLIAM JAMES

Presuppositions of method

The arguments I am about to urge all proceed on two suppositions: first, when we make theories about the world and discuss them with one another, we do so in order to attain a conception of things which shall give us subjective satisfaction; and, second, if there be two conceptions, and the one seems to us, on the whole, more rational than the other, we are entitled to suppose that the more rational one is the truer of the two. I hope that you are all willing to make these suppositions with me; for I am afraid that if there be any of you here who are not, they will find little edification in the rest of what I have to say. I cannot stop to argue the point; but I myself believe that all the magnificent achievements of mathematical and physical science—our doctrines of evolution, of uniformity of law, and the rest—proceed from our indomitable desire to cast the world into a more rational shape in our minds than the shape into which it is thrown there by the crude order of our experience.

The world has shown itself, to a great extent, plastic to this demand of ours for rationality. How much farther it will show itself plastic no one can say. Our only means of finding out is to try; and I, for one, feel as free to try conceptions of moral as of mechanical or of logical rationality. If a certain formula for expressing the nature of the world violates my moral demand, I shall feel as free to throw it overboard, or at least to doubt it, as if it disappointed my demand for uniformity of sequence, for example; the one demand being, so far as I can see, quite as subjective and emotional as the

---

* From William James, "The Dilemma of Determinism" (a lecture given in 1884). Published in *The Will to Believe, and Other Essays in Popular Philosophy* (Longmans, Green, 1896). Reprinted by courtesy of the publisher.

other is. The principle of causality, for example,—what is it but a postulate, an empty name covering simply a demand that the sequence of events shall some day manifest a deeper kind of belonging of one thing with another than the mere arbitrary juxtaposition which now phenomenally appears? It is as much an altar to an unknown god as the one that Saint Paul found at Athens. All our scientific and philosophic ideals are altars to unknown gods. Uniformity is as much so as is free-will. If this be admitted, we can debate on even terms. But if any one pretends that while freedom and variety are, in the first instance, subjective demands, necessity and uniformity are something altogether different, I do not see how we can debate at all. . . .

The idea of chance[1]

The stronghold of the deterministic sentiment is the antipathy to the idea of chance. As soon as we begin to talk indeterminism to our friends, we find a number of them shaking their heads. This notion of alternative possibility, they say, this admission that any one of several things may come to pass, is, after all, only a roundabout name for chance; and chance is something the notion of which no sane mind can for an instant tolerate in the world. What is it, they ask, but barefaced crazy unreason, the negation of intelligibility and law? And if the slightest particle of it exist anywhere, what is to prevent the whole fabric from falling together, the stars from going out, and chaos from recommencing her topsy-turvy reign?

Remarks of this sort about chance will put an end to discussion as quickly as anything one can find. I have already told you that "chance" was a word I wished to keep and use. Let us then examine exactly what it means, and see whether it ought to be such a terrible bugbear to us. I fancy that squeezing the thistle boldly will rob it of its sting.

The sting of the word "chance" seems to lie in the assumption that it means something positive, and that if anything happens by chance, it must needs be something of an intrinsically irrational and preposterous sort. Now, chance means nothing of the kind. It is a purely negative and relative term, giving us no information about that of which it is predicated, except that it happens to be

---

[1] The reader is advised to compare James' use of the word "chance" with the present book's definition of "spontaneity" (p. 123).

disconnected with something else—not controlled, secured, or necessitated by other things in advance of its own actual presence. As this point is the most subtle one of the whole lecture, and at the same time the point on which all the rest hinges, I beg you to pay particular attention to it. What I say is that it tells us nothing about what a thing may be in itself to call it "chance." It may be a bad thing, it may be a good thing. It may be lucidity, transparency, fitness incarnate, matching the whole system of other things, when it has once befallen, in an unimaginably perfect way. All you mean by calling it "chance" is that this is not guaranteed, that it may also fall out otherwise. For the system of other things has no positive hold on the chance-thing. Its origin is in a certain fashion negative: it escapes, and says, Hands off! coming, when it comes, as a free gift, or not at all.

This negativeness, however, and this opacity of the chance-thing when thus considered *ab extra,* or from the point of view of previous things or distant things, do not preclude its having any amount of positiveness and luminosity from within, and at its own place and moment. All that its chance-character asserts about it is that there is something in it really of its own, something that is not the unconditional property of the whole. If the whole wants this property, the whole must wait till it can get it, if it be a matter of chance. That the universe may actually be a sort of joint-stock society of this sort, in which the sharers have both limited liabilities and limited powers, is of course a simple and conceivable notion.

Nevertheless, many persons talk as if the minutest dose of disconnectedness of one part with another, the smallest modicum of independence, the faintest tremor of ambiguity about the future, for example, would ruin everything, and turn this goodly universe into a sort of insane sand-heap or nulliverse, no universe at all. Since future human volitions are as a matter of fact the only ambiguous things we are tempted to believe in, let us stop for a moment to make ourselves sure whether their independent and accidental character need be fraught with such direful consequences to the universe as these.

The open future

What is meant by saying that my choice of which way to walk home after the lecture is ambiguous and matter of chance as far as the present moment is concerned? It means that both Divinity Avenue and Oxford Street are called; but that only one, and that one *either* one, shall be chosen. Now, I ask you seriously to suppose that this ambiguity of my choice is real; and then to make the impossible hypothesis that the choice is made twice over, and each time falls on a different street. In other words, imagine that I first walk through Divinity Avenue, and then imagine that the powers governing the universe annihilate ten minutes of time with all that it contained, and set me back at the door of this hall just as I was before the choice was made. Imagine then that, everything else being the same, I now make a different choice and traverse Oxford Street. You, as passive spectators, look on and see the two alternative universes—one of them with me walking through Divinity Avenue in it, the other with the same me walking through Oxford Street. Now, if you are determinists you believe one of these universes to have been from eternity impossible: you believe it to have been impossible because of the intrinsic irrationality or accidentality somewhere involved in it. But looking outwardly at these universes, can you say which is the impossible and accidental one, and which the rational and necessary one? I doubt if the most ironclad determinist among you could have the slightest glimmer of light on this point. In other words, either universe *after the fact* and once there would, to our means of observation and understanding, appear just as rational as the other. There would be absolutely no criterion by which we might judge one necessary and the other matter of chance. Suppose now we relieve the gods of their hypothetical task and assume my choice, once made, to be made forever. I go through Divinity Avenue for good and all. If, as good determinists, you now begin to affirm, what all good determinists punctually do affirm, that in the nature of things I *couldn't* have gone through Oxford Street—had I done so it would have been chance, irrationality, insanity, a horrid gap in nature,—I simply call your attention to this, that your affirmation is what the Germans call a *Machtspruch*, a mere conception fulminated as a dogma and based on no insight into details. Before my choice, either street seemed as natural to you as to me. Had I happened to take Oxford Street, Divinity Avenue would have figured in your philosophy as the gap in nature; and you would have so proclaimed it with the best deterministic conscience in the world.

But what a hollow outcry, then, is this against a chance which, if it were present to us, we could by no character whatever distinguish from a rational necessity! I have taken the most trivial of examples, but no possible example could lead to any different result. For what are the alternatives which, in point of fact, offer themselves to human volition? What are those futures that now seem matters of chance? Are they not one and all like the Divinity Avenue and Oxford Street of our example? Are they not all of them *kinds* of things already here and based in the existing frame of nature? Is anyone ever tempted to produce an *absolute* accident, something utterly irrelevant to the rest of the world? Do not all the motives that assail us, all the futures that offer themselves to our choice, spring equally from the soil of the past; and would not either one of them, whether realized through chance or through necessity, the moment it was realized, seem to us to fit that past, and in the completest and most continuous manner to interdigitate with the phenomena already there?

A favorite argument against free-will[2] is that if it be true, a man's murderer may as probably be his best friend as his worst enemy, a mother be as likely to strangle as to suckle her first-born, and all of us be as ready to jump from fourth-story windows as to go out of front doors, etc. Users of this argument should properly be excluded from debate till they learn what the real question is. "Free-will" does not say that everything that is physically conceivable is also morally possible. It merely says that of alternatives that really *tempt* our will more than one is really possible. Of course, the alternatives that do thus tempt our will are vastly fewer than the physical possibilities we can coldly fancy. Persons really tempted often do murder their best friends, mothers do strangle their first-born, people do jump out of fourth-story windows, etc. . . .

And this at last brings us within sight of our subject. We have seen what determinism means: we have seen that indeterminism is rightly described as meaning chance; and we have seen that chance, the very name of which we are urged to shrink from as from a metaphysical pestilence, means only the negative fact that no part of the world, however big, can claim to control absolutely the destinies of the whole. . . .

[2] James published this paragraph as a footnote.

The character of a deterministic world

I wish first of all to show you just what the notion that this is a deterministic world implies. The implications I call your attention to are all bound up with the fact that it is a world in which we constantly have to make what I shall, with your permission, call judgments of regret. Hardly an hour passes in which we do not wish that something might be otherwise. . . .

Now, it is undeniable that most of these regrets are foolish. . . . Even from the point of view of our own ends, we should probably make a botch of remodelling the universe. How much more then from the point of view of ends we cannot see! Wise men therefore regret as little as they can. But still some regrets are pretty obstinate and hard to stifle—regrets for acts of wanton cruelty or treachery, for example, whether performed by others or by ourselves. Hardly anyone can remain *entirely* optimistic after reading the confession of the murderer at Brockton the other day: how, to get rid of the wife whose continued existence bored him, he inveigled her into a desert spot, shot her four times, and then, as she lay on the ground and said to him, "You didn't do it on purpose, did you, dear?" replied, "No, I didn't do it on purpose," as he raised a rock and smashed her skull. Such an occurrence, with the mild sentence and self-satisfaction of the prisoner, is a field for a crop of regrets, which one need not take up in detail. We feel that, although a perfect mechanical fit to the rest of the universe, it is a bad moral fit, and that something else would really have been better in its place.

But for the deterministic philosophy the murder, the sentence, and the prisoner's optimism were all necessary from eternity; and nothing else for a moment had a ghost of a chance of being put into their place. To admit such a chance, the determinists tell us, would be to make a suicide of reason; so we must steel our hearts against the thought. And here our plot thickens, for we see the first of those difficult implications of determinism and monism which it is my purpose to make you feel. If this Brockton murder was called for by the rest of the universe, if it had to come at its preappointed hour, and if nothing else would have been consistent with the sense of the whole, what are we to think of the universe? Are we stubbornly to stick to our judgment of regret, and say, though it *couldn't* be, yet it *would* have been a better universe with something different from this Brockton murder in it? That, of course, seems the natural and spontaneous thing for us to do; and yet it is nothing short of deliberately espousing a kind of pessimism. The judgment of regret calls the murder bad. Calling a thing bad means, if it mean anything at all, that the thing ought not to be, that something else ought to be in its stead. Determinism, in denying that anything else can be in its stead, virtually defines the universe as a place in which what ought to be is impossible—in other words, as an organism whose constitution is afflicted with an incurable taint, an irremediable flaw. The pessimism of a Schopenhauer says no more than this—that the murder is a symptom; and that it is a vicious symptom because it belongs to a vicious whole, which can express its nature no otherwise than by bringing forth just such a symptom as that at this particular spot. Regret for the murder must transform itself, if we are determinists and wise, into a larger regret. It is absurd to regret the murder alone. Other things being what they are, *it* could not be different. What we should regret is that whole frame of things of which the murder is one member. I see no escape whatever from this pessimistic conclusion, if, being determinists, our judgment of regret is to be allowed to stand at all....

Solution by action

The only escape is by the practical way. And since I have mentioned the nowadays much-reviled name of Carlyle, let me mention it once more, and say it is the way of his teaching. No matter for Carlyle's life, no matter for a great deal of his writing. What was the most important thing he said to us? He said: "Hang your sensibilities! Stop your snivelling complaints, and your equally snivelling raptures! Leave off your general emotional tomfoolery and get to WORK like men!" But this means a complete rupture with the subjectivist philosophy of things. It says conduct, and not sensibility, is the ultimate fact for our recognition. With the vision of certain works to be done, of certain outward changes to be wrought or resisted, it says our intellectual horizon terminates. No matter how we succeed in doing these outward duties, whether gladly and spontaneously, or heavily and unwillingly, do then we somehow must; for the leaving of them undone is perdition. No matter how we feel; if we are only faithful in the outward act and refuse to do wrong, the world will in so far be safe, and we quit of our debt toward it. Take, then, the yoke upon our shoulders; bend our neck beneath the heavy legality of its weight; regard something else than our feeling as our limit, our master, and our law; be willing to live and die in its service—and, at a stroke, we have passed from the subjective into the objective philosophy of things, much as one awakens from some feverish dream, full of bad lights and noises, to find one's self bathed in the sacred coolness and quiet of the air of the night. . . .

A world of real possibilities

But this brings us right back, after such a long detour, to the question of indeterminism and to the conclusion of all I came here to say tonight. For the only consistent way of representing a pluralism and a world whose parts may affect one another through their conduct being either good or bad is the indeterministic way. What interest, zest, or excitement can there be in achieving the right way, unless we are enabled to feel that the wrong way is also a possible and a natural way—nay, more, a menacing and an imminent way? And what sense can there be in condemning ourselves for taking the wrong way, unless we need have done nothing of the sort, unless the right way was open to us as well? I cannot understand the willingness to act, no matter how we feel, without the belief that acts are really good and bad. I cannot understand the belief that an act is bad, without regret at its happening. I cannot understand regret without the admission of real, genuine possibilities in the world. Only *then* is it other than a mockery to feel, after we have failed to do our best, that an irreparable opportunity is gone from the universe, the loss of which it must forever after mourn.

*Private Reflections**

I think that yesterday was a crisis in my life. I finished the first part of Renouvier's second *Essais* and see no reason why his definition of Free Will—"the sustaining of a thought *because I choose to*

* From *The Letters of William James,* Vol. I (Atlantic Monthly Press, 1920), pp. 147–148. Reprinted by courtesy of the publisher. An extract from James' diary, written at the age of twenty-seven after a period of illness and pessimistic doubt. The writing by Charles Renouvier (1815–1903) which so deeply influenced James' philosophy was the second part (Volumes III and IV) of his *Essais de critique générale.*

when I might have other thoughts"—need be the definition of an illusion. At any rate, I will assume for the present—until next year—that it is no illusion. My first act of free will shall be to believe in free will. For the remainder of the year, I will abstain from the mere speculation and contemplative *Grüblei* [grubbing among subtleties] in which my nature takes most delight, and voluntarily cultivate the feeling of moral freedom, by reading books favorable to it, as well as by acting. After the first of January, my callow skin being somewhat fledged, I may perhaps return to metaphysical study and skepticism without danger to my powers of action. For the present then remember: care little for speculation; much for the *form* of my action; recollect that only when habits of order are formed can we advance to really interesting fields of action—and consequently accumulate grain on grain of willful choice like a very miser; never forgetting how one link dropped undoes an indefinite number. . . . Hitherto, when I have felt like taking a free initiative, like daring to act originally, without carefully waiting for contemplation of the external world to determine all for me, suicide seemed the most manly form to put my daring into; now, I will go a step further with my will, not only act with it, but believe as well; believe in my individual reality and creative power. My belief, to be sure, *can't* be optimistic—but I will posit life (the real, the good) in the self-governing *resistance* of the ego to the world. Life shall be built on doing and suffering and creating.

To Shadworth Hodgson*

As for the Free Will article, I have very little to say, for it leaves entirely untouched what seems to me the only living issue involved. The paper is an exquisite piece of literary goldsmith's work—nothing like it in that respect since Berkeley,—but it hangs in the air of speculation and touches not the earth of life, and the beautiful distinctions it keeps making gratify only the understanding which has no end in view but to exercise its eyes by the way. The distinc-

* From *The Letters of William James,* Vol. I, pp. 244-247. Hodgson was an English philosopher who tried in "Dialogue on Free Will" to solve the problem of freedom vs. determinism by distinguishing between compulsion (*vis impressa*) and determination or reaction (*vis insita*)—between deterministic necessity operating from without and deterministic necessity operating from within.

tions between *vis impressa* and *vis insita*, and compulsion and "reaction" *mean* nothing in a monistic world; and any world is a monism in which the parts to come are, as they are in your world, absolutely involved and presupposed in the parts that are already given. Were such a monism a palpable optimism, no man would be so foolish as to care whether it was predetermined or not, or to ask whether he was or was not what you call a "real agent." He would acquiesce in the flow and drift of things, of which he found himself a part, and rejoice that it was such a whole. The question of free will owes its entire being to a difficulty you disdain to notice, namely that we *cannot* rejoice in such a whole, for it is *not* a palpable optimism, and yet, if it be predetermined, we *must treat* it as a whole. Indeterminism is the only way to *break* the world into good parts and into bad, and to stand by the former as against the latter. . . .

For life *is* evil. Two souls are in my breast; I see the better, and in the very act of seeing it I do the worse. To say that the molecules of the nebula implied this and *shall have implied it* to all eternity, so often as it recurs, is to condemn me to that "dilemma" of pessimism or subjectivism of which I once wrote, and which seems to have so little urgency to you, and to which all talk about abstractions erected into entities; and compulsion vs. "freedom" are simply irrelevant. What living man cares for such niceties, when the real problem stares him in the face of how practically to meet a world foredone, with no possibilities left in it?

What a mockery then seems your distinction between determination and compulsion, between passivity and an "activity" every minutest feature of which is preappointed, both as to its *whatness* and as to its *thatness,* by what went before! What an insignificant difference then the difference between "impediments from within" and "impediments from without"!—between being fated to do the thing *willingly* or not! The point is not as to how it is done, but as to its being done at all. It seems a wrong complement to the rest of life, which rest of life (according to your precious "free-will determinism," as to any other fatalism), whilst shrieking aloud at its *whatness*, nevertheless exacts rigorously its *thatness* then and there. Is that a reasonable world from the moral point of view? And is it made more reasonable by the fact that when I brought about the *thatness* of the evil *whatness*, decreed to come by the *thatness* of all else beside, I did so consentingly and aware of no "impediments outside of my own nature"? With what can I *side* in such a world as this? this monstrous indifferentism which brings forth everything *eodem jure*? Our nature demands something *objective* to take sides with. If the world is a Unit of this sort there *are* no sides—there's the moral rub! And you don't see it!

Ah, Hodgson, Hodgson *mio!* from whom I hoped so much! Most spirited, most clean, most thoroughbred of philosophers! *Perchè di tanto inganni i figli tuoi?* ["Why so heartlessly deceive your sons?"—Leopardi, *To Sylvia.*] If you want to reconcile us rationally to Determinism, write a Theodicy, reconcile us to *Evil*, but don't talk of the distinction between impediments from within and without when the within and the without of which you speak are both within that *Whole* which is the only real agent in your philosophy. There is no such superstition as the idolatry of the *Whole*. . . .

Our Knowledge of Other Selves*

W. K. CLIFFORD

Distinction of object and eject

There are, however, some inferences which are profoundly different from those of physical science. When I come to the conclusion that *you* are conscious, and that there are objects in your consciousness similar to those in mine, I am not inferring any actual or possible feelings of my own, but *your* feelings, which are not, and cannot by any possibility become, objects in my consciousness. The complicated processes of your body and the motions of your brain and nervous system, inferred from evidence of anatomical researches, are all inferred as things possibly visible to me. However remote the inference of physical science, the thing inferred is always a part of me, a possible set of changes in my consciousness

* From the essay, "On the Nature of Things-in-Themselves," in W. K. Clifford (1845-1879), *Lectures and Essays,* Vol. II, (Macmillan, 1879).

bound up in the objective order with other known changes. But the inferred existence of your feelings, of objective groupings among them similar to those among my feelings, and of a subjective order in many respects analogous to my own,—these inferred existences are in the very act of inference *thrown out* of my consciousness, recognized as outside of it, as *not* being a part of me. I propose, accordingly, to call these inferred existences *ejects,* things thrown out of my consciousness, to distinguish them from *objects,* things presented in my consciousness, phenomena.

It is to be noticed that there is a set of changes of my consciousness symbolic of the eject, which may be called my conception of you; it is (I think) a rough picture of the whole aggregate of my consciousness, under imagined circumstances like yours; *qua* group of my feelings, this conception is like the object in substance and constitution, but differs from it in implying the existence of something that is not itself, but corresponds to it, namely, of the eject. The existence of the object, whether perceived or inferred, carries with it a group of beliefs; these are always beliefs in the future sequence of my feelings. The existence of this table, for example, as an object in my consciousness, carries with it the belief that if I climb up on it I shall be able to walk about on it as if it were the ground. But the existence of my conception of you in my consciousness carries with it a belief in the existence of you outside of my consciousness, a belief which can never be expressed in terms of the future sequence of my feelings. How this inference is justified, how consciousness can testify to the existence of anything outside of itself, I do not pretend to say; I need not untie a knot which the world has cut for me long ago. It may very well be that I myself am the only existence, but it is simply ridiculous to suppose that anybody else is. The position of absolute idealism may, therefore, be left out of count, although each individual may be unable to justify his dissent from it.

Formation of the social object

The belief, however, in the existence of other men's consciousness, in the existence of ejects, dominates every thought and every action of our lives. In the first place, it profoundly modifies the object. This room, the table, the chairs, your bodies, are all objects in my consciousness; as simple objects, they are parts of me. But I somehow infer the existence of similar objects in your consciousness, and these are not objects to me, nor can they ever be made so; they are ejects. This being so, I bind up with each object as it exists in my mind the thought of similar objects existing in other men's minds; and I thus form the complex conception, "this table, as an object in the minds of men,"—or, as Mr. Shadworth Hodgson puts it, an object of consciousness in general. This conception symbolizes an indefinite number of ejects, together with one object which the conception of each eject more or less resembles. Its character is therefore mainly ejective in respect of what it symbolizes, but mainly objective in respect of its nature. I shall call this complex conception the *social object*; it is a symbol of one thing (the *individual object*, it may be called for distinction's sake) which is in my consciousness, and of an indefinite number of other things which are ejects and out of my consciousness.

Now, it is probable that the individual object, as such, never exists in the mind of man. For there is every reason to believe that we were gregarious animals before we became men properly so called. And a belief in the eject—some sort of recognition of a kindred consciousness in one's fellow-beings—is clearly a condition of gregarious action among animals so highly developed as to be called conscious at all. Language, even in its first beginnings, is impossible without that belief; and any sound which, becoming a sign to my neighbor, becomes thereby a mark to myself, must by the nature of the case be a mark of the social object, and not of the individual object. But if not only this conception of the particular social object, but all those that have been built up out of it, have been formed at the same time with, and under the influence of, language, it seems to follow that the belief in the existence of other men's minds like our own, but not part of us, must be inseparably associated with every process whereby discrete impressions are built together into an object. I do not, of course, mean that it presents itself in consciousness as distinct; but I mean that as an object is formed in my mind, a fixed habit causes it to be formed as a social object, and insensibly embodies in it a reference to the minds of other men. And this sub-conscious reference to supposed ejects is what constitutes the impression of *externality* in the object, whereby it is described as *not-me*. At any rate, the formation of the social object supplies an account of this impression of outness, without requiring me to assume any ejects or things outside my consciousness except the minds of other men.

Consequently, it cannot be argued from the impression of outness that there is anything outside of my consciousness except the minds of other men. I shall argue presently that we have grounds for believing in non-personal ejects, but these grounds are not in any way dependent on the impression of outness, and they are not included in the ordinary or common-sense view of things. It seems to me that the prevailing belief of uninstructed people is merely a belief in the social object, and not in a non-personal eject, somehow corresponding to it; and that the question whether the latter exists or not is one which cannot be put to them so as to convey any meaning without considerable preliminary training. On this point I agree entirely with Berkeley, and not with Mr. Spencer.

I and Thou*

MARTIN BUBER

To MAN the world is twofold, in accordance with his twofold attitude.

The attitude of man is twofold, in accordance with the twofold nature of the primary words which he speaks.

The primary words are not isolated words, but combined words.

The one primary word is the combination *I-Thou*.

The other primary word is the combination *I-It*; wherein, without a change in the primary word, one of the words *He* and *She* can replace *It*.

Hence the *I* of man is also twofold.

* From Martin Buber (1875—), *I and Thou* (published in German, 1923; the English translation by Ronald Gregor Smith published by T. and T. Clark, Edinburgh, 1937). Selections reprinted by courtesy of Charles Scribner's Sons, the American publisher.

For the *I* of the primary word *I-Thou* is a different *I* from that of the primary word *I-It*.

* * *

Primary words do not signify things, but they intimate relationships.

Primary words do not describe something that might exist independently of them, but being spoken they bring about existence.

Primary words are spoken from the being.

If *Thou* is said, the *I* of the combination *I-Thou* is said along with it.

If *It* is said, the *I* of the combination *I-It* is said along with it.

The primary word *I-Thou* can only be spoken with the whole being.

The primary word *I-It* can never be spoken with the whole being.

* * *

There is no *I* taken in itself, but only the *I* of the primary word *I-Thou* and the *I* of the primary word *I-It*.

When a man says *I* he refers to one or other of these. The *I* to which he refers is present when he says *I*. Further, when he says *Thou* or *It*, the *I* of one of the two primary words is present.

The existence of *I* and the speaking of *I* are one and the same thing.

When a primary word is spoken the speaker enters the word and takes his stand in it.

* * *

The spheres in which the world of relation arises are three.

First, our life with nature. There the relation sways in gloom, beneath the level of speech. Creatures live and move over against us, but cannot come to us, and when we address them as *Thou*, our words cling to the threshold of speech.

Second, our life with men. There the relation is open and in the form of speech. We can give and accept the *Thou*.

Third, our life with intelligible forms. There the relation is clouded, yet it discloses itself; it does not use speech, yet begets it. We perceive no *Thou*, but none the less we feel we are addressed and we answer—forming, thinking, acting. We speak the primary word with our being, though we cannot utter *Thou* with our lips.

But with what right do we draw what lies outside speech into relation with the world of the primary word?

In every sphere in its own way, through each process of becoming that is present to us we look out toward the fringe of the eternal *Thou*; in each we are aware of a breath from the eternal *Thou*; in each *Thou* we address the eternal *Thou*.

* * *

If I face a human being as my *Thou*, and say the primary word *I-Thou* to him, he is not a thing among things, and does not consist of things.

This human being is not *He* or *She*, bounded from every other *He* and *She*, a specific point in space and time within the net of the world; nor is he a nature able to be experienced and described, a loose bundle of named qualities. But with no neighbor, and whole in himself, he is *Thou* and fills the heavens. This does not mean that nothing exists except himself. But all else lives in *his* light.

Just as the melody is not made up of notes nor the verse of words nor the statue of lines, but they must be tugged and dragged till their unity has been scattered into these many pieces, so with the man to whom I say *Thou*. I can take out from him the color of his hair, or of his speech, or of his goodness. I must continually do this. But each time I do it he ceases to be *Thou*.

And just as prayer is not in time but time in prayer, sacrifice not in space but space in sacrifice, and to reverse the relation is to abolish the reality, so with the man to whom I say *Thou*. I do not meet with him at some time and place or other. I can set him in a particular time and place; I must continually do it; but I set only a *He* or a *She*, that is an *It*, no longer my *Thou*.

So long as the heaven of *Thou* is spread out over me the winds of causality cower at my heels, and the whirlpool of fate stays its course.

I do not experience the man to whom I say *Thou*. But I take my stand in relation to him, in the sanctity of the primary word. Only when I step out of it do I experience[1] him once more. In the act of experience *Thou* is far away.

---

[1] The German language affords two words for "experience": *Erfahrung*, "casual, external experience," and *Erlebnis*, "living experience." Dr. Buber employs the former word in *I and Thou*, contrasting it with *Beziehung*, "relation" or perhaps more accurately "relationship."

Even if the man to whom I say *Thou* is not aware of it in the midst of his experience, yet relation may exist. For *Thou* is more than *It* realizes. No deception penetrates here; here is the cradle of the Real Life.

* * *

The *Thou* meets me through grace—it is not found by seeking. But my speaking of the primary word to it is an act of my being, is indeed *the* act of my being.

The *Thou* meets me. But I step into direct relation with it. Hence the relation means being chosen and choosing, suffering and action in one; just as any action of the whole being, which means the suspension of all partial actions and consequently of all sensations of actions grounded only in their particular limitation, is bound to resemble suffering.

The primary word *I-Thou* can be spoken only with the whole being. Concentration and fusion into the whole being can never take place through my agency, nor can it ever take place without me. I become through my relation to the *Thou*; as I become *I*, I say *Thou*. All real living is meeting.

* * *

Feelings accompany the metaphysical and metapsychical fact of love, but they do not constitute it. The accompanying feelings can be of greatly differing kinds. The feeling of Jesus for the demoniac differs from his feeling for the beloved disciple; but the love is the one love. Feelings are "entertained": love comes to pass. Feelings dwell in man; but man dwells in his love. That is no metaphor, but the actual truth. Love does not cling to the *I* in such a way as to have the *Thou* only for its "content," its object; but love is *between* *I* and *Thou*. The man who does not know this, with his very being know this, does not know love; even though he ascribes to it the feelings he lives through, experiences, enjoys, and expresses. Love ranges in its effect through the whole world. In the eyes of him who takes his stand in love, and gazes out of it, men are cut free from their entanglement in bustling activity. Good people and evil, wise and foolish, beautiful and ugly, become successively real to him; that is, set free they step forth in their singleness, and confront him as *Thou*. In a wonderful way, from time to time, exclusiveness arises—and so he can be effective, helping, healing, educating, raising up, saving. Love is responsibility of an *I* for a *Thou*. In this lies the likeness—impossible in any feeling whatsoever—of all who love, from the smallest to the greatest and from the blessedly protected man, whose life is rounded in that of a loved being, to him who is all his life nailed to the cross of the world, and who ventures to bring himself to the dreadful point—to love *all men*. . . . Believe in the simple magic of life, in service in the universe, and the meaning of that waiting, that alertness, that "craning of the neck" in creatures will dawn upon you. Every word would falsify; but look! round about you beings live their life, and to whatever point you turn you come upon being.

* * *

"You speak of love as though it were the only relation between men. But properly speaking, can you take it even only as an example, since there is such a thing as hate?"

So long as love is "blind," that is, so long as it does not see a *whole* being, it is not truly under the sway of the primary word of relation. Hate is by nature blind. Only a part of a being can be hated. He who sees a whole being and is compelled to reject it is no longer in the kingdom of hate, but is in that of human restriction of the power to say *Thou*. He finds himself unable to say the primary word to the other human being confronting him. This word consistently involves an affirmation of the being addressed. . . .

Yet the man who straightforwardly hates is nearer to relation than the man without hate and love.

* * *

In the beginning is relation.

Consider the speech of "primitive" peoples, that is, of those that have a meagre stock of objects, and whose life is built up within a narrow circle of acts highly charged with presentness. The nuclei of this speech, words in the form of sentences and original pre-grammatical structures (which later, splitting asunder, give rise to the many various kinds of words), mostly indicate the wholeness of a relation. We say "far away"; the Zulu has for that a word which means, in our sentence form, "There where someone cries out: 'O mother, I am lost.' " The Fuegian soars above our analytic wisdom with a seven-syllabled word whose precise meaning is, "They stare at one another, each waiting for the other to volunteer to do what both wish, but are not able to do." In this total situation the persons, as expressed both in nouns and pronouns, are embedded, still only in relief and without finished independence. The chief concern is not with these products of analysis and reflection but with the true original unity, the lived relation.

We greet the man we meet, wishing him well or assuring him of our devotion or commending him to God. But how indirect these worn-out formulas are! What do we discern even dimly in "Hail!" of the original conferring of power? Compare these with the ever fresh Kaffir greeting, with its direct bodily relation, "I see you!" or with its ridiculous and sublime American Indian variant, "Smell me!"

* * *

"But you believe then in the existence of a paradise in the earliest days of mankind?"

Even if it was a hell—and certainly that time to which I can go back in historical thought was full of fury and anguish and torment and cruelty—at any rate it was not unreal.

The relational experiences of man in earliest days were certainly not tame and pleasant. But rather force exercised on being that is really lived than shadowy solicitude for faceless numbers! From the former a way leads to God, from the latter only one to nothingness.

PART FOUR

Values

CHAPTER XII

The Nature of Value

We all know what it is to make an appraisal, to set a value on something. "That was a delicious dinner!" "What a dull movie!" "Such a lovely woman!" "You'd better read that book!" "He behaves admirably in a crisis." "You ought to drive more carefully." And so on. Each of these utterances expresses a *normative* judgment. Its primary intent is not to communicate a fact, although there are factual implications in each instance, but to affirm that some person or thing or action or relationship is, in one manner or another, *good* or *bad*. The branch of philosophy which studies the different ways in which something can be good or bad—i.e., have positive or negative value—and the relation of value to valuing on the one hand, and to the facts of objective existence on the other, is called *axiology*.

i. Types of Value

Since value is so strongly bound up with the act of valuing, and therefore with the shifting currents of human passions and interests, it is a somewhat fluid concept, and men's judgments concerning it are rarely beyond dispute. The following classification is offered not as anything final, but instrumentally as a means of reflecting upon the problems more clearly:

A. Values of possession
   1. Pleasure, comfort, security
   2. Health, or bodily well-being
   3. Wealth, or economic well-being
   4. Repute, or social well-being
B. Values of action
   1. Dynamic values: action and achievement for their own sake—acting *intensely*
   2. Eudaimonistic values: self-fulfillment
   3. Loyalty values: emulation—acting *worthily*
   4. Deontological values: doing what one ought—acting *rightly*
   5. Release values: acting *playfully*
C. Values of contemplation
   1. Aesthetic: the beautiful
   2. Intellectual: the true
D. Values of existence
   1. Individual: being one's self; privacy
   2. Social: love, shared play, coöperation
   3. Religious: sense of connection with a Something More, a higher entity than man

To be, to know, to do, and to have: these four basic aspects of the human situation correspond, in reverse order, to the four main types of value here distinguished. Has anything essential been left out? Nothing that cannot be assigned a place in the schema by suitable analysis. Some of the more important interconnections of the several categories may be judged from the following comments, others may be disclosed by the reader's own reflections.

Having and being

Admittedly the line between what a man *is* and what he *has* is not always clear. The values of individual existence (D1) are not always sharply distinguishable from the values of possessing bodily, and to an even greater degree psychic health (A2). Nor is the boundary between bodily health and psychic health always perfectly clear. Again, the values of social existence (D2)—the sheer immediate joy of sharing, communing, and coöperating with fellow-beings—are often hard to distinguish from the value of possessing a good reputation (A4). Therefore, since the values of existence are usually *continuous* with the values of possession, and since it is easier to speak clearly about the objects we possess than about the subjects that we are, it is not surprising that certain philosophers have taken the values of possession to be the only basic values, interpreting all other values as either instrumental to or derivative from them. Once that first reductive step is taken, of explaining all values as ultimately values of possession, it is usual to go a step farther and postulate that all values of possession—and hence all values whatever—are for the sake of pleasure and the avoidance of pain. Any value theory that takes this second step, of setting up pleasure and pain as the positive and negative poles of all valuation, is characterized as *hedonistic*.

Pleasure and pain

If we employ the convenient term "comfort" to mean "absence of pain," hedonism may be defined as the axiological doctrine that pleasure and comfort are the only fundamental values, of which all others are but derivatives. Hedonistic philosophies are of two main kinds. Egoistic hedonism identifies ultimate value with the pleasure and comfort of the individual valuator; altruistic or universalistic hedonism, with the pleasure and comfort of all human, or even all sentient beings. Jeremy Bentham, the English legal philosopher who has given universalistic hedonism its fullest exposition and most vigorous defense, employs the word "happiness," somewhat misleadingly, to denote "pleasure together with absence of pain"; and it is in this strictly defined sense of the word that "the greatest happiness of the greatest number" becomes Bentham's formula for what is fundamentally, rather than derivatively, good. The uncompromising character of his hedonism shows itself in the following typical statements:

Take away pleasures and pains: not only happiness, but justice, and duty, and obligation, and virtue—all which have been so elaborately held up to view as independent of them—are so many empty sounds.

Destitute of reference to the ideas of *pain* and *pleasure*, whatever ideas are annexed to the words *virtue* and *vice* amount to nothing more than that of groundless approbation and disapprobation. All language in which these appelatives are employed, is no better than empty declamation.

Whatever appears likely to produce an increase of pleasure or a decrease of pain (preferably both, no doubt) constitutes an *interest*; and as there are various types of pleasure and of pain, so there are correspondingly different types of interest. Bentham particularizes the correspondence in the following table:

Table of the Springs of Action[1]

(1) Pleasures and pains of the taste, the palate, the alimentary canal. . . . Corresponding interest: Interest of the Palate, Interest of the Bottle.

(2) Pleasures and pains of the sexual appetite, or of the sixth sense.—Sexual Interest.

(3) Pleasures and pains of sense, or of the senses: viz., generically or collectively considered.—Interest of Sense, of the Senses, Sensual Interest.

(4) Pleasures and pains derived from the matter of wealth.—Interest of the Purse.

(5) Pleasures and pains derived from power.—Interest of the Sceptre.

(6) Pleasures and pains of curiosity.—Interest of the Spying-Glass.

(7) Pleasures and pains of amity: viz., pleasures derivable from the good will, thence from the free services, of this or that individual; pains derivable from the loss or non-acquisition of ditto.—Interest of the Closet.

---

[1] Jeremy Bentham (1748-1832), *Works,* Vol. I, pp. 195ff.

(8) Pleasures and pains of the moral or popular sanction: of reputation, of good or ill repute.—Interest of the Trumpet.

(9) Pleasures and pains of the religious sanction.—Interest of the Altar.

(10) Pleasures and pains of sympathy.—Interest of the Heart.

(11) Pleasures and pains of antipathy, of ill-will, of the irascible appetite; including the pleasures of revenge, and the pains of unsatisfied vindictiveness.—Interest of the Gall-Bladder.

(12) Pains of labor, toil, fatigue.—Interest of the Pillow.

(13) Pains of death, and bodily pains in general.—Interest of Existence, of Self-Preservation.

(14) Pleasures and pains of the self-regarding class, generically or collectively considered: i.e., of all the above sorts except (10) and (11).—Self-Regarding Interest.

This table supplies Bentham with a schema for the analysis of the more complex interests and motives that shape human conduct. The pleasures of inebriation, for example, may be analyzed into pleasure of the palate (1), pleasure of exhilaration (3), and pleasure of sympathy or good will (10) "towards the co-partakers, the compotators." A *sense of justice* is analyzed into five component elements: desire of self-preservation (13); sympathy (10) for particular sufferers from injustice; sympathy (10) for the community at large, considered "as being liable, in an indefinite extent, to become a sufferer by injustice"; antipathy (11) towards any persons considered as profiting, or as being in a way to profit, by the opposite injustice; and antipathy (11) towards any person, such as a judge, "considered as concerned, or about to be concerned, in giving existence or effect to the injustice."

While a hedonistic analysis may perhaps adequately explain one's motives in drinking a cocktail, it proves much less adequate for so distinctively human and rational an interest as the love of justice. Bentham's failure to explain justice hedonistically becomes clear when it is observed that four of the five elements of his explanation are circular, since they employ the undefined word "injustice." By his analysis the love of justice is nothing more than a desire of self-preservation joined with a sympathy for the actual and possible victims of *injustice,* and an antipathy towards all actual and likely perpetrators of it. Now a love of justice cannot be desire of self-preservation alone, for that desire is admittedly active in other forms too; yet Bentham provides no further account of it except in terms of its opposite, injustice. To equate love of justice with antipathy towards injustice explains nothing: the equivalence is a matter of logic, not of ethics. What is wanted is a definition of the sentiment of justice that will give its positive essence: as in Wilbur M. Urban's definition of it as "the feeling for moral symmetry." This *structural* characteristic, not only with respect to justice but with respect to good and bad generally, is just what Bentham's account omits.

While it would be foolish to deny the important role that pleasure and comfort *in some sense or other* play in all valuation, it makes all the difference in just what sense, and with what implications for specific preference and choice, these words are taken. Aristotle puts the significant point as follows:

> Moreover, the life of those active in virtue is intrinsically pleasant. For besides the fact that pleasure is something belonging to the soul, each man takes pleasure in what he is said to love—the horse-lover in horses, the lover of sights in public spectacles, and similarly the lover of justice in just acts, and more generally, the lover of virtue in virtuous acts. But while most men take pleasure in things which, as they are not truly pleasant by nature, create warring factions in the soul, the lovers of what is noble take pleasure in things that are truly pleasant in themselves. Virtuous actions are things of this kind; hence they are pleasant for such men, as well as pleasant intrinsically. The life of such men, therefore, requires no adventitious pleasures, but finds its own pleasure within itself.[2]

Axiological pluralism

The fact that the different types of value interpenetrate and overlap is not sufficient reason for declaring them identical. The

---

[2] Aristotle, *The Nicomachean Ethics,* Bk. I, Chap. viii (p. 171 of the Odyssey Press edition of selections from Aristotle).

distinctions between one type and another are important both for clear thinking and decisive choice, even though there are many situations which are axiologically ambiguous. Moreover, the fact that objects of possession can usually be described more clearly than subjects of existence is not sufficient reason for declaring them more fundamental. The most important things in human experience are not always the clearest and most easily definable. Despite the many difficulties that will crop up in particular cases, the best method is to start by recognizing the chief differences among types of value, and thereby be in a position to discover their many forms of interpenetration. Axiological pluralism offers a more promising basis for the study of values than any species of axiological monism.

The values of non-possession

Once we have agreed not to beg the question of values by assuming in advance that possessive values are fundamental, it then becomes possible to understand the aim to which many philosophers have devoted their lives—of surmounting the ordinary enticements of life, and taking the path of "dispossession." Three centuries ago Spinoza wrote:

All the objects pursued by the multitude, not only bring no remedy that tends to preserve our being, but even act as hindrances, causing the death not seldom of those who possess them, and always of those who are possessed by them. There are many examples of men who in pursuit of wealth have exposed themselves to so many dangers, that they have paid their life as a penalty for their folly. Examples are no less numerous of men who have endured the utmost wretchedness for the sake of gaining or preserving their reputation. Lastly, there are innumerable cases of men who have hastened their death through overindulgence in sensual pleasure. All these evils seem to have arisen from the fact that happiness or unhappiness is made wholly to depend on the quality of the object which we love. When a thing is not loved, no quarrels will arise concerning it—no sadness will be felt if it perishes—no envy if it is possessed by another—no fear, no hatred, in short no disturbances of the mind. All these fears arise from the love of what is perishable, such as the objects already mentioned.[3]

To read Spinoza attentively is to see that his philosophic aim is not a negative one. It is not "asceticism" in the popular, caricatured, masochistic sense of the word. The fundamental aim in life—for all of us, if we but know it—is "to preserve our being," and possessions are discounted not because they are bad in themselves, but because they become hindrances and distractions to that primary aim. Spinoza denies that anything external is either good or evil in itself; its worth is determined by the use we make of it. In seeking to attain pleasure or wealth, or even health or repute, for their own sakes, we stake our happiness on gratifications which depend largely on circumstance. The gratification of appetite finally brings satiety and boredom, while frustration of appetite brings disappointment and restlessness. Our error—Spinoza concludes—consists in loving what is external and accidental, whereas the real good of man, and his only true source of unchallenged happiness, is found within himself—in the developing of a mature and disciplined character.

In a similar vein the Stoic philosophers taught and practiced the search for values of being, rather than of possessing. Epictetus begins his *Encheiridion,* or Manual of the Good Life, with the significant statement: "Of the things that exist, some lie within our power, while others do not." Our body, our property, our reputation—in a word everything that we ordinarily say we possess—lie really outside our control. They are not ours to possess, but only on loan.

Remember, therefore, that if what is really bound by circumstance you think to be free, and what is not your own to be your own, you will be hampered, will grieve, will be in turmoil, and will blame both gods and men; while if you think only what is your own to be

---

[3] From Spinoza, *On the Improvement of the Understanding* (translated by Elwes), p. 5.

your own, and what is not your own to be, as it really is, not your own, then no one will ever be able to exert compulsion upon you, no will will hinder you, you will blame no one, will find fault with no one, will do absolutely nothing against your will, you will have no personal enemy, no one will harm you, for neither is there any harm that can touch you.[4]

The aesthetic and the moral

A most important distinction in the realm of values has to do with the way in which they are related to the demand for action. In the classification on p. 402 the values of action—i.e., values judged to lie within action for its own sake—were recognized as forming a distinct class. A different question now arises. Even when a value is found in something other than action, it is likely to entail action of one kind rather than another. If you value health more highly than wealth, your choice of actions will be different in some respects than if the axiological comparison is reversed. According as a higher valuation is put upon privacy or upon the sharing of experiences with others, a man's choice of daily occupations and amusements will be largely guided. Even when the quietude of contemplation is valued above all else, a demand with respect to action is implied. For in the first place, contemplation is a kind of action, although less overt than other kinds. And in the second place, in order to be free for contemplation, steps have to be taken and arrangements have to be made. When Buddha taught the Noble Eightfold Way to supreme blessedness, he included various right actions, right desires, right resolves, and right living arrangements among the early stages of the way, although the eighth and last stage was the joy of devoted, unruffled contemplation.

Nevertheless, although all values doubtless have some relevance to the choice of one action rather than another when the conditions are approximate, yet the degree and kind of relevance

---

[4] From Epictetus, *Encheiridion*, translated by W. A. Oldfather (Loeb Classical Library). By courtesy of Harvard University Press.

in different instances may vary greatly. The judgment "What a dull movie!" may involve, as a secondary implication, "I advise you not to see it"; but not necessarily. It may be that the person addressed has different tastes in the matter, so that direct advice would be inappropriate. The judgment is primarily *aesthetic*—a judgment of values found in the quality and structure of the perceptible world. Similarly with the judgment "Such a lovely woman!" To judge a woman lovely does not necessarily lead to courtship, nor even to any attempt to see her again.

On the other hand, suppose one formed the value-judgment: "The profession of medicine is better (for one with my abilities) than a business career." Or the value-judgment: "There is nothing so important as getting rich." Or again, the value-judgment: "Father's advice is wise." The relation of valuation to action is more direct and more clearly marked in such instances as these. Either the values are such as lie at least partly within our power to achieve, or they entail actions which do so. This capability of being realized directly or indirectly through action is the first differentia of moral value from value in general. What else is needed? The answer can be found by examining a case where *only* the first differentia is present. "It would be more fun to join the picnic than to stay at home and watch television." Here is a judgment of value (in a particular and personal situation) which clearly points the way to appropriate action. Yet it is not a moral judgment; for the fun of joining the picnic, although a real enough value no doubt, is a relatively trifling one. Ordinarily it would have no important consequences for other persons than the doer, nor for him beyond the time of the picnic itself. If, however, he had given his promise to someone who would be disappointed and perhaps discommoded by his absence; or, on the other hand, if by going he would break a pledge made to himself to keep regular hours of work: the value of attending the picnic would then be positively or negatively consequential in a significant way, and the value would accordingly be, in that context, a *moral* one.

The conditions of moral valuation

What are the distinguishing characteristics of a moral value—that is, of moral good and bad—as distinguished from goods and bads which lie outside the moral context, and may be designated *non-moral* or *amoral*? Or—what amounts to the same thing—what are the conditions of moral valuation? Five such differentiae seem especially prominent.

1. A moral value is *not wholly actual*. A man in process of repaying a debt is in a moral situation because it is good to get the debt paid off and it is not yet paid off. When the process of payment is completed, then that moral situation is closed. The debtor *was* moral, and his action of repayment may have given evidence of a continuing moral character, but he is no longer making moral choices and behaving morally in *that* respect. It is good, of course, that the debt is now paid. But this new good is not a moral good. The good had a moral character during the process of its realization; it became a general axiological good when the process was completed.

2. A moral value lies at least partly *within someone's power* to achieve and realize. It implies some possibility of choice. A simple case will show this. Suppose we condemn a man for failing to rescue another from drowning, and afterwards learn that the man we criticized could not swim. Would we not withdraw our moral judgment? No one is held morally bound to do something which he is unable to do. "Ought" in the moral sense implies "can."

3. A moral value therefore stands *in potential conflict* with some other real and attainable value. A choice has moral value in relation to opposing choices which could have been made in place of this one. But if none of those choices had even the slightest attraction for the chooser, his freedom with respect to them was an empty freedom. In all moral choice there is an element of contrary temptation, however well controlled. A really moral man, as distinguished from a pompous pretender, will be

able to look at the opposite line of action and avow with Martin Luther, "There but for the grace of God go I!"

4. A moral value is significantly *consequential*. The value which has not yet been attained but which lies within someone's power to attain, is a moral value only if it counts for something beyond the immediate action which it prompts. If, for instance, the conflict of choice is simply between skating and skiing, where no ulterior effects or obligations are involved, the situation is not a moral one. The alternatives are simply ends in themselves, and the values which are chosen and rejected—the fun of skating vs. the fun of skiing—terminate with the termination of the act. Such a choice, between doing this or that merely for fun, is not moral because it has no significance beyond the act of enjoyment. If, however, the idea of skating presents itself to the doer as the more attractive of the two when he has already promised to go skiing with someone, the consequences of the act are indefinitely more extensive. To break a promise is more likely to entail bad consequences than good. For not only are there the effects on the present occasion to be considered; there is the yielding to moral slovenliness in oneself, and there is the possible weakening of the respect for truth in others. The values of skating vs. skiing in this new context are not isolated but *organic*. They are interrelated with other values, positive and negative, which have greater permanence. And as the values involved are consequential, so the choice made with respect to them must be more *responsible*. Consequentiality of the values at stake and responsibility of the choice between them are essential to the kind of situation we call moral.

5. A moral value has a *potentially social dimension*. There are, to be sure, private moral choices which may seem at the time to have personal consequences but few if any social ones. A youth struggling to overcome his own timidity, for example, may be thinking only of the kind of character he wishes to make *of himself*, and that effort of character-building may be undertaken with a real enough moral intensity. But on the other hand, even

though the social aspects are hidden at the time, yet no one is insulated from his fellow mortals, and eventually the kind of character which is developed is going to affect for better or worse one's relations with others. Taste can be highly idiosyncratic, morality not. Let one person have a passion for the music of Bach or the art of Mondrian while another detests them, and with a little effort at tolerance they can still manage to live together in social harmony. But let them disagree fundamentally on the principle of respecting one another's rights, and the situation is quite different. There is continuity—more marked in some situations than in others—between the private and public aspects of moral value.

ii. Absolutism vs. Relativism

One of the most disputed questions about values concerns the degree to which, and the sense in which, they are objective. On the one hand, people's valuations do differ and are likely to undergo change: that is one of the undeniable facts with which any theory of values must begin. The wide differences between the standards of beauty which find expression in native African art, ancient Greek art, and the art of twentieth century America need no demonstration. We bridge the gaps to some degree by conscious borrowings, but fundamental differences remain. Differences in standards of moral valuation are scarcely less conspicuous. Even within two generations the manners and morals of Americans have changed in striking respects.

The question of axiological objectivity, then, is not the factual question of how people make valuations, for that can be answered with tolerable success by statistics. Over and above the differences of actual valuations there looms the *normative* question: Is there any *standard* by which some of those valuations, and the objects they evaluate, can be judged to be objectively and intrinsically better than others? Extreme *absolutism* or *dogmatism* answers yes, and specifies such a standard as valid for all persons and nations everywhere—if they would but recognize it! Extreme *relativism* or *subjectivism* answers no, and explains away standards as accidents of taste and circumstance which have become perpetuated by custom and so "rationalized."[5] Between these two extreme views certain intermediate positions are possible. In order to arrive at a suitable and valid answer to this problem of the status of values, let us first make a critical examination of the two extremes, and then see what intelligible possibilities there are of steering between them.

Absolutism

A plausible case can be made out for a dogmatic attitude toward values. It can be argued that people cannot live happily or well without a secure faith in what they are living *for*; that such security requires an acceptance of values that are not subject to the vicissitudes of circumstance and whim; that where such an acceptance and such security are lacking, both the individual and the society to which he contributes tend to become vacillating, anarchic, and weak. So much on the practical side.

But it is a lame defense of absolutism that rests on such pragmatic grounds alone. The honest absolutist promotes a set of values not only because he believes them useful but because he believes them true. How is absolute truth established? Obviously not by each person's intuition, for intuitive discoveries, outside of purely logical relations, are apt to be highly individual. Empirical induction will not serve. Its method and aim are factual, not normative. Hence, it is self-limited to discovering the facts about the diverse valuations that people actually make; it disavows the very question of whether any of those values are absolute. Can absolute truth about values be attained, then, by reasoning? But philosophers who have professed to be guided by reason at each step of the way have sometimes arrived at incom-

---

[5] See Glossary for the proper meaning of the words "rationalize" and "rationalization." Do not confuse them with "reason," "reasoning," and "rational."

patible results. Immanuel Kant and Bertrand Russell have each made a great show of their devotion to rational method, but the one argues logically that there must be no suicides and no divorces, the other argues with apparently equal logic that suicides and divorces are sometimes justified.

Since the private powers of discovery, whether outward or inward, when exercised by individuals, lead to such diverse results, the absolutist argues that truth must have been revealed to men in some special and authoritative way. Whether such revelation was given once for all and transmitted through a sacred Book, as Protestant fundamentalists believe, or whether there is a continuing revelation through an instituted Church, as Catholics believe, the revelation is regarded as authoritative in either case. It may well be, as Catholic Dominicans teach, that the revealed truths can be independently confirmed by one or more of man's other means of forming beliefs. But such a concession is qualified by the requirement that one's reasoning, or one's mystical intuitions, or one's interpretation of nature, will yield truth concerning valuational matters only if they are carried out rightly; and as their rightness must eventually be judged by whether or not their conclusions are in accord with the authoritarian doctrine, we are led back to the position that the sole source of absolute truth must be *revelation preserved and interpreted by authority.*

The truths thus taken as absolute are of two kinds—theological and axiological. The most fundamental belief of the former kind will be considered in Chapter XV; the axiological side of the question is what interests us now. What is there to be said against an absolutism of values?

The first and most obvious reply is that dogmas and the authorities which uphold them are often in conspicuous disagreement with one another. Catholics and Protestant fundamentalists disagree as to the total pattern of authoritarian teaching; and the disagreement cuts even deeper between Christians as a whole and Moslems; deeper still between Christians and Moslems on the one hand and dogmatic Marxists on the other. How can there be an authority by which to decide between the claims of conflicting authorities? Each sect of dogmatists points to its own authority in reply, as the sole recognized arbiter, and so we are back where we started. The only actual solutions are three: mutual insulation (which becomes increasingly difficult in our global age), compromise (moderately effective so long as there is an approximate balance of power), and mutual attempt at suppression, which is to say war.

Extreme relativism

The case for relativism in its extreme form (as distinguished from the more moderate positions sometimes designated "objective relativism," "contextual relativism," etc., to be considered later) is usually built upon a plain sociological fact. "He that will carefully peruse the history of mankind," John Locke wrote three centuries ago, ". . . will be able to satisfy himself that there is scarce that principle of morality to be named, or rule of virtue to be thought on . . . which is not, somewhere or other, slighted and condemned by the general fashion of whole societies of men, governed by practical opinions and rules of living quite opposite to others." What Locke says about moral judgments can be extended to aesthetic and religious judgments also. That value-judgments in all fields show much diversity and fluctuation is admitted by all who examine the evidence. In short, there is the undeniable fact of valuational relativity. Men's ways of valuing are historically and culturally conditioned.

Relativity of valuation is found not only between one society and another, separated in place or time, but in more limited ways between individual and individual within a society. Within the framework of valuational encouragements and pressures which every society consciously and unconsciously sets up, there is room for individual differences and fluctuations. The social allowance of such differences itself fluctuates. In mid-twentieth-century America there is probably more room allowed for disagreement about aesthetic and religious values than there was a century ago; less room, however, for disagreement about political values. These observations all give evidence of the general fact of valuational relativity. Individuals share in a general way the historical conditioning which molds their society; they are further conditioned by the more particular factors of physical inheritance, early upbringing, the clutch of circumstance, and the accumulation of character through repeated individual choices.

What distinguishes the extreme relativist is not his acceptance of the acknowledged fact that valuations differ widely, but the way in which he uses this fact of *valuational relativity* as a prop for *axiological relativism*. The extreme position so far as moral values are concerned is summarized in John Graham Sumner's phrase, "The *mores* can make everything right"; in the aesthetic sphere by Bernard Heyl's declaration "that differing though equally sensitive persons will respond to music in differing ways and that, therefore, more than a single critical attitude is justified." The logical link between the first and second clauses is made explicit in an earlier declaration that an individual's critical judgment and attitude "can reasonably be binding only for those people who, as a result of fundamental similarities in their temperament, education, and environment, basically resemble him."[6] The step from plain statement of fact to axiological judgment becomes particularly clear from an analysis of Professor Heyl's language. That persons do respond to music in different ways is plain fact; that such persons are "equally sensitive" is a judgment of appraisal, the grounds of which are not specified. That most people do not feel themselves bound by the critical judgment of those whose temperament and background are basically dissimilar is a plain fact; but the word "reasonably" brings in Heyl's axiological judgment of that situation. Sumner's position allows

---

[6] William Graham Sumner, *Folkways* (1907), Chap. XV. Bernard C. Heyl, *New Bearings in Esthetics and Art Criticism* (Yale University Press, 1943), pp. 140, 137.

no logical possibility of criticizing the *mores* of one's age as dissolute. Heyl's position, although more carefully formulated, does not do justice to the axiological situation in which a person recognizes the limits of his own sensitivity and asks, "Are there not aesthetic values in Chinese art, or Gregorian music, or whatever it may be, that I have not yet perceived but which, by educating and extending my aesthetic perceptions, I might be able to perceive?" As a teacher of art Professor Heyl is well aware of the possibility and importance of such *self*-criticism. But self-criticism, in a reasonable sense, is only possible if one is willing to recognize the existence of standards that transcend one's present taste and understanding.

Semantic relativism

In recent years the development of the science of semantics has enabled relativists to claim an additional support for their theory. Semantics is the science of *meanings*—the investigation of how language operates to express and communicate what is meant. The extreme relativist in axiology is likely to be a positivist in semantics. The position of semantic positivism is (1) *that only those terms are meaningful which publicly designate*, and (2) *that only those statements are true* (a statement being an assertable relation between terms) *which are publicly verifiable—in principle if not in fact*. The term "good" does not designate anything that can be publicly agreed on, but a description of men's actions and utterances does. Accordingly the semantic positivist proposes that a normative statement about what is "good" be translated into descriptive statements about how people behave—including, of course, their verbal behavior and their sometimes concealed but always discoverable emotional behavior. Moreover, a statement such as "Marital fidelity is good" is not publicly verifiable. It might be possible to verify such a descriptive proposition as "Marital fidelity promotes social cohesion in a majority of cases," but how should we reply to a critic who retorted, "I don't think social cohesion is the main *good* in question"? A descriptive statement of what fidelity *leads to* may be true or false, but a normative statement of whether fidelity and what it leads to are good in themselves, or better than something else, is not publicly verifiable and *therefore neither true nor false*. Thus by semantic analysis the axiological relativist claims to have reinforced his position, that there can be no such thing as a value over and beyond the shifting facts of human valuation.

The consequence of relativism is that all valuations are reduced to subjective matters of taste. The old adage, *De gustibus non est disputandum*—"There's no disputing about tastes"—or Max Beerbohm's whimsical variation of it, "For people who like that sort of thing, that is the sort of thing they like"—becomes the final word on any question of what is good or bad, right or wrong, beautiful or ugly, and the like. Instrumental or contributing values can be discussed—e.g., whether an axe is sharp enough to be *valuable for* chopping wood, or whether honest behavior is valuable in the sense of *contributing to* a good reputation, business success, personal self-satisfaction, and the like. For questions of instrumental value merely ask, "Will this act or object whose value is in question lead to a certain desired result, or won't it?" They are therefore questions of fact to begin with. But questions of intrinsic value—the value of the ends for their own sakes—must be reduced to factual questions in another way before they can be significantly considered. They must be translated into the questions of one of two types: (1) Does so-and-so *actually want* (hence, set a value on) pleasure or success or whatever it may be, and at what price in money, energy, or sacrifice? (2) Statistically determined, how much is a certain kind of thing *actually wanted* (valued) by a given social collective at a given time? The prominence of this latter type of question among contemporary sociologists has given rise to the relativist formula, "The only norm is the normal."

Meeting of extremes

Thus extreme relativism, no less than extreme absolutism, rules out discussion of what is really valuable in itself. Extreme absolutism says, "You cannot discuss questions of ultimate value because the answers are already authoritatively fixed." Extreme relativism says, "You cannot discuss questions of ultimate value because such questions are meaningless." Both extreme positions tend to transform questions of value into questions of fact, in opposite ways. Relativism makes the transformation openly, declaring that the only significant questions are factual, including the factual question of whether something is or is not valuable *instrumentally*—e.g., whether an axe is (factually) sharp enough to be valuable for chopping wood. Absolutism retains the axiological vocabulary, but in putting certain questions beyond the reach of free discussion it turns their answers into virtual statements of fact. Thus, for both the orthodox and the conservative branches of Jewry it is virtually a fact that it is wrong for Jews to eat pork and to do unnecessary labor on Saturday (the Sabbath); for certain Protestant sects it is virtually a fact that it is wrong to play cards on Sunday; while for Roman Catholics it is virtually a fact that secular marriage, contraception, and divorce are wrong. The *word* "fact" may be avoided in this connection, but the nature of the question is semantically transformed nevertheless. In short, each of the two extreme positions tends, in one way or another, to make the vitally important question, "What is most really valuable?" disappear.

iii. Contextual Objectivism

Somehow we must find a middle axiological ground. Against the extreme relativist we must insist that values are real and that questions concerning what is valuable in itself are meaningful. Against the absolutist we must insist that the form in which values appear to this or that individual, and to this or that society, are physically, culturally, and historically conditioned, so that any particular formulation of a value-judgment is of limited (though real) validity and hence open to possible discussion.

That values are objective

It is evident to anyone who examines the problem reflectively that diversity and fluctuation of value-judgments is no logical disproof that values may objectively exist. Take two analogous cases. First, size. There are sometimes marked differences of size between two people's retinal images of what they acknowledge to be "the same object." When such is discovered to be the case hardly anyone concludes that the object itself has no size. Rather, each person willingly checks his individual impression by measuring "the object itself." Again, take color or temperature. Here, too, if there is real dispute as to the exact shade of blue in paint or the exact degree of warmth in a room, measurement is again resorted to. The measurement of color and temperature, however, is less direct than the measurement of size. To discover the physical size of an ordinary object like a table it is enough to superimpose upon its surface another object—say a yardstick—whose length has been accepted as standard. Whatever the retinal discrepancies of two persons, they will usually be able to agree accurately on such a physical comparison. Quite possibly the table looks bigger to Dick than to Tom, but if so, then the yardstick looks bigger also. And both by sight and by touch the two observers can agree on where the notches on the yardstick and the ends of the table coincide. When the dispute has to do with secondary qualities, on the other hand, such as color and warmth, the observers cannot resolve their differences by so simple a physical maneuver as superimposition of one surface upon another. A more complicated device is needed—a photometer in the one case, a thermometer in the other—which gives a quantitative substitute for a certain kind of quality.

Can the "tertiary qualities," as they are sometimes called, of good and bad, beautiful and ugly, humorous, dull, noble, vile, etc. be referred to an objective standard in any analogous way? Plato repeatedly sought to discover and justify such a standard, and in *The Statesman* he has his spokesman, the Eleatic Stranger, declare:

> The very existence of the arts must be held to depend on the possibility of measuring what is more and what is less, not only in relation to one another, but especially with a view to the attainment of the mean. . . . For if there are arts, there is a standard of measure, and if there is a standard of measure, there are arts: but if either is lacking, there is neither.[7]

The speaker is anxious that the word "measure" should not be crudely misunderstood, however, and accordingly he proceeds to distinguish between those arts (developed in the technology of our day) "which measure number, length, depth, breadth, swiftness, and their opposites" and the arts of another kind which guide their measurements by the standard of the golden mean, the fit, the appropriate. Whereas the former arts (e.g., physical dynamics) measure quantitatively by standards drawn from outside us and accepted by convention or stipulation, the latter arts (e.g., music) measure qualitatively by standards drawn from within us, and which are the products not of convention or chance but of a healthy and well-regulated soul. When arts of the latter kind employ measurement and standards of the former kind they deteriorate. Plato's example in the *Republic* is that of a musician who tries to outdo other musicians in some trick of his art and thereby fails to be a good artist. Think, for instance, of the artistic badness of a singer who exults in being able to hold a high note longer than anyone else, regardless of what the character of the music calls for. The music itself, Plato believes, makes an objective requirement, and the good musician is one who submits to that requirement, neither going beyond nor falling short of it, and thereby observing the golden mean.

In several well-known passages in the Dialogues Plato pushes

[7] Plato, *The Statesman*, 284 D-E, based on Jowett's translation.

his objectivism too far, and defends or at least explores the view that values are eternally valid forms, which the soul of man knew before its rebirth in the present body, but which were blotted from his memory at birth, so that the acquiring of standards is neither invention nor discovery, but recollection. We need not follow Plato so far. But it would be wise to agree with him that values are known as values; that this type of knowledge is at least as fundamental and real as any factual or statistical knowledge of how people under given conditions want and strive and verbalize their wants and strivings. Most of all, from the standpoint of philosophical inquiry, let us agree with Plato, against both of the extreme standpoints, that values *can be significantly discussed*.

That value-statements are meaningful

But we cannot overlook the relativist's appeal to semantics. What of his claim that a value-question has no meaning other than a strictly factual one? What of his claim that "Treachery is evil" means no more than one or both of the factual judgments: (1) "I dislike treachery, and I wish that everyone else would dislike it too"; (2) "A majority of people dislike treachery and are disposed to show their disapproval when it is practiced." Is the translation of "Treachery is evil" into (1) and (2) semantically adequate? Probably most readers will not think so. When we judge something to be "bad" or "wrong," we surely think we mean something more than that we ourselves, or society in general, disapprove of it. What is that something more?

According to Charles L. Stevenson's analysis,[8] the something more is an imperative or hortatory ingredient. To say "Treachery is wrong" means two things:

(1) I dislike treachery. (implicit statement)
(2) Come now, don't be treacherous! (implicit command)

---

[8] Charles L. Stevenson, *Ethics and Language* (Yale University Press, 1944), Chap. II.

The importance of Professor Stevenson's interpretation is that it recognizes other than declarative elements in what appears to be, grammatically, a statement. His proof that there is a non-declarative element in value-judgments is ingenious and, so far as it goes, a valid step toward the solution of the problem. He asks us to consider the nature of *disagreement*. If A and B disagree about a question of value, the situation can be represented by the following model:

    A. "This is good."
    B. "No, this is bad."

B's word "No" is appropriate as indicating his disagreement with what A has said. Now suppose that this model is translated into a pair of purely descriptive propositions—pure declarations of fact:

    A. "I approve of this, and want you to do so as well."
    B. "No, I disapprove of this, and want you to do so as well."

The word "No" has now become inappropriate, because there is no real disagreement between what A says and what B says. That A approves and that B disapproves are two independent facts; that A wants B to approve and that B wants A to disapprove are also independent facts. A asserts a double fact about A's subjective experience; B asserts a double fact about B's subjective experience. Their assertions are not in the least incompatible, and the word "No" is as badly out of place as if A had said, "It is raining in Omaha" and B had replied, "No, it is clear weather in Tucson." For it is the nature of disagreement that A and B shall give different answers *to the same question*. In the first model this is done; A and B are giving answers to the single question, "Is this good?" Therefore B can say "No" to A's answer. In the second model, on the other hand, there is not one question involved, but two. A is replying to the question, "What is A's attitude in the matter?" while B is replying to the different question, "What is B's attitude in the matter?" Clearly, then, the second model is a mistranslation of the first.

Stevenson's solution is to formulate a third model, which he believes is a correct translation of the first:

A. "I approve of this; do so as well."
B. "No, I disapprove of this; do so as well."

The "No" refers, of course, to the second part of A's statement, not to the first. B does not doubt that A approves; as Stevenson puts it, there is no disagreement *about* attitudes, there is disagreement *in* attitude. B's disagreement is not with the declarative but with the hortatory part of A's utterance. The word "No" is appropriate here because it indicates a real hortatory opposition. It is as if A had said, "Come on, share my approval, won't you?" and B had replied, "No, *you* come on, and share my *dis*approval." This third model, then, Professor Stevenson concludes to be a correct translation of the first; from which it follows that the first model—and by extension every value-statement—has two implicit components: the one declarative, stating that the speaker does like or dislike a certain object in a certain way, the other hortatory.

There is a non-declarative element, then, implicit in every value-judgment. But is that non-declarative element only hortatory? I would say not, and as I am not sure how far Professor Stevenson's agreement can be counted on in what follows, I will speak independently from here on.

In a real value-judgment there is not only command, there is yielding—i.e., being on the receiving end of a command—and there is *self*-command as a result of this. Let each reader test this for himself by introspective reflection. Think of some *discovery* of value and consequent obligation—e.g., when one recognizes what one owes to a friend in need and accepts the obligation to help him. In a practical situation like this the value at issue is perhaps never formulated in words. Whether it is or not, it involves more than the factual discovery, "I *want* to help my friend." Of course there is this too. But there may be an even stronger contrary pull—"It is so inconvenient to give him the help he needs!" The question is not the factual one of which motive is, at the moment of considering them, stronger. The reasoner does not reduce the question to the simple factual form, "Which do I actually want to do more?" Even if he uses that form of words, there is a surplus of meaning which they do not express. That additional element of meaning comes not as a discovery of fact, but as a discovery of command; and not a command issued by one individual to another, but a command issuing somehow out of the situation, or it may be from beyond the situation, and which the reasoner beholds as an obligation to be fulfilled—or better, as a vocation, a *being called*. A real value-judgment is always in part an answer to command, a "So be it!"

Who or what issues the command? The question carries us outside the sphere of axiology, and must be postponed until the latter part of Chapter XV. Let us for the present try not to prejudge that question. In axiological context it is enough to say: Values are known *in the guise of* commands to acquiesce and (when the values are moral ones) to act, or become disposed to act.

That value-statements are contextual

The first two assertions of contextual realism—that values are objective and real, and that value-statements are meaningful—were made as against the extreme axiological relativist and subjectivist. The third assertion, that values are contextual, sets limits to the claims of the absolutist. How can a value be declared objectively real and yet at the same time contextually conditioned? Let us take a concrete example.

Consider the meaning of a lover's judgment: "Mary is the loveliest of women." What is the judgment *about*? Evidently about Mary, and not about the lover's own state of mind and heart. If a wooer were to think merely, "What pleasurable feelings I enjoy in Mary's presence! How deliciously Mary affects me!" he would be no lover, but an arrant egotist, and Mary would be well advised to reject him. For if that were his attitude, he would not be caring about Mary herself, he would be merely using her as a means to his own enjoyment and comfort. His essential relation toward her would be *I-it,* not *I-thou.*

The real lover, on the other hand, is interested primarily in Mary, not in his feelings toward her. The feelings must be there, of course. They are a main contributor to the *perspective* in which John sees and knows Mary, and thereby to the *context* in which it is true that Mary is so lovely. Doubtless no one else shares John's perspective fully. If John is a typical lover he proudly acknowledges his perspectival isolation. "No one else can see Mary's admirable qualities as I can; they don't know her as I do!" What John "sees in Mary" he sees as something in Mary and not in his own psyche. The state of his psyche is a contextualizing factor of his vision, but Mary's loveliness is the objective content of that vision.

Concluding comment

The position of contextual realism, or objectivism, as distinguished from relativism on the one hand and from absolutism on the other, has the great advantage of keeping the search for values and the discussion of value-judgments fruitfully open. If there are no objective values, there is nothing to discuss; and if one simple code of values is absolute, we cannot fundamentally discuss it, we can only learn what it is. The intermediate position, here espoused, accepts the postulate that some values are inherently better than others—as mutual aid, for example, is inherently better than cut-throat competition—but recognizes the large admixture of human partisanship and error that qualifies any attempt to formulate them in theory or realize them in living. Nevertheless the search for them is not doomed to hopeless frustration. Socrates has shown the way. By recognizing how limited our knowledge is, we can step a little beyond those former limits. By acknowledging that our valuations are partisan, both individually and collectively, we are a little better able to appreciate other value-perspectives which we do not share. For the various perspectives are not atomically distinct; they are different paths, sometimes oddly circuitous ones, toward a goal that is beyond human reach, but that still gives validation to the pilgrimage, and even furnishes here and there a blurred signpost.

For Further Study

RALPH BARTON PERRY, *General Theory of Value* (Longmans, Green, 1926). Value defined by interests.

WOLFGANG KOEHLER, *The Place of Value in a World of Facts* (Liveright, 1934). By the leader of the Gestalt school of psychology.

CLARENCE I. LEWIS, *An Analysis of Knowledge and Valuation* (Open Court, 1946), Chaps. XII-XVII.

GEORGE H. PALMER, *The Nature of Goodness* (Houghton Mifflin, 1903).

H. OSBORNE, *Foundations of the Philosophy of Value* (Cambridge University Press, 1933). From the standpoint of philosophical idealism.

CHARLES L. STEVENSON, *Ethics and Language* (Yale University Press, 1944).

EVERETT W. HALL, *What Is Value?* (Humanities Press, 1952). Semantic approach.

A. L. HILLIARD, *The Forms of Value* (Columbia University Press, 1950). Analytic method applied to value study.

JOHN LAIRD, *The Idea of Value* (Cambridge University Press, 1929). Gives more than usual attention to economic value.

STEPHEN C. PEPPER, *A Digest of Purposive Values* (University of California Press, 1947).

SAMUEL L. HART, *Treatise on Values* (Philosophical Library, 1949).

RAY LEPLEY, editor, *Value; A Coöperative Inquiry* (Columbia University Press, 1949).

MAURICE PICARD, *Values, Immediate and Contributory* (New York University Press, 1920).

BERNARD C. HEYL, *New Bearings in Esthetics and Art Criticism* (Yale University Press, 1943). A defense of value relativism.

Questions for Discussion

1. "We do in fact hold that when one man approves of a certain act while another disapproves, one of them is mistaken, which would not be the case with a mere emotion. If one man likes oysters and another dislikes them, we do not say that either of them is mistaken." Santayana, quoting this earlier opinion of Bertrand Russell, comments: "In other words, we are to maintain our prejudices, however absurd, lest it should become unnecessary to quarrel about them! Truly the debating society has its idols, no less than the cave and the theatre."—GEORGE SANTAYANA, "The Philosophy of Bertrand Russell," in *Winds of Doctrine* (1913).

On which side of the controversy do you stand? Why?

2. What are the intellectual and moral disadvantages of maintaining without qualification:

   a) We discover values, we do not create them?
   b) We create values, we do not discover them?

3. Examine the classification of values in Section i with these two questions in mind:

   a) Which of them do you judge to be *ethically* more fundamental—i.e., to be preferred, on the whole, in situations where they conflict with others?
   b) Which of them do you judge to be *logically* more fundamental—i.e., more basic in the sense that others can be explained in terms of them?

4. "The silence of the desert is without value, until some wanderer finds it lonely and terrifying; the cataract, until some human sensibility finds it sublime, or until it is harnessed to satisfy human needs."—RALPH BARTON PERRY, General *Theory of Value*, p. 125.

Can you discover any significant sense in which the cataract may be said to have the quality of sublimity even at those times when no human sensibility is responding to it? Cf. Question 3 in Chapter 6.

5. Test whether Professor Stevenson's analysis can be applied satisfactorily to the following cases.

   a) A qualified ethical judgment of the type: "It is my duty to carry out this project that I have undertaken. I'm not saying that anyone else in my position should feel similarly obligated; my own duty is all that I can judge of."

b) The aesthetic judgment of an explorer who delights in a view which he does not expect or wish anyone to share.

6. Everett W. Hall argues that not all normatives conceal imperatives, for there are normatives in the past tense, but no imperatives in the past tense. Thus we can say "Chamberlain ought not to have yielded to Hitler at Munich," but we cannot now command or urge Chamberlain not to have done so. (Everett W. Hall, *What Is Value?*, p. 156.)

Do you see any way of interpreting the preterit "ought" consistently with the semantic analysis of normatives given in the present chapter? If not, how will you interpret the meaning of "I (or you, or he) ought (or ought not) to have done so-and-so"?

7. What is your judgment of Windelband's view that accountability is present not only in the moral field, but also in the fields of thought and feeling—i.e., that there is not only a moral conscience, but also a logical and an aesthetic conscience?—Discussed by MAURICE PICARD, *Values, Immediate and Contributory*, Chap. VII.

8. When *A* calls a certain poem beautiful, admirable, delightful, or by some other adjective expressing positive aesthetic value, while *B* declares it worthless or insipid or banal or in some other way lacking in positive and perhaps even possessing negative aesthetic value, is there any objective method of determining which of them is right, or more nearly right than the other? A. L. Hilliard answers yes, and defends his objectivism as follows:

"When we ask the quite legitimate question, is the poetry of Leonidas of Tarentum beautiful or is it not? we certainly do not mean to determine our answer simply by *A*'s, *B*'s, or our own idiosyncrasies. What then is the universe of discourse within which we ask the question and expect the answer? I should suggest that it is determined in this interest by the character of a particular type of individual: the individual, namely, who has attained a certain degree of cultural maturity in the Western tradition, who has evinced interest in the creations of poetry, who is of a discriminating turn of mind, and perhaps who has a command of the Greek language. When we ask if the poetry of Leonidas is beautiful, we are asking whether or not the majority of connoisseurs, in something of the preceding sense, derives positive terminal value from reading it. If it does and if A is of this type and B is not, B is declared to be mistaken in his judgment, notwithstanding the truth of the proposition, 'Leonidas' poetry is not beautiful for B.' "—A. L. HILLIARD, *The Forms of Value*, p. 285.

Do you agree? If not, on what ground can you justify the teaching of art and literature, or the study of critical writings?

If, on the other hand, you accept Hilliard's criterion, how can you reconcile it with the wide disagreement among experts? Moreover, who are the experts? On that question, too, experts disagree. By what criterion can an ordinary man decide among them when their testimonies conflict?

CHAPTER XIII

Aesthetic Values

We all pass judgment from time to time that certain things are beautiful or ugly. Unfortunately the *word* "beautiful," being longer and clumsier than such equivalents as the German *"schön"* and the French *"beau,"* is not easy to use without a trace of self-consciousness. But there are other words which do service for it more colloquially. When we characterize something as pretty, charming, lovely, fine, superb, and the like, we are pronouncing, with one connotative emphasis or another, a favorable aesthetic judgment. Figures of speech and current slang provide further ways of expressing aesthetic approval or disapproval: to call someone a gorilla or a scarecrow suggests that the speaker finds a lack of certain specific aesthetic qualities in him.

It should be remembered that an aesthetic judgment is a judgment of intrinsic, not instrumental value. Its reference is to a quality that is regarded as an end in itself, not to some course of action for the attaining of that end. "That is a beautiful stretch of land" is an aesthetic judgment to the extent that the word "beautiful" conceals no implication for suggested behavior. If you tacitly add, "Just the place to start a real estate development," your judgment turns out to have been mainly utilitarian.

I have taken aesthetic *judgment* as the starting point of discussion because judgment is the stage at which experience becomes articulate. But if the judgment is honest, there must be or have been a real experience on which it is based. In Prall's words, "Aesthetic judgment is distinguished from aesthetic experience as such by the simple fact that it follows and records such experience after the experience has been had and with reference to what was experienced. . . . It is always a record of direct aesthetic experience, of the fact that in the presence of some objects beauty has been felt."[1] Prall warns, accordingly, against the practice of basing apparent aesthetic judgments on hearsay or authority. To declare the Parthenon frieze beautiful or *Paradise Lost* a majestically great poem merely because the consensus of competent opinion supports such judgments is to do little more than repeat a memorized phrase. Other people's critical approval is relevant only when we use it as a guide to explore new possibilities of aesthetic experience for ourselves.

i. The Aesthetic Experience

What are the principal ingredients of the aesthetic experience and of the object that excites it? The two questions cannot be separated. Experience and object are not sharply distinguishable, but stand in a mutually conditioning relation: sometimes the inquiry will be focused on the one, sometimes on the other, but always both will be involved. When the aesthetic object is manmade it may be defined as a "work of art" (with no implication as yet as to whether it is good or bad), and the special group of problems that then arise will be considered in Section ii. For the present our inquiry is aimed at the nature of the aesthetic experience and the aesthetic object in general, independently of any question as to how the object came into existence.

Pleasure and aesthetic surface

Some kind of pleasure is always involved in an aesthetic experience, but its role is prone to be misunderstood and misem-

[1] D. W. Prall, *Aesthetic Judgment* (Crowell, 1929), p. 5.

phasized. On the one hand it is clear that an aesthetic experience must be pleasurable. To say, "It is lovely music but I heartily dislike it," is either a contradiction or else represents a confusion of two different standards. A more accurate and more honest statement would be: "It is widely agreed to be lovely music and therefore it doubtless produces a pleasurable sense of loveliness in some persons, but it does not do so in me." On the other hand, while all genuine aesthetic experiences are pleasurable, it does not follow that all pleasurable experiences are aesthetic. Pleasures connected with the satisfaction of gross bodily needs —for food, sex, nerve-tingling excitement, simple release from strain—are not aesthetic in themselves, although under proper conditions they may be disciplined, stylized, and sublimated in such a way that they become aesthetic: as when a simple greed of the palate is educated into a pleasurable interest in the tasteful (not merely tasty) blending of flavors, or as when animal lust is elevated into the ritual of courtship. What, then, differentiates aesthetic from other kinds of pleasures?

Let us consider first the simplest manifestation of aesthetic pleasure—that which is stirred by a simple quality not involving any pattern or composition. As you gaze into an unclouded sky taking quiet delight in the pure limpid blue, or as you listen contentedly to the rustle of leaves and warblings of birds, the joy that you feel is, in this primitive way, an aesthetic one. Why? What distinguishes it? I think the answer is that joys of this kind involve none of the grosser discharges of bodily energy; they are experienced in quietude—not, however, the quietude of apathy, but rather a quietude combined with fully conscious awareness. Such calm receptivity on the subjective side corresponds, on the objective, to what Prall calls *aesthetic surface*.

Discriminating perception focused upon an object as it appears directly to sense, without ulterior interest to direct that perception inward to an understanding of the actual forces or underlying structure giving rise to this appearance, or forward to the purpose to which the object may be turned or to the events its presence and movement may presage, or outward to its relations in the general structure and the moving flux—such free attentive activity may fairly be said to mark the situation in which beauty is felt. It is the occurrence of such activity that makes possible the records put down in what we have called aesthetic judgments. Only the red that has caught our attention fully, and upon which that attention has actually rested, is more than merely red—bright or glaring or harsh or stirring, or lovely and rich and glowing, or fresh and clear and happy, or harsh or muddy or dull or distressing, ugly or beautiful in any one of a thousand determinate and specific meanings of those words.[2]

It is the full catching of awakened sensuous attention that counts. If someone asks me to hand him a red book, I notice its redness pragmatically, merely in order to perform a specified action. But when no action is involved, or when in spite of action my visual awareness is calm and free, I can attend to the redness with a certain quiet enjoyment. It may then become lovingly experienced for its own sake. It assumes a fuller and more concrete appearance, which might be approximately expressed by some such phrase as "cherry red" or "red like a smear of blood" or "a warm lush red," or the like. Of course, no words are precise enough to discriminate the subtlest shade of difference between one experience of red and another. But these several attempts at description are reminders of how an aesthetic contemplation of redness involves at once a greater concretion in the object—to such an extent that words can no longer do justice to it—and a greater intrusion of subjectivity, involving to some degree a willing fusion of subject and object. An aesthetic experience is subjective to the degree that the quality of it is conditioned (we never know just how far) by the sensitivity and emotional predisposition of the beholder. But at the same time it is objective: not only in the logically self-evident respect that some precise sensuous quality is presented as the object of the beholder's conscious enjoyment, but dynamically also, in that he submits

[2] Prall, *op. cit.*, p. 57. By courtesy of Thomas Y. Crowell Company.

voluntarily to the spell of that aesthetic object, and allows his senses and emotions to be guided by the unique particular nature that it displays.

Form

Except in limiting cases such as those just cited, the characteristic object of aesthetic delight is something more than a simple quality. It involves arrangement. Compare, to begin with, two very simple arrangements: a triangle resting on its base and the same triangle inverted and resting on its apex. As you contemplate the one you get a sense of stability, as you contemplate the other with full attention you enter imaginatively into its precarious balance. Consequently, while painters have frequently used the first triangle as a ground plan for the composition of a painting, the second would have to be used more cautiously—either as a component in a larger whole or else as a pendant with a suggestion of being fastened from above. In any case, our aesthetic apprehension of the two designs would be quite different, and this formal difference would play a substantial part in affecting the aesthetic response of an observer. Of course it must be understood that the form is never as simple as geometrical triangularity. There is a strong suggestion of triangularity, for example, in Raphael's celebrated painting, "The Garden Madonna," which hangs in the Louvre and reproductions of which can be found in many anthologies; but the base of Raphael's triangle is a living base, to which the skirt of the Madonna and the figures of the infants Jesus and John the Baptist variously contribute. The formal composition is more flowing than any geometry, because it is not independent of the sensuous content.

The presence of form thus introduces a new dimension of aesthetic pleasure. Such pleasure as comes from balance, symmetry combined with novelty, identity in difference, is not simply an addition to what we get from pure aesthetic surface, it is different. To let the mind and senses take in the noble proportions of a Poussin painting or the stately progression of a Bach fugue is another kind of experience from that of simply enjoying the cool greens or warm flesh tints in a painting or the pleasant sound of the cellos in the orchestra. The two kinds of factor are complementary and variously combined: a proper enjoyment of a painting will embrace the greens and flesh tints along with the arrangement in which they are composed; a delight in the formal pattern of a symphony or a fugue need not cancel out one's appreciation of the tonal beauty of the instruments.

Participation

Active enjoyment of beauty involves a certain paradox. Detachment is required, and yet the attitude of the detached observer, sensing the surface and discerning the form of an aesthetic object, is not enough. Pure detachment is aesthetically barren. Enjoyment of beauty involves love, and love involves a reaching out toward union with what is loved. Now love may have many stages and many degrees of refinement. At its most physical stage the union it desires is carnal; but such urgency is lust rather than love. What personal love involves is an intense interest in, and contemplation of, and craving to be closely associated with another *person*. Where "John loves Mary" is more than a perfunctory joke chalked on a fence, John wants to be involved in Mary's concerns, to become a part of the life of her thought and feelings, and thus to participate in her personhood. At the same time he probably sees Mary as an aesthetic object, delightful to behold. The outreaching toward participation *in* the object and the joyous contemplation *of* the object are two main complementary factors in the experience of love.

When the aesthetic object is not a person, in what sense can we still be said to participate in it? Theodor Lipps, an eminent German psychologist of half a century ago, declared that the imagination always feels its way into any object in which it takes aesthetic delight. Lipps named the process *Einfühlung*, the current English word for which is *empathy*. The following is an American psychologist's account of it:

> When we listen to a song, we have a tendency to move in time to the rhythm, and to repeat the notes with accompanying tension in the throat. In silent reading, the tendency to movement often goes over into actual movement of the lips or muscles of the larynx. The act of unity itself, fundamental to experience, is conceived in motor terms as a bringing of things together. . . . These motor sets may be, and in fact most frequently are, subconscious. The object observed, whether through the eye, ear, or another of the senses, arouses the memory of former movements, which are so revived that they form a nervous pattern; that is, the nerve paths going to the necessary muscle groups are opened, and those to opposed muscle groups are closed, and this pattern, which is ready on additional stimulation to produce actual movement, is sufficient to give us our perception of space, weight, form, smoothness, delicacy, and many of our other experiences.[3]

What the quotation stresses is the motor basis of empathy, which can be described in the technical language of experimental psychology, whereas the actual experience of empathy cannot. Some persons feel the empathic experience more fully than others: with the former, to admire a snow-covered pine tree is to feel the joy of communion or affinity with it. Such participation appears to have been far more widespread in earlier societies, when man's daily activities were more constantly in harmony with nature's pulsations, than now.

Significance

An aesthetic experience may consist largely of sheer delight in the surfaces of things, or it may give intimations of something more, of which the surfaces are a kind of *threshold symbol*. Where this latter condition is realized the aesthetic object strikes us as having not only beauty but also significance.

[3] Herbert Sidney Langfeld, *The Aesthetic Attitude* (Harcourt, Brace, 1920), pp. 110-111.

The growth of personal acquaintance supplies a familiar type of example. Recall the impression that some attractive person first made on you. Before you got to know him or her, the impression was largely an affair of aesthetic surface. Afterwards, if you found the person intelligent, sympathetic, and alert, the aesthetic impression was altered and deepened, for the aesthetic surface-pleasure of beholding a well-formed face and graceful carriage has now merged with the remembered and expected pleasures of lively and illuminating conversation. The face and form and voice have become threshold symbols for other in-interesting experiences that might be in store just beyond the threshold. The experience has acquired a dimension of *aesthetic depth*.

Even a face that had originally looked ugly can acquire aesthetic depth from our developing acquaintance with its owner in such a way that we later find it "striking" or "interesting": even the surface itself catches, by a happy contagion, some of the quality that attaches to the person. Thus you come to feel an affection for the very lineaments of a beloved friend: you wouldn't want them other than they are, however ugly they may be by conventional standards. This truth was memorably crystallized in Jean Cocteau's movie version of *Beauty and the Beast*, which has been exhibited in a number of American cities. In the standard child's version of the old fairy tale the ugly Beast, who is a handsome prince bewitched, wins Beauty's sympathy, then her love, whereupon the spell of enchantment is broken and he is transformed back into his original shape. The child reader is given to understand that Beauty is unreservedly delighted with the changed appearance and that all ends happily. In Cocteau's version the psychology is more subtle and more realistic. The moment of transformation is a moment of restrained shock: Beauty looks dazed and doubtful, for her beloved Beast has vanished; then, recovering, she accepts the situation and the prince with good grace, and with the lightest overtone of irony the film story "ends happily." But the spectator is left to wonder whether Beauty's future happiness will occasionally be touched by a wistful remembrance of the homely Beast who had been her first love.

Is significance involved in aesthetic objects that are neither actual persons nor man-made works of art? The answer will vary both with the nature of the object and the attitude of the spectator. Two spectators may enjoy a landscape aesthetically in different ways. The one may enjoy looking at what is simply, for him, a lovely pattern of forms, colors, and recognizable objects. The other may contemplate it with a more visionary eye —with a sensitivity to the haunting suggestions of nature's tendencies, pulsations, and mysteries that always elude direct grasp and logical formulation.

> For I would walk alone
> Under the quiet stars, and at that time
> Have felt whate'er there is of power in sound
> To breathe an elevated mood, by form
> Or image unprofaned; and I would stand,
> If the night blackened with a coming storm,
> Beneath some rock, listening to notes that are
> The ghostly language of the ancient earth,
> Or make their dim abode in distant winds.[4]

Because the depth dimension can never be made completely explicit without distorting its experiential nature, it will always have an ingredient of mystery. When we contemplate anything with full mind we feel our own finitude measured against the infinity of possibles that surround us. We feel stirred with both wonder and humility in the presence of the great Unknown, and the fused emotion that contains these two as its components is *awe*. Awe is the subjective correlative of mystery, as mystery is the objective correlative of awe; the terms are thus mutual indicators. But of course no definition can do more than

[4] William Wordsworth, *The Prelude* (1850 edition), Bk. II, lines 302-310.

set us down at the door of an idea; it is the experiential realization of awe in the presence of mystery that counts.

Psychic renewal

Where the preceding elements of aesthetic experience have been realized, the effect is likely to be a beneficent one. Our faculties are refreshed and reinvigorated, a new zest is felt, we become partialy re-created. To speak of "recreation" as synonymous with any kind of play or pastime is to overlook the important meaning which the word conceals. Not all of the so-called "recreations" in which we habitually indulge contribute much toward re-creating us. The role of pleasure as a component of aesthetic experience has already been acknowledged, but the *kind* of pleasure is more important than its sheer intensity. There are pleasures that stupefy the mind, pleasures that awaken it, and pleasures that leave scarcely any effect one way or the other. Each individual must supply his own instances. In any case a pleasure that is truly aesthetic—say a walk through the country on a clear fresh spring morning—always provides something of a release from tensions and a sustained sense of renewed joyous life. It involves what the Greeks called a *katharsis*—a spiritual purgation, or cleansing—of the old self; for the partial death of the old is always a factor in, and condition of, the creation of anything significantly new.

ii. Artistic Creation

The foregoing discussion has dealt with the aesthetic experience and the aesthetic object quite generally, without reference to how an aesthetic object may have come into existence. It is applicable, therefore, to natural and man-made beauty alike. Let us now examine certain questions which arise when we limit our attention specifically to man-made aesthetic objects, i.e., to works of art. The former dyadic relation becomes in this context a triadic relation: our discussion must now have three points of reference—the artist, the work of art, and the aesthetic observer. An aesthetic observer is more than a merely perceptual observer: he not only observes, he also enjoys; he not merely perceives, he is perceptive. A perceptive observer is one who discriminates, whose discriminations are relevant to the experience in question, and who still enjoys the original experience in its totality when the discriminations have been made. He is conscious not merely of liking or disliking a certain object or situation, but also of the characteristics, the qualities and relations and suggestive potencies in it, on which his judgment is based. An aesthetic observer is therefore to some degree a critic, and it will sometimes be convenient to employ the single word "critic" for any person, such as you or me, in so far as he enjoys a work of art with reasonable discrimination.

Art, to be sure, is a generic term. There are various arts, and there are distinctive problems arising out of each of them. Moreover, the word is of ambiguous extent. If you hear it said that someone is "studying art" you normally infer that he is taking up either painting or sculpture. On the other hand, when an educational institution is described as a "college of the arts and sciences," a broader meaning is implied. In order to delimit the subject matter suitably to a short discussion, while at the same time doing justice to the breadth of the major artistic problems, let us allow the term "art" here to comprise what are generally regarded as the six major arts—painting, sculpture, architecture, literature, music, and the dance. Of these, the first three are primarily spatial, the next two primarily temporal, and the last, the dance, spatial and temporal combined. One of them, moreover, architecture, is inseparable from functional considerations; the others not. To discuss the various interpretative and critical problems peculiar to each of the six major arts would require a separate volume; for indications in that direction the student is referred to some of the rewarding books listed at the end of the chapter. The present discussion is limited to a consideration of certain issues regarding the general nature of art as a sphere of human interest.

Functional utility

Architecture is the art most clearly connected with the idea of utility; it is the only one of the six major arts of which one can reasonably ask, what is it *for*? There are those who emphasize this aspect to the point of declaring that architecture should be exclusively functional, and that any departure from the functional needs of a building is architecturally bad. It must be admitted that functionalism contains a substantial amount of truth. Architectural customs tend to lag over from former ages, even though new functional requirements and newly available building materials with new properties invite drastic revision. The contribution of the American architect Frank Lloyd Wright has been to conceive of a building not as a pretty or conventional exterior which happens also to have an inside, but as an enclosed pattern of functionally understood spaces, the external enclosure in turn being suitably related both to the major function of the building and to the character of the terrain. To understand the function of the interior spaces an architect must enter imaginatively into the domestic life, profession, business, or other activity that is to be carried on within. Moreover, it is distasteful, from a functional standpoint, to see an office building surmounted with turrets and spires suggesting a mediaeval castle or Gothic cathedral, or to see a filling station trying to disguise itself as a mosque. As regards terrain, a house built on a rocky hillside, a house in a wood, and a house on an open plain should each be designed with discriminating reference to its respective site.

On the other hand, the functional idea in architecture need not be pressed to the farthest limit. A die-hard functionalist has been heard to condemn the magnificent bronze doors of the Florentine Baptistery on the ground that the function of a door is simply to open and shut and therefore a bas-relief of Biblical scenes is out of place on it. What this stubborn critic overlooks is that the function of those doors, as the Renaissance artist and his contemporaries conceived them, was not simply to open and shut, but symbolically to open the way into heaven. Analogously the high-vaulted nave of a Gothic church may be viewed quasi-functionally, since it draws the worshiper's thoughts upward, and "up" is a commonly shared symbol for one attribute of the Divine. In designing rooms in a private house an architect may well think functionally, but let him remember that a room functions in more ways than one. The late Katharine E. Gilbert distinguishes seven different ways, variously intermingling, in which a room can be conceived and enjoyed: as a cell or fortress, where our delight is in its protecting bounds and the sense of privacy it bestows; as a "porch"—where, as in Chinese dwellings and in some contemporary houses designed for warm climates, there is organic connection with the world outside; as an impalpable essence, offering delight by its mood, to which the prevailing color tone, the lighting, and numerous small touches are likely to contribute; as exhibiting harmony and satisfying proportions; as offering elements of surprise, unexpectedness and humor; as a reminder and symbol—by means of pictures and other art objects, which bring an effluence of remote or nonexistent worlds into the room; and finally as functional in the restricted sense—where the form and furnishings are controlled by prospective use, whether for entertaining, sleeping, working, or whatever else. Dr. Gilbert draws the reasonable conclusion:

> What after all is function? Activity directed to an end; and of these man has an uncounted number. It is a mistake to associate "functional building" with the more obvious physical usages of man, basic as these are. A man may need a spacious room not only to breathe in but to think in. Any want that genuinely stems from within is a "function" whether it is a temperamental order for gay fantastic decoration, or for a library full of emblem books.[5]

Certain theorists have tried to show that all the arts have their roots in utility. Painting, they say, goes back to the sign language

---

[5] Katharine E. Gilbert, "Seven Senses of a Room," *Journal of Aesthetics and Art Criticism,* September, 1949 (Vol. VIII, No. 1)

of pictograms and to pictures drawn with magical intent—like those of bison with arrows through the heart in the paleolithic caves of Spain and France; the earliest Egyptian sculptures appear to have been made in the likeness of the dead Pharaoh and placed in his tomb in order that his spirit might return and partake of the food and drink placed there for him; poetry arose because in the days when traditional tales were handed down by word of mouth it was easier to remember them if they were declaimed rhythmically; tribal dances were held to arouse the fighting spirit or magically to assist the cycle of the seasons and the growth of crops. What such considerations prove is that there is an important utility *element* in much early art. But utility is only one factor among several. Authentic art, primitive or civilized, exhibits a spontaneity, a love of form, and a precision of workmanship which go far beyond anything that practical necessity requires, and in many cases has no discoverable relation to it whatever.

Imitation

Aristotle has given the classical statement of the view that art, at least in the forms to which he gives consideration, involves imitation or miming (*mimêsis*) of something found in nature. In *The Art of Poetry* he writes:

Broadly considered, the origin of poetry may be traced to two causes, each of them inherent in man's nature. On the one hand the desire to imitate or represent is instinctive in man from childhood; in fact one of man's distinguishing marks is that he is the most mimetic of all animals, and it is through his mimetic activity that he first begins to learn. Moreover, such imitating and representing is always a source of delight, as experience plainly shows: for even where the objects themselves are disagreeable to behold—repulsive animals, for instance, or dead bodies—we take delight in artistically exact reproductions of them.[6]

[6] Aristotle, *The Art of Poetry (Poetics)*, Sec. 4. The other factor in the origin of poetry, although left rather obscure at this point in the text, is evidently the instinct to stylize—i.e., to arrange the imitations in rhythmic and patterned forms.

Three centuries later Lucretius explains the origin of music as having arisen from men's attempt to imitate the liquid notes of birds with their mouths and the whistlings of the wind among the reeds by blowing through hollow stalks.[7]

And there is no doubt that the imitative impulse plays an important role. In the prehistoric caves of the Upper Paleolithic Period, cited above, the animals are drawn with such attention to detail that the brown bear is still distinguishable from the cave bear and three distinct breeds of horses can be recognized. The bison's head is realistically lowered and his hair is correctly drawn long and thick on neck and back, short and smooth on the belly. The prehistoric artist has observed and reproduced the grace of the horse's foreleg, the reindeer's cautious turn of the head, the stretched necks of cattle. In the primitive dance, too, imitation is an important formative factor. In Mexico at the present day one can see mimetic dances in which the participants wear skins or feathers and imitate rhythmically the characteristic attitudes and movements of certain animals. Other mimetic dances simulate the movements of love or war or such daily activities as stalking game.

But how far should the imitative role of art be carried? Probably no one would maintain that art should strictly copy nature on the one hand, while very few would say that it should have no recognizable relation to nature on the other. Even the paleolithic cave artist deliberately exaggerated certain qualities in the animals he was drawing—great strength and force in the bison's body together with exquisite grace in the preternaturally thin legs—no doubt because these qualities stirred a responsive feeling in him which he felt impelled to express. And perhaps there was another motive too, at once objective and dynamic. Aristotle supplemented his doctrine of imitation and offered a more organic conception of the artist's function when he declared that art gives the finishing touches to what nature has left incomplete. The paleolithic caves, of which Aristotle knew nothing,

---

[7] Lucretius, *De Rerum Natura*, Bk. V, lines 1379-1384.

lend incidental confirmation to this view. One thing that those prehistoric artists have frequently done is utilize natural formations of rock and stalagmite deposit to make the ribs and legs of a horse or bison, and affix stag's horns to a natural skull-shaped depression in the rock. Gertrude R. Levy, who has made an intensive study of the Period, takes the practice to indicate that nature's markings on the rock appeared to primitive man as indications of animal souls residing there.[8] What nature offered to the prehistoric artist—as it offers to every artist, and to the artistic faculty hidden in each one of us—was not a completed model to be imitated in prescribed detail, but a raw material, potent with suggestive possibilities, to be molded into an expressive and artistically effective form.

Self-expression

It is sometimes said that art must be an expression of deep feeling or it is nothing. Friedrich Nietzsche, Benedetto Croce, Eugene Véron, and Oscar Wilde are among the well-known writers who have espoused an expressionist theory of art. Véron declares that the artist is "free, absolutely free in his own province, on the one condition of absolute sincerity. He must seek to express the ideas, sentiments, and emotions proper to himself, and must copy no one." For, Véron argues, a work may have many acknowledged faults and yet win our admiration "solely by the personality of its author which shines through it with powerful originality, and by the energy with which it manifests the character and constitution of an individual impression." Accordingly he defines art as "the manifestation of an emotion" which obtains external interpretation through "expressive arrangement" of the lines, forms, and colors, or of the sounds and words or other elements of the chosen medium.[9]

Now it would seem that there is a limited sense in which

[8] Gertrude R. Levy, *The Gate of Horn* (London: Faber and Faber, 1948).
[9] Eugene Véron, *Aesthetics* (Eng. tr., 1879), pp. vii-viii, 53, 97.

Véron is right and another in which he is dangerously misleading. Art must originate in a genuine and individual feeling on the part of the artist toward the thing he is creating. If his feeling toward it is superficial or hackneyed or fuzzy and vague—a mere play upon the surface of his mind or a mere echo of other men's emotional clichés or an obscure yearning for undisciplined expression—his product will be mediocre. The German novelist Jakob Wassermann has written about his craft:

> The problem that confronts us in art is always this: at what level of intensity and renewal can the outer world, with all it offers of experience and life, be transferred to the inner world and there be recast in such a way that the resultant abbreviations, which are constructive and of the order of phantasy, can comprise on a higher level what our immediate experiences offer at first hand? That is exactly the problem of form, which is nothing more than the problem of the artist.[10]

To see or hear anyone merely "express himself" is likely to be boring, except to a sympathetic friend. An artist wins his right to a general hearing by having a real wealth of significant experience and interests, long reflected on, to express; and by developing a skill whereby he can mould his self-expressive urge into a form that is effectively communicative and aesthetically interesting.

Formalization

The problem of form is different for each of the arts. In painting, for instance, it involves not only a general pictorial pattern, but relationships of line and mass, of light and shade, of one color to another, and the like. In literature it is not merely the overt structure that is in question—the metrical beat, the regular or irregular lines of a poem, the three or five acts of a drama—but the entire confluence of rhythm (which is more subtle and

[10] Jakob Wassermann, "Attempt at a Spiritual Autobiography" *(Versuch einer geistigen Autobiographie)*, in *Die Literarische Welt*, June 26, 1931.

varied than meter), imagery, idea, and emotive evocation which builds up and lets down in some kind of patterned way. In music and the dance the dominant element of form is rhythm. Gross rhythms tend to victimize the organism that submits to them, as may be seen from the uncontrolled swaying or jerking bodies and tapping feet of juke box addicts. Subtler rhythms, such as the master composers know how to employ, do not stimulate an overt physical effect, but stir the listener by heightening his power of sensitive receptivity. By their varying but somehow related modulations they invite the intelligence to be awake instead of lulling it to sleep. Musical rhythm is not the steady ticktock of the metronome, but the pulsing expression of an idealized inner life, conceived by the composer's auditory imagination. Larger units of form—such as sonata, fugue, symphonic poem, or theme and variations—constitute the structure of the musical composition, and give the listener a satisfying sense of unity persisting through diversity and making the diversity significant and purposeful.

Certain modern movements in art have tended to stress formal elements to what would seem, by more conservative standards, an exaggerated degree. The Russian painter Kandinsky found that in painting a picture the "inner necessity" of the composition required him to distort the forms of objects until they lost their identities. So he gradually acquired the gift of no longer noticing the given object, or at least of overlooking it. And he declares as a kind of manifesto: "No more external reality—dogs, vases, naked women—but instead, the 'material' reality of pictural means and resources which calls for the complete transformation of all vehicles of expression, and even technique itself. A picture is the synthetic unity of all its parts."[11] It is reasonable and valid to affirm that the critical appraisal of a painting should be based not on its subject matter but on the

---

[11] Wassily Kandinsky, quoted in Frances B. Blanshard, *Retreat from Likeness in the Theory of Painting* (Columbia University Press, 1949), p. 133.

way in which the subject matter is given expressive form; it does not in the least follow from this that a painting need have no subject matter whatever. Abstract art is often a useful laboratory exercise for the painter testing out the effect of certain combinations of lines and colors, and it may stimulate new visual perceptiveness in the observer, but it is not sufficiently integral to wear the mark of greatness.

Communication of meaning

An artist, to be of any interest, must "have something to say." What he has to say is uniquely related to the language and context of his art; it cannot be said in any other way than he has said it. His quick perception detects some quality in a scene or event that he wishes to commemorate by his art and so immortalize by withdrawing it from the stream of time. A landscape under a certain light, a series of tones heard by the inner ear, a peculiar mood of exaltation, a smile on a child's face—whatever it may be, or in whatever combination, it is some freshly envisaged patch of outer or inner experience that asserts itself as too valuable to let slip away. On hearing such a work as Beethoven's Ninth Symphony one can hardly doubt that it expresses a certain vision of life, a way of apprehending the totality of experience, even though any attempt to say in words what it means must necessarily fail.

In literature the problem of meaning is complicated, and its possibilities are enriched, by the fact that the medium of expression here is *words,* which, when suitably combined into *language,* have incomparably greater meaning-potentialities than colors and masses, or tones and harmonies. For the technique by which words are linguistically combined is *syntax*; and what syntax can express, which the entirely fluid devices of music and the presentational devices of painting cannot, is *the relational structure of what is meant.*

On the other hand the syntax of *expressive* language, which distinguishes literature, is not limited to the forms of syntax which constitute *logical* language—although it does not entirely lose connection with these. Even where the grammatical syntax follows the accepted conventions, the inner semantic syntax (i.e., the operation of word-groupings to produce meanings) is likely to be more freely explorative. Whereas strictly logical language is content to designate the general characteristics of an object—those which give it membership in a class-concept—expressive language—which, when controlled by deliberate art, may be called *poetic* language—draws the hearer's attention to what is most concrete, particular, and distinctive about some actual or proposed experience taken in its wholeness.

> The trees are in their autumn beauty,
> The woodland paths are dry,
> Under the October twilight the winter
> Mirrors a still sky;
> Upon the brimming water among the stones
> Are nine-and-fifty swans.[12]

Again, where the logical use of language stays close to the conventional or else explicitly stipulated meaning of a word, the expressive use of language exploits the controlled associations of a word: as may be illustrated by the difference between the literal meaning of the word "concave," as a draughtsman or physicist might use it, and the glowing suggestiveness of Wordsworth's

> Beneath the concave of an April sky . . .

Whereas in the logical or "literal" use of language the meaning of a word can be stipulated by definition, and hence can and should be kept invariant throughout a given frame of reference, the problem is somewhat different when language functions poetically. For since one aim of expressive language is to do

---

[12] William Butler Yeats, "The Wild Swans at Coole," from *Collected Poems*. Reprinted by courtesy of the Macmillan Company, publisher.

fullest possible justice to the ever-changing character of experience as actually lived and concretely imagined, its meanings will reflect to some degree, although never adequately, the fluctuations of life itself. Hence a word or phrase functioning poetically, although never entirely out of relation to its prose-and-dictionary meaning, acquires fresh connotations, fresh overtones of suggestiveness, from each new context into which it enters. The result is that there are likely to be tensions of meaning—*semantic tensions*—between what I. A. Richards has called the "scenario meaning" of an expressive passage and the connotations which the context calls into being, or even between one such set of connotations and another. It would be roughly true to say that whereas logical-literal meanings are characteristically *stipulative*, expressive-poetic meanings are characteristically *contextual*.

There is a price to be paid for linguistic expressiveness, and that is the greater hazard of communication. To the extent that meanings are subtler, more concrete, more fluid, and more richly suggestive, they are correspondingly more difficult to control; with the result that a person who has not disciplined and advanced his powers of expression often feels frustrated by his inability to communicate what he deeply but inarticulately means. The development of a command of language, therefore, not only as a pragmatic tool, but as an instrument for conveying and receiving the fullest possible semantic content in one's relationships with fellow-beings, stands among the highest of man's intrinsic values.

For Further Study

ANDRÉ MALRAUX, *The Voices of Silence* (Doubleday, 1953).
SUSANNE K. LANGER, *Feeling and Form* (Scribner, 1953).
LOUIS W. FLACCUS, *The Spirit and Substance of Art* (F. S. Crofts, 1926).
E. F. CARRITT, *The Theory of Beauty* (Macmillan, 1914).
BERNARD BOSANQUET, *Three Lectures on Aesthetics* (Macmillan, 1915).

John Dewey, *Art as Experience* (Minton, Balch, 1934).
Stephen C. Pepper, *Principles of Art Appreciation* (Harcourt, Brace, 1949).
Stephen C. Pepper, *Aesthetic Quality* (Scribner, 1937).
Brewster Thiselin, *The Creative Process* (University of California Press, 1952). Thirty-eight artists in different fields describe the creative process as they have experienced it.
Frances M. Blanshard, *Retreat from Likeness in the Theory of Painting* (Columbia University Press, 1949).
Helen H. Parkhurst, *Beauty* (Harcourt, Brace, 1931).
Herbert S. Langfeld, *The Aesthetic Attitude* (Harcourt, Brace, 1920).
Jacques Maritain, *Creative Intuition in Art and Poetry* (Bollingen Series, Pantheon Press, 1953).
Theodore M. Greene, *The Arts and the Art of Criticism* (Princeton University Press, 1940).
Erich Auerbach, *Mimesis: The Representation of Reality in Western Literature* (Princeton University Press, 1953).
Katharine E. Gilbert and Helmut Kuhn, *A History of Esthetics* (Indiana University Press, 1953).

Anthologies

Eliseo Vivas and Murray Krieger, *The Problems of Aesthetics* (Rinehart, 1953).
Melvin Rader, *A Modern Book of Aesthetics* (Holt, rev. ed., 1952).
Edwin B. Burgum, *The New Criticism* (Prentice-Hall, 1930).

Questions for Discussion

1. May "aesthetic experience" be defined as "experience of the beautiful," or is this too narrowing a definition? Can there be aesthetic experiences of non-beautiful objects—e.g., of the grotesque and the comic? If you answer yes, then (*a*) how will you define "aesthetic," and (*b*) how will you distinguish the beautiful from other species of aesthetic object?

2. Is successful imitation important as an element in painting and sculpture? If you answer yes, must the abstractions of Picasso and

Brancusi be condemned wholesale? If you answer no, what do you make of the following statements by two great poets?

a) Homer, describing the shield of Achilles, says: "And behind the plough the earth went black, and looked like ploughed ground, though it was made of gold; that was a very miracle of his craft."

b) Dante praising the sculptures on the marble of Purgatory says that the smoke was so faithfully represented as to set his eyes and nose at variance as to whether it was real.

Examine Bosanquet's view that the miracle which both poets admire lies here: "that without the heavy matter and whole natural process of the reality, man's mind possesses a magic by which it can extract the soul of the actual thing or event, and confer it on any medium which is convenient to him, the wall of a cave, or a plate of gold, or a scrap of paper."—BERNARD BOSANQUET, *Three Lectures on Aesthetics,* p. 50.

3. "The materialistic doctrine that has most influenced aesthetic theory is the doctrine that the artist's perceptions give us no knowledge of the nature of reality."—J. W. N. SULLIVAN, *Beethoven: His Spiritual Development* (Knopf, 1927; reprinted in Mentor Books).

Is there any relation between this philosophical predisposition and the greater emphasis on distortion and technical experiment in modern art?

4. "Unless there is com-pression, nothing is ex-pressed."—JOHN DEWEY, *Art as Experience,* p. 66. Compare the ancient Hindu myth that the creator god Prajapati "first practiced austerities upon himself" and thus there grew up within him the power to create the worlds.

But Dewey explains the compression as resulting when "inner impulse and contact with environment, in fact or in idea, meet and create a ferment." And he cites in illustration the war dance and harvest dance of the savage which "do not issue from within except there be an impending hostile raid or crops are to be gathered." Is it true that artistic creation requires such external incentives? What counter-suggestion is contained in Wordsworth's phrase, "recollection in tranquillity"?

5. Discuss Dewey's statement that "insincerity in art . . . is found wherever substance and form fall apart" (*op. cit.*, p. 127). How would it apply to the use of Gothic spires on an office building? to

the playing of Brahms or Wagner as an accompaniment to radio or video commercials? Can you suggest other illustrations?

6. "A work of genius is not a thing of utility. To be useless is its very patent of nobility. It exists for itself alone."—SCHOPENHAUER.

Are these three sentences interdependent? Are they all equally true?

CHAPTER XIV

Values in Action: the Realm of Ethics

WHEN WE PASS from value in general to moral value in particular we raise the question, *What to do?* Aesthetic values are beheld and enjoyed; moral values are taken as criteria and guides of action. The study of moral values falls under the general topic of *ethics*—in the philosophical sense of the word. Ethics, then, may be provisionally defined as "the systematic study of reflective choice, the standards of right and wrong by which it may be guided, and the attainable goods towards which it may be directed."[1] The problem of standards and goods and their interrelations will receive attention in the sections that follow. As a preliminary step let us consider what reflective choice mainly involves.

The nature of ethical choice

To choose implies that there are *significant alternatives*, each of which *can be*, but *is not certain of being* realized. The italicized words correspond to the third, second, and first (in this order) of the conditions of moral valuation stated on pp. 411-413. Underlying all ethical discussion, therefore, and conditioning its very possibility, are the postulates that some values are real and significant; that human choices can sometimes be effective in molding a future which is not entirely fixed; and that the effort

[1] Philip Wheelwright, *A Critical Introduction to Ethics* (Odyssey Press, rev. ed., 1949), p. 3.

of decision is needful, since the world to which it can be applied is imperfect. These postulates are metaphysical rather than ethical, but they must be at least tacitly acknowledged by anyone to whom ethics is more than an academic game.

Now the choice, to be truly ethical, must be reflective. Of course many human actions are "ethical" in the conventional sense of following a prescribed pattern of behavior, or in the negative sense that they harm no one. These more colloquial uses of the word should not be allowed to confuse the main meaning. To be ethical in the best sense is to act with a kind of open honesty toward the question, *Why?* It does not require us to postpone further action until all the *whys* are answered. Philosophy is not moral paralysis. But even in the acting—from whatever urgency or habit or interest or loyalty or whim—the ethical man, which is to say the honest lover of philosophy, stands always ready to look both motive and results in the face, using his previous experience, both outer and inner, as a guide to wiser choosing at the next opportunity.

In thus examining himself and thereby taking more effective command of his actions in the future a man acts on the human as distinguished from the merely animal level. For while man is certainly an animal, he is a very distinctive kind of animal—the animal who can think and reflect. The ability to think—in its ethical as distinguished from its purely contemplative aspect—finds fullest expression in those moments of conscious stock-taking when a man faces the perennial question: "What kind of a life do I choose to lead, and why?" That is, in fact, the central question of ethical philosophy.

There are three main ways in which the ethical problem can be envisaged, and consequently three main interpretations or translations of the question just put. Ethics may concern itself primarily with satisfactions, with duties, or with self-realization. The first type of ethics takes the basic question to mean, "What do I most want to *get* out of life?" The second takes it to mean: "What are my principal *duties* in life? What ought I to *do*?" The third: "What kind of a person do I really want to *be*?" In practice these three concepts—getting, doing, and being—are variously interrelated and sometimes hard to distinguish. Nevertheless they represent different basic perspectives. In fact it can be said that the main differences among ethical philosophies arise out of the way in which one or another of the concepts is emphasized and interpreted. Accordingly we shall examine the three perspectives, one by one, in the three sections that follow.

i. *The Ethics of Satisfactions*

The method of the first type of ethics usually consists of the following steps:

(1) To discover the things most wanted for their own sakes —e.g., friendship, harmonious family relations, a congenial occupation, attractive surroundings, adequate wealth, a proper balance of adventure and security, a favorable reputation, intellectual interests, an occasional sense of power, a well-adjusted sex life, tasty meals, pleasant forms of exercise and recreation, a feeling of security toward the future, and so on. All such things are postulated as *intrinsic goods*.

(2) To analyze their common character, and to postulate this as the dominant intrinsic good. Such goods, when set in clear distinction from the actions designed to produce them, are usually conceived hedonistically—i.e., in terms of pleasure, together with its more tepid associates comfort and security. Thus Bentham sets up the pleasure and comfort of mankind as the dominant intrinsic good, Epicurus the cultivated pleasures which a man can share with his friends; while Callicles, the cynical man-about-town in Plato's Dialogue *Gorgias*, holds that a sensible fellow will devote his life to securing the maximum of pleasurable sensations *for himself*, artificially stimulating his appetites in order to increase their capacity for enjoyment.

(3) Having discovered or postulated the dominant intrinsic good, the next step is to recognize its contrary as intrinsically bad, or (although some reject the word) evil. The dominant bad-in-

itself, or evil-in-itself, according to virtually all hedonists, is pain —interpreted broadly enough to include such vaguely unpleasurable states as boredom, fatigue, etc.

(4) Having discovered by reflection the intrinsic goods, and by analysis the dominant quality which pervades them all, the last main step is to discover empirically both the means and the hindrances to their attainment. Such means and hindrances are *instrumental* goods and bads respectively.

The theory of hedonism

That pleasure and comfort (by which word we may designate absence of pain) are intrinsic goods is evident from the fact that anyone would reject as foolish the question "Why do you want them?" The only answer would be the child's answer, "Because I do." And that, of course, is no answer at all. If you were asked, "Why would you like an income of $50,000 a year?" you might perhaps reasonably answer, "Because of all the pleasurable things I could buy with it," or "Because of the comfort and security it would give me"—where security denotes the prospect of comfort in the future. We can justify our choices as instrumentalities of pleasure or comfort or both; but pleasure and comfort, when they are wanted, are wanted for their own sakes.

Now the hedonist assumes that pleasure and comfort, in some proportion or other, are wanted all the time. This assumption is a psychological one, since it represents a theory about the motives, or psychological causes, of why people act as they do. It involves a one-sided interpretation of the facts, as was argued in Section i of Chapter XII. Moreover it propounds a two-sided riddle. For in the first place, why is there any need for a code of ethics, if it is known in advance that everyone will act in such a way as to procure his own pleasure and comfort? Since pleasure and absence of pain are the two sides of man's dominant intrinsic *good*, and since they are also the constant object of every man's *actual* pursuit, isn't ethics thereby rendered superfluous? Why not just coast along?

Bentham's reply to this first side of the riddle, and his justification of the ethics, is that people are often unwise in their pursuit of those desirable ends. Through ignorance, sloth, rash impulse, prejudice, and conventionality they make many wrong choices—which is to say, choices that lead to less pleasure and more pain than would have been got by other means. The hedonistic "ought" is therefore always a *prudential* one. "You ought to keep your promises, pay your bills, etc." means, to the hedonist, "It is prudent to do so; you'd better do these things because you're likely to get pleasant results if you do, painful ones if you do not." Ethics thus becomes a science of calculation; Bentham even goes so far as to call it "moral arithmetic."

The social quandary

But there is another side to the hedonistic riddle. Bentham's theory of all obligation as prudential gives ethics a content, to be sure, but a purely egoistic one. Now people do have to live together in society, and how is this possible if everyone is really concerned only with getting the most favorable credit balance of pleasures over pains *for himself*? As a matter of fact, Bentham's personal disposition was strongly benevolent, and he had relinquished a private law practice in order to devote himself to social reform—that is, to producing a greater amount of "happiness" (by which word he denotes the double meaning of pleasure and absence of pain) *for the greatest number of people*. No doubt he could justify his own benevolent activities to himself, on the ground that a man of such disposition receives more "happiness" from ameliorating the lot of others than from a life devoted either to private study or to competitive greed. But most people have far less active concern for others than a public-spirited man like Bentham. What *they* get most pleasure and comfort from is their eating and drinking, their lusts, and their petty amusements. A man like Bentham, who happens to enjoy social welfare work, will engage in it simply because it is pleasurable *to him*; other men, who happen not to enjoy it particularly, will let it go by default.

The problem is intensified when we look at the reverse side of the matter. Not only are most people slothful about helping others; there are moments in most people's lives when it is tempting to secure pleasure or comfort for oneself even at the cost of injuring someone else. Now Bentham declares outspokenly that in *all* actions *every* human being pursues the line of conduct which "according to his view of the case, taken by him at the moment" will yield the greatest amount of pleasure and comfort *to himself*—"whatsoever be the effect of it, in relation to the happiness of other similar beings, any or all of them taken together."[2] In other words, men are so constituted, that every one of them will injure his fellows when it appears to be to his benefit to do so. Here, then, is the second side of the hedonistic riddle. In the private sphere we had to ask, "Why is ethics needed?" and we have seen Bentham's reply. In the social sphere we must raise the more formidable question, "How is ethics possible?" If it is possible, it is certainly needed, for society can hardly survive unless its members are somehow induced to respect one another's claims to happiness as well as pursuing individually their own. But how, if men are unmitigated egoists, can they be so induced?

Bentham replies with his doctrine of "sanctions." As his own statement of the doctrine is given in the Readings (pp. 513-523), it will be sufficient here to speak of two types of sanction only, "the political or legal," and the "popular or moral." The former of these has two branches, "the judicial acting almost exclusively by punishments, the administrative mostly by rewards." Bentham's theory of penal jurisprudence is a logical outcome of his hedonism. The only justification of legal punishment, he argues, is to set up penalties as deterrents against anti-social offenses. In hedonistic language, a prospect of pain is set before the potential wrongdoer, just harsh enough to overbalance the prospect of pleasure attached to the deed. The potential burglar (not, of course, the habitual one) will apply the hedonistic calculus by

[2] Bentham, *Works*, Vol. IX, p. 5.

balancing the pleasure of getting loot against the discomfort of going to prison; if the law is rightly designed and efficiently enforced, the amount and high probability of that discomfort will counteract the attraction of burglarizing. Of course Bentham does not mean that the wavering burglar employs such academic language or such a deliberate thought-process, but only that some such hedonistic logic implicitly and perhaps inarticulately affects his course of action.

The "popular or moral sanction" operates more widely and on the whole more effectively than the legal. Everyone desires to be thought well of by someone or other, by some group or other, in some respect or other. If we fail to achieve repute in some desired respect we may cover our chagrin with a show of bravado, or we may transfer our efforts into another channel. Hitler failed to impress Viennese art dealers with his paintings as a young man; his need of recognition, frustrated in one respect, found a wider and more disastrous scope in the seizure of political control. On the more favorable side, a concern for public opinion prevents a man from many actions injurious to his neighbors, and stirs him to some degree of social coöperation.

Is hedonism enough?

There is a good deal in hedonism, both practically and theoretically, that invites approval. On the practical side, let us agree that to learn the art of full enjoyment is a large part of the wisdom of life. Montaigne observes that "man foolishly exercises his ingenuity in lessening the number and sweetness of the pleasures that we have a right to; as he industriously and successfully employs his artifices in tricking out and disguising the ills and alleviating the sense of them."[3] Thus the appeal of hedonism is in part legitimate. It need not invite to depraved kinds of pleasure; for these, by the hedonist's own logic, can be rejected as tending to produce eventually disagreeable effects. It

[3] Michel de Montaigne (1533-1592), *Essays*, Bk. I, Chap. XXX. (Trechmann's translation: Oxford University Press.)

may be a useful device for awakening the mind to explore the richnesses that life offers, and to attend with full sensuous enjoyment to the qualities of each experience that comes.

There is the practical danger, however, that in pursuing pleasures we may become dependent on them. And the result of that is continual insecurity, for pleasures (in the word's usual sense) are externally as well as internally conditioned, and in the former respect they lie essentially outside of our control. The Stoic philosophy draws attention to this harsh fact, and concludes that pleasures, since they merely *happen* to us, must be a matter of complete indifference to the wise man; and that a more reasonable objective is perfected self-discipline, since that does lie within the doer's power. Since enjoyment and self-discipline—*eros* and *askêsis*—are necessary complementaries in a wise pattern of human living, neither complete acceptance nor complete rejection of the hedonistic ideal seems advisable.

On the theoretical side, hedonism makes its appeal probably for two main reasons. In the first place, it brings into the open an element which it would be hypocritical to deny. Pleasure and comfort do motivate us to a larger degree than we are sometimes ready to admit, and a deflation of idealistic pretensions is sometimes a mark of honesty. It can be carried too far, however, and the sort of bravado which prompts a man to assign ignoble motives to his generous or courageous acts may be almost as much a distortion of the truth as the hypocrisy against which it is reacting. A less distasteful falsehood no doubt, but a falsehood still.

Secondly, hedonism has the lure of simplicity. Human motives are complex, elusive, and variable; to understand them in the full manifoldness of their actuality defies even the hardiest intelligence. Hedonism therefore does what, essentially, every theory does: it selects a prominent set of characteristics which can be systematized and somewhat objectively explored, and allows these to stand as symbol and representative of all else. An analogous selectivity was noted in the kinetic theory of physical nature (Chapters V and VI). Here, as there, it is wise to remember the limits of effective theorizing. The progress of intelligence consists not in systematizing alone, but of systematization and exploration in dialectical mutuality. As the mediaeval schoolman's reliance on Aristotle was valuable as far as it led him to explore the natural world's diverse potencies but self-defeating when it prevented his discovery of physical and physiological laws that Aristotle's science did not embrace, so too with hedonism. Its value as a theory depends on a willingness to recognize its limits of effective application. How are those limits determined?

A theory outruns its usefulness, I would say, when the identities and distinctions which it sets up as primary turn out, in a given application, to be unimportant ones, and hence distract the mind from what is really important. For instance, when Bernard Mandeville argues that "there is no merit in saving an innocent babe ready to drop into the fire" on the ground that "we only obliged ourselves, for to have seen it fall, and not strove to hinder it, would have caused a pain, which self-preservation compelled us to prevent,"[4]—when he argues thus, and declares such an action "neither good nor bad," is he not failing (in Plato's metaphor) to carve at the joints of the argument? Surely it is of major importance whether a bystander rescues the innocent babe in this harrowing situation or with a shrug of the shoulders lets it drop. To lump the contrary alternatives under one category and declare them both morally indifferent because the bystander simply pleased himself in either case is to pretend an identity where no significant identity exists. Similarly to explain a soldier's bravery in battle, a mother's devotion to her child, a traveler's love of adventure, and a libertine's unbridled lusts by the same single "principle of self-preference," as Bentham calls it, is to smudge over the important distinctions in order to maintain a position.

[4] Bernard Mandeville (1670-1733), *An Enquiry into the Origin of Moral Virtue.*

Let us turn now to another, radically different conception of ethics, and see what can be said for taking such terms as *right, ought, duty,* and *obligation* as fundamental and primary in ethical inquiry.

ii. The Idea of Duty

That the *idea* of duty exists is an undeniable fact. Nearly everybody recognizes some duties or other, and implicitly approves or condemns himself according as he performs or neglects them. But how is the idea of duty to be explained and justified? In appearance it is quite a different sort of thing from impulse. A conflict between impulses takes the form, "Which would I rather do—go to the dance or go to a movie?" The question there is one of actual preference, and the purpose of deliberation is simply to find out, in view of the probable outcome of each alternative, which of the two impulses is actually the stronger.

The nature of temptation

A conflict between impulse and duty seems to be essentially different. We do not ask ourselves which impulse is actually stronger, but which one, regardless of its present strength, we ought to try to make prevail. Everyone has known what it is to be tempted. In a case of strong temptation the conflict within us seems to be between an impulse which it would be easier to yield to, and a conviction that it is our duty to resist this impulse and act in another way. The conviction of duty is not an abstraction, it has some impulsive power, but its actual power as an impulse is often slighter than that of its rival, so that it must be reinforced by an extra effort on the doer's part. The question of whether this extra effort is something added to the situation or was really there latent all the time has been discussed in Chapter X. Our present question is about the nature of the sense of duty that stirs the effort. And the first point to be clear about is that the prompting of the "ought" is not so much a drive as an inner exhortation, not so much impulsive as imperative—a sort of unspoken command to master the stronger impulse.

The strongest actual propensity at a given moment is often towards a course of action contrary to the one towards which duty beckons. An effort is required to break away from the fascination of the immediate. The sense that such an effort is required, that it *can* be made, and that it would be better to make it because the result would be an eventually greater good, are conditions of a feeling of "ought."[5]

Can an ethics of satisfactions explain the phenomenon of temptation? After a fashion. A hedonist interprets all such apparent conflicts between pleasure and duty as really conflicts between a nearer, more obvious pleasure and a more remote pleasure which, by the illusion of distance, looks less attractive to the beholder although intellectually he has calculated it to be greater. The hedonist does not suppose us to be always moved by what is actually the greatest pleasure, but by what strikes us as such at the moment of decision. Ideas must be vivid in order to strike us forcibly, and propinquitous results (as Bentham calls them) are likely to be imagined more vividly than remote ones. To be tempted, then, the hedonist explains, is to be moved by a vividly imagined idea of pleasure even though we know intellectually that a larger amount of pleasure or a lesser amount of pain would eventually be got from following the opposite course. To "overcome temptation" is, for the hedonist, to succeed in imagining the remoter pleasures and pains more vividly, so that a more accurate hedonistic calculus can be computed.

Now even if the hedonist's account seems fairly plausible for cases of private temptation, where only one's own future is at stake, how does it apply to the temptation to be selfish at someone else's expense? By hypothesis we are all completely selfish in everything we do; how then explain the sense of duty to others? In the temptation to be selfish at another's expense, the conflict is not, as in the former case, between a present and a

[5] Wheelwright, *op. cit.*, p. 16.

future pleasure or pain of one's own, but between my pleasures or pains and yours. Bentham's five sanctions do not operate perfectly enough to equalize such conflicts of interest. The best of calculations may indicate a probable deficit of pleasures for me from performing a certain act, and yet the conviction of a duty to perform it is not lessened thereby. There have been cases of soldiers who allowed themselves to be tortured to death by the enemy rather than betray their own comrades-at-arms. Is their "pleasure" of imagining how their sacrifice will benefit the army *gerater in amount* than the physical agony of the ordeal?

The plain fact seems to be that duty is essentially distinct from pleasure, however much the two may be commingled in concrete instances. Correspondingly, on the subjective side, conscience is essentially distinct from impulse—with the same qualification. For conscience and duty are subjective and objective correlatives in a moral situation. Duty is *what* one ought to do, and conscience is one's moral *discernment* of that duty. How is such discernment to be explained?

In general there are four types of explanation which still preserve the distinctive character of duty as something more than impulse: the authoritarian, the rationalistic, the humanistic, and the religious. The authoritarian answer requires no discussion, for if one accepts a given authority as absolute in moral matters—a holy Book, or a Church, or a dictator's commands—the only questions to be asked are: "What does the authority say on a given matter?" and, if there is no pronouncement on the matter in question, then: "How should the authority's words be interpreted so as to apply?" The humanistic answer will be examined in Section iii, and the religious answer is implicit in the argument of the next chapter. We turn, now, then, to the answer propounded by rationalism.

Kant: duty as commitment to a universal

One of the most uncompromising of all theories of moral duty is that espoused by Immanuel Kant. The first essential fact about duty, as Kant rightly sees, is its *autonomy*. It does not take orders from impulse nor yet from calculated self-interest. Its difference from impulse in general has just been discussed. Where an impulse becomes transferred into a long-range objective—e.g., where a man's acquisitive urge, his desire for pleasure and security, and his love of power combine into the long-range interest of amassing a fortune—a sense of duty, an imperative, develops. But it is a prudential, or as Kant calls it a "hypothetical" imperative, not an intrinsic or "categorical" one. It has no binding power in itself; it only says, "If you wish to achieve so-and-so, then do this as a necessary means." If you wish to win scholastic honors you'd better study, if you wish to amass a fortune you'd better sweat and save. The "you'd better" is sometimes masked as an "ought," but it is essentially no different from such idiomatic uses as "You're on the wrong road; you ought to have turned right." Is there any imperative that is binding in itself—any purely *categorical* one?

Kant's answer is yes, and his argument is briefly this. Man's impulsive nature can produce no morally binding imperatives, the source of these must be independent of the impulses, and therefore must lie in man's *power to act rationally,* which Kant calls his "rational will." Now what distinguishes a rational will from merely rationalized impulse? Perfect consistency. To will rationally is to will without contradicting yourself, for the Law of Contradiction is a primary axiom of logic, and logic is the science of valid reasoning. Very well, then: how shall the principle of consistency be applied to problems of right action? By applying the same rule to myself as to others, and the same rule on difficult occasions as on easy ones. Our impulsive nature tempts us to make an exception of the present instance, and to make an exception of our own case. Against such irrational partisanship, reason supplies the corrective maxim: "Act always in such a way that you could will your action to become a universal law."

But it is not the external action that counts, for that may have been done from a wrong motive. A man may repay a debt not simply because he owes the money, but in order to establish his credit as a basis for further borrowings. His action is right but the maxim from which it proceeds is self-interest, not duty. Hence on other occasions, when nothing would be gained by repayment, he may feel free to ignore his debts. The maxim from which he acts is all-important. If he acts from the maxim stated above, he is acting from duty, and his action is a moral one; if he does not, then even though his action may be in accordance with duty on a particular occasion, it is but accidentally so, and has no moral worth. In order to incorporate this idea of rational motive Kant reformulates his statement of the moral law to read: *"Act always in such a way that you can will the maxim on which you act to be adopted as a universal law."* Shall I repay the debt if I need the money and think I shall come to no harm by default? Self-interest perhaps answers no. Reason requires that we ask: Can I wish it to be a general rule that nobody should repay a debt unless he should happen to find it convenient? Obviously we cannot wish such a state of affairs, for it would mean the breakdown of all credit and of men's faith in one another. Far from wishing debt default to become a universal policy, I wish only to make it *my* policy in *this* particular case. The action is thus irrational; and being irrational it is immoral.

The worth of persons

From the principle just stated a second can be deduced. For not only is the law of conduct a rational law; it is a law which is binding upon rational selves. Consequently the intrinsic worth which belongs to the law must also be an attribute of rational selves. All men are potentially rational: they have in themselves the power of reason to choose between right and wrong. Hence every man is an end in himself and should be so treated. Thus a second categorical imperative arises as a corollary from the first: *"So act as to treat humanity, whether in your own person or in that of another, always as an end and never as merely a means."*

Critical observations

Kant's two basic imperatives express two indispensable elements in the conception of duty. First, a moral duty has the character of a law, as binding on me as on anyone else, and as binding when inconvenient as when in accordance with inclination. Secondly, a moral duty must always involve an absolute respect for persons as persons, one's own personhood included. Nevertheless the authority of reason, although a necessary part of ethics, is not the whole of it. Of the two ethical philosophies so far considered, the one belittles man's power of reason by making it a mere servant of impulse, while the other isolates it from all collaboration with impulse. Moreover, a great deal depends on how the work of reason is understood. A man can think out his actions conscientiously and recognize the binding force of an "ought" distinct from his readiest and strongest impulses, without accepting the proposition that the same "ought" must be equally binding upon everybody. In short, he can accept both moral responsibility and moral individuality as basic complementary notions indispensable to his moral outlook. The ethics of self-realization gives theoretical expression to this possibility.

iii. The Ethics of Self-Realization

The third main type of ethics focuses primary attention not upon what a man gets, nor upon what he does, but upon what he is and makes of himself—the kind of character he develops. How is this to be judged? Obviously not by a single particular model, for the nature of the ideal self—i.e., the self which it is most important to realize—cannot be the same for all. Not only do individuals differ as to the kind of self which seems to be potentially theirs, but there are also great differences in the ideals peculiar to one and another nation and epoch. The human qualities most admired in contemporary America are not identical with those that were most admired when America was a group of pioneering colonies, nor with those most admired in France, in England, in ancient Greece. There are changing conceptions of the ideal self, as well as changing conditions for its development, and no authentic philosophy of self-realization can be narrowly doctrinaire. Are we then thrown back upon ethical relativism?

The escape from relativism—as Socrates, Plato, and Aristotle agreed in opposition to the relativism taught by the Sophists—is to distinguish what is essential from what is incidental or secondary, and to discover the conception of goodness which it implies. Now man is many things, and the differences that separate one group of men from another are of many kinds. How, then, is man's *essential* nature to be determined?

Good defined by function

Aristotle, who was the most systematic of the three leading Greek philosophers, replied to this question as biologist and logician at once. His logic had, in fact, grown largely out of his vast interest in biology, and the need of classifying structures and functions according to an intelligible principle. The present question is about man's function—the main function which distinguishes him as a biological species. This is his reason. Man shares with other animals the capacities of "sensation and locomotion," or more generally sensation and impulse; he differs from them in his ability to reflect upon his sensations and impulses and thus put them at the disposal of ends which he himself has conceived. Man, then, is briefly defined as the rational animal.

Having determined what man is, how can we proceed to discover wherein his excellence lies? Aristotle here introduces his humanistic postulate of valuation. *Find the proper function of a thing, and the specific excellence of that thing will consist in performing its function well.* The proper function of a pruning hook (a useful implement among the olive-, fig-, and lemon-growing Hellenes) is to clip the branches of trees and vines. Accordingly we consider it a good pruning hook if it can do this effectively, a bad one if it becomes dull or broken so that it cannot.

Organisms differ from pruning hooks and other man-made objects in that they were not made, but grew; and consequently their function is inherent in them, not imposed upon them by a maker. They are *"entelechies"* in this precise sense that their *telos,* or end, is within themselves, and thus is essentially self-determined. But with that important difference the humanistic postulate of valuation still applies to them. Man's distinctively human virtues—his excellences as a man—are derived from the nature of his distinctive function, his ability to reason.

The two functions of reason

Broadly speaking there are two ways in which reason is exercised: in contemplation and in deliberation. The contemplative exercise of reason, which Aristotle considers the nobler, consists in knowing for knowing's sake, out of a sense of wonder toward the world around us and the intelligible forms and relations which it reveals. The deliberative exercise consists in knowing for the sake of doing. For man is not a disembodied reasoner, but an animal with many impulses, and the function of deliberative reason is to control and direct those impulses for the sake of the man as a whole. As there are two main species of reasoning, so correspondingly there are two types of human virtue (or excellence). A man has intellectual virtue so far as he actualizes and develops his natural ability to engage in reasoning for its own sake—as in the "disinterested" study of philosophy, science, history, literature. He has moral virtue (or excellence) so far as he actualizes and develops his natural ability to control his impulses and appetites. But since it is the *whole* man that concerns us, it is not enough that his ability should find expression only once or only now and then. He achieves moral excellence to the extent that his rational control of appetite becomes a habit, and so becomes the expression of an enduring *character*.

The golden mean

How, precisely, does reason operate in the control of animal impulse? Aristotle's reply is, that while no natural impulse is evil in itself, its tendency is to go to an extreme and to seek satisfaction indiscriminately. To act according to reason is first of all to act moderately, to follow the middle way, the ideal of the golden mean. "The man who flees and fears everything and never stands his ground is a coward, while he who fears nothing at all and is ready to face everything is rash." True courage is destroyed by excess and deficiency alike, but preserved by moderation.

Nevertheless, Aristotle does not offer the doctrine of the mean as a simple formula or foolproof rule. The moderate course suitable to one occasion may not serve on another. More courage is required in a crisis than at ordinary times; when fellow lives are at stake it becomes proper to take risks which at other times would be condemned as rash. Moral virtue consists not only in steering between contrary vices, but in doing so "at the right time, on the right occasions, toward the right persons, in a right manner, and with a right aim in view." In short, the moderate way is to be determined on each occasion as a man of prudence and highly developed character would determine it.

Harmony and happiness

The law of moderation is at the same time a law of harmony. To be immoderate, whether in drink or sex or money-making or anything else, is to allow one set of impulses to tyrannize over all the rest; to follow the middle way is, on the affirmative side, to allow for the harmonious development of the various potentialities and needs that make up one's nature. This can be done only when the most humanly distinctive of them, the potentiality of reason, takes precedence over the rest, and establishes a regulative principle for their proper subordination.

The harmony which moderate living promotes is social and political also. As strong impulses and passions tend to tyrannize within each personality, so the persons who are dominated by them tend to tyrannize in one way or another in the state. The art of statecraft is the art of enabling men to live together in a community, no one of them demanding more than his proper share, and each of them performing the role for which his special abilities fit him and which his station in society requires. Thus it is that harmoniously constituted individuals tend to produce a harmonious society.

Through such double harmony men achieve the goal of human desire, which is happiness. The Greek word *eudaimonia,* which we customarily translate "happiness," had both an inward and an outward reference. Etymologically the word connotes "possession of a good genius," which is to say, first and most essentially, possession of a good inner working principle of choice and avoidance. But a man's *daimon* or "genius" also signified what we sometimes call "his lucky star"—prosperity and a fortunate outcome of his endeavors. There is an inescapable factor of luck in the achievement of happiness. Do what we may, disaster may overwhelm us, and a man cannot be called completely happy if, despite a virtuous character, he has been overwhelmed by one disaster after another. Nevertheless, while circumstances can mar happiness in exceptional cases, they are not the sole determinants, and in most cases not even the most important ones. For the most part man is a self-directive animal who can choose his own path, and is himself mainly responsible for the harmony and happiness, or lack of them, which he brings into his life.

There is, to be sure, a further meaning of happiness and harmony which takes us beyond the purely ethical perspective into the religious. The Chinese sage Chuang Tzu says of the wise men of old that they were perfectly free in mind, grave yet cheerful in demeanor, because "their passions occurred in quiet rhythm, like the seasons. They were in harmony with all creation—of which no man can know the limit. This is what is called not leading the heart astray from Tao."[6] Perhaps the harmony that man seeks for his fullest blessedness is not confined to his own psychic economy nor to his relations with fellow men, important though both of these types are, but concerns his relationship with a Reality that transcends the world of mundane experience. That is a question which we must investigate in the next chapter.

For Further Study

Radoslav A. Tsanoff, *The Moral Ideals of Our Civilization* (Dutton, 1942).
Warner Fite, *Moral Philosophy* (Dial Press, 1925).
W. David Ross, *Foundations of Ethics* (Oxford University Press, 1939).
Hastings Rashdall, *The Theory of Good and Evil* (Oxford University Press, 2 vols., 1907). Advanced.
Philip Wheelwright, *A Critical Introduction to Ethics* (Odyssey Press, rev. ed., 1951).
Lucius Garvin, *A Modern Introduction to Ethics* (Houghton Mifflin, 1953).
Cecil De Boer, *The Ifs and Oughts of Ethics* (William B. Eerdmans, 1936).
A. C. Ewing, *The Definition of Good* (Macmillan, 1947).
Paul Weiss, *Man's Freedom* (Yale University Press, 1950).

Anthologies

A. I. Melden, *Ethical Theories* (Prentice-Hall, 1950).
G. H. Clark and T. V. Smith, *Readings in Ethics* (Crofts, rev. ed., 1935).

---

[6] *Chuang Tzu, Mystic, Moralist, and Social Reformer:* selections from his writings, translated from the Chinese by Herbert A. Giles (Shanghai, 1926), Chap. VI.

Questions for Discussion

1. Review the five conditions of moral valuation in Chapter XII (pp. 411-413). Imagine some instance of moral deliberation, such as whether or not to withdraw from college. Assume that each one of the conditions is false in turn. How is the nature of the situation affected?

2. Suppose that "I want what I want when I want it" were made one's dominant or only rule of action. Would there be any moral questions left?

3. Can you think of any experience that you would regard as good *in itself* which is not a pleasant experience? Conversely, are there any pleasant experiences which, *ignoring their effects,* you would be unwilling to consider good?

4. Compare the Golden Rule—"Do unto others as you would have them do unto you"—with each of Kant's two categorical imperatives.

5. Can either of Kant's categorical imperatives be held and reasonably put into practice without some reference to the other?

6. Can a humanistic philosophy of self-realization be practiced while ignoring the principle of moderation? In other words, can Aristotle's postulate of valuation (pp. 471-472) be separated from his doctrine of the mean?

CHAPTER XV

Value and Belief: the Religious Problem

In an essay entitled "Man against Darkness," which stirred a lively controversy several years ago, Professor Walter T. Stace offered a restatement of the atheistic position. Characterizing religious beliefs as childish fantasies which have served men hitherto as props and crutches, he urges us to face frankly the vision of a purposeless universe—one in which, beyond man himself, there is "no spirituality, no regard for values, no friend in the sky, no help or comfort for man of any sort." Our only hope for the future, he believes, is to "grow up as a race in the same sense as individual men grow up." And he concludes with the challenge:

Can man put away childish things and adolescent dreams? Can he grasp the real world as it actually is, stark and bleak, without its romantic or religious halo, and still retain his ideals, striving for great ends and noble achievements? If he cannot, he will probably sink back into the savagery and brutality from which he came, taking a humble place once more among the lower animals.[1]

i. The Meaning of Religious Belief

Two questions distinguished

It is always well to have a position honestly stated, and whatever defects Professor Stace's argument may show on careful

[1] *The Atlantic Monthly*, Vol. 182 (1948), p. 55.

examination, I think he deserves a real though limited praise for pushing his beliefs to their logical conclusion in so forthright a manner. "Does civilization need religion?" is a familiar and frequently repeated question. One group of thinkers begins with that question, answers it affirmatively, and concludes that we had better find grounds for believing in religion's essential tenets. Another group of thinkers, of whom Auguste Comte was the most eminent, contraposes the argument. Starting with the proposition that the essential tenets of religion are false, they conclude that mankind will therefore be better off without them, and that the hope of the future lies in a thoroughly secularized world. The one group reasons from the desirability of a fact to the fact itself, or at any rate to a self-induced belief in it; the other group reasons from the denial of that fact to its undesirability. Mr. Stace makes no compromise with either of these easy roads to optimism. He admits the possibility that man perhaps cannot behold the real world in its purposeless, godless emptiness and still retain his ideals in full strength. He admits, therefore, that facing the truth about the world may have disastrous consequences. But he believes that it is a mark of honesty and courage to face the truth in any event. For the truth or falsity of religious belief is one kind of question, and the human consequences of believing or disbelieving in religion is another kind of question. Accordingly the kinds of evidence relevant to the two questions are essentially different, although perhaps not entirely separate.

Evidence regarding the *results* of belief or disbelief is partly psychological, partly sociological and historical. Since it concerns a future that has not yet been tried, and since historical precedents are notoriously inexact, a prediction based on such evidence is of doubtful validity. Nevertheless, a qualified prediction may still be possible. If we were to find some degree of historical correlation between periods of religious disbelief and cultural decline, repeated by rough analogy in different civilizations and different ages, we could conclude the probability of some causal connection between the two sets of phenomena—although which was cause and which was effect we might still hesitate to say. *Are* there such correlations in history, and are they sufficiently frequent and typical to be evidentially valid? This is a hard question to answer with assurance: not only because of the complexity and sometimes conflicting nature of historical evidence, but also for at least two other reasons. The one is the different forms which religious phenomena take in different stages of the rise and decline of civilizations. The other is the lag between cause and effect in large-scale historical phenomena. It may be—and there seems to be some evidence for the suggestion—that the early effects of sceptical questionings in religion are often socially and spiritually advantageous, acting as a needed stimulant to beliefs and practices that have grown lethargic and smug; but that the long-range effects become increasingly injurious, as the scepticism gathers momentum and passes like a contagion from cosmology to morals and affects not only man's far-flung beliefs about the universe but the very texture of his daily activities and interrelationships.

But whatever opinion we may hold and however we interpret the evidence as regards that historical question, it is important, in the interests of clear thinking and honest inquiry to investigate the other question, of whether or not religion is *true,* by an independent route. Our primary method here cannot be statistical and historically empirical, but dialectical. We must first determine, with as much accuracy as the subject-matter allows, the nature of the belief whose truth or falsity is in question; and then proceed to examine the strongest reasons that can be offered both for accepting and for rejecting it.

Granted that religion is more than belief, that in its full sense it also involves a way of living and of worshiping, both outwardly and inwardly, and that the formulated creed is an abstraction when drawn apart from this existential context; nevertheless the belief element is what gives significance and justification to the other aspects. Moreover it is the belief element which we are eyeing when we ask whether, and in what sense, religion in general, or a certain religion in particular, is true. Let us then inquire what is the essential content of religious belief.

Religion basically defined

The words "essential content" warn us against the opposite dangers of narrowness and excessive breadth in our primary definition. If we identify religious belief with the creed of a particular church or sect, or even with the doctrines distinguishing one world religion from another, we shall have missed what is essential to religion as a whole. If, on the other hand, in our zeal for tolerance we broaden the notion of religious belief to include all basic and large-scale views of things—permitting even the paradox that "the atheist's religion is his atheism"—then we have emptied the notion of all distinctive content, and have left ourselves without any question of truth to discuss. There is a middle way here, as in all things; and it consists in being explicit without being doctrinaire. There have been a number of attempts by philosophers to define the content of religion in a way that meets both requirements. That of William James is given in the Readings, p. 576; William Temple's may be cited in the present connection. Archbishop Temple believes that religion in its higher forms is characterized by three central convictions, which "are perhaps different expressions of one truth," but at any rate need to be stated and understood separately in an analytical approach:

First is the conviction that Spirit is a true source of initiation of processes;

Second is the conviction that all existence finds its source in a Supreme Reality of which the nature is Spirit;

Third is the conviction that between that Spirit and ourselves there can be, and to some extent already is, true fellowship, at least such as is involved in our conscious dependence on that Spirit.[2]

[2] William Temple, late Archbishop of Canterbury, *Nature, Man and God* (Gifford Lectures for 1932-1933 and 1933-1934; Macmillan, 1934), p. 35.

It may be objected that the foregoing definition is too narrow because by speaking of a "Supreme Reality" it rules out polytheism from the domain of religion. James' definition is more cautious in this respect; but in any case the objection is more specious than real, as the important religious phenomenon known as "henotheism" tends to show. For what is the nature of worship in a society whose official religion is polytheistic? The outward ceremonies, especially those of a public character, are likely to be polytheistic also. It is sound public policy to give each god and goddess his just due in sacrifice and honor. But in the higher forms of polytheistic religion there seems to be an increasing disposition, in the more meditative individuals, to regard each god or goddess, at the moment of worship, as an embodiment of the universal Spirit. Such has been the case in India since at least 800 B.C., for the ancient Upanishads express the doctrine that the universal spirit, Brahma, is the reality of which the many deities in the Vedic mythology are manifestations. In modern India, although the transcendency of Brahma is still an article of faith, another henotheistic doctrine has come into prominence—namely, that Vishnu, the World Preserver and the spirit of divine love, comes to earth in *avatars* or "descents," appearing at different times of Hindu history in one or another heroic or godlike incarnation. In ancient Greece the henotheistic tendency finds typical expression in the prayer of the tragic chorus in Aeschylus' *Agamemnon,* beginning "O Zeus or Pan or Apollo, by whatever name you are called. . . .!" The attitude variously expressed in these instances cannot be called montheism (*mono,* "alone"), for the formal acceptance of polytheism still persists; the name *henotheism* (from the Greek *hen,* "one") has therefore come into use for the purpose of designating it. At all events the phenomenon illustrates the tendency of faith to reach out beyond the particular to the universal, and to shake off the endless diversities of myth for the unitive contemplation that is worship.

With the foregoing qualification, then, we may take the second of Archbishop Temple's three convictions as the focal one, although it must be understood in the context of the first and third. The first implicitly defines "Spirit" by extension of the direct knowledge that each of us has of himself as spirit, which is to say "as a true source of initiation of processes." Of course the Spirit which is the supreme object of worship is unimaginably *more* than the finite spirits we are. The reasoning here is by *hyperlogy*—i.e., it starts with a familiar notion and then says, with the Hindu teachers of the Upanishads, "*Neti neti*—not quite that!" Taken by itself the content of the second conviction is chronically elusive; for the Infinite cannot be comprehended by the finite. It requires the third, therefore, to complete it. The relation between the second and third convictions is not a logical one, for it is by no means logically evident how there can be "fellowship" between a finite spirit and an Infinite Spirit which eludes comprehension. God's absolute transcendence on the one hand and the particularity of his relationship to individuals on the other constitute a fundamental paradox which is part of the very life of religion.

Nevertheless, since our present approach to the problem must be as logical as we can make it, we cannot ignore the question of logical priority. Temple's second proposition is logically prior to his third, in the obvious sense that you cannot have true fellowship with something that doesn't exist. The next two sections, therefore, will consider respectively what can be said against, and what can be said in support of, the belief that God exists.

ii. The Grounds of Disbelief

It is necessary at the outset to distinguish grounds from causes. If we were to investigate the "causes" of the weakening of religious belief in our time the inquiry would be a sociological and historical one. Prominent among them are probably such factors as the changing conditions of family life, the greater mobility of populations, the increasing dependence upon technology both in occupations and in pastimes, and the widespread dissemination of standardized opinions through mass media of communication. Whether or not this is a correct and adequate account need not detain us, for to halt or redirect such Gargantuan trends does not lie within any individual's power.

But while an individual cannot master the cultural trends of his time, he need not, on the other hand, be wholly enslaved by them. In a rational being such factors are not so much causes as *influences*. It is the nature of an influence that while it has a *tendency* to produce one result rather than another, the possibility of an alternative outcome remains open. Whether the difference between cause and influence is real or only apparent is another way of formulating the questions of spontaneity (cf. Chapter IV) and freedom (Chapter X). At all events, as a basis of rational inquiry and discussion we shall postulate our freedom to remold our beliefs by considering the *reasons* for believing or disbelieving, instead of submitting them passively to the operation of *causes*. And when we inquire first into the reasons for rejecting the central tenets of religion, there are two which are likely to present themselves with especial force. For brevity they may be called the anthropological and psychological objections to religious belief.

The anthropological objection

The general nature of the anthropological attack upon religious belief consists in discovering that men's religious opinions have evolved; then stressing one or another of the more conspicuous factors which operated at an early stage of that evolution —magic, or fear of ghosts, or frustrated curiosity about natural phenomena—and assigning causal preëminence to it; finally, denying the objective truth of the belief on the ground that it can be quite satisfactorily explained by such anthropological beginnings. Let us see briefly how this method is employed by an anthropologist of high eminence.

The late Sir James G. Frazer, in the most celebrated of his writings, *The Golden Bough*, gives a unity of perspective to his vast number of anthropological facts by making one dominant assumption—namely, that religion can be explained as a product of magic. More specifically his hypothesis is this. The most primitive men had no otherworldly beliefs, but they did have an imperious need to control nature and yoke her to their own uses. Now to control nature requires an ability to discover causal relations, and such discovery in turn requires the patience and skill to make controlled observations. That is to say we validly, though not of course infallibly, infer a causal relation between A and B when we have observed, in a number of quite different situations, the presence or absence, respectively, of the one or the other. The earliest men had not learned to think in this analytic manner; their mode of thinking was by spontaneous association. Two principles are especially prominent in the spontaneous association of ideas—similarity and contiguity. A perception of A tends to stir a thought of B when A and B are alike in some way that appeals to the beholder; or again, when A and B have previously been found existing together. These two native tendencies of association gave rise, Frazer believes, to the two principal forms of magic, "homeopathic" and "contagious." The one works by similars, as when a savage makes a waxen image of his enemy and melts it, in order to cause his enemy to waste away; or as when the Navajo Indians seek to attract rain clouds by making clouds of tobacco smoke. The other works with things that have an affinity through previous contact, as when a magician seeks to injure a man by burning his shorn hair or nail parings, or to heal him by anointing the weapon by which he was wounded. Primitive man interprets such operations by the notion of a vague semi-animate force or potency, called *mana* by the Melanesians, pervading all things to greater or less degree. The magician's task is to coerce this force, in one or both of the ways described, and thereby to produce the desired changes in nature.

Now, Frazer argues, the incidence of failure in the practice of magic must have been high. Gradually, therefore, in the long slow course of prehistoric time there must have developed the realization that nature is stubborn and cannot be very successfully coerced. Simultaneously, the pre-animistic notion of *mana* tended to evolve into the more definite animistic notion of souls inhabiting this or that area of nature. The result of this double intellectual development was that early man began to substitute *supplication* for attempts at coercion. As he developed the art of petitionary prayer, he began to ascribe more exalted characteristics to the beings he was addressing, so that they arose more and more to the status of gods. Thus there evolved polytheism. And out of polytheism, in the further course of time, there sometimes developed a movement towards monotheism—mythologically, by one god's conquest over his rivals; psychologically, by the worshiper's growing need of a unified world-outlook.

Frazer's theory can be criticized on two grounds. In the first place, many anthropologists, while admiring his erudition and organization of facts, challenge his overemphasis upon the factor of magic in primitive phenomena. That magic is widely employed cannot be doubted. But we are in danger of begging the question by calling activities "magic" because of an apparently magical element in them and then ignoring other elements that may have been more important in fashioning the primitive man's outlook. Much that an outsider calls magical is, to the participant, *sacramental*—a way of expressing through appropriate ritual, gesture, and words his sense of reverence towards a Something Other, in which he vaguely but none the less vitally believes. Primitive reverence may, to be sure, contain a large admixture of more earthy emotional qualities, notably fear, frustrated curiosity, and desire for benefits. But these were probably not the whole story. Giving them a special tone, distinguishing them as religious rather than secular, there may have been something more transcendental—a half-formed and crudely symbolized belief in spiritual presences, to whom allegiance and worship are due—not only because they expect it and reward the worshiper, but also because they are felt to be worthy of it.

The other ground of criticism is more universal, applying not only against Frazer's magical theory but against all attempts to explain away religious truth by reference to the supposed origins of religious belief. The fallacy is evident to anyone who reflects, and it is usually named the *genetic fallacy*. It consists in judging the validity of a belief by the conditions of its genesis. We do not judge the truth or falsity of the atomic theory by pointing out certain crudities and doubtful motives in the first attempts at an atomistic way of thinking by Leucippus and Democritus in ancient Greece. We recognize that those older scientists had caught an imperfect glimpse of a truth which later became known more adequately. In short, we acknowledge, in the case of the sciences, the validity of the concept of *intellectual development*—which is to say, the possibility of a gradual discovery of truth, not just a perpetuation of error. Why may we not acknowledge the same possibility in the history of religion? Those who dispute such a possibility may proceed to rest their case upon the psychological argument—to which we turn next.

The psychological objection

The prestige of Freud in contemporary psychology has drawn attention to his theory that the idea of God is a pure illusion, without any ground in reality. In *The Psychopathology of Everyday Life* he writes:

> I believe that a large proportion of the mythological conception of the world which reaches far into the most modern religions is nothing but Psychology projected into the outer world. The dim perception of psychic factors and relations of the Unconscious was taken as a model in the construction of a transcendental reality which is destined to be changed again by science into the psychology of the Unconscious. We venture to explain in this way the myth of paradise, and the fall of man, of God, of Good and Evil, of immortality and the like.[3]

[3] Sigmund Freud (1856-1939), *The Psychopathology of Everyday Life* (Macmillan, 1917), p. 310. Reprinted in Mentor Books.

Other passages expressing the same theory are found in a number of Freud's writings.

Similarly Freud's most eminent successor and in many respects his sharp critic, Carl G. Jung, has declared that God "is nothing but a projected complex of the representation of the sum of the libido"; and again, that "God is . . . a function of the unconscious, namely the manifestation of a split-off sum of libido, which has activated the God-*imago*."[4]

Jung's readiness in these passages to reduce God to a mere projection of human subjectivity jars harshly with a more reasonable and more careful statement which he had made in a British medical periodical. In the course of discussing the relation of analytical psychology to poetic art, and having laid down the excellent principle that "the problem what is art in itself can never be the object of a psychological, but only of an aesthetico-artistic mode of approach," he goes on to declare:

> A similar distinction must also be made in the realm of religion; there also a psychological consideration is permissible only in respect of the emotional and symbolical phenomena of a religion, wherein the essential nature of religion is in no way involved, as indeed it cannot be. For were this possible, not religion alone, but art also could be treated as a mere subdivision of psychology. In saying this I do not mean to affirm that such an encroachment has not actually taken place.[5]

The limitations of psychology for an understanding of religion have been indicated more fully and accepted more consistently by William James. Remarking as a psychologist that "modern psychology, finding definite psychophysical connections to hold good, assumes as a convenient hypothesis that the dependence of mental states upon bodily conditions must be thoroughgoing and complete," he continues in an ironic vein:

[4] Carl G. Jung (1875—), *Psychology of the Unconscious,* Chap. I; *Psychological Types,* Chap. V. These are being republished as part of Jung's complete writings, in the Bollingen Series, Pantheon Press.

[5] "On the Relation of Analytical Psychology to Poetic Art," *British Journal of Medical Psychology,* Vol. III, Part III, p. 213.

According to the general postulate of psychology just referred to, there is not a single one of our states of mind, high or low, healthy or morbid, that has not some organic process as its condition. Scientific theories are organically conditioned just as much as religious emotions are; and if we only knew the facts intimately enough, we should doubtless see "the liver" determining the dicta of the sturdy atheist as decisively as it does those of the Methodist under conviction anxious about his soul. When it alters in one way the blood that percolates it, we get the Methodist, when in another way, we get the atheist form of mind. So of all our raptures and our drynesses, our longings and pantings, our questions and beliefs. They are equally organically founded, be they of religious or of non-religious content.[6]

James proceeds, in a later chapter of the same book (see Readings, pp. 576-590) to develop the positive side of his hypothesis. The gist of it is that the subconscious self need not be, as Freud and for the most part Jung assume, a mere product and projection of man's—or, in Jung's later theory, mankind's—subjective wishes and fears; but it may be, in addition, the actual area of contact between the individual self and a higher, transcendental power. Psychology can neither prove nor disprove this hypothesis decisively; for as a science it is limited to describing the phenomena of the psyche and the structures of connection in which they are found to occur. Any speculation as to their ultimate significance is not psychology but metaphysics. James and Freud stand as perhaps the two most eminent psychologists in modern times, and each of them speaks consistently with the observable facts of his science; but each of them interprets his empirical observations in the light of his own intuitive hunch about the way things ultimately shape up. The difference in their perspectives is a reminder of the necessary limits of psychological method with respect to questions of religious truth.

---

[6] William James (1842-1910), *The Varieties of Religious Experience*, (Longmans, Green, 1916), p. 14.

iii. The Religious Hypothesis

In using the word "hypothesis," with its connotation of something tentative and probable rather than final and certain, I do not mean that the central beliefs of religion can be no more than this. But the philosophical method cannot assume more at the outset. The arguments for and against the existence of God must be given a fair hearing, and surely this is impossible if one has decided the issue in advance. Nor do I mean by this that a personal precommitment is necessarily wrong. The eager responsiveness of what James calls our "passional nature" to the sparse indications of a Something More on which we can pin our ultimate loyalty and faith is an evidence of partisanship indeed, and the partisanship is one that a real believer will neither wish nor be able to renounce. Where the belief in a Something Other goes marrow-deep, the arguments favoring its existence are certain to be weighted in advance. Let us admit this—only adding that disbelievers, quite as much as believers, have their emotional predispositions. So perhaps an altogether fair hearing is impossible, after all. Nevertheless, we should strive for as much objectivity as possible in philosophical discussion, even though it cannot be perfectly attained; and by regarding the belief in God as a hypothesis we enable the theist and the atheist to achieve that prerequisite of all genuine discussion, a meeting of minds and a friendly examination, pro and con, of the arguments.

Each of the four arguments for God's existence which follow is presented in dialectical fashion. First the argument is stated in its more elementary and probably better known form (A); the weakness of this form is then exposed (B); and finally the argument is reformulated and recontextualized in such a way (C) as to bring out what I take to be its inherent (though partial, not coercive) validity.

The cosmological argument

A. In its simplest form the cosmological argument runs as follows. Nature as a whole at each moment is the effect of what it was at each preceding moment. Thus the changing states of the universe form a causal series extending indefinitely backward in time. That such a series should be infinite is inconceivable; for whatever is past is actual, and an actual infinite is a contradiction in terms. There must therefore have been a first cause, and, since it must have been endowed with unlimited power in order to create the entire universe, it may be called "God."

B. Two objections can readily be raised against this version of the argument. The first is crudely expressed by the familiar question, "If God made the world, then who made God?" For either the Creator God is conceived as having a place in the series of natural events—as being, in fact, the first event in that series—or he is not. If he (or it) is so conceived, the question of a further cause is legitimate. If, on the other hand, the Creator God is *not* so conceived, then he does not provide an answer to the question posed in the argument. For the scientific postulate, from which the argument sets out, is that nature at each moment is a totality of simultaneous *events*, the cause of which must be the *events* at a preceding moment, and so on. If God is not such an event, he is not a "cause" in the sense on which this argument rests. The objection can therefore be summed up in the dilemma: "Either the supposed First Cause is an event or it is not. If so, it is not first (for there must be previous events which caused it); and if not, it is not a cause in the sense that the argument postulates."

The other objection consists in asking what *kind* of a God the argument would prove, if the proof were valid. The one attribute he must necessarily have had, if he created the universe, is power. But power alone does not constitute divinity. We have a poor opinion of a man who would worship power merely because it is powerful; such an attitude is that of the toady and bootlicker, not of the free man. Perhaps, however, (as certain theologians have urged) we owe God our gratitude and worship because he brought us into existence and without his creative act we would have been nothing. Is this really a convincing argument? For my part I think not. It sounds too much like the claim sometimes made by an old-fashioned parent: "You should be grateful to me for having brought you into the world." Most children resent such a remark, and rightly so. We can feel gratitude to someone who relieves us of some worse state of existence by helping us to a better one, for we can remember or imagine ourselves going through the transition from the one to the other. The passage from poverty to affluence, or from sickness to health, has an imaginatively concrete meaning for us. It is impossible, on the other hand, (except by artificial effort) to be grateful for the gift of bare existence—because it is impossible to imagine ourselves in the state preceding it—namely, non-existence—and impossible, therefore, to form any imaginatively concrete idea of what the passage from non-existence to existence can be like. Consequently, if the only attribute we could ascribe to God were that creative power which the cosmological argument tries to establish, he would not be the God of religion at all, but merely an impersonal force. The cosmological argument indicates nothing about the *goodness* of God, and can only seem to do so when it is allied or fused with certain other arguments, notably the teleological and moral ones.

C. Although I do not regard the cosmological argument as having more than a limited validity, there is another form of it which merits more respect than the one which has been considered, and perhaps even a qualified acquiescence. The note is struck in Archbishop Temple's observation: "That the world should give rise to minds which know the world involves a good deal concerning the nature of the world." Involvement is less definite and less certain than implication. Nothing is logically demonstrated, for the possibility remains (as we saw in Chapter VII) that minds simply "emerged"—just happened!—and I do not see any way of decisively disproving that possibility. Nevertheless, there is involvement—in the sense that a troublesome question is raised, which might be put thus: *What kind of a* universe would have to be supposed in order to explain the existence of creatures with minds and consciences? The crucial word here is "explain." The theory of emergence does not explain; it merely restates, in philosophical language, the order of evolutionary occurrences, and adds, in effect, that no explanation is forthcoming. The hypothesis of a creative power not less but greater than minds as we know them would be more in the nature of an explanation, if we could accept it as true. The facts of human existence do not prove the hypothesis, but they point to it as a suggestive possibility.

The teleological argument

A. The teleological argument, in its more elementary form, runs somewhat as follows. Nature shows innumerable evidences of adaptation—too many to be the product of mere chance.

> The curious adapting of means to ends, throughout all nature, [Cleanthus in Hume's *Dialogues* declares] resembles exactly, though it much exceeds, the productions of human contrivance—of human design, thought, wisdom, and intelligence. Since, therefore, the effects resemble each other, we are led to infer, by all the rules of analogy, that the causes also resemble, and that the Author of Nature is somewhat similar to the mind of man, though possessed of much larger faculties, proportioned to the grandeur of the work which he has executed.[7]

B. There are several ways of replying to the argument from design. In Hume's Dialogue Philo points out the weakness of any such reasoning by analogy. We employ analogy validly enough in countless cases of perception, where the similarity of the things compared is so close that we infer from one to the other without the slightest hesitation. That a stone will fall, that fire will burn, that the earth will support our feet we have observed thousands of times, and the similarity of the next instance to the preceding ones is all the evidence we ask for complete assurance. The same principle applies to ascriptions of purpose. If we were to explore

---

[7] David Hume (1711-1776), *Dialogues concerning Natural Religion.*

an unknown island and discover a house we would conclude with the greatest certainty that it had a builder, "because this is precisely that species of effect which we have experienced to proceed from that species of cause." But the universe does not resemble a house in at all the same way that one house resembles another, or even in the same way that a house resembles some other man-made product. Indeed, "the dissimilitude is so striking, that the utmost you can here pretend to is a guess, a conjecture, a presumption concerning a similar cause."

Moreover, if we are willing to be content with so shaky a conjecture, what *kind* of a cosmic designer would the available evidence suggest? John Stuart Mill observes:

> If there are any marks at all of special design in creation, one of the things most evidently designed is that a large proportion of all animals should pass their existence in tormenting and devouring other animals. They have been lavishly fitted out with the instruments necessary for that purpose; their strongest instincts impel them to it, and many of them seem to have been constructed incapable of supporting themselves by any other food.[8]

If foxes could reason there would doubtless be teleologists among them who would find evidences of cosmic design in the fact that rabbits were so plentiful and so admirably adapted to the foxes' needs. But what of the rabbits' point of view? And shall it be said that at any rate the benefits of such competitive living outweigh the evils? Schopenhauer retorts to any such optimist by advising him to imagine and compare the respective feelings of two animals, one of whom is engaged in eating the other up. If anything so definite as the happiness or well-being of sentient creatures is to be taken as the standard, the evidence from design might seem to point to a malevolent monster in charge of cosmic operations, quite as much as to a beneficent God worthy of our worship.

Suppose, on the other hand, the teleologist qualifies his posi-

---

[8] John Stuart Mill (1806-1873), *Three Essays on Religion*, first essay, "Nature."

tion by declaring that pleasure and pain, happiness and misery, as we know them, are conceptions too limited to attribute to the Purpose that guides the universe. What is then left of his argument? What is now meant by asserting that there are evidences of adaptation in nature, and therefore of conscious design? The assertion becomes a tautology. For in the broadest sense everything is adapted to something else; nothing to everything else. Millions of years ago, the earth was not adapted to civilized life, but it was sufficiently well adapted to the more elementary species which then inhabited it. Millions of years hence, when the earth will probably either have cooled or have dried up, it will again become incapable of sustaining human life, but it will then be better adapted to whatever forms of existence, living or lifeless, succeed us. Consequently, William R. Dennes argues, "coherence in things is no evidence of a controlling intelligence, for *with or without such an intelligence there could be nothing that was not coherent.*"[9] The fact that the order of nature does, in certain stretches, suit man, Professor Dennes continues, no more constitutes evidence of a controlling and benevolent intelligence "than does the 'suitableness' of the disintegration of a comet to the being and career of the derivative meteors constitute such evidence. All stretches of natural process that occur at all are perfectly suited to their ingredients and their 'environment,' and to say so much of any existent is to say no more than that it exists as what it is."

C. There are at least two main ways of readmitting the teleological argument, however, which avoid the defects pointed out in the elementary form of it. The conception of a purposeful but limited God, as proposed by Mill and James, opens up one way. If, as Mill suggests in the passage quoted in the Readings (p. 575), the Creator is limited by the materials with which he must work and by the instruments at his disposal to employ, then the evils which we discover in the universal economy need not be

---

[9] William R. Dennes, "Preface to an Empiricist Philosophy of Religion," in College of the Pacific, *Publications in Philosophy,* Vol. III (1934).

attributed to either malevolence or indifference; there remains the possibility that his "creative skill, wonderful as it is, was not sufficiently perfect to accomplish his purposes more thoroughly."

The other higher form of the teleological argument represented in the Readings (p. 561) is Aristotle's. Each thing in the universe, and each species of thing, he teaches, is drawn toward some good or other; he defines the good, in fact, as that towards which a thing is fundamentally drawn. Not every good harmonizes with every other: the good of the fox and the good of the hare, the good of the invading Persians and the good of the Greeks defending their homeland, he perceived to be in raw conflict. Accident, chance, good luck and bad, exist as an inescapable corollary of this plurality of ends, which is to say of goods. But while he thus acknowledges a relativity of goods— since each is relative to the organism which strives towards it— he does not retreat into relativism. For the particular good towards which each thing strives is a partial view of the ultimate good which is God. God is thus the ultimate producer of motion—not by pushing it into existence, nor by cunning contrivance, but through the sheer fact of being loved. Aristotle describes God, therefore, as the "Unmoved Mover." As a wise parent moves his children to good conduct not by trying to force them all into one mold but through being loved, so that each child feels stirred to emulate him in its own individual way; in like manner Aristotle conceives God as the ultimate goodness which all things emulate, although with different degrees of adequacy according to their various natures. Man, by virtue of his reason, stands higher in the scale than the other animals, and thus can approximate God's nature more nearly than they. The manner in which he can best do so was described in Chapter XIV. There, as in Aristotle's own ethical writings, the good was treated as an ideal. It is that of course, but, as Aristotle goes on to declare in his *Metaphysics*, it is actually existent as well. It "energizes" (to draw Aristotle's own word over into English vocabulary), and in that active and actual sense it is not only good, but God.

The moral argument

A. Immanuel Kant, whose ethical philosophy was outlined in the preceding chapter, employs the categorical imperative as a premise for his demonstration that God exists. A rational agent, Kant argues, "ought to seek to promote the highest good, and therefore the highest good must be possible. He must therefore postulate the existence of a cause of nature as a whole, which is distinct from nature, and which is able to connect happiness and morality in exact harmony with each other."[10] As the argument here stands it is a shocking *non sequitur*, which Kant's long rambling paragraph from which it is taken does little to clarify. The explanation is that Kant is building on an assumption which he had stated in an earlier paragraph, namely that happiness should be in proportion to morality. He still holds that a moral agent should not *aim* at happiness—"the moral law, being a law of free beings, commands us to act from motives that are entirely independent of nature and of the harmony of nature with our desires." But although we should not aim at such a result, such a result ought nevertheless to *be*. Well, let us grant that it ought; what then? Kant concludes:

> The highest good is thus capable of being realized in the world, only if there exists a supreme cause of nature whose causality is in harmony with the moral character of the agent. Now, a being that is capable of acting from the consciousness of law is a rational being, an *intelligence,* and the causality of that being, proceeding as it does from the consciousness of law, is a *will.* There is therefore implied, in the idea of the highest good, a being who is the supreme cause of nature, and who is the cause or author of nature through his intelligence and will, that is, *God.* If, therefore, we are entitled to postulate the highest *derivative* good, or the best world, we must also postulate the actual existence of the highest *original* good, that is, the existence of God.[11]

---

[10] Immanuel Kant (1704-1804), *The Critique of Practical Reason,* translated by John Watson in his volume of extracts, *The Philosophy of Kant* (Glasgow, 1888), Bk. II, Chap. V.

[11] Kant, *loc. cit.*

The conclusion, obviously, stands or falls according as we are or are not entitled to postulate that this is "the best world." Since the best world is defined as one in which morality and happiness are exactly proportioned and harmonized, there is plenty of evidence that the world we live in, however leniently you judge it, is pretty far from being "the best." Kant's reply is that the supreme harmony must nevertheless be true, appearances notwithstanding. Why? Because, as he argued a chapter earlier, the moral law is a command to produce in the world "the highest good"; the highest good can be achieved only if there *is* that harmony just spoken of; and the possibility of its achievement is "implied in the command to promote that object." Consequently, since that perfect harmony is not found in this life, Kant draws two conclusions: (*a*) immortality of the individual self, as allowing enough time for such perfect harmony to be brought about, and (*b*) the existence of God as the guarantee that it will be.

B. The main weaknesses in Kant's argument are not hard to discover. In the first place, his assumption that there exists a perfect harmony between moral action and happiness begs the question at issue; for such harmony is not discovered in actual experience, and to assume it is virtually the same thing as to assume that perfect wisdom and benevolence—which is to say God—are at work in the world. The real gist of the conclusion that is sought—that a cosmic guarantee of ultimate justice exists—has already been presupposed.

Or, if you prefer, take that proposition about perfect harmony not as an assumption but as deduced from the prior assumption that the command to promote an object implies the possibility of its achievement. Now let us grant (*a*) that a moral law does operate in us, and (*b*) that the law would be empty and meaningless unless there were *some* possibility of its achievement. But "some" is not good enough for Kant; he demands the possibility not of its partial but of its *perfect* achievement. And I do not see that this idea is necessarily implied in the nature of a command. Indeed, what is more characteristic of man's condition, in its most spiritual aspect, than the tragic tension between the high destiny to which we are repeatedly called and the often crippling limitations which prevent that vocation from being more than partially realized?

Finally, there is an internal inconsistency in Kant's argument. Examine once more his premise that the command to promote an object implies the possibility of its achievement. What is the object in question? Evidently, the harmony we have been speaking of. Is that, then, what the moral law requires us to promote? The logic of the argument requires us to say yes, but Kant has expressly and repeatedly declared that the motive from which we are commanded to act is entirely free of such considerations—"entirely independent of nature and of the harmony of nature with our desires." His argument, therefore, breaks into two pieces having no logical connection.

C. Can the moral argument be reformulated in such a way as to avoid the fallacies committed by Kant? I think it can, provided we avoid confusing (as Kant has done) moral considerations with teleological. The following statement of the moral argument by Hastings Rashdall seems to me to meet this requirement, and consequently to have a far greater validity than Kant's. It will repay careful and reflective study.

We say that the Moral Law has a real existence, that there is such a thing as an absolute Morality, that there is something absolutely true or false in ethical judgments, whether we or any number of human beings at any given time actually think so or not. Such a belief is distinctly implied in what we mean by Morality. The idea of such an unconditional, objectively valid, Moral Law or ideal undoubtedly exists as a psychological fact. The question before us is whether it is capable of theoretical justification. We must then face the question *where* such an ideal exists, and what manner of existence we are to attribute to it. Certainly it is to be found, wholly and completely, in no individual human consciousness. Men actually think differently about moral questions, and there is no empirical reason for supposing that they will ever do otherwise. Where then and how does the moral ideal really exist?

As regards matters of fact or physical law, we have no difficulty in satisfying ourselves that there is an objective reality which is what it is irrespectively of our beliefs or disbeliefs about it. For the man who supposes that objective reality resides in the things themselves, our ideas about them are objectively true or false so far as they correspond or fail to correspond with this real and independent archetype, though he might be puzzled to give a metaphysical account of the nature of this "correspondence" between experience and a Reality whose *esse* is something other than to be experienced. In the physical region the existence of divergent ideas does not throw doubt upon the existence of a reality independent of our ideas.

But in the case of moral ideals it is otherwise. On materialistic or naturalistic assumptions the moral ideal can hardly be regarded as a real thing. Nor could it well be regarded as a property of any real thing: it can be no more than an aspiration, a product of the imagination, which may be useful to stimulate effort in directions in which we happen to want to move, but which cannot compel respect when we feel no desire to act in conformity with it. An absolute Moral Law or moral ideal cannot exist *in* material things. And it does not (we have seen) exist in the mind of this or that individual. Only if we believe in the existence of a Mind for which the true moral ideal is already in some sense real, a Mind which is the source of whatever is true in our own moral judgments, can we rationally think of the moral ideal as no less real than the world itself. Only so can we believe in an absolute standard of right and wrong, which is as independent of this or that man's actual ideas and actual desires as the facts of material nature. . . . A moral ideal can exist nowhere and nohow but in a mind; an absolute moral ideal can exist only in a Mind from which all Reality is derived. Our moral ideal can only claim objective validity in so far as it can rationally be regarded as the revelation of a moral ideal eternally existing in the mind of God.[12]

The ontological argument

A. The ontological argument for God's existence is associated most closely with the name of Anselm of Canterbury, eleventh

---

[12] Hastings Rashdall, *The Theory of Good and Evil* (Oxford University Press, 1924), Vol. II, pp. 211-212. Reprinted by courtesy of the publisher.

century abbot of the Abbey of Bec, Normandy, and afterwards archbishop of Canterbury. In the preface to his *Proslogium* he tells that after long meditation upon the grounds of faith and upon the relations of one argument to another, he began to ask himself "whether there might be found a single argument which would require no other for its proof than itself alone; and alone would suffice to demonstrate that God truly exists." At length he discovered the argument which he thought would serve as this focus of demonstration. The form in which he put it is devotional, addressed in prayer to the God whose existence he is seeking to establish. He writes:

> We certainly believe that thou art a being than which nothing greater can be conceived. Or is there no such nature, since the fool hath said in his heart, there is no God? But, at any rate, this very fool, when he hears of this being of which I speak—a being than which nothing greater can be conceived—understands what he hears, and what he understands is in his understanding, although he does not understand it to exist. Hence, even the fool is convinced that something exists in the understanding, at least, than which nothing greater can be conceived. . . .
>
> Now assuredly that, than which nothing greater can be conceived, cannot exist in the understanding alone. For suppose this were the case; then something still greater could be conceived. For to exist in reality is greater than to exist only in the understanding. Therefore, if that, than which nothing greater can be conceived, exists in the understanding alone, it follows that a greater can be conceived, than that, than which no greater can be conceived. But this is manifestly impossible.
>
> Hence there is no further room for doubt that there exists a being, than which nothing greater can be conceived, and it exists both in the understanding and in reality.[13]

B. Many refutations of Anselm's celebrated argument have been offered, some of them very subtle. But the one central

---

[13] St. Anselm of Canterbury (1033-1109), *Proslogium, or Discourse on the Existence of God,* Chap. II. The translation is based on that of Sidney N. Deane (Open Court, 1910), but I have retranslated two sentences rather freely for the sake of clarity.

fallacy in it, which everyone can understand, and which an acute reader can discover for himself, is the illicit passage from idea to reality. What Anselm's argument proves is that *if I think of God as existing in reality*, I think of him as something greater than *if I think of him as merely existing in my understanding*. I cannot compare pure thought with pure reality; when I try to do this, what I really compare is *my thought of a thought* with *my thought of a reality*. And so the argument as Anselm formulated it is plainly invalid.

C. But we cannot stop there. As a trick of reasoning the argument fails. There is a deeper sense, however, in which it is profoundly suggestive as a clue to the meaning and validity of religious truth. In this deeper sense it matters little whether we still describe the argument as ontological, or whether we adopt a more expressive word that is now current and call it *existential*. I shall call it existential by way of making a fresh start, but the analogy of the argument in its new form to the old ontological argument can be detected.

The religious hypothesis existentially considered

What is a thought, an idea? The trouble with the question is that it tends to throw an unwary reader into an *either-or* frame of mind. He may unconsciously interpret "idea" to mean *"merely an idea"*; which is to say, something subjective and therefore not objective. This is an error. All our thoughts and ideas are subjective in the psychological sense that *as occurrences* they take place in some conscious subject. On the other hand, our different ideas are objective to a greater or less degree, in the semantic sense that *as meanings* they point, refer, intend beyond themselves.

It is the natural character of an idea to mean more than it is. If you say to me, "We've missed our train; how shall we reach our destination on time?" and I reply, "I've got an idea . . ." it is clear to both of us that my idea (say of hiring an automobile) refers to a situation beyond itself, which we hope to realize in the immediate future. The idea in this case refers to a set of somewhat definite experiences which will either occur or not occur within a fairly definite span of time. Hence the hypothesis which the idea involves—namely that I shall be able to hire a car—can be definitely verified or refuted. The difference between *having the idea* and *having the appropriate experience* is clear cut, and in this simple relationship the former standing by itself is subjective, while the latter by contrast is objective.

Not all ideas, however, are separable in this way from the experience to which they refer. Consider in this framework once again the two great dominant postulative ideas earlier discussed: the existence of a material world and the existence of other conscious minds. Unlike my idea of hiring a car, my idea that there is an external world cannot be verified or refuted by one or a few experiences. It is present in nearly all of them as a silent partner. Berkeley has demonstrated the purely logical possibility of discarding that idea of an external world (i.e., independent of anyone's experiencing it). The solipsist has gone a step farther and shown the logical possibility of treating other persons in the same way. After a schooling in the subjectivist and solipsistic schools of philosophy we become aware that it is *logically possible* to treat all experiences whatever as simply animated pictures and sounds in the mind's private theater. But whether it is logically possible is one question; whether it is a reasonable attitude for reasonable men to take is another.

For the mind is naturally self-transcendent; it reaches out toward that which is other than itself. It does not naturally say, "I won't believe in anything until it is proved." Its natural attitude, as the young child and the pre-civilized man both attest, is to say, "I'm ready to believe almost anything, because life is full of interesting possibilities, but gradually I'll discard particular beliefs because of their failure to harmonize with experience as a whole." There is, however, an opposite and more pathological method, which people and civilizations often adopt without realizing it—that of discarding a great area of possible experience because it fails to harmonize with a particular belief.

Now one way in which the mind naturally tends to reach out is toward that which stands infinitely beyond itself and yet seems to give a meaning to existence and a sense of direction to our acts of responsible choice. Is this idea a deceptive one? The ontological argument, interpreted existentially, replies as follows. To doubt the testimony of the deepest intuitions "involves so pervasive a 'scepticism of the instrument' as to render all conviction impossible, and all opinion temerarious. If I may not trust what seems to me more sure than sight, more convincing than touch, I find no reason to accept any data of experience whatever."[14] The idea which is greater and more pervasive than all other ideas, giving greater life and richer significance to all the rest, bears the mark of reality if any ideas do. Hence it is to be trusted if any ideas are to be trusted.

There are two possible ways of replying to this neo-ontological, or existential argument. One is the way that has just been dealt with—the way of denying that *any* pervasive intuitions are to be trusted. It may be called the way of doctrinaire scepticism. It cannot be refuted, but if carried out consistently to the bitter end (which it rarely or never is) it would leave no ground for believing in either an independent world or the independent existence of other people.

The other way of reply is a more modest and more reasonable one. The second type of critic does not challenge the major premise that our most basic and pervasive intuitions are to be trusted. He may agree that the intuitions of an outer world, of people in it, and of certain primary moral standards, are such basic presuppositions of all our living and thinking that to doubt them would be both impractical and inconsistent. But he may report that he does not find the idea of God, a divine Other, an object of ultimate loyalty, fundamental and necessary in the same way.

To one who replies in this way we must give credit for honesty. But on one condition: That he take care not to let his

[14] William Temple, *op. cit.*, p. 255.

honest avowal of ignorance become an excuse or a cloak for sloth. It makes a world of difference whether one says "I have no such intuitions, so those who claim to have them must be self-deluded," or "I have had no such intuitions as yet, but it may be that there is a certain blindness in me, and I would like to learn how to be more alert."

The problem, then, when the doctrinaire objections have been discarded, is one of spiritual alertness. For as Martin Buber remarks, "The waves of the aether roar on always, but for the most part we have turned off our receivers."[15] Spiritual alertness is above all a listening, and so a readiness to commune. Between man and man it makes possible the highest form of *I-thou* relationship—wherein each of two communicants is alert not only to what the other may say but even more to the shades of unspoken meaning which an active sympathy may detect and respond to. But can the *I-thou* relationship become effective not only with another human being but with That which is ungraspably beyond man? The religious hypothesis is a perhaps tentative, but receptive and responsive affirmation that it can.

"How do I know it is not self-delusion?" asks the sceptic. We do not know with demonstrative certainty; there is always, as James says, a "moral risk." But that the moral risk is a reasonable one, consistent enough with the authentic facts of psychology, James shows by his discussion of the role of the subconscious in the God-man relation (pp. 585-587). Our deepest relationships are not confined to the conscious surface of the mind; and *if* the main religious hypothesis is true, and there is a divine Other with whom we may enter into significant relationship, then it may well be that our "trans-marginal states"—the elements of our selfhood just beyond the boundaries of consciousness—offer channels through which such relationship may become effective.

---

[15] Martin Buber, *Between Man and Man* (London: Kegan Paul, 1947), the essay entitled "Dialogue."

For Further Study

CHARLES HARTSHORNE and WILLIAM L. REESE, *Philosophers Speak of God* (University of Chicago Press, 1953). A critical anthology covering virtually all shades of opinion.

JOHN B. NOSS, *Man's Religions* (Macmillan, 1949).

E. O. JAMES, *The Concept of Deity: A Comparative and Historical Study* (London: Hutchinson, 1950).

ALAN W. WATTS, *The Supreme Identity; "An Essay on Oriental Metaphysic and the Christian Religion"* (Pantheon, 1950). *The Wisdom of Insecurity* (Pantheon, 1951).

JOHN R. EVERETT, *Religion in Human Experience* (Holt, 1950).

ABRAHAM J. HESCHEL, *Man Is Not Alone: A Philosophy of Religion* (Farrar, Strauss and Young, 1951).

WILLIAM ERNEST HOCKING, *The Meaning of God in Human Experience* (Yale University Press, 1912), especially Chapts. XII ("The Knowledge of God and the Knowledge of Man," which connects the present topic with that discussed above in Chapter 12), XXII, and XXIII.

WILLIAM TEMPLE, *Nature, Man and God* (Gifford Lectures for 1932-1933 and 1933-1934; Macmillan, 1934).

ARCHIBALD ALLAN BOWMAN, *Studies in the Philosophy of Religion* (Macmillan, 2 vols., 1938).

H. RICHARD NIEBUHR, *The Meaning of Revelation* (Macmillan, 1941).

REINHOLD NIEBUHR, *Faith in History* (Scribner, 1949).

EUGEN ROSENSTOCK-HUESSY, *The Christian Future* (Scribner, 1946).

PAUL TILLICH, *The Protestant Era* (University of Chicago Press, 1948).

WILLIAM JAMES, *Varieties of Religious Experience* (Longmans, Green, 1902).

JAMES B. PRATT, *The Religious Consciousness* (Macmillan, 1920).

SYDNEY H. MELLONE, *The Bearings of Psychology on Religion* (Oxford: Basil Blackwell, 1941).

THOMAS H. HUGHES, *The New Psychology and Religious Experience* (London: Allen and Unwin, 1933).

A. RUDOLPH UREN, *Recent Religious Psychology* (Scribner, 1928).

Peter A. Bertocci, *Introduction to the Philosophy of Religion* (Prentice-Hall, 1951).

Roger Hazelton, *On Proving God* (Harper, 1952).

D. Elton Trueblood, *The Logic of Belief* (Harper, 1942).

William R. Dennes, "Preface to an Empiricist Philosophy of Religion," in College of the Pacific, *Publications in Philosophy*, Vol. III (1934). A semantic attack upon theism.

Questions for Discussion

1. Should a reasonable man accept any religious belief which, so far as he can see,

a) cannot be verified or at least rendered probable by scientific method?

b) is inconsistent with empirical probabilities?

c) is not *self*-consistent?

Can you think of specific religious beliefs (or at any rate beliefs which have been widely accepted as religious) which are lacking in one or another of these respects?

2. How would you rate the following in order of importance for a religious outlook?

a) a belief in God?

b) belief in the established creed of some religious body?

c) ritual?

d) private prayer, worship, and meditation?

e) a feeling of reverence?

f) an ethical way of life?

g) active benevolence?

3. If you considered it to be proved beyond reasonable doubt that religious beliefs had evolved out of such primitive phenomena as magic, superstitious fear of ghosts, and tribal celebration of harvest, would that weaken, in your opinion, the validity of such beliefs?

4. "The evidence of the existence of a God and of a devil is substantially the same. Both of these deities are inferences; each one is a perhaps. . . . Now no intelligent man believes in the existence of a devil."—Robert Green Ingersoll, "Superstition" (*Ingersoll's Greatest Lectures*, republished by Freethought Press Association, 1944).

Complete the argument, examine its validity, and consider what replies are possible.

5. Professor Dennes (*op. cit.*) argues against the moral argument for God's existence, declaring that the hypothesis of a divine authority adds nothing to the security of values, "since the choice and the very authoritativeness of authorities themselves derives, and can derive, from no other source than our loves and hopes."

Test the effectiveness of this refutation by applying it successively to (*a*) de Burgh's argument given below, (*b*) Kant's and (*c*) Rashdall's arguments as given in Section iii.

"In contrast to the irrational, blind, and purely subjective belief that the universe will supply what we want simply because we want it, stands the faith of reason that is assured of satisfaction because the truth and the goodness in which its trust is set are the objects of a desire independent of the play of personal inclination."—W. G. DE BURGH, *Towards a Religious Philosophy* (London: Macdonald and Evans, 1937).

6. Maimonides, the great Jewish theologian of the Middle Ages, declares: "The term *one* is just as inapplicable to God as the term *many*; for both unity and plurality are categories of quantity, and are therefore as inapplicable to God as crooked and straight in reference to sweetness, or salted and savorless in reference to a voice."—*The Guide of the Perplexed*, I, 57. Dr. Heschel proposes a way out of the paradox, by adopting from Rabbinic literature the phrase *Yehido shel olam*, "The Unique of the universe."

What, if anything, is gained by substituting "Unique" for "One"?

7. How real do you consider the danger indicated in the following quotations? How can a genuinely religious attitude best avoid it?

a) "You will not see the sky if you cover your glasses with blue paint."—ALAN W. WATTS, *The Wisdom of Insecurity*.

b) "We must beware lest we violate the holy, lest our dogmas overthink the mystery, lest our psalms sing it away."—A. J. HESCHEL, *Man Is Not Alone*.

CHAPTER XVI

Epilogue: On Choosing a Philosophy

The end of a first course in philosophy should be a time of personal stock-taking. You have passed in review a number of philosophical questions and a diversity of answers to them, and you have learned something of the arguments by which a given position can be defended and can be assailed. But philosophy is not merely a collection of moves in an abstract intellectual game. The game has its uses, to be sure; for by throwing light on points of view, actual and possible, which might have been overlooked, it shakes the mind out of contentment with a limited horizon and a narrow outlook. Nevertheless, discontent is not a good in itself. Its value lies in the new mental efforts which it energizes, and these in turn are justified at length by the new insights that are precariously won. I say "precariously" in the Socratic vein; for an insight has continuing vitality only when it is accompanied by the recognition that other, even contrary, insights may be quite as valid for other times, to other persons, and in other contexts. There is, as James has said, a "moral risk" in every outreach of the mind toward new wisdom. If it were not so the philosophic quest would be dull, for who wants a journey without adventures? And when have honest adventures not entailed some risk? The risk of inquiry is a real one, for if one's thinking goes deep it will make a difference not only in the kind of thinker but in the kind of person that one is gradually to become. Nor can the risk be avoided by simply closing one's mind against philosophic doubts. There is one kind of risk in the cat's curiosity, another in the tactics of the ostrich.

At any rate, by the time you are reading these words, it may be presumed, you have already decided in favor of the philosophic enterprise, or at least in favor of giving it a sustained trial. And like a mountain-climber who reaches a ledge you are now in a position to pause for breath and survey the landscape which your climb has at length brought into view. It is the same countryside that you knew before you started to mount, but it wears a different look. As a matter of fact, in order to adapt the simile to the situation under discussion, we shall have to modify it by supposing not one ledge but several, each of which shows the landscape in a somewhat different perspective. And we shall have to suppose not one but a party of mountaineers, who inspect the different ledges and disagree as to which of their several outlooks reveals the character of the countryside most truly. Some of them praise the view from one vantage point, others from another. They contemplate the familiar but strangely modified outlines of houses and fields, and argue for their respective positions without avail. Finally one of their number proposes that they reserve judgment until they have explored further; suggesting that perhaps they may find another ledge higher up, from where they can more easily agree on what the landscape is really like. Unfortunately, however, if they climb too high, their distancing vision will eventually lose the bright particularities of landscape altogether and see only the gray haziness of cloud. The end of the parable sounds pessimistic, but it is not. It simply reminds us that our present task is always to interpret the world as best as we can from the ledge we have reached; that, in the words of the adage, "it is better to milk a standing cow than to chase after cows that are running away." The simile and the adage represent only half-truths—as what similes and adages do not? —but even half-truths serve as useful reminders when the half which they contain is something prone to be overlooked. Let us, then, stop our climbing and our chasing for a moment and face the question, which each must put to himself individually: "Where, really, do I stand on the main issues that have been raised?"

In the last resort, of course, no one can settle that question for anyone else. It lies beyond the frontier of possible teaching. What teaching and learning can do, at most, is to supply materials and suggestions, and models of how other men have thought. With these limitations understood, then, I recall your attention to the threefold division of philosophies which was proposed at the end of Chapter I. The problems that most deeply concern us as rational human beings invite possible answers of three main kinds, which (whatever their variations in detail) I have summarily designated the materialistic, the humanistic, and the transcendental. If your readings and reflections have convinced you of the inadequacy of this and of any other brief schematization, all the better; such devices are merely signposts, not crutches. Nevertheless, the problem of basic intellectual allegiance remains. When a question concerns you deeply and comprehensively—which is to say existentially—what is to be the dominant direction in which you will look for an answer? Toward the processes and tendencies of the sub-human world? Toward a Being that is infinitely superior to men, and in relation to Which (or to Whom) one may find both the right direction of moral effort and the ultimate ground of existence? Or toward man himself, in all his varied expressions and ramifications, not excluding either the material components or the transcendental aspirations from the total definition, but reserving the right to interpret both of them in the light of man as he knows himself and his fellows? These are, in a rough and broad way, the three major attitudes and points of view which reveal themselves variously in philosophical controversy. If you can discover, with sturdy metaphysical integrity, where you stand on this most basic issue, you will possess a helpful, though not infallible, criterion for meeting particular problems with a more alert and more independent mind.

Readings for Part Four

Letter to a Friend*

EPICURUS

WE MUST consider that of desires some are natural, others empty; that of the natural some are necessary, others not; and that of the necessary some are necessary for happiness, others for bodily comfort, and others for life itself. A right understanding of these facts enables us to direct all choice and avoidance toward securing the health of the body and tranquillity of the soul; this being the final aim of a blessed life. For the aim of all actions is to avoid pain and fear; and when this is once secured for us the tempest of the soul is entirely quelled, since the living animal no longer needs to wander as though in search of something he lacks, hunting for that by which he can fulfill some need of soul or body. We feel a need of pleasure only when we grieve over its absence; when we stop grieving we are in need of pleasure no longer. Pleasure, then, is the beginning and end of the blessed life.[1] For we recognize it as a good which is both primary and kindred to us. From pleasure we begin every act of choice and avoidance; and to pleasure we return again, using the feeling as the standard by which to judge every good.

Now since pleasure is the good that is primary and most natural to us, for that very reason we do not seize all pleasures indiscriminately; on the contrary we often pass over many pleasures, when greater discomfort accrues to us as a result of them. Similarly we not infrequently judge pains better than pleasures, when the long endurance of a pain yields us a greater pleasure in the end. Thus every pleasure because of its natural kinship to us is good, yet not every pleasure is to be chosen; just as every pain also is an evil, yet that

---

* From Epicurus' Letter to Menoecius, preserved in Diogenes Laertius, *Lives of the Philosophers*, Bk. X.

[1] I.e., since it is a product of that health of body and tranquility of soul mentioned above.

does not mean that all pains are necessarily to be shunned. It is by a scale of comparison and by the consideration of advantages and disadvantages that we must form our judgment on these matters. On particular occasions we may have reason to treat the good as bad, and the bad as good.

Independence of circumstance we regard as a great good: not because we wish to dispense altogether with external advantages, but in order that, if our possessions are few, we may be content with what we have, sincerely believing that those enjoy luxury most who depend on it least, and that natural wants are easily satisfied if we are willing to forego superfluities. Plain fare yields as much pleasure as a luxurious table, provided the pain of real want is removed; bread and water can give exquisite delight to hungry and thirsty lips. To form the habit of a simple and modest diet, therefore, is the way to health: it enables us to perform the needful employments of life without shrinking, it puts us in better condition to enjoy luxuries when they are offered, and it renders us fearless of fortune.

Accordingly, when we argue that pleasure is the end and aim of life, we do not mean the pleasure of prodigals and sensualists, as some of our ignorant or prejudiced critics persist in mistaking us. We mean the pleasure of being free from pain of body and anxiety of mind. It is not a continual round of drunken debauches and lecherous delights, nor the enjoyment of fish and other delicacies of a wealthy table, which produce a pleasant life; but sober reasoning, searching out the motives of choice and avoidance, and escaping the bondage of opinion, to which the greatest disturbances of spirit are due.

The first step and the greatest good is prudence—a more precious thing than philosophy even, for all the other virtues are sprung from it. By prudence we learn that we can live pleasurably only if we live prudently, honorably, and justly, while contrariwise to live prudently, honorably, and justly guarantees a life that is pleasurable as well. The virtues are by nature bound up with a pleasant life, and a pleasant life is inseparable from them in turn.

Is there any better and wiser man than he who holds reverent beliefs about the gods, is altogether free from the fear of death, and has serenely contemplated the basic tendencies (*telos*) of natural law? Such a man understands that the limit of good things is easy to attain, and that evils are slight either in duration or in intensity. He laughs at Destiny, which so many accept as all-powerful. Some things, he observes, occur of necessity, others by chance, and still others through our own agency. Necessity is irresponsible, chance is inconstant, but our own actions are free, and it is to them that praise and blame are properly attached. It would be better even to believe the myths about the gods than to submit to the Destiny which the natural philosophers teach. For the old superstitions at least offer some faint hope of placating the gods by worship, but the Necessity of the scientific philosophers is absolutely unyielding. As to chance, the wise man does not deify it as most men do; for if it were divine it would not be without order. Nor will he accept the view that it is a universal cause even though of a wavering kind; for he believes that what chance bestows is not the good and evil that determine a man's blessedness in life, but the starting-points from which each person can arrive at great good or great evil. He esteems the misfortune of the wise above the prosperity of a fool; holding it better that well chosen courses of action should fail than that ill chosen ones should succeed by mere chance.

Meditate on these and like precepts day and night, both privately and with some companion who is of kindred disposition. Thereby shall you never suffer disturbance, waking or asleep, but shall live like a god among men. For a man who lives constantly among immortal blessings is surely more than mortal.

The Nature and Sanctions of Moral Action*

JEREMY BENTHAM

The principle of utility

Nature has placed mankind under the governance of two sovereign masters, *pain* and *pleasure*. It is for them alone to point out

* The first two sections are from Jeremy Bentham (1748–1832), *An Introduction to the Principles of Morals and Legislation*, Chaps. I and IV. The remainder is from Bentham's *Deontology* (published posthumously, 1834), Chap. VII. It should be kept in mind that Bentham employs the words "happiness" and "utility" in a special sense. Happiness denotes surplus in the total amount of pleasures over pains; utility, the character which an action has of promoting such happiness.

what we ought to do, as well as to determine what we shall do. On the one hand the standard of right and wrong, on the other the chain of causes and effects, are fastened to their throne. They govern us in all we do, in all we say, in all we think: every effort we can make to throw off our subjection, will serve but to demonstrate and confirm it. In words a man may pretend to abjure their empire, but in reality he will remain subject to it all the while. The *principle of utility* recognizes this subjection, and assumes it for the foundation of that system, the object of which is to rear the fabric of felicity by the hands of reason and of law. Systems which attempt to question it deal in sounds instead of sense, in caprice instead of reason, in darkness instead of light.

But enough of metaphor and declamation: it is not by such means that moral science is to be improved.

The principle of utility is the foundation of the present work: it will be proper therefore at the outset to give an explicit and determinate account of what is meant by it. By the principle of utility is meant that principle which approves or disapproves of every action whatsoever, according to the tendency which it appears to have to augment or diminish the happiness of the party whose interest is in question: or, what is the same thing in other words, to promote or to oppose that happiness. I say of every action whatsoever; and therefore not only of every action of a private individual, but of every measure of government. . . .

Computation of pleasures and pains

Pleasures then, and the avoidance of pains, are the *ends* which the legislator has in view: it behooves him therefore to understand their *value*. Pleasures and pains are the *instruments* he has to work with: it behooves him therefore to understand their force, which is again, in another point of view, their value.

To a person considered *by himself*, the value of a pleasure or pain considered *by itself,* will be greater or less according to the four following circumstances:

(1) Its *intensity*.
(2) Its *duration*.
(3) Its *certainty* or *uncertainty*.
(4) Its *propinquity* or *remoteness*.

These are the circumstances which are to be considered in estimating a pleasure or a pain considered each of them by itself. But when the value of any pleasure or pain is considered for the purpose of estimating the tendency of any *act* by which it is produced, there are two other circumstances to be taken into account. These are:

(5) Its *fecundity,* or the chance it has of being followed by sensations of the *same* kind: that is, pleasures, if it be a pleasure; pains, if it be a pain.

(6) Its *purity,* or the chance it has of *not* being followed by sensations of the *opposite* kind: that is, pains, if it be a pleasure; pleasures, if it be a pain.

These two last, however, are in strictness scarcely to be deemed properties of the pleasure or the pain itself; they are not, therefore, in strictness to be taken into the account of the value of that pleasure or that pain. They are in strictness to be deemed properties only of the act, or other event, by which such pleasure or pain has been produced; and accordingly are only to be taken into the account of the tendency of such act or such event.

To a *number* of persons, with reference to each of whom the value of a pleasure or a pain is considered, it will be greater or less, according to seven circumstances: to wit, the six preceding ones; *viz.,*

(1) Its *intensity.*
(2) Its *duration.*
(3) Its *certainty* or *uncertainty.*
(4) Its *propinquity* or *remoteness.*
(5) Its *fecundity.*
(6) Its *purity.*

And one other; to wit:

(7) Its *extent;* that is, the number of persons to whom it *extends,* or (in other words) who are affected by it.

To take an exact account then of the general tendency of any act by which the interests of a community are affected, proceed as follows. Begin with any one person of those whose interests seem most immediately to be affected by it, and take an account:

(1) Of the value of each distinguishable *pleasure* which appears to be produced by it in the *first* instance.

(2) Of the value of each *pain* which appears to be produced by it in the *first* instance.

(3) Of the value of each pleasure which appears to be produced by it *after* the first. This constitutes the *fecundity* of the first *pleasure* and the *impurity* of the first *pain*.

(4) Of the value of each *pain* which appears to be produced by it after the first. This constitutes the *fecundity* of the first *pain*, and the *impurity* of the first *pleasure*.

(5) Sum up all the values of all the pleasures on the one side, and those of all the pains on the other. The balance, if it be on the side of pleasure, will give the *good* tendency of the act upon the whole, with respect to the interests of that *individual* person; if on the side of pain, the *bad* tendency of it upon the whole.

(6) Take an account of the *number* of persons whose interests appear to be concerned, and repeat the above process with respect to each. *Sum up* the numbers expressive of the degrees of *good* tendency which the act has, with respect to each individual in regard to whom the tendency of it is *good* upon the whole; do this again with respect to each individual in regard to whom the tendency of it is *bad* upon the whole. Take the *balance;* which, if on the side of *pleasure,* will give the general *good tendency* of the act, with respect to the total number or community of individuals concerned; if on the side of *pain*, the general *evil tendency*, with respect to the same community.

It is not to be expected that this process should be strictly pursued previously to every moral judgment, or to every legislative or judicial operation. It may, however, be always kept in view; and as near as the process actually pursued on these occasions approaches to it, so near will such process approach to the character of an exact one.

The problem of sanctions

Respice finem. The end of action being defined, that end must be steadily kept in view, and no inquiry can be more important than as to the most efficient means of promoting that end. Those means present themselves in the shape of the inducements which operate on conduct. They bring conduct and its consequences into the regions of hopes and fears—of hopes which present a balance of pleasure, of fears which anticipate a balance of pain. These inducements may be conveniently called sanctions.

The strength of a temptation to a misdeed is in the ratio of the excess of the pleasure of the misdeed (as it stands in the idea of the person tempted) above the intensity of the pain which is to follow, compounded with its apparent proximity and probability.

Sanctions, as has been said, are inducements to action. They suppose the existence of temptations. Temptations are the evil; sanctions the remedy. But neither are sanctions nor temptations anything but pains and pleasures, acting singly in the case of temptations, acting as sanctions in groups.

(1) *Physical sanction*

The physical sanction concerns a man's person physically and psychologically considered, as experienced in the pains and pleasures affecting the body. It is derived from the physical construction of man in general, and will be modified by the peculiar sensibilities of the individual. Generally speaking, the physical sanction may be considered as that influence growing out of the ordinary course of things, which is brought to bear upon any action or actions, without reference to the will of others. It is that influence which is independent of motives derived from sources foreign to the individual: it is the sanction which would exist, in all its force, if a man were isolated from the world, if he had no communion with his fellow-men, and no belief in the superintendence of Providence. It represents those pains and pleasures which do not directly emanate from his social, political, or religious position; though it is the groundwork of the power of all other inducements, for it is only by their influence on man's physical organization, only by their power of producing suffering or enjoyment in the individual, that they can become motives to action.

(2) *Social sanction*

The social or sympathetic sanction is that which grows out of a man's personal or domestic relations; it is a sort of mixture of the selfish with the social regard. To some extent its judgment is created by his own influences; it is the application to himself of that domestic code of which he has been one of the framers. If he be a father, his children will, in the ratio of their respect for his opinions and practice, recognize his authority, and adopt his standard of right and wrong. The domestic sanction may be more or less efficient, more or less enlightened than the popular sanction: its operation is more direct and immediate than the popular can be, in as far as a man's happiness, for the most part, depends more on those who are near him, habitually or frequently, than upon those who are remote. The social and the popular sanction act and re-act upon each other; the popular sanction being, in fact, the great recipient of all the social sanctions.

(3) *Popular sanction*

The moral or popular sanction is that which is commonly called public opinion; it is the received decision of society on conduct. . . .

Among the pleasures and pains growing out of the moral or popular sanction, and exercising a vast influence on virtue and vice, and thence on happiness and misery, are a group of factitious entities, which demand attention. Reputation, honor, renown, fame, glory, and dignity, may serve as a sample of them. They have this in common, that they are, though factitious, the objects of possession. They are distinguished from other objects of possession in this, that pursuit of them, to any extent, is not deemed improper. The love of money, everyone admits, may be carried to excess, but not so the pursuit of these attractions.

But in the mistakes made respecting them, in the eulogiums poured on those who pursue and those who possess them, will be found one of the most fruitful sources of improbity and mischief. The means a man has at his disposal he will employ, not only to keep that which he possesses, but to obtain that which he desires. These possessions are the instruments of influence, and that influence is liable to be baneful, according to its extent. The mischief is at its minimum where confined to an individual; it is at its maximum when it operates on a national or international field. . . .

The more men live in public, the more amenable they are to the moral sanction. The greater dependence men are in to the public, that is, the more equality there is among them, the more it has of certainty in its results. The liberty of the press throws all men into the public presence. The liberty of the press is the greatest coadjutor of the moral sanction. Under such influence, it were strange if men grew not every day more virtuous than on the former day. I am satisfied they do. I am satisfied they will continue so to do, till, if ever, their nature shall have arrived at its perfection. Shall they stop?

Shall they turn back? The rivers shall as soon make a wall, or roll up the mountains to their source....

The constitution of the human mind being opened by degrees, the labyrinth is explored, a clue is found out for it. That clue is the influence of interest; of interest, not in that partial and sordid sense in which it is the tyrant of sordid souls, but in the enlarged and beneficent sense in which it is the common master of all spirits, and especially of the enlightened. It is put into the hands of every man. The designs by which short-sighted iniquity would mask its projects, are every day laid open. There will be no moral enigmas by and by.

Who knows but even I, an instrument as mean as I, may be found to have done something towards a work so glorious, and this my prophecy itself, like so many others, be in a certain degree the cause of its own completion?

(4) *Political sanction*

The political, or legal sanction. It has two branches, the judicial and the administrative. The judicial acting almost exclusively by punishments, the administrative mostly by rewards. This sanction becomes law, and is called into operation upon all those acts which legislation makes penal, or those which legislation deems worthy of public recompense. In other words, the political sanction belongs to those vices which, being deemed misdemeanors or crimes, are taken cognizance of by the official authorities, as meet subjects for penal visitation, or to those virtues which are marked out for state reward. It is the legislator, rather than the moralist, who is armed with the political sanction; but it was necessary to mention it as one of the sources of action.

Scandal is to the moral sanction what perjury is to the political.

(5) *Religious sanction*

The religious or superhuman sanction. It has two principal sources of influence, which, when they can be brought to bear upon human action, necessarily invest the sanction with high authority and power. For, first, it supposes the Divine Being to be thoroughly cognizant of the existence of every misdeed in question; and, secondly, to have perfect knowledge of the exact quantity and quality of its malignity, from the knowledge of all the aggravating and extenuating circumstances. Thence all those chances of escape from observation or from punishment, which diminish the efficiency of the other sanctions, are removed from this, which at once brings the offender into the presence of an all-seeing, all-knowing, all-weighing, and equitably awarding judge. . . .

To what is the inefficiency of the religious sanction to be attributed? For if its power be as it is represented, it ought to be the most influential of instruments, inasmuch as infinite is greater than finite, and the pains and pleasures it proposes are intense and permanent beyond all others; and let it be said, once for all, that it is not intended here to supersede its authority, but merely to supply auxiliaries which may add to its beneficial influence. The enjoyments and sufferings of a future life being inaccessible to experience, whether our own or that of others, no man having hitherto reported, for the information of his fellows, what had happened to him beyond the grave, and no man having hitherto learned it for himself, those enjoyments and sufferings represent nothing which our experience has shown to be either pleasurable or painful. Being remote as to distance, uncertain and unimmediate as to their contingency on any particular action, undefined as to their character, and indivisible in their operation, it is not to be wondered at that they so often lose their power in the presence of adjacent, certain, palpable influences. Events placed so far beyond the limits of life and knowledge are not, it must be admitted, susceptible of being brought into the mind with the vividness of that which is propinquitous. As in receding from the loftiest and sublimest objects, however substantial, they gradually diminish; so the tremendous hopes and fears with which it is the province of religion to agitate us, fail in their influence, and become obscured in the remoteness of eternity. . . .

Another main quality on which the effect of a punishment depends is its celerity. No man ever thrusts his hand into the fire. Why? Because the suffering follows instantaneously upon the act.

There are certain consequences which follow almost as certainly the acts calculated to produce them, as the pain of burning from thrusting the hand into the fire. Yet these acts are committed. Why? Because the penal consequence is distant.

Delay gives room for obstacles to intervene. Apparent diminution of *certainty* therefore follows necessarily from abatement of celerity.

Pity, too, has more time to operate, to prevent or mitigate the punishment. And pity destroys a proportion of its effect.

The religious sanction is eminently deficient in the article of celerity. . . .

The religious sanction is founded, and can only be founded, on the moral attributes of God, and those moral attributes cannot oppose happiness.

Justice is of use no farther than as the handmaid of benevolence.

Justice is one of those means for compassing the ends that benevolence proposes.

If God is just, it is because he is benevolent.

If there is no benevolent Being that looks to us, we must look to ourselves; we must procure our own happiness by ourselves, as far as we can. What other resource is left to us?

If there is a Being that watches over us, but is not benevolent, he is not just: there is no guessing what will please him; there is no guessing what will not please him; there is no knowing how to please him: our only wisdom is to please ourselves.

If there is a benevolent Being that watches over us, that rewards and punishes in the exercise of that benevolence, he, at least, cannot be displeased at our procuring our happiness to the utmost; for the disposition to contribute to it is what we mean by benevolence, when we mean anything, and in the very proportion of our love and reverence will our conviction of his benevolence be.

By a given instance, however, the operation of the different sanctions upon conduct may be best traced.

A story with a moral

Timothy Thoughtless and Walter Wise are fellow prentices. Thoughtless gave in to the vice of drunkenness; Wise abstained from it. Mark the consequence.

1. Physical sanction. For every debauch, Thoughtless was rewarded by sickness in the head; to recruit himself he lay in bed the next morning, and his whole frame became enervated by relaxation; and when he returned to his work, his work ceased to be a source of satisfaction to him.

Walter Wise refused to accompany him to the drinking table. His health had not been originally strong, but it was invigorated by temperance. Increasing strength of body gave increasing zest to every satisfaction he enjoyed: his rest at night was tranquil, his risings in the morning cheerful, his labor pleasurable.

2. Social sanction. Timothy had a sister, deeply interested in his happiness. She reproved him at first, then neglected, then abandoned him. She had been to him a source of great pleasure—it was all swept away.

Walter had a brother, who had shown indifference to him. That brother had watched over his conduct, and began to show an interest in his well-being—the interest increased from day to day. At last he became a constant visitor, and a more than common friend, and did a thousand services for his brother, which no other man in the world would have done.

3. Popular sanction. Timothy was a member of a club, which had money and reputation. He went thither one day in a state of inebriety; he abused the secretary, and was expelled by an unanimous vote.

The regular habits of Walter had excited the attention of his master. He said one day to his banker—The young man is fitted for a higher station. The banker bore it in mind, and on the first opportunity, took him into his service. He rose from one distinction to another, and was frequently consulted on business of the highest importance by men of wealth and influence.

4. Legal sanction. Timothy rushed out from the club whence he had been so ignominiously expelled. He insulted a man in the streets, and walked penniless into the open country. Reckless of everything, he robbed the first traveler he met; he was apprehended, prosecuted, and sentenced to transportation.

Walter had been an object of approbation to his fellow-citizens. He was called, by their good opinion, to the magistracy. He reached its highest honors, and even sat in judgment on his fellow apprentice, whom time and misery had so changed, that he was not recognized by him.

5. Religious sanction. In prison, and in the ship which conveyed Timothy to Botany Bay, his mind was alarmed and afflicted with the apprehension of future punishment—an angry and avenging Deity was constantly present to his thoughts, and every day of his existence was embittered by the dread of the Divine Being.

To Walter the contemplation of futurity was peaceful and pleasurable. He dwelt with constant delight on the benign attributes of the Deity, and the conviction was ever present to him that it must be well, that all ultimately must be well, to the virtuous. Great, indeed, was the balance of pleasure which he drew from his existence, and great was the sum of happiness to which he gave birth.

Crito*

PLATO

SOCRATES. Why have you come at this hour, Crito? Is it not still early?

CRITO. Yes, very early.

SOCRATES. About what time is it?

CRITO. It is just day-break.

SOCRATES. I wonder that the jailor was willing to let you in.

CRITO. He knows me now, Socrates, I come here so often; and besides, I have done him a service.

SOCRATES. Have you been here long?

CRITO. Yes; some time.

SOCRATES. Then why did you sit down without speaking? why did you not wake me at once?

CRITO. Indeed, Socrates, I wish that I myself were not so sleepless and sorrowful. But I have been wondering to see how sweetly you sleep. And I purposely did not wake you, for I was anxious not to disturb your repose. Often before, all through your life, I have thought that your temper was a happy one; and I think so more than ever now, when I see how easily and calmly you bear the calamity that has come to you.

---

* Plato's Dialogue *Crito,* complete, in the F. J. Church translation. The time is 399 B.C.; the scene, an Athenian prison. Socrates has been sentenced to death on the charge of having corrupted the minds of the young men of Athens by teaching radical religious doctrines.

SOCRATES. Nay, Crito, it would be absurd if at my age I were angry at having to die.

CRITO. Other men as old are overtaken by similar calamities, Socrates; but their age does not save them from being angry with their fate.

SOCRATES. That is so; but tell me, why are you here so early?

CRITO. I am the bearer of bitter news, Socrates: not bitter, it seems, to you; but to me, and to all your friends, both bitter and grievous: and to none of them, I think, is it more grievous than to me.

SOCRATES. What is it? Has the ship come from Delos, at the arrival of which I am to die?

CRITO. No, it has not actually arrived: but I think that it will be here today, from the news which certain persons have brought from Sunium, who left it there. It is clear from their news that it will be here today; and then, Socrates, tomorrow your life will have to end.

SOCRATES. Well, Crito, may it end fortunately. Be it so, if so the gods will. But I do not think that the ship will be here today.

CRITO. Why do you suppose not?

SOCRATES. I will tell you. I am to die on the day after the ship arrives, am I not?

CRITO. That is what the authorities say.

SOCRATES. Then I do not think it will come today, but tomorow. I judge from a certain dream which I saw a little while ago in the night: so it seems to be fortunate that you did not wake me.

CRITO. And what was this dream?

SOCRATES. A fair and comely woman, clad in white garments, seemed to come to me, and call me and say, "O Socrates—

'The third day hence shalt thou fair Phthia reach.' "[1]

CRITO. What a strange dream, Socrates!

SOCRATES. But its meaning is clear; at least to me, Crito.

CRITO. Yes, too clear, it seems. But, O my good Socrates, I beseech you for the last time to listen to me and save yourself. For to me your death will be more than a single disaster: not only shall I lose a friend the like of whom I shall never find again, but many persons, who do not know you and me well, will think that I might have

[1] Homer, *Iliad,* ix. 363.

saved you if I had been willing to spend money, but that I neglected to do so. And what character could be more disgraceful than the character of caring more for money than for one's friends? The world will never believe that we were anxious to save you, but that you yourself refused to escape.

SOCRATES. But, my excellent Crito, why should we care so much about the opinion of the world? The best men, of whose opinion it is worth our while to think, will believe that we acted as we really did.

CRITO. But you see, Socrates, that it is necessary to care about the opinion of the world too. This very thing that has happened to you proves that the multitude can do a man not the least, but almost the greatest harm, if he be falsely accused to them.

SOCRATES. I wish that the multitude were able to do a man the greatest harm, Crito, for then they would be able to do him the greatest good too. That would have been well. But, as it is, they can do neither. They cannot make a man either wise or foolish: they act wholly at random.

CRITO. Well, be it so. But tell me this, Socrates. You surely are not anxious about me and your other friends, and afraid lest, if you escape, the informers should say that we stole you away, and get us into trouble, and involve us in a great deal of expense, or perhaps in the loss of all our property, and, it may be, bring some other punishment upon us besides? If you have any fear of that kind, dismiss it. For of course we are bound to run those risks, and still greater risks than those if necessary, in saving you. So do not, I beseech you, refuse to listen to me.

SOCRATES. I am anxious about that, Crito, and about much besides.

CRITO. Then have no fear on that score. There are men who, for no very large sum, are ready to bring you out of prison into safety. And then, you know, these informers are cheaply bought, and there would be no need to spend much upon them. My fortune is at your service, and I think that it is sufficient: and if you have any feeling about making use of my money, there are strangers in Athens, whom you know, ready to use theirs; and one of them, Simmias of Thebes, has actually brought enough for this very purpose. And Cebes and many others are ready too. And therefore, I repeat, do not shrink from saving yourself on that ground. And do not let what you said in the Court, that if you went into exile you would not know what to do with yourself, stand in your way; for there are many places for you to go to, where you will be welcomed. If you choose to go to Thessaly, I have friends there who will make much of you, and shelter you from any annoyance from the people of Thessaly.

And besides, Socrates, I think that you will be doing what is wrong, if you abandon your life when you might preserve it. You are simply playing the game of your enemies; it is exactly the game of those who wanted to destroy you. And what is more, to me you seem to be abandoning your children too: you will leave them to take their chance in life, as far as you are concerned, when you might bring them up and educate them. Most likely their fate will be the usual fate of children who are left orphans. But you ought not to beget children unless you mean to take the trouble of bringing them up and educating them. It seems to me that you are choosing the easy way, and not the way of a good and brave man, as you ought, when you have been talking all your life long of the value that you set upon virtue. For my part, I feel ashamed both for you, and for us who are your friends. Men will think that the whole of this thing which has happened to you—your appearance in court to take your trial, when you need not have appeared at all; the very way in which the trial was conducted; and then lastly this, for the crowning absurdity of the whole affair, is due to our cowardice. It will look as if we had shirked the danger out of miserable cowardice; for we did not save you, and you did not save yourself, when it was quite possible to do so, if we had been good for anything at all. Take care, Socrates, lest these things be not evil only, but also dishonorable to you and to us. Consider then; or rather the time for consideration is past; we must resolve; and there is only one plan possible. Everything must be done tonight. If we delay any longer, we are lost. O Socrates, I implore you not to refuse to listen to me.

SOCRATES. My dear Crito, if your anxiety to save me be right, it is most valuable: but if it be not right, its greatness makes it all the more dangerous. We must consider then whether we are to do as you say, or not; for I am still what I always have been, a man who will listen to no voice but the voice of the reasoning which on consideration I find to be truest. I cannot cast aside my former arguments because this misfortune has come to me. They seem to me to be as true as ever they were, and I hold exactly the same ones in honor and esteem as I used to: and if we have no better reasoning to substitute for them, I certainly shall not agree to your proposal, not even though the power of the multitude should scare us with fresh terrors, as children are scared with hobgoblins, and inflict upon us new fines, and imprisonments, and deaths. How then shall we most fitly examine the question? Shall we go back first to what you say about the opinions of men, and ask if we used to be right in thinking that we ought to pay attention to some opinions, and not to others? Used we to be right in saying so before I was condemned to die, and has it now become apparent that we were talking at random, and arguing for the sake of argument, and that it was really nothing but play and nonsense? I am anxious, Crito, to examine our former reasoning with your help, and to see whether my present position will appear to me to have affected its truth in any way, or not; and whether we are to set it aside, or to yield assent to it. Those of us who thought at all seriously, used always to say, I think, exactly what I said just now, namely, that we ought to esteem some of the opinions which men form highly, and not others. Tell me, Crito, if you please, do you not think that they were right? For you, humanly speaking, will not have to die tomorrow, and your judgment will not be biased by that circumstance. Consider then: do you not think it reasonable to say that we should not esteem all the opinions of men, but only some, nor the opinions of all men, but only of some men? What do you think? Is not this true?

CRITO. It is.

SOCRATES. And we should esteem the good opinions, and not the worthless ones?

CRITO. Yes.

SOCRATES. But the good opinions are those of the wise, and the worthless ones those of the foolish?

CRITO. Of course.

SOCRATES. And what used we to say about this? Does a man who is in training, and who is in earnest about it, attend to the praise and blame and opinion of all men, or of the one man only who is a doctor or a trainer?

CRITO. He attends only to the opinion of the one man.

SOCRATES. Then he ought to fear the blame and welcome the praise of this one man, not of the many?

CRITO. Clearly.

SOCRATES. Then he must act and exercise, and eat and drink in whatever way the one man who is his master, and who understands the matter, bids him; not as others bid him?

CRITO. That is so.

SOCRATES. Good. But if he disobeys this one man, and disregards his opinion and his praise, and esteems instead what the many, who understand nothing of the matter, say, will he not suffer for it?

CRITO. Of course he will.

SOCRATES. And how will he suffer? In what direction, and in what part of himself?

CRITO. Of course in his body. That is disabled.

SOCRATES. You are right. And, Crito, to be brief, is it not the same, in everything? And, therefore, in questions of right and wrong, and of the base and the honorable, and of good and evil, which we are now considering, ought we to follow the opinion of the many and fear that, or the opinion of the one man who understands these matters (if we can find him), and feel more shame and fear before him than before all other men? For if we do not follow him, we shall cripple and maim that part of us which, we used to say, is improved by right and disabled by wrong. Or is this not so?

CRITO. No, Socrates, I agree with you.

SOCRATES. Now, if, by listening to the opinions of those who do not understand, we disable that part of us which is improved by health and crippled by disease, is our life worth living, when it is crippled? It is the body, is it not?

CRITO. Yes.

SOCRATES. Is life worth living with the body crippled and in a bad state?

CRITO. No, certainly not.

SOCRATES. Then is life worth living when that part of us which is maimed by wrong and benefited by right is crippled? Or do we consider that part of us, whatever it is, which has to do with right and wrong to be of less consequence than our body?

CRITO. No, certainly not.

SOCRATES. But more valuable?

CRITO. Yes, much more so.

SOCRATES. Then, my excellent friend, we must not think so much of what the many will say of us; we must think of what the one man, who understands right and wrong, and of what Truth herself will say of us. And so you are mistaken to begin with, when you invite us to regard the opinion of the multitude concerning the right and the honorable and the good, and their opposites. But, it may be said, the multitude can put us to death?

CRITO. Yes, that is evident. That may be said, Socrates.

SOCRATES. True. But, my excellent friend, to me it appears that the conclusion which we have just reached, is the same as our conclusion of former times. Now consider whether we still hold to the belief, that we should set the highest value, not on living, but on living well?

CRITO. Yes, we do.

SOCRATES. And living well and honorably and rightly mean the same thing: do we hold to that or not?

CRITO. We do.

SOCRATES. Then, starting from these premises, we have to consider whether it is right or not right for me to try to escape from prison, without the consent of the Athenians. If we find that it is right, we will try: if not, we will let it alone. I am afraid that considerations of expense, and of reputation, and of bringing up my children, of which you talk, Crito, are only the reflections of our friends, the many, who lightly put men to death, and who would, if they could, as lightly bring them to life again, without a thought. But reason, which is our guide, shows us that we can have nothing to consider but the question which I asked just now: namely, shall we be doing right if we give money and thanks to the men who are to aid me in escaping, and if we ourselves take our respective parts in my escape? Or shall we in truth be doing wrong, if we do all this? And if we find that we should be doing wrong, then we must not take any account either of death, or of any other evil that may be the consequence of remaining quietly here, but only of doing wrong.

CRITO. I think that you are right, Socrates. But what are we to do?

SOCRATES. Let us consider that together, my good sir, and if you can contradict anything that I say, do so, and I will be convinced: but if you cannot, do not go on repeating to me any longer, my dear friend, that I should escape without the consent of the Athenians. I am very anxious to act with your approval: I do not want you to think me mistaken. But now tell me if you agree with the doctrine from which I start, and try to answer my questions as you think best.

CRITO. I will try.

SOCRATES. Ought we never to do wrong intentionally at all; or may we do wrong in some ways, and not in others? Or, as we have often agreed in former times, is it never either good or honorable to do wrong? Have all our former conclusions been forgotten in these few days? Old men as we were, Crito, did we not see, in days gone by, when we were gravely conversing with each other, that we were no better than children? Or is not what we used to say most assuredly the truth, whether the world agrees with us or not? Is not wrong-doing an evil and a shame to the wrong-doer in every case, whether we incur a heavier or a lighter punishment than death as the consequence of doing right? Do we believe that?

CRITO. We do.

SOCRATES. Then we ought never to do wrong at all?

CRITO. Certainly not.

SOCRATES. Neither, if we ought never to do wrong at all, ought we to repay wrong with wrong, as the world thinks we may?

CRITO. Clearly not.

SOCRATES. Well then, Crito, ought we to do evil to anyone?

CRITO. Certainly I think not, Socrates.

SOCRATES. And is it right to repay evil with evil, as the world thinks, or not right?

CRITO. Certainly it is not right.

SOCRATES. For there is no difference, is there, between doing evil to a man, and wronging him?

CRITO. True.

SOCRATES. Then we ought not to repay wrong with wrong or do harm to any man, no matter what we may have suffered from him. And in conceding this, Crito, be careful that you do not concede more than you mean. For I know that only a few men hold, or ever will hold this opinion. And so those who hold it, and those who do not, have no common ground of argument; they can of necessity only look with contempt on each other's belief. Do you therefore consider very carefully whether you agree with me and share my opinion. Are we to start in our inquiry from the doctrine that it is never right either to do wrong, or to repay wrong with wrong, or to avenge ourselves on any man who harms us, by harming him in return? Or do you disagree with me and dissent from my principle? I myself have believed in it for a long time, and I believe in it still. But if you differ in any way, explain to me how. If you still hold to our former opinion, listen to my next point.

CRITO. Yes, I hold to it, and I agree with you. Go on.

SOCRATES. Then, my next point, or rather my next question, is this: Ought a man to perform his just agreements, or may he shuffle out of them?

CRITO. He ought to perform them.

SOCRATES. Then consider. If I escape without the state's consent, shall I be injuring those whom I ought least to injure, or not? Shall I be abiding by my just agreements or not?

CRITO. I cannot answer your question, Socrates. I do not understand it.

SOCRATES. Consider it in this way. Suppose the laws and the commonwealth were to come and appear to me as I was preparing to run away (if that is the right phrase to describe my escape) and were to ask, "Tell us, Socrates, what have you in your mind to do? What do you mean by trying to escape, but to destroy us the laws, and the whole city, so far as in you lies? Do you think that a state can exist and not be overthrown, in which the decisions of law are of no force, and are disregarded and set at nought by private individuals?" How shall we answer questions like that, Crito? Much might be said, especially by an orator, in defense of the law which makes judicial decisions supreme. Shall I reply, "But the state has injured me: it has decided my cause wrongly." Shall we say that?

CRITO. Certainly we will, Socrates.

SOCRATES. And suppose the laws were to reply, "Was that our agreement? or was it that you would submit to whatever judgments the state should pronounce?" And if we were to wonder at their words, perhaps they would say, "Socrates, wonder not at our words, but answer us; you yourself are accustomed to ask questions and to answer them. What complaint have you against us and the city, that you are trying to destroy us? Are we not, first, your parents? Through us your father took your mother and begat you. Tell us, have you any fault to find with those of us that are the laws of marriage?" "I have none," I should reply. "Or have you any fault to find with those of us that regulate the nurture and education of the child, which you, like others, received? Did not we do well in bidding your father educate you in music and gymnastic?" "You did," I should say. "Well then, since you were brought into the world and nurtured and educated by us, how, in the first place, can you deny that you are our child and our slave, as your fathers were before you? And if this be so, do you think that your rights are on a level with ours? Do you think that you have a right to retaliate upon us if we should try to do anything to you? You had not the same rights that your father had, or that your master would have had, if you had been a slave. You had no right to retaliate upon them if they ill-treated you, or to answer them if they reviled you, or to strike them back if they struck you, or to repay them evil with evil in any way. And do you think that you may retaliate on your country and its laws? If we try to destroy you, because we think it right, will you in return do all that you can to destroy us, the laws, and your country, and say that in so doing you are doing right, you, the man, who in truth thinks so much of virtue? Or are you too wise to see that your country is worthier, and more august, and more sacred, and holier, and held in higher honor both by the gods and by all men of understanding, than your father and your mother and all your other ancestors; and that it is your bounden duty to reverence it, and to submit to it, and to approach it more humbly than you would approach your father, when it is angry with you; and either to do whatever it bids you to do or to persuade it to excuse you; and to obey in silence if it orders you to endure stripes or imprisonment, or if it send you to battle to be wounded or to die? That is what is your duty. You must not give way, nor retreat, nor desert your post. In war, and in the court of justice, and everywhere, you must do whatever your city and your country bids you do, or you must convince them that their commands are unjust. But it is against the law of God to use violence to your father or to your mother; and much more so is it against the law of God to use violence to your country." What answer shall we make, Crito? Shall we say that the laws speak truly, or not?

CRITO. I think that they do.

SOCRATES. "Then consider, Socrates," perhaps they would say, "if we are right in saying that by attempting to escape you are attempting to injure us. We brought you into the world, we nurtured you, we educated you, we gave you and every other citizen a share of all the good things we could. Yet we proclaim that if any man of the Athenians is dissatisfied with us, he may take his goods and go away whithersoever he pleases; we give that permission to every man who chooses to avail himself of it, so soon as he has reached man's estate, and sees us, the laws, and the administration of our city. No one of us stands in his way or forbids him to take his goods and go wherever he likes, whether it be to an Athenian colony, or to any foreign country, if he is dissatisfied with us and with the city. But we say that every man of you who remains here, seeing how we administer justice, and how we govern the city in other matters, has agreed, by the very fact of remaining here, to do whatsoever we bid him. And, we say, he who disobeys us, does a threefold wrong: he disobeys us who are his parents, and he disobeys us who fostered him, and he disobeys us after he has agreed to obey us, without persuading us that we are wrong. Yet we did not bid him sternly to do whatever we told him. We offered him an alternative; we gave him his choice, either to obey us, or to convince us that we were wrong: but he does neither.

"These are the charges, Socrates, to which we say that you will expose yourself, if you do what you intend; and that not less, but more than other Athenians." And if I were to ask, "And why?" they might retort with justice that I have bound myself by the agreement with them more than other Athenians. They would say, "Socrates, we have very strong evidence that you were satisfied with us and with the city. You would not have been content to stay at home in it more than other Athenians, unless you had been satisfied with it more than they. You never went away from Athens to the festivals, save once to the Isthmian games, nor elsewhere except on military service; you never made other journeys like other men; you had no desire to see other cities or other laws; you were contented with us and our city. So strongly did you prefer us, and agree to be governed by us: and what is more, you begat children in this city, you found it so pleasant. And besides, if you had wished, you might at your trial have offered to go into exile. At that time you could have done with the state's consent, what you are trying now to do without it. But then you gloried in being willing to die. You said that you preferred death to exile. And now you are not ashamed of those words: you do not respect us the laws, for you are trying to destroy us: and you are acting just as a miserable slave would act, trying to run away, and breaking the covenant and agreement which you made to submit to our government. First, therefore, answer this question. Are we right, or are we wrong, in saying that you have agreed not in mere words, but in reality, to live under our government?" What are we to say, Crito? Must we not admit that it is true?

CRITO. We must, Socrates.

SOCRATES. Then they would say, "Are you not breaking your covenants and agreements with us? And you were not led to make them by force or by fraud: you had not to make up your mind in a hurry. You had seventy years in which you might have gone away, if you had been dissatisfied with us, or if the agreement had seemed to you unjust. But you preferred neither Lacedaemon nor Crete, though you are fond of saying that they are well governed, nor any other state, either of the Hellenes, or the Barbarians. You went away from Athens less than the lame and the blind and the cripple. Clearly you, far more than other Athenians, were satisfied with the city, and also with us who are its laws: for who would be satisfied with a city which had no laws? And now will you not abide by your agreement? If you take our advice, you will, Socrates: then you will not make yourself ridiculous by going away from Athens.

"For consider: what good will you do yourself or your friends by thus transgressing, and breaking your agreement? It is tolerably certain that they, on their part, will at least run the risk of exile, and of losing their civil rights, or of forfeiting their property. For yourself, you might go to one of the neighboring cities, to Thebes or to Megara for instance—for both of them are well governed—but, Socrates, you will come as an enemy to these commonwealths; and all who care for their city will look askance at you, and think that you are a subverter of law. And you will confirm the judges in their opinion, and make it seem that their verdict was a just one. For a man who is a subverter of law may well be supposed to be a corrupter of the young and thoughtless. Then will you avoid well-governed states and civilized men? Will life be worth having, if you do? Or will you consort with such men, and converse without shame

—about what, Socrates? About the things which you talk of here? Will you tell them that virtue, and justice, and institutions, and law are the most precious things that men can have? And do you not think that that will be a shameful thing in Socrates? You ought to think so. But you will leave these places; you will go to the friends of Crito in Thessaly: for there there is most disorder and license: and very likely they will be delighted to hear of the ludicrous way in which you escaped from prison, dressed up in peasant's clothes, or in some other disguise which people put on when they are running away, and with your appearance altered. But will no one say how you, an old man, with probably only a few more years to live, clung so greedily to life that you dared to transgress the highest laws? Perhaps not, if you do not displease them. But if you do, Socrates, you will hear much that will make you blush. You will pass your life as the flatterer and the slave of all men; and what will you be doing but feasting in Thessaly? It will be as if you had made a journey to Thessaly for an entertainment. And where will be all our old sayings about justice and virtue then? But you wish to live for the sake of your children? You want to bring them up and educate them? What? Will you take them with you to Thessaly, and bring them up and educate them there? Will you make them strangers to their own country, that you may bestow this benefit on them too? Or supposing that you leave them in Athens, will they be brought up and educated better if you are alive, though you are not with them? Yes; your friends will take care of them. Will your friends take care of them if you make a journey to Thessaly, and not if you make a journey to Hades? You ought not to think that, at least if those who call themselves your friends are good for anything at all.

"No, Socrates, be advised by us who have fostered you. Think neither of children, nor of life, nor of any other thing before justice, that when you come to the other world you may be able to make your defense before the rulers who sit in judgment there. It is clear that neither you nor any of your friends will be happier, or juster, or holier in this life, if you do this thing, nor will you be happier after you are dead. Now you will go away wronged, not by us, the laws, but by men. But if you repay evil with evil, and wrong with wrong in this shameful way, and break your agreements and covenants with us, and injure those whom you should least injure, yourself, and your friends, and your country, and us, and so escape, then we shall be angry with you while you live, and when you die our brethren, the laws in Hades, will not receive you kindly; for they will know that on earth you did all that you could to destroy us. Listen then to us, and let not Crito persuade you to do as he says."

Know well, my dear friend Crito, that this is what I seem to hear, as the worshippers of Cybele seem, in their frenzy, to hear the music of flutes: and the sound of these words rings loudly in my ears, and drowns all other words. And I feel sure that if you try to change my mind you will speak in vain; nevertheless, if you think that you will succeed, say on.

CRITO. I can say no more, Socrates.

SOCRATES. Then let it be, Crito: and let us do as I say, seeing that God so directs us.

The Nature of Virtue*

PLATO

WOULD you agree to define the function of anything as that work, for the accomplishment of which it is either the only or the best instrument?

I don't understand.

Take an example. Can you see with anything besides eyes? Can you hear with anything besides ears?

No.

Then wouldn't it be right to say that seeing and hearing are the respective functions of these organs?

Yes, certainly.

Again, you might cut off a vine-shoot with a dagger or a chisel

---

* From Plato, *Republic,* Bk. I, 352 D–254 A. Based in part upon the Davies and Vaughan translation (1858), but somewhat abridged, and one pair of sentences interchanged for greater clarity.

or many another tool; but with nothing so well as with the pruning-knife made for that purpose. May we not, then, define pruning to be the function of the pruning-knife?

Yes, I agree.

Good. Then you are now able to understand what I meant when I offered to define the function of a thing as the work for the accomplishment of which it is either the only or the best instrument. Now let's take a further step. Does everything which has a proper function have also an appropriate excellence, or "virtue"? Let's reconsider our instances. We have said that the eyes and the ears have their respective functions. Have they their virtues also? Do you suppose that the eyes could perform their function well if their specific virtue were lost and were replaced by the corresponding vice?

Certainly not, if I understand you rightly. Do you mean, if sight is replaced by blindness?

I mean, whatever their virtue be. Don't jump ahead of the argument. All I am asking now is this. Is it through their own peculiar virtue that things perform their proper functions well, and through their own peculiar defect or "vice" that they perform them ill?

It is. I cannot dispute you so far.

And does what we say apply not only to the ears and other bodily organs but quite universally?

I think it does.

Then let us apply this generalization to the soul. Has the soul any function which could be performed by nothing else? What about such actions as superintending, deliberating and making decisions? Is there anything other than the soul which can perform activities of this kind?

Nothing else whatever.

And above all, what of living? Isn't that a function peculiar to the soul?

Decidedly.

Now do we agree also that the soul has a proper excellence—a proper virtue? Have we not, in fact, granted that justice is the specific virtue of the soul, and injustice its specific evil?

Yes, all this has been granted.

Then by our former principle, Thrasymachus, can it ever happen that a soul performs its functions well when destitute of its peculiar virtue? Or is that impossible?

Quite impossible.

In other words a just soul, which is to say a just man, deliberates and makes decisions and manages his life well, while an unjust one performs all such activities badly? In short a just man has learned the art of living well, and hence living happily, while an unjust man, lacking this art, is fundamentally wretched?

Suppose I grant it; then what?

Simply this. You had maintained that injustice is more profitable than justice. But only what leads to happiness can be called profitable; what leads to wretchedness surely cannot be?

Of course.

Let us never say, then, friend Thrasymachus, that injustice is more profitable than justice.

Reason and Duty*

IMMANUEL KANT

NOTHING in the whole world, or even outside of the world, can possibly be regarded as good without limitation except a *good will*. No doubt it is a good and desirable thing to have intelligence, sagacity, judgment, and other intellectual gifts, by whatever name they may be called; it is also good and desirable in many respects to possess by nature such qualities as courage, resolution, and perseverance; but all these gifts of nature may be in the highest degree pernicious and hurtful, if the will which directs them, or what is called the *character,* is not itself good. The same thing applies to *gifts of fortune.* Power, wealth, honor, even good health, and that

---

* From Immanuel Kant (1724–1804), *The Metaphysic of Morality,* Section I. The translation and extracts are those of the late Dr. John Watson (the Canadian philosopher, not the American behaviorist) as published in his volume *The Philosophy of Kant* (Glasgow, 1891).

general well-being and contentment with one's lot which we call *happiness*, give rise to pride and not infrequently to insolence, if a man's will is not good; nor can a reflective and impartial spectator ever look with satisfaction upon the unbroken prosperity of a man who is destitute of the ornament of a pure and good will. A good will would therefore seem to be the indispensable condition without which no one is even worthy to be happy.

A man's will is good, not because the consequences which flow from it are good, nor because it is capable of attaining the end which it seeks, but it is good in itself, or because it wills the good. By a good will is not meant mere well-wishing; it consists in a resolute employment of all the means within one's reach, and its intrinsic value is in no way increased by success or lessened by failure.

This idea of the absolute value of mere will seems so extraordinary that, although it is endorsed even by the popular judgment, we must subject it to careful scrutiny.

The supreme good an intrinsically good will

If nature had meant to provide simply for the maintenance, the well-being, in a word the happiness, of beings which have reason and will, it must be confessed that, in making use of their reason, it has hit upon a very poor way of attaining its end. As a matter of fact the very worst way a man of refinement and culture can take to secure enjoyment and happiness is to make use of his reason for that purpose. Hence there is apt to arise in his mind a certain degree of *misology,* or hatred of reason. Finding that the arts which minister to luxury, and even the sciences, instead of bringing him happiness, only lay a heavier yoke on his neck, he at length comes to envy, rather than to despise, men of less refinement, who follow more closely the promptings of their natural impulses, and pay little heed to what reason tells them to do or to leave undone. It must at least be admitted, that one may deny reason to have much or indeed any value in the production of happiness and contentment, without taking a morose or ungrateful view of the goodness with which the world is governed. Such a judgment really means that life has another and a much nobler end than happiness, and that the true vocation of reason is to secure that end.

The true object of reason then, in so far as it is practical, or capable of influencing the will, must be to produce a will which is *good in itself,* and not merely good *as a means* to something else. This will is not the only or the whole good, but it is the highest good, and the condition of all other good, even of the desire for happiness itself. It is therefore not inconsistent with the wisdom of nature that the cultivation of reason which is essential to the furtherance of its first and unconditioned object, the production of a good will, should, in this life at least, in many ways limit, or even make impossible, the attainment of happiness, which is its second and conditioned object.

"From" duty vs. "in accordance with" duty

To bring to clear consciousness the conception of a will which is good in itself, a conception already familiar to the popular mind, let us examine the conception of *duty,* which involves the idea of a good will as manifested under certain subjective limitations and hindrances.

I pass over actions which are admittedly violations of duty, for these, however useful they may be in the attainment of this or that end, manifestly do not proceed *from* duty. I set aside also those actions which are not actually inconsistent with duty, but which yet are done under the impulse of some natural inclination, although *not a direct inclination* to do these particular actions; for in these it is easy to determine whether the action that is consistent with duty, is done *from duty* or with some selfish object in view. It is more difficult to make a clear distinction of motives when there is a *direct* inclination to do a certain action, which is itself in conformity with duty. The preservation of one's own life, for instance, is a duty; but, as everyone has a natural inclination to preserve his life, the anxious care which most men usually devote to this object, has no intrinsic value, nor the maxim from which they act any moral import. They preserve their life *in accordance with* duty, but not *because of* duty. But, suppose adversity and hopeless sorrow to have taken away all desire for life; suppose that the wretched man would welcome death as a release, and yet takes means to prolong his life simply from a sense of duty: then his maxim has a genuine moral import.

But, secondly, an action that is done from duty gets its moral value, *not from the object* which it is intended to secure, but from the maxim by which it is determined. Accordingly, the action has the same moral value whether the object is attained or not, if only the *principle* by which the will is determined to act is independent of every object of sensuous desire. What was said above makes it clear, that it is not the object aimed at, or, in other words, the consequences which flow from an action when these are made the end and motive of the will, that can give to the action an unconditioned and moral value. In what, then, can the moral value of an action consist, if it does not lie in the will itself, as directed to the attainment of a certain object? It can lie only in the principle of the will, no matter whether the object sought can be attained by the action or not. For the will stands as it were at the parting of the ways, between its *a priori* principle, which is formal, and its *a posteriori* material motive. As so standing it must be determined by something, and, as no action which is done from duty can be determined by a material principle, it can be determined only by the formal principle of all volition.

Duty as reverence for law

From the two propositions just set forth a third directly follows, which may be thus stated: *Duty is the obligation to act from reverence for law.* Now, I may have a natural *inclination* for the object that I expect to follow from my action, but I can never have *reverence* for that which is not a spontaneous activity of my will, but merely an effect of it; neither can I have reverence for any natural inclination, whether it is my own or another's. If it is my own, I can at most only approve of it; if it is manifested by another, I may regard it as conducive to my own interest, and hence I may in certain cases even be said to have a love for it. But the only thing which I can reverence or which can lay me under an obligation to act, is the law which is connected with my will, not as a consequence, but as a principle; a principle which is not dependent upon natural inclination, but overmasters it, or at least allows it to have no influence whatever in determining my course of action. Now if an action which is done out of regard for duty sets entirely aside the influence of natural inclination and along with it every object of the will, nothing else is left by which the will can be determined but objectively the *law* itself, and subjectively *pure reverence* for the law as a principle of action. Thus there arises the maxim, to obey the moral law even at the sacrifice of all my natural inclinations.

The supreme good which we call moral can therefore be nothing but the *idea of the law* in itself, in so far as it is this idea which determines the will, and not any consequences that are expected to follow. Only a *rational* being can have such an idea, and hence a man who acts from the idea of the law is already morally good, no matter whether the consequences which he expects from his action follow or not.

Now what must be the nature of a law, the idea of which is to determine the will, even apart from the effects expected to follow, and which is therefore itself entitled to be called good absolutely and without qualification? As the will must not be moved to act from any desire for the results expected to follow from obedience to a certain law, the only principle of the will which remains is that of the conformity of actions to universal law. In all cases I must act in such a way *that I can at the same time will that my maxim should become a universal law*. This is what is meant by conformity to law pure and simple; and this is the principle which serves, and must serve, to determine the will, if the idea of duty is not to be regarded as empty and chimerical. As a matter of fact the judgments which we are wont to pass upon conduct perfectly agree with this principle, and in making them we always have it before our eyes.

May I, for instance, under the pressure of circumstances, make a promise which I have no intention of keeping? The question is not, whether it is prudent to make a false promise, but whether it is morally right. To enable me to answer this question shortly and conclusively, the best way is for me to ask myself whether it would satisfy me that the maxim to extricate myself from embarrassment by giving a false promise should have the force of a universal law, applying to others as well as to myself. And I see at once, that, while I can certainly will the lie, I cannot will that lying should be a universal law. If lying were universal, there would, properly speaking, be no promises whatever. I might say that I intended to do a certain thing at some future time, but nobody would believe me, or if he did at the moment trust to my promise, he would afterwards pay me back in my own coin. My maxim thus proves itself to be self-destructive, so soon as it is taken as a universal law.

Duty, then, consists in the obligation to act from *pure* reverence for the moral law. To this motive all others must give way, for it is the condition of a will which is good *in itself,* and which has a value with which nothing else is comparable.

Moral philosophy vs. natural dialectic

There is, however, in man a strong feeling of antagonism to the commands of duty, although his reason tells him that those commands are worthy of the highest reverence. For man not only possesses reason, but he has certain natural wants and inclinations, the complete satisfaction of which he calls happiness. These natural inclinations clamorously demand to have their seemingly reasonable claims respected; but reason issues its commands inflexibly, refusing to promise anything to the natural desires, and treating their claims with a sort of neglect and contempt. From this there arises a *natural dialectic,* that is, a disposition to explain away the strict laws of duty, to cast doubt upon their validity, or at least, upon their purity and stringency, and in this way to make them yield to the demands of the natural inclinations.

Thus men are forced to go beyond the narrow circle of ideas within which their reason ordinarily moves, and to take a step into the field of *moral philosophy,* not indeed from any perception of speculative difficulties, but simply on practical grounds. The practical reason of men cannot be long exercised any more than the theoretical, without falling insensibly into a dialectic, which compels it to call in the aid of philosophy; and in the one case as in the other, rest can be found only in a thorough criticism of human reason.

The Philosophy of Happiness*

ARISTOTLE

Nature of good

Every art and every scientific investigation, as well as every action and purposive choice, appears to aim at some good; hence the good has rightly been declared to be that at which all things aim. A difference is observable, to be sure, among the several ends: some of them are activities, while others are products over and above the activities that produce them. Wherever there are certain ends over and above the actions themselves, it is the nature of such products to be better than the activities.

As actions and arts and sciences are of many kinds, there must be a corresponding diversity of ends: health, for example, is the aim of medicine, ships of ship-building, victory of military strategy, and wealth of domestic economics. Where several such arts fall under some one faculty—as bridle-making and the other arts concerned with horses' equipment fall under horsemanship, while this in turn along with all other military matters falls under the head of strategy, and similarly in the case of other arts—the aim of the master art is always more choiceworthy than the aims of its subordinate arts, inasmuch as these are pursued for its sake. And this holds equally good whether the end in view is just the activity itself or something distinct from the activity, as in the case of the sciences above mentioned.

Primacy of statecraft

If in all our conduct, then, there is some end that we wish on its own account, choosing everything else as a means to it; if, that is to say, we do not choose everything as a means to something else (for at

* From Aristotle, *The Nicomachean Ethics,* parts of Bk. I, Chaps. i, ii, iv, v, vii, xiii; Bk. II, Chaps. i, iii, v, vi, ix; Bk. X, Chap. vii. Based on *Aristotle: Selections* (Odyssey Press, 1951).

that rate we should go on *ad infinitum,* and our desire would be left empty and vain); then clearly this one end must be the good—even, indeed, the highest good. Will not a knowledge of it, then, have an important influence on our lives? Will it not better enable us to hit the right mark, like archers who have a definite target to aim at? If so, we must try to comprehend, in outline at least, what the highest end is, and to which of the sciences or arts it belongs.

Evidently the art or science in question must be the most absolute and most authoritative of all. Statecraft answers best to this description; for it prescribes which of the sciences are to have a place in the state, and which of them are to be studied by the different classes of citizens, and up to what point; and we find that even the most highly esteemed of the arts are subordinated to it, *e.g.*, military strategy, domestic economics, and oratory. So then, since statecraft employs all the other sciences, prescribing also what the citizens are to do and what they are to refrain from doing, its aim must embrace the aims of all the others; whence it follows that the aim of statecraft is man's proper good. Even if we suppose the chief good to be eventually the same for the individual as for the state, that of the state is evidently of greater and more fundamental importance both to attain and to preserve. The securing of even one individual's good is cause for rejoicing, but to secure the good of a nation or of a city-state is nobler and more divine. This, then, is the aim of our present inquiry, which is in a sense the study of statecraft.

The good as happiness[1]

Since all knowledge and all purpose aims at some good, what is it that we declare to be the aim of statecraft? In other words, what is the highest of all realizable goods? As to its name there is pretty general agreement. The majority of men, as well as the cultured few, speak of it as happiness; and they would maintain that to live well and to do well are the same thing as to be happy.

As there is evidently a plurality of ends, and as some of these are chosen only as means to ulterior ends (*e.g.*, wealth, flutes, and instruments in general), it is clear that not all ends are final. But the supreme good must of course be something final. Accordingly, if there is only one final end, this will be the good that we are seeking;

[1] From Bk. I, Chaps. iv and vii combined.

and if there is more than one such end, the most complete and final of them will be this good. Now we call what is pursued as an end in itself more final than what is pursued as a means to something else; and what is never chosen as a means we call more final than what is chosen both as an end in itself and as a means; in fact, when a thing is chosen always as an end in itself and never as a means we call it absolutely final. Happiness, more than anything else, seems to answer to this description: for it is something we choose always for its own sake and never for the sake of something else; while honor, pleasure, reason, and all the virtues, though chosen partly for themselves (for we might choose any one of them without heeding the result), are chosen also for the sake of the happiness which we suppose they will bring us. Happiness, on the other hand, is never chosen for the sake of any of these, nor indeed as a means to anything else at all.

We seem to arrive at the same conclusion if we start from the notion of self-sufficiency; for the final good is admittedly self-sufficient. To be self-sufficient we do not mean that an individual must live in isolation. Parents, children, wife, as well as friends and fellow-citizens generally, are all permissible; for man is by nature political. To be sure, some limit has to be set to such relationships, for if they are extended to embrace ancestors, descendants, and friends of friends, we should go on *ad infinitum*. But this point will be considered later on; provisionally we may attribute self-sufficiency to that which taken by itself makes life choiceworthy and lacking in nothing. Such a thing we conceive happiness to be. Moreover, we regard happiness as the most choiceworthy of all things; nor does this mean that it is merely one good thing among others, for if that were the case it is plain that the addition of even the least of those other goods would increase its desirability; since the addition would create a larger amount of good, and of two goods the greater is always to be preferred. Evidently, then, happiness is something final and self-sufficient, and is the end and aim of all that we do.

Conflicting views of happiness

People differ, however, as to what happiness is, and the mass of mankind give a different account of it from philosophers. The former take it to be something palpable and obvious, like pleasure or wealth or fame; they differ, too, among themselves, nor is the same man always of one mind about it: when ill he identifies it with health.

when poor with wealth; then growing aware of his ignorance about the whole matter he feels admiration for anyone who proclaims some grand ideal above his comprehension. And to add to the confusion, there have been some philosophers who held that besides the various particular good things there is an absolute good which is the cause of all particular goods. As it would hardly be worth while to examine all the opinions that have been entertained, we shall confine our attention to those that are the most popular or that appear to have some rational foundation.

To judge from men's actual lives, one would say that the majority of them, being vulgarians, identify happiness with pleasure, and find no higher aim in life than to enjoy themselves. For there are three outstanding types of life: the one just mentioned, the political, and thirdly, the contemplative. The mass of men reveal their utter slavishness by preferring a life fit only for cattle; yet their views have a certain plausibility from the fact that many of those in high places share the tastes of Sardanapalus.[2] Men of superior refinement and active disposition, on the other hand, identify happiness with honor, this being more or less the aim of a statesman's life. It is evidently too superficial, however, to be the good that we are seeking: for it appears to depend rather on him who bestows than on him who receives it, while we may suppose the chief good to be something peculiarly a man's own, of which he is not easily deprived. Besides, men seem to pursue honor primarily in order to assure themselves of their own merit; at any rate, apart from personal acquaintances, it is by those of sound judgment that they seek to be appreciated, and on the score of virtue. Clearly, then, they imply that virtue is superior to honor: and so, perhaps, we should regard this rather than honor as the end and aim of the statesman's life. Yet even about virtue there is a certain incompleteness; for it is supposed that a man may possess it while asleep or during lifelong inactivity, or even while suffering the greatest disasters and misfortunes; and surely no one would call such a man happy, unless for the sake of a paradox. But we need not further pursue this subject, which has been sufficiently treated of in current discussions. Thirdly, there is the contemplative life, which we shall examine at a later point.

As for the life of money-making, it is something unnatural. Wealth

[2] An ancient Assyrian king to whom is attributed the saying, "Eat, drink, and be merry: nothing else is worth a snap of the fingers."

is clearly not the good that we are seeking, for it is merely useful as a means to something else. Even the objects above mentioned come closer to possessing intrinsic goodness than wealth does, for they at least are cherished on their own account. But not even they, it seems, can be the chief good, although much labor has been lost in attempting to prove them so.

Functional analysis of man's highest good

It may be objected, then, that to call happiness the supreme good is a mere truism, and that a clearer account of it is still needed. We can give this best, probably, if we ascertain the proper function of man. Just as the excellence and good performance of a flute-player, a sculptor, or any kind of artist, and generally speaking of anyone who has a function or business to perform, lies always in that function, so man's good would seem to lie in the function of man, if he has one. But can we suppose that while a carpenter and a cobbler each has a function and mode of activity of his own, man qua man has none, but has been left by nature functionless? Surely it is more likely that as his several members, eye and hand and foot, can be shown to have each its own function, so man too must have a function over and above the special functions of his various members. What will such a function be? Not merely to live, of course: he shares that even with plants, whereas we are seeking something peculiar to himself. We must exclude, therefore, the life of nutrition and growth. Next comes sentient life, but this again is had in common with the horse, the ox, and in fact all animals whatever. There remains only the practical life of his rational nature; and this has two aspects, one of which is rational in the sense that it obeys a rational principle, the other in the sense that it possesses and exercises reason. To avoid ambiguity let us specify that by rational we mean the exercise or activity, not the mere possession, of reason; for it is the former that would seem more properly entitled to the name. Thus we conclude that man's function is an activity of the soul in conformity with, or at any rate involving the use of, rational principle.

An individual and a superior individual who belong to the same class we regard as sharing the same function: a harpist and a good harpist, for instance, are essentially the same. This holds true of any class of individuals whatever; for superior excellence with respect to a function is nothing but an amplification of that selfsame function: *e.g.*, the function of a harpist is to play the harp, while that of a good harpist is to play it well. This being so, if we take man's proper function to be a certain kind of life, *viz.*, an activity and conduct of the soul that involves reason, and if it is the mark of a good man to perform such activities well and nobly, and if a function is well performed when it is performed in accordance with its own proper excellence: we may conclude that the good of man is an activity of the soul in accordance with virtue, or, if there be more than one virtue, in accordance with the best and most perfect of them. And we must add, in a complete life. For one swallow does not make a spring, nor does one fine day; and similarly one day or brief period of happiness does not make a man happy and blessed.

Divisions of the soul

Since happiness is a certain activity of the soul in accordance with perfect virtue, we must inquire into the nature of virtue. It goes without saying that the virtue we are to study is human virtue, just as the good that we have been inquiring about is a human good, and the happiness a human happiness. By human virtue we mean virtue not of the body but of the soul, and by happiness too we mean an activity of the soul. This being the case, it is not less evident that the student of statecraft must have some knowledge of the soul, than that a physician who is to heal the eye or the whole body must have some knowledge of these organs; more so, indeed, in proportion as statecraft is superior to and more honorable than medicine. Now all physicians who are educated take much pains to know about the body. Hence as students of statecraft, too, we must inquire into the nature of the soul; but we must do so with reference to our own distinctive aim and only to the extent that it requires, for to go into minuter detail would be more laborious than is warranted by our subject-matter.

We may adopt here certain doctrines about the soul that have been adequately stated in our public discourses: as that the soul may be distinguished into two parts, one of which is irrational while the other possesses reason. Whether these two parts are actually distinct like the parts of the body or any other divisible thing, or are distinct only in a logical sense, like convex and concave in the circumference of a circle, is immaterial to our present inquiry.

Of the irrational part, again, one division is apparently of a vegetative nature and common to all living things: I mean that which is the cause of nutrition and growth. It is more reasonable to postulate a vital faculty of this sort, present in all things that take nourishment, even when in an embryo stage, and retained by the full-grown organism, than to assume a special nutritive faculty in the latter. Hence we may say that the excellence belonging to this part of the soul is common to all species, and not specifically human: a point that is further confirmed by the popular view that this part of the soul is most active during sleep. For it is during sleep that the distinction between good men and bad is least apparent; whence the saying that for half their lives the happy are no better off than the wretched. This, indeed, is natural enough, for sleep is an inactivity of the soul in those respects in which the soul is called good or bad. (It is true, however, that to a slight degree certain bodily movements penetrate to the soul; which is the reason why good men's dreams are superior to those of the average person.) But enough of this subject: let us dismiss the nutritive principle, since it has by nature no share in human excellence.

There seems to be a second part of the soul, which though irrational yet in some way partakes of reason. For while we praise the rational principle and the part of the soul that manifests it in the case of the continent and the incontinent men alike, on the ground that it exhorts them rightly and urges them to do what is best; yet we find within these men another element different in nature from the rational element, and struggling against and resisting it. Just as ataxic limbs, when we choose to move them to the right, turn on the contrary to the left, so it is with the soul: the impulses of the incontinent man run counter to his ruling part. The only difference is that in the case of the body we see what it is that goes astray, while in the soul we do not. Nevertheless the comparison will doubtless suffice to show that there is in the soul something besides the rational element, opposing and running counter to it. (In what sense the two elements are distinct need not detain us.) But this other element, as we have said, seems also to have some share in a rational principle: at any rate, in the continent man it submits to reason, while in the man who is at once temperate and courageous it is presumably all the more obedient; for in him it speaks on all matters harmoniously with the voice of reason.

Evidently, then, the irrational part of the soul is twofold. There is the vegetative element, which has no share in reason, and there is the concupiscent, or rather the appetitive element, which does in a sense partake of reason, in that it is amenable and obedient to it: *i.e.*, it is rational in the sense that we speak of "having *logos* of" (paying heed to) father and friends, not in the sense of "having *logos* of" (having a rational understanding of) mathematical truths. That this irrational element is in some way amenable to reason is shown by our practice of giving admonishment, and by rebuke and exhortation generally. If on this account it is deemed more correct to regard this element as also possessing reason, then the rational part of the soul, in turn, will have two subdivisions: the one being rational in the strict sense as actually possessing reason, the other merely in the sense that a child obeys its father.

Virtue, too, is differentiated in accordance with this division of the soul: for we call some of the virtues intellectual and others moral: wisdom, understanding, and sagacity being among the former, liberality and temperance among the latter. In speaking of a man's character we do not say that he is wise or intelligent, but that he is gentle or temperate; yet we praise the wise man too for the disposition he has developed within himself, and praiseworthy dispositions we call virtues.

How moral virtue is acquired[3]

Virtue, or excellence, then, being of two kinds, intellectual and moral, intellectual excellence owes its birth and its growth mainly to teaching, and so requires experience and time, while moral excellence is the product of habit, and in fact has derived its name, by a slight variation from that word. Hence it is plain that none of the moral virtues is implanted in us by nature, for no natural property can be changed by habit. A stone, for instance, which has the natural property of falling, can never be habituated to rise, even though we made innumerable attempts to train it by throwing it into the air; nor can fire be habituated to move downwards, nor can any-

[3] Here begins Book II.

thing else that has a natural property of behaving in one way be habituated to behave differently. The virtues, then, are not engendered in us either by nature or in opposition to nature: rather nature gives us the capacity for receiving them, and this capacity is developed through habit.

Moreover, in the case of our natural endowments we first receive a certain power, to which we later give expression by acting in a certain way. The senses offer an illustration of this: they are not acquired as a result of seeing and hearing; on the contrary, instead of being acquired by practice they had first to be possessed before they could be used. The virtues, on the other hand, are acquired by first giving them expression in actual practice, and this is true of the arts as well. To learn an art it is first necessary to perform those actions that pertain to it: *e.g.*, we become builders by building, and harpists by playing the harp. Similarly we become just by performing just actions, temperate by temperate actions, brave by brave actions. This is confirmed by what goes on in our city-states, where it is by training that legislators make people good; at any rate that is the aim of legislation, and if it is not achieved the legislation is a failure. By such legislation a good constitution is distinguished from a bad.

From the same causes and by the same means that a moral virtue is produced it may also be destroyed. This is equally true of the arts. It is by playing the harp that both good and bad harpists are produced, and so of builders and the rest; for men become good or bad builders according as they practice building well or badly. If this were not so, they would require no instruction, but would all have been born good or bad at their trades. So too in the case of the virtues. It is by our actual conduct in our intercourse with other men that we become just or unjust, and it is by our conduct in dangerous situations, accustoming ourselves there to feel fear or confidence, that we become cowardly or brave. So, too, with our appetites and angry impulses: it is by behaving in one way or another on the appropriate occasions that we become either temperate and gentle or profligate and irascible. In short, a particular kind of moral disposition is produced by a corresponding kind of activities. That is why we ought to take care that our activities are of the right sort, inasmuch as our moral dispositions will vary in accordance with them. It is no small matter, then, what habits we form even from early youth; rather this is of great, indeed of paramount importance.

Pleasure and pain in relation to virtue

The best index to our dispositions is found in the pleasure or pain that accompanies our actions. A man who abstains from bodily indulgence and finds enjoyment in doing so is temperate, but he who abstains reluctantly is licentious; and he who faces danger gladly, or at any rate without pain, is brave, while he who does it with pain is a coward. Thus pleasure and pain are matters that deeply concern the question of moral virtue. This is evident, first, from the fact that it is pleasure which prompts us to base deeds, and pain which deters us from noble ones; and therefore men ought, as Plato observes, to be trained from youth to find pleasure and pain in the right objects—which is just what we mean by a sound education. It is evident again from the fact that punishment is inflicted through the medium of pains, by reason of their curative property; and a cure must naturally be the opposite of the disease to which it is applied.

Again, as we have said before, every disposition of the soul realizes its nature through being related to and concerned with those things that influence it for better or worse. But it is through pleasures and pains that our dispositions are corrupted—*i.e.*, through pursuit or avoidance of pleasures and pains of the wrong sort, or at the wrong time, or in the wrong manner, or wrongly in some other specific respect. This is why some people go so far as to define the virtues as states of quietude without feeling; but they make a mistake when they use these terms in an absolute sense instead of qualifying them by adding, "in the right or wrong manner," "at the right or wrong time," etc.

There are three sorts of thing that move us to choice, and three that move us to avoidance: on the one side, the nobly beautiful (*kalos*), the advantageous, and the pleasant; on the other their opposites, the basely ugly, the injurious, and the painful. The good man is apt to go right and the bad man to go wrong about all of these, but especially about pleasure: for pleasure is experienced by men and animals alike; also it is an accompaniment of all objects of choice; and, as a matter of fact, even the nobly beautiful and the advantageous may be regarded as in a sense pleasant.

We may conclude, then, that virtue of a moral sort involves the doing of what is best in matters of pleasure and pain, while vice has the opposite effect; that the same actions which have produced virtue will also develop it; and that it finds full expression in activities of the same kind as those by which it was produced.

The genus of moral virtue

We may now attempt a formal definition of moral virtue. First as to its genus.

Every state of the soul is one of three things: a feeling (*pathos*), an ability or faculty (*dynamis*), or a developed disposition, which may also be called a state of character. By "feelings" I mean appetite, anger, fear, confidence, envy, joy, friendly affection, hatred, longing, emulation, pity, and in general whatever is accompanied by pleasure or pain; by "faculties" I mean the capacities by which we are said to be capable of any of these feelings—the ability, for instance, to feel anger or pity or pain; and by "dispositions" I mean the possession of a certain attitude, whether good or bad, with reference to the passions—e.g., we are badly disposed with respect to anger if our angry feelings are either too violent or too slack, well disposed if they are moderate, and similarly in the case of the other feelings.

Now the virtues and vices cannot be feelings. For, in the first place, we are called good or bad in respect of our virtues or vices, whereas we are not called so in respect of our feelings. Then too, we are praised and blamed for our virtues and vices, but not for our feelings: it is not simply for being frightened or angry that a man is praised, nor is it for that alone that he is blamed, but for being so in a particular way. Furthermore, fear and anger are not the result of deliberate choice, but the virtues are a kind of choice, or at any rate are impossible without it. Finally, in the case of feelings we are said to be impelled, while in the case of virtues and vices we are not said to be impelled but to be disposed in a certain way.

The same kind of considerations show that the virtues cannot be faculties; we are not called good or bad for being merely *capable* of feeling, nor are we praised or blamed for this. And further, while faculties are given to us by nature, we are not made good or bad by nature—a point already treated of.

Consequently, as the virtues are neither feelings nor faculties, the only thing that remains for them to be is dispositions; and therein we have stated what virtue is in respect of its genus.

Differentia of moral virtue: doctrine of the mean

But to say that virtue is a disposition is not enough; we must specify what kind of a disposition it is.

The virtue, or excellence, of anything must be acknowledged to have a twofold effect on the thing to which it belongs: it renders the thing itself good, and causes it to perform its function well. The excellence of the eye, for instance, makes both the eye and its work good, for it is by the excellence of the eye that we see well. Likewise the proper excellence of horse at once makes a particular horse what he should be, and also makes him good at running and at carrying his rider and at facing the enemy. Hence, if this is universally true, the virtue or proper excellence of man will be just that formed disposition which both makes him good and enables him to perform his function well. We have already indicated how this is accomplished; but we may clarify the matter by examining wherein the nature of virtue consists.

Of everything that is both continuous and divisible it is possible to take a greater, a less, or an equal amount; and this may be true either objectively with respect to the thing in question or else relatively to ourselves. By equal I denote that which is a mean between excess and deficiency. By the objective mean I denote that which is equidistant from both extremes, and this will always be the same for everybody. By the mean that is relative to ourselves I denote that which is neither too much nor too little, and this is not one and the same for everybody. For instance, if ten is many and two is few, then six is the mean considered in terms of the object; for it exceeds and is exceeded by the same amount, and is therefore the mean of an arithmetical proportion. But the mean considered relatively to ourselves cannot be determined so simply: if ten pounds of food is too much for a certain man to eat and two pounds is too little, it does not follow that the trainer will prescribe six pounds, for this may be too much or too little for the man in question—too little for Milo the wrestler, too much for the novice at athletics. This is equally true of running and wrestling.

So it is that an expert in any field avoids excess and deficiency, and seeks and chooses the mean—that is, not the objective mean, but the mean relatively to himself. If, then, every sort of skill perfects its work in this way, by observing the mean and bringing its work up to this standard (which is the reason why people say of a good work of art that nothing could be either taken from it or added to it, implying that excellence is destroyed by excess or deficiency but is preserved by adherence to the mean; and good artists, we say, observe this standard in their work), and if furthermore virtue, like nature, is more exact and better than any art, it follows that virtue will have the property of aiming at the mean. I am speaking, of course, of moral virtue, for it is moral virtue that has to do with feelings and actions, and it is in respect of these that excess, deficiency, and moderation are possible. That is to say, we can feel fear, confidence, desire, anger, pity, and in general pleasure and pain, either too much or too little, and in either case not well; but to feel them at the right times, with reference to the right objects, toward the right people, with the right motive, and in the right manner, is to strike the mean, and therein to follow the best course—a mark of virtue. And in the same way our outward acts admit of excess, deficiency, and the proper mean. Now virtue has to do with feelings and also with outward acts; in both of these excess and deficiency are regarded as faults and are blamed, while a moderate amount is both praised and regarded as right—palpable signs of virtue. Virtue, then, is a kind of moderation, in that it aims at the mean. This conclusion is further confirmed by the fact that while there are numerous ways in which we can go wrong (for evil, according to the Pythagorean figure of speech, belongs to the class of the unlimited, good to that of the limited), there is only one way of going right. That is why the one is easy, the other hard—easy to miss the mark, but hard to hit it. And this offers further evidence that excess and deficiency are characteristic of vice while hitting the mean is characteristic of virtue: "for good is simple, badness manifold."

We may conclude, then, that virtue is an habitual disposition with respect to choice, the characteristic quality of which is moderation judged relatively to ourselves according to a determinate principle, *i.e.,* according to such a principle as a man of insight would use. The quality of moderation belongs to virtue in a double sense: as falling between two vices, the one of which consists in excess, the other in deficiency; and also in the sense that while these vices respectively fall short of and exceed the proper standard both of feelings and of actions, virtue both finds and chooses the mean. Hence, in respect of its essence and according to the definition of its basic nature, virtue is a state of moderation; but regarded in its relation to what is best and right it is an extreme.

Accordingly it is not every action nor every feeling to which the principle of the mean is applicable. There are some whose very names imply badness: *e.g.,* malevolence, shamelessness, envy, and among actions, adultery, theft, and murder. These and everything else like them are condemned as being bad in themselves and not merely when in excess or deficiency. To do right in performing them is therefore impossible; their performance is always wrong. Rightness or wrongness in any of them (*e.g.,* in adultery) does not depend on the rightness or wrongness of person and occasion and manner, but on the bare fact of doing it at all. It would be absurd to distinguish moderation, excess, and deficiency in action that is unjust or cowardly or profligate; for we should then have moderation of excess and deficiency, excess of excess, and deficiency of deficiency. The truth of the matter is that just as there can be no excess and deficiency of temperance and courage (for the proper mean is, in its own way, an extreme), so these opposite kinds of conduct likewise do not admit of moderation, excess, and deficiency: they are always wrong, no matter how they are done.

Difficulty of attaining the mean

We have now sufficiently shown that moral virtue consists in observance of a mean, and in what sense this is so: in the sense, namely, of holding a middle position between two vices, one of which involves excess and the other deficiency, and also in the sense of being the kind of a disposition which aims at the middle point both in feelings and in actions. This being the case, it is a hard thing to be good, for it is hard to locate the mean in particular instances, just as to locate the mean point (*i.e.,* the center) of a circle is not a thing that everybody can do, but only the man of science. So, too, anyone can get angry—that is easy—or spend money or give it away; but to do all this to the right person, to the right extent, at the right time, with the right motive, and in the right manner, is not a thing that everyone can do, and is not easy; and that is why good conduct is at once rare and praiseworthy and noble.

Accordingly, whoever aims at the mean should first of all strive to avoid that extreme which is more opposed to it, as in Calypso's advice to "keep the ship well clear of that foaming surf."[4] For of the two extremes one will be more of an evil, the other less; therefore, as it is hard to hit the exact mean, we ought to choose the lesser of the two evils and sail, as the saying goes, in the second best way, and this is accomplished most successfully in the manner stated. But we must bear in mind as well the errors to which we personally are prone. These will be different for different individuals, and each may discover them in his own case by noting the occasions on which he feels pleasure or pain. Having discovered them, let him bend himself in the opposite direction; for by steering wide of error we shall strike a middle course, as warped timber is straightened by bending it backwards. Especially and in all cases we must guard against pleasure and what is pleasant, because we cannot estimate it impartially. Hence we ought to feel toward pleasure as the elders of the people felt toward Helen, and on every occasion repeat their saying;[5] for if we dismiss pleasure thus we are less likely to go wrong.

Happiness and contemplation[6]

If happiness is activity in accordance with virtue, we may reasonably suppose that it must be in accordance with the highest type of virtue—*i.e.*, with such virtue as is distinctive of the best part of us. This best part of us (call it reason or what you will), which seems by nature disposed to rule and guide us and to take thought of noble and divine objects (whether it be a divine principle residing in us or only the most nearly divine part of our nature), is the thing whose activity, when in accordance with its own proper virtue, constitutes happiness. Such activity, as already stated, consists in contemplation.

Our present conclusion seems to agree both with our previous deductions and with known truths. (1) To contemplate is the noblest

---

[4] Odysseus' order to his steersman (*Odyssey*, xii, 219–220), quoting the advice earlier given by Circe (not Calypso) to steer rather toward the monster Scylla, who will devour only a few of the men, than toward the whirlpool Charybdis, which will engulf them all.

[5] "She is wondrously like the immortal goddesses to look upon. But be that as it may, let her depart on the ships, rather than be left here as a bane to us and our children after us." (*Iliad*, Bk. III, 158–160.)

[6] Bk. X, Chap. vii.

of activities; for our reason is the noblest part of us, and the objects of reason are the best of all knowable things. Again, (2) contemplation exhibits continuity in the highest degree, for we can contemplate truth more continuously than we can do anything else whatever. Again, (3) we hold that happiness ought to contain an admixture of pleasure; and activity in accordance with wisdom is the most pleasant of all virtuous activities—at any rate, the pursuit of wisdom admittedly offers pleasures of remarkable purity and duration, and it is reasonable to assume that those who know are more pleasantly occupied than those who merely inquire. Again, (4) the activity of contemplation is peculiarly characterized by what is called self-sufficiency. That is not to say, of course, that possession of wisdom, any more than possession of justice, will enable a man to dispense with the necessaries of life. Nevertheless, when these have been supplied, the just man will still need persons toward whom and in whose company he may behave justly; so, too, the man who is temperate, or brave, or the like. The wise man, on the contrary, will be able to contemplate truth quite alone, and the wiser he is the better able he will be. Doubtless his speculations would be improved if he had other persons with whom to share them; but at any rate he is more truly self-sufficient than anyone else. Again, (5) the activity of contemplation seems to be the only one that is loved for its own sake: it yields no result apart from the contemplating. From practical activities, on the contrary, we expect to achieve some result, whether great or small, beyond the activities themselves.

Finally, (6) happiness is thought to involve leisure; for we toil in order to get leisure, as we make war in order to get peace. But the activity of the practical virtues has to do either with the ordinary affairs of state or with war, and activities concerned with either of these must be accounted unleisurely. Particularly is this true of war: no one chooses to be at war or provokes a war for the sake of war alone; indeed, we should call a man downright bloodthirsty who made enemies of friends in order to bring about battles and slaughter. But it is true also of a statesman's peacetime activities. The statesman aims at something more than the practice of statecraft itself: at despotic powers and honors, perhaps, or else at the happiness of himself and his fellow-citizens. That the happiness at which he aims is something over and above the art of statecraft which he practices is shown by the fact that we investigate the two fields independently. Inasmuch as politics and war, then, while surpassing in nobility and grandeur all other practical expressions of human excellence, are unleisurely and aim at an ulterior end instead of being chosen for their own sakes, while the activity of reason is acknowledged to be superior in seriousness (since it is contemplative), to aim at nothing beyond itself, to entail a peculiar pleasure of its own (which in turn promotes the activity), and to be characterized by self-sufficiency, leisureliness, and as much unwearied diligence as is possible to mankind, together with whatever other attributes are ascribed to the supremely happy man: it evidently follows that complete human happiness will consist in the exercise of reason—provided that we postulate also a complete term of life, for happiness admits of nothing incomplete.

Such a life as this would be superior to anything merely human. He who leads such a life will do so not in his strictly human capacity, but only so far as there is in him an element of the divine. To just the extent that this divine element is superior to our composite human nature, its proper activity will be superior to ordinary virtuous conduct. In short, if reason is divine as compared with the whole man, then the life of reason is divine as compared with ordinary human life. Instead of listening to those who advise us to express our human and mortal nature by giving our attention to human and mortal things, we ought, so far as we can, to become immortal by making every effort to live in accordance with the best that is in us; for though this best part of us be small in bulk, it surpasses all the rest in power and worth. It may even be designated a man's real self, since it is his sovereign and better part. And it would be strange, surely, if one were to prefer some other way of life to the life of his real self.

We may apply here, too, the principle already laid down, that whatever is proper to the nature of each thing is best and pleasantest for that thing. Since it is reason that is most truly man, a life according to reason must be at once best and pleasantest for man. Such a life, therefore, will be the most truly happy.

On the Existence of God*

ARISTOTLE

Evidence for God's existence

Whatever produces motion while itself in motion is intermediate, not ultimate. There must therefore be something which operates without being in motion—something eternal which is at once essentially existent and in actual operation. How it operates may be explained as follows.

The ultimate objects of desire and of thought are the same. For it is the apparent good that is the object of appetite and the real good that is the object of rational deliberation. We desire because of our opinions rather than form opinions because of our desires; and this shows that thought can be an initiating principle. Now thought is moved by what is intelligible, and the essentially existent stands first in the list of intelligible entities. (By "essentially" we mean without qualification, not in this or that respect; and by "existent" we mean fully actual.)

That which is the object of thought and desire together produces motion without being moved. Can that for whose sake something else is stirred be motionless? A distinction will show that it can. That for whose sake anything occurs (*i.e.*, that towards which any process is drawn) is in some sense good. It may be good for an ulterior purpose, or it may be good simply and entirely as that at which the action or occurrence aims. In the latter sense, though not in the former, it can be something immutable. It produces motion *through being loved,* whereas other things produce motion through being in motion themselves.

Now if anything is in motion (i.e., in process) it is capable of being otherwise than it is. In so far, then, as a thing's actuality

---

* From Aristotle, *Metaphysics,* Bk. XII (Lambda), Chap. vii, into which one paragraph of Chap. viii has been transposed. Based on *Aristotle: Selections* (Odyssey Press, 1951).

consists in motion—even though it be the primary form of motion, which is spherical—then, in respect of that motion, the thing can be otherwise than it is—in respect of place at least, whether or not in respect of essence. But since there must be Something which, existing in full actuality, produces motion without being moved, that Something cannot be otherwise than it is in any respect. Consequently that Something must necessarily exist. It is necessary as the initiating principle of all things, being the ultimate good towards which all things strive.

Such, then, is the initiating principle upon which the phenomena of sky and earth depend. It enjoys such a life as we may enjoy in our best moments, and it lives perpetually in that state, as we cannot do. Since all actuality as such yields pleasure—as shown by the fact that waking, perception, and thinking are pleasurable in themselves, while hopes and memories derive their pleasant character from them—it is evident that to be actual in that highest state is supremely pleasurable.

In what way does God think?

What further attribute must the Supreme Mind[1] have in order to be divine? If Supreme Mind thinks of nothing, how could it have any majesty, being in the condition of one who sleeps? If, on the other hand, Mind thinks of something other than itself, so that its thinking is governed by the nature of that something else, then its specific essence would lie not in its thinking but in its *capacity* to think, and this would not be the most excellent sort of nature, for the act of thinking is more estimable than the mere capacity. Of what, then, does thought think?

Now thought in its intrinsic nature deals with what is intrinsically best, and where thought is most completely present its object is most completely present. Consequently, perfect thought may be said to "think itself," in the sense that it participates completely in the object it is thinking of. That is to say, perfect thought apprehends and thinks its object in such a way that the thought and its object become one, and thus the thought becomes its own object.

---

[1] That the supreme Something has the character of Mind is implicit in the foregoing statements that it is fully actual (for there is a higher degree of actuality in mind than in sub-mental things) and that it is the object of universal love (of which nothing *less* than mind would be worthy).

Moreover, perfect thought is fully active. For all thought consists in responsiveness to the specific nature of its object; and in thus possessing the essence of its object thought becomes fully active. Hence to be active, not passive, would seem to characterize the divine aspect of thought, and its contemplative activity is at once its best and its most highly pleasurable state. If, then, God is perpetually in that condition of contemplative activity to which we occasionally attain, it is wonderful enough; if in an even higher condition, it is still more wonderful. And this is indeed the case. Life, too, belongs to God. For the actuality of thought is what constitutes life, and God is that actuality—in the intrinsic and best and eternal sense. We declare, then, that God is a living being of the highest kind and eternal; so that life and continuous eternal duration belong to God—*are* God, in fact.

Five Arguments for God's Existence*

THOMAS AQUINAS

Objections examined

We proceed to the Third Article as follows. It may be objected (1) that God does not exist. For, in the first place, if one of two contraries be infinite, the other must be destroyed altogether. Now the very word "God" means a Being of infinite goodness. Accordingly, if God existed no evil would be found anywhere. But evil *is* found in the world. Therefore God does not exist.

Furthermore, (2) when something can be explained by fewer principles it is superfluous to explain it by more. Now it seems that everything that manifests itself in the world can be adequately explained by other principles, supposing that God did not exist. For whatever is natural can be reduced to one principle, which is nature;

---

* Thomas Aquinas (1225–1274), *Summa Theologica*, Part I ("God"), Question 2, Article 3. The third Article, entitled "Whether God Exists" (*Utrum Deus Sit*) is here translated in its entirety.

and whatever is voluntary can be reduced to one principle, which is human reason or will. Therefore there is no need to suppose that God exists.

On the other hand, there is that which God speaks in his own person, in the Book of Exodus (3:14): "I am who am."

The five arguments

I answer that the existence of God can be proved in five ways.

The first and most evident way of proof is that which proceeds from the fact of motion. It is certain, by the evidence of our senses, that some things in the world are in motion. Now whatever is in motion must be moved by something other than itself: for nothing is in motion except as it is in a state of potentiality with respect to that towards which it is in motion; whereas whatever produces the motion is in a state of actuality. For to produce motion is nothing else than to draw something out of a state of potentiality into a state of actuality. But nothing can be drawn from potentiality to actuality except by a state of being that is already actual. Thus fire, which is actually hot, makes wood, which is potentially hot, to be actually hot, and thereby moves and changes it. Now it is not possible that the same thing should be actual and potential in the same respect, but only in different respects. For what is actually hot cannot at the same time be potentially hot; it is, however, at the same time potentially cold. Consequently it is impossible that the same thing should be both mover and moved in the same respect —i.e., that it should move itself. Whatever is in motion, therefore, must be moved by something else. If that by which it is moved is itself in motion, then it also must be moved by something other than itself, and that, in turn, by something other. But this cannot keep going on to infinity, because if it did there would be no first mover, and consequently nothing would be imparting motion to anything else. For secondary movers do not produce motion except as they are put in motion by a primary mover—as a staff produces motion [in other things] only when it is moved by the hand. Thus the argument necessarily leads to a first mover who is not put in motion by anything else; and this is what all mean by "God."

The second way of proof is from the nature of the propelling cause (*causa efficiens*). We find in the world as we perceive it, that propelling causes are arranged in serial order. Nothing is ever found to be a propelling cause of itself; nor indeed is that possible, for in order to be a propelling cause of itself a thing would have to be prior to itself, which is impossible. Moreover, it is not possible that there should be an infinite regress of propelling causes. The order of a set of propelling causes is such that the first event in the series is the cause of an intermediate event, and the intermediate event is the cause of an ultimate event—whether the intermediate events be several or only one. Now if the cause is taken away the effect is taken away likewise. Therefore, if there be no first term in a series of propelling causes, neither will there be any ultimate nor intermediate terms. But if a series of propelling causes goes back to infinity, there will be no first propelling cause, and hence there will be neither any intermediate propelling causes nor any ultimate effect: a consequence which is plainly false. Therefore it is necessary to affirm a first propelling cause; and this is universally called God.

The third way is drawn from the ideas of the possible and the necessary, and is as follows. We find in nature certain things that can exist and yet can be non-existent. For we discover them being generated and destroyed, and from this it follows that they are the kind of thing that can exist and can be non-existent. That such things should exist perpetually is impossible, for if it is possible for a thing not to exist there must be some time or other when it actually does not exist. Therefore, if everything were such as might possibly not exist, then there must have been a time when nothing existed. In that case there would be nothing in existence even now; because that which does not exist only begins to exist by virtue of something already existing. Therefore, if there was ever a time when nothing existed, it would have been impossible for anything to have begun to exist, and thus there would have been nothing existing even now—which is plainly false. Not all things are merely possible, therefore; there is need that something should exist necessarily. Now whatever is necessary either has its necessity caused by something else, or it has not. Even as we have proved that the series of propelling causes cannot be infinite, so it is impossible that there should be an infinite series of necessary things, each having its necessity caused by something else. Therefore we must postulate that there is something which exists by the necessity of its own nature, not by a necessity imposed from without, and which is the cause[1] of whatever necessity there is in other things.

The fourth way is taken from the gradations which are found in things. We find in the world instances of better and worse, more and less true, more and less noble, and the like. But "more" and "less" are predicated of different things according as they approximate in different ways to something which is "most." E.g., a thing is hotter when it approximates more nearly to the condition of what is hottest. Hence in like manner there is something which is truest, and best, and noblest, and consequently of uttermost being; for whatever is most fully true has greatest fullness of being, as is declared in the *Metaphysics*, Book II. Now that which has the greatest fullness of being of a given kind is the cause of all else of that kind; as fire, which is most fully hot, is the cause of all other hot states of being. Therefore there must be something which is the cause of the goodness and whatever grade of perfection may be found in various things; and this we call God.

The fifth way is taken from the governance of the world. We see that things which lack awareness (*cognitio*), such as natural bodies, act with reference to ends; and this is shown by the fact that they act, either always or usually, in the same way, and in such a way as to produce the best result. It is plain, then, that they achieve this end not by chance but by design (*intentio*). Now things which lack awareness cannot tend toward an end unless directed by some being who is aware and has understanding. E.g., an arrow flies toward its mark only because it has been aimed by an archer. Consequently there must be some being by whom, with understanding, all natural things are directed to their respective ends.

The objections answered

To the first objection reply must be made according to the words of Augustine in the *Enchiridion* [Chap. XI]: "Since God is good in the highest sense, he would certainly not permit any evil to exist in his works, unless his omnipotence and goodness were such as to produce good out of evil." It is a mark of God's infinite goodness,

---

[1] The "cause" intended in this paragraph is the *formal* cause, or formal factor in any situation (cf. Aristotle, in the Readings, p. 214), and may therefore also be translated "rational ground."

therefore, that he permits evils to exist and turns them to good results.

To the second objection it must be replied, that since [as we have now proved] nature works toward a definite end under the direction of a higher agent, everything which is done by nature must also be traceable to God as its first cause. Similarly, whatever is done as a voluntary act must also be traceable back to some higher cause than the human reason and will: for these are variable and capable of defect, and whatever partakes of variation and defect must be traceable to an unchanging and intrinsically necessary first principle, as we have demonstrated.

A Plea for Atheism*

BARON D'HOLBACH

Origin of the idea of gods

The first theology of man was grounded on fear, modeled by ignorance: either afflicted or benefited by the elements, he adored these elements themselves, and extended his reverence to every material, coarse object; he afterwards rendered his homage to the agents he supposed presiding over these elements—to powerful genii; to inferior genii; to heroes, or to men endowed with great qualities. By dint of reflection, he believed he simplified the thing in submitting the entire of nature to a single agent—to a sovereign intelligence, to a spirit, to a universal soul, which put this nature and its parts in motion. In recurring from cause to cause, man finished by losing sight of every particular, and in this obscurity, in this dark abyss, he placed his God, and formed new chimeras which will afflict him until a knowledge of natural causes undeceives him with regard to those phantoms he had always so stupidly adored.

If a faithful account was rendered of man's ideas upon the Divinity, he would be obliged to acknowledge, that the word "God"

---

* Baron d'Holbach (1723-1789), *The System of Nature;* from Vol. I, Chap. XIX; Vol. II, Chaps. I, IV, XI.

had only been used to express the concealed, remote, unknown causes of the effects he witnessed; he uses this term only when the spring of natural and known causes ceases to be visible: as soon as he loses the thread of these causes, or as soon as his mind can no longer follow the chain, he solves the difficulty, terminates his research, by ascribing it to God; thus giving a vague definition to an unknown cause, at which either his idleness, or his limited knowledge, obliges him to stop. When, therefore, he ascribes to God the production of some phenomenon, of which his ignorance precludes him from unravelling the true cause, does he, in fact, do anything more than substitute for the darkness of his own mind, a sound to which he has been accustomed to listen with reverential awe?

The rise of monotheism

By dint of meditation and reflection some, who gave the subject more consideration than others, reduced the whole to one all-powerful Divinity, whose power and wisdom sufficed to govern it. This God was looked upon as a monarch jealous of nature. They persuaded themselves that to give rivals and associates to the monarch to whom all homage was due would offend him; that he could not bear a division of empire; that infinite power and unlimited wisdom had no occasion for a division of power nor for any assistance. Thus some thinkers who would be thought profound have admitted one God, and in doing so have flattered themselves with having achieved a most important discovery.

And yet, they must at once have been most sadly perplexed by the contradictory actions of this *one* God; so much so that they were obliged to heap on him the most incompatible and extravagant qualities to account for those contradictory effects which so palpably and clearly gave the lie to some of the attributes they assigned to him. In supposing a God, the author of everything, man is obliged to attribute to him unlimited goodness, wisdom, and power, agreeable to the beneficence and order he fancied he saw in the universe, and according to the wonderful effects he witnessed; but, on the other hand, how could he avoid attributing to this God malice, improvidence, and caprice, seeing the frequent disorders and numberless evils to which the human race is so often liable? How can man avoid taxing him with improvidence, seeing that he is continually employed in destroying the work of his own hands? How is it possible not to suspect his impotence, seeing the perpetual non-performance of those projects of which he is supposed to be the contriver?

The paradox of God's goodness

Farfetched and endless torments are, by the justice of a merciful and compassionate God, reserved for fragile beings, for transitory offenses, for false reasonings, for involuntary errors, for necessary passions, which depend on the temperament this God has given them; circumstances in which he has placed them, or, if they will, the abuse of this pretended liberty, which a provident God ought never to have accorded to beings capable of abusing it. Should we call that father good, rational, just, clement, or compassionate, who should arm with a dangerous and sharp knife the hands of a petulant child, with whose imprudence he was acquainted, and who should punish him all his life, for having wounded himself with it? Should we call that prince just, merciful, and compassionate, who did not proportion the punishment to the offense, who should put no end to the torments of that subject who in a state of inebriety should have transiently wounded his vanity, without however causing him any real injustice—above all, after having himself taken pains to intoxicate him? Should we look upon that monarch as all-powerful, whose dominions should be in such a state of anarchy, that, with the exception of a small number of faithful subjects, all the others should have the power every instant to despise his laws, insult him, and frustrate his will? O theologians! confess that your God is nothing but a heap of qualities, which form a whole as perfectly incomprehensible to your mind as to mine; by dint of overburdening him with incompatible qualities, ye have made him truly a chimera, which all your hypotheses cannot maintain in the existence you are anxious to give him.

They will, however, reply to these difficulties, that goodness, wisdom, and justice, are, in God, qualities so eminent, or have such little similarity to ours, that they have no relation with these qualities when found in men. But I shall answer, how shall I form to myself ideas of these divine perfections, if they bear no resemblance to those of the virtues which I find in my fellow-creatures, or to the dispositions which I feel in myself? If the justice of God is not that of men;

if it operates in that mode of which men call injustice, if his goodness, his clemency, and his wisdom do not manifest themselves by such signs that we are able to recognize them; if all his divine qualities are contrary to received ideas; if in theology all the human actions are obscured or overthrown, how can mortals like myself pretend to announce them, to have a knowledge of them, or to explain them to others?

In short, theology invests its God with the incommunicable privilege of acting contrary to all the laws of nature and of reason, whilst it is upon his reason, his justice, his wisdom and his fidelity in the fulfilling his pretended engagements, that they are willing to establish the worship which we owe him, and the duties of morality. What an ocean of contradictions! A being who can do everything, and who owes nothing to anyone, who, in his eternal decrees, can elect or reject, predestinate to happiness or to misery, who has the right of making men the playthings of his caprice, and to afflict them without reason, who could go so far as even to destroy and annihilate the universe, is he not a tyrant or a demon? Is there anything more frightful than the immediate consequences to be drawn from these revolting ideas given to us of their God, by those who tell us to love him, to serve him, to imitate him, and to obey his orders? Would it not be a thousand times better to depend upon blind matter, upon a nature destitute of intelligence, upon chance, or upon nothing, upon a God of stone or of wood, than upon a God who is laying snares for men, inviting them to sin, and permitting them to commit those crimes which he could prevent, to the end that he may have the barbarous pleasure of punishing them without measure, without utility to himself, without correction to them, and without their example serving to reclaim others?

The paradox of God's immateriality

Man is a material being; he cannot have any ideas whatever but of that which is material like himself—that is to say, of that which can act upon his organs, or of that which, at least, has qualities analogous to his own. In despite of himself, he always assigns material properties to his God, which the impossibility of compassing has made him suppose to be spiritual, and distinguished from nature or the material world. Indeed, either he must be content not to understand himself, or he must have material ideas of a God, who is supposed to be the creator, the mover, the conserver of matter; the human mind may torture itself as long as it will, it will never comprehend that material effects can emanate from an immaterial cause, or that this cause can have any relation with material beings. Here is, as we have seen, the reason why men believe themselves obliged to give to God those moral qualities, which they have themselves; they forget that this being, who is purely spiritual, cannot, from thence, have either their organization, or their ideas, or their modes of thinking and acting, and that, consequently, he cannot possess that which they call intelligence, wisdom, goodness, anger, justice, etc. Thus, in truth, the moral qualities which have been attributed to the Divinity, suppose him material, and the most abstract theological notions are founded upon a true and undeniable *anthropomorphism*.

The theologians, in despite of all their subtleties, cannot do otherwise; like all the beings of the human species, they have a knowledge of matter alone, and have no real idea of a pure spirit. When they speak of intelligence, of wisdom, and of design in the Divinity, it is always those of men which they ascribe to him, and which they obstinately persist in giving to a being, of whom the essence they ascribe to him does not render him susceptible. How shall we suppose a being, who has occasion for nothing, who is sufficient for himself, whose projects must be executed as soon as they are formed, to have wills, passions, and desires? How shall we attribute anger to a being who has neither blood nor bile? . . . In short, a God, such as he has been depicted to us, cannot have any of the human qualities, which always depend on our peculiar organization, on our wants, on our institutions, and which are always relative to the society in which we live. The theologians vainly strive to aggrandize, to exaggerate in idea, to carry to perfection, by dint of abstractions, the moral qualities which they assign to their God; in vain they tell us that they are in him of a different nature from what they are in his creatures; that they are *perfect, infinite, supreme, eminent*; in holding this language, they no longer understand themselves; they have no one idea of the qualities of which they are speaking to us, seeing that a man cannot conceive them but inasmuch as they bear an analogy to the same qualities in himself.

It is thus that by subtilizing, mortals have not one fixed idea of the God to whom they have given birth. But little contented with a physical God, with an active nature, with matter capable of producing everything, they must despoil it of the energy which it possesses in virtue of its essence, in order to invest it in a pure spirit, which they are obliged to remake a material being, as soon as they are inclined to form an idea of it themselves, or make it understood by others. In assembling the parts of man, which they do no more than enlarge and spin out to infinity, they believe they form a God. It is upon the model of the human soul that they form the soul of nature, or the secret agent from which she receives impulse. After having made man double, they make nature double, and they suppose that this nature is vivified by an intelligence. In the impossibility of knowing this pretended agent, as well as that which they have gratuitously distinguished from their own body, they have called it spiritual, that is to say, of an unknown substance; from this, of which they have no ideas whatever, they have concluded that the spiritual substance was much more noble than matter, and that its prodigious subtility, which they have called *simplicity,* and which is only an effect of their metaphysical abstractions, secured it from decomposition, from dissolution, and from all the revolutions to which material bodies are evidently exposed.

It is thus that men always prefer the marvelous to the simple; that which they do not understand, to that which they can understand; they despise those objects which are familiar to them, and estimate those alone which they are not capable of appreciating: from that of which they have only had vague ideas, they have concluded that it contains something important, supernatural, and divine. In short, they need mystery to move their imagination, to exercise their mind, to feed their curiosity, which is never more in labor than when it is occupied with enigmas impossible to be guessed at, and which they judge, from thence, extremely worthy of their researches.

Nature is self-explanatory

Nevertheless, a deliberate study of nature is sufficient to undeceive every man who will calmly consider things: he will see that everything in the world is connected by links invisible to the superficial and to the too impetuous observer, but extremely intelligible to him who views things with coolness. He will find that the most unusual, and the most marvelous, as well as the most trifling and ordinary effects are equally inexplicable; but that they must flow from natural causes; and that supernatural causes, under whatever name they may be designated, with whatever qualities they may be decorated, will do no more than increase difficulties, and make chimeras multiply. The simplest observation will incontestably prove to him that everything is necessary, that all the effects which he perceives are material, and can only originate in causes of the same nature, even when he should not be able, by the assistance of the senses, to recur to these causes. Thus his mind will everywhere show him nothing but matter acting sometimes in a manner which his organs permit him to follow, and sometimes in a mode imperceptible to him: he will see that all beings follow constant and invariable laws, by which all combinations form and destroy themselves, all forms change, whilst the great whole ever remains the same. Then cured of the notions with which he was imbued, undeceived in those erroneous ideas which, from habit, he attached to imaginary beings, he will cheerfully consent to be ignorant of that which his organs cannot compass; he will know that obscure terms, devoid of sense, are not calculated to explain difficulties; and guided by reason, he will throw aside all hypotheses of the imagination, to attach himself to those realities which are confirmed by experience.

The Case for a Limited God*

JOHN STUART MILL

External limitations

It is next to be considered, given the indications of a Deity, what *sort* of a Deity do they point to? What attributes are we warranted, by the evidence which Nature affords of a creative mind, in assigning to that mind?

* From John Stuart Mill (1806–1873), *Three Essays in Religion:* third essay, "Theism," Part II.

It needs no showing that the power if not the intelligence, must be so far superior to that of man, as to surpass all human estimate. But from this to omnipotence and omniscience there is a wide interval. And the distinction is of immense practical importance.

It is not too much to say that every indication of design in the Cosmos is so much evidence against the omnipotence of the Designer. For what is meant by design? Contrivance: the adaptation of means to an end. But the necessity for contrivance—the need of employing means—is a consequence of the limitation of power. Who would have recourse to means if to attain his end his mere word was sufficient? The very idea of means implies that the means have an efficacy which the direct action of the being who employs them has not. Otherwise they are not means, but an incumbrance. A man does not use machinery to move his arms. If he did, it could only be when paralysis had deprived him of the power of moving them by volition. But if the employment of contrivance is in itself a sign of limited power, how much more so is the careful and skilful choice of contrivances? Can any wisdom be shown in the selection of means, when the means have no efficacy but what is given them by the will of him who employs them, and when his will could have bestowed the same efficacy on any other means? Wisdom and contrivance are shown in overcoming difficulties, and there is no room for them in a Being for whom no difficulties exist. The evidences, therefore, of Natural Theology[1] distinctly imply that the author of the Cosmos worked under limitations; that he was obliged to adapt himself to conditions independent of his will, and to attain his ends by such arrangements as those conditions admitted of. . . .

Limits of power and knowledge

Omnipotence, therefore, cannot be predicated of the Creator on grounds of natural theology. The fundamental principles of natural religion as deduced from the facts of the universe, negative his omnipotence. They do not, in the same manner, exclude omniscience: if we suppose limitation of power, there is nothing to contradict the supposition of perfect knowledge and absolute wisdom. But neither is there anything to prove it. The knowledge of the powers and properties of things necessary for planning and executing the arrange-

[1] I.e., as distinguished from theology based on revelation.

ments of the Cosmos, is no doubt as much in excess of human knowledge as the power implied in creation is in excess of human power. And the skill, the subtlety of contrivance, the ingenuity as it would be called in the case of a human work, is often marvelous. But nothing obliges us to suppose that either the knowledge or the skill is infinite. We are not even compelled to suppose that the contrivances were always the best possible. If we venture to judge them as we judge the works of human artificers, we find abundant defects. The human body, for example, is one of the most striking instances of artful and ingenious contrivance which nature offers, but we may well ask whether so complicated a machine could not have been made to last longer, and not to get so easily and frequently out of order. We may ask why the human race should have been so constituted as to grovel in wretchedness and degradation for countless ages before a small portion of it was enabled to lift itself into the very imperfect state of intelligence, goodness and happiness which we enjoy. The divine power may not have been equal to doing more; the obstacles to a better arrangement of things may have been insuperable. But it is also possible that they were not. The skill of the Demiourgos was sufficient to produce what we see; but we cannot tell that this skill reached the extreme limit of perfection compatible with the material it employed and the forces it had to work with. I know not how we can even satisfy ourselves on grounds of natural theology, that the Creator foresees all the future; that he foreknows all the effects that will issue from his own contrivances. There may be great wisdom without the power of foreseeing and calculating everything; and human workmanship teaches us the possibility that the workman's knowledge of the properties of the things he works on may enable him to make arrangements admirably fitted to produce a given result, while he may have very little power of foreseeing the agencies of another kind which may modify or counteract the operation of the machinery he has made. Perhaps a knowledge of the laws of nature on which organic life depends, not much more perfect than the knowledge which man even now possesses of some other natural laws, would enable man, if he had the same power over the materials and the forces concerned which he has over some of those of inanimate nature, to create organized beings not less wonderful nor less adapted to their conditions of existence than those in Nature.

The Nature and Validity of Religious Experience

WILLIAM JAMES

Five characteristics of the religious life

Summing up in the broadest possible way the characteristics of the religious life, as we have found them, it includes the following beliefs:—

1. That the visible world is part of a more spiritual universe from which it draws its chief significance;

2. That union or harmonious relation with that higher universe is our true end;

3. That prayer or inner communion with the spirit thereof—be that spirit "God" or "law"—is a process wherein work is really done, and spiritual energy flows in and produces effects, psychological or material, within the phenomenal world.

Religion includes also the following psychological characteristics:—

4. A new zest which adds itself like a gift to life, and takes the form either of lyrical enchantment or of appeal to earnestness and heroism.

5. An assurance of safety and a temper of peace, and, in relation to others, a preponderance of loving affections.

More than one valid perspective

... Ought it to be assumed that in all men the mixture of religion with other elements should be identical? Ought it, indeed, to be assumed that the lives of all men should show identical religious elements? In other words, is the existence of so many religious types and sects and creeds regrettable?

To these questions I answer "No" emphatically. And my reason is that I do not see how it is possible that creatures in such different positions and with such different powers as human individuals are,

* From William James, *The Varieties of Religious Experience* (Longmans, Green, 1902), Lecture XX, with omissions. Reprinted by courtesy of the publisher.

should have exactly the same functions and the same duties. No two of us have identical difficulties, nor should we be expected to work out identical solutions. Each, from his peculiar angle of observation, takes in a certain sphere of fact and trouble, which each must deal with in a unique manner. One of us must soften himself, another must harden himself; one must yield a point, another must stand firm —in order the better to defend the position assigned him. If an Emerson were forced to be a Wesley, or a Moody forced to be a Whitman, the total human consciousness of the divine would suffer. The divine can mean no single quality, it must mean a group of qualities, by being champions of which in alternation, different men may all find worthy missions. Each attitude being a syllable in human nature's total message, it takes the whole of us to spell the meaning out completely. So a "god of battles" must be allowed to be the god for one kind of person, a god of peace and heaven and home the god for another. We must frankly recognize the fact that we live in partial systems, and that parts are not interchangeable in the spiritual life. If we are peevish and jealous, destruction of the self must be an element of our religion; why need it be one if we are good and sympathetic from the outset? If we are sick souls, we require a religion of deliverance; but why think so much of deliverance if we are healthy-minded? Unquestionably, some men have the completer experience and the higher vocation, here just as in the social world; but for each man to stay in his own experience, whate'er it be, and for others to tolerate him there, is surely best. . . .

Is religion an anachronism?

The conclusions of the science of religions are as likely to be adverse as they are to be favorable to the claim that the essence of religion is true. There is a notion in the air about us that religion is probably only an anachronism, a case of "survival," an atavistic relapse into a mode of thought which humanity in its more enlightened examples has outgrown; and this notion our religious anthropologists at present do little to counteract.

This view is so widespread at the present day that I must consider it with some explicitness before I pass to my own conclusions. Let me call it the "Survival theory" for brevity's sake.

The pivot round which the religious life, as we have traced it, revolves, is the interest of the individual in his private personal destiny. Religion, in short, is a monumental chapter in the history of human egotism. The gods believed in—whether by crude savages or by men disciplined intellectually—agree with each other in recognizing personal calls. Religious thought is carried on in terms of personality, this being, in the world of religion, the one fundamental fact. Today, quite as much as at any previous age, the religious individual tells you that the divine meets him on the basis of his personal concerns.

Science, on the other hand, has ended by utterly repudiating the personal point of view. She catalogues her elements and records her laws, indifferent as to what purpose may be shown forth by them, and constructs her theories quite careless of their bearing on human anxieties and fates. Though the scientist may individually nourish a religion and be a theist in his irresponsible hours, the days are over when it could be said that for Science herself the heavens declare the glory of God and the firmament showeth his handiwork. Our solar system, with its harmonies, is seen now as but one passing case of a certain sort of moving equilibrium in the heavens, realized by a local accident in an appalling wilderness of worlds where no life can exist. In a span of time which as a cosmic interval will count but as an hour, it will have ceased to be. The Darwinian notion of chance production, and subsequent destruction, speedy or deferred, applies to the largest as well as to the smallest facts. It is impossible, in the present temper of the scientific imagination, to find in the driftings of the cosmic atoms, whether they work on the universal or on the particular scale, anything but a kind of aimless weather, doing and undoing, achieving no proper history, and leaving no result. Nature has no one distinguishable ultimate tendency with which it is possible to feel a sympathy. In the vast rhythm of her processes, as the scientific mind now follows them, she appears to cancel herself. The books of natural theology which satisfied the intellects of our grandfathers seem to us quite grotesque, representing, as they did, a God who conformed the largest things of nature to the paltriest of our private wants. The God whom science recognizes must be a God of universal laws exclusively, a God who does a wholesale, not a retail business. He cannot accommodate his processes to the convenience of individuals. The bubbles on the foam which coats a stormy sea are floating episodes, made and unmade by the forces of the wind and water. Our private selves are like those bubbles—epiphenomena, as Clifford, I believe, ingeniously called them; their destinies weigh nothing and determine nothing in the world's irremediable currents of events.

You see how natural it is, from this point of view, to treat religion as a mere survival, for religion does in fact perpetuate the traditions of the most primeval thought. To coerce the spiritual powers, or to square them and get them on our side, was, during enormous tracts of time, the one great object in our dealings with the natural world. For our ancestors, dreams, hallucinations, revelations, and cock-and-bull stories were inextricably mixed with facts. Up to a comparatively recent date such distinctions as those between what has been verified and what is only conjectured, between the impersonal and the personal aspects of existence, were hardly suspected or conceived. Whatever you imagined in a lively manner, whatever you thought fit to be true, you affirmed confidently; and whatever you affirmed, your comrades believed. Truth was what had not yet been contradicted, most things were taken into the mind from the point of view of their human suggestiveness, and the attention confined itself exclusively to the aesthetic and dramatic aspects of events.

How indeed could it be otherwise? The extraordinary value, for explanation and prevision, of those mathematical and mechanical modes of conception which science uses, was a result that could not possibly have been expected in advance. Weight, movement, velocity, direction, position—what thin, pallid, uninteresting ideas! How could the richer animistic aspects of Nature, the peculiarities and oddities that make phenomena picturesquely striking or expressive, fail to have been first singled out and followed by philosophy as the more promising avenue to the knowledge of Nature's life? Well, it is still in these richer animistic and dramatic aspects that religion delights to dwell. It is the terror and beauty of phenomena, the "promise" of the dawn and of the rainbow, the "voice" of the thunder, the "gentleness" of the summer rain, the "sublimity" of the stars, and not the physical laws which these things follow, by which the religious mind still continues to be most impressed; and just as of yore, the devout man tells you that in the solitude of his room or of the fields he still feels the divine presence, that inflowings of help come in reply to his prayers, and that sacrifices to this unseen reality fill him with security and peace.

Pure anachronism! says the survival-theory;—anachronism for which deanthropomorphization of the imagination is the remedy required. The less we mix the private with the cosmic, the more we dwell in universal and impersonal terms, the truer heirs of Science we become.

Religion and concrete reality

In spite of the appeal which this impersonality of the scientific attitude makes to a certain magnanimity of temper, I believe it to be shallow, and I can now state my reason in comparatively few words. That reason is that, so long as we deal with the cosmic and the general, we deal only with the symbols of reality, but *as soon as we deal with private and personal phenomena as such, we deal with realities in the completest sense of the term.* I think I can easily make clear what I mean by these words.

The world of our experience consists at all times of two parts, an objective and a subjective part, of which the former may be incalculably more extensive than the latter, and yet the latter can never be omitted or suppressed. The objective part is the sum total of whatsoever at any given time we may be thinking of, the subjective part is the inner "state" in which the thinking comes to pass. What we think of may be enormous—the cosmic times and spaces, for example—whereas the inner state may be the most fugitive and paltry activity of mind. Yet the cosmic objects, so far as the experience yields them, are but ideal pictures of something whose existence we do not inwardly possess but only point at outwardly, while the inner state is our very experience itself; its reality and that of our experience are one. A conscious field *plus* its object as felt or thought of *plus* an attitude towards the object *plus* the sense of a self to whom the attitude belongs—such a concrete bit of personal experience may be a small bit, but it is a solid bit as long as it lasts; not hollow, not a mere abstract element of experience, such as the "object" is when taken all alone. It is a *full* fact, even though it be an insignificant fact; it is of the *kind* to which all realities whatsoever must belong; the motor currents of the world run through the like of it; it is on the line connecting real events with real events. That unsharable feeling which each one of us has of the pinch of his individual destiny as he privately feels it rolling out on fortune's wheel may be disparaged for its egotism, may be sneered at as unscientific, but it is the one thing that fills up the measure of our concrete actuality, and any would-be existent that should lack such a feeling, or its analogue, would be a piece of reality only half made up.

If this be true, it is absurd for science to say that the egotistic elements of experience should be suppressed. The axis of reality runs solely through the egotistic places—they are strung upon it like so many beads. To describe the world with all the various feelings of the individual pinch of destiny, all the various spiritual attitudes, left out from the description—they being as describable as anything else—would be something like offering a printed bill of fare as the equivalent for a solid meal. Religion makes no such blunder. The individual's religion may be egotistic, and those private realities which it keeps in touch with may be narrow enough; but at any rate it always remains infinitely less hollow and abstract, as far as it goes, than a science which prides itself on taking no account of anything private at all.

A bill of fare with one real raisin on it instead of the word "raisin," with one real egg instead of the word "egg," might be an inadequate meal, but it would at least be a commencement of reality. The contention of the survival-theory that we ought to stick to non-personal elements exclusively seems like saying that we ought to be satisfied forever with reading the naked bill of fare. I think, therefore, that however particular questions connected with our individual destinies may be answered, it is only by acknowledging them as genuine questions, and living in the sphere of thought which they open up, that we become profound. But to live thus is to be religious; so I unhesitatingly repudiate the survival-theory of religion, as being founded on an egregious mistake. It does not follow, because our ancestors made so many errors of fact and mixed them with their religion, that we should therefore leave off being religious at all. By being religious we establish ourselves in possession of ultimate reality at the only points at which reality is given us to guard. Our responsible concern is with our private destiny, after all.

Ambiguity of "fact"[1]

Even the errors of fact may possibly turn out not to be as wholesale as the scientist assumes. The religious conception of the universe seems to many mind-curers "verified" from day to day by their experience of fact. "Experience of fact" is a field with so many things in it that the sectarian scientist, methodically declining, as he does, to recognize such "facts" as mind-curers and others like them experience, otherwise than by such rude heads of classification as "bosh," "rot," "folly," certainly leaves out a mass of raw fact which, save for the industrious interest of the religious in the more personal aspects of reality, would never have succeeded in getting itself recorded at all. We know this to be true already in certain cases; it may, therefore, be true in others as well. Miraculous healings have always been part of the supernaturalist stock in trade, and have always been dismissed by the scientist as figments of the imagination. But the scientist's tardy education in the facts of hypnotism has recently given him an apperceiving mass for phenomena of this order, and he consequently now allows that the healings may exist, provided you expressly call them effects of "suggestion." Even the stigmata of the cross on Saint Francis's hands and feet may on these terms not be a fable. Similarly, the time-honored phenomenon of diabolical possession is on the point of being admitted by the scientist as a fact, now that he has the name of "hystero-demonopathy" by which to apperceive it. No one can foresee just how far this legitimation of occultist phenomena under newly found scientist titles may proceed—even "prophecy," even "levitation," might creep into the pale.

Thus the divorce between scientist facts and religious facts may not necessarily be as eternal as it at first sight seems, nor the personalism and romanticism of the world, as they appeared to primitive thinking, be matters so irrevocably outgrown. The final human opinion may, in short, in some manner now impossible to foresee, revert to the more personal style, just as any path of progress may follow a spiral rather than a straight line. If this were so, the rigorously impersonal view of science might one day appear as having been a temporarily useful eccentricity rather than the definitively triumphant

---

[1] This section was published by James as a footnote.

position which the sectarian scientist at present so confidently announces it to be.

The subjective aspect of religion

Let us agree, then, that Religion, occupying herself with personal destinies and keeping thus in contact with the only absolute realities which we know, must necessarily play an eternal part in human history. The next thing to decide is what she reveals about those destinies, or whether indeed she reveals anything distinct enough to be considered a general message to mankind. . . .

First, is there, under all the discrepancies of the creeds, a common nucleus to which they bear their testimony unanimously? And second, ought we to consider the testimony true?

I will take up the first question first, and answer it immediately in the affirmative. The warring gods and formulas of the various religions do indeed cancel each other, but there is a certain uniform deliverance in which religions all appear to meet. It consists of two parts:—

1. An uneasiness; and
2. Its solution.

1. The uneasiness, reduced to its simplest terms, is a sense that there is *something wrong about us* as we naturally stand.

2. The solution is a sense that *we are saved from the wrongness* by making proper connection with the higher powers.

In those more developed minds which alone we are studying, the wrongness takes a moral character, and the salvation takes a mystical tinge. I think we shall keep well within the limits of what is common to all such minds if we formulate the essence of their religious experience in terms like these:—

The individual, so far as he suffers from his wrongness and criticizes it, is to that extent consciously beyond it, and in at least possible touch with something higher, if anything higher exist. Along with the wrong part there is thus a better part of him, even though it may be but a most helpless germ. With which part he should identify his real being is by no means obvious at this stage; but when stage 2 (the stage of solution or salvation) arrives, the man identifies his real being with the germinal higher part of himself; and does so in the following way. *He becomes conscious that this higher part is conterminous and continuous with a* MORE *of the same quality, which is operative in the universe outside of him, and which he can keep in working touch with, and in a fashion get on board of and save himself when all his lower being has gone to pieces in the wreck.* . . .

The hypothesis of objective truth

So far, however, as this analysis goes, the experiences are only psychological phenomena. They possess, it is true, enormous biological worth. Spiritual strength really increases in the subject when he has them, a new life opens for him, and they seem to him a place of conflux where the forces of two universes meet; and yet this may be nothing but his subjective way of feeling things, a mood of his own fancy, in spite of the effects produced. I now turn to my second question: What is the objective "truth" of their content?

The part of the content concerning which the question of truth most pertinently arises is that "MORE of the same quality" with which our own higher self appears in the experience to come into harmonious working relation. Is such a "more" merely our own notion, or does it really exist? If so, in what shape does it exist? Does it act, as well as exist? And in what form should we conceive of that "union" with it of which religious geniuses are so convinced?

It is in answering these questions that the various theologies perform their theoretic work, and that their divergencies most come to light. They all agree that the "more" really exists; though some of them hold it to exist in the shape of a personal god or gods, while others are satisfied to conceive it as a stream of ideal tendency embedded in the eternal structure of the world. They all agree, moreover, that it acts as well as exists, and that something really is effected for the better when you throw your life into its hands. It is when they treat of the experience of "union" with it that their speculative differences appear most clearly. Over this point pantheism and theism, nature and second birth, works and grace and karma, immortality and reincarnation, rationalism and mysticism, carry on inveterate disputes.

At the end of my lecture on Philosophy I held out the notion that an impartial science of religions might sift out from the midst of their discrepancies a common body of doctrine which she might also formulate in terms to which physical science need not object. This, I said, she might adopt as her own reconciling hypothesis, and recommend it for general belief. I also said that in my last lecture I should have to try my own hand at framing such an hypothesis.

The time has now come for this attempt. Who says *"hypothesis"* renounces the ambition to be coercive in his arguments. The most I can do is, accordingly, to offer something that may fit the facts so easily that your scientific logic will find no plausible pretext for vetoing your impulse to welcome it as true.

The role of the subconscious

The "more," as we called it, and the meaning of our "union" with it, form the nucleus of our inquiry. Into what definite description can these words be translated, and for what definite facts do they stand? It would never do for us to place ourselves offhand at the position of a particular theology, the Christian theology, for example, and proceed immediately to define the "more" as Jehovah, and the "union" as his imputation to us of the righteousness of Christ. That would be unfair to other religions, and, from our present standpoint at least, would be an over-belief.

We must begin by using less particularized terms; and, since one of the duties of the science of religions is to keep religion in connection with the rest of science, we shall do well to seek first of all a way of describing the "more," which psychologists may also recognize as real. The *subconscious self* is nowadays a well-accredited psychological entity; and I believe that in it we have exactly the mediating term required. Apart from all religious considerations, there is actually and literally more life in our total soul than we are at any time aware of. The exploration of the transmarginal field has hardly yet been seriously undertaken, but what Mr. Myers said in 1892 in his essay on the Subliminal Consciousness is as true as when it was first written: "Each of us is in reality an abiding psychical entity far more extensive than he knows—an individuality which can never express itself completely through any corporeal manifestation. The Self manifests through the organism; but there is always some part of the Self unmanifested; and always, as it seems, some power of organic expression in abeyance or reserve." Much of the content of this larger background against which our conscious being stands out in relief is insignificant. Imperfect memories, silly jingles, inhibitive timidities, "dissolutive" phenomena of various sorts, as Myers calls them, enter into it for a large part. But in it many of the performances of genius seem also to have their origin; and in our study of conversion, of mystical experiences, and of prayer, we have seen how striking a part invasions from this region play in the religious life.

Let me then propose, as an hypothesis, that whatever it may be on its *farther* side, the "more" with which in religious experience we feel ourselves connected is on its *hither* side the subconscious continuation of our conscious life. Starting thus with a recognized psychological fact as our basis, we seem to preserve a contact with "science" which the ordinary theologian lacks. At the same time the theologian's contention that the religious man is moved by an external power is vindicated, for it is one of the peculiarities of invasions from the subconscious region to take on objective appearances, and to suggest to the Subject an external control. In the religious life the control is felt as "higher"; but since on our hypothesis it is primarily the higher faculties of our own hidden mind which are controlling, the sense of union with the power beyond us is a sense of something, not merely apparently, but literally true.

This doorway into the subject seems to me the best one for a science of religions, for it mediates between a number of different points of view. Yet it is only a doorway, and difficulties present themselves as soon as we step through it, and ask how far our transmarginal consciousness carries us if we follow it on its remoter side. Here the over-beliefs begin: here mysticism and the conversion-rapture and Vedantism and transcendental idealism bring in their monistic interpretations and tell us that the finite self rejoins the absolute self, for it was always one with God and identical with the soul of the world. Here the prophets of all the different religions come with their visions, voices, raptures, and other openings, supposed by each to authenticate his own peculiar faith.

Those of us who are not personally favored with such specific revelations must stand outside of them altogether and, for the present at least, decide that, since they corroborate incompatible theological doctrines, they neutralize one another and leave no fixed result. If we follow any one of them, or if we follow philosophical theory and embrace monistic pantheism on non-mystical grounds, we do so in the exercise of our individual freedom, and build out our religion in the way most congruous with our personal susceptibilities. Among these susceptibilities intellectual ones play a decisive part. Although the religious question is primarily a question of life, of living or not living in the higher union which opens itself to us as a gift, yet the spiritual excitement in which the gift appears a real one will often fail to be aroused in an individual until certain particular intellectual beliefs or ideas which, as we say, come home to him, are touched. These ideas will thus be essential to that individual's religion;—which is as much as to say that over-beliefs in various directions are absolutely indispensable, and that we should treat them with tenderness and tolerance so long as they are not intolerant themselves. As I have elsewhere written, the most interesting and valuable things about a man are usually his over-beliefs.

Disregarding the over-beliefs, and confining ourselves to what is common and generic, we have in *the fact that the conscious person is continuous with a wider self through which saving experiences come,* a positive content of religious experience which, it seems to me, *is literally and objectively true as far as it goes.* If I now proceed to state my own hypothesis about the farther limits of this extension of our personality, I shall be offering my own over-belief—though I know it will appear a sorry under-belief to some of you—for which I can only bespeak the same indulgence which in a converse case I should accord to yours.

The pragmatic test

The further limits of our being plunge, it seems to me, into an altogether other dimension of existence from the sensible and merely "understandable" world. Name it the mystical region, or the supernatural region, whichever you choose. So far as our ideal impulses originate in this region (and most of them do originate in it, for we find them possessing us in a way for which we cannot articulately account), we belong to it in a more intimate sense than that in which we belong to the visible world, for we belong in the most intimate sense wherever our ideals belong. Yet the unseen region in question is not merely ideal, for it produces effects in this world. When we commune with it, work is actually done upon our finite personality, for we are turned into new men, and consequences in the way of conduct follow in the natural world upon our regenerative change. But that which produces effects within another reality must be termed a reality itself, so I feel as if we had no philosophic excuse for calling the unseen or mystical world unreal.

God is the natural appellation, for us Christians at least, for the supreme reality, so I will call this higher part of the universe by the name of God. We and God have business with each other; and in opening ourselves to his influence our deepest destiny is fulfilled. The universe, at those parts of it which our personal being constitutes, takes a turn genuinely for the worse or for the better in proportion as each one of us fulfils or evades God's demands. As far as this goes, I probably have you with me, for I only translate into schematic language what I may call the instinctive belief of mankind: God is real since he produces real effects.

The farther reach of faith

The real effects in question, so far as I have as yet admitted them, are exerted on the personal centres of energy of the various subjects, but the spontaneous faith of most of the subjects is that they embrace a wider sphere than this. Most religious men believe (or "know," if they be mystical) that not only they themselves, but the whole universe of beings to whom the God is present, are secure in his parental hands. There is a sense, a dimension, they are sure, in which we are *all* saved, in spite of the gates of hell and all adverse terrestrial appearances. God's existence is the guarantee of an ideal order that shall be permanently preserved. This world may indeed, as science assures us, some day burn up or freeze; but if it is part of his order, the old ideals are sure to be brought elsewhere to fruition, so that where God is, tragedy is only provisional and partial, and shipwreck and dissolution are not the absolutely final things. Only when this farther step of faith concerning God is taken, and remote objective consequences are predicted, does religion, as it seems to me, get wholly free from the first immediate subjective experience, and bring a *real hypothesis* into play. A good hypothesis in science must have other properties than those of the phenomenon it is immediately invoked to explain, otherwise it is not prolific enough. God, meaning only what enters into the religious man's experience of union, falls short of being an hypothesis of this more useful order. He needs to enter into wider cosmic relations in order to justify the subject's absolute confidence and peace.

Conclusion

That the God with whom, starting from the hither side of our own extra-marginal self, we come at its remoter margin into commerce should be the absolute world-ruler, is of course a very considerable over-belief. Over-belief as it is, though, it is an article of almost every one's religion. Most of us pretend in some way to prop it upon our philosophy, but the philosophy itself is really propped upon this faith. What is this but to say that Religion, in her fullest exercise of function, is not a mere illumination of facts already elsewhere given, not a mere passion, like love, which views things in a rosier light? It is indeed that, as we have seen abundantly. But it is something more, namely, a postulator of new *facts* as well. The world interpreted religiously is not the materialistic world over again, with an altered expression; it must have, over and above the altered expression, a *natural constitution* different at some point from that which a materialistic world would have. It must be such that different events can be expected in it, different conduct must be required.

This thoroughly "pragmatic" view of religion has usually been taken as a matter of course by common men. They have interpolated divine miracles into the field of nature, they have built a heaven out beyond the grave. It is only transcendentalist metaphysicians who think that, without adding any concrete details to Nature, or subtracting any, but by simply calling it the expression of absolute spirit, you make it more divine just as it stands. I believe the pragmatic way of taking religion to be the deeper way. It gives it body as well as soul, it makes it claim, as everything real must claim, some characteristic realm of fact as its very own. What the more characteristically divine facts are, apart from the actual inflow of energy in the faith-state and the prayer-state, I know not. But the over-belief on which I am ready to make my personal venture is that they exist. The whole drift of my education goes to persuade me that the world of our present consciousness is only one out of many worlds of consciousness that exist, and that those other worlds must contain experiences which have a meaning for our life also; and that although in the main their experiences and those of this world keep discrete, thing is sought: actually there is no such thing as seeking God, for there is nothing in which He could not be found. How foolish and hopeless would be the man who turned aside from the course of his life in order to seek God; even though he won all the wisdom of solitude and all the power of concentrated being he would miss God. Rather is it as when a man goes his way and simply wishes that it might be the way: in the strength of his wish his striving is expressed. Every relational event is a stage that affords him a glimpse into the consummating event. So in each event he does not partake, but also (for he is waiting) does partake, of the one event. Waiting, not seeking, he goes his way; hence he is composed before all things, and makes contact with them which helps them. But when he has *found,* his heart is not turned from them, though everything now meets him in the one event. He blesses every cell that sheltered him, and every cell into which he will yet turn. For this finding is not the end, but only the eternal middle, of the way.

* * *

You know always in your heart that you need God more than everything; but do you not know too that God needs you—in the fulness of His eternity needs you? How would man be, how would you be, if God did not need him, did not need you? You need God, in order to be—and God needs you, for the very meaning of your life. In instruction and in poems men are at pains to say more, and they say too much—what turgid and presumptuous talk that is about the "God who becomes"; but we know unshakably in our hearts that there is a becoming of the God that is. The world is not divine sport, it is divine destiny. There is divine meaning in the life of the world, of man, of human persons, of you and of me.

Creation happens to us, burns itself into us, recasts us in burning —we tremble and are faint, we submit. We take part in creation, meet the Creator, reach out to Him, helpers and companions.

Two great servants pace through the ages, prayer and sacrifice. The man who prays pours himself out in unrestrained dependence, and knows that he has—in an incomprehensible way—an effect upon God, even though he obtains nothing from God; for when he no longer desires anything for himself he sees the flame of his effect burning at its highest. And the man who makes sacrifice? I cannot despise him, this upright servant of former times, who believed that God yearned for the scent of his burnt-offering. In a foolish but powerful way he knew that we can and ought to give to God. This is known by him, too, who offers up his little will to God and meets Him in the grand will. "Thy will be done," he says, and says no more; but truth adds for him "through me whom Thou needest."

What distinguishes sacrifice and prayer from all magic? Magic desires to obtain its effects without entering into relation, and practices its tricks in the void. But sacrifice and prayer are set "before the Face," in the consummation of the holy primary word that means mutual action: they speak the *Thou*, and then they hear.

* * *

The spheres in which the world of relation is built are three.

First, our life with nature, in which the relation clings to the threshold of speech.

Second, our life with men, in which the relation takes on the form of speech.

Third, our life with intelligible forms, where the relation, being without speech, yet begets it.

In every sphere in its own way, through each process of becoming that is present to us, we look out toward the fringe of the eternal *Thou*; in each we are aware of a breath from the eternal *Thou*; in each *Thou* we address the eternal *Thou*.

Every sphere is compassed in the eternal *Thou*, but it is not compassed in them.

Through every sphere shines the one present.

We can, however, remove each sphere from the present.

From our life with nature we can lift out the "physical" world, the world of consistency, from our life with men the "psychical" world, the world of sensibility, and from our life with spiritual beings the "noetic" world, the world of validity. But now their transparency, and with it their meaning, has been taken from them; each sphere has become dull and capable of being used—and remains dull even though we light it up with the names of Cosmos and Eros and Logos. For actually there is a cosmos for man only when the universe becomes his home, with its holy hearth whereon he offers sacrifice; there is Eros for man only when beings become for him pictures of the eternal, and community is revealed along with them; and there is Logos for man only when he addresses the mystery with work and service for the spirit.

Form's silent asking, man's loving speech, the mute proclamation of the creature, are all gates leading into the presence of the Word.

But when the full and complete meeting is to take place, the gates are united in one gateway of real life, and you no longer know through which you have entered.

Glossary

These definitions are intended to elucidate philosophical terms either unfamiliar or used in a special sense. Terms that have been adequately explained in the text are usually omitted. Students wishing to pursue such inquiries further are referred to the following works of reference: *Dictionary of Philosophy and Psychology*, edited by James Mark Baldwin (two volumes); *Encyclopedia of Religion and Ethics*, edited by James Hastings (many volumes); *Dictionary of Philosophy*, edited by Dagobert D. Runes (single volume); *Encyclopaedia of Religion*, edited by Vergilius Ferm (single volume).

Several of the definitions have been adapted from *A Vocabulary of the Philosophical Sciences*, edited by Charles P. Krauth (1878).

Absolute

1. What exists in its own right—e.g., a man, a tree—vs. what exists only relatively to something else—e.g., "father." One of the great philosophical questions is whether such universals as justice, beauty, and goodness are absolute in this sense. Plato gave an affirmative answer; the philosophy of nominalism answers negatively.

2. What can be taken as true without restriction vs. what must be understood in a qualified sense (*"secundum quid"*). E.g., molecular activity is physical *absolutely* (since it is so defined—cf. definition of "physical"); man, however, is physical only with respect to his bodily manifestations.

3. What comprises all finite and relative things as parts or aspects of itself (Hegel).

4. What is underived, or self-caused. A basic theological question is whether it is necessary to postulate a cosmic Absolute in the third and fourth senses.

Abstract

"When we draw off and *contemplate separately* any part of an object presented to the mind, disregarding the rest of it, we are said to abstract that part of it. Thus, a person might, when a rose was before his eye or his mind, make the scent a distinct object of attention, laying aside all thought of the color, form, etc."—Archbishop Whately, *Logic*.

Accident

1. In an ontological sense: any property of a substance which could be removed without changing the essential nature of the substance. E.g., man's ability to see is one of the "accidents" of his human nature. Because the adjective "accidental" is nearly always used in Sense 2, the ontological meaning is usually expressed by the adjective "incidental." Cf. "attribute."

2. In a cosmological sense: that which fulfills or thwarts some real or imagined purpose without having been actually brought about by that purpose. The word is virtually a synonym of "chance" as indicated in Chap. IV, p. 124.

Analogy

Not simple resemblance, but the similarity or identity of *relations*. When A (one kind of thing or situation) is related to m in much the same way that B (another kind of thing or situation) is related to n, an analogy is said to exist between the two relationships. Ordinarily A and B must differ in kind, not only in degree: e.g., the lungs of a man are not usually said to be analogous to the lungs of an ape, but lungs in general are analogous to the gills of a fish and to the spiracula of insects.

Analogy never constitutes proof (Socrates notwithstanding), but may be useful (1) in the elucidation of something already known, and (2) in the suggestion of a new hypothesis.

Analysis

The mental division of a whole into its constituent parts or aspects, in order to study these separately or in their relations to one another.

Animatism

The belief that nature is filled with a kind of potency (called *mana* by the Melanesians), more marked in some things than in others, and existing to a superior degree in certain privileged persons (shamans, medicine men, wizards, magicians), as well as in certain magical words, symbols, implements (such as a magician's wand) and totemic beasts. Cf. "magic."

Animism

The belief that nature is peopled by innumerable spirits, having more or less distinct, although perhaps shadowy, individualities.

Anthropomorphic

"In the likeness of man." Applied to transcendent notions when they are conceived in human terms or visualized in a human form. Ernst Haeckel's characterization of the popular Christian God as "a gaseous vertebrate" is an ironic reminder of this tendency in religion.

Antinomy

A pair of mutually contradictory propositions, each of which seems to be logically demonstrable from evident premises, but which cannot both

GLOSSARY

be true. Two examples from Kant's *Critique of Pure Reason*, where the term is used prominently: (i) Time must have had a beginning, yet time could not have had a beginning; (ii) All human actions must be entirely predetermined by causes external to themselves, yet (if moral duty has any real meaning) some human actions must be partly free from external causes. The method of dealing with an antinomy is dialectical (*q.v.*): to define the opposing standpoints by formulating the hidden postulates on which they rest; to consider the full human significance and worth of each standpoint; and to specify the exact sense in which each of the postulates may be considered true.

Apriori
Non-empirical. An apriori proposition is one whose truth or falsity depends entirely upon its meaning, and hence cannot be either established or refuted by particular experiences. For examples see Chap. II, Sec. ii. Sometimes written *"a priori."*

As such
In so far as meant without qualification.

Attribute
Any property of a substance without which the substance would not exist. E.g., equality of radii is an attribute of the circle.

Autonomous
Having the right or power of making its own laws, or of determining its own nature.

Categorical
Unconditional, without qualification. Kant's doctrine of the Categorical Imperative is stated in Chap. XIV, Sec. ii.

Category
One of the most general classes to which the elements or aspects of experience can be referred. Thus, *person* and *thing* are opposing categories within everyday experience; *value* and *duty* are categories of ethics; *space, quantity,* and *law* are categories of experimental science. The adjective is *categorial*.

Catharsis
The Greek word *katharsis* (the spelling of which is frequently retained) meant "purgation," with a twofold reference: *medical*, as connoting the purgation of superfluous bodily elements which had caused any ailment, and the consequent restoration of health; *religious*, as connoting the purgation of mundane desires and ambitions, preparatory to initiation into a life of the spirit. In Aristotle's *Poetics* the word is employed by metaphoric extension to connote the quasi-purgative effect that tragic drama may have upon loose psychic feelings.

Cause

In the most general sense, a cause is that without which something else (the effect) cannot be. Aristotle distinguishes four kinds of "cause" thus broadly conceived: the material cause—e.g., the stones and other substances out of which a house is built; the efficient (or propelling) cause—the activity of the workmen; the formal cause—the plan by which they are guided; and the final (telic) cause—the goal toward which they are striving, which is the house as it will be when it is finished.

In a more restricted, and generally speaking a more modern sense: an event preceding another event, and at once necessary and sufficient to account for it.

Common sense

"A phrase employed to denote that degree of intelligence, sagacity, and prudence which is common to all men."—KRAUTH.

This same primary understanding also enables us to distinguish what is true and what is false in matters which are self-evident, such as those instanced in Chap. II, Sec. ii. Moreover it is by this same means that we recognize differences in similar things and identities in things different. In these latter aspects common sense is virtually the same as intuition (*q.v.*). The tendency to claim as common sense what is really prejudice was noticed in Chap. II.

Connotation

1. In traditional logic the *denotation* of a term refers to the class of instances to which it properly refers, the *connotation* to the characteristics which distinguish the instances and make them a class rather than a motley collection. Thus the denotation of "man" is the totality of individual specimens, at all times and places, which are designated by that word; the connotation of "man" is the set of essential characteristics—notably, having the power of independent thought—by virtue of which we include certain specimens in the class and not others.

2. In critical discourse generally, the denotation of a word or phrase or larger unit of language is considered to be its core of logical meaning (including both denotation and connotation in Sense 1), while the connotations are the meanings implicitly suggested by context and association. From a semantic standpoint poetry may be said to function by making adroit use of the connotative overtones of language.

Context

The general mass of ideas, presuppositions and expectancies which surround a given idea or problem and influence our way of interpreting it. Sometimes used almost interchangeably with *perspective* (*q.v.*). But contexts may properly be spoken of as wider and narrower; perspectives (because of the different metaphorical connotation) as sharp and clear or the reverse.

Contradiction

Two propositions stand in logical contradiction to each other, and are called logical contradictories, when they are so related that the truth or falsity of either one implies respectively the falsity or truth of the other.

Two terms are contradictory when any situation to which they are applicable must be characterized by one or the other of them and cannot be characterized by both.

Contrapose

A verb meaning to perform the logical process of contraposition: i.e., to reverse the terms or component clauses of an affirmative proposition without changing the logical meaning. This is done by substituting for the component terms or clauses their respective contradictories. E.g., (i) "All good citizens contribute something to their country's welfare." Contrapositive: "Those who contribute nothing to their country's welfare are not good citizens." (ii) "If there is complete divine foreknowledge of every human act, men's choices must be always completely predetermined." Contrapositive: "If men's choices are ever to any degree free from predetermination, there cannot be complete divine foreknowledge of every human act."

Cosmology

That branch of philosophical inquiry which treats of the structure, relations, and tendencies of the existent universe.

Daimon

An intermediate spiritual nature between the divine and the human. In Plato's *Symposium* its function is said to consist in transmitting and interpreting to the gods the prayers and sacrifices of men, and in revealing to men and impressing upon their inner consciousness the divine will. The English word "demon," connoting a power intrinsically and preeminently evil, has grown out of early Christian misunderstandings of the Greek religious teaching.

Demiourgos

The ancient Greek word for a workman, craftsman, or architect. Plato, in the *Timaeus*, applied the term to the creative divinity who made the universe.

Denotation

See *Connotation*

Deontology

That aspect of ethics which is concerned with the problem of duty.

Dialectic

1. Derived from the Greek word meaning "to converse," the word *dialektikê*, which we translate "dialectic," is employed by Socrates and Plato to mean the attempt to discover truth through the give-and-take of

conversation, instead of by straight linear deduction. Plato's use of the Dialogue as a medium of philosophical expression indicates the importance he attaches to this conception.

2. According to Xenophon (*Memorabilia*, IV. 5. 11) Socrates declared that dialectic is so called not only because it is an inquiry pursued by men taking counsel together, but because it follows the method "of separating the subjects considered according to their kinds" (*dialegontas*). Three further elements are: the search for exact definition of terms; the free use of analogy, drawing particularly upon such basic concerns as sickness and health and human functions generally; and revelation of the weakness of an opinion by forcing one's opponent to make a series of admissions leading up to one that is logically inconsistent with the opinion in question or with some corollary of it.

3. In Aristotle's *Organon*: the logic of plausibility—i.e., of winning and rebutting arguments against an opponent—as distinguished from demonstration, which proceeds from premises established as true.

4. In Hegel: the process of discovering hidden oppositions in a situation, formulating them as thesis and antithesis, which together are then seen to be "sublated" in a higher synthesis, i.e., in a concept which includes but transcends them. Hegel interpreted all history as following an analogous dialectic pattern.

Dilemma

An argument purporting to show that either of two contradictory propositions leads, by independent steps, to the same logical consequence. Since one or the other of two contradictory propositions must necessarily be true, it follows (if there are no loopholes or ambiguities in the argument) that the final consequence must be true. Example: "Everyone is either interested or not interested in studying philosophy. If anyone is interested, he should be encouraged to take a course in the subject, because one's intellectual interests should not be stifled. If anyone is not interested, his intellectual interests are unduly narrow, and a course in philosophy will be valuable in helping to broaden them. Therefore—?"

Dogmatism

The attitude of maintaining certain propositions or a certain point of view to be indubitable, when there is in fact contrary evidence which the dogmatist refuses to examine fairly.

Dynamic

Pertaining to events and movement; hence to the physical world. E.g., "In its logical aspect Aristotle conceives of matter as the substance in which qualities inhere; in its dynamic (or dynamical) aspect, as a potentiality of some specific development."

Dynamism

1. In metaphysics, a doctrine such as that of Leibniz, or of Schopenhauer, that all substance is essentially force, tendency, or will.

2. In ethics, the valuing of power, activity, or novelty for their own sakes, rather than as means to a static goal. Schopenhauer is a dynamist in the first sense only; Nietzsche in both senses.

Eclecticism
A philosophy prominent at Alexandria in the third and fourth centuries of our era, professing to gather and unite into one body of doctrine what was true in all systems of philosophy. From the Greek *ek-lego*, "choose out, select."

Ecstasy
Derived from *ek-stasis*, "a standing out." A transport of the soul by which it seems as if it were out of the body. Plotinus declared that four times in his life he had experienced an "ecstatic" union with the Divine. St. Bonaventura (*Itinerarium Mentis in Deum*) recommends certain methods of contemplative self-discipline which may lead to a state of philosophical ecstasy as the goal. John Locke, on the other hand, doubts the validity of the method: "Whether that which we call ecstasy be not dreaming with the eyes open, I leave to be examined" (*Essay Concerning Human Understanding*, Bk. II, Chap. 19).

Eidolon
An image supposed by certain ancient Greek philosophers to emanate from an object and pass through the eyes into the head, thus producing visual perceptions.

Empathy
An experience of seeming identification with another person or object, consisting (according to the most common psychological hypothesis) of kinaesthetic feelings which in turn are produced by muscular tensions and motor attitudes.

Empiricism
The philosophy that nothing should be accepted as true save what is given by sense-experience, or by inductions from sense-experience.

Epistemology
The branch of philosophy that inquires into the grounds upon which knowledge may be accepted as valid.

Eschatology
The study of matters pertaining to the nature of existence after death.

Essence
The essence of anything comprises those properties (qualities or relationships) without which a thing would not exist or would be of a fundamentally different nature. The properties themselves are called attributes (*q.v.*).

GLOSSARY

Existential
An existential question is one that is conceived not as a pastime, a conundrum, or a means to some end, but as an authentic expression of one's existence in the full human sense as a responsible maker of decisions.

Experiential
Pertaining to experience as a whole. A broader term than *empirical*. Whereas empirical evidence for a belief is confined to such sense-experiences as can be shared by all normal observers, experiential evidence may include the more private sorts of awarenesses as well.

Faculty
Any native human power, potentially rational, which shows a tendency towards some characteristic type of expression. E.g., the reasoning faculty; the faculty of making friends.

Genetic
Having to do with the origin or early stages of a developing thing.

Gestalt
The German word for "form, configuration." The Gestalt school of psychology stresses the integral and relational character of psychic phenomena.

Henotheism
In a polytheistic culture, an attitude of worship which consists of taking now one god, now another as the Supreme Deity of which all the other gods are but manifestations.

Homogeneous
Similar in essential type. Opposed to *heterogeneous*, which connotes an irreducible difference of type. Thus the color blue and the sound of a violin are heterogeneous; but the light-waves emanating from the one and the sound-waves from the other are homogeneous.

Hylozoism
The view that all matter (*hylê*) contains life (*zoê*) or potencies of life.

Hypostatize
To treat an abstract quality or relation as if it were a thing or substance.

Implication
One proposition is said to imply another when their relation is such that if the first is true the second must also be true. One concept implies another if in any proposition in which the first is asserted of anything the second can logically be substituted for it.

Inference
"To infer is nothing but by virtue of one proposition laid down as true, to draw in another as true."—LOCKE, *op. cit.* Whereas implication is a strictly logical relation, inference is a mental operation based on it.

Introspection
The experience, and more particularly the psychological method, of looking inward at one's own thoughts, feelings, and volitions, with a view to learning about one's own nature.

Intuition
Immediate, direct apprehension of a truth, in contrast to forms of knowledge which are mediated by a discursive process. John Locke writes (*op. cit.*, Bk. IV, Chap. 2): "Sometimes the mind perceives the agreement or disagreement of two ideas immediately by themselves, without the intervention of any other; and this, I think, we may call intuitive knowledge. For in this the mind is at no pains of proving or examining, but perceives the truth as the eye doth the light, only by being directed towards it. Thus, the mind perceives that white is not black, that a circle is not a triangle, that three is more than two, and equal to one and two."

Law
"Laws in their most extended signification are the necessary relations arising from the nature of things; and, in this sense, all beings have their laws, the Deity has his laws, the material world has its laws, . . . the beasts have their laws, and man has his laws."—MONTESQUIEU, *Spirit of Laws*, Bk. I, Chap. i.

Original signification: a command or prohibition addressed by one having authority to subjects conceived as having the freedom to obey or disobey. Statute laws, laws of custom, laws of morality, and laws of religion come under this head. But the word has become transferred to mean, not an order commanded or prescribed, but simply an order discovered in nature; an invariant connection between one type of event and another.

Magic
Any method (real or supposed) of producing effects in nature by direct control over the hidden force, the *mana*, within her.

Mana
A Melanesian word signifying the living force supposedly pervading all nature. Objects which are felt and believed to partake of this force to an extraordinary degree are likely to be taboo (*q.v.*).

Metaphysics
The study of the most general character and relations of things, particularly as subsisting between various major realms of discourse (*q.v.*) and between the categories and first principles essential to each realm. Any

judgment of the form, "x is more real than y," is a metaphysical judgment. When a metaphysical judgment is put in the exclusionist form, "x alone is real" (e.g., "Only minds are real," or "Only what can be verified scientifically is real"), it becomes a metaphysical dogma. Metaphysics is usually regarded as comprising ontology and cosmology as its branches.

Metascientific
Pertaining to questions and propositions which are suggested by scientific ways of thinking but which are universal and therefore metaphysical in scope. Thus whereas it is a legitimate postulate of science that every scientific hypothesis should be open to public verification, the assertion that every valid belief must have this character is metascientific.

Monism
Any philosophy which holds that there is one single reality—whether God, mind, matter, force, blind will, or something unknown—of which all apparent diversities are but manifestations.

Monotheism
The doctrine that there is only one God.

Mysticism
The philosophy which holds that reality is truly known only by relinquishing one's separate individuality and experiencing a union with the divine ground of all existence.

Naturalism
The philosophy which identifies reality with "nature"—usually as this is defined and discovered scientifically.

Objective
1. Derived from *objicio*, "throw against," the word was formerly applied to things in their character of being presented to the mind. Thus Descartes distinguishes between the sun as *actually* or *formally* in the sky and as *objectively* in our idea of it. This meaning is apparent in the following passage from Berkeley's *Siris*: "Natural phenomena are only natural appearances. They are, therefore, such as we see and perceive them. Their *real* and *objective* natures are, therefore, one and the same."
2. Having a reality independent of our ideas of it.
3. Methodologically: that which has been tested and confirmed by repeated and controlled observations.

Organicism
The cosmological theory which interprets the universe on the analogy of a biological organism, particularly involving the subordination of parts to wholes and (in some forms of the doctrine) of means to ends.

Ormuzd and Ahriman
The ancient Iranian (Persian) cosmic principles of good and evil, regarded as engaged in a constant warfare in which every man takes part,

choosing for himself which side he will be on. The name Ormuzd is a contraction of Ahura Mazda, "Lord of Light." Ahriman, "the Lie," is probably a prototype of the Hebraeo-Christian Satan.

Panpsychism
The doctrine that all (*pan*) is really and inwardly of the same nature as our own selves, or souls (*psyché*).

Pantheism
The doctrine that God (*theos*) is all, and hence that the entire universe is but an outward manifestation of divine substance.

Parsimony
The principle of Parsimony, usually regarded as one of the requirements of scientific method, declares that in explaining any phenomenon we should choose that explanation which requires the fewest qualifications and gratuitous assumptions.

Pejorative
Having an unfavorable connotation.

Personalism
The philosophy which declares that living persons are the most real of all entities, and cannot be adequately explained by anything else.

Perspective
The word is implicitly metaphorical, connoting an angle of vision. In an intellectual context it refers to the way in which a problem is envisaged as a result of the point of view adopted. Thus in historical perspective we would consider how such a doctrine as materialism arose and developed; in logical perspective, what arguments may be adduced for its support or refutation; in sociological perspective, its likely effects upon social behavior.

Phenomenalism
The doctrine that we can know only phenomena (*q.v.*), not ultimate reality.

Phenomenology
The philosophical method developed by Edmund Husserl (1859-1938) and his school. It consists in "bracketing off" the abstract concepts and assumptions employed by science, common sense, and traditional metaphysics—e.g., "matter," "physical cause," "objective fact"—and in attempting to describe and classify the various aspects and types of experience as they actually appear rather than as they have been interpreted by preconceived theories.

Phenomenon
Whatever actually appears to the senses, in its apparent character. The plural is *phenomena*.

Physical
Pertaining to the world of space, time, and objectively verifiable existence.

Plenitude
Fullness. The Principle of Plenitude is philosophically complementary to the Principle of Parsimony (*q.v.*). It asserts that an adequate philosophy should take full account of the qualitative diversity of things, and not intellectually reduce this to the logical simplicity of a theory.

Polytheism
Belief in a number of gods. Cf. *henotheism*.

Positivism
The doctrine that valid knowledge must be based exclusively upon the methods of the sciences, and that neither the speculations of metaphysics nor the insights of intuition can make any real contribution.

Postulate
A proposition accepted as true in order that other propositions may be derived from it, or in order that inquiries and investigations of a certain type may be guided by it.

Pragmatism
The doctrine that the meaning of an idea or theory is to be found in its total consequences for human living; and that its truth is to be measured by the degree to which those consequences are ultimately satisfactory.

Propaedeutic
Applied to what is studied in advance of some main subject-matter as a means to understanding it.

Proposition
The type of meaning which can be meaningfully affirmed or denied, and hence be meaningfully judged true or false. Normally but not always expressed in a declarative sentence. Thus the declarative sentence, "Everyone really believes in the existence of an external world," and the rhetorical interrogative, "Does anyone really doubt that an external world exists?" express an identical proposition.

Qua
Shortened form of the Latin *quatenus*, "in so far as"; "to just the extent of being." Example: Physics studies men qua bodies obeying the causal laws of motion, biology studies them qua living organisms, and ethics studies them qua potentially moral agents.

Q.v.

From the Latin *quod vide*, "which see." I.e., look up the word just given or the matter just referred to. Used repeatedly in the present Glossary.

Rationalize

To invent plausible reasons for a belief which is held independently of those reasons. The verb "to rationalize" is pejorative, and should not be employed where "to reason" is meant.

Realm of discourse

A major branch of inquiry, distinguished by the categories which it employs and the first principles (axioms or postulates) on which it rests.

Reductio ad absurdum

Establishing a proposition as true by assuming its negative and demonstrating that the consequences of that assumption are inadmissible.

Reduction

Denial of some characteristic of experience on the ground that it can be adequately explained by something else. E.g., the extreme behaviorist's contention that thought is nothing more than a vibration of the larynx; Berkeley's argument that the physical world is but a coherent pattern of ideas; the pantheist's belief that the entire mundane world is only a manifestation of God's effulgent nature.

Scepticism

1. An attitude of questioning doubt; refusal to accept any belief until the evidence for it is adequate.

2. The philosophical position that no knowledge is possible; that there are only opinions.

Scientizing

Appealing to the prestige of science in support of a philosophical theory which cannot actually be established by scientific method. The quotations from Hugh Elliot in Chapter VI furnish a lively example.

Solipsism

The notion that only I (i.e., the solipsist) exist; that other persons have no independent existence of their own but exist solely as objects of my consciousness, when and in so far as I am conscious of them.

Soul

The self, conceived as substantial—i.e., as somehow more than the bare totality of its changing states.

Spiritual

Having to do with man's highest values: the beautiful, the good, the true, and the holy.

Subjective
1. In the mind without reference to an outer object.
2. Applied to beliefs held for private, usually emotional reasons, without confirmation by objective inquiry.

Subsist
A verb designating the mode of being of such entities as have no location in space and time but are nevertheless real: chiefly universals, relations, numbers, and values.

Substance
That which is and abides. The nature of a thing which is conceived to remain the same despite changes in its accidents (*q.v.*); and which can be adequately conceived in abstraction from its accidents.

Syllogism
Two propositions (premises) so related that they logically imply a third proposition (the conclusion).

Synoptic
Lit., envisioned altogether. Applied to the attitude which emphasizes wholeness rather than merely parts.

Taboo
The modern colloquial meaning, "prohibited," is only a part of the primitive meaning. An object or action or place or person is taboo when it is felt to have an extraordinary degree of *mana* (*q.v.*) potentially dangerous and not susceptible to magical (*q.v.*) control. It is then regarded as sacred: i.e., withheld from ordinary usage and reserved for ritualistic observances on special occasions.

Tautology
Restatement in the predicate of a meaning already implicit in the subject. E.g., "Every effect must have had a cause." Here the idea of "having had a cause" is already implicit in the meaning of "effect"; for if there were an event that had not had a cause, it would not be spoken of as an effect.

Technosophy
The view of life constituted by technological habits of thought—i.e., thought in the triple aspect of explanation, expectation, and valuation.

Teleology
The interpretation of phenomena in terms of tendencies, aims, or implicit purposes.

Telepathy
Transfer of thoughts from one mind to another without the use of external means of communication.

Telic
Pertaining to an end, aim, goal, towards which a process is directed, as distinguished from the previous causes which initiated it or conditioned its beginning.

Theology
The study of God's existence and nature. Also, any organized body of doctrines concerning Him.

Totem
Said to be from an Ojibwa Indian word signifying brother-sister relation. The word is applied when this relation is established ritually between a certain group within a primitive tribe and a certain species of animal.

Transcendent
Beyond the reach of ordinary experience and strictly natural explanation.

Universals
General characteristics which inhere in an indefinitely large number of particulars and thereby constitute them a logical class.

Universe
The totality of all that exists. The term "universe of discourse" is sometimes employed as a synonym of "realm of discourse" (*q.v.*).

Validity
An argument is called valid when its conclusion is strictly implied by its premises. More generally and loosely, a belief or set of beliefs is said to be valid when it is both coherent in itself and consistent with known evidence.

Wholistic
Or (from the Greek spelling) *holistic*. Stressing wholes rather than parts. Thus Aristotle studied animal and plant organisms wholistically, whereas a bio-chemist does not. Cf. *Gestalt; organicism*.

Will
The power of determining and disposition to determine our actions—to whatever extent this may be possible.
"Appetite is the will's solicitor, and will is the appetite's controller; what we covet according to the one, by the other we often reject."
—RICHARD HOOKER (1554-1600).

Index

Absolutism, see Dogmatism
Abstraction, 9, 10, 14, 21, 102-104
Accident, see Chance
Acquaintance, 25-27; cf. Experience, Knowledge
ADLER, ALFRED, 276-277
AESCHYLUS, 481
Aesthetic, 16, 410, 432-452; aesthetic surface, 433-437
ALEXANDER, SAMUEL, 72, 343
Ambiguity, 19-20, 28-29, 50, 88, 185-186
ANAXAGORAS, 130-131, 352
ANAXIMANDER, 133-134
ANSELM, SAINT, 499-501
Anthropology, 483-486
Appreciation, 6; cf. Value
Apriori, 33-36; cf. Axiom
AQUINAS, see THOMAS AQUINAS
ARCHIMEDES, 353
ARISTOTLE, 12, 36, 49, 56, 57, 66-68, 117, 125, 131-132, 133, 139, 140, 192, 199, 212-221, 247, 248, 272-273, 302-304, 350-353, 406, 445, 446, 471-473, 495, 544-563
ARRHENIUS, 202
Art, 66, 118, 217, 417-418, 422, 441-452
Associationism, 269-271
Assurance, see Belief
Atheism, 486-488, 567-573
AUGUSTINE, SAINT, 304, 566
Authority, 29-31, 415

AUROBINDO, SRI, 208-209
Axiom, 60, 142, 468

BACH, JOHANN SEBASTIAN, 437
BACON, FRANCIS, 28, 31, 80-91, 151
Beauty, see Aesthetic
BECK, LEWIS W., 50
Becoming, see Process
BEERBOHM, MAX, 419
BEETHOVEN, LUDWIG VAN, 450
Behaviorism, 186, 263-265, 285-287, 325-327
Belief, 5-6, 26-27, 28-42, 75-76, 477-482, 502
BENTHAM, JEREMY, 61, 403-406, 458, 459-462, 464, 466, 513-523
BERGSON, HENRI, 64, 207, 373-375
BERKELEY, BISHOP GEORGE, 72-73, 169-174, 181, 188, 328, 502
Biology, 190-210
BLANC, LOUIS, 51
BOAS, MARIE, 133
BOHR, NIELS, 157
BORGIA, [CESARE], 81
BOSANQUET, BERNARD, 248, 454
BOYLE, ROBERT, 133, 134, 136, 165
BRADLEY, F. H., 223-224
Brahma, 208-209, 481
BROAD, C. D., 70-80, 227-233
BRIDGMAN, P. W., 176-178

BUBER, MARTIN, 337-339, 392-397, 504, 590-594
BURBANK, LUTHER, 199

CALDIN, E. F., 179-180, 183, 234-235
CALVIN, JOHN, 304
CANTOR, GEORG, 75
CARLYLE, THOMAS, 385
CARNOT, SADI, 146-148
CARROLL, LEWIS, 336
CASSIRER, ERNST, 119, 121-122
Category, see Concept, basic
Catharsis, 441
Cause, 123, 136-137, 155-156, 306-309, 317, 373-376, 379, 490
CEZANNE, PAUL, 185
Chance, 124, 135, 380-383
Change, see Process
Chemistry, 8, 163, 194-195, 205
Choice, 11, 15, 299, 303, 312-313, 319, 385-387, 456-458
CHUANG TZU, 474-475
CLAUSIUS, RUDOLF, 147-148
CLIFFORD, W. K., 283, 389-392, 579, 590
COCTEAU, JEAN, 439
COLLINGWOOD, R. G., 135, 140, 142
COMPTON, ARTHUR H., 313, 317
COMTE, AUGUSTE, 478
Concept, 26, 118, 122; basic (category), 58-59, 74-75, 102-106, 185, 222-224
CONKLIN, EDWIN G., 247
Conscience, 275, 277
Conservation laws, 141-145
Consistency, 21, 52-54, 468-469
Contemplation, 13, 20-21, 558-560, 562-563
Contextualism (or Contextual realism), 162, 181-187, 420-423, 425-426
Contingency, 125-126
Continuity, 115-116

COPERNICUS, 139-140
Cosmology, 17, 119, 128-158, 561-562, 564-566; cosmological argument for God, 489-492
Critical attitude, 5-6, 54-58, 62-63, 76-77
CROCE, BENEDETTO, 447

D'ABRO, A., 156-157
DANTE ALIGHIERI, 454
DARWIN, CHARLES R., 197, 200, 247
DARWIN, CHARLES GALTON, 157-158
DE BURGH, W. G., 507
Deduction, 36, 38-39
DEMOCRITUS, 13-14, 113, 162
DENNES, WILLIAM R., 494, 507
DESCARTES, RENÉ, 37, 91-99, 133, 165-167, 171, 261-262, 282-283, 288, 324, 353-359
Determinism, 155, 164-165, 306-311, 314-316, 372-378, 384-385
DE VRIES, HUGO, 201
DEWEY, JOHN, 37 n., 69, 454
D'HOLBACH, BARON, 567-573
Dialectic, 18, 35-54, 55, 61-63
Dogmatism, 30-31, 35, 90, 195, 382, 413-416
DRIESCH, HANS, 247, 324
Dualism, 165-167
DUNS SCOTUS, JOHN, 127
Duty, 465-470, 526-536, 538-543

Economics, 8-9
EDDINGTON, ARTHUR S., 236-245
Egoism, moral, 21, 458-461; metaphysical, see Solipsism
EINSTEIN, ALBERT, 146, 154
Eject, 389-392
ELLIOT, HUGH, 163, 188, 307-308
Emergence, theory of, 204, 205-207, 209
EMERSON, RALPH WALDO, 20
Empathy, 437-438
EMPEDOCLES, 216

INDEX

Empirical method, 37-40, 80-81, 234-235
Energy, 144-145, 236, 283-284
End and means, 13, 17, 21, 460, 474
Entropy, 146-149
EPICTETUS, 408
EPICURUS, 113, 164, 458, 511-513
Epiphenomenism, 287-292
Epistemology, 17-18, 24, 169-174, 181-186
Error, 26, 32-33
Esthetic, see Aesthetic
Ethics, 13, 15, 59, 61, 96-99, 409-413, 423-426, 456-475
Evil, 384-385, 388-389, 493, 563, 566-567, 569-570
Evolution, 196-209
Excellence: see Virtue
Existential method: 14-16, 21, 501-504, 510
Experience, 6, 11, 111-122, 129, 184-185, 221-222, 312, 313, 502, 581
Experiment, 176-178, 190
Explanation, 122-126, 130, 131, 214-216, 317
Extrospection, 336-337

Fatalism, 301-302, 388
FÉNÉLON, FRANÇOIS, 323, 324
Fiction, 175-178
Field theory, 154-156
FISKE, JOHN, 311
Fitzgerald contraction, 152
FLÜGEL, J. C., 277
Force, 175; cf. Energy
FRANCIS, SAINT, 582
FRAZER, JAMES G., 484-486
Freedom, psychological and moral, 15, 299-320, 372-389, 408
FREUD, SIGMUND, 265-266, 274-276, 277, 486-487, 488
Function, 443-445, 471-472, 536-538

GALILEI, GALILEO, 71, 142
GEDDES, PATRICK, 201
Genetic fallacy, 487
GHOSE, SRI AUROBINDO, see AUROBINDO
GILBERT, WILLIAM, 135
GILBERT, KATHERINE E., 444
Goal, see End and means, Telic principle
Good, see Value

HAECKEL, ERNST, 188-204
HALL, EVERETT W., 430
Happiness, 473-475, 513 n., 558-560
Health, 192, 273-274, 528-529
Hearsay, 28-29
Heat, 133-134
Hedonism, 403-405, 458-464, 466, 511-525
HEGEL, GEORG W. F., 52, 65
HEISENBERG, WERNER, 157, 317
Henotheism, 481
HERACLITUS, 23, 49, 82, 113, 220
HERRICK, C. JUDSON, 310-311
HESCHEL, ABRAHAM J., 507
HEYL, BERNARD, 417-418
HILBERT, DAVID, 154
HILLIARD, A. L., 430-431
HIPPOCRATES, 192, 273
History, 305-306, 479
HITLER, ADOLF, 462
HOBBES, THOMAS, 162-163
HOCKING, WILLIAM ERNEST, 318
HODGSON, SHADWORTH, 387-389, 391
HOMER, 454, 524
Humanism, 19-22; cf. ARISTOTLE, JAMES, etc.
HUME, DAVID, 270, 492
Humor, 244-245
HUXLEY, THOMAS, 287-290
HUYGENS, CHRISTIAN, 149
Hypothesis, 37-40, 77, 489, 588; cf. Theory

Idealism, 6, 169-174
Idols, Baconian, 28, 31, 81-89
Imitation, 217, 445-447
Implication, 34
Indeterminacy, 156-158, 316-317
INFELD, LEOPOLD, 146, 154
INGE, W. R., 321
INGERSOLL, ROBERT G., 506
Instrumentalism, see Pragmatism
Interactionism, 281-285, 297, 311, 357-359
Introspection, 322, 336-337, 360-367
Intuition, 40; rational, 33-37, 336-337, 414-415
Involution, 208
I-thou relation, 337-341, 427, 590-594; cf. Other selves

JAMES, WILLIAM, 5, 6, 25, 53, 69-70, 221-224, 290-291, 319, 359-371, 379-389, 480-481, 487-488, 489, 494, 504, 508, 576-590
JASPERS, KARL, 53
JEVONS, F. B., 9, 10
JOHNSON, SAMUEL, 188-189
Judgment, of value, 423-427; implicit, 25-27
JUNG, CARL G., 287, 288

KANDINSKY, WASSILY, 449
KANT, IMMANUEL, 20, 319, 415, 467-470, 496-498, 538-543
Katharsis, 441
KEPLER, JOHANNES, 40, 135-136
Kinetic principle, 132-134, 168, 179
Knowledge, 25-27, 66, 162, 166, 207, 244-245

LANGFELD, HERBERT S., 438
Language, 104-106, 333-335, 450-452; cf. Semantics, Ambiguity, Poetry
LAPLACE, PIERRE S., 164, 307

Law, logical, 34, 468; scientific, 62, 156, 183, 234-235, 236-239, 244, 315-316, 373-376; moral, 467-470, 541-543; political, 532-535
LEIBNIZ, GOTTFRIED WILHELM, 279, 321
LENIN, NICOLAI, 305
LEOPARDI, GIACOMO, 389
LEWIS, CLARENCE I., 185-186
LEVY, GERTRUDE RACHEL, 447
Libertarianism, 301, 303, 312-319
Life, 190, 191-196, 350, 387; cf. Evolution
Light, 149-152
Limited god, 573-575
LINDEMANN, F. A., 156
LIPPS, THEODOR, 437-438
LOCKE, JOHN, 24-25, 43, 165-166, 171, 362, 416
LOEB, JACQUES, 194, 195, 205
Logical positivism, 285
LORENTZ, H. A., 153-154, 230
LUCRETIUS, 446
LUTHER, MARTIN, 412

MACMURRAY, JOHN, 343
Magic, 483-485
MAIMONIDES, MOSES, 507
Mana, 484
MANDEVILLE, BERNARD, 464
MARCEL, GABRIEL, 53, 337, 340-341
MARX, KARL, 266
Mass, 142-144, 241, 244
Mathematics, 58, 95, 151-154
Materialism, 6, 17-20, 155, 162-169, 172
Matter, 133, 163, 166, 208-209, 213, 232, 243
Mean, golden, 473, 555-558
Meaning, 6, 36, 73-75, 285, 438-441, 450-452
Means, see End and means
Measurement, 132, 141-142, 421-423

Mechanism, 145, 194-196, 204-205, 227-233, 309-311; cf. Behavorism, Materialism
Meditation, see Reflection
MERCIER, CHARLES, 283
Metaphysics, 13-14, 54-60, 163, 187, 301
Metapsychology, see Self
Metascientific, 31
Method, philosophical, 9-11, 21-22, 29, 94-95; scientific, 37-40, 224-227
MILL, JOHN STUART, 136, 137, 156, 160, 172-173, 330, 331, 493, 494, 573-575
Mimesis, see Imitation
Mind, 209, 238-239, 280, 283-284, 289-297, 326, 352-357
MINKOWSKI, H., 156
MONTAIGNE, MICHEL DE, 462
MORGAN, C. LLOYD, 206-207
Motion, see Kinetic principle; self-motion, see Spontaneity
Music, 417-418, 422, 434, 449, 450, 536
MYERS, F. H., 585-586
Mystery, 6, 22, 341, 591-593

Nature, 128, 135, 253-257; cf. World
Necessity, 218-219; cf. Determinism
NEWTON, ISAAC K., 40, 62, 138, 140, 149, 224-227, 313
NIETZSCHE, FRIEDRICH, 53, 59, 447
Norm, 51, 413-414, 468-470, 473, 514, 528-531, 542

Observation, 31-33, 37-40; cf. Experience, Empirical method
Occam (Ockham), William of, see William
Ontology, 17, 161-187; ontological argument, 499-501
Operationalism, see Pragmatism
Opinion, see Belief
Organism, 17, 140, 248-249
Other selves, 16, 322-341, 369-371, 389-397
Ought, see Duty

Painting, 436-437, 446-447, 449
Panpsychism, 294-296
Paradox, 149-152, 482
Parallelism, 292-294, 296
PARMENIDES, 19
Parsimony, Law of, 183, 210, 285
Participation, see Empathy
PASCAL, BLAISE, 65
PAULSEN, FRIEDRICH, 293-296
PEIRCE, CHARLES, 127
Perception, 32, 117-118, 166, 231-232, 421
PERRY, RALPH BARTON, 429
Person, see Self
Pessimism, 327-328, 385, 388, 477, 493
Philosophy, its nature, 3-12, 69-70, 72-79, 100-101; as critical method, 5-6, 31, 37, 59-63, 76-77; choice of, 508-510; difficulty of, 68; errors of, 90, 104; main standpoints, 19-22, 510; motive for, 67, 69-70; objections against, 69-73; typical problems, 12-18
Physiology, 7-8
Physics, 7-8, 60, 132-158, 163, 176-180, 183, 236-244, 248-249
PICARD, MAURICE, 430
PLANCK, MAX, 149-150, 317
Planetary movement, 39-40, 226
PLATO, 3, 36, 46-48, 50-51, 52, 59, 139, 143, 192, 268-269, 271-272, 274, 276, 303, 344-350, 422-423, 458, 464, 471, 523-538
Pleasure (and pain), 403-405, 434, 458-465, 511-516, 553, 559
Plenitude (ontological), see Wholeness
Poetry, 440, 445, 451

Pointer readings, 241-243
Positivism, logical, see Logical positivism
Postulate, 59-60, 132, 224-227
POUSSIN, NICOLAS, 437
Potentiality (or potency), 116-117, 132, 208-209, 302-304
Pragmatism, 174-181, 587-588
Prajapati, 454
PRALL, DAVID W., 433, 434-435
Predestination, 304-305
Prejudice, 28-29; cf. Belief, Idols
PRICE, H. H., 333-334, 336, 337, 343
Primitive outlook, 119, 121, 129, 190, 339, 391-397, 446-447
Process, 114-116, 131, 134-136, 212-214, 347-349, 362, 364-366
Propaedeutic, 18
Psychoanalysis, 265-267, 274-277
Psychology, 263-278

Quality, 112-114, 129-131, 141, 145, 162, 165-167, 170, 184-185, 206, 231, 421
Quantity, see Measurement

RAPHAEL, 436
RASHDALL, HASTINGS, 498-499
Reality, 13-14, 57-58, 161-186; cf. Metaphysics
Realms of discourse, 54-58
Reason, 30, 33-37, 41-42, 61-63, 102-106; contemplative vs. deliberative, 12-13
Reflection, 5-7, 11, 21-22, 30, 45, 91, 101, 456-457, 508-510
Relation (relatedness), 9-11, 15, 34-36, 206, 393, 590, 593; cf. Wholeness
Religion, 16, 21-22, 402, 477-504, 519-521, 576-590; cf. Theology
RENOUVIER, CHARLES, 59, 386
RICHARDS, I. A., 452
RICHTER, JEAN PAUL, 327-328

Right (and wrong), 13, 414-416, 465-470, 526-536
Rights, basic human, 16, 20, 300; cf. Other selves
RUSSELL, BERTRAND, 160, 372-378, 415, 429
RYLE, GILBERT, 326-327, 328

Sanctions, ethical, 516-523
SANTAYANA, GEORGE, 429
SARDANAPALUS, 547
SARTRE, JEAN-PAUL, 53
Scepticism, 27, 63, 161, 353-354, 479
SCHMIDT, CARL, 59
SCHOPENHAUER, ARTHUR, 65, 100-107, 251-257
Science, 8-10, 21, 30-31, 62, 132-158, 174, 182-184, 224-227, 234-235, 240, 578-587; cf. Physics, Biology, etc.
Self, 15, 261-278, 359-371, 458, 469-471; cf. Other selves, Soul
Self-evidence, 33-36, 60
Self-motion, see Spontaneity
Semantics, 18, 29, 418-419; cf. Language, Ambiguity
Significance, see Meaning
SINNOTT, EDMUND W., 211
SOCRATES, 3, 23, 45, 46-48, 49, 50-51, 52, 53, 192, 268-269, 273-274, 303, 471, 523-536
Solipsism, 323-329
SOPHOCLES, 302
Soul, 135, 136, 166-167, 267-269, 344-353, 357-359, 528, 549-551
Space, 113, 117-120, 138-140, 154-155, 166, 169, 184-185
Speculation, see Theory
SPINOZA, BARUCH, 37, 52, 53, 61, 182, 309, 312, 407-408
Spontaneity, 123, 347-349
STACE, WALTER T., 343, 477-478
Standard, see Norm

Statement, 423-437
STEVENSON, CHARLES L., 423-435
SULLIVAN, J. W. N., 454
Syllogism, 37

TAYLOR, ALFRED E., 332
Telic principle, 16, 123-124, 131, 215, 216-218, 247-250, 472; teleological argument, 492-495
TEMPLE, WILLIAM, 480, 482, 491, 503
Temptation, 465-466
Theology, 304-305, 415, 561-567
Theory, 54, 78-79, 175, 179
Thing, 112-117
THOMAS AQUINAS, SAINT, 37, 52, 563-567
THOMPSON, D'ARCY, 245-250
THOMSON, J. ARTHUR, 195-196, 201
THURBER, JAMES, 277
Time, 120-122, 138, 151-156, 315, 363
Transcendentalism, 19-20, 510
TROTZKY, LEON, 305-306

Understanding, 24-25, 80, 83-85; cf. Knowledge, Concept, Philosophy
Universals, 467-469; cf. Concept
URBAN, WILBUR M., 406

VAIHINGER, HANS, 175-176, 180-181
Value, 11, 13, 187, 401-429, 539, 545-549; cf. End and means
Velocity, 151-154
VÉRON, EUGENE, 447-448

Virtue, 46-49, 406, 551-557
Vitalism, 204, 207-209

WASSERMANN, JAKOB, 448
WATSON, JOHN (Canadian philosopher), 538 n.
WATSON, JOHN B. (American behaviorist), 263-264, 286, 288
WATTS, ALAN W., 507
Wave-motion, 149-151
WELLS, H. G., 168
WEYL, HERMANN, 156
WHEELWRIGHT, PHILIP (quoted), 456, 466
WHITEHEAD, ALFRED N., 52, 155-156, 195, 230, 316
WHITTAKER, E. T., 154-155
Wholeness, 8-11, 51, 54, 206, 271-273, 472
Will, freedom of, see Freedom; will to live, 205, 207, 252-257; ethical will, 539-540
WILLIAM OF OCCAM, 183
WINDELBAND, WILHELM, 430
WISTER, RICHARD, 159, 189
Wonder, 3, 6, 30, 67, 70
WORDSWORTH, WILLIAM, 440, 451, 454
World, everyday, 111-126; physical, 128-158; vital, 190-210; cf. Nature, Reality
WRIGHT, FRANK LLOYD, 443
WUNDT, WILHELM, 284

YEATS, WILLIAM BUTLER, 451

ZENO OF ELEA, 188
Zoology, 219-220, 246; cf. Biology, Evolution

Date Due			
DEC 14 59			
JAN 5 '60			
JAN 21 60			
MAY 4 62 F			
NOV 20 '78			
RESERVE			
RESERVE			
RESERVE			
RESERVE			
	PRINTED	IN U.S.A.